Collins

COBUILD
Essential
English
Dictionary

HarperCollins Publishers
Westerhill Road
Bishopbriggs
Glasgow
G64 2QT

Second edition 2014

10 9 8 7 6 5 4 3

© HarperCollins Publishers 2010, 2014

ISBN 978-0-00-755653-3

Collins ® is a registered trademark of
HarperCollins Publishers Limited

www.collinsdictionary.com/COBUILD
www.collinselt.com

A catalogue record for this book is
available from the British Library

Printed in Italy by GRAFICA VENETA
S.p.A.

Typeset by Davidson Publishing Solutions
Artwork and colour supplement by
Q2A Media and Aptara

Editorial staff for the second edition

Contributors
Rosalind Combley
Laura Wedgeworth
Kate Woodford

For the publisher
Kate Ellis
Gavin Gray
Lily Khambata
Lisa Sutherland

Contents

Key Themes in Pictures:

These pictures are in the middle of the dictionary.

Guide to dictionary entries

The main form of the word is in blue.

butterfly /ˈbʌtəflaɪ/ *noun* (**butterflies**)
an insect with large coloured wings:
Butterflies are attracted to the wild flowers.

Plurals: to make a plural form, the general rule is to add 's'. Where a word does not follow this rule, the plural form is shown.

These symbols show you how to say the word. See page xxii for an explanation of these.

set¹ /set/ *noun*
1 a number of things that belong together:
The table and chairs are normally bought as a set.
□ *I got a chess set for my birthday.*
2 the place where a film is made: *The place looked like the set of a James Bond movie.*

This tells you the word class of a word (for example, if it is a noun, an adjective or a verb).

The forms of all verbs are given.

Blue boxes show the most common and useful words to know.

set² /set/ *verb* (**sets, setting, set**)
1 to put something somewhere carefully:
She set the vase down gently on the table.
2 to make a clock ready to use: *I set my alarm clock for seven o'clock every morning.*
3 to decide what a date or a price will be:
They have finally set the date of their wedding.
4 when the sun sets, it goes down in the sky: *They watched the sun set behind the hills.*
5 to prepare the table for a meal by putting plates, glasses, knives, forks, and spoons on it: *Could you set the table for dinner, please?*

Words with the same spelling but different word classes have different numbers.

Where a word has several meanings, these are ordered according to how common they are.

set fire to something/set something on fire to make something burn: *Angry protestors threw stones and set cars on fire.*
□ *I struck a match and set fire to the papers.*
set off to start going somewhere: *Nick set off for his farmhouse in Connecticut.*
set someone free to cause someone to be free: *They agreed to set the prisoners free.*
set something up to start or arrange something: *He plans to set up his own business.*

Idioms and phrasal verbs are shown below the definitions for the main word.

Example sentences show you typical uses of words, and help you to understand them.

Related words are shown in blue within entries.

sad /sæd/ *adjective* (**sadder, saddest**)
1 unhappy: *I'm sad that Jason's leaving.*
▸**sadly** *adverb* '*My girlfriend is moving away*', he said sadly.
▸ **sadness** *uncountable noun* *I left with a mixture of sadness and joy.*
2 making you feel unhappy: *It was a sad ending to a great story.* □ *I have some sad news for you.*

Comparative and superlative forms are given, unless they are formed with *more* or *most*.

baton /ˈbætɒn/ *noun*
1 a light, thin stick that is used by a conductor (= a person who directs musicians)
2 a short stick that one runner passes to another in a race

We use simple words in definitions, but where a difficult word is necessary, a short explanation is given.

You will find lots of words in this dictionary to help you with your schoolwork. There is a list of all the school subject words in the reference section on page 10.

bacteria /bæk'tɪəriə/ *plural noun*
very small living things that can make people ill: *There were high levels of dangerous bacteria in the water.*
▸ **bacterial** *adjective* *Tuberculosis is a bacterial disease.*

skate¹ /skeɪt/ *noun*
1 (*also* **ice-skate**) a boot with a long, sharp piece of metal on the bottom, for moving quickly and smoothly on ice
2 (*also* **roller-skate**) a boot with wheels on the bottom, for moving quickly on the ground

> This information shows that there is another way of expressing the word.

board² /bɔːd/ *verb* (**boards, boarding, boarded**)
to get into a train, a ship or an aircraft to travel somewhere (*formal*): *I boarded the plane to Boston.*

> A *formal* label means that this word is usually used in more serious or official situations.

> An *informal* label means that this word is not usually used in more serious situations or in serious writing.

stuff¹ /stʌf/ *uncountable noun*
things in general (*informal*): *He pointed to a bag. 'That's my stuff.'* □ *There is a huge amount of useful stuff on the Internet.*

'shop ,assistant (*American:* **clerk**) *noun*
a person who works in a shop
→ Look at picture on P7

> Common American words are shown.

angry /'æŋgri/ *adjective* (**angrier, angriest**)
feeling a strong emotion when someone has done something bad, or someone has treated you unfairly: *We are very angry about the decision to close the school.* □ *An angry crowd gathered.*

> **LANGUAGE HELP**
> If someone is very angry, you can say they are **furious**. If they are less angry, you can say they are **annoyed** or **irritated**.

> Language Help boxes show related words for vocabulary building.

already /ɔːl'redi/ *adverb*
1 used for showing that one thing happened before another thing: *The meeting had already finished when we arrived.*
2 used for showing that a situation exists now or that it started earlier than expected: *We've already spent most of the money.* □ *Most of the guests have already left.*

> **LANGUAGE HELP**
> **already** or **yet**? In British English, you usually use **already** and **yet** with the perfect tenses. *I've already seen that film. Have they arrived yet?* In American English, people often use a past tense. *She already told us about the party. I didn't have any breakfast yet.*

> Language Help boxes show differences between words that are often confused.

Grammatical labels used in the dictionary

Nearly all the words that are explained in this dictionary have grammar information given about them. For each word, its word class is shown after the headword. Examples of word classes are *adjective*, *noun*, *verb* and *preposition*.

The sections below contain more information about each word class.

adjective

An adjective is a word that is used for telling you more about a person or thing. You would use an adjective to talk about appearance, colour, size, or other qualities:

> **angry:** An **angry** woman appeared at the door.
> **brown:** She has **brown** eyes.
> **wet:** My gloves are **wet**.

adverb

An adverb is a word that gives more information about when, how, or where something happens:

> **tomorrow:** Bye; see you **tomorrow**.
> **slowly:** He spoke **slowly** and clearly.
> **down:** I want to get **down** now.

article

An article is one of the words *a*, *an*, or *the* that is used before a noun. It shows whether you are talking about a particular thing or a general example of something:

> **a:** I need **a** drink.
> **an:** You'll need **an** umbrella; it's raining outside.
> **the:** You should never look directly at **the** sun.

auxiliary verb

An auxiliary verb is a verb that is used with another verb to show its tense, to form questions, or to form the passive. The main auxiliary verbs in English are *be*, *have* and *do*:

> **be:** **Is** it snowing?
> **have:** I **have** never been to China.
> **do:** We **don**'t have a computer at home.

conjunction

A conjunction is a word such as *and*, *but*, *if*, and *since*. Conjunctions are used for linking two words or two parts of a sentence together:

> **but:** I enjoyed my holiday, **but** it wasn't long enough.
> **and:** James **and** Ewan came to the party.
> **if:** **If** you miss your bus, you'll have to walk home.

exclamation

An exclamation is a word or phrase which is spoken suddenly or loudly in order to express a strong emotion:

> **oh:** '**Oh**!' Kenny said. 'Has everyone gone?'
> **wow:** **Wow**; this is so exciting!

modal verb

A modal verb is a verb such as *may*, *must*, or *would*. A modal verb is used before the infinitive form of a verb:

> You **must** see a doctor.

In questions, it comes before the subject:

> **May** we come in?

In negatives, it comes before the negative word:

> I **can't** play the piano.

Modal verbs do not add an -s in the third person singular (with *he*, *she*, and *it*):

> He **could** win if he tried harder.

noun

A noun is a word that refers to a person, a thing, or a quality. In this dictionary, the label *noun* is given to all countable nouns, and all nouns that can be both countable and uncountable (see below). A countable noun is used for talking about things that can be counted, and that have both singular and plural forms. When a countable noun is used in the singular, it must normally have a word like *a*, *an*, *the*, or *her* in front of it:

> **head:** She turned her **head** away.
> **room:** Go to my **room**, and fetch my bag, please.

uncountable noun

An uncountable noun is used for talking about things that are not normally counted, or that we do not think of as single items. Uncountable nouns do not have a plural form, and they are used with a singular verb:

> **help:** He shouted for **help**.
> **rain:** We got very wet in the **rain**
> **bread:** She bought a loaf of **bread**.

plural noun

A plural noun is always plural, and it is used with plural verbs:

> **pyjamas:** What colour are your **pyjamas**?
> **scissors:** Be careful; these **scissors** are very sharp.

preposition

A preposition is a word such as *by*, *with*, or *from* which is always followed by a noun group or the *-ing* form of a verb:

> **near:** He stood **near** the door.
> **of:** Alice is a friend **of** mine.

pronoun

A pronoun is a word that you use instead of a noun, when you do not need or want to name someone or something directly:

> **it:** John took the book and opened **it**.
> **her:** He rang Mary and invited **her** to dinner.

verb

A verb is a word that is used for saying what someone or something does, or what happens to them, or to give information about them:

> **sleep:** She **slept** till 10 o'clock in the morning.
> **eat:** I **ate** my breakfast quickly.

Using your dictionary

The exercises in these study pages will help you to understand and use fully all the different features of this dictionary, and to practise your dictionary skills. You will find answers to all the exercises in the Answer Key on pages xiv-xv.

Order of entries

The main part of the dictionary is made up of entries from A to Z. An **entry** is a complete explanation of a word and all its meanings. For example, the first three entries on page 1 are 'a', 'abandon' and 'abbreviation'. You will find each entry under the first letter of that word.

Guide words

At the top of every page you will see two words. These words are **guide words**. The guide words show what the first and last entry on that page is. For example, on page 2, the first entry is 'abroad', and the last entry is 'accept'.

Exercise 1

Put the words on the left between the appropriate guide words. The first one has been done for you as an example.

1	~~amount~~	a	apartment .... apply
2	answer	b	admiration .... advanced
3	apparently	c	assemble .... astronomy
4	assistance	d	ambitious ......*amount*...... analyse
5	admit	e	annoy .... anticlockwise

Inflected forms

Inflected forms are the different forms that a word can have, such as the past form for a verb, or a plural form for a noun. These forms are shown after the pronunciations.

At verb entries, you can see the 3rd person singular, the *-ing* form, the past tense, and, if it is different from the past tense, the past participle.

do¹ /də, STRONG duː/ *auxiliary verb* (does, doing, did, done)

At adjective and adverb entries, you can see their comparative forms.

pretty /'prɪti/ *adjective, adverb* (prettier, prettiest)

Most nouns add an -s in the plural, but for those that follow a different pattern, you can see their plural forms.

woman /ˈwʊmən/ *noun* (women)
an adult female human being: *She was
a tall, dark woman, with an unusual face.*

Exercise 2

Which headword would you look at to find these words? The first one has been done for you.

1   beaches ......*beach*.......   6   secretaries ....

2   seemed   7   nicest ....

3   living   8   women ....

4   clearer   9   forgotten ....

5   geese   10   parties ....

Definitions and examples

Definitions are written using simple words. Examples show typical ways of using the word, and they also give more information about its grammatical patterns.

Exercise 3

Decide what is wrong with each of the following sentences by looking up the word printed in bold. Use the information in the entry to write down the correct sentence.

1   *He hasn't made his* **homework**.

2   *The prime minister did a* **speech** *to the nation.*

3   *Sally* **graduated** *Edinburgh University in the summer.*

4   *He* **asked** *to me my name.*

5   *The price of petrol has* **fallen** *down.*

Grammar information

Each headword has a label that shows its grammatical word class, for example whether it is a noun, a verb, or an adjective. A list of these labels is shown on pages vi-vii.

accent /'æksənt/ (noun)
1 the particular way that someone pronounces words, which shows where the person comes from: *He had an Irish accent.*
2 a mark written above a letter to show how it is pronounced: *The word 'café' has an accent on the 'e'.*

Exercise 4

Write a correct word class from the box next to each word. The first one has been done for you.

~~noun~~	pronoun	modal verb	verb	adjective	noun
preposition	exclamation	adverb	adjective		

1 pool ......*noun*............   6 accident ....

2 woolly ....   7 mad ....

3 grind ....   8 wow ....

4 concerning ....   9 me ....

5 must ....   10 hardly ....

Some words have more than one word class. These words have separate 'entries' for each word class. These entries have a small number after the headword, for example, at answer:

answer¹ /'ɑːnsə/ *verb* (answers, answering, answered)
1 to say something back to someone who has spoken to you: *I asked him but he didn't answer.* □ *Williams answered that he didn't know.*
2 to pick up the telephone when it rings: *Why didn't you answer when I phoned?* □ *She didn't answer the telephone.*

answer² /'ɑːnsə/ *noun*
1 a way to solve a problem: *There are no easy answers to this problem.*
2 the information that you give when you are doing a test: *I got three answers wrong.*

Exercise 5

Read the following sentences. In the first column, write the word class of the bold word.

Look for the word in the dictionary, and write the headword and its number in the second column.

		word class	headword
1	I **hope** you can come to my party.	....verb.......	.....hope¹....
2	I don't know the **answer** to this question.	....	....
3	In the afternoon, we looked **around** the shops.	....	....
4	Amy was very **upset** when she heard the news.	....	....
5	I'm **backing** France in the final.	....	....

Style labels

Some words are used in particular situations.

In this dictionary, the label *formal* shows that a word is used mainly in official situations such as politics and business.

The label *informal* shows that a word is used mainly in relaxed conversations and personal letters or emails.

Exercise 6

Write the correct style label ('formal' or 'informal') next to these words. Use your dictionary to help you.

1	appliance	....
2	hang on	....
3	exceed	....
4	notify	....
5	weird	....
6	reckon	....

Exercise 7

Look at the sentences below. The *bold italic* word in each one is informal. Use the dictionary to help you re-write the sentence in a less informal way.

1   *She's had a nasty shock, but she's **okay**.*

_____

2   *Have you got any **kids**?*

_____

3   *Who's that **guy** with Katie?*

_____

4   *Tony was my best **mate** at school.*

_____

5   *'Remember to turn the computer off.' 'Oh, **yeah**.'*

_____

Exercise 8

This dictionary is written in British English, but it also contains common American English words.

Look at the sentences below. For each, say whether the word in *bold italic* is British or American English, using the dictionary to help you. Then write the American or British English word with the same meaning (the 'equivalent') next to it in the space provided.

Examples	British or American?	Equivalent
1 *There was a long **queue** of people at the post office.*		
2 *Could you take the **garbage** out, please?*		
3 *I'm wearing a red shirt and black **trousers**.*		
4 *Please send us your **CV**.*		
5 *Don't park your car on the **sidewalk**.*		

Language Help

Language Help boxes give you extra information about words and meanings.
For example, they tell you how to avoid common mistakes or when to use a related
word. They are the blue boxes that appear after the entry or meaning they relate to.
Look at the entry for 'news' to find an example of a Language Help box.

Exercise 9

Use the Language Help boxes in the dictionary to help you to correct the mistakes in
these sentences.

1   *My parents **educated** me very strictly.*

_____

2   *Mum was downstairs **hearing** the radio.*

_____

3   *These vegetables need **little** salt to improve their taste.*

_____

4   *How many **luggages** have you got?*

_____

5   *Was anyone **wounded** in the car accident?*

_____

Answer Key

Exercise 1

1d, 2e, 3a, 4c, 5b

Exercise 2

1	beach	6	secretary
2	seem	7	nice
3	live	8	woman
4	clear	9	forget
5	goose	10	party

Exercise 3

1 *He hasn't **done** his homework.*
2 *The prime minister **gave** a speech to the nation.*
3 *Sally **graduated from** Edinburgh University in the summer.*
4 *He **asked** me my name.*
5 *The price of petrol has **fallen**.*

Exercise 4

1	noun	6	noun
2	adjective	7	adjective
3	verb	8	exclamation
4	preposition	9	pronoun
5	modal verb	10	adverb

Exercise 5

1 verb, **hope¹**
2 noun, **answer²**
3 preposition, **around¹**
4 adjective, **upset¹**
5 verb, **back³**

Exercise 6

1 formal
2 informal
3 formal
4 formal
5 informal
6 informal

Exercise 7

1   She's had a nasty shock, but she's **safe and well**.
2   Have you got any **children**?
3   Who's that **man** with Katie?
4   Tony was my best **friend** at school.
5   'Remember to turn the computer off.' 'Oh, **yes**.'

Exercise 8

Examples	British or American?	Equivalent
1 There was a long **queue** of people at the post office.	British	line
2 Could you take the **garbage** out, please?	American	rubbish
3 I'm wearing a red shirt and black **trousers**.	British	pants
4 Please send us your **CV**.	British	résumé
5 Don't park your car on the **sidewalk**.	American	pavement

Exercise 9

1   My parents **brought** me **up** very strictly.
2   Mum was downstairs **listening to** the radio.
3   These vegetables need **a little** salt to improve their taste.
4   How many **pieces of luggage** have you got?
5   Was anyone **injured** in the car accident?

Punctuation

● **full stop** (*American*: **period**)
A full stop is used at the end of a sentence, unless it is a question or an exclamation.

> *It's not your fault.*
> *Cook the rice in salted water.*

? **question mark**
If a sentence is a question, you put a question mark at the end.

> *Why did you do that?*
> *He's very good at maths, isn't he?*

! **exclamation mark** (*American*: **exclamation point**)
You put an exclamation mark at the end of a sentence that expresses surprise, excitement, enthusiasm, or horror.

> *What a lovely smell!*
> *How awful!*

, **comma**
You put a comma between things on a list. You do not need a comma if the items are separated by 'and' or 'or'.

> *We came to a small, dark room.*
> *We ate fish, steak and fruit.*

You put a comma after or in front of someone's name, or the word you use when you speak to them.

> *Jenny, I'm sorry.*
> *I love you, darling.*

You put a comma between the name of a place and the country, state, or county it is in.

> *She was born in Richmond, Surrey, in 1913.*

You put a comma before a part of a sentence that gives extra information.

> *We sat in the living room, which was rather small.*

You put a comma before a question tag.

> *You're American, aren't you?*

; **semi-colon**
You use a semi-colon to separate clauses that are closely related.

> *He knew everything about me; I knew nothing about him.*

colon

You use a colon before a list or explanation, where the list or explanation relates to the previous clause.

> *These clothes are made of natural materials: cotton, silk, wool, and leather.*

apostrophe

You use an apostrophe with *s* to show that a person or thing belongs to someone or something. When the noun is singular, or is plural, but does not end in an *s*, the apostrophe is placed before the *s*.

> *I stayed at Fiona's house last night.*
> *Here are the children's rooms.*

When the noun is a regular plural (with an *s*), the apostrophe is placed after the *s*.

> *Those are the dogs' bowls.*

Note: You do not use an apostrophe before the s of the possessive pronouns *yours*, *hers*, *ours*, *theirs*, or *its*.

You use an apostrophe in shortened forms of *be*, *have*, *would*, and *not*.

> *I'm very sorry.*
> *I've got two brothers and two sisters.*
> *I'd like a coffee and a ham sandwich, please.*
> *I can't see anything.*

hyphen

You use a hyphen to join together two words to make another word.

> *He was forty-three years old.*
> *At half-time, the score was 2-1.*

quotation marks (or quotes, or inverted commas)

You put quotation marks at the beginning and end of direct speech. You start direct speech with a capital letter and you end it with a full stop, a question mark, or an exclamation mark.

> *"What happened?"*

If you put something like 'he said' after the direct speech, you put a comma in front of the second inverted comma, not a full stop.

> *'We have to go home,' she told him.*
> *'Yes,' he replied. 'He'll be all right.'*

Times and dates

Talking about time

If you want to talk about the time that you can see on a clock or a watch, you use the verb *be*.

> *What's the time now? It's three thirty.*
> *Can you tell me the time? It's twenty-five past twelve.*
> *The time is six forty-five.*
> *It's five to eight and breakfast's at eight o'clock.*

You also use these prepositions to indicate a specific time.

at	on	past	to

> *I'll meet you at seven o'clock.*
> *He mentioned it to me on Friday.*
> *It was four minutes past midnight.*
> *At exactly five minutes to nine, Ann left her car.*

You use these prepositions to relate events to a non-specific time.

after	before	by	during	following	over

> *The match started again after lunch.*
> *She woke up during the night.*
> *Several demonstrations have been held over the past few weeks.*
> *I have to finish this essay by Monday.*
> *We arrived before lunch.*
> *Following the storm, the sun came out.*

Dates

Writing dates

There are several different ways of writing a date.

20 April	April 20
20th April	April 20th

say 'the twentieth of April' or 'April the twentieth')

If you want to give the year, you put it last.

> *She was born on December 15th 2009.* ('December the fifteenth, two thousand and nine')

You can write a date in figures.

> *15/12/09*   *15.12.09*

Note that in American English, you put the month in front of the day.

12/15/09   12.15.09

Days of the week

| Monday | Tuesday | Wednesday | Thursday | Friday | Saturday | Sunday |

The exam is on Friday afternoon.
We meet here every Tuesday morning.
He took a flight to Nairobi last Thursday.
Aunty Margaret is coming to stay next Tuesday.

Months of the year

| January | February | March | April | May | June | July |
| August | September | October | November | December | | |

Here are the most common ways of talking about months.

We always have snow in January.
The new shop opens on 5 February.
I flew to Milan in early March.
I've been here since last June.
I'm going to Paris next November.

Seasons

| spring | summer | autumn | winter |

Here are the most common ways of talking about seasons.

In winter the nights are cold and long.
Richard is starting university next autumn.
We met again in the spring of 2007.

American speakers often use *fall* instead of autumn.

He begins teaching in the fall.

Telling the time

Here are the most common ways of saying and writing the time.

four o'clock
four
4.00

nine o'clock
nine
9.00

twelve o'clock
twelve
12.00

 four in the
morning
4 a.m.

 nine in the
morning
9 a.m.

 twelve in the
morning
12 a.m.
midday
noon

four in the
afternoon
4 p.m.

nine in the
evening
9 p.m.

twelve at night
12 p.m.
midnight

half past eleven (*British*)
half-eleven (*British*)
eleven-thirty
11.30

a quarter to one (*British*)
quarter to one (*British*)
twelve forty-five
12.45
(a) quarter of one (*American*)

 a quarter past twelve (*British*)
quarter past twelve (*British*)
12.15
quarter after twelve (*American*)

 ten to eight (*British*)
ten minutes to eight (*British*)
seven-fifty
7.50
ten of eight (*American*)

 twenty-five past two (*British*)
twenty-five minutes past two (*British*)
two twenty-five
2.25
twenty-five after two (*American*)

 twenty to eleven (*British*)
twenty minutes to eleven (*British*)
ten-forty
10.40
twenty of eleven (*American*)

Saying hello and goodbye

Saying hello

The usual way of greeting someone is by saying *hello*. After you have greeted someone, you often say their name, or ask how they are.

> *'Hello, it's Molly.' – 'Oh, hello love.'*
> *'Hello, Mike.' – 'Hello. How are you today?'*

To greet someone more informally, you can say *hello there*, *hi*, or *hiya*.

To greet someone at a particular time of day, you can use the expressions *good morning*, *good afternoon*, and *good evening*.

Good morning is used before twelve o'clock midday.

Good afternoon is used between midday and about six o'clock.

Good evening is used after that.

With people you know, these greetings are often shortened to *morning*, *afternoon*, and *evening*.

Note: *Good night* is only used to say goodbye to someone before you or they go to bed.

Saying goodbye

When two people part, they usually say *goodbye*, *bye*, or *bye bye*. People who know each other are more likely to say *bye* than *goodbye*. People do not usually say *bye* or *bye bye* in very formal situations.

To say goodbye more informally, people use the expressions *see you* and *see you later*. They also sometimes say *take care* and *all the best*.

In British English, people sometimes say *cheers*, *cheerio*, or *look after yourself*.

If you have just met someone for the first time, you can say *it was nice to meet you* when you leave them.

> *Thanks for coming along here. It was very nice to meet you.*

Responding to greetings

You can respond to a greeting or goodbye by repeating the expression that the other person has used, or with another appropriate expression.

> *'Hello Colin.' – 'Hello.'*
> *'Hello Colin.' – 'Good evening, how are you?'*

Pronunciation

In this dictionary the International Phonetic Alphabet (IPA) is used to show how the words are pronounced. The symbols used in the International Phonetic Alphabet are shown in the table below.

IPA Symbols

Vowel sounds		Consonant sounds	
ɑː	calm, ah	b	bed, rub
æ	act, mass	d	done, red
aɪ	dive, cry	f	fit, if
aɪə	fire, tyre	g	good, dog
aʊ	out, down	h	hat, horse
aʊə	flour, sour	j	yellow, you
e	met, lend, pen	k	king, pick
eɪ	say, weight	l	lip, bill
eə	fair, care	m	mat, ram
ɪ	fit, win	n	not, tin
iː	seem, me	p	pay, lip
ɪə	near, beard	r	run, read
ɒ	lot, spot	s	soon, bus
əʊ	note, coat	t	talk, bet
ɔː	claw, more	v	van, love
ɔɪ	boy, joint	w	win, wool
ʊ	could, stood	x	loch
uː	you, use	z	zoo, buzz
ʊə	sure, pure	ʃ	ship, wish
ɜː	turn, third	ʒ	measure, leisure
ʌ	fund, must	ŋ	sing, working
ə	the first vowel in about	tʃ	cheap, witch
		θ	thin, myth
		ð	then, bathe
		ðʒ	joy, bridge

Notes

Primary and secondary stress are shown by marks above and below the line, in front of the stressed syllable. For example, in the word abbreviation, /əˌbriːvɪˈeɪʃən/, the second syllable has secondary stress and the fourth syllable has primary stress.

We do not normally show pronunciations for compound words (words which are made up of more than one word). Pronunciations for the words that make up the compounds are usually found at their entries at other parts of the dictionary. However, compound words do have stress markers.

Aa

a /ə, STRONG eɪ/ or **an** /ən, STRONG æn/ *article*

an is used before words that begin with the sound of **a, e, i, o** or **u**

1 used before a noun when people may not know which particular person or thing you are talking about: *A waiter came in with a glass of water.* □ *He started eating an apple.*

2 used when you are talking about any person or thing of a particular type: *You should leave it to an expert.* □ *Bring a sleeping bag.*

3 used instead of the number 'one' before some numbers or measurements: *a hundred miles*

4 each; for each: *Cheryl goes to London three times a month.* □ *This cheese costs £12.25 a kilo.*

abandon /əˈbændən/ *verb* (**abandons, abandoning, abandoned**)

1 to leave a place, a person or a thing, especially when you should not: *His parents abandoned him when he was a baby.*
▶ **abandoned** *adjective* *They found an abandoned car.*

2 to stop doing an activity or a piece of work before it is finished: *After several hours they abandoned their search.*

abbreviation /ə,briːviˈeɪʃən/ *noun*
a short form of a word or phrase: *The abbreviation for 'page' is 'p.'*

abdomen /ˈæbdəmən/ *noun*

1 the part of your body below your chest: *The pain in my abdomen is getting worse.*
▶ **abdominal** /æbˈdɒmɪnəl/ *adjective* the abdominal muscles

2 the back part of the three parts that an insect's body is divided into

ability /əˈbɪlɪti/ *noun* (**abilities**)
a quality or a skill that makes it possible for you to do something: *Her drama teacher*

noticed her acting ability. □ *His mother had strong musical abilities.*

able /ˈeɪbəl/ *adjective*
be able to do something

1 to have skills or qualities that make it possible for you to do something: *A 10-year-old should be able to prepare a simple meal.* □ *The company says they're able to keep prices low.*

2 to have enough freedom, power, time or money to do something: *Are you able to help me?* □ *If I get this job, I'll be able to buy a new car.*

abnormal /æbˈnɔːməl/ *adjective*
unusual, especially in a way that is a problem: *She has an abnormal heartbeat.*

aboard /əˈbɔːd/ *preposition*
on, in or onto a ship, plane, train or bus: *He invited us aboard his boat.* □ *There were about 600 passengers aboard the train.*

abolish /əˈbɒlɪʃ/ *verb* (**abolishes, abolishing, abolished**)
to officially end a system or practice: *The committee voted on Thursday to abolish the death penalty.*
▶ **abolition** /,æbəˈlɪʃən/ *uncountable noun* the abolition of slavery

about¹ /əˈbaʊt/ *preposition*
used for introducing a particular subject: *He knows a lot about architecture.* □ *He never complains about his wife.*

about² /əˈbaʊt/ *adverb*
used in front of a number to show that the number is not exact: *The child was about eight years old.* □ *It got dark at about six o'clock.*
be about to do something to be going to do something very soon: *I think he's about to leave.*

When you are talking about a number that is not exact, you can use **around** and **round** as well as **about**.

above /əˈbʌv/ *preposition*
1 over or higher than another thing:

a

He lifted his hands above his head. □ Their flat is above a clothes shop. □ There was a mirror above the fireplace.

2 greater than a particular level: The temperature rose to just above 40 degrees.

3 in a higher position than you at work, or in a higher class than you at school: The bosses above us make all the decisions. □ She was in the year above me at school.

abroad /ə'brɔːd/ *adverb*
in or to a foreign country: Many students go abroad to work for the summer. □ I lived abroad for five years when I was a child.

abrupt /ə'brʌpt/ *adjective*
very sudden, often in a way that is unpleasant: His career came to an abrupt end in 1998.
▶ **abruptly** *adverb* The horses stopped abruptly.

absence /'æbsəns/ *noun*
the fact of not being present in a particular place: Her absence from work is becoming a problem.

absent /'æbsənt/ *adjective*
not at a place or an event: Anna was absent from the meeting. □ 'Was he at school yesterday?' — 'No, he was absent.'

'absent-m'inded *adjective*
often forgetting things or not paying attention to what you are doing: She looked around the room in an absent-minded dream.
▶ **absent-mindedly** *adverb* Elliot absent-mindedly scratched his head.

absolute /'æbsəluːt/ *adjective*
total and complete: No one knows anything with absolute certainty. □ We provide French courses for absolute beginners.

absolutely /ˌæbsə'luːtli/ *adverb*
1 totally and completely: Joan is absolutely right. □ I absolutely refuse to get married.
2 used as a way of saying yes or of agreeing with someone strongly: 'Do you think I should call him?' — 'Absolutely.'

absorb /əb'zɔːb/ *verb* (absorbs, absorbing, absorbed)
to take in a substance: Cook the rice until it absorbs the water.
▶ **absorbent** /əb'zɔːbənt/ *adjective* A real sponge is softer and more absorbent.

absorbing /əb'zɔːbɪŋ/ *adjective*
very interesting and using all your

attention and energy: This is a very absorbing game.

abstract /'æbstrækt/ *adjective*
1 based on general ideas rather than on real things: The students are intelligent and good at abstract thought.
2 using shapes and patterns rather than showing people or things: Mondrian's abstract paintings, with their heavy black lines and bright blocks of colour

abuse¹ /ə'bjuːs/ *noun*
1 cruel treatment of a person: The court found her guilty of child abuse.
2 *uncountable* very rude things that people say when they are angry: He shouted abuse as the car drove away.
3 the use of something in a wrong way or for a bad purpose: This disease results from alcohol abuse.

abuse² /ə'bjuːz/ *verb* (abuses, abusing, abused)
to treat a person cruelly: The film is about a woman who was abused as a child.

academic /ˌækə'demɪk/ *adjective*
relating to the work done in schools, universities and colleges: The university has a reputation for academic excellence.

academy /ə'kædəmi/ *noun* (academies)
a word that is sometimes used in the names of schools: She's a second-year student at the Royal Academy of Music.

accelerate /æk'seləreɪt/ *verb* (accelerates, accelerating, accelerated)
1 to get faster: Her heartbeat accelerated when she saw him in the crowd.
2 to go faster: Suddenly the car accelerated.

accelerator /æk'seləreɪtə/ *noun*
the part in a car that you press with your foot to make the car go faster: He took his foot off the accelerator.

accent /'æksənt/ *noun*
1 the particular way that someone pronounces words, which shows where the person comes from: He had an Irish accent.
2 a mark written above a letter to show how it is pronounced: The word 'café' has an accent on the 'e'.

accept /æk'sept/ *verb* (accepts, accepting, accepted)
1 to say yes to something that someone offers you, or to agree to take or do

something: *She accepted his offer of marriage.* ▫ *Doctors may not accept gifts.*

▸ **acceptance** /æk'septəns/ *uncountable noun* We listened to his acceptance speech for the Nobel Peace Prize.

2 to recognize that an unpleasant fact or situation cannot be changed: *People often accept noise as part of city life.*

3 to recognize that you are responsible for something: *Accept the fact that the accident was your fault!*

acceptable /æk'septəbəl/ *adjective*

1 considered to be normal by most people: *Asking people for money is not acceptable behaviour.*

▸ **acceptably** *adverb* They try to teach children to behave acceptably.

2 good enough for a particular purpose: *There was one restaurant that looked acceptable.*

access¹ /'ækses/ *uncountable noun*

1 permission to go into a particular place: *The general public does not have access to the White House.*

2 when you are able or allowed to see or use information or equipment: *Patients have access to their medical records.*

access² /'ækses/ *verb* (**accesses, accessing, accessed**)
to find information on a computer: *Parents can see which sites their children have accessed.*

accessible /æk'sesɪbəl/ *adjective*
easy for people to reach or enter: *The city centre is easily accessible to the general public.* ▫ *Most of the bedrooms and bathrooms are accessible for wheelchairs.*

accessory /æk'sesəri/ *noun* (**accessories**)
a small thing such as a belt or a scarf that you wear with your clothes: *We shopped for handbags, scarves and other accessories.*

accident /'æksɪdənt/ *noun*

1 when a vehicle hits something and causes injury or damage: *He broke his right leg in a motorbike accident.*

2 when something bad happens to a person by chance, sometimes causing injury or death: *The boy was injured in an accident at a swimming pool.*

by accident by chance: *We met by accident at a party in Los Angeles.*

accidental /,æksɪ'dentəl/ *adjective*
happening by chance or as the result of

an accident: *The police said that the fire was accidental.*

▸ **accidentally** /,æksɪ'dentəli/ *adverb* They accidentally removed the names from the computer.

accommodation /ə,kɒmə'deɪʃən/ *uncountable noun*
buildings or rooms where people live or stay: *They always pay extra for luxury accommodation.*

accompany /ə'kʌmpəni/ *verb* (**accompanies, accompanying, accompanied**)

1 to go somewhere with someone (*formal*): *Ken agreed to accompany me on a trip to Africa.*

2 to play one part of a piece of music while a singer or a musician sings or plays the main tune: *Her singing teacher accompanied her on the piano.*

accomplish /ə'kʌmplɪʃ/ *verb* (**accomplishes, accomplishing, accomplished**)
to succeed in doing something: *If we all work together, I think we can accomplish our goal.*

accomplishment /ə'kʌmplɪʃmənt/ *noun*
something unusual or special that you have made or achieved: *This book is an amazing accomplishment.*

accord /ə'kɔːd/ *noun*

of your own accord because you want to, and not because someone has asked you: *He left his job of his own accord.*

ac'cording to *preposition*

1 used when you are saying where some information comes from: *They drove away in a white van, according to police reports.*

2 used when you are saying which way something should be done: *They played the game according to the British rules.*

according to plan happening in the way that you intended: *Everything is going according to plan.*

accordion
/ə'kɔːdɪən/
noun
a musical
instrument
in the shape
of a box,
which you
hold in your
hands. You
play it by

accordion

a

pressing keys and buttons on the side, while moving the two ends in and out.

account¹ /əˈkaʊnt/ *noun*
1 an arrangement you have with a bank. The bank looks after your money, and you can take some out when you need it: *I have £3,000 in my bank account.*
2 an arrangement you have with a company to use a service they provide: *an email account*
3 a report of something that has happened: *He gave the police a detailed account of the events.*

take something into account/take account of something to consider something when you are trying to make a decision: *You have to take people's feelings into account.*

account² /əˈkaʊnt/ *verb* (**accounts, accounting, accounted**)
account for something to explain something or give the reason for it: *How do you account for these differences?*

accountant /əˈkaʊntənt/ *noun*
a person whose job is to keep financial accounts

accounts /əˈkaʊnts/ *plural noun*
records of all the money that a person or a business receives and spends: *He kept detailed accounts of all the money he spent.*

accurate /ˈækjʊrət/ *adjective*
1 correct: *I can't give an accurate description of the man because it was too dark.*
▶ **accuracy** *uncountable noun Don't trust the accuracy of weather reports.*
▶ **accurately** *adverb He described it quite accurately.*
2 able to work without making a mistake: *The car's steering is accurate, and the brakes are powerful.*
▶ **accuracy** *uncountable noun Your accuracy will improve with practice.*
▶ **accurately** *adverb He hit the golf ball powerfully and accurately.*

accuse /əˈkjuːz/ *verb* (**accuses, accusing, accused**)
to say that someone did something wrong or dishonest: *They accused her of lying.*

ache /eɪk/ *verb* (**aches, aching, ached**)
to feel a steady pain in a part of your body: *Her head was hurting and she ached all over (= in every part of her body).* □ *My leg still aches*

when I stand for a long time. ● **ache** *noun A hot bath will take away all your aches and pains.*

achieve /əˈtʃiːv/ *verb* (**achieves, achieving, achieved**)
to succeed in doing something, usually after a lot of effort: *He worked hard to achieve his goals.*

achievement /əˈtʃiːvmənt/ *noun*
something that you have succeeded in doing, especially after a lot of effort: *Being chosen for the team was a great achievement.*

acid /ˈæsɪd/ *noun*
a chemical, usually a liquid, that can burn your skin and cause damage to other substances: *As you can see, the acid damaged the metal bowl.*

ˌacid ˈrain *noun*
rain that contains acid that can harm the environment. The acid comes from pollution in the air.

acknowledge /əkˈnɒlɪdʒ/ *verb* (**acknowledges, acknowledging, acknowledged**)
to agree that something is true or that it exists (*formal*): *He acknowledged that he was wrong.* □ *At last, the government has acknowledged the problem.*

acknowledgments /əkˈnɒlɪdʒmənts/ also **acknowledgements** *plural noun*
in a book, the names of all the people who helped the writer: *There are two pages of acknowledgments at the beginning of the book.*

acquaintance /əˈkweɪntəns/ *noun*
someone you have met, but who you don't know well: *He spoke to the owner of the bookshop, who was an old acquaintance of his.*

acquire /əˈkwaɪə/ *verb* (**acquires, acquiring, acquired**)
1 to get or buy something (*formal*): *The club wants to acquire new sports equipment.*
2 to learn or develop something: *Students on this programme will acquire a wide range of skills.*

acre /ˈeɪkə/ *noun*
a unit for measuring an area of land: *William farms a hundred acres of land in Wales.*

across /əˈkrɒs/ *preposition*
1 from one side of something to the other side of it: *She walked across the floor and sat down.* □ *He watched Karl run across the street.*
● **across** *adverb Richard stood up and walked across to the window.*

2 going from one side of something to the other side of it: *The bridge across the river was closed.* □ *He wrote his name across the cheque.*

acrylic /ə'krılık/ *adjective*
used for describing a type of artist's paint that dries very quickly: *Most people prefer acrylic paint because it dries faster.*

acrylics /ə'krılıks/ *plural noun*
acrylic paints: *This book is a great introduction to painting with acrylics.*

act¹ /ækt/ *verb* (**acts, acting, acted**)
1 to do something for a particular purpose: *The police acted to stop the fight.*
2 to behave in a particular way: *The youths were acting suspiciously.* □ *He acts as if I'm not there.*
3 to have a part in a play or a film: *He acted in many films, including 'Reds'.*

act² /ækt/ *noun*
1 a single thing that someone does (*formal*): *I will never forget his act of kindness.* □ *This was an appalling act of violence.*
2 a law passed by the government: *The organization was set up by an Act of Congress in 1998.*
3 one of the main parts that a play is divided into: *Act two has a really funny scene.*

acting /'æktıŋ/ *uncountable noun*
the activity or profession of performing in plays or films: *I'd like to do some acting some day.*

action /'ækʃən/ *noun*
1 *uncountable* when you do something for a particular purpose: *The government is taking emergency action.*
2 something that you do on a particular occasion: *Peter could not explain his actions.*

active¹ /'æktıv/ *adjective*
moving around a lot; doing a lot of different things: *We've got three very active little kids.* □ *As you get older, it's important to keep active.*

'active² *noun*
in grammar, the form of a verb that you use to show that the subject performs the action. For example, in 'I saw him', the verb **see** is in the active. Compare with **passive**.

activity /æk'tıvıti/ *noun* (**activities**)
1 *uncountable* when people are doing things and there is a lot happening:

Children are supposed to get physical activity every day.
2 something that you spend time doing: *At our hotel, there were lots of activities for small children.*

actor /'æktə/ *noun*
someone whose job is acting in plays or films: *His father was an actor.*
→ Look at picture on P7

actress /'æktrəs/ *noun* (**actresses**)
a woman whose job is acting in plays or films: *She's a really good actress.*
→ Look at picture on P7

actual /'æktʃʊəl/ *adjective*
real, exact or genuine: *The stories in this book are based on actual people.*

> **LANGUAGE HELP**
> **Actual** is **not** used for talking about something that is happening now. For this meaning, use **current** or **present**.

actually /'æktʃʊəli/ *adverb*
really; in fact: *People call me Will, but I'm actually called William.*

> **LANGUAGE HELP**
> **Actually** is **not** used for talking about something that is happening now. For this meaning, use **currently** or **now**.

acute /ə'kju:t/ *adjective*
very severe or serious: *He was in acute pain.*

acute accent /ə'kju:t 'æksənt/ *noun*
a symbol that you put over vowels (= the letters a, e, i, o and u) in some languages to show how to pronounce that vowel. For example, there is an acute accent over the letter 'e' in the French word 'café'.

acute angle /ə'kju:t 'æŋgəl/ *noun*
an angle of less than 90°.

ad /æd/ *noun*
an advertisement (*informal*): *It costs £175 to place an ad in the newspaper for 30 days.*

AD /,eı 'di:/
used in dates to show the number of years that have passed since the year in which Jesus Christ was born. Compare with **BC**: *The church was built in 600 AD.*

adapt /ə'dæpt/ *verb* (**adapts, adapting, adapted**)
1 to change your ideas or behaviour in order to deal with a new situation:

The world will be different in the future, and we will have to adapt to the change.

2 to change something so that you can use it in a different way: *They adapted the library for use as an office.*

adaptable /əˈdæptəbəl/ *adjective*
able to deal with new situations: *Dogs and cats are easily adaptable to new homes.*

add /æd/ *verb* (**adds, adding, added**)
1 to put one thing with another thing: *Add the grated cheese to the sauce.*
2 to calculate the total of various numbers or amounts: *Add all the numbers together, and divide by three.*
3 to say something more: *'He's very angry,' Mr Smith added.*

add something up to find the total of various numbers or amounts: *Add up the number of hours you spent on the task.*

add up to something to form a total: *Altogether, the three bills add up to £2,456.*

addict /ˈædɪkt/ *noun*
1 someone who cannot stop doing something harmful or dangerous, such as using drugs: *His girlfriend is a former drug addict.*
2 someone who likes a particular activity very much (*informal*): *She is a TV addict.*

addicted /əˈdɪktɪd/ *adjective*
unable to stop taking or doing something that is harmful to you: *Many of the women are addicted to heroin.*

addiction /əˈdɪkʃən/ *noun*
1 when someone is unable to stop taking drugs, alcohol or some other harmful substance: *She helped him fight his drug addiction.*
2 a strong need to do a particular activity for as much time as possible: *We discussed our children's addiction to computer games.*

addition /əˈdɪʃən/ *uncountable noun*
the process of calculating the total of two or more numbers: *She can count to 100, and do simple addition problems.*

in addition/in addition to something used when you want to mention another thing relating to the subject you are discussing: *In addition to meals, drinks will be provided.*

address¹ /əˈdres/ *noun* (**addresses**)
1 the number of the building, the name of the street, and the town or city where you live or work: *'What's your address?' — 'It's 24 Cherry Road, Cambridge, CB1 5AW'.*
2 the location of a website on the Internet, for example, http://www.harpercollins.com: *Our website address is at the bottom of this page.*

address² /əˈdres/ *verb* (**addresses, addressing, addressed**)
1 to write a person's name and address on a letter: *One of the letters was addressed to her.*
2 to speak to a group of people formally: *He addressed the crowd of 17,000 people.*

a'ddress book *noun*
1 a book in which you write people's names and addresses
2 a computer program that you use to record people's email addresses and telephone numbers

adequate /ˈædɪkwət/ *adjective*
having enough of something; good enough: *One in four people worldwide do not have adequate homes.* □ *The food in the hotel was adequate, but plain.*

adhesive /ædˈhiːsɪv/ *noun*
a substance used for making things stick together: *Attach the mirror to the wall with a strong adhesive.*

adjective /ˈædʒɪktɪv/ *noun*
a word such as 'big' or 'beautiful' that describes a person or thing. Adjectives usually come before nouns or after verbs like 'be' and 'feel'.

adjust /əˈdʒʌst/ *verb* (**adjusts, adjusting, adjusted**)
to make a small change to something: *The company adjusts gas prices once a year.* □ *You can adjust the height of the table.*

administration /ædˌmɪnɪˈstreɪʃən/ *noun*
1 *uncountable* the job of managing a business or an organization: *A private company took over the administration of the local jail.*
2 the government of a country (*American*): *Three officials in the administration have resigned.*

administrative /ædˈmɪnɪstrətɪv/ *adjective*
relating to the management of a business or an organization: *Administrative costs were high.*

administrator /ædˈmɪnɪstreɪtə/ *noun*
a person whose job is to help manage

a business or an organization: *Tom has worked as a university administrator for 20 years.*

admiration /ˌædmɪˈreɪʃən/ *uncountable noun*

a strong feeling of liking and respect: *I have great admiration for him.*

admire /ədˈmaɪə/ *verb* (**admires, admiring, admired**)

to like and respect someone or something very much: *I admired her when I first met her.*

▶ **admirer** *noun* *He was an admirer of her paintings.*

admission /ædˈmɪʃən/ *noun*

1 *uncountable* permission to enter a place: *One man was refused admission to the restaurant.*

2 when you admit that you have done something wrong: *By the footballer's own admission, he is not playing well this season.*

3 *uncountable* the amount of money that you pay to enter a museum, park or other place: *Gates open at 10.30 a.m. and admission is free.*

admit /ædˈmɪt/ *verb* (**admits, admitting, admitted**)

1 to agree that you have done something wrong: *I am willing to admit that I made a mistake.*

2 to allow someone to enter a place or an organization: *She was admitted to law school.* ▫ *Security officers refused to admit him to the building.*

adolescent /ˌædəˈlesənt/ *adjective*

relating to young people who are no longer children but who have not yet become adults: *Her music is popular with adolescent girls.* ● **adolescent** *noun* *Adolescents don't like being treated as children.*

▶ **adolescence** /ˌædəˈlesəns/ *uncountable noun* *Adolescence is often a difficult period for young people.*

adopt /əˈdɒpt/ *verb* (**adopts, adopting, adopted**)

1 to begin to behave or live in a new way: *You need to adopt a more positive attitude.* ▫ *Try to adopt a healthy lifestyle.*

2 to take someone else's child into your own family and make them legally your son or daughter: *There are hundreds of people who want to adopt a child.*

▶ **adoption** *uncountable noun* *They gave their babies up for adoption.*

adore /əˈdɔː/ *verb* (**adores, adoring, adored**)

1 to feel strong love and admiration for someone: *She adored her parents and would do anything to please them.*

2 to like something very much (*informal*): *Richard adores university life.*

adult /ˈædʌlt/ *noun*

a fully grown person or animal: *Tickets cost £20 for adults and £10 for children.* ● **adult** *adjective* *I am the mother of two adult sons.*

adult

child

advance¹ /ædˈvɑːns/ *verb* (**advances, advancing, advanced**)

1 to move forward, often in order to attack someone: *Soldiers are advancing towards the capital.*

2 to make progress, especially in your knowledge of something: *Science has advanced greatly in the last 100 years.*

advance² /ædˈvɑːns, -ˈvæns/ *noun*

1 a movement forward, usually as part of a military operation: *Hitler's army began its advance on Moscow in June 1941.*

2 progress in understanding a subject or an activity: *There have been many advances in medicine and public health.*

in advance before a particular date or event: *We bought our tickets for the show in advance.*

advanced /ædˈvɑːnst/ *adjective*

1 modern: *This is one of the most advanced phones available.*

a

2 relating to people who are very good at something: *a dictionary for advanced learners of English*

advantage /æd'vɑ:ntɪdʒ/ *noun*

1 something that puts you in a better position than other people: *Being small gives our company an advantage.*

2 a way in which one thing is better than another: *The advantage of home-grown vegetables is their great flavour.*

take advantage of someone to unfairly get what you want from someone, especially when they are being kind to you: *She took advantage of him — borrowing money and not paying it back.*

take advantage of something to make good use of something while you can: *People are taking advantage of lower prices.*

adventure /æd'ventʃə/ *noun*

an experience that is unusual, exciting and perhaps dangerous: *I'm planning a new adventure in Alaska.*

adverb /'ædvɜːb/ *noun*

a word such as 'slowly', 'now', 'very' or 'happily' that adds information about an action, event or situation

advert /'ædvɜːt/ *noun*

information that tells you about something such as a product, an event or a job (*informal*): *Have you seen that new advert for Pepsi?*

advertise /'ædvətaɪz/ *verb* (**advertises, advertising, advertised**)

to tell people about something in newspapers, on television, on signs, or on the Internet: *They are advertising houses for sale in this magazine.* □ *The company advertises on radio stations.*

advertisement /æd'vɜːtɪsmənt/ *noun*

information that tells you about something such as a product, an event, or a job (*formal*): *They saw an advertisement for a job on a farm.* □ *an advertisement for a new film*

advertising /'ædvətaɪzɪŋ/ *uncountable noun*

the business of creating information that tells people about a product or an event: *I work in advertising.*

advice /æd'vaɪs/ *uncountable noun*

what you say to someone when you are telling them what you think they should do: *Take my advice and stay away from him!* □ *I'd like to ask you for some advice.*

advise /æd'vaɪz/ *verb* (**advises, advising, advised**)

to tell someone what you think they should do: *Passengers are advised to check in two hours before their flight.* □ *His lawyers advised him to plead guilty.*

adviser /æd'vaɪzə/ also **advisor** *noun*

an expert whose job is to give advice: *You should ask your financial adviser for advice.*

aerial /'eəriəl/ (*American:* **antenna**) *noun*

a piece of equipment that receives television or radio signals

aerobics /eə'rəʊbɪks/ *uncountable noun*

a form of exercise that makes your heart and lungs stronger: *I'd like to join an aerobics class to improve my fitness.*

aeroplane /'eərəpleɪn/ (*American:* **airplane**) *noun*

→ see **plane**

aerosol /'eərəsɒl/ *noun*

a metal container with liquid in it. When you press a button, the liquid comes out strongly in a lot of very small drops: *an aerosol spray can*

aesthetic /iːs'θetɪk/ *adjective*

relating to beauty and art: *We chose the flowers for their aesthetic value.*

▶ **aesthetically** /iːs'θetɪkli/ *adverb We want our products to be aesthetically pleasing.*

affair /ə'feə/ *noun*

1 an event or a group of related events: *She has handled the whole affair badly.* □ *Our wedding was a simple affair.*

2 a sexual relationship between two people who are not married to each other: *He was having an affair with the woman next door.*

affairs /ə'feəz/ *plural noun*

1 things in your life that you consider to be private: *Why are we so interested in the private affairs of famous people?*

2 important events and situations: *She is an expert on international affairs.*

affect /ə'fekt/ *verb* (**affects, affecting, affected**)

to cause someone or something to change

in some way: *This problem affects all of us.*
□ *This area was badly affected by the earthquake.*

affection /ə'fekʃən/ *uncountable noun*
the feeling of loving or liking someone a lot: *She thought of him with affection.*

affectionate /ə'fekʃənət/ *adjective*
showing that you love or like someone very much: *She's very affectionate, and she's always hugging the kids.*
▸ **affectionately** *adverb* *He looked affectionately at his niece.*

afford /ə'fɔːd/ *verb* (**affords, affording, afforded**)
can afford something to have enough money to pay for something: *Some people can't even afford a new TV.*

afloat /ə'fləʊt/ *adverb*
floating: *They tried to keep the ship afloat for several hours.*

afraid /ə'freɪd/ *adjective*
1 worried that something unpleasant may happen: *I was afraid that nobody would believe me.*
2 frightened because you think that something very unpleasant is going to happen to you: *I was afraid of the other boys.*
□ *Don't be afraid to ask for help.*

after /'ɑːftə/ *preposition*
1 happening later than a particular date or event: *He died after a long illness.* □ *After breakfast, Amy took a taxi to the station.*
● **after** *conjunction* *The phone rang two seconds after we arrived.*
2 following or chasing someone: *Why don't you go after him? He's your son.*

afternoon /,ɑːftə'nuːn/ *noun*
the part of each day that begins at lunchtime and ends at about six o'clock: *He's arriving in the afternoon.* □ *He stayed in his room all afternoon.*

aftershave /'ɑːftəʃeɪv/ *uncountable noun*
a liquid with a pleasant smell that men put on their faces after shaving

afterwards /'ɑːftəwʊd/ *adverb*
in the time after a particular event or time that you have already mentioned: *Shortly afterwards, the police arrived.*

again /ə'gen, ə'geɪn/ *adverb*
1 one more time: *He kissed her again.*
□ *Again there was a short silence.*
2 used for saying that something is now

in the same state it was in before: *He opened his case, took out a folder, then closed it again.*

against /ə'genst, ə'geɪnst/ *preposition*
1 touching someone or something: *She leaned against him.* □ *The rain was beating against the window panes.*
2 used for showing that you think that something is wrong or bad: *He was against the war.* ● **against** *adverb* *66 people voted in favour of the decision and 34 voted against.*
3 on the other side in a sports game or a competition: *This is the first of two games against Liverpool.*
4 used for talking about who or what you are trying to stop: *The security forces used violence against opponents of the government.*
□ *Vitamin E protects against heart disease.*
5 in opposition to: *She left the hospital against the doctors' advice.*
against the law/rules not according to a law or a rule: *It is against the law to use your mobile phone while you are driving.*

age¹ /eɪdʒ/ *noun*
1 the number of years that you have lived: *Diana left school at the age of 16.*
2 *uncountable* the state of being old: *He refuses to let age slow him down.*
3 a period in history: *the age of silent films*

age² /eɪdʒ/ *verb* (**ages, aging** or **ageing, aged**)
1 to cause someone to look much older than before: *Worry has aged him.*
2 to start to look older than before: *She has aged dramatically in recent months.*

aged /eɪdʒd/ *adjective*
of a particular age: *They have two children: Julia, aged 8, and Jackie, aged 10.*

agency /'eɪdʒənsi/ *noun* (**agencies**)
a business that provides a service: *I work in an advertising agency.*

agenda /ə'dʒendə/ *noun*
1 a set of things that you want to do: *They support the president's education agenda.*
2 a list of things to be discussed at a meeting: *I'll add it to the agenda for Monday's meeting.*

agent /'eɪdʒənt/ *noun*
a person whose job is to do business for another person or company: *I am buying direct, not through an agent.*

aggressive /ə'gresɪv/ *adjective*
behaving angrily or violently towards

other people: *Some children are much more aggressive than others.*

▶ **aggressively** *adverb* *They may react aggressively.*

ago /ə'gəʊ/ *adverb*
in the past; before now: *I got your letter a few days ago.*

agony /'ægəni/ *noun*
great physical or mental pain: *He tried to move, but screamed in agony.*

agree /ə'gri:/ *verb* (**agrees, agreeing, agreed**)
1 to have the same opinion as someone else about something: *I agree with you.* □ *Do we agree that there's a problem?*
2 to say that you will do something, or to accept something: *He agreed to pay me for the drawings.* □ *She agreed to my suggestion.*

agreement /ə'gri:mənt/ *noun*
a plan or a decision that two or more people have made: *After two hours' discussion, they finally reached an agreement.*

agriculture /'ægrɪkʌltʃə/ *uncountable noun*
the business or activity of taking care of crops and farm animals
▶ **agricultural** /,ægrɪ'kʌltʃərəl/ *adjective*
agricultural land

ah /ɑ:/ *exclamation*
a word used for showing that you understand something or that you are surprised or pleased: *Ah, I see what you mean.*

aha /ɑ:'hɑ:/ *exclamation*
a word used for showing that you finally understand something: *Aha! Here is the answer to my question.*

ahead /ə'hed/ *adverb*
1 in front of someone or something: *The road ahead was blocked.* □ *Dad went ahead to fetch the car.*
2 directly in front of you: *Brett looked straight ahead.*
3 winning in a competition: *Chelsea was ahead all through the game.*
4 in the future: *There are exciting times ahead.*

ahead of someone/something in front of you: *I saw a man thirty metres ahead of me.*
go ahead used when you are giving someone permission to do something: *'Can I borrow your dictionary?' — 'Sure, go ahead.'*

aid /eɪd/ *uncountable noun*
money, equipment or services that are

given to a country or to people, often after something very bad has happened to them: *They have promised billions of dollars in aid.*

in aid of someone/something in order to make money to help a particular organization: *We held a concert in aid of the Red Cross.*

AIDS /eɪdz/ *uncountable noun*
a disease that destroys the body's ability to fight other diseases: *Twenty-five per cent of adults there have AIDS.*

aim¹ /eɪm/ *verb* (**aims, aiming, aimed**)
1 to plan or hope to do something: *He is aiming for the 100-metre world record.* □ *The booklet aims to help pupils choose a career.*
2 to point something toward a person or a thing: *He was aiming the gun at Wright.*

aim² /eɪm/ *noun*
the purpose of something: *The aim of the event is to bring parents and children together.*

ain't /eɪnt/
short for 'am not', 'are not', 'is not', 'have not' and 'has not'. Many people think this use is wrong. (*informal*)

air¹ /eə/ *noun*
1 *uncountable* the mixture of gases all around us that we breathe: *Keith opened the window and felt the cold air on his face.*
2 the space around things or above the ground: *He was waving his arms in the air.*

air² /eə/ *adjective*
travel in aircraft: *Air travel will continue to grow at around 6% per year.*

'air-cond'itioned *adjective*
having a special piece of equipment that makes the air in a room or a vehicle colder: *All the rooms are air-conditioned, with en suite and satellite TV.*

'air-cond'itioning *uncountable noun*
a system for keeping the air cool and dry in a building or a vehicle

aircraft /'eəkrɑ:ft/ *noun* (**aircraft**)
an aeroplane or a helicopter: *The aircraft landed safely.*

'air force *noun*
a military force that uses aeroplanes: *the United States Air Force*

airline /'eəlaɪn/ *noun*
a company that carries people or goods in aeroplanes: *Most low-cost airlines do not serve food.*

airplane /'eəpleɪn/ *noun* (*American*)
→ see **aeroplane**

'air po‚llution *uncountable noun*
chemicals or other substances that have
a harmful effect on the air: *We think that air
pollution may be the cause of the illness.*

airport /'eəpɔːt/ *noun*
a place where aeroplanes come and go,
with buildings and services for
passengers: *Heathrow Airport is the busiest
international airport in the world.*

aisle /aɪl/ *noun*
a long narrow passage where people can
walk between rows of seats or shelves:
You'll find the peas in the frozen food aisle.
□ *Please do not leave bags in the aisle.*

alarm /ə'lɑːm/ *noun*
1 a piece of equipment that warns you of
danger, for example, by making a noise:
The fire alarm woke us at 5 a.m.
2 → see **alarm clock**: *Dad set the alarm for
eight the next day.*

a'larm clock *noun*
a clock that makes a noise to wake you up:
I set my alarm clock for 4.30.

album /'ælbəm/ *noun*
1 a collection of songs on a CD: *The band
released their new album on July 1.*
2 → see **book** in which you keep things
that you have collected: *Theresa showed me
her photo album.*

alcohol /'ælkəhɒl/ *uncountable noun*
1 drinks that can make people drunk:
Alcohol will not be served on the flight.
2 a liquid that is found in drinks such as
beer and wine. It is also used as a
chemical for cleaning things: *Clean the
wound with alcohol.*

alcoholic ¹ /‚ælkə'hɒlɪk/ *noun*
someone who drinks alcohol too often
and cannot stop: *He admitted that he is an
alcoholic.*

alcoholic ² /‚ælkə'hɒlɪk/ *adjective*
containing alcohol: *Wine and beer are
alcoholic drinks.*

alert ¹ /ə'lɜːt/ *adjective*
paying attention and being ready to deal
with anything that might happen: *We all
have to stay alert.*

alert ² /ə'lɜːt/ *verb* (**alerts, alerting,
alerted**)
to tell someone about a dangerous

situation: *He wanted to alert people to the
danger.*

A level /'eɪ ‚levəl/ *noun*
a British qualification that people
take when they are seventeen or eighteen
years old: *Laura is taking her A levels next
summer.*

algebra /'ældʒɪbrə/ *uncountable noun*
a type of mathematics in which letters
and signs are used to represent numbers

alien /'eɪliən/ *noun*
a creature from another planet: *Robin
Williams plays the part of an alien from the
planet 'Ork'.*

alike /ə'laɪk/ *adjective, adverb*
1 similar: *They all look alike to me.*
2 in a similar way: *They even dressed alike.*

alive /ə'laɪv/ *adjective*
living; not dead: *Is your father still alive?*

alkali /'ælkə‚laɪ/ *noun*
a substance that is the opposite of an
acid, which can burn your skin

all ¹ /ɔːl/ *adjective*
1 used for talking about everyone or
everything of a particular type: *Hugh and
all his friends came to the party.* □ *He loves all
literature.*
2 used for talking about the whole of
something: *Someone's used all the milk.* □ *Did
you eat all of it?*
all day/all night during the whole day,
or the whole night: *He watches TV all day.*
at all used for making negative sentences
stronger: *I never really liked him at all.*

all ² /ɔːl/ *adverb*
completely: *I went away and left her all alone.*

Allah /'ælə, 'ælɑ:/ *noun*
the name of God in Islam: *We thank Allah
that the boy is safe.*

allergic /ə'lɜːdʒɪk/ *adjective*
becoming ill when you eat, touch or
breathe something that does not usually
affect people in this way: *I'm allergic to cats.*

allergy /'ælədʒi/ *noun* (**allergies**)
a condition in which you become ill
when you eat, touch or breathe
something that does not usually affect
people in this way: *He has an allergy to nuts.*

alley /'æli/ *noun*
a narrow street between buildings

alliance /ə'laɪəns/ *noun*
a group of people, countries,

a

organizations, or political parties that work together: *The two parties formed an alliance.*

alligator /'ælɪgeɪtə/ *noun*
a long animal with rough skin, big teeth and short legs: *Do not feed the alligators.*

alligator

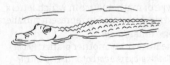

allocate /'æləkeɪt/ *verb* (**allocates, allocating, allocated**)
1 to give something to someone: *Some of the tickets will be allocated to students.*
2 to use something for a particular purpose: *They allocated one billion dollars for malaria research.*

allow /ə'laʊ/ *verb* (**allows, allowing, allowed**)
1 to give someone permission to do something: *We allow the children to watch TV after school.*
2 if you are allowed to do or have something, you have permission to do or have it: *I'm not allowed to go to the party.*
3 to give permission for something to happen: *Mobile phone use is not allowed in this carriage.*

all right¹ *adjective*
1 satisfactory or acceptable: *'What's your new teacher like?' – 'He's all right.'*
2 well or safe: *Are you all right?*

all right² *exclamation*
used for saying that you agree to something: *'I think you should go now.' – 'All right.'*

ally /'ælaɪ/ *noun* (**allies**)
1 a country that supports another country, especially in a war: *the Western allies*
2 someone who helps and supports another person: *He is a close ally of the president.*

almond /'ɑːmənd/ *noun*
a type of nut that you can eat or use in cooking: *She made a cake flavoured with almonds.*

almost /'ɔːlməʊst/ *adverb*
nearly but not completely: *We have been married for almost three years.* ◻ *He caught flu, which almost killed him.*

alone /ə'ləʊn/ *adjective, adverb*
1 without any other people: *She wanted to be alone.* ◻ *We were alone together.* ◻ *He lived alone in this house for almost five years.*
2 without help from other people: *Raising a child alone is very difficult.*

along¹ /ə'lɒŋ/ *preposition*
1 towards one end of a road or other place: *Pedro walked along the street.*
2 in or beside a road or another long narrow place: *There were traffic jams all along the roads.*

along² /ə'lɒŋ/ *adverb*
1 forwards: *He was talking as they walked along.*
2 with you: *Bring along your friends and family.*

alongside /ə,lɒŋ'saɪd/ *preposition*
1 next to: *He crossed the street and walked alongside Central Park.*
2 in the same place as: *He worked alongside Frank and Mark.*

aloud /ə'laʊd/ *adverb*
in such a way that other people can hear you: *When we were children, our father read aloud to us.*

alphabet /'ælfəbet/ *noun*
a set of letters that is used for writing words: *The Russian alphabet has 31 letters.*

alphabetical /,ælfə'betɪkəl/ *adjective*
following the normal order of the letters in the alphabet: *The books are arranged in alphabetical order.*

already /ɔːl'redi/ *adverb*
1 used for showing that one thing happened before another thing: *The meeting had already finished when we arrived.*
2 used for showing that a situation exists now or that it started earlier than expected: *We've already spent most of the money.* ◻ *Most of the guests have already left.*

> **LANGUAGE HELP**
> **already** or **yet**? In British English, you usually use **already** and **yet** with the perfect tenses. *I've already seen that film. Have they arrived yet?* In American English, people often use a past tense. *She already told us about the party. I didn't have any breakfast yet.*

also /'ɔːlsəʊ/ *adverb*
used for giving more information about something: *The book also includes an index of*

all US presidents. ☐ *We've got a big table and also some stools and benches.*

alter /'ɔːltə/ *verb* (**alters, altering, altered**)
to change: *World War II altered life in many ways.* ☐ *His appearance had altered since their last meeting.*

alternate¹ /'ɔːltəneɪt/ *verb* (**alternates, alternating, alternated**)
1 to do one and then the other: *Alternate between walking and running.*
2 to repeatedly happen or come one after another: *Rain alternated with snow.*

alternate² /ɔːl'tɜːnət/ *adjective*
1 repeatedly happening or coming one after another
2 happening on one day, week, etc, and not on the next day, week etc: *We go skiing on alternate years.*

alternative¹ /ɔːl'tɜːnətɪv/ *noun*
something that you can use or do instead of another thing: *The new treatment may provide an alternative to painkillers.*

alternative² /ɔːl'tɜːnətɪv/ *adjective*
1 different from something that you already have: *Alternative methods of travel were available.* ☐ *We are working on alternative proposals.*
2 different from the usual thing: *Have you considered alternative health care?*

alternatively /ɔːl'tɜːnətɪvli/ *adverb*
used for mentioning something different from what you have just said: *Hotels are not too expensive. Alternatively you could stay in a flat.*

although /ɔːl'ðəʊ/ *conjunction*
1 used for introducing an idea that may seem surprising: *Their system worked, although no one knew how.* ☐ *Although I was only six, I can remember seeing it on TV.*
2 used for introducing information that slightly changes what you have already said: *They all play basketball, although on different teams.*

altitude /'æltɪtjuːd/ *noun*
a measurement of height above the level of the sea: *The aircraft reached an altitude of*

about 39,000 feet. ☐ *The illness does not occur in areas of high altitude.*

altogether /ˌɔːltə'geðə/ *adverb*
including everyone or everything: *There were eleven of us altogether.*

aluminium /ˌælʊ'mɪniəm/ *uncountable noun*
a light metal used for making things such as cooking equipment and cans for food and drink: *We recycle aluminium cans.*

always /'ɔːlweɪz/ *adverb*
1 at all times; every time: *She's always late for school.* ☐ *She always gave me socks for my birthday.*
2 for ever: *I'll always love him.*
3 used when you are talking about something that someone does a lot and which annoys you: *Why are you always interrupting me?*

am /əm, STRONG æm/ → see **be**

a.m. /ˌeɪ 'em/ also **am**
used after a number when you are talking about a time between midnight and noon. Compare with **p.m.**: *I start work at 9 a.m. and I usually finish at 6 p.m.*

amateur /'æmətə/ *noun*
someone who does an activity as a hobby and not as a job ● **amateur** *adjective an amateur golfer*

amaze /ə'meɪz/ *verb* (**amazes, amazing, amazed**)
to surprise someone very much: *He amazed us with his knowledge of Italian history.*
▶ **amazed** *adjective I was amazed at how difficult it was.*

amazement /ə'meɪzmənt/ *uncountable noun*
the feeling you have when something surprises you very much: *I looked at her in amazement.*

amazing /ə'meɪzɪŋ/ *adjective*
very surprising, in a way that you like: *It's amazing what we can remember if we try.*
▶ **amazingly** *adverb She was an amazingly good cook.*

ambassador /æm'bæsədə/ *noun*
an important official person who lives in a foreign country and represents his or her own country there: *We met the ambassador to Poland.*

ambition /æm'bɪʃən/ *noun*
1 the feeling that you want very much to

do something at some time in the future: *His ambition is to sail around the world.*

2 *uncountable* the desire to be successful, rich or powerful: *These young people have hopes for the future and great ambition.*

ambitious /æm'bɪʃəs/ *adjective*

1 having a strong feeling that you want to be successful, rich or powerful: *Chris is very ambitious.*

2 needing a lot of work or money: *He has ambitious plans for the firm.*

ambulance /'æmbjʊləns/ *noun*
a vehicle for taking people to hospital

ambulance

amendment /ə'mendmənt/ *noun*
a change that is added to a law: *They have proposed an amendment to the bill.*

among /ə'mʌŋ/ *preposition*

1 in the middle of a group of people or things: *There were teenagers sitting among adults.*

2 included in a particular group: *We discussed it among ourselves.* □ *Don't worry; you're among friends.*

3 used for saying that most people in a group have a particular opinion or feeling: *There is concern among parents about teaching standards.*

4 used for saying that something is given to all of the people in a particular group: *The money will be shared among family members.*

> **LANGUAGE HELP**
> **among** or **between**? If there are more than two people or things, use **among**. If there are only two people or things, use **between**.

amount¹ /ə'maʊnt/ *noun*
how much of something that there is; how much of something that you have, need or get: *He needs that amount of money to live.* □ *I still do a certain amount of work for them.*

amount² /ə'maʊnt/ *verb* (amounts, amounting, amounted)
amount to something to add up to a particular total: *The payment amounted to £42 billion.*

amplifier /'æmplɪfaɪə/ *noun*
a piece of electrical equipment that makes sounds louder

amuse /ə'mjuːz/ *verb* (amuses, amusing, amused)
to make you laugh or smile: *The thought amused him.*
amuse yourself to do something so that you do not become bored: *As a child he amused himself listening to the radio.*

amused /ə'mjuːzd/ *adjective*
wanting to laugh or smile because of something: *For a moment, Jackson looked amused.* □ *Alex looked at me with an amused expression on his face.*

amusement /ə'mjuːzmənt/ *noun*
1 *uncountable* the feeling that you have when you think that something is funny: *Tom watched them with amusement.*
2 a way of passing the time pleasantly: *People did not have many amusements to choose from in those days.*

a'musement park *noun*
a place where people pay to ride on machines for fun

amusing /ə'mjuːzɪŋ/ *adjective*
making you laugh or smile: *It's an amusing programme that the whole family can enjoy.*

an /ən, STRONG æn/ *article*
used instead of 'a' before words that begin with vowel sounds

anaesthetic /ˌænɪs'θetɪk/ *noun*
a substance that doctors use to stop you feeling pain: *The operation was performed under a general anaesthetic.*

analogue also **analog** /'ænəlɒg/ *adjective*
used for describing a clock or a watch that shows the time using hands (= the long parts that move around and show the time) instead of numbers. Compare with **digital**.

analyse /'ænəlaɪz/ *verb* (analyses, analysing, analysed)
to consider something carefully in order to fully understand it or to find out what is in it: *We need more time to analyse the decision.* □ *They haven't analysed those samples yet.*

analysis /ə'nælɪsɪs/ *noun* (**analyses** /ə'nælɪsiːz/)
1 the process of considering something carefully in order to understand it or explain it: *Our analysis shows that the treatment was successful.*
2 *uncountable* the scientific process of finding out what is in something: *They collect blood samples for analysis.*

ancestor /'ænsestə/ *noun*
one of the people in your family who lived before you: *Our daily lives are so different from those of our ancestors.*

anchor /'æŋkə/ *noun*
a heavy object that you drop into the water from a boat to stop it moving away

ancient /'eɪnʃənt/ *adjective*
very old, or from a long time ago: *ancient Jewish traditions*

and /ənd, STRONG ænd/ *conjunction*
1 used for connecting two or more words or phrases: *She and Simon have already gone.* □ *I'm 53 and I'm very happy.*
2 used for connecting two words that are the same, in order to make the meaning stronger: *Learning becomes more and more difficult as we get older.* □ *We talked for hours and hours.*
3 used when one event happens after another: *I waved goodbye and went down the steps.*
4 used for showing that two numbers are added together: *Two and two makes four.*

angel /'eɪndʒəl/ *noun*
1 a being that some people believe can bring messages from God. In pictures, angels often have wings.
2 someone who is very kind and good: *Thank you so much; you're an angel.*

anger /'æŋgə/ *uncountable noun*
the strong emotion that you feel when you think that someone has behaved badly or has treated you unfairly: *Parents expressed anger at the decision.* ● **anger** *verb* (**angers, angering, angered**) *The decision angered some parents.*

angle /'æŋgəl/ *noun*
the space between two lines or surfaces that meet in one place. Angles are measured in degrees: *a 30 degree angle*

angle

45°　　90°

at an angle leaning, not straight: *He wore his hat at an angle.*

angry /'æŋgri/ *adjective* (**angrier, angriest**)
feeling a strong emotion when someone has done something bad, or someone has treated you unfairly: *We are very angry about the decision to close the school.* □ *An angry crowd gathered.*

LANGUAGE HELP
If someone is very angry, you can say they are **furious**. If they are less angry, you can say they are **annoyed** or **irritated**.

animal /'ænɪməl/ *noun*
1 a creature such as a dog or a cat, but not a bird, fish, insect or human: *He was attacked by wild animals.*
2 any living creature, including a human

animation /ˌænɪ'meɪʃən/ *uncountable noun*
the process of making films in which drawings appear to move: *computer animation*

ankle /'æŋkəl/ *noun*
the part of your body where your foot joins your leg: *John twisted his ankle badly.*

anniversary /ˌænɪ'vɜːsəri/ *noun* (**anniversaries**)
a date that is remembered because something special happened on that date in an earlier year: *They just celebrated their fiftieth wedding anniversary.*

announce /ə'naʊns/ *verb* (**announces, announcing, announced**)
to tell people about something officially: *He will announce tonight that he is resigning.* □ *She was planning to announce her engagement.*

announcement /ə'naʊnsmənt/ *noun*
information that someone tells to a lot of people: *The president is expected to make an announcement about his future today.* □ *An announcement told us that the train was going to be late.*

announcer /ə'naʊnsə/ *noun*
someone whose job is to talk between programmes on radio or television: *The radio announcer said it was nine o'clock.*

a

annoy /ə'nɔɪ/ *verb* (**annoys, annoying, annoyed**)

to make someone angry and upset: *Rosie said she didn't mean to annoy anyone.* □ *It annoyed me that she believed him.*

annoyed /ə'nɔɪd/ *adjective*

angry about something: *She was annoyed that Sasha was there.*

annoying /ə'nɔɪɪŋ/ *adjective*

making you feel angry and upset: *It's very annoying when this happens.*

annual /'ænjʊəl/ *adjective*

1 happening once every year: *They held their annual meeting on 20th May.*

▶ **annually** *adverb* *The prize is awarded annually.*

2 for a period of one year: *The company has annual sales of about £80 million.*

▶ **annually** *adverb* *El Salvador produces 100,000 tons of copper annually.*

anonymous /ə'nɒnɪməs/ *adjective*

without giving your name or saying who you are: *You can speak to a police officer at any time, and you can choose to remain anonymous.*

▶ **anonymously** *adverb* *The photographs were sent anonymously to the magazine's offices.*

another /ə'nʌðə/ *adjective*

1 one more person or thing of the same type: *We're going to have another baby.*

● **another** *pronoun* *'These biscuits are delicious.' – 'Would you like another?'*

2 a different person or thing: *I'll deal with this problem another time.* ● **another** *pronoun* *He said one thing and did another.*

one another used for showing that each member of a group does something to or for the other members: *These children are learning to help one another.*

answer¹ /'ɑːnsə/ *verb* (**answers, answering, answered**)

1 to say something back to someone who has spoken to you: *I asked him but he didn't answer.* □ *Williams answered that he didn't know.*

2 to pick up the telephone when it rings: *Why didn't you answer when I phoned?* □ *She didn't answer the telephone.*

3 to open the door when you hear a knock or the bell: *I knocked and Mary answered the door.* ● **answer** *noun* *I knocked at the front door and there was no answer.*

4 to write or say what you think is the correct answer to a question in a test: *Before you start to answer the questions, read the whole exam carefully.*

answer² /'ɑːnsə/ *noun*

1 a way to solve a problem: *There are no easy answers to this problem.*

2 the information that you give when you are doing a test: *I got three answers wrong.*

'answering machine or **answerphone** *noun*

a small machine that records telephone messages

ant /ænt/ *noun*

a small crawling insect that lives in large groups

antenna /æn'tenə/ *noun* (**antennae /æn'teniː/** or **antennas**)

> **LANGUAGE HELP**
> **Antennas** is the usual plural form for meaning **2**.

1 one of the two long, thin parts attached to the head of an insect that it uses to feel things with

antenna

2 (*American*) → see **aerial**

antibiotic /ˌæntibaɪ'ɒtɪk/ *noun*

a drug that is used for killing bacteria and treating infections: *Your doctor may prescribe antibiotics.*

anticipate /æn'tɪsɪpeɪt/ *verb* (**anticipates, anticipating, anticipated**)

to think about an event and prepare for it before it happens: *Organizers anticipate an even bigger crowd this year.*

anticipation /ænˌtɪsɪ'peɪʃən/ *uncountable noun*

a feeling of excitement about something that you know is going to happen: *The days before Christmas were filled with anticipation and excitement.*

in anticipation of something done because you believe that an event is going to happen: *Some schools were closed in anticipation of the bad weather.*

anticlockwise /ˌænti'klɒkwaɪz/ *adjective, adverb*

moving in the opposite direction to the direction in which the hands of a clock move

antiperspirant /ˌæntiˈpɜːspərənt/ *noun*
a substance that you put on your skin to stop you from sweating (= producing liquid through your skin when you are hot) *adjective* *Try using an antiperspirant for sensitive skin.*

antique /ænˈtiːk/ *noun*
an old object that is valuable because of its beauty or because of the way it was made: *Jill started collecting antiques as a hobby about a year ago.*

antisocial /ˌæntiˈseʊʃəl/ *adjective*
not friendly towards other people: *antisocial behaviour*

ˈanti-ˈviˈrus also **antivirus** *adjective*
protecting a computer from attack by viruses (= programs that enter your computer and stop it from working properly): *antivirus software*

antler /ˈæntlə/ *noun*
one of the two horns that are shaped like branches on the head of a male deer (= a large brown animal with long thin legs)

antonym /ˈæntənɪm/ *noun*
a word that means the opposite of another word

anus /ˈeɪnəs/ *noun* (**anuses**)
the hole from which solid waste matter leaves a person's body

anxiety /æŋˈzaɪɪti/ *noun* (**anxieties**)
a feeling of being nervous and worried: *Her voice was full of anxiety.*

anxious /ˈæŋkʃəs/ *adjective*
nervous or worried about something: *She became very anxious when he didn't come home.*
▶ **anxiously** *adverb* *They are waiting anxiously for news.*

any /ˈeni/ *adjective*
1 used in negative sentences to show that no person or thing is involved: *I don't have any plans for the summer holidays yet.* □ *We made this without any help.* • **any** *pronoun The children needed new clothes and we couldn't afford any.*
2 used in questions to ask if there is some of a particular thing: *Do you speak any foreign languages?* • **any** *pronoun I will stay and answer questions if there are any.*
3 used in positive sentences when you want to say that it does not matter which person or thing you choose: *I'll take any advice.*

any more/any longer used with negative sentences to say that something has stopped happening or is no longer true: *I couldn't hide the tears any longer.*

anybody /ˈenibɒdi/ *pronoun*
→ see **anyone**

anyhow /ˈenihaʊ/ *adverb*
→ see **anyway**

anyone /ˈeniwʌn/ *pronoun*

LANGUAGE HELP
You can also say **anybody**.

1 used in negative statements and questions instead of 'someone' or 'somebody': *I won't tell anyone I saw you here.* □ *Why would anyone want that job?*
2 used for talking about someone when the exact person is not important: *It's not a job for anyone who is slow with numbers.*
3 used for talking about all types of people: *Anyone could do what I'm doing.*

anything /ˈeniθɪŋ/ *pronoun*
1 used in negative statements and questions instead of 'something': *We can't do anything.* □ *She couldn't see or hear anything at all.* □ *Did you find anything?*
2 used for talking about something when the exact thing is not important: *More than anything else, he wanted to become a teacher.*
3 used for showing that you are talking about a very large number of things: *He is young and ready for anything.*

anyway /ˈeniweɪ/ *adverb*
used for suggesting that something is true despite other things that have been said: *I'm not very good at golf, but I play anyway.*

anywhere /ˈeniweə/ *adverb*
1 used in negative statements and questions instead of 'somewhere': *Did you try to get help from anywhere?* □ *I haven't got anywhere to live.*
2 used for talking about a place, when the exact place is not important: *I can meet you anywhere you want.*

apart /əˈpɑːt/ *adverb*
some distance from each other: *Ray and his sister lived just 25 miles apart.* □ *Jane and I live apart now.*

apart from someone/something
except for: *She's feeling better, apart from a slight headache.*

take something apart to separate something into parts: *He likes taking bikes apart and putting them together again.*

apartment /əˈpɑːtmənt/ *noun* (American)
→ see **flat**

ape /eɪp/ *noun*
a type of animal like a monkey that lives among trees in hot countries and has long, strong arms and no tail: *wild animals such as monkeys and apes*

apologize /əˈpɒlədʒaɪz/ *verb* (apologizes, apologizing, apologized)
to say that you are sorry: *He apologized to everyone.*
I apologize used as a formal or polite way of saying sorry: *I apologize for being late.*

apology /əˈpɒlədʒi/ *noun* (apologies)
something that you say or write in order to tell someone that you are sorry: *I didn't get an apology.* □ *We received a letter of apology.*

apostrophe /əˈpɒstrəfi/ *noun*
the mark (') that shows that one or more letters have been removed from a word, as in "isn't" and "we'll". It is also added to nouns to show possession, as in "Mike's car".

app /æp/ *noun*
a computer program with one main purpose, especially one that you use on a mobile phone: *The app translates conversations while you speak.*

apparent /əˈpærənt/ *adjective*
clear and obvious: *It's apparent that standards have improved.*

apparently /əˈpærəntli/ *adverb*
used for talking about something that seems to be true, although you are not sure whether it is: *Apparently, he has left.*

appeal /əˈpiːl/ *verb* (appeals, appealing, appealed)
1 to seem attractive or interesting to someone: *The idea appealed to him.*
2 to make a serious and urgent request to someone: *Police appealed to the public for help.*
□ *The president appealed for calm.* ● **appeal** *noun* *The police made an urgent appeal for help.*

appealing /əˈpiːlɪŋ/ *adjective*
pleasant and attractive: *The restaurant serves an appealing mix of Asian dishes.*

appear /əˈpɪə/ *verb* (appears, appearing, appeared)
1 to come into sight or begin to be seen:

A woman appeared at the far end of the street. □ *These small white flowers appear in early summer.*
2 to seem: *The boy appeared to be asleep.*

appearance /əˈpɪərəns/ *noun*
the way that someone or something looks: *He didn't mention her appearance.*

appendix /əˈpendɪks/ *noun* (appendixes)

LANGUAGE HELP
The plural form **appendices** /əpˈendɪsiːz/ is usually used for meaning **2**.

1 a small closed tube in the right side of your body: *They had to remove his appendix.*
2 extra information that is placed after the end of the main text of a book or a document: *an appendix to the main document*

appetite /ˈæpɪtaɪt/ *noun*
the feeling that you want to eat: *He had a healthy appetite, so I cooked huge meals.*

applaud /əˈplɔːd/ *verb* (applauds, applauding, applauded)
to clap your hands together to show that you like something: *The audience laughed and applauded.*

applause /əˈplɔːz/ *uncountable noun*
the noise that a group of people make when they all clap their hands together to show that they like something: *The crowd greeted the couple with loud applause.*

apple /ˈæpəl/ *noun*
a firm round fruit with green, red or yellow skin: *a crisp green apple*
→ Look at picture on P2

appliance /əˈplaɪəns/ *noun*
a machine that you use to do a job in your home (formal): *You can buy a DVD player from any shop that sells electronic appliances.*

applicant /ˈæplɪkənt/ *noun*
someone who formally asks to be considered for a job or a course: *The company keeps records on every job applicant.*

application /ˌæplɪˈkeɪʃən/ *noun*
1 a written request to be considered for a job or a course: *I filled in an application form.*
2 a piece of software that is designed to do a particular task in computing: *a software application*

apply /əˈplaɪ/ *verb* (applies, applying, applied)
1 to write a letter or write on a form in

order to ask for something such as a job: *I am applying for a new job.*

2 to be about a person or a situation: *This rule does not apply to you.*

appoint /əˈpɔɪnt/ *verb* (**appoints, appointing, appointed**)

to choose someone for a job or a position: *The bank appointed Kenneth Conley as manager of its office in Birmingham.*

appointment /əˈpɔɪntmənt/ *noun*

1 an arrangement to see someone at a particular time: *She has an appointment with her doctor.*

2 a job or a position of responsibility: *I decided to accept the appointment as music director.*

appreciate /əˈpriːʃieɪt/ *verb* (**appreciates, appreciating, appreciated**)

1 to like something: *Everyone can appreciate this kind of art.*

2 to be grateful for something that someone has done for you: *Peter helped me so much. I really appreciate that.*

▶ **appreciation** *noun He wants to show his appreciation for her support.*

apprentice /əˈprentɪs/ *noun*

a young person who works for someone in order to learn their skill: *Their son Dominic is an apprentice woodworker.*

approach /əˈprəʊtʃ/ *verb* (**approaches, approaching, approached**)

1 to move closer to something: *He approached the front door.* ☐ *When I approached, the girls stopped talking.*

2 to deal with a task, a problem or a situation, or to think about it in a particular way: *The bank has approached the situation in a practical way.* ● **approach** *noun* (**approaches**) *There are two approaches: spend less money or find a new job.*

appropriate /əˈprəʊpriət/ *adjective*

correct for a particular situation: *Is it appropriate that they pay for it?* ☐ *Wear clothes that are appropriate for the occasion.*

▶ **appropriately** *adverb Try to behave appropriately and ask intelligent questions.*

approval /əˈpruːvəl/ *uncountable noun*

1 when someone agrees to something: *The chairman gave his approval for an investigation.*

2 when you like and admire someone or something: *She wanted her father's approval.*

approve /əˈpruːv/ *verb* (**approves, approving, approved**)

1 to like someone or something or think they are good: *My father approves of you.*

2 to formally agree to a plan: *The directors have approved the change.*

approximate /əˈprɒksɪmət/ *adjective*

near the correct number, time or position, but not exact: *The approximate value of the flat is £300,000.*

▶ **approximately** *adverb They've spent approximately £150 million.*

apricot /ˈeɪprɪkɒt/ *noun*

a small, soft, round fruit with yellow flesh and a large seed inside: *a bag of dried apricots*

April /ˈeɪprɪl/ *noun*

the fourth month of the year: *I'm getting married in April.*

apron /ˈeɪprən/ *noun*

a piece of clothing that you wear over the front of your normal clothes, especially when you are cooking, in order to prevent your clothes from getting dirty

aquarium /əˈkweəriəm/ *noun*

1 a building where fish and sea animals live

2 a glass box filled with water, in which people keep fish

arch /ɑːtʃ/ *noun* (**arches**)

a structure that is curved at the top and is supported on either side: *The bridge is 65 feet high at the top of the main arch.*

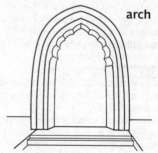

arch

archaeology /ˌɑːkiˈɒlədʒi/ *uncountable noun*

the study of the past that is done by examining the things that remain, such as buildings and tools

▶ **archaeological** /ˌɑːkiəˈlɒdʒɪkəl/ *adjective This is one of the region's most important archaeological sites.*

▶ **archaeologist** /ˌɑːkiˈɒlədʒɪst/ *noun*
Archaeologists discovered buildings from an ancient culture in Mexico City.

architect /ˈɑːkɪtekt/ *noun*
a person whose job is to design buildings

architecture /ˈɑːkɪtektʃə/ *uncountable noun*
1 the art of designing buildings: He studied architecture in Rome.
2 the style of the design of a building: modern architecture

are /ə, STRONG ɑː/ → see **be**

area /ˈeəriə/ *noun*
1 a particular part of a town, a country, a region or the world: There are 11,000 people living in the area.
2 a piece of land or a part of a building that is used for a particular activity: We had lunch in the picnic area.
3 the amount of flat space that a surface covers, measured in square units: What's the area of this triangle? □ The islands cover a total area of 400 square miles.

arena /əˈriːnə/ *noun*
a place where sports or entertainments take place: This is the largest indoor sports arena in the world.

aren't /ɑːnt/
short for 'are not'

argue /ˈɑːgjuː/ *verb* (**argues, arguing, argued**)
1 to disagree with someone about something: He was arguing with his wife about money. □ They are arguing over details.
2 to give the reasons why you think something is true: Employers argue that the law should be changed.

argument /ˈɑːgjʊmənt/ *noun*
1 a conversation in which people disagree with each other: Annie had an argument with one of the other girls.
2 what you say in order to try to convince people that your opinion is correct: This is a strong argument against nuclear power.

arise /əˈraɪz/ *verb* (**arises, arising, arose, arisen** /əˈrɪzən/)
to begin to exist: When the opportunity finally arose, thousands of workers left.

arithmetic /əˈrɪθmɪtɪk/ *uncountable noun*
basic number work, for example adding or multiplying: We teach the young children reading, writing and arithmetic.

arm¹ /ɑːm/ *noun*
1 one of the two parts of your body between your shoulders and your hands: She stretched her arms out.
2 the part of a chair on which you rest your arm when you are sitting down: Mack held the arms of the chair.
3 the part of a piece of clothing that covers your arm: The coat was short in the arms.

arm² /ɑːm/ *verb* (**arms, arming, armed**)
to provide someone with a weapon: She was so frightened that she armed herself with a rifle.

armchair /ˈɑːmtʃeə/ *noun*
a big comfortable chair that supports your arms: She was sitting in an armchair in front of the TV.
→ Look at picture on P5

armed /ɑːmd/ *adjective*
carrying a weapon, usually a gun: City police said the man was armed with a gun.
□ There were armed guards in the street outside their house.

armed forces *plural noun*
a country's military forces, who fight on the land, the sea, or in the air: members of the armed forces

armour /ˈɑːmə/ *uncountable noun*
special metal clothing that soldiers wore in the past for protection in battles: a suit of armour

armpit /ˈɑːmpɪt/ *noun*
the area of your body under your arm where your arm joins your shoulder: The water came up to my armpits.

arms /ɑːmz/ *plural noun*
weapons, especially bombs and guns: Soldiers searched the house for illegal arms.

army /ˈɑːmi/ *noun* (**armies**)
a large group of soldiers who are trained to fight battles on land: Perkins joined the Army in 1990.

arose /əˈrəʊz, əˈraʊz/ → see **arise**

around¹ /əˈraʊnd/ *preposition*
1 surrounding a place or an object or on all sides of it: She looked at the people around her.
2 along the edge of something, and back to the point where you started: We went for a walk around the lake. • **around** *adverb* They live in a little village with hills all around.

▢ They celebrated their win by running around on the football pitch.

3 to the other side of something: The man turned back and hurried around the corner.

4 on the other side of something: I looked around the door but the hall was empty.

5 in different parts of a place or area: Police say ten people have been arrested around the country.

around² /əˈraʊnd/ adverb

1 into different places: She moved things around so the table was under the window.

2 present in a place: Have you seen my wife anywhere around?

3 approximately: My salary was around £35,000.

arrange /əˈreɪndʒ/ verb (**arranges, arranging, arranged**)

1 to make plans for an event to happen: She arranged an appointment for Friday afternoon. ▢ I've arranged to see him on Thursday.

2 to carefully place things in a particular position: She enjoys arranging dried flowers.

arrangement /əˈreɪndʒmənt/ noun

1 a plan that someone makes so that something can happen: They're working on final arrangements for the meeting.

2 a group of things that have been placed in a particular position: a flower arrangement

arrest /əˈrest/ verb (**arrests, arresting, arrested**)

to take someone to a police station, because they may have broken the law: Police arrested five young men in the city.

● **arrest** noun Police later made two arrests.

arrival /əˈraɪvəl/ noun

when you arrive somewhere: It was the day after his arrival in Glasgow.

arrive /əˈraɪv/ verb (**arrives, arriving, arrived**)

to come to a place from somewhere else: Their train arrived on time. ▢ After a couple of hours, we arrived at the airport.

arrogant /ˈærəɡənt/ adjective

behaving in an unpleasant way towards other people because you believe that you are more important than them: Some rather arrogant people think they know everything.

▸ **arrogance** uncountable noun the arrogance of powerful people

arrow /ˈærəʊ/ noun

1 a long thin weapon that is sharp and pointed at one end: They were armed with bows and arrows.

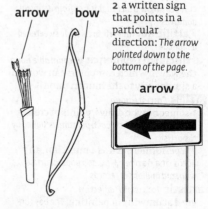

arrow   **bow**

2 a written sign that points in a particular direction: The arrow pointed down to the bottom of the page.

arrow

art /ɑːt/ noun

1 uncountable pictures or objects that are created for people to look at: modern American art

2 uncountable the activity of creating pictures or objects for people to look at: She decided she wanted to study art. ▢ Edinburgh College of Art and Design

3 plural activities such as music, painting, literature, film, theatre and dance: She knew she wanted a career in the arts.

artery /ˈɑːtəri/ noun (**arteries**)

one of the tubes in your body that carry blood from your heart to the rest of your body. Compare with vein: Many patients suffer from blocked arteries.

'art ˌgallery noun (**art galleries**)

a place where people go to look at art: It is the most famous art gallery in the world.

arthritis /ɑːˈθraɪtɪs/ uncountable noun

a medical condition in which the joints in your body swell and become painful: I have arthritis in my wrist.

artichoke /ˈɑːtɪtʃəʊk/ noun

a round green vegetable that has thick leaves and looks like a flower

article /ˈɑːtɪkəl/ noun

1 a piece of writing in a newspaper or magazine: I read about it in a newspaper article.

a

2 a word like 'a', 'an' or 'the', which shows whether you are talking about a particular thing or things in general

artificial /ˌɑːtɪˈfɪʃəl/ *adjective*
made by people, instead of nature: *The city has many small lakes, natural and artificial.*
□ *Try to follow a diet that is free from artificial additives.*
▸ **artificially** *adverb* *artificially sweetened lemonade*

artificial in'telligence *uncountable noun*
the way in which computers can work in a similar way to the human mind

artist /ˈɑːtɪst/ *noun*
1 someone who draws, paints or creates other works of art: *Each painting is signed by the artist.*
2 a performer such as a musician, an actor or a dancer: *He was a popular artist, who sold millions of records.*

artistic /ɑːˈtɪstɪk/ *adjective*
good at drawing or painting: *The boys are sensitive and artistic.*

as¹ /əz, STRONG æz/ *conjunction*
1 at the same time as something else happens: *We shut the door behind us as we entered.*
2 used for saying how something happens or is done: *Today, as usual, he was wearing a suit.* □ *Please do as you're asked first time.*
3 because: *As I was so young, I didn't have to pay.*

as² /əz, STRONG æz/ *preposition*
1 used when you are talking about someone's job: *She works as a nurse.*
2 used when you are talking about the purpose of something: *The fourth bedroom is used as a study.*

as...as used when you are comparing things, or saying how large or small something is: *It's not as easy as I expected.* □ *I'm nearly as big as you.*

as if used when you are saying that something appears to be the case: *Anne stopped, as if she didn't know what to say next.*

asap /ˌeɪ es eɪ ˈpiː/ *adverb*
short for 'as soon as possible'

ash /æʃ/ *noun* (**ashes**)
the grey powder that remains after something is burned: *the cold ashes of a log fire*

ashamed /əˈʃeɪmd/ *adjective*
feeling embarrassed or guilty because of someone or something: *I was ashamed of myself for getting so angry.*

ashore /əˈʃɔː/ *adverb*
from the sea onto the land: *The hurricane came ashore south of Miami.*

ashtray /ˈæʃtreɪ/ *noun*
a small dish for cigarette ash

aside /əˈsaɪd/ *adverb*
1 to one side of someone: *Sarah closed the book and put it aside.*
2 so that someone can pass you: *She stepped aside to let them pass.*

ask /ɑːsk, æsk/ *verb* (**asks, asking, asked**)
1 to say something to someone in the form of a question: *'How is Frank?' he asked.* □ *I asked him his name.* □ *She asked me if I was enjoying my dinner.*
2 to tell someone that you want them to do something: *We politely asked him to leave.*
3 to say that you would like to know or have something: *She asked for my address.*
4 to invite someone to go to an event or a place: *I asked Juan to the party.*

asleep /əˈsliːp/ *adjective*
sleeping: *My daughter was asleep on the sofa.*
fall asleep to start sleeping: *Sam soon fell asleep.*

asparagus /əˈspærəgəs/ *uncountable noun*
a long, thin, green vegetable

asparagus

aspect /ˈæspekt/ *noun*
a quality or a part of something: *He was interested in all aspects of the work here.*

aspirin /ˈæspɪrɪn/ *noun*
a mild drug that reduces pain

assassinate /əˈsæsɪneɪt/ *verb* (**assassinates, assassinating, assassinated**)
to murder someone for political reasons: *Robert Kennedy was assassinated in 1968.*
▸ **assassination** /əˌsæsɪˈneɪʃən/ *noun*
Pope John Paul survived an assassination attempt in 1981.

assault /əˈsɔːlt/ *noun*
a physical attack on a person: *There has been a series of assaults in the university area.*
● **assault** *verb* (**assaults, assaulting,**

assaulted) *The gang assaulted him with baseball bats.*

assemble /ə'sembəl/ *verb* (**assembles, assembling, assembled**)
1 to come together in a group: *The students assembled in the hall before classes.*
2 to collect something together or to fit the different parts of it together: *Workers were assembling aeroplanes.*

assembly /ə'sembli/ *noun* (**assemblies**)
1 a group of people gathered together for a particular purpose: *She made the announcement during a school assembly.*
2 *uncountable* the process of fitting the different parts of something together: *a car assembly line*

assess /ə'ses/ *verb* (**assesses, assessing, assessed**)
to consider a person, thing or situation in order to make a judgment about them: *I looked around and assessed the situation.* □ *The doctor is assessing whether I am well enough to travel.*
▶ **assessment** *noun* *We carry out an annual assessment of senior managers.*

asset /'æset/ *noun*
someone or something that is considered to be useful or valuable: *He is a great asset to the company.*

assignment /ə'saınmənt/ *noun*
a task that you are given to do, especially as part of your studies: *We give written assignments as well as practical tests.*

assist /ə'sıst/ *verb* (**assists, assisting, assisted**)
to help someone: *He was assisting elderly passengers with their luggage.*

assistance /ə'sıstəns/ *uncountable noun*
when you help someone: *Please let us know if you need any assistance.*

assistant /ə'sıstənt/ *noun*
a person who helps someone in their work: *Mr Johnson asked his assistant to answer the phone while he went out.*

associate¹ /ə'səusıeıt/ *verb* (**associates, associating, associated**)
to connect someone or something in some way with something else in your mind: *Some people associate money with happiness.*

associate² /ə'səusıət/ *noun*
a person you are closely connected with, especially at work: *business associates*

association /ə,səusi'eıʃən/ *noun*
an official group of people who have the same job, aim or interest: *We're all members of the National Basketball Association.*

assorted /ə'sɔːtıd/ *adjective*
different from each other in some way: *We have a selection of cotton jumpers in assorted colours.*

assortment /ə'sɔːtmənt/ *noun*
a group of things that are different from each other in some way: *There was an assortment of books on the shelf.*

assume /ə'sjuːm/ *verb* (**assumes, assuming, assumed**)
to suppose that something is true: *I assumed it was an accident.*

assure /ə'ʃuə/ *verb* (**assures, assuring, assured**)
to tell someone that something is true or will happen: *He assured me that there was nothing wrong.* □ *'Are you sure it's safe?' she asked anxiously. 'It couldn't be safer,' Max assured her.*

asterisk /'æstərısk/ *noun*
the sign *

asthma /'æsmə/ *uncountable noun*
a lung condition that causes difficulty in breathing

astonish /ə'stɒnıʃ/ *verb* (**astonishes, astonishing, astonished**)
to surprise someone very much: *The news astonished them.*
▶ **astonished** *adjective* *They were astonished to find the driver was a young boy.*

astonishing /ə'stɒnıʃıŋ/ *adjective*
very surprising: *She found that fact astonishing.*
▶ **astonishingly** *adverb* *Andrea was an astonishingly beautiful young woman.*

astonishment /ə'stɒnıʃmənt/ *uncountable noun*
a feeling of great surprise: *He looked at her in astonishment.*

astronaut /'æstrənɔːt/ *noun*
a person who is trained for travelling in space

astronomy /ə'strɒnəmi/ *uncountable noun*
the scientific study of

astronaut

a

the stars, planets and other natural objects in space

▶ **astronomer** *noun* an amateur astronomer

at /ət, STRONG æt/ *preposition*

1 used for saying where something happens or is situated: *He will be at the airport to meet her.* □ *I didn't like being alone at home.* □ *They agreed to meet at a restaurant.*

2 used for saying when something happens: *The funeral will take place this afternoon at 3.00 p.m.*

3 used for saying how fast, how far or how much: *I drove back down the motorway at normal speed.* □ *There were only two houses at that price.*

4 used when you direct an action towards someone: *He looked at Michael and laughed.*

5 used for saying that someone or something is in a particular state or condition: *The two nations are at war.*

6 used for saying what someone is reacting to: *Mum was annoyed at the mess.*

good at something doing something well: *I'm good at my work.*

ate /et, eɪt/ → see **eat**

athlete /ˈæθliːt/ *noun*

a person who is good at any type of physical sports, exercise or games, especially in competitions: *Jesse Owens was one of the greatest athletes of the twentieth century.*

athletic /æθˈletɪk/ *adjective*

relating to athletes and athletics: *He comes from an athletic family.*

atlas /ˈætləs/ *noun* (**atlases**)

a book of maps

ATM /ˌeɪ tiː ˈem/ *noun* (**ATMs**) (American)
→ see **cash machine**

atmosphere /ˈætməsfɪə/ *noun*

1 the layer of air or other gases around a planet: *The shuttle Columbia will re-enter the Earth's atmosphere tomorrow morning.*

▶ **atmospheric** /ˌætməsˈferɪk/ *adjective*
atmospheric gases

2 the general feeling that you get when you are in a place: *The rooms are warm and the atmosphere is welcoming.*

atom /ˈætəm/ *noun*

the very smallest part of something

atomic /əˈtɒmɪk/ *adjective*

relating to atoms or to power that is produced by splitting atoms: *atomic energy* □ *the atomic number of an element*

attach /əˈtætʃ/ *verb* (**attaches, attaching, attached**)

1 to fasten something to an object: *There is usually a label with instructions attached to the plant.* □ *Please use the form attached to this letter.*

2 to send a file with an email message: *I'm attaching the document to this email.*

attached /əˈtætʃt/ *adjective*

liking someone or something very much: *She is very attached to her family and friends.*

attachment /əˈtætʃmənt/ *noun*

a file that is attached to an email message and sent with it: *You can send your CV as an attachment to an email.*

attack¹ /əˈtæk/ *verb* (**attacks, attacking, attacked**)

1 to try to hurt someone: *I thought he was going to attack me.* □ *He was in the garden when the dog attacked.*

2 to use violence to enter a building or a town: *An armed gang attacked the bank.*

attack² /əˈtæk/ *noun*

1 an occasion when someone tries to hurt someone: *There have been several attacks on police officers.*

2 when you suffer badly from an illness: *an asthma attack*

attempt /əˈtempt/ *noun*

an occasion when you try to do something, often without success: *He made three attempts to rescue his injured colleague.* ● **attempt** *verb* (**attempts, attempting, attempted**) *She attempted to rescue the boy from the river.*

attend /əˈtend/ *verb* (**attends, attending, attended**)

1 to be present at an event: *Thousands of people attended the wedding.* □ *I was invited but I was unable to attend.*

2 to go to a school, college or church regularly: *They attended college together.*

▶ **attendance** *uncountable noun*
Attendance at the school is always high.

attendant /əˈtendənt/ *noun*

someone whose job is to serve people in a public place: *Tony Williams was working as a car park attendant in Leeds.*

attention /əˈtenʃən/ *uncountable noun*

1 when you look at someone or something, listen to them or think about them carefully: *Can I have your attention?*

2 when someone is dealing with you or

caring for you: *Each year more than two million people need medical attention.*

pay attention to watch and listen carefully: *Are you paying attention to what I'm saying?*

attic /'ætɪk/ *noun*
a room at the top of a house just under the roof

attitude /'ætɪtjuːd/ *noun*
the way that you think and feel about something: *You need to change your attitude to life.*

attract /ə'trækt/ *verb* (**attracts, attracting, attracted**)
1 to cause someone or something to come to a place: *The museum is attracting many visitors.*
2 used for describing how one object causes a second object to move towards it: *Opposite ends of a magnet attract each other.*
be attracted to someone/something to like someone or something, and to be interested in knowing more about them: *I was attracted to her immediately.*

attraction /ə'trækʃən/ *noun*
1 *uncountable* a feeling of liking someone: *His attraction to her was growing.*
2 something that people can visit for interest or enjoyment: *DisneyWorld is an important tourist attraction.*

attractive /ə'træktɪv/ *adjective*
pleasant to look at: *She's a very attractive woman.* ◻ *The flat was small but attractive.*

aubergine /'əʊbəʒiːn/ (American: **eggplant**) *noun*
a vegetable with a smooth, dark purple skin

auction /'ɔːkʃən/ *noun*
a public sale where items are sold to the person who offers the most money: *The painting sold for £400,000 at auction.*
● **auction** *verb* (**auctions, auctioning, auctioned**) *Eight drawings by French artist Jean Cocteau will be auctioned next week.*

audience /'ɔːdiəns/ *noun*
all the people who are watching or listening to a performance, a film or a television programme: *There was a TV audience of 35 million.*

audio /'ɔːdiəʊ/ *adjective*
used for recording and producing sound: *audio and video files*

audition /ɔː'dɪʃən/ *noun*
a short performance that an actor, a dancer or a musician gives so that someone can decide if they are good enough to be in a play, film or orchestra: *She went to an audition for a Broadway musical.*

August /'ɔːgəst/ *noun*
the eighth month of the year: *The film comes out in August.* ◻ *My new job starts on 22 August.*

aunt /ɑːnt/ *noun*
the sister of your mother or father, or the wife of your uncle: *She wrote to her aunt in Manchester.* ◻ *Aunt Margaret is coming to visit next week.*
→ Look at picture on P8

authentic /ɔː'θentɪk/ *adjective*
real: *They serve authentic Italian food.*

author /'ɔːθə/ *noun*
1 the person who wrote a piece of writing: *Jill Phillips is the author of the book 'Give Your Child Music'.*
2 a person whose job is writing books: *Haruki Murakami is Japan's best-selling author.*

authority /ɔː'θɒrɪti/ *noun* (**authorities**)
1 *uncountable* the power to control other people: *Only the police have the authority to close roads.* ◻ *He is now in a position of authority.*
2 *plural* the people who are in charge of everyone else: *The authorities are investigating the attack.*
3 an official organization or government department: *the Local Education Authority*

authorize /'ɔːθəraɪz/ *verb* (**authorizes, authorizing, authorized**)
to give your permission for something to happen: *Only the president could authorize its use.*
▶ **authorization** /ˌɔːθəraɪ'zeɪʃən/ *uncountable noun* *We didn't have authorization from the general to leave.*

autobiography /ˌɔːtəbaɪ'ɒgrəfi/ *noun* (**autobiographies**)
the story of your life, that you write yourself: *He published his autobiography last autumn.*
▶ **autobiographical** /ˌɔːtəbaɪə'græfɪkəl/ *adjective* *an autobiographical novel*

autograph /'ɔːtəɡrɑːf/ *noun*
the signature of someone famous: *He asked for her autograph.*

automatic /ˌɔːtəˈmætɪk/ *adjective*
1 an automatic machine works when no one is operating it: *Modern trains have automatic doors.*
2 done without thinking: *All of the automatic body functions, even breathing, are affected.*
▸ **automatically** /ˌɔːtəˈmætɪkəli/ *adverb* *You will automatically wake up after 30 minutes.*

automobile /ˈɔːtəməbiːl/ *noun* (American) → see **car**

autumn /ˈɔːtəm/ (American: **fall**) *noun* the season between summer and winter when the weather becomes cooler and the leaves fall off the trees

auxiliary verb /ɔːɡˈzɪljəri ˌvɜːb/ *noun* a verb that you can combine with another verb to change its meaning slightly. In English, 'be', 'have' and 'do' are auxiliary verbs.

available /əˈveɪləbəl/ *adjective*
1 that you can find or get: *Breakfast is available from 6 a.m.*
2 not busy and free to do something: *Mr Leach is not available for interviews today.*

avalanche /ˈævəlɑːntʃ/ *noun* a large amount of snow or earth that falls down the side of a mountain

avenue /ˈævɪnjuː/ *noun*
1 sometimes used in the names of streets. The written short form 'Ave.' is also used: *They live on Park Avenue.*
2 a straight road, especially one with trees on either side

average ¹ /ˈævərɪdʒ/ *noun*
1 the result that you get when you add two or more amounts together and divide the total by the number of amounts you added together: *'What's the average of 4, 5 and 6?' — '5.'* ● **average** *adjective* *The average price of goods went up by just 2.2%.*
2 the normal amount or quality for a particular group: *Rainfall was twice the average for this time of year.* ● **average** *adjective* *The average adult man burns 1,500 to 2,000 calories per day.*

average ² /ˈævərɪdʒ/ *adjective* ordinary: *He seemed to be a pleasant, average guy.*

avocado /ˌævəˈkɑːdəʊ/ *noun* a fruit with dark green skin and a large seed in the middle: *crab and avocado salad*

avoid /əˈvɔɪd/ *verb* (**avoids, avoiding, avoided**)
1 to do something in order to stop something unpleasant from happening: *It was a last-minute attempt to avoid a disaster.*
2 to choose not to do something: *I avoid working in public places.*
3 to keep away from a person or thing: *She went to the women's toilets to avoid him.*

> **LANGUAGE HELP**
> Remember that you **cannot** say that you 'avoid to do something'.

awake /əˈweɪk/ *adjective* not sleeping: *I stayed awake until midnight.*

award /əˈwɔːd/ *noun* a prize that a person is given for doing something well: *He won the National Book Award for fiction.* ● **award** *verb* (**awards, awarding, awarded**) *She was awarded the prize for both films.*

aware /əˈweə/ *adjective* knowing about something: *They are well aware of the danger.*
▸ **awareness** *uncountable noun* *We are trying to raise awareness of the pollution problem.*

away /əˈweɪ/ *adverb*
1 moving in a direction so that you are no longer in a place: *He walked away from his car.*
2 not in the place where people expect you to be: *Jason was working away from home for a while.*
3 due to happen after a particular period of time: *Christmas is now only two weeks away.*
4 not near a person or place: *Remember to stay a safe distance away from the car in front.*
5 at an opponent's sports ground. Compare with **home**: *Canada's Davis Cup team will play away against the Netherlands in February.* □ *Charlton are about to play an important away match.*
put something away to put something where it should be: *I put my book away and went to bed.*

awesome /ˈɔːsəm/ *adjective*
1 very powerful or frightening: *I love the awesome power of the ocean waves.*
2 very good or special (*informal*): *We all agreed the game was awesome.*

awful /ˈɔːfʊl/ *adjective*
very bad: *I thought he was an awful actor.*
▫ *There was an awful smell of paint.*

awkward /ˈɔːkwəd/ *adjective*
1 embarrassing and difficult to deal with:
He kept asking awkward questions.
▸ **awkwardly** *adverb* There was an
awkwardly long silence.
2 difficult to use or carry: *The bicycle was
small but awkward to carry.*
3 looking strange or uncomfortable:
*Amy made an awkward movement with
her hands.*
▸ **awkwardly** *adverb* He fell awkwardly.

axe /æks/ *noun*
a tool with a heavy metal blade and a long
handle that is used for cutting wood

axis /ˈæksɪs/ *noun* (**axes**)
1 an imaginary line through the middle
of something: *The Earth spins around its axis.*
2 one of the two lines on which you mark
points to show measurements or
amounts: *We can label the axes: time is on the
vertical axis and money is on the horizontal one.*

axis

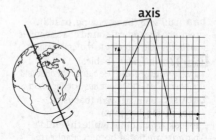

Bb

baa /bɑː/ *verb* (**baas, baaing, baaed**)
to make the typical sound of a sheep: *He sat by the tent, listening to the lambs baaing.*

baby /'beɪbi/ *noun* (**babies**)
a very young child: *He bathed the baby and put her to bed.* □ *My wife has just had a baby.*

babysit /'beɪbɪsɪt/ *verb* (**babysits, babysitting, babysat**)
to look after a child while the child's parents are not at home: *I promised to babysit for Mrs Plunkett.*

babysitter /'beɪbɪˌsɪtə/ *noun*
a person who looks after a child while the child's parents are not at home: *It can be difficult to find a good babysitter.*

bachelor /'bætʃələ/ *noun*
a man who has never married

back¹ /bæk/ *adverb*
1 in the direction that is behind you: *She stepped back from the door.*
2 in or to the place where someone or something was before: *I went back to bed.* □ *I'll be back as soon as I can.* □ *Put the meat back in the freezer.*
3 used when you are talking about phoning or writing to someone after they have phoned or written to you: *I'll call you back after dinner.* □ *I wrote to Anna last week but she hasn't written back yet.*
back and forth in one direction and then in the opposite direction: *He paced back and forth.*

back² /bæk/ *noun*
1 the part of your body from your neck to your waist that is on the opposite side to your chest: *Her son was lying on his back.*
→ Look at picture on P1
2 the side or part of something that is furthest from the front: *She was in a room at the back of the shop.* ● **back** *adjective She opened the back door.* □ *Ann sat in the back seat of their car.*
back to front with the back where the front should be: *You're wearing your t-shirt*
back to front. □ *He wears his cap back to front.*
say/do something behind someone's back to say or do something when someone is not there, so that they do not know what you have said or done: *You shouldn't criticize her behind her back.*

back³ /bæk/ *verb* (**backs, backing, backed**)
1 to move a vehicle backwards: *He backed his car out of the driveway.*
2 to support someone: *We told them what we wanted to do, and they agreed to back us.*
back away to move away from someone or something, often because you are frightened: *James stood up, but the girl backed away.*
back off to move away from someone or something, in order to avoid problems: *When she saw me she backed off, looking worried.*
back out to decide not to do something that you had agreed to do: *They've backed out of the project.*
back something up
1 to show evidence to suggest that something is true: *He didn't have any proof to back up his story.*
2 to make a copy of a computer file so that you can use it if the original file is lost: *Make sure you back up your files every day.*

backbone /'bækbəʊn/ *noun*
the line of bones down the middle of your back

background /'bækgraʊnd/ *noun*
1 the type of family you come from and the type of education and experiences you have had: *He came from a very poor background.*
2 sounds, such as music, that you can hear but that you are not listening to with your full attention: *I heard the sound of music in the background.*
3 the part of a picture that is behind the main things or people in it. Compare with **foreground**: *I looked at the man in the background of the photograph.*

backpack /ˈbækpæk/ *noun*
a bag that you carry on your back

backstroke /ˈbækstrəʊk/ *uncountable noun*
a way of swimming on your back: *Linda swam backstroke and Isabelle swam breaststroke.*

backup /ˈbækʌp/ also **back-up** *noun*
1 *uncountable* extra help that you can get if you need it: *If you need backup, just call me.*
2 a copy of a computer file that you can use if the original file is lost or damaged: *It is very important to make backups of your data.*

backward /ˈbækwəd/ *adjective*
1 in the direction that is behind you: *He walked away without a backward glance.*
2 without modern industries and machines: *backward nations*

backwards /ˈbækwədz/ *adverb*
1 towards the direction that is behind you: *He took two steps backwards.*
2 in the opposite way to the usual way: *Kate counted backwards from ten to zero.*
backwards and forwards in one direction and then in the opposite direction over and over again: *Jennifer moved backwards and forwards in time with the music.*

backyard /bækˈjɑːd/ also **back yard** *noun* (American)
the land at the back of a house: *The house has a large backyard.*

bacon /ˈbeɪkən/ *uncountable noun*
strips of salted or smoked meat that comes from a pig: *We had bacon and eggs for breakfast.*

bacteria /bækˈtɪəriə/ *plural noun*
very small living things that can make people ill: *There were high levels of dangerous bacteria in the water.*
▸ **bacterial** *adjective Tuberculosis is a bacterial disease.*

bad /bæd/ *adjective* (**worse, worst**)
1 unpleasant or harmful: *When the weather was bad, I stayed indoors.* ◻ *When Ross and Judy heard the bad news, they were very upset.* ◻ *Too much coffee is bad for you.*
2 of a very low standard, quality or amount: *bad housing* ◻ *The school's main problem is that teachers' pay is so bad.*
3 unable to do something well: *He's a bad driver.*

4 painful or not working properly because of illness or injury: *Joe has a bad back.*
5 rude or offensive: *I don't like to hear bad language in the street.*
be bad at something/be bad at doing something to be unable to do something well: *I'm bad at football.* ◻ *He's bad at making decisions.*
feel bad about something to feel sorry or guilty about something: *I feel bad that he's doing most of the work.*
go bad to become too old to eat: *I think this fish has gone bad.*
not bad quite good (*informal*): *'How are you feeling?' — 'Not bad.'*

badge /bædʒ/ *noun*
a small piece of metal or plastic that you wear on your clothes to show people who you are: *I showed him my police badge.*

badger /ˈbædʒə/ *noun*
a wild animal, with a white head with two wide black stripes, that lives beneath the ground and comes out to feed at night

badger

badly /ˈbædli/ *adverb* (**worse, worst**)
1 in a way that is not successful or effective: *I was angry because I played so badly.* ◻ *The whole project was badly managed.*
2 seriously or severely: *The fire badly damaged a church.* ◻ *One man was killed and another was badly injured.*
3 very much: *Why do you want to go so badly?*

badminton /ˈbædmɪntən/ *uncountable noun*
a game played by two or four players in which the players get points by hitting a small object (= a shuttlecock) across a high net using a racket

bag /bæg/ *noun*
a container made of paper, plastic or leather, used for carrying things: *He ate a whole bag of sweets.* ◻ *The old lady was carrying a heavy shopping bag.*

baggage /ˈbægɪdʒ/ *uncountable noun*
all the bags that you take with you when you travel: *He collected his baggage and left the airport.*

bags

backpack

carrier bag

handbag

baggy /'bægi/ *adjective* (**baggier, baggiest**)
big and loose: *He wore baggy trousers and no shirt.*

bait /beɪt/ *noun*
food that you put on a hook or in a trap to catch fish or animals: *This shop sells fishing bait.*

bake /beɪk/ *verb* (**bakes, baking, baked**)
to cook food in an oven: *How did you learn to bake cakes?* □ *Bake the fish in the oven for 20 minutes.*

baked 'beans *plural noun*
small white beans cooked in tomato sauce, sold in a tin: *baked beans on toast*

baker /'beɪkə/ *noun*
1 a person whose job is to make and sell bread and cakes
2 (*also* **baker's**) a shop where you can buy bread and cakes: *If you're going to the baker's, could you get me some bread, please?*

bakery /'beɪkəri/ *noun* (**bakeries**)
a place where bread and cakes are baked or sold: *The town has two bakeries.*

baking /'beɪkɪŋ/ *uncountable noun*
the activity of cooking bread or cakes in an oven: *The children want to do some baking.*

balance¹ /'bæləns/ *verb* (**balances, balancing, balanced**)
1 to keep yourself or something else steady, to avoid falling: *I balanced on Mark's shoulders.* □ *She balanced the chair on top of the table.*
2 to give the same importance to two different things: *Bob has difficulty balancing the demands of his work with the needs of his family.*

balance² /'bæləns/ *noun*
1 *uncountable* the ability to stay steady and not to fall over: *Dan lost his balance and started to fall.*
2 when all the different parts of something have the same importance: *It is important to have a balance between work and play.*
3 the amount of money you have in your bank account: *I'll need to check my bank balance first.*

balanced /'bælənst/ *adjective*
fair and reasonable: *Journalists should present balanced reports.*
a balanced diet a diet containing the right amounts of different foods to keep your body healthy: *Eat a healthy, balanced diet and get regular exercise.*

balcony /'bælkəni/ *noun* (**balconies**)
1 a place where you can stand or sit on the outside of a building, above the ground
2 the seats upstairs in a theatre

bald /bɔːld/ *adjective* (**balder, baldest**)
with no hair, or very little hair, on the top of your head: *He rubbed his hand across his bald head.*

ball /bɔːl/ *noun*
1 a round object that you kick, throw or hit in some sports and games: *Two young boys were kicking a ball.* □ *a tennis ball*
2 anything that has a round shape: *Form the butter into small balls.*
3 a large formal party where people dance: *My parents go to a New Year's ball every year.*

ballet /'bæleɪ/ *noun*
1 *uncountable* a type of dancing with carefully planned movements: *We saw a film about a boy who becomes a ballet dancer.*
2 a performance of this type of dancing that tells a story: *My favourite ballet is 'Swan Lake'.*

balloon /bəˈluːn/ *noun*
1 a small, thin, brightly-coloured rubber bag that you blow air into so that it becomes larger. Balloons are used for decoration at parties: *Large balloons floated above the crowd.*
2 (*also* **hot-air balloon**) a large bag full of hot air, with a basket attached that people can stand in and ride through the air

ballpark figure /ˈbɔːlpɑːk ˈfɪgə/ *noun*
an approximate figure: *I can't tell you the exact cost, but £500 is a ballpark figure.*

bamboo /bæmˈbuː/ *uncountable noun*
a tall plant that grows in hot countries, with hard, hollow stems that are sometimes used for making furniture: *We sat on big bamboo chairs with soft cushions.*

ban /bæn/ *verb* (**bans, banning, banned**)
to say officially that something must not be done, shown or used: *Ireland was the first country to ban smoking in all workplaces.* □ *The film was banned by the French government.*
● **ban** *noun The report proposes a ban on plastic bags.*

banana /bəˈnɑːnə/ *noun*
a long curved fruit with yellow skin: *I bought milk, bread and a bunch of bananas.*
→ Look at picture on P2

band /bænd/ *noun*
1 a group of people who play music together: *Matt's a drummer in a rock band.*
2 a flat, narrow strip of material that you wear around your head or wrists, or that is part of a piece of clothing: *Before treatment, doctors and nurses should always check the patient's wristband.*
3 a strip or circle of metal or another strong material that makes something stronger, or that holds several things together: *He took out a white envelope with a rubber band around it.*

bandage /ˈbændɪdʒ/ *noun*
a long strip of cloth that is wrapped around an injured part of your body to protect or support it: *We put a bandage on John's knee.* ● **bandage** *verb* (**bandages, bandaging, bandaged**) *Mary finished bandaging her sister's hand.*

Band-Aid *also* **band-aid** *noun* (*trademark, American*)
→ see **plaster**: *She had a Band-Aid on her ankle.*

bang /bæŋ/ *verb* (**bangs, banging, banged**)
to hit something hard, making a loud noise: *Lucy banged on the table with her fist.* □ *The toddler was sitting on the floor, banging two pots together.* ● **bang** *noun I heard four or five loud bangs.*

bangs /bæŋz/ *plural noun* (*American*)
→ see **fringe**: *Both of them had blond bangs.*

banister /ˈbænɪstə/ *noun*
a long narrow piece of wood that you hold on to when you are walking down stairs

banjo /ˈbændʒəʊ/ *noun*
a musical instrument that looks like a guitar, with a round body, a long neck and four or more strings

bank¹ /bæŋk/ *noun*
1 a place where people can keep their money: *He had just £14 in the bank when he died.*
2 a raised area of ground along the edge of a river: *We walked along the east bank of the river.*

bank² /bæŋk/ *verb* (**banks, banking, banked**)
bank on someone/something to rely on someone or something: *Everyone is banking on his recovery.*

ˈbank acˌcount *noun*
an arrangement with a bank where they look after your money for you

ˈbank card or **ATM card** *noun*
a plastic card that your bank gives you so that you can get money from your bank account using a cash machine

bankrupt /ˈbæŋkrʌpt/ *adjective*
without enough money to pay your debts: *If the company cannot sell its products, it will go bankrupt.*

banner /ˈbænə/ *noun*
a long strip of cloth or plastic with something written on it: *The crowd danced and sang, and waved banners reading 'No War'.*

baptism /ˈbæptɪzəm/ *noun*
a Christian ceremony in which a person is baptized: *Father Wright regularly performs weddings and baptisms.*

baptize /bæpˈtaɪz/ *verb* (**baptizes, baptizing, baptized**)
to touch or cover someone with water, to show that they have become a member of the Christian church: *Mary decided to become a Christian and was baptized.*

bar /bɑː/ *noun*

1 a long, straight piece of metal: *The building had bars on all of the windows.*

2 a small block of something: *What is your favourite chocolate bar?*

3 a place where you can buy and drink alcoholic drinks: *Lyndsay met her boyfriend at a local bar.*

4 a place where you can buy drinks and snacks: *a coffee bar*

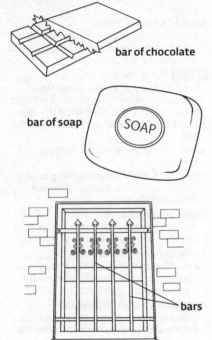

bar of chocolate

bar of soap

bars

barbecue /'bɑːbɪkjuː/ *also* **barbeque, BBQ** *noun*

1 a piece of equipment that you use for cooking outdoors

2 a party where you cook food on a barbecue outdoors: *On Saturday we had a barbecue on the beach.* ●**barbecue** *verb* (**barbecues, barbecuing, barbecued**) *Tuna can be grilled, fried or barbecued.*

barber /'bɑːbə/ *noun*

1 a person whose job is to cut men's hair

2 (*also* **barber's**) a shop where men can have their hair cut

bare /beə/ *adjective* (**barer, barest**)

1 not covered by any clothing: *Jane's feet were bare.*

2 not covered or decorated with anything: *The flat has bare wooden floors.*

3 empty: *His refrigerator was bare.*

barefoot /'beəfʊt/ *adjective*

not wearing shoes or socks: *He walked 10 miles barefoot to find help.*

barely /'beəli/ *adverb*

only just true or possible: *Anna could barely remember the ride to the hospital.*

bargain /'bɑːgɪn/ *noun*

something that is being sold at a lower price than usual: *At this price the dress is a bargain.*

barge /bɑːdʒ/ *noun*

a long, narrow boat with a flat bottom, used for carrying heavy loads: *The barges carried water, food and medicines.*

bark¹ /bɑːk/ *verb* (**barks, barking, barked**)

to make the short, loud noise that a dog makes: *Don't let the dogs bark.* ●**bark** *noun* *Your child may be afraid of a dog's bark, or its size.*

bark² /bɑːk/ *uncountable noun*

the rough surface of a tree

barn /bɑːn/ *noun*

a building on a farm where animals and crops are kept

barracks /'bærəks/ *noun*

a building where soldiers live and work: *an army barracks*

barrel /'bærəl/ *noun*

1 a large container, with curved sides and flat ends, for storing liquids: *The U.S. uses about 20 million barrels of oil a day.*

2 the long metal part of a gun

barricade /'bærɪkeɪd/ *noun*

a line of things that have been put across a road to stop people from passing: *The street was blocked by a barricade.*

●**barricade** *verb* (**barricades, barricading, barricaded**) *Police barricaded all entrances to the square.*

barrier /'bæriə/ *noun*

a fence or a wall that prevents people or things from moving from one area to another: *A police barrier blocked the road.*

bartender /'bɑːtendə/ *noun*

a person who makes and serves drinks in a bar

base¹ /beɪs/ *noun*

1 the lowest part of something, or the part that it stands on: *They planted flowers around the base of the tree.* □ *The base of the statue weighs four tons.*

2 a place where soldiers live and work: *The army base is close to the airport.*

3 the main place where you work or live: *In the summer her base is her home in London.*

base² /beɪs/ *verb* (**bases, basing, based**)
be based on something to be made by using an idea or material from another thing : *The film is based on a novel by Alexander Trocchi.*

baseball /'beɪsbɔːl/ *uncountable noun*
a game, played with a bat and a ball on a large field by two teams of nine players, in which players must hit the ball and run around four bases to score

'baseball cap *noun*
a cap with a curved part at the front that sticks out above your eyes: *Joe often wears a baseball cap.*

basement /'beɪsmənt/ *noun*
a part of a building below ground level: *They put the old toys in the basement.*

bases
1 the plural of **base**
2 the plural of **basis**

bash /bæʃ/ *verb* (**bashes, bashing, bashed**)
to hit someone or something very hard (*informal*): *I bashed him on the head.*

bashful /'bæʃfʊl/ *adjective*
shy and easily embarrassed: *She gave a little bashful smile.*

basic /'beɪsɪk/ *adjective*
1 relating to the simplest and most important part of something: *Everyone needs the basic skills of reading and writing.*
2 relating to the essential things that everyone needs: *There were shortages of the most basic foods.*

basically /'beɪsɪkli/ *adverb*
used when you are talking about the most important part of someone or something: *Basically, he is a nice boy.* □ *The film is basically a love story.*

basin /'beɪsən/ *noun*
1 → see **washbasin**
2 a deep bowl used for holding liquids: *Water dripped into a basin at the back of the room.*

basis /'beɪsɪs/ *noun* (**bases** /'beɪsiːz/)
1 the particular way that something is done: *We meet here for lunch on a regular basis.*
2 the most important part of something that other things can develop from:
The UN plan is a possible basis for peace talks.

basket /'bɑːskɪt/ *noun*
a container made from thin strips of wood, plastic or metal, that is used for carrying or storing objects: *The picnic basket was filled with sandwiches and fruit.*

basketball /'bɑːskɪtbɔːl/ *uncountable noun*
a game in which two teams of five players each try to throw a large ball through a round net hanging from a high metal ring
→ Look at picture on P6

bass /beɪs/ *adjective*
making a very deep sound: *Dee Murray plays bass guitar in the band.*

bassoon /bə'suːn/ *noun*
a large musical instrument, shaped like a tube, that you play by blowing into a curved metal pipe

bat¹ /bæt/ *noun*
1 a long piece of wood that is used for hitting the ball in games such as cricket or baseball: *a cricket bat*
2 a small animal, like a mouse with wings, that sleeps upside down during the day and comes out to fly at night

bat² /bæt/ *verb* (**bats, batting, batted**)
to hit the ball with a bat in games such as cricket or baseball: *Paxton hurt his elbow while he was batting.*

batch /bætʃ/ *noun* (**batches**)
a group of things or people of the same type: *I baked a batch of cakes this morning.*

bath¹ /bɑːθ/ *noun* (*American*: **bathtub**)
a long container that you fill with water and sit or lie in to wash your body: *She was lying in the bath.*
have/take a bath to sit or lie in a bath filled with water, and wash your body: *He had a bath before he went to bed.*
→ Look at picture on P8

bath² /bɑːθ/ *verb* (**baths, bathing, bathed**)
to wash a young child in a bath: *Would you like me to bath the baby?*

b

bathe /beɪð/ *verb* (**bathes, bathing, bathed**)
1 to swim in the sea or a lake or river: *Every morning, we bathed in the river.*
2 to wash a part of your body carefully: *Bathe the wound in warm water.*

bathrobe /'bɑːθrəʊb/ *noun*
a loose coat that you wear indoors after having a bath or a shower

bathroom /'bɑːθruːm/ *noun*
a room that contains a toilet: *She asked if she could use the bathroom.*
→ Look at picture on P4

bathtub /'bɑːθtʌb/ *noun* (*American*)
→ see **bath**: *She was lying in a huge pink bathtub.*

baton /'bætɒn/ *noun*
1 a light, thin stick that is used by a conductor (= a person who directs musicians)
2 a short stick that one runner passes to another in a race

batter /'bætə/ *noun*
1 *uncountable* a mixture of flour, eggs and milk, that is used for making cakes: *Pour the cake batter into a round baking tin.*
2 in sports such as baseball, a person who hits the ball: *The batter hit the ball toward second base.*

battery /'bætəri/ *noun* (**batteries**)
1 a small object that provides electricity for things such as radios: *The game requires two AA batteries.*
2 a box containing acid that provides the electricity that is needed to start a car: *Wendy can't take us because her car's battery is flat.*

battle /'bætəl/ *noun*
1 a violent fight between groups of people, especially between armies during a war: *The battle of Gettysburg took place in July 1863.*
2 a struggle for success or control over something: *Lance Armstrong won his battle against cancer.* ● **battle** *verb* (**battles, battling, battled**) *Doctors battled all night to save her life.*

bay /beɪ/ *noun*
a part of a coast where the land goes in and forms a curve: *We sailed across the bay in the morning.*

BC /ˌbiː ˈsiː/ also **B.C.**
used in dates to show the number of years before the year in which Jesus Christ was born. Compare with **AD**: *He probably lived in the fourth century BC.*

be¹ /bi, STRONG biː/ *auxiliary verb* (**am, are, is, being, was, were, been**)
1 used with another verb to form the past or present continuous: *This is happening everywhere in the country.* □ *She was driving to work when the accident happened.*
2 used with another verb to form the passive: *Her husband was killed in a car crash.*
3 used with an infinitive to show that something is planned to happen: *The talks are to begin tomorrow.*

be² /bi, STRONG biː/ *verb* (**am, are, is, being, was, were, been**)
1 used for introducing more information about a subject: *She's my mother.* □ *He is a very kind man.* □ *He is fifty years old.* □ *The sky was black.* □ *Dad's in the garden.*
2 used with 'it' when you are giving your opinion on a situation: *It was too cold for swimming.* □ *Sometimes it is necessary to say no.* □ *It's nice having friends to talk to.*
3 used in expressions like 'there is' and 'there are' to say that something exists: *There is very little traffic this morning.*

beach /biːtʃ/ *noun* (**beaches**)
an area of sand or stones next to a lake or the sea: *The children played on the beautiful sandy beach.*

bead /biːd/ *noun*
a small piece of coloured glass, wood or plastic that is used for making jewellery: *Victoria was wearing a purple bead necklace.*

beak /biːk/ *noun*
the hard, pointed part of a bird's mouth: *She pointed to a black bird with a yellow beak.*

beam¹ /biːm/ *verb* (**beams, beaming, beamed**)
to have a big happy smile on your face: *Lucy was waiting at the door, beaming.* □ *Frances beamed at her friend.*

beam² /biːm/ *noun*
1 a line of light that shines from something bright
2 a long thick bar of wood or metal that supports the roof of a building: *The ceilings are supported by oak beams.*

bean /biːn/ *noun*
the seed of a plant that you can eat as a

vegetable: *'More green beans, anyone?'* Mrs Parkinson asked.
→ Look at picture on P2

bear¹ /beə/ *verb* (**bears, bearing, bore, borne**)
1 to accept an unpleasant experience: *The loneliness was hard to bear.*
2 to be able to support your weight: *The ice was not thick enough to bear their weight.*
can't bear someone/something to dislike someone or something very much: *I can't bear people being late.* □ *I can't bear rudeness.*

bear² /beə/ *noun*
a large, strong wild animal with thick fur and sharp claws

bearable /'beərəbəl/ *adjective*
that you can deal with without too much difficulty: *A cool breeze made the heat bearable.*

beard /bɪəd/ *noun*
the hair that grows on a man's chin and cheeks: *He's 60 years old, with a long white beard.*

beast /biːst/ *noun*
a large and dangerous animal: *He told the children that there were wild beasts in the woods.*

beat¹ /biːt/ *verb* (**beats, beating, beat, beaten**)
1 to hit someone or something very hard: *They beat him, and left him on the ground.* □ *We could hear the rain beating against the windows.*
2 to make a regular sound and movement: *I felt my heart beating faster.*
• **beat** *noun* *He could hear the beat of his heart.*
3 to mix food quickly with a spoon or a fork: *Beat the eggs and sugar together.*
4 to defeat someone in a competition or an election: *The Red Sox beat the Yankees 5-2 last night.*

beat² /biːt/ *noun*
the rhythm of a piece of music: *Play some music with a steady beat.*

beautiful /'bjuːtɪfʊl/ *adjective*
1 very attractive to look at: *She was a very beautiful woman.*
2 pleasant to look at, listen to or experience: *The countryside is beautiful in the autumn.* □ *It was a beautiful morning.*
▶ **beautifully** /'bjuːtɪfli/ *adverb* *Karen sings beautifully.*

LANGUAGE HELP
Sense 1 is usually used for talking about women and girls. You can describe an attractive man as **handsome** or **good-looking**.

beauty /'bjuːti/ *uncountable noun*
the quality of being beautiful: *The hotel is in an area of natural beauty.*

beaver /'biːvə/ *noun*
an animal with thick fur, a big flat tail and large teeth

became /bɪ'keɪm/ → see **become**

because /bɪ'kɒz/ *conjunction*
used when you are giving the reason for something: *He is called Mitch because his name is Mitchell.* □ *I'm sad because he didn't ask me to his birthday party.*
because of something as a result of something: *He's retiring because of ill health.*

become /bɪ'kʌm/ *verb* (**becomes, becoming, became, become**)
to start to be something or someone: *The weather became cold and wet in October.* □ *Teresa wants to become a teacher.*

bed /bed/ *noun*
1 a piece of furniture that you lie on when you sleep: *We went to bed at about 10 p.m.* □ *Nina was already in bed.*
→ Look at picture on P5
2 the ground at the bottom of the sea or of a river

bedroom /'bedruːm/ *noun*
a room that is used for sleeping in: *Emma, please tidy your bedroom.*
→ Look at picture on P5

bedspread /'bedspred/ *noun*
a decorative cover that you put on a bed

bedtime /'bedtaɪm/ *noun*
the time when someone usually goes to bed: *It was eight-thirty, Peter's bedtime.*

bee /biː/ *noun*
a yellow-and-black striped flying insect that makes a sweet food (= honey) and can sting you: *Bees buzzed in the flowers.*

beef /biːf/ *uncountable noun*
meat from a cow: *We had roast beef for lunch.*

beefburger /'biːfbɜːgə/ *noun* (British)
→ see **hamburger**: *beefburgers and chips*

beehive /'biːhaɪv/ *noun*
a container for bees to live in

b

been [1] /bɪn, biːn/ → see **be**

been [2] /bɪn, biːn/ *verb*
   have been to to have visited a place: *Have you ever been to Paris?*

beep [1] /biːp/ *noun*
   1 a short, high sound made by a piece of electronic equipment: *Please leave a message after the beep.*
   2 a short, loud sound made by a car horn

beep [2] /biːp/ *verb* (**beeps, beeping, beeped**)
   1 to make a short, high sound: *My mobile phone beeps when I receive a text message.*
   2 to make a short, loud sound: *He beeped the horn and waved.* □ *When the microwave beeped, he took out his meal and ate it quickly.*

beer /bɪə/ *uncountable noun*
   an alcoholic drink made from grain: *He sat in the kitchen drinking beer.*

beetle /'biːtəl/ *noun*
   an insect with a hard, shiny black body

beetroot /'biːtruːt/ *noun*
   a dark red root, eaten as a vegetable, that is often preserved in vinegar (= a liquid with a strong sharp taste): *Thinly slice the beetroot.*

before [1] /bɪ'fɔː/ *preposition*
   earlier than a particular date, time or event: *Annie was born a few weeks before Christmas.* ● **before** *conjunction* *Brush your teeth before you go to bed.*

before [2] /bɪ'fɔː/ *adverb*
   in the past: *I've never been here before.* □ *Have you met Professor Lewis before?*

beforehand /bɪ'fɔːhænd/ *adverb*
   earlier than something else: *If you want to come to the party, please tell me beforehand.*

beg /beg/ *verb* (**begs, begging, begged**)
   1 to ask someone to do something in a way that shows that you want them to do it very much: *I begged him to come to New York with me.* □ *I begged for help but no one listened.*
   2 to ask people for food or money because you are very poor: *Homeless people were begging on the streets.*

began /bɪ'gæn/ → see **begin**

beggar /'begə/ *noun*
   someone who lives by asking people for money or food: *There are no beggars on the streets in Vienna.*

begin /bɪ'gɪn/ *verb* (**begins, beginning, began, begun**)
   1 to start doing something: *Jack stood up and began to move around the room.* □ *David began to look angry.*
   2 to start to happen, or to start something: *The problems began last November.* □ *He has just begun his second year at college.*

beginner /bɪ'gɪnə/ *noun*
   someone who has just started to do or to learn something: *The course is for both beginners and advanced students.*

beginning /bɪ'gɪnɪŋ/ *noun*
   the first part of something: *This was the beginning of her career.* □ *The wedding will be at the beginning of March.*

begun /bɪ'gʌn/ → see **begin**

behalf /bɪ'hɑːf/ *noun*
   on someone's behalf/on behalf of someone for somebody; in place of somebody: *She thanked us all on her son's behalf.*

behave /bɪ'heɪv/ *verb* (**behaves, behaving, behaved**)
   1 to do and say things in a particular way: *I couldn't believe Molly was behaving in this way.*
   2 to act in the way that people think is correct and proper: *Remember to behave yourselves, children!*

behaviour /bɪ'heɪvjə/ *uncountable noun*
   the way that a person or an animal behaves: *Parents should always reward good behaviour.*

behind /bɪ'haɪnd/ *preposition*
   1 at the back of someone or something: *I put a cushion behind his head.* □ *They were parked behind the lorry.*
   2 following someone or something: *Keith walked along behind them.* ● **behind** *adverb* *The other police officers followed behind in a second vehicle.*
   be behind/be behind schedule to be slower or later doing something than you planned: *The work is 22 weeks behind schedule.*
   leave someone/something behind to not take someone or something with you when you go somewhere: *The soldiers escaped into the mountains, leaving behind their weapons.*

beige /beɪʒ/ *adjective*
   pale brown in colour: *The walls are beige.*

●**beige** *noun* I like beige more than dark brown.

being [1] /'biːɪŋ/ → see **be**

being [2] /'biːɪŋ/ *noun*
a person or a living thing: Remember you are dealing with a living being — consider the horse's feelings too.

belief /bɪ'liːf/ *noun*
a powerful feeling that something is real or true: Benedict has a deep belief in God.

believable /bɪ'liːvəbəl/ *adjective*
able to be believed: Mark's excuse was not very believable.

believe /bɪ'liːv/ *verb* (**believes, believing, believed**)
1 to think that something is true (*formal*): Scientists believe that life began around 4 billion years ago. □ We believe that the money is hidden here in this flat.
2 to feel sure that someone is telling the truth: Never believe what you read in the newspapers.
3 to feel sure that something exists: I don't believe in ghosts.

bell /bel/ *noun*
1 a metal object that makes a ringing sound: I was eating my lunch when the bell rang.
2 a hollow metal object with a loose piece hanging inside it that hits the sides and makes a pleasant sound: It was a Sunday, and all the church bells were ringing.

belly /'beli/ *noun* (**bellies**)
the stomach of a person or an animal: She put her hands on her swollen belly.

belong /bɪ'lɒŋ/ *verb* (**belongs, belonging, belonged**)
1 to be owned by someone: The house has belonged to her family for three generations.
2 to be a member of a particular group or organization: I used to belong to the tennis club.
3 to be in the right place: After ten years in New York, I really feel that I belong here.
□ 'Where do these plates belong?' – 'In that cupboard.'

belongings /bɪ'lɒŋɪŋz/ *plural noun*
the things that you own: I gathered my belongings and left.

below /bɪ'ləʊ/ *preposition*
1 in or to a lower position than someone

or something else: He came out of the flat below Leonard's. □ We watched the sun sink below the horizon. ●**below** *adverb* I could see the street below.
2 less than a particular amount, rate or level: Night temperatures can drop below zero.
●**below** *adverb* Daytime temperatures were at zero or below.

belt /belt/ *noun*
a strip of leather or cloth that you wear around your waist: He wore a belt with a large brass buckle.

bench /bentʃ/ *noun* (**benches**)
a long seat made of wood or metal: Tom sat down on a park bench.

bend /bend/ *verb* (**bends, bending, bent**)
1 to move the top part of your body down and forward: I bent over and kissed her cheek. □ She bent down and picked up the toy.
2 to change the position of a part of your body so that it is no longer straight: Remember to bend your legs when you do this exercise.
3 to change direction to form a curve: The road bends slightly to the right. ●**bend** *noun* The accident happened on a sharp bend in the road.

beneath /bɪ'niːθ/ *preposition*
below; under: She could see the muscles of his shoulders beneath his T-shirt. □ There is a car park beneath the shopping centre.

benefit /'benɪfɪt/ *verb* (**benefits, benefiting, benefited**)
to help you or improve your life: These projects will benefit the poor. ●**benefit** *noun* Parents need to educate their children about the benefits of exercise.
benefit from something to get help or an advantage from something: You would benefit from a change in your diet.

bent [1] /bent/ → see **bend**

bent [2] /bent/ *adjective*
not straight: Keep your knees slightly bent. □ He found a bent nail on the ground.

berry /'beri/ *noun* (**berries**)
a small, round fruit that grows on a bush or a tree

beside /bɪ'saɪd/ *preposition*
next to someone or something: Can I sit beside you?

besides [1] /bɪ'saɪdz/ *preposition*
in addition to someone or something:

b

besides – bicycle

38

She has many good qualities besides being very beautiful.

besides² /bɪˈsaɪdz/ *adverb*
used when you want to give another reason for something: *The house is far too expensive. Besides, I don't want to leave our little apartment.*

best¹ /best/ *adjective*
a form of the adjective **good**, used to show that one thing is better than all the others: *Who is your best friend?* □ *Drink regularly through the day — water is best.*

best² /best/ *adverb*
a form of the adverb **well**, used to show that something is done or happens in a way that is better than all the others: *I did best in physics in my class.* □ *J. R. R. Tolkien is best known as the author of 'The Hobbit'.*

best³ /best/ *noun*
do your best to try very hard to do something as well as possible: *If you do your best, no one can criticize you.*
the best someone or something that is better than all other people or things: *We offer only the best to our clients.*

bet /bet/ *verb* (**bets, betting, bet**)
to give someone some money and say what you think that the result of a race or a sports game will be. If you are correct, they give you your money back with some extra money, but if you are wrong they keep your money: *I bet £20 on a horse called Bright Boy.* ● **bet** *noun Did you make a bet on the horse race?*
▸ **betting** *uncountable noun Betting is illegal in many countries.*
I bet used for showing that you are sure something is true (*informal*): *I bet you are good at sports.*

better¹ /ˈbetə/ *adjective*
1 a form of the adjective **good**, used for saying that one thing is of a higher standard than another thing: *This book is better than her last one.*
2 no longer ill or injured: *When I'm better, I'll talk to him.*
3 feeling less ill: *He is feeling much better today.*

better² /ˈbetə/ *adverb*
1 a form of the adverb **well**, used to show that one thing is done or happens in a way that is of a higher standard than another thing: *You play football better than I do.*

2 more: *I like your poem better than mine.*
had better should; ought to: *I think we had better go home.*

between /bɪˈtwiːn/ *preposition*
1 with one person or thing on one side of you and another person or thing on the other side of you: *Nicole was standing between the two men.*
2 from one place to the other and back again: *I spend a lot of time travelling between Edinburgh and London.*
3 greater than the first amount mentioned and smaller than the second amount: *Try to exercise between 15 and 20 minutes every day.*
4 after the first time or date mentioned and before the second time or date: *The house was built between 1793 and 1797.* □ *I came home between three o'clock and four.*
5 used to say how many people share something: *There is only one bathroom shared between eight people.*

LANGUAGE HELP
If there are only two people or things, use **between**. If there are more than two people or things, use **among**.

beware /bɪˈweə/ *verb*
beware of someone/something to be careful because a person or a thing is dangerous: *Beware of the dog.*

bewildered /bɪˈwɪldəd/ *adjective*
very confused and unable to decide what to do: *The shoppers looked bewildered by the huge variety of goods for sale.*

beyond /bɪˈjɒnd/ *preposition*
on the other side of something; further away than something: *On his right was a garden and beyond it a large house.* ● **beyond** *adverb The house had a fabulous view out to the sea beyond.*

the Bible /ðə ˈbaɪbəl/ *noun*
the holy book of the Christian and Jewish religions: *He reads the Bible in bed every day.*

biceps /ˈbaɪseps/ *plural noun*
the large muscles at the front of the upper part of your arms

bicycle /ˈbaɪsɪkəl/ *noun*
a vehicle with two wheels that you ride by sitting on it and using your legs to make the wheels turn

bid /bɪd/ *verb* (bids, bidding, bid)
to promise that you will pay a certain amount of money for something that is being sold: *Lily wanted to bid for the painting.*
● **bid** *noun* Bill made the winning £620 bid for the statue.

big /bɪg/ *adjective* (bigger, biggest)
1 large in size: *Australia is a big country.* □ *Her husband was a big man.* □ *The crowd included a big group from Cambridge.*
2 important or serious: *He owns one of the biggest companies in Italy.* □ *Mandy's problem was too big for her to solve alone.*
3 older: *I live with my big brother, John.*

big ˈbang ˌtheory *noun*
a theory that states that the universe was created after an extremely large explosion

bike /baɪk/ *noun*
a bicycle or a motorcycle (*informal*): *When you ride a bike, you exercise all your leg muscles.*

bikini /bɪˈkiːni/ *noun*
a piece of clothing with two parts that women wear for swimming

bilingual /ˌbaɪˈlɪŋgwəl/ *adjective*
1 able to speak two languages equally well: *He is bilingual in French and English.*
2 written or spoken in two languages: *a bilingual dictionary*

bill /bɪl/ *noun*
1 (*American*: **check**) a document that shows how much money you must pay for something: *They couldn't afford to pay their bills.*
2 (*American*) a piece of paper money: *The case contained a large quantity of U.S. dollar bills.*
3 an official document produced by a government containing a suggestion for a new law: *The bill was approved by a large majority.*

billboard /ˈbɪlbɔːd/ *noun*
a very large board for advertisements at the side of the road

billion /ˈbɪljən/

> **LANGUAGE HELP**
> The plural form is **billion** after a number.

the number 1,000,000,000: *The country's debt has risen to 3 billion dollars.* □ *The game was watched by billions of people around the world.*

billionaire /ˌbɪljəˈneə/ *noun*
an extremely rich person who has money

or property worth at least a billion pounds

bin /bɪn/ *noun*
1 a container that you put rubbish in: *I took the letter and threw it in the bin.*
2 a container that you keep things in: *a plastic storage bin*

bind /baɪnd/ *verb* (binds, binding, bound)
to tie rope or string around something to hold it firmly: *They bound his hands behind his back.*

binoculars /bɪˈnɒkjʊləz/ *plural noun*
special glasses that you use to look at things that are a long distance away

binoculars

biodiesel /ˈbaɪəʊˌdiːzəl/ *uncountable noun*
a fuel that is made from things such as vegetable and animal oils and that can be used instead of diesel

biofuel /ˈbaɪəʊˌfjuːəl/ *noun*
a fuel that is made from things such as vegetable and animal oils: *Biofuels can be mixed with conventional fuels.*

biography /baɪˈɒgrəfi/ *noun* (biographies)
the story of the life of a person that has been written by another person: *I am reading a biography of Franklin D. Roosevelt.*

biological /ˌbaɪəˈlɒdʒɪkəl/ *adjective*
relating to the scientific study of living things: *biological processes such as reproduction and growth*

biology /baɪˈɒlədʒi/ *uncountable noun*
the scientific study of living things
▶ **biologist** /baɪˈɒlədʒɪst/ *noun* The marine biologist was killed by a shark while diving.

bipolar /ˌbaɪˈpəʊlə/ *adjective*
having a mental illness in which you are sometimes very happy and excited and sometimes very sad

bird /bɜːd/ *noun*
an animal with feathers and wings: *a bird's nest* □ *The bird flew away as I came near.*

birdhouse /ˈbɜːdhaʊs/ *noun*
a box placed in a tree or other high place

b

that birds can build a nest in: *He showed us how to build a birdhouse.*

birth /bɜ:θ/ *noun*
the moment when a baby is born: *They are celebrating the birth of their first child.* □ *Alice weighed 5 lb 7 oz at birth.*
give birth to produce a baby from your body: *She's just given birth to a baby girl.*

birthday /'bɜ:θdeɪ, -di/ *noun*
the day of the year that you were born: *We called David on his birthday.*

biscuit /'bɪskɪt/ (American: **cookie**) *noun*
a kind of hard, dry cake that is usually sweet and round in shape: *a chocolate biscuit*
→ Look at picture on P3

bishop /'bɪʃəp/ *noun*
a leader in the Christian church whose job is to look after all the churches in a particular area

bit¹ /bɪt/ *noun*
a unit of information that can be stored on a computer

bit² /bɪt/ *noun*
a bit a small amount of something, or a small part or section of something: *I did a bit of work.* □ *Only a bit of the cake was left.*
a bit a little: *This girl was a bit strange.* □ *I think people feel a bit happier now.*
a bit/for a bit for a short time: *Let's wait a bit.*
quite a bit quite a lot (*informal*): *Things have changed quite a bit.*

bit³ /bɪt/ → see bite

bite¹ /baɪt/ *verb* (**bites, biting, bit, bitten**)
1 to use your teeth to cut into or through something: *William bit into his sandwich.*
2 if a snake or an insect bites, it makes a mark or a hole in your skin with a sharp part of its body: *Do these flies bite?* □ *He was bitten by a snake.*

bite² /baɪt/ *noun*
1 a small piece of food that you cut into with your teeth: *Dan took another bite of apple.*
2 a painful mark on your body where an animal, a snake or an insect has bitten you: *a dog bite*

bitten /'bɪtən/ → see bite

bitter /'bɪtə/ *adjective* (**bitterest**)
1 tasting unpleasantly sharp and sour: *The medicine tasted bitter.*

2 very angry and upset about something that has happened: *She is very bitter about the way she lost her job.*
▶ **bitterly** *adverb* 'And he didn't even try to help us,' Grant said bitterly.
3 extremely cold: *A bitter east wind was blowing.*
▶ **bitterly** *adverb* *It's bitterly cold here.*

bizarre /bɪ'zɑ:/ *adjective*
very strange: *They were all surprised by their boss's bizarre behaviour.*
▶ **bizarrely** *adverb* *She dresses bizarrely.*

black¹ /blæk/ *adjective* (**blacker, blackest**)
1 with the colour of the sky at night: *She was wearing a black coat with a white collar.* □ *He had thick black hair.*
2 belonging to a race of people with dark skins, especially a race originally from Africa: *He worked for the rights of black people.*
3 without milk: *A cup of black coffee contains no calories.*

black² /blæk/ *noun*
1 the colour of the sky at night: *She was wearing black.*
2 a person who belongs to a race of people with dark skins: *There are about 31 million blacks in the U.S.*

black and 'white also **black-and-white** *adjective*
with the colours black, white and grey only: *old black and white films* □ *a black-and-white photo*

blackberry /'blækbəri/ *noun* (**blackberries**)
a small, soft black or dark purple fruit

Blackberry /'blækbəri/ *noun* (**Blackberries**)
a mobile phone with a small keyboard and with its own special system for sending messages (*trademark*)

blackboard /'blækbɔ:d/ (American: **chalkboard**) *noun*
a big, dark-coloured board for writing on in a classroom

black 'eye *noun*
a dark-coloured mark around a person's eye because they have been hit there by someone or something: *Jan arrived at the hospital with a broken nose and a black eye.*

blackmail /'blækmeɪl/ *uncountable noun*
saying that you will say something bad about someone if they do not do what you tell them to do or give you money: *Mr Stanley was accused of blackmail.*
● **blackmail** *verb* (**blackmails, blackmailing, blackmailed**) *Jeff suddenly realized that Linda was blackmailing him.*

blacksmith /'blæksmɪθ/ *noun*
a person whose job is making things out of metal

bladder /'blædə/ *noun*
the part of your body where liquid waste is stored until it leaves your body

blade /bleɪd/ *noun*
the flat, sharp edge of a knife that is used for cutting: *The axe blade cut deep into the log.*

blame [1] /bleɪm/ *verb* (**blames, blaming, blamed**)
to say that someone or something made something bad happen: *Police blamed the bus driver for the accident.*

blame [2] /bleɪm/ *noun*
get the blame for something to have people say that you made something bad happen: *I always got the blame for the trouble that my sister caused.*
take the blame for something to accept that you made something bad happen, even if this is not true: *Jan always took the blame for Alan's mistakes.*

bland /blænd/ *adjective* (**blander, blandest**)
1 dull and not interesting: *Their music is bland and boring.*
2 with very little flavour: *The pizza tasted bland, like warm cardboard.*

blank /blæŋk/ *adjective*
1 with no writing or pictures: *He tore a blank page from his notebook.*
2 showing no reaction: *Albert looked blank. 'I don't know him, sir.'*
▶ **blankly** *adverb* *Ellie stared at him blankly.*

blanket /'blæŋkɪt/ *noun*
a large, thick piece of cloth that you put on a bed to keep you warm

blast /blɑːst, blæst/ *noun*
a big explosion, especially one caused by a bomb: *250 people were killed in the blast.*

blaze /bleɪz/ *noun*
a large fire that destroys a lot of things:

More than 4,000 firefighters are battling the blaze. ● **blaze** *verb* (**blazes, blazing, blazed**) *Three people died as the building blazed.*

blazer /'bleɪzə/ *noun*
a type of jacket that people wear as part of a uniform

bleach /bliːtʃ/ *uncountable noun*
a chemical that is used for making cloth white, or for making things very clean: *Only use bleach on white fabrics.* ● **bleach** *verb* (**bleaches, bleaching, bleached**) *I bleached the kitchen sink.*

bleak /bliːk/ *adjective* (**bleaker, bleakest**)
1 not hopeful or likely to be successful: *The future looks bleak.*
2 cold, dull and unpleasant: *The weather can be quite bleak here.*

bleed /bliːd/ *verb* (**bleeds, bleeding, bled**)
to lose blood from a part of your body: *Ian's lip was bleeding.*
▶ **bleeding** *uncountable noun* *We tried to stop the bleeding from the cut on his arm.*

blend /blend/ *verb* (**blends, blending, blended**)
1 to mix substances together: *Blend the butter with the sugar.* ◻ *Blend the ingredients together until you have a smooth mixture.*
2 to look or sound attractive together: *All the colours blend perfectly together.*
● **blend** *noun* *Their music is a blend of jazz and rock'n'roll.*

bless /bles/ *verb* (**blesses, blessing, blessed**)
to ask for God's protection for someone or something: *The pope blessed the crowd.*
Bless you something polite that you say to someone when they sneeze (= blow out air through their nose and mouth suddenly and noisily)

blew /bluː/ → see **blow**

blind [1] /blaɪnd/ *adjective*
unable to see: *My grandfather is going blind.*
the blind people who are blind: *He's a teacher of the blind.*

blind [2] /blaɪnd/ *noun*
a piece of cloth or other material that you can pull down over a window to cover it: *Susan pulled the blinds up to let the bright sunlight into the room.*

blindfold /'blaɪndfəʊld/ *noun*
a strip of cloth that is tied over someone's

eyes so that they cannot see • **blindfold** *verb* (**blindfolds, blindfolding, blindfolded**) *Mr Li was handcuffed and blindfolded.*

blink /blɪŋk/ *verb* (**blinks, blinking, blinked**)
to shut your eyes and very quickly open them again: *I stood blinking in bright light.*

blister /'blɪstə/ *noun*
a raised area of skin filled with a clear liquid: *I get blisters when I wear these shoes.*

blizzard /'blɪzəd/ *noun*
a very bad storm with snow and strong winds

blob /blɒb/ *noun*
a small amount of a thick liquid (*informal*): *Denise wiped a blob of jelly off Edgar's chin.*

block¹ /blɒk/ *noun*
1 a large, solid piece of a substance that has straight sides: *Elizabeth carves animals from blocks of wood.*
2 a large building with offices inside it: *an office block*
3 a group of buildings in a town or a city with streets on all sides: *He walked around the block three times.* □ *She walked four blocks down High Street.*

block² /blɒk/ *verb* (**blocks, blocking, blocked**)
to stop someone or something from passing along a road: *The police blocked all the streets in the centre of the city.* □ *A tree fell down and blocked the road.*

blocked /blɒkt/ or **blocked up** *adjective*
completely closed so that nothing can get through: *The pipes are blocked and the water can't get through.*

blog /blɒg/ *noun*
a website that describes the daily life of the person who writes it, and also their thoughts and ideas: *His blog was later published as a book.*
▶ **blogger** *noun* *Loewenstein is a freelance author, blogger and journalist.*
▶ **blogging** *uncountable noun* *Blogging is very popular.*

blogosphere /'blɒgəsfɪə/ or **blogsphere** /'blɒgsfɪə/ *noun*
all the blogs (= personal records) on the Internet: *The blogosphere continues to expand.*

blonde¹ /blɒnd/ *adjective* (**blonder, blondest**)
1 with pale-coloured hair: *My sister has blonde hair.*
2 with blonde hair: *He's blonder than his brother.*

blonde² /blɒnd/ *noun*
a person, especially a woman, with pale-coloured hair: *She's a blonde with blue eyes.*

blood /blʌd/ *uncountable noun*
the red liquid that flows inside your body: *His shirt was covered in blood.*

blood vessel /'blʌd ˌvesəl/ *noun*
one of the narrow tubes that your blood flows through

bloom /blu:m/ *verb* (**blooms, blooming, bloomed**)
to produce flowers; to open out into flowers: *This plant blooms between May and June.* □ *Although it was late autumn, roses were still blooming in the garden.*

blossom /'blɒsəm/ *uncountable noun*
the flowers that appear on a fruit tree: *The cherry blossom lasts only a few days.*
• **blossom** *verb* (**blossoms, blossoming, blossomed**) *The peach trees will blossom soon.*

blouse /blaʊz/ *noun*
a shirt for a girl or a woman

blow¹ /bləʊ/ *verb* (**blows, blowing, blew, blown**)
1 when a wind or breeze blows, the air moves: *A cold wind was blowing.*
2 to move something using the power of the wind: *The wind blew her hair back from her forehead.*
3 to send out air from your mouth: *Danny blew on his fingers to warm them.*
4 to send air from your mouth into an object so that it makes a sound: *When the referee blows his whistle, the game begins.*

blow something out to blow at a flame so that it stops burning: *I blew out the candle.*

blow something up
1 to destroy something by an explosion: *He was jailed for trying to blow up a plane.* □ *Three cars in the car park blew up.*
2 to fill something with air: *Can you help me blow up the balloons?*

blow your nose to force air out of your

nose in order to clear it: *He took out a handkerchief and blew his nose.*

blow ² /bləʊ/ *noun*
1 a hard hit from someone's hand or from an object: *He went to the hospital after a blow to the face.*
2 an event that makes you feel very unhappy or disappointed: *The increase in tax was a blow to the industry.*

blown /bləʊn/ → see **blow**

blue /bluː/ *adjective* (**bluer, bluest**)
having the colour of the sky on a sunny day: *We looked up at the cloudless blue sky.*
□ *She has pale blue eyes.* ● **blue** *noun Julie and Angela wore blue.*

blueberry /'bluːbəri/ *noun* (**blueberries**)
a small dark blue fruit

the blues /ðə 'bluːz/ *plural noun*
a type of slow, sad music that developed among African-American musicians in the southern United States: *I grew up singing the blues at home with my mum.*

Bluetooth /'bluːtuːθ/ *uncountable noun*
a type of technology that allows devices such as mobile phones and computers to communicate with each other without being connected by wires (*trademark*): *This is the latest Bluetooth technology.*

blunt /blʌnt/ *adjective* (**blunter, bluntest**)
1 saying exactly what you think, without trying to be polite
2 not sharp or pointed: *a blunt pencil*

blurred /blɜːd/ *adjective*
not clear: *She showed me a blurred photograph.*

blush /blʌʃ/ *verb* (**blushes, blushing, blushed**)
to become red in the face because you are ashamed or embarrassed: *'Hello, Maria,' he said, and she blushed again.*

board ¹ /bɔːd/ *noun*
1 a flat, thin piece of wood: *There were wooden boards over the doors and windows.*
2 a flat piece of wood or plastic that you use for a special purpose: *The picture was on the staff noticeboard.* □ *A wooden chopping board can be very heavy.*
3 the group of people who organize and make decisions about a company: *The board meets today, and it will announce its decision tomorrow.*

on board on a train, a ship or an aircraft: *All 25 people on board the plane were killed.*

board ² /bɔːd/ *verb* (**boards, boarding, boarded**)
to get into a train, a ship or an aircraft to travel somewhere (*formal*): *I boarded the plane to Boston.*

'boarding pass *noun* (**boarding passes**)
a card that a passenger must show when they are entering an aircraft or a boat

boast /bəʊst/ *verb* (**boasts, boasting, boasted**)
to talk about something that you have done or that you own too proudly, in a way that annoys other people: *He boasted that the police would never catch him.* □ *Carol boasted about her new job.*

boat /bəʊt/ *noun*
a small ship: *One of the best ways to see the area is in a small boat.* □ *a fishing boat*

body /'bɒdi/ *noun* (**bodies**)
1 all the physical parts of a person or an animal: *Yoga creates a healthy mind in a healthy body.*
2 the main part of a person's or an animal's body, but not their arms, head and legs: *Lying flat on your back, twist your body onto one side.*
3 a dead person or animal: *Two days later, her body was found in a wood.*

bodyguard /'bɒdigɑːd/ *noun*
someone whose job is to protect an important person: *Three of his bodyguards were injured in the attack.*

boil /bɔɪl/ *verb* (**boils, boiling, boiled**)
1 to produce bubbles and start to change into steam: *I stood in the kitchen, waiting for the water to boil.* □ *Boil the water in the saucepan and add the salt.*
2 to cook food in boiling water: *Wash and boil the rice.* □ *I peeled potatoes and put them in a pot to boil.*

boiling /'bɔɪlɪŋ/ *adjective*
very hot: *It's boiling in here.*

'boiling point *uncountable noun*
the temperature at which a liquid starts to change into steam

bold /bəʊld/ *adjective* (**bolder, boldest**)
1 not afraid to do dangerous things; confident: *Their bold plan almost worked.*
2 very bright: *Jill's dress was patterned with bold flowers.*

b

bolt /bəʊlt/ *noun*

1 a long piece of metal that you use with another small piece of metal with a hole in it (= a nut) to fasten things together: *Tighten any loose bolts and screws on your bicycle.*

2 a piece of metal that you move across to lock a door: *Taylor went to the door and opened it.* ● **bolt** *verb* (**bolts, bolting, bolted**) *He locked and bolted the kitchen door.*

bomb¹ /bɒm/ *noun*

a weapon that explodes and damages things nearby: *Bombs went off at two London train stations.* □ *The police do not know who planted the bomb.*

bomb² /bɒm/ *verb* (**bombs, bombing, bombed**)

to attack a place with bombs: *Military airplanes bombed the airport.*

▶ **bombing** *noun* *The bombing of Pearl Harbor started World War II.*

bond /bɒnd/ *noun*

a strong feeling of friendship or love between people: *The experience created a special bond between us.* ● **bond** *verb* (**bonds, bonding, bonded**) *Belinda quickly bonded with her new baby.*

bone /bəʊn/ *noun*

one of the hard white parts inside your body: *Many passengers suffered broken bones in the accident.*

bonfire /'bɒnfaɪə/ *noun*

a large fire that you make outside: *Bonfires are not allowed in many areas.*

bonnet /'bɒnɪt/ *noun*

1 (*American*: **hood**) the front part of a car that covers the engine

2 a soft hat that you tie under your chin

bonus /'bəʊnəs/ *noun* (**bonuses**)

1 an extra amount of money that you earn, usually because you have worked very hard: *Each member of staff received a £100 bonus.*

2 something good that you would not usually expect to get: *As a bonus, the CD comes with a free DVD.*

book¹ /bʊk/ *noun*

a number of pieces of paper, usually with words printed on them, that are fastened together and fixed inside a cover: *Her* second book was an immediate success. □ *I've just read a new book by Rosella Brown.*

book² /bʊk/ *verb* (**books, booking, booked**)

to arrange to have or use something, such as a hotel room or a ticket to a concert, at a later time: *Laurie booked a flight home.*

bookcase /'bʊkkeɪs/ *noun*

a piece of furniture with shelves that you keep books on

→ Look at picture on P5

booklet /'bʊklət/ *noun*

a very thin book that has a paper cover and that gives you information about something: *The travel office gave us a booklet about places to visit in Venice.*

bookmark /'bʊkmɑːk/ *noun*

the address of a website that you add to a list on your computer so that you can return to it easily: *Use bookmarks to give you quick links to your favourite websites.*

● **bookmark** *verb* (**bookmarks, bookmarking, bookmarked**) *Do you want to bookmark this page?*

bookshelf /'bʊkʃelf/ *noun* (**bookshelves**)

a shelf that you keep books on

bookshop /'bʊkʃɒp/ *noun*

a shop where books are sold

boom¹ /buːm/ *noun*

an increase in the number of things that people are buying: *an economic boom*

boom² /buːm/ *verb* (**booms, booming, boomed**)

to make a loud, deep sound: *The wind roared and the thunder boomed above them.* □ *'Ladies,' boomed Helena. 'We all know why we're here tonight.'*

boost /buːst/ *verb* (**boosts, boosting, boosted**)

to cause something to increase, improve or be more successful: *Lower prices will boost sales.*

boost someone's confidence to make someone feel more confident: *If the team wins, it will boost their confidence.* ● **boost** *noun* *Scoring that goal gave me a real boost.*

boot¹ /buːt/ *noun*

1 a shoe that covers your whole foot and the lower part of your leg: *He sat down and took off his boots.*

2 (*American*: **trunk**) the space at the back of a car that is used for carrying things in

boot ^{2} /buːt/ *verb* (**boots, booting, booted**)
to make a computer ready to start working: *Put the CD into the drive and boot the machine.* ● **boot up** *Go over to your computer and boot it up.*

border /ˈbɔːdə/ *noun*
1 an imaginary line that divides two countries: *They drove across the border.* □ *Soldiers closed the border between the two countries.*
2 a decoration around the edge of something: *The curtains were white with a red border.*

bore /bɔː/ *verb* (**bores, boring, bored**)
to make someone feel uninterested in something, usually by talking about it too much: *Dick bored me with stories of his holiday.*

bored /bɔːd/ *adjective*
not interested in something; having nothing to do: *I am getting very bored with this television programme.* □ *Many children get bored during the long school summer holidays.*

boring /ˈbɔːrɪŋ/ *adjective*
not interesting: *Washing dishes is boring work.*

born ^{1} /bɔːn/ *verb*
be born to come out of your mother's body and begin life: *She was born in Milan on April 29, 1923.*

born ^{2} /bɔːn/ *adjective*
having a natural ability to do a particular activity or job: *Jack was a born teacher.*

borne /bɔːn/ → see **bear**

borrow /ˈbɒrəʊ/ *verb* (**borrows, borrowing, borrowed**)
to use something that belongs to another person for a period of time and then return it: *Can I borrow a pen please?*

boss /bɒs/ *noun* (**bosses**)
the person in charge of you at the place where you work: *He likes his new boss.*

bossy /ˈbɒsi/ *adjective*
always telling people what to do, in an annoying way: *Susan is a bossy little girl.*

botany /ˈbɒtəni/ *uncountable noun*
the scientific study of plants
▸ **botanical** /bəˈtænɪkəl/ *adjective* The area is of great botanical interest.

both /bəʊθ/ *adjective*
1 used when you are saying that something is true about two people or things: *Stand up straight with both arms at your sides.* □ *Both men were taken to hospital.*
● **both** *pronoun* Miss Brown and her friend are both from York. □ They both worked at Harvard University.
2 used for showing that you are talking about two people or things: *Both of them have to go to London regularly.*
both...and... used to show that each of two facts is true: *Now women work both before and after having their children.*

bother /ˈbɒðə/ *verb* (**bothers, bothering, bothered**)
1 to try to talk to someone when they are busy: *I'm sorry to bother you, but there's someone here to speak to you.*
2 to make you feel worried or angry: *Is something bothering you?*
can't be bothered to do something to not want to do something because it is too much work: *I can't be bothered to cook this evening; let's order a pizza.*
not bother to do something to not do something because you think it is not necessary: *Lots of people don't bother to get married these days.*

bottle /ˈbɒtəl/ *noun*
a glass or plastic container in which drinks and other liquids are kept: *There were two empty water bottles on the table.* □ *She drank half a bottle of apple juice.*

bottom /ˈbɒtəm/ *noun*
1 the lowest or deepest part of something: *He sat at the bottom of the stairs.* □ *Answers can be found at the bottom of page 8.* ● **bottom** *adjective* There are pencils in the bottom drawer of the desk.
2 the part of your body that you sit on → Look at picture on P1

bought /bɔːt/ → see **buy**

bounce /baʊns/ *verb* (**bounces, bouncing, bounced**)
1 to hit a surface and immediately move away from it again: *The ball bounced across the floor.* □ *Matthew came into the kitchen bouncing a rubber ball.*
2 to jump up and down on a soft surface: *Some children were playing football; others were riding scooters or bouncing on the trampoline.*
3 if an email bounces, it is returned to the person who sent it because of a problem

bounce

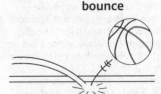

The ball bounced across the floor.

bound ¹ /baʊnd/ → see **bind**

bound ² /baʊnd/ *adjective*
bound to certain to happen or to do something: *There are bound to be price increases next year.*

boundary /ˈbaʊndəri/ *noun* (**boundaries**)
an imaginary line that separates one area of land from another area of land: *The river forms the western boundary of my farm.*

bouquet /bəʊˈkeɪ, buː-/ *noun*
a bunch of flowers that have been cut: *The bride carried a beautiful bouquet of roses.*

bout /baʊt/ *noun*
a short period of illness: *Dominic had a really bad bout of flu before the holidays.*

boutique /buːˈtiːk/ *noun*
a small shop that sells fashionable clothes, shoes or jewellery: *She found a beautiful black dress in a little boutique.*

bow ¹ /baʊ/ *verb* (**bows, bowing, bowed**)
to bend your head or body towards someone as a formal way of greeting them or showing respect: *They bowed low to the king.* ● **bow** *noun* *I gave a theatrical bow and waved.*

bow ² /bəʊ/ *noun*
1 a knot with two round parts and two loose ends that is used in tying shoelaces and ribbons: *Add some pretty ribbon tied in a bow.*
2 a weapon for shooting arrows: *Some of the men were armed with bows and arrows.*
3 a long thin piece of wood with threads stretched along it that you move across the strings of a musical instrument: *I drew the bow across the strings of the violin.*

bowels /ˈbaʊəlz/ *plural noun*
the tubes in your body where digested food from your stomach is stored before you pass it from your body: *Eating plenty of fruit and vegetables can help to keep your bowels healthy.*

bowl ¹ /bəʊl/ *noun*
a round container that is used for mixing and serving food: *Put the soup in a bowl.* □ *a bowl of hot soup*

bowl ² /bəʊl/ *verb* (**bowls, bowling, bowled**)
to throw the ball in a game of cricket, so that someone can hit it

bowling /ˈbəʊlɪŋ/ *uncountable noun*
a game in which you roll a heavy ball down a narrow track toward a group of wooden objects and try to knock down as many of them as possible: *We go bowling every Saturday afternoon.*

bow 'tie *noun*
a tie in the form of a bow (= a knot with two round parts) that men sometimes wear on formal occasions

box ¹ /bɒks/ *noun* (**boxes**)
1 a container with a hard bottom, hard sides and usually a lid: *He packed his books into the cardboard box beside him.* □ *They sat on wooden boxes.*
2 a square shape that is printed on paper: *For more information, just tick the box and send us the form.*

box ² /bɒks/ *verb* (**boxes, boxing, boxed**)
to fight someone according to the rules of boxing: *At school I boxed and played baseball.*
▶ **boxer** *noun* *He wants to be a professional boxer.*

'boxer shorts *plural noun*
loose underwear that boys and men wear on the lower part of their body: *a pair of boxer shorts*

boxing /ˈbɒksɪŋ/ *uncountable noun*
a sport in which two people fight following special rules

'box ˌoffice also **box-office** *noun*
the place in a theatre where the tickets are sold: *There was a long queue of people outside the box office.*

boy /bɔɪ/ *noun*
a male child: *Did you have any pets when you were a little boy?*

boy band *noun*
a music group made up of young men who sing popular music and dance: *He was in a very successful boy band in the nineties.*

boycott /ˈbɔɪkɒt/ *verb* (**boycotts, boycotting, boycotted**)
to refuse to be involved with a country,

an organization or an activity because you disapprove of it: *Some groups threatened to boycott the meeting.*

boyfriend /'bɔɪfrend/ *noun*
a man or a boy that someone is having a romantic relationship with: *Brenda came with her boyfriend, Anthony.*

Boy Scout /ˌbɔɪ 'skaʊt/ *noun*
→ see **scout**: *He was a Boy Scout in his youth.*
the Boy Scouts → see **the Scouts**: *I joined the Boy Scouts when I was ten years old.*

bra /brɑː/ *noun*
a piece of underwear that women wear to support their breasts

bracelet /'breɪslɪt/ *noun*
a piece of jewellery that you wear around your wrist

brackets /'brækɪts/ *plural noun*
curved ( ) or square [ ] marks that you can place around words, letters or numbers when you are writing: *There's a telephone number in brackets under his name.*

brain /breɪn/ *noun*
1 the organ inside your head that controls your body's activities and allows you to think and to feel things
2 your mind and the way that you think: *Sports are good for your brain as well as your body.*
have brains to have the ability to learn and understand things quickly: *These scientists have brains and imagination.*

brake /breɪk/ *noun*
the part in a vehicle that makes it go slower or stop: *He stepped on the brake as the light turned red.* ● **brake** *verb* (**brakes, braking, braked**) *The driver braked to avoid an accident.*

branch /brɑːntʃ/ *noun* (**branches**)
1 one of the parts of a tree that have leaves, flowers and fruit: *We picked apples from the upper branches of a tree.*
2 one of the offices or shops that form part of a bigger company: *Sadly, we are closing some of our smaller branches.*

brand /brænd/ *noun*
the name of a product that a particular company makes: *This shop doesn't sell my favourite brand of biscuits.*

'brand-'new *adjective*
completely new: *Yesterday he bought a brand-new car.*

brandy /'brændi/ *noun* (**brandies**)
a strong alcoholic drink made from wine

brass /brɑːs/ *uncountable noun*
1 a yellow-coloured metal: *Ritchie lifted the shiny brass door knocker.*
2 musical instruments that are made of brass: *a piece of music for brass*
3 all the musical instruments in an orchestra that are made of brass: *Suddenly the brass comes in with great power and intensity.*

brave /breɪv/ *adjective* (**braver, bravest**)
willing to do things that are dangerous, without showing fear: *A brave 12-year-old boy tried to help his friends.*
▶ **bravely** *adverb* *The army fought bravely.*

bravery /'breɪvəri/ *uncountable noun*
the ability to do things that are dangerous without showing fear: *He received an award for his bravery.*

bread /bred/ *noun*
a food made mostly from flour and water: *She bought a loaf of bread at the shop.*
□ *I usually just have bread and butter for breakfast.*
→ Look at picture on P3

break[1] /breɪk/ *verb* (**breaks, breaking, broke, broken**)
1 to separate suddenly into pieces often after falling or hitting something: *The plate broke.* □ *The plane crashed into the trees and broke into three pieces.* □ *Rachel's right arm broke when she was hit by a car.*
2 to make something separate into pieces, often by dropping or hitting it: *I'm sorry. I've broken a glass.* □ *After the match, I found out I had broken a bone in my left foot.*
3 to damage something so that it stops working: *I've broken my mobile phone so I need a new one.*
4 to do something that you should not do because it is against a law, or because it goes against something that you have agreed or promised to do: *We didn't know we were breaking the law.* □ *She says you broke a promise to her.*

break down
1 to stop working: *Their car broke down.*
2 to start crying: *I broke down and cried.*
break in (*also* **break into something**) to get into a building by force: *The robbers broke in and stole £8,000.* □ *There was someone trying to break into the house.*

break out to begin suddenly: *He was 29 when war broke out.*

break something off to remove one part of a thing from the rest of it by breaking it: *Grace broke off a large piece of bread.*

break up
1 to end a relationship: *I was married for eight years but we broke up last year.* □ *My girlfriend has broken up with me.*
2 to start the school holidays: *We break up at the end of June.*

break² /breɪk/ *noun*
a short period of time when you have a rest: *We get a 15-minute break for coffee.*

breakdown /ˈbreɪkdaʊn/ *noun*
1 the failure of a relationship, a plan or a discussion: *Newspapers reported the breakdown of talks between the U.S. and European Union officials.* □ *Arguments about money led to the breakdown of their marriage.*
2 when a car or a piece of machinery stops working: *You should be prepared for breakdowns and accidents.*

breakfast /ˈbrekfəst/ *noun*
the first meal of the day: *Would you like eggs for breakfast?*

breakthrough /ˈbreɪkθruː/ *noun*
an important discovery that is made after a lot of hard work: *The scientist described a medical breakthrough in cancer treatment.*

breast /brest/ *noun*
1 one of the two soft, round parts on a woman's chest that can produce milk to feed a baby
2 a piece of meat that is cut from the front of a bird: *For dinner I cooked chicken breast with vegetables.*

breaststroke /ˈbreststrəʊk/ *uncountable noun*
a way of swimming in which you pull both of your arms back at the same time, and kick your legs with your knees bent: *I'm learning to swim breaststroke.*

breath /breθ/ *noun*
the air that you let out through your mouth when you breathe: *His breath smelled of onion.*
be out of breath to be breathing very quickly because your body has been working hard: *She was out of breath from running.*
take a breath to breathe in once: *He took a deep breath, and began to climb the stairs.*

breathe /briːð/ *verb* (**breathes, breathing, breathed**)
to take air into your lungs and let it out again: *He was breathing fast.*
▶ **breathing** *uncountable noun* *Her breathing became slow.*

breathless /ˈbreθləs/ *adjective*
having difficulty breathing properly, because you have been running, for example: *I was breathless after the race.*

breed¹ /briːd/ *noun*
a particular type of animal: *There are about 300 breeds of horse.*

breed² /briːd/ *verb* (**breeds, breeding, bred**)
1 to keep male and female animals so that they will produce babies: *He breeds dogs for the police.*
2 to produce babies: *Birds usually breed in the spring.*

breeze /briːz/ *noun*
a gentle wind: *We enjoyed the cool summer breeze.*

bribe /braɪb/ *verb* (**bribes, bribing, bribed**)
to offer someone money or something valuable in order to persuade them to do something dishonest: *He was accused of bribing a bank official.* ● **bribe** *noun The police took bribes from criminals.*

bribery /ˈbraɪbəri/ *uncountable noun*
the act of offering someone money or something valuable in order to persuade them to do something dishonest for you: *He was arrested for bribery.*

brick /brɪk/ *noun*
a rectangular block used in the building of walls: *a brick wall*

bride /braɪd/ *noun*
a woman on her wedding day, or a woman who is about to get married or has just got married

bridegroom /ˈbraɪdɡruːm/ *noun*
a man who is getting married

bridesmaid /ˈbraɪdzmeɪd/ *noun*
a woman or a girl who helps the bride on her wedding day

bridge /brɪdʒ/ *noun*
a structure that is built over a river or a road so that people or vehicles can cross from one side to the other: *He walked over the bridge to get to school.*

bridge

brief /bri:f/ *adjective* (**briefer, briefest**)

1 lasting for only a short time: *She once made a brief appearance on television.*

2 without many words or details: *The book begins with a brief description of his career.*

briefcase /'bri:fkeɪs/ *noun*

a small suitcase for carrying business papers in

briefly /'bri:fli/ *adverb*

for a very short period of time: *He smiled briefly.*

briefs /bri:fs/ *plural noun*

men's or women's underwear that they wear on the lower part of their body: *a pair of briefs*

bright /braɪt/ *adjective* (**brighter, brightest**)

1 strong and noticeable in colour: *She wore a bright red dress.*

2 shining strongly: *He looked pale and tired under the bright lights of the TV studio.*

▸ **brightly** *adverb* *The sun shone brightly in the sky.*

3 full of light: *There was a bright room where patients could sit with their visitors.*

4 clever and able to learn things quickly: *He seems brighter than most boys.*

brighten /'braɪtən/ *verb* (**brightens, brightening, brightened**)

1 to suddenly look happier: *Seeing him, she seemed to brighten a little.*

2 to make something more colourful and attractive: *Pots planted with flowers brightened the area outside the door.*

brilliant /'brɪliənt/ *adjective*

1 very clever or skilful: *She had a brilliant mind.* □ *He was a brilliant pianist.*

▸ **brilliantly** *adverb* *The film was brilliantly*

written and acted – a really great production.

2 extremely bright in light or colour: *The woman had brilliant green eyes.*

3 very good (*informal*): *That film was brilliant.*

brim /brɪm/ *noun*

the part of a hat that sticks out around the bottom: *Rain dripped from the brim of his old hat.*

bring /brɪŋ/ *verb* (**brings, bringing, brought**)

1 to have someone or something with you when you come to a place: *Remember to bring an old shirt to wear when we paint.* □ *Can I bring Susie to the party?*

2 to get something that someone wants and take it to them: *He poured a glass of milk for Sarah and brought it to her.*

bring someone up to take care of a child until it is an adult: *She brought up four children.* □ *He was brought up in Nebraska.*

bring something back to return something: *Please could you bring back those books that I lent you?*

bring something in to earn money: *My job brings in about £24,000 a year.*

bring something up to introduce a particular subject into a conversation: *Her mother brought up the subject of going back to work.*

LANGUAGE HELP

bring or take? **Bring** gives the idea of movement towards the speaker and **take** gives the idea of movement away from the speaker.

brisk /brɪsk/ *adjective* (**brisker, briskest**)

quick and using a lot of energy: *He gave me a brisk handshake.*

▸ **briskly** *adverb* *Eve walked briskly through the park.*

bristle /'brɪsəl/ *noun*

1 one of the short hairs that grow on a man's face

2 a short thick hair on a brush

brittle /'brɪtəl/ *adjective*

hard but easily broken: *I have very brittle fingernails.*

broad /brɔːd/ *adjective* (**broader, broadest**)

1 wide: *His shoulders were broad and his waist was narrow.*

a broad smile/grin a big, happy smile or grin: *He greeted them with a wave and a broad smile.*

2 including a large number of different things: *The library had a broad range of books.*

broadband /'brɔːdbænd/ *uncountable noun*

a method of sending many electronic messages at the same time over the Internet: *They've announced big price cuts for broadband customers.*

broadcast /'brɔːdkɑːst/ *verb* (**broadcasts, broadcasting, broadcast**)

to send out a programme so that it can be heard on the radio or seen on television: *The concert will be broadcast live on television and radio.* ● **broadcast** *noun We saw a live television broadcast of Saturday's football game.*

broccoli /'brɒkəli/ *uncountable noun*

a vegetable with thick green stems and small green flowers on top
→ Look at picture on P2

brochure /'brəʊʃə/ *noun*

a thin magazine with pictures that gives you information about a product or a service: *The city looked beautiful in the travel brochures.*

broke¹ /brəʊk/ → see **break**

broke² /brəʊk/ *adjective*

without any money (*informal*): *I don't have a job, and I'm broke.*

broken¹ /'brəʊkən/ → see **break**

broken² /'brəʊkən/ *adjective*

in pieces or not working: *She was taken to hospital with a broken leg.* □ *a broken window* □ *My watch is broken.*

bronze¹ /brɒnz/ *uncountable noun*

a yellowish-brown metal that is a mixture of copper and tin: *a bronze statue of a ballet dancer*

bronze² /brɒnz/ *adjective*

yellowish-brown in colour: *The sky began to fill with bronze light.*

bronze medal *noun*

an award made of brown metal that you get as third prize in a competition

brooch /brəʊtʃ/ *noun* (**brooches**)

a piece of jewellery that has a pin on the back so that you can fasten it to your clothes

brood /bruːd/ *verb* (**broods, brooding, brooded**)

to feel sad or worry a lot about something: *She constantly broods about having no friends.*

broom /bruːm/ *noun*

a type of brush with a long handle used for sweeping the floor

brother /'brʌðə/ *noun*

a boy or a man who has the same parents as you: *Are you Peter's brother?*
→ Look at picture on P8

brother-in-law *noun* (**brothers-in-law**)

the brother of your husband or wife, or the man who is married to your sister
→ Look at picture on P8

brought /brɔːt/ → see **bring**

brow /braʊ/ *noun*

your forehead: *He wiped his brow with the back of his hand.*

brown /braʊn/ *adjective* (**browner, brownest**)

having the colour of earth or wood: *He looked into her brown eyes.* ● **brown** *noun Colours such as dark brown and green will be popular in the fashion world this autumn.*

brownie /'braʊni/ *noun*

a small flat chocolate cake: *She put a tray of chocolate brownies on the table.*

Brownie /'braʊni/ *noun*

a girl who is a member of the Brownies
the Brownies an organization for girls between the ages of seven and ten

browse /braʊz/ *verb* (**browses, browsing, browsed**)

1 to look at things in a shop, without buying anything: *I stopped in several bookshops to browse.*

2 to look through a book or a magazine: *She was sitting on the sofa browsing through the TV magazine.*

3 to search for information on the Internet: *The software allows you to browse the Internet on your mobile phone.*

browser /'braʊzə/ *noun*

a piece of computer software that allows you to search for information on the Internet: *You need an up-to-date Web browser.*

bruise /bruːz/ *verb* (**bruises, bruising, bruised**)

to injure a part of your body so that a purple mark appears there: *I bruised my knee on a desk drawer.* ● **bruise** *noun How did you get that bruise on your arm?*
▶ **bruised** *adjective a bruised knee*

brush¹ /brʌʃ/ *noun* (**brushes**)
an object with a lot of bristles or hairs attached to it that you use for painting, cleaning things and making your hair tidy: *We gave him paint and brushes.* □ *He brought soapy water and brushes to clean the floor.*

brush² /brʌʃ/ *verb* (**brushes, brushing, brushed**)
1 to clean something or make it tidy using a brush: *Have you brushed your teeth?* □ *You need to brush your hair.*
2 to remove something with movements of your hands: *He brushed the snow off his suit.*
3 to touch something lightly: *The cat brushed against her leg.*

brushes

toothbrush

dustpan and brush

hairbrush

paintbrush

brussels sprout /ˌbrʌsəlz ˈspraʊt/ *noun*
a small round vegetable made of many leaves

brutal /ˈbruːtəl/ *adjective*
very cruel and violent: *a brutal military dictator* □ *brutal punishment*
▶ **brutally** *adverb* *Her parents were brutally murdered.*

BTW
short for 'by the way' in an email or a text message

bubble¹ /ˈbʌbəl/ *noun*
1 a small ball of air or gas in a liquid: *Air bubbles rise to the surface.*
2 a hollow ball of soapy liquid that is floating in the air or standing on a surface: *With soap and lots of bubbles children love bathtime.*

bubble² /ˈbʌbəl/ *verb* (**bubbles, bubbling, bubbled**)
to produce bubbles: *Heat the soup until it is bubbling.*

bubbly /ˈbʌbli/ *adjective*
1 very lively and cheerful: *Sue is a bubbly girl who loves to laugh.*
2 with a lot of bubbles: *When the butter is melted and bubbly, add the flour.*

bucket /ˈbʌkɪt/ *noun*   **bucket**
a round metal or plastic container with a handle, used for holding and carrying water: *She threw a bucket of water on the fire.*

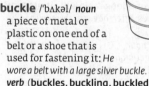

buckle /ˈbʌkəl/ *noun*
a piece of metal or plastic on one end of a belt or a shoe that is used for fastening it: *He wore a belt with a large silver buckle.* ● **buckle** *verb* (**buckles, buckling, buckled**) *The girl sat down to buckle her shoes.*

buckle

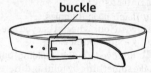

bud /bʌd/ *noun*
a new growth on a tree or plant that develops into a leaf or flower: *Small pink buds were beginning to form on the bushes.*

Buddhism /ˈbʊdɪzəm/ *uncountable noun*
a religion that teaches that the way to end suffering is by controlling your desires

Buddhist /ˈbʊdɪst/ *noun*
a person whose religion is Buddhism
● **Buddhist** *adjective* *Buddhist monks*

budge /bʌdʒ/ *verb* (**budges, budging, budged**)

not budge

1 to refuse to change your mind about something: *The government will not budge on this point.*

2 to be impossible to move: *I tried to open the window, but it wouldn't budge.*

budget¹ /'bʌdʒɪt/ *noun*

1 the amount of money that you have available to spend: *She will design a new kitchen for you within your budget.* □ *The actress will star in a low-budget film.*

2 a formal speech made by a government in some countries in which the people are told how much money the government will spend on services in the next year

budget² /'bʌdʒɪt/ *verb* (**budgets, budgeting, budgeted**)

to decide how much money you can afford to spend: *The company has budgeted £10 million for advertising.*

buffalo /'bʌfələʊ/ *noun* (**buffalo**)

a wild animal like a large cow with horns that curve upwards

buffet /'bʌfeɪ/ *noun*

a meal at a party where the food is arranged on a long table and guests serve themselves: *After the event, there will be a buffet.*

bug /bʌg/ *noun*

1 an insect (*informal*)

2 a mild illness (*informal*): *I think I have a stomach bug.*

3 a mistake in a computer program: *There is a bug in the software.*

buggy /'bʌgi/ *noun* (**buggies**)

a chair with four wheels that you use for pushing a small child along

build¹ /bɪld/ *verb* (**builds, building, built**)

to make something by joining different things together: *They are going to build a hotel here.* □ *The house was built in the early 19th century.*

build² /bɪld/ *noun*

the particular shape of a person's body: *He's six feet tall and of medium build.*

builder /'bɪldə/ *noun*

a person whose job is to build or repair houses and other buildings: *The builders have finished the roof.*

→ Look at picture on P7

building /'bɪldɪŋ/ *noun*

a structure that has a roof and walls: *They lived on the top floor of the building.*

built /bɪlt/ → see **build**

bulb /bʌlb/ *noun*

1 the glass part inside a lamp that gives out light: *A single bulb hangs from the ceiling.*

2 a root of a flower or a plant: *tulip bulbs*

bulge /bʌldʒ/ *verb* (**bulges, bulging, bulged**)

to stick out: *His pockets were bulging with coins.* ● **bulge** *noun The police officer noticed a bulge under the man's coat and realized that he had a gun.*

bulk /bʌlk/ *noun*

in bulk in large amounts: *It is cheaper to buy supplies in bulk.*

the bulk of something most of: *The bulk of the money will go to the children's hospital in Dublin.*

bulky /'bʌlki/ *adjective* (**bulkier, bulkiest**)

large and heavy: *The shop can deliver bulky items like lawnmowers.*

bull /bʊl/ *noun*

a male animal of the cow family, and some other animals

bulldog /'bʊldɒg/ *noun*

a short dog with a large square head

bulldozer /'bʊldəʊzə/ *noun*

a large vehicle with a broad metal blade at the front that is used for moving large amounts of earth

bullet /'bʊlɪt/ *noun*

a small piece of metal that is shot out of a gun: *A bullet hit the wall behind him, narrowly missing him.*

'bulletin board *noun*

in computing, a system that allows users to send and receive messages: *The Internet is the largest computer bulletin board in the world.*

bully /'bʊli/ *noun* (**bullies**)

someone who uses their strength or power to frighten other people: *He was the class bully.* ● **bully** *verb* (**bullies, bullying, bullied**) *I wasn't going to let him bully me.*

bumblebee /'bʌmbəlˌbiː/ also **bumble bee** *noun*

a large bee

bump¹ /bʌmp/ *verb* (**bumps, bumping, bumped**)

to accidentally hit something or someone while you are moving: *They stopped walking and I almost bumped into them.* □ *She bumped her head on a low branch.*

bump into someone to meet someone you know by chance: *I bumped into Lisa in the supermarket yesterday.*

bump² /bʌmp/ *noun*
an injury that you get if you hit something or if something hits you: *She fell over and got a large bump on her head.*

bumper /'bʌmpə/ *noun*
a heavy bar at the front and back of a vehicle that protects the vehicle if it hits something: *I felt something hit the rear bumper of my car.*

bumpy /'bʌmpi/ *adjective* (**bumpier, bumpiest**)
not smooth or flat: *We rode our bicycles down the bumpy streets.*

bun /bʌn/ *noun*
1 a small bread roll: *He had a bun and a glass of milk.*
2 a style of arranging your hair so that it is attached tightly at the back of your head in the shape of a ball

bunch /bʌntʃ/ *noun* (**bunches**)
1 a number of flowers with their stems held together: *He left a huge bunch of flowers in her hotel room.*
2 a number of bananas or grapes growing together

bunch of flowers

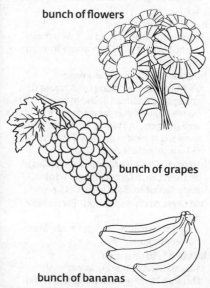

bunch of grapes

bunch of bananas

3 a group or a number of people or things (*informal*): *They're a great bunch of kids.*

bundle /'bʌndəl/ *noun*
a number of things that are tied or wrapped together so that they can be carried or stored: *He left a bundle of papers on the floor.*

bungalow /'bʌŋgələʊ/ *noun*
a house that has only one level, and no stairs

bunk /bʌŋk/ *noun*
a narrow bed that is usually attached to a wall, especially in a ship: *Sally was lying on her narrow wooden bunk.*

'bunk beds *plural noun*
two single beds that are built one on top of the other: *The children slept in bunk beds.*

bunny /'bʌni/ *noun* (**bunnies**)
a child's word for a rabbit (*informal*)

buoy /bɔɪ/ *noun*
an object floating in the sea or a lake that shows ships and boats where they can go safely

burden /'bɜːdən/ *noun*
something that causes people a lot of worry or hard work: *I don't want to become a burden on my family when I get old.*

burger /'bɜːgə/ *noun* (*also* **hamburger**)
meat that is cut into very small pieces and pressed into a flat round shape, often eaten between two pieces of bread: *I ordered a burger for lunch.*

burglar /'bɜːglə/ *noun*
someone who enters a building by force in order to steal things: *Specially-trained dogs often help the police to catch burglars.*

burglary /'bɜːgləri/ *noun* (**burglaries**)
the crime of entering a building by force and stealing things: *An 11-year-old boy committed a burglary.*

burgle /'bɜːgəl/ *verb* (**burgles, burgling, burgled**)
to enter a building by force and steal things: *My flat was burgled today.*

burial /'beriəl/ *noun*
the act or ceremony of putting a dead body into a grave in the ground: *Charles and his two sons attended the burial.*

burn /bɜːn/ *verb* (**burns, burning, burned or burnt**)
1 to destroy or damage something with fire: *She burned her old love letters.*

2 to injure a part of your body by fire or by something very hot: *Take care not to burn your fingers.* ● **burn** *noun* *She suffered burns to her back.*

3 to produce heat or fire: *Forty forest fires were burning in Alberta yesterday.*

4 to be destroyed by fire: *When I arrived, one of the vehicles was still burning.*

5 to copy something onto a CD: *I have the equipment to burn audio CDs.*

burnt /bɜ:nt/ → see **burn**

burp /bɜ:p/ *verb* (**burps, burping, burped**)
to make a noise because air from your stomach has been forced up through your throat ● **burp** *noun* *a loud burp*

burqa /'bɜ:kə/ also **burka** *noun*
a long dress that covers the head and body and is traditionally worn by some women in Islamic countries

burst /bɜ:st/ *verb* (**bursts, bursting, burst**)
to suddenly break open and release air or another substance: *The driver lost control of his car when a tyre burst.*
burst out to suddenly start laughing, crying or making another noise: *The class burst out laughing.*

bury /'beri/ *verb* (**buries, burying, buried**)
1 to put something into a hole in the ground and cover it up: *Some animals bury nuts and seeds.*
2 to put the body of a dead person into a grave and cover it with earth: *Soldiers helped to bury the dead.*

bus /bʌs/ *noun* (**buses**)
a large motor vehicle that carries passengers: *He missed his last bus home.*

bush /bʊʃ/ *noun* (**bushes**)
a plant with leaves and branches that is smaller than a tree: *a rose bush*
the bush an area in a hot country that is far from cities and where very few people live: *the Australian bush*

busily /'bɪzɪli/ *adverb*
in a very active way: *Workers were busily trying to repair the damage.*

business /'bɪznɪs/ *noun* (**businesses**)
1 *uncountable* work that is related to producing, buying and selling things: *He had a successful career in business.* □ *She attended Harvard Business School.*
2 an organization that produces and sells

goods or that provides a service: *The bakery is a family business.*

businessman /'bɪznɪsmən/ *noun* (**businessmen**)
a man who works in business: *He's a rich businessman.*
→ Look at picture on P7

businesswoman /'bɪznɪswʊmən/ *noun* (**businesswomen**)
a woman who works in business: *She's a successful businesswoman who manages her own company.*
→ Look at picture on P7

busy /'bɪzi/ *adjective* (**busier, busiest**)
1 working hard, so that you are not free to do anything else: *What is it? I'm busy.* □ *They are busy preparing for a party on Saturday.*
2 full of people who are doing things: *We walked along a busy city street.*
3 when a telephone line is busy, it is being used by someone else: *I tried to reach him, but the line was busy.*

but¹ /bət, STRONG bʌt/ *conjunction*
used to introduce something that is different from what you have just said: *I really enjoyed my holiday, but now it's time to get back to work.* □ *Heat the milk until it is very hot, but not boiling.*

but² /bət, STRONG bʌt/ *preposition*
except: *You've done nothing but complain all day.*

butcher /'bʊtʃə/ *noun*
1 someone who cuts up and sells meat
2 (*also* **butcher's**) a shop where you can buy meat

butter /'bʌtə/ *uncountable noun*
a soft yellow food made from cream that you spread on bread or use in cooking: *The waitress brought us bread and butter.* ● **butter** *verb* (**butters, buttering, buttered**) *She put two pieces of bread on a plate and buttered them.*
→ Look at picture on P3

butterfly /'bʌtəflaɪ/ *noun* (**butterflies**)
an insect with large coloured wings: *Butterflies are attracted to the wild flowers.*

butterscotch /'bʌtəˌskɒtʃ/ *uncountable noun*
a type of hard brown sweet made from butter and sugar

button¹ /'bʌtən/ *noun*
1 a small hard object that you push through holes (= buttonholes) to fasten

your clothes: *I bought a blue jacket with silver buttons.*

2 a small object on a piece of equipment that you press to make it work: *He put in a DVD and pressed the 'play' button.*

button² /ˈbʌtən/ *verb* (**buttons, buttoning, buttoned**)

to fasten a piece of clothing by pushing its buttons through the buttonholes: *Ferguson stood up and buttoned his coat.*

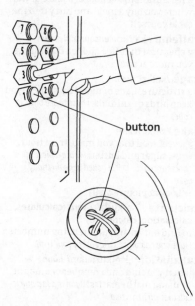

button

buy /baɪ/ *verb* (**buys, buying, bought**)
to get something by paying money for it:

He could not afford to buy a house. □ *Lizzie bought herself a bike.*

▶ **buyer** *noun* *Car buyers are more interested in safety than speed.*

buzz /bʌz/ *verb* (**buzzes, buzzing, buzzed**)
to make a sound like a bee: *There was a fly buzzing around my head.* ● **buzz** *noun* *The annoying buzz of an insect kept us awake.*

by /baɪ/ *preposition*

1 used for showing which person or thing did or made something: *The dinner was served by his mother and sisters.* □ *She was woken by a loud noise in the street.* □ *Here's a painting by Van Gogh.*

2 used for showing what you use to do something: *We usually travel by car.* □ *You can pay by credit card, cheque or cash.*

3 beside; close to: *Judith was sitting in a chair by the window.* □ *Jack stood by the door, ready to leave.*

4 past: *He waved as he drove by the house.*

● **by** *adverb* *They were very polite and would always say hello as they walked by.*

5 at or before a particular time: *I'll be home by eight o'clock.*

by yourself

1 alone: *A man was sitting by himself in a corner.*

2 without help from anyone else: *I can do it by myself.*

bye /baɪ/ or **bye-bye**
a way of saying goodbye (*informal*): *Bye, Daddy.*

byte /baɪt/ *noun*
a unit of information in computing: *two million bytes of data*

Cc

c

cab /kæb/ *noun*
→ see **taxi**

cabbage /ˈkæbɪdʒ/ *noun*
a round vegetable with white, green or
purple leaves
→ Look at picture on P2

cabin /ˈkæbɪn/ *noun*
1 a small wooden house in the woods or
mountains: *We stayed in a log cabin.*
2 a small room on a boat: *He showed her to
a small cabin.*
3 the part of a plane where people sit:
He sat in the first-class cabin.

cabinet /ˈkæbɪnɪt/ *noun*
1 a piece of furniture with shelves, used
for storing things in: *I looked in the medicine
cabinet.*
→ Look at picture on P4
2 a group of important members of the
government who give advice to the prime
minister: *The issue was discussed at the
cabinet's weekly meeting.*

cable /ˈkeɪbəl/ *noun*
1 a very strong, thick rope, made of metal:
They used a cable made of steel wire.
2 a thick wire that carries electricity: *The
island gets its electricity from underground
power cables.*

cable television *uncountable noun*
a television system in which signals
travel along wires: *We don't have cable TV.*

cactus /ˈkæktəs/ *noun*
(**cacti** /ˈkæktaɪ/)
a plant with lots of
sharp points that
grows in hot, dry
places

café /ˈkæfeɪ/
also **cafe** *noun*
a place where
you can buy
drinks and
small meals

cactus

cafeteria /ˌkæfɪˈtɪəriə/ *noun*
a restaurant in a school or a place of work
where you buy a meal and carry it to the
table yourself

caffeine /ˈkæfiːn/ *uncountable noun*
a chemical in coffee and tea that makes
you more active

cage /keɪdʒ/ *noun*
a structure made of metal bars where you
keep birds or animals: *I hate to see birds in
cages.*

cake /keɪk/ *noun*
a sweet food that you make from flour,
eggs, sugar and butter: *He ate a piece of
chocolate cake.* □ *We baked her a birthday
cake.*
→ Look at picture on P3

calculate /ˈkælkjʊleɪt/ *verb* (**calculates,
calculating, calculated**)
to find out an amount by using numbers:
Have you calculated the cost of your trip?

calculation /ˌkælkjʊˈleɪʃən/ *noun*
when you find out a number or amount
by using mathematics: *Ryan made a quick
calculation in his head*

calculator /ˈkælkjʊˌleɪtə/ *noun*
a small electronic machine that you use
to calculate numbers: *He takes a pocket
calculator to school.*

calendar /ˈkælɪndə/ *noun*
a list of days, weeks and months for a
particular year: *There was a calendar on the
wall.*

calf /kɑːf/ *noun* (**calves** /kɑːvz/)
1 a young cow
2 the thick part at the back of your leg,
between your ankle and your knee
→ Look at picture on P1

call /kɔːl/ *verb* (**calls, calling, called**)
1 to give someone or something a
particular name: *I wanted to call the dog
Mufty.* □ *Her daughter is called Charlotte.*
2 to say something in a loud voice:

Someone called his name.
3 to telephone someone: *Call me when you find out.* □ *I will call the doctor.* ● **call** *noun I made a phone call to my grandmother.*
4 to make a short visit somewhere: *A salesman called at the house.* ● **call** *noun The doctor was out on a call.*
call for someone to go to someone's home so that you can both go somewhere else together: *I'll call for you at seven o'clock.*
call on someone to visit someone for a short time: *I called on Ava.*
call someone back to telephone someone in return for a call they made to you: *I'll call you back.*
call something off to cancel an event that has been planned: *He called off the trip.*

callback /ˈkɔːl,bæk/ *noun*
an occasion when your telephone rings when a number that you have been trying to call becomes available

caller /ˈkɔːlə/ *noun*
a person who is making a telephone call: *A caller told police what happened.*

calm¹ /kɑːm/ *adjective* (**calmer, calmest**)
1 not worried, angry or excited: *She is a calm, patient woman.* □ *Try to keep calm.*
▶ **calmly** *adverb Alan said calmly, 'I don't believe you.'*
2 not moving much: *The sea was very calm.*
3 without much wind: *It was a fine, calm day.*

calm² /kɑːm/ *verb* (**calms, calming, calmed**)
calm down to become less upset or excited: *Calm down and listen to me.*
calm someone down to make someone less upset or excited: *I'll try to calm him down.*

calorie /ˈkæləri/ *noun*
a unit that is used for measuring the amount of energy in food: *These sweet drinks have a lot of calories in them.*

came /keɪm/
→ see **come**

camel /ˈkæməl/ *noun*
an animal with one or two large lumps on its back

camel

camera /ˈkæmrə/ *noun*
a piece of equipment for taking photographs or

making films: *a digital camera*

'camera phone *noun*
a mobile phone that can take photographs

camp¹ /kæmp/ *noun*
a place where people live or stay in tents: *an army camp*

camp² /kæmp/ *verb* (**camps, camping, camped**)
to stay somewhere in a tent: *We camped near the beach.*
▶ **camping** *uncountable noun They went camping in Devon.*

campaign /kæmˈpeɪn/ *noun*
a number of things that you do over a period of time in order to get a particular result: *January marks the start of the election campaign.* ● **campaign** *verb* (**campaigns, campaigning, campaigned**) *We are campaigning for better health services.*

camper /ˈkæmpə/ *noun*
a person who is staying in a tent, for example on holiday: *The campers packed up their tents.*

campfire /ˈkæmpfaɪə/ *noun*
a fire that you light outdoors when you are camping

campsite /ˈkæmpsaɪt/ *noun*
a place where you can stay in a tent

campus /ˈkæmpəs/ *noun* (**campuses**)
an area of land that contains the main buildings of a university or college

can¹ /kən, STRONG kæn/ *modal verb*

LANGUAGE HELP
Use the form **cannot** in negative statements. When you are speaking, you can use the short form **can't**, pronounced /kɑːnt/.

1 used for saying that you have the ability to do something: *I can take care of myself.* □ *Can you swim yet?*
2 used for showing that something is sometimes true: *Exercise can be fun.*
3 used with words like 'smell', 'see' and 'hear': *I can smell smoke.*
4 used for saying that you are allowed to do something: *Can I go to the party at the weekend?* □ *Sorry. We can't answer any questions.*
5 used for making requests or offers: *Can I have a look at that book?* □ *Can I help you?*

can² /kæn, kæn/ *noun*
a metal container for food, drink or paint: *a can of cola*

canal /kə'næl/ *noun*
a long narrow river made by people for boats to travel along: *The canals of Venice are very beautiful.*

cancel /'kænsəl/ *verb* (**cancels, cancelling, cancelled**)
to say that something that has been planned will not happen: *We cancelled our trip to Washington.*
▶ **cancellation** /kænsə'leɪʃən/ *noun The cancellation of his visit upset many people.*

cancer /'kænsə/ *noun*
a serious disease that makes groups of cells in the body grow when they should not: *Jane had cancer when she was 25.*

candidate /'kændɪdeɪt/ *noun*
someone who is trying to get a particular job, or trying to win a political position: *He is a candidate for the job.*

candle /'kændəl/ *noun*
a long stick of wax with a piece of string through the middle, that you burn to give you light: *The only light in the bedroom came from a candle.*

candlestick /'kændəl,stɪk/ *noun*
an object that holds a candle

candy /'kændi/ *noun* (American) (**candies**)
sweet food such as chocolate or toffee: *I gave him a piece of candy.*

cane /keɪn/ *noun*
the long hollow stem of a plant such as bamboo: *cane furniture*

cannon /'kænən/ *noun*
a large heavy gun on wheels that was used in battles in the past: *The soldiers stood beside the cannons.*

cannot /'kænɒt, kə'nɒt/
the negative form of **can 1**

canoe /kə'nu:/ *noun*
a small, narrow boat that you move through the water using a short pole (= a paddle)

canoe

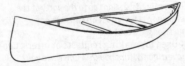

can't /kɑ:nt/
short for 'cannot'

canteen /kæn'ti:n/ *noun*
a place in a school or college where students can buy and eat lunch: *Rebecca ate her lunch in the canteen.*

canvas /'kænvəs/ *noun* (**canvases**)
1 *uncountable* a strong, heavy material that is used for making tents and bags: *a canvas bag*
2 a piece of this material that you paint on: *an artist's canvas*

canyon /'kænjən/ *noun*
a long, narrow valley with very steep sides: *the Grand Canyon*

cap /kæp/ *noun*
1 a soft, flat hat with a curved part at the front: *He wore a dark blue baseball cap.*
2 the lid of a bottle: *She took the cap off her water bottle and drank.*

capable /'keɪpəbəl/ *adjective*
1 able to do something: *He was not even capable of standing up.*
2 able to do something well: *She's a very capable teacher.*

capacity /kə'pæsɪti/ *noun* (**capacities**)
1 the maximum amount that something can hold: *The stadium has a capacity of 50,000.*
2 *uncountable* someone's ability to do something: *Every human being has the capacity for love.*

cape /keɪp/ *noun*
1 a large piece of land that sticks out into the sea: *the Cape of Good Hope*
2 a long coat without sleeves, that covers your body and arms

capital /'kæpɪtəl/ *noun*
1 the city where the government of a country meets: *Berlin is the capital of Germany.*
2 the large letter that you use at the beginning of sentences and names: *He wrote his name in capitals.*

> **LANGUAGE HELP**
> Note that you must always use a capital letter with days of the week and months of the year.

3 *uncountable* money that you use to start a business: *They provide capital for small businesses.*

capitalism /'kæpɪtə,lɪzəm/ *uncountable noun*

an economic and political system in which property, business and industry are privately owned and not owned by the state

capitalist /'kæpɪtəlɪst/ *noun*

someone who believes in a system where industry is owned by private companies rather than by the government
• **capitalist** *adjective* Banks play an important part in the capitalist system.

,**capital 'punishment** *uncountable noun*

when a criminal is killed legally as a punishment: *Capital punishment is not used in some countries.*

captain /'kæptɪn/ *noun*

1 an officer of middle rank in the army or navy: *He was a captain in the army.*
2 the leader of a sports team: *Mickey Thomas is the captain of the tennis team.*
3 the person who is in charge of an aeroplane or a ship: *Who is the captain of this boat?*

caption /'kæpʃən/ *noun*

a piece of writing next to a picture, that tells you something about the picture: *The photo had the caption 'John, aged 6 years'.*

captive /'kæptɪv/ *noun*

a person or animal who is kept in a place and not allowed to leave: *The captives were treated with respect.* • **captive** *adjective* Scientists are studying the behaviour of the captive birds.

captivity /kæp'tɪvɪti/ *uncountable noun*

when a person or animal is kept in a place and not allowed to leave: *The birds were kept in captivity.*

capture /'kæptʃə/ *verb* (**captures, capturing, captured**)

to catch someone or something and keep them somewhere so that they cannot leave: *The enemy shot down the aeroplane and captured the pilot.*

car /kɑː/ *noun*

1 (*American*: **automobile**) a motor vehicle with space for about 5 people: *They arrived by car.*
2 (*American*) → see **carriage**

caramel /'kærəmel/ *uncountable noun*

a type of sweet food made from burnt sugar, butter and milk

caravan /'kærəvæn/ (*American*: **trailer**) *noun*

a large vehicle that is pulled by a car. You can sleep and eat in a caravan on holiday.

carbohydrate /,kɑːbəʊ'haɪdreɪt/ *noun*

a substance in food that provides the body with energy: *You need to eat more carbohydrates such as bread, pasta or potatoes.*

carbon dioxide /,kɑːbən daɪ'ɒksaɪd/ *uncountable noun*

a gas that animals and people produce when they breathe out

carbon monoxide /,kɑːbən mə'nɒksaɪd/ *uncountable noun*

a poisonous gas that is produced by engines that use petrol

card /kɑːd/ *noun*

1 a piece of stiff paper with a picture and a message, that you send to someone on a special occasion: *She sends me a card on my birthday.*
2 a small piece of cardboard or plastic that has information about you written on it: *Please remember to bring your membership card.*

cards

birthday card

credit card

playing card

3 a small piece of plastic that you use to pay for things: *He paid the bill with a credit card.*

4 a piece of stiff paper with numbers or pictures on it that you use for playing games: *They enjoy playing cards.*

5 *uncountable* strong, stiff paper: *You will need three pieces of strong card.*

cardboard /'kɑ:dbɔ:d/ *uncountable noun*
thick, stiff paper that is used for making boxes: *a cardboard box*

cardigan /'kɑ:dɪgən/ *noun*
a jumper that opens at the front like a jacket

care¹ /keə/ *verb* (**cares, caring, cared**)
to be interested in someone or something, or to think they are very important: *We care about the environment.*
care for someone
1 to love someone: *He still cares for you.*
2 to look after someone: *A nurse cares for David in his home.*

care² /keə/ *uncountable noun*
when you do something very carefully so that you do not make any mistakes: *He chose his words with care.*
take care of something/someone to look after someone: *There was no one to take care of the children.*

career /kə'rɪə/ *noun*
a job that you do for a long time, or the years of your life that you spend working: *She had a long career as a teacher.*

careful /'keəfʊl/ *adjective*
thinking a lot about what you are doing so that you do not make any mistakes: *Be very careful with this liquid, it can be dangerous.*
▶ **carefully** *adverb* *Have a nice time, and drive carefully.*

careless /'keələs/ *adjective*
not giving enough attention to what you are doing, and so making mistakes: *Some of my students were very careless with homework.*

caretaker /'keəteɪkə/ *noun*
someone who looks after a building such as a school and the area around it

cargo /'kɑ:gəʊ/ *noun* (**cargoes**)
the things that a ship or a plane is carrying: *The ship was carrying a cargo of bananas.*

carnation /kɑ:'neɪʃən/ *noun*
a plant with white, pink or red flowers

carnival /'kɑ:nɪvəl/ *noun*
a celebration in the street, with music and dancing

carnivore /'kɑ:nɪvɔ:/ *noun*
an animal that eats mainly meat. Compare with **herbivore** and **omnivore**.

carol /'kærəl/ *noun*
a song that Christians sing at Christmas: *The children all sang carols as loudly as they could.*

'car park *noun*
an area of ground or a building where people can leave their cars for a period of time

carpenter /'kɑ:pɪntə/ *noun*
a person whose job is to make and repair wooden things
→ Look at picture on P7

carpet /'kɑ:pɪt/ *noun*
a thick, soft covering for the floor: *He picked up the clothes and vacuumed the carpets.*

carriage /'kærɪdʒ/ *noun*
one of the sections of a train where people sit: *He found his seat in the carriage and sat down.*

carrier bag /'kæriə bæg/ *noun*
a plastic or paper bag with handles that you use for carrying shopping

carrot /'kærət/ *noun*
a long, thin, orange-coloured vegetable: *We had chicken with potatoes, peas and carrots.*
→ Look at picture on P2

carry /'kæri/ *verb* (**carries, carrying, carried**)
1 to hold something in your hand and take it with you: *He was carrying a briefcase.*
2 to always have something with you: *You have to carry a passport.*
3 to take someone or something somewhere: *Lorries carrying food and medicine left the capital city yesterday.*
carry on to continue to do something: *The teacher carried on talking.*
carry something out to do something: *They carried out tests in the laboratory.*

cart /kɑ:t/ *noun*
1 an old-fashioned wooden vehicle that is usually pulled by a horse
2 (*American*) → see **trolley**

carton /'kɑːtən/ *noun*
a plastic or cardboard container for food or drink: *a carton of milk*

cartoon /kɑːˈtuːn/ *noun*
1 a funny drawing, often in a magazine or newspaper: *cartoon characters*
2 a film that uses drawings for all the characters and scenes instead of real people or objects: *We watched children's cartoons on TV.*

carve /kɑːv/ *verb* (**carves, carving, carved**)
1 to cut an object out of wood or stone: *He carved the statue from one piece of rock.*
2 to cut slices from meat: *Andrew began to carve the chicken.*

case /keɪs/ *noun*
1 a particular situation, especially one that you are using as an example: *In some cases, it can be very difficult.*
2 a crime that police are working on: *a murder case*
3 a container that is designed to hold or protect something: *He uses a black case for his glasses.*
in any case said when you are adding another reason for something: *The concert was sold out, and in any case, most of us could not afford a ticket.*
in case/just in case because a particular thing might happen: *I've brought some food in case we get hungry.*
in that/which case if that is the situation: *'It's raining.' — 'Oh, in that case we'll have to stay in.'*

cash ¹ /kæʃ/ *uncountable noun*
money in the form of notes and coins: *two thousand pounds in cash*

cash ² /kæʃ/ *verb* (**cashes, cashing, cashed**)
to take a cheque to a bank and get money for it: *I stopped at the bank to cash a cheque.*

'cash desk *noun*
the place in a shop where you pay

cashew /kəˈʃuː, ˈkæʃuː/ *noun* (*also* **cashew nut**)
a curved nut that you can eat

cashier /kæˈʃɪə/ *noun*
a person whose job is to take customers' money in shops or banks

'cash ma,chine (*American*: **ATM**) *noun* (*also* **cash dispenser**)
a machine in the wall outside a bank or other building where you can get money, using a special plastic card

casino /kəˈsiːnəʊ/ *noun*
a place where people gamble (= risk money) by playing games

cassette /kəˈset/ *noun*
a small, flat plastic case containing tape that is used for recording and playing sound or pictures: *a small cassette recorder*

cast /kɑːst/ *noun*
1 all the people who act in a play or a film: *The show is very amusing and the cast is very good.*
2 a hard cover for protecting a broken arm or leg: *His arm is in a cast.*

castle /'kɑːsəl/ *noun*
a large building with thick, high walls that was built in the past to protect people during wars and battles

casual /ˈkæʒʊəl/ *adjective*
1 relaxed and not worried about what is happening: *She tried to sound casual, but she was frightened.*
▶ **casually** *adverb* '*No need to hurry,' Ben said casually.*
2 worn at home or on holiday, and not on formal occasions: *I also bought some casual clothes for the weekend.*
▶ **casually** *adverb* *They were casually dressed.*

casualty /ˈkæʒʊəlti/ *noun* (**casualties**)
1 a person who is injured or killed in a war or in an accident: *Helicopters bombed the town, causing many casualties.*
2 *uncountable* the place in a hospital where people go for emergency treatment if they have a bad accident or a sudden illness

cat /kæt/ *noun*
a small animal covered with fur that people in some countries keep as a pet: *The cat sat on my lap, purring.*

catalogue /ˈkætəlɒg/ *noun*
a list of things you can buy from a particular company: *The website has an on-line catalogue of products.*

catastrophe /kəˈtæstrəfi/ *noun*
a sudden event that causes a lot of

cat

tail

fur

claw

paw

suffering or damage: *They learn how to deal with major catastrophes, including earthquakes.*
▶ **catastrophic** /ˌkætə'strɒfɪk/ *adjective*
A storm caused catastrophic damage to the houses.

catch /kætʃ/ *verb* (**catches, catching, caught**)
1 to find a person or animal and hold them: *Police say they are confident of catching the man.* □ *Where did you catch the fish?*
2 to take and hold an object that is moving through the air: *I jumped up to catch the ball.* ● **catch** *noun* (**catches**) *That was a great catch.*
3 to get part of your body stuck somewhere accidentally: *I caught my finger in the car door.*
4 to get on a bus, train or plane in order to travel somewhere: *We caught the bus on the corner of the street.*
5 to see or find someone doing something wrong: *They caught him with £30,000 cash in a briefcase.*
6 to become ill with an illness: *Keep warm, or you'll catch a cold.*

catch up or **catch up with someone**
1 to reach someone by walking faster than they are walking: *I stopped and waited for her to catch up.* □ *She hurried to catch up with him.*
2 to reach the same level as someone else: *You'll have to work hard to catch up.*

categorize /'kætɪgəˌraɪz/ *verb* (**categorizes, categorizing, categorized**)
to say which group or type people or things belong to: *Their music is usually categorized as jazz.*

category /'kætɪgri/ *noun* (**categories**)
a group of people or things are that are similar: *Their music falls into the category of 'jazz'.*

caterpillar /'kætəpɪlə/ *noun*
a small animal with a long body that develops into a butterfly (= an insect with large coloured wings)

cathedral /kə'θiːdrəl/ *noun*
a large and important church: *We visited some of the great cathedrals of Madrid.*

Catholic /'kæθlɪk/ *adjective* (*also* **Roman Catholic**)
belonging to a section of the Christian Church that has the Pope as its leader: *a Catholic priest* ● **Catholic** *noun His parents are Catholics.*

cattle /'kætəl/ *plural noun*
cows that are kept for their milk or meat

caught /kɔːt/ → see **catch**

cauliflower /'kɒliflaʊə/ *noun*
a large, round, white vegetable surrounded by green leaves
→ Look at picture on P2

cause¹ /kɔːz/ *noun*
1 what makes an event happen: *We still don't know the exact cause of the accident*
2 an aim that some people support or fight for: *A strong leader will help our cause.*

cause² /kɔːz/ *verb* (**causes, causing, caused**)
to make something happen: *Stress can cause headaches.*

caution /'kɔːʃən/ *uncountable noun*
great care to avoid danger: *Always cross the street with caution.*

cautious /'kɔːʃəs/ *adjective*
very careful, because there might be danger: *Doctors are cautious about using this new medicine.*
▶ **cautiously** *adverb David moved cautiously forward and looked down into the water.*

cave /keɪv/ *noun*
a large hole in the side of a hill or under the ground

caveman /'keɪvmæn/ *noun* (**cavemen**)
a person in the past who lived mainly in caves

cc /ˌsiː 'siː/
used at the beginning of emails or at the end of a business letter to show that a copy is being sent to another person: *cc j.jones@harpercollins.co.uk*

CD /ˌsiː 'diː/ *noun* (**CDs**)
a disc for storing music or computer information. **CD** is short for **compact disc**.

CD burner /ˌsiː 'diː ˌbɜːnə/ *noun*
a piece of equipment that you use for copying information or music from a computer onto a CD

CD player *noun*
a machine that plays CDs

CD-ROM /ˌsiː diː 'rɒm/ *noun* (**CD-ROMs**)
a CD that stores a very large amount of information that you can read using a computer

cease /siːs/ *verb* (ceases, ceasing, ceased)
to stop (*formal*): *At one o'clock the rain ceased.*

cease-fire /'siːsfaɪə/ also **ceasefire** *noun*
an agreement to stop fighting a war:
They have agreed to a ceasefire after three years of war.

ceiling /'siːlɪŋ/ *noun*
the top inside part of a room: *The rooms all had high ceilings.*

celebrate /'selɪˌbreɪt/ *verb* (celebrates, celebrating, celebrated)
to do something enjoyable for a special reason: *I passed my test and wanted to celebrate.* □ *Dick celebrated his 60th birthday on Monday.*
▸ **celebration** /ˌselɪ'breɪʃən/ *noun There was a celebration in our house that night.*

celebrity /sɪ'lebrɪti/ *noun* (celebrities)
someone who is famous: *Kylie Minogue will be our celebrity guest.*

celery /'seləri/ *uncountable noun*
a vegetable with long, pale-green sticks that you can cook or eat raw (= without cooking): *Cut a stick of celery into small pieces.*

cell /sel/ *noun*
1 the smallest part of an animal or plant: *We are studying blood cells.*
2 a small room with a lock in a prison or a police station: *How many prisoners were in the cell?*

cellar /'selə/ *noun*
a room underneath a building: *He kept the boxes in the cellar.*

cello /'tʃeləʊ/ *noun*
a musical instrument that is like a large violin. You sit behind it and rest it on the floor.
▸ **cellist** /'tʃelɪst/ *noun He is a great cellist.*

cellphone /'selfəʊn/ *noun* (American)
→ see **mobile phone**

Celsius /'selsiəs/ *adjective*
used for describing a way of measuring temperature. Water freezes at 0° Celsius and boils at 100° Celsius: *11° Celsius is 52° Fahrenheit.*

cement /sɪ'ment/ *uncountable noun*
a grey powder that becomes very hard when you mix it with sand and water and leave it to dry

cemetery /'semətri/ *noun* (cemeteries)
a place where dead people are buried

census /'sensəs/ *noun* (censuses)
an occasion when a government counts all the people in a country: *That census counted a quarter of a billion Americans.*

cent /sent/ *noun*
a small coin that is used in many countries. There are one hundred cents in a dollar or a euro: *The book cost six dollars and fifty cents.*

centilitre /'sentɪˌliːtə/ *noun*
a unit for measuring liquid. There are ten millilitres in a centilitre and one hundred centilitres in a litre

centimetre /'sentɪˌmiːtə/ *noun*
a unit for measuring length. There are ten millimetres in a centimetre and one hundred centimetres in a metre: *This tiny plant is only a few centimetres high.*

central /'sentrəl/ *adjective*
in the middle part of a place: *They live in Central America.*

central 'heating *uncountable noun*
a heating system that uses hot air or water to heat every part of a building

centre /'sentə/ *noun*
1 the middle of something: *We sat in the centre of the room.*
2 a place where people can take part in a particular activity, or get help: *The building is now a health centre.*

centrifugal force /'sentrɪfˌjuːgəl fɔːs/ *uncountable noun*
the force that makes objects move away from the centre when they are moving around a central point: *The juice is removed by centrifugal force.*

century /'sentʃəri/ *noun* (centuries)
one hundred years: *The story started a century ago.* □ *She was one of the most important painters of the nineteenth century.*

ceramic /sɪ'ræmɪk/ *adjective*
made from clay (= a type of earth) that has been heated to a very high temperature so that it becomes hard: *The wall is covered with ceramic tiles.*

ceramics /sə'ræmɪks/ *plural noun*
objects made from clay (= a type of earth) that has been heated to a very high temperature so that it becomes hard: *The museum has a huge collection of Chinese ceramics.*

c

cereal /'sɪəriəl/ *noun*
1 *uncountable* a food made from grain, that you can mix with milk and eat for breakfast: *I have a bowl of cereal every morning.*
→ Look at picture on P3
2 a plant that produces grain for food: *Rice is similar to other cereal grains such as corn and wheat.*

ceremonial /ˌserɪ'məʊniəl/ *adjective*
used or done at a ceremony: *The children watched the ceremonial dances.*

ceremony /'serɪməni/ *noun* (**ceremonies**)
a formal event: *a wedding ceremony*

certain /'sɜːtən/ *adjective*
1 sure: *She's absolutely certain that she's going to recover.* □ *One thing is certain, both players are great sportsmen.*
2 particular: *He calls me at a certain time every day.*
for certain without any doubt at all: *She didn't know for certain if he was at home.*
make certain to check something so that you are sure: *Parents should make certain that children do their homework.*

certainly /'sɜːtənli/ *adverb*
1 definitely, without any doubt: *The meeting will certainly last an hour.*
2 used when you are agreeing or disagreeing strongly with what someone has said: *'Are you still friends?' – 'Certainly.'* □ *'Perhaps I should go now.' – 'Certainly not!'*

certainty /'sɜːtənti/ *uncountable noun*
the feeling of having no doubts at all about something: *I can tell you this with absolute certainty.*

certificate /sə'tɪfɪkət/ *noun*
an official document that proves that the facts on it are true: *You must show your birth certificate.* □ *I have a certificate signed by my teacher.*

chain¹ /tʃeɪn/ *noun*
a line of metal rings that are connected together: *He wore a gold chain around his neck.*

chain² /tʃeɪn/ *verb* (**chains, chaining, chained**)
to attach a person or thing to something with a chain: *The dogs were chained to a fence.*

chair¹ /tʃeə/ *noun*
a piece of furniture for one person to sit on, with a back and four legs: *He suddenly got up from his chair.*

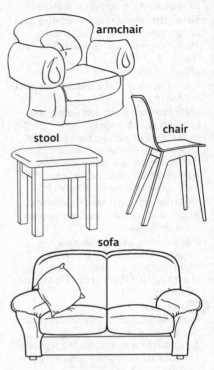

chairs

armchair

stool

chair

sofa

chair² /tʃeə/ *verb* (**chairs, chairing, chaired**)
to be the person who controls a meeting: *They asked him to chair the committee meeting.*

chairman /'tʃeəmən/ *noun* (**chairmen**)
the person who controls a meeting or an organization: *He is chairman of the committee that wrote the report.*

chairperson /'tʃeəpɜːsən/ *noun*
the person who controls a meeting or an organization: *She's the chairperson of the planning committee.*

chairwoman /'tʃeəwʊmən/ *noun* (**chairwomen**)
the woman who controls a meeting or an organization: *The chairwoman welcomed us and opened the meeting.*

chalk /tʃɔːk/ *uncountable noun*
1 a type of soft white rock
2 small sticks of chalk that you use for writing or drawing: *Now use a piece of*

coloured chalk to write your name.

chalkboard /'tʃɔːkbɔːd/ *noun* (American)
→ see **blackboard**

challenge¹ /'tʃælɪndʒ/ *noun*
something that is difficult to do: *His first challenge was learning the rules of the game.*

challenge² /'tʃælɪndʒ/ *verb* (**challenges, challenging, challenged**)
to invite someone to fight or play a game with you: *Jackson challenged O'Meara to another game.*

champagne /ʃæm'peɪn/ *uncountable noun*
an expensive French white wine with bubbles in it

champion /'tʃæmpiən/ *noun*
the winner of a sports competition or game: *He was an Olympic champion twice.* □ *Kasparov became the world champion.*

championship /'tʃæmpiənʃɪp/ *noun*
a competition to find the best player or team in a particular sport or game: *The world chess championship was on TV last night.*

chance /tʃɑːns/ *noun*
1 a possibility that something will happen: *There is a good chance that we can win the game against Australia.*
2 a time when you can do something: *Everyone gets a chance to vote.* □ *Millions of children never get the chance to go to school.*
by chance not planned by anyone: *He met Justin by chance in the street.*

change¹ /tʃeɪndʒ/ *noun*
1 an occasion when something becomes different: *There will soon be some big changes in our company.*
2 *uncountable* the money that you get back when you pay with more money than something costs: *'There's your change.' — 'Thanks very much.'*
3 *uncountable* coins: *I need 36 pence. Do you have any change?*

change² /tʃeɪndʒ/ *verb* (**changes, changing, changed**)
1 to become different: *The colour of the sky changed from pink to blue.* □ *She changed into a happy woman.*
2 to make something different: *They should change the law.*
3 to replace something with something new or different: *They decided to change the*

name of the band. □ *He changed to a different medication.*
4 to put on different clothes: *Ben changed his shirt.* □ *They let her shower and change.* □ *You can get changed in the bedroom.*
5 to get off one bus, train or plane, and get on to another in order to continue your journey: *I changed planes in Chicago.*

channel /'tʃænəl/ *noun*
1 a television station: *There is a huge number of television channels in America.*
2 a narrow passage that water can flow along: *a shipping channel*

chant /tʃɑːnt/ *noun*
a word or group of words that is repeated again and again: *Then the crowd started the chant of 'U-S-A!'* ● **chant** *verb* (**chants, chanting, chanted**) *The people chanted his name.* □ *The crowd chanted 'We are with you.'*

chaos /'keɪɒs/ *uncountable noun*
when there is no order or organization: *The race ended in chaos.*

chaotic /keɪ'ɒtɪk/ *adjective*
completely confused and without order: *The city seemed to be a chaotic place to me.*

chapel /'tʃæpəl/ *noun*
a room or part of a church that people pray in: *She went to the chapel on the hillside to pray.*

chapter /'tʃæptə/ *noun*
a part of a book: *For more information, see Chapter 4.*

character /'kærɪktə/ *noun*
1 all the things that make a person or place different from other people or places: *It's difficult to understand the change in her character.*
2 one of the people in a story: *Collard himself plays the main character.*

characteristic /,kærɪktə'rɪstɪk/ *noun*
a quality that is typical of someone or something: *The twins already had their own characteristics.*

charcoal /'tʃɑːkəʊl/ *uncountable noun*
burnt wood that you can use for drawing: *We all did charcoal drawings of the building.*

charge¹ /tʃɑːdʒ/ *verb* (**charges, charging, charged**)
1 to ask someone to pay money for something: *The driver only charged us £2 each.* □ *How much do you charge for printing photos?*
2 to formally tell someone that they have done something wrong: *The police have*

enough evidence to charge him.

3 to put electricity into a battery: *Alex forgot to charge his mobile phone.* □ *I left my MP3 player charging.*

charge something to something
to pay for something you are buying using your credit card (= a plastic card that you use to buy things and pay for them later): *I'll charge it to my Visa.*

charge² /tʃɑːdʒ/ *noun*
1 an amount of money that you have to pay for a service: *We can arrange this for a small charge.*
2 the amount or type of electrical force that something has: *an electrical charge*

in charge of someone/something
to be responsible for someone or something: *Who is in charge here?* □ *He was in charge of the campaign.*

charity /'tʃærɪti/ *noun* (**charities**)
an organization that collects money for people who need help: *Michael is working for a children's charity.* □ *She gives a lot of money to charity.*

charm /tʃɑːm/ *uncountable noun*
the quality of being pleasant and attractive: *This nineteenth century hotel has real charm.*

charming /'tʃɑːmɪŋ/ *adjective*
very pleasant and attractive: *He seemed to be a charming young man.*

chart /tʃɑːt/ *noun*
a diagram or graph that shows information: *See the chart on next page for more details.*

charter /'tʃɑːtə/ *noun*
a formal document that describes the rights or principles of an organization: *the United Nations Charter*

chase /tʃeɪs/ *verb* (**chases, chasing, chased**)
to run after someone in order to catch them: *A policeman chased him but couldn't catch him.* □ *The dog was chasing a squirrel.*
• **chase** *noun* *The chase ended at about 10.30 p.m. on the M1 motorway.*

chat /tʃæt/ *verb* (**chats, chatting, chatted**)
to talk in an informal, friendly way: *The women sit and chat at coffee time.* □ *I was chatting to him the other day.* • **chat** *noun* *I had a chat with John.*

'chat room also **chatroom** *noun*

a website where people can exchange messages

chat show *noun*
a television or radio show in which a person asks famous people questions about themselves: *I saw her once on a chat show.*

chatter /'tʃætə/ *verb* (**chatters, chattering, chattered**)
1 to talk quickly about things that are not important: *Erica chattered about her grandchildren.* • **chatter** *uncountable noun* *The students stopped their noisy chatter.*
2 used for describing how your teeth keep knocking together if you are cold: *She was so cold her teeth chattered.*

chauffeur /'ʃəʊfə, ʃəʊˈfɜː/ *noun*
a person whose job is to drive for another person: *She has a chauffeur to drive her around.*

chav /tʃæv/ *noun*
a rude word for a young person who speaks or dresses in a style that educated people do not like

cheap /tʃiːp/ *adjective* (**cheaper, cheapest**)
1 costing little money or less than you expected: *I'm going to rent a room if I can find somewhere cheap enough.* □ *People who own cars are demanding cheaper petrol.*
▸ **cheaply** *adverb* *You can deliver more food more cheaply by ship.*
2 costing less money than similar products but often of bad quality: *Don't buy any of those cheap watches.*

cheat /tʃiːt/ *verb* (**cheats, cheating, cheated**)
to do something that is not honest or fair, often because you want to get something: *Students sometimes cheated in order to get into top schools.* • **cheat** *noun* *Are you calling me a cheat?.*

check¹ /tʃek/ *verb* (**checks, checking, checked**)
1 to make sure that something is correct: *Check the meanings of the words in a dictionary.* □ *I think there might be an age limit, but I'll check.* □ *She checked whether she had a clean shirt.*
2 (*American*) → see **tick**

check in to tell the person at the desk of an airport or a hotel that you have arrived: *We checked in early and walked around* the airport. ◻ *I checked in at a small hotel on the village square.*

check out to pay the bill at a hotel and leave: *They packed and checked out of the hotel.* ◻ *They checked out yesterday morning.*

check² /tʃek/ *noun*
1 when you make sure that something is correct: *We need to do some quick checks before the plane leaves.*
2 (*American*) the **bill** in a restaurant
3 (*American*) → see **cheque**

checked /tʃekt/ *adjective*
with a pattern of small squares, usually of two colours: *The waiter had a checked shirt.*

'check-in *noun*
the counter or desk at an airport where you show your ticket and give someone your luggage

'checking a,ccount *noun* (*American*)
→ see **current account**

'check mark *noun* (*American*)
→ see **tick**

checkout /'tʃekaʊt/ *noun*
the place where you pay in a supermarket or other shop

'check-up *noun*
a general examination by your doctor or dentist

cheek /tʃiːk/ *noun*
one of the two sides of your face below your eyes: *The tears started rolling down my cheeks.*

cheeky /'tʃiːki/ *adjective* (**cheekier, cheekiest**)
rude, often in an amusing way: *David was a very cheeky little boy who loved to play jokes on people.*

cheer /tʃɪə/ *verb* (**cheers, cheering, cheered**)
to shout loudly to show that you are pleased or to encourage someone: *We cheered as she went up the steps to the stage.*
● **cheer** *noun* *The audience gave him a loud cheer.*

cheer someone up to make someone feel happier: *Stop trying to cheer me up.*
cheer up to become happier: *Cheer up. Life could be worse.*

cheerful /'tʃɪəfʊl/ *adjective*
happy: *Paddy was always smiling and cheerful.*
▶ **cheerfully** *adverb* *'We've got good news,' Pat said cheerfully.*

▶ **cheerfulness** *uncountable noun* *I liked his natural cheerfulness.*

cheerleader /'tʃɪəliːdə/ *noun*
one of a group of people who encourage the crowd to shout support for their team at a sports event

cheers /tʃɪəz/ *exclamation*
1 used just before people drink to celebrate something (*informal*)
2 goodbye (*informal*)
3 thank you (*informal*)

cheese /tʃiːz/ *noun*
a solid food made from milk which is usually white or yellow: *We had bread and cheese for lunch.* ◻ *This shop sells delicious French cheeses.*
→ Look at picture on P3

chef /ʃef/ *noun*
a cook in a restaurant
→ Look at picture on P7

chemical¹ /'kemɪkəl/ *adjective*
relating to chemistry or chemicals: *Do you know what caused the chemical reaction?*
◻ *Almost all of the natural chemical elements are found in the ocean.*

chemical² /'kemɪkəl/ *noun*
a substance that is used in a chemical process or made by a chemical process: *The programme was about the use of chemicals in farming.*

chemist /'kemɪst/ *noun*
1 a person who prepares and sells medicines
2 (*also* **chemist's**) a shop that sells medicines, make-up and some other things
3 a scientist who studies chemistry

chemistry /'kemɪstri/ *uncountable noun*
the science of the structure of gases, liquids and solids, and how they change

cheque /tʃek/ (*American*: **check**) *noun*
a printed piece of paper from a bank. You write an amount of money on it and use it to pay for things: *He gave me a cheque for £1500.*

chequebook /'tʃekbʊk/ *noun*
a book containing a number of cheques

cherry /'tʃeri/ *noun* (**cherries**)
a small, round fruit with red skin
→ Look at picture on P2

chess /tʃes/ *uncountable noun*
a game for two people, played on a board

with black and white squares on it, using different shaped pieces: *He was playing chess with his uncle.*

chest /tʃest/ *noun*
1 the top part of the front of your body: *He folded his arms across his broad chest.* □ *He was shot in the chest.*
→ Look at picture on P1
2 a large, strong box for storing things: *We know she has money locked in a chest somewhere.*

chest of 'drawers *noun*
a piece of furniture with drawers that you use for keeping clothes in
→ Look at picture on P5

chew /tʃuː/ *verb* (**chews, chewing, chewed**)
to break up food with your teeth: *Always chew your food well.*

'chewing gum *uncountable noun*
a type of sweet that you can chew for a long time: *a packet of chewing gum*

chick /tʃɪk/ *noun*
a baby bird

chicken /'tʃɪkɪn/ *noun*
1 a bird that is kept on a farm for its eggs and meat
2 *uncountable* the meat of this bird: *We had chicken sandwiches.*

chief¹ /tʃiːf/ *noun*
the leader of a group: *The police chief has said very little.*

chief² /tʃiːf/ *adjective*
most important: *Sunburn is the chief cause of skin cancer.*

chiefly /'tʃiːfli/ *adverb*
not completely, but especially or mostly: *Rhodes is chiefly known for her fashion designs.*

child /tʃaɪld/ *noun* (**children**)
1 a young boy or girl: *When I was a child I lived in a village.* □ *The show is free for children age 6 and under.*
2 someone's sons and daughters: *They have three young children.*

childhood /'tʃaɪldhʊd/ *noun*
the time when someone is a child: *She had a happy childhood.*

childish /'tʃaɪldɪʃ/ *adjective*
behaving like a child: *Paco had a childish smile on his face.*

children /'tʃɪldrən/
the plural of **child**

chill /tʃɪl/ *verb* (**chills, chilling, chilled**)
to make something cold: *Chill the fruit salad in the fridge.*

chill out to relax (*informal*): *After school, we chill out and watch TV.*

chilli /'tʃɪli/ *noun* (**chillies** or **chillis**) also **chili**
a small red or green pepper that tastes very hot
→ Look at picture on P2

chilly /'tʃɪli/ *adjective* (**chillier, chilliest**)
rather cold: *It was a chilly afternoon.*

chimney /'tʃɪmni/ *noun*
a pipe above a fire that lets the smoke travel up and out of the building: *Smoke from chimneys polluted the skies.*
→ Look at picture on P5

chimpanzee /,tʃɪmpæn'ziː/ *noun*
a type of small African animal, like a monkey with no tail

chin /tʃɪn/ *noun*
the part of your face below your mouth

china /'tʃaɪnə/ *uncountable noun*
a hard white substance that is used for making expensive cups and plates: *He ate from a small bowl made of china.*

chip¹ /tʃɪp/ *noun*
1 (*American*: **fry**) a long thin piece of potato, cooked in oil and eaten hot: *fish and chips*
→ Look at picture on P3
2 (*American*) → see **crisp**
3 a very small part that controls a piece of electronic equipment: *a computer chip*
4 a small piece that has been broken off something: *It contains real chocolate chips.*

chip² /tʃɪp/ *verb* (**chips, chipping, chipped**)
to break a small piece off something: *The toffee chipped the woman's tooth.*
▶ **chipped** *adjective* *The paint on the door was badly chipped.*

chocolate /'tʃɒklət/ *noun*
1 *uncountable* a sweet food made from cocoa: *We shared a bar of chocolate.*
2 (*also* **hot chocolate**) a hot drink made from chocolate: *The visitors can buy tea, coffee and chocolate.*
3 a small sweet or nut covered with chocolate: *The class gave the teacher a box of chocolates.*

choice /tʃɔɪs/ *noun*
1 a situation when there are several

things and you can choose the one you want: *It comes in a choice of colours.* □ *There's a choice between meat or fish.*
2 the thing or things that you choose: *Her husband didn't really agree with her choice.*
have no choice to be unable to choose to do something else: *We had to agree - we had no choice.*

choir /'kwaɪə/ *noun*
a group of people who sing together: *He sang in his church choir for years.*

choke /tʃəʊk/ *verb* (**chokes, choking, choked**)
to be unable to breathe because there is not enough air, or because something is blocking your throat: *A small child may choke on the toy.* □ *The smoke was choking her.*

cholesterol /kə'lestərɒl/ *uncountable noun*
a substance that exists in your blood. Too much cholesterol in the blood can cause heart disease: *He has a dangerously high cholesterol level.*

choose /tʃuːz/ *verb* (**chooses, choosing, chose, chosen**)
1 to decide to have a person or thing: *Each group will choose its own leader.* □ *You can choose from several different patterns.*
2 to do something because you want to: *Many people choose to eat meat at dinner only.* □ *You can remain silent if you choose.*

chop /tʃɒp/ *verb* (**chops, chopping, chopped**) (*also* **chop something up**)
to cut something into pieces with a knife: *Chop the butter into small pieces.* □ *We started chopping wood for a fire.*

chop something down to cut through the trunk of a tree with an axe: *Sometimes they chop down a tree for firewood.*

chop something off to remove something using scissors or a knife: *Chop off the fish's heads and tails.*

chop something up same meaning as chop

chopsticks /'tʃɒpstɪks/ *plural noun*
a pair of thin sticks that people in East Asia use for eating food: *She had no idea how to use chopsticks.*

chord /kɔːd/ *noun*
a number of musical notes played or sung at the same time: *I can play a few chords on the guitar.*

chore /tʃɔː/ *noun*
a job that you have to do, for example, cleaning the house: *After I finished my chores, I could go outside and play.*

chorus /'kɔːrəs/ *noun* (**choruses**)
1 a part of a song that you repeat several times: *Caroline sang two verses and the chorus of her song.*
2 a large group of people who sing together: *The Harvard orchestra and chorus performed Beethoven's Ninth Symphony.*

chose /tʃəʊz/ → see **choose**

chosen /'tʃəʊzən/ → see **choose**

christen /'krɪsən/ *verb* (**christens, christening, christened**)
to give a baby a name during a Christian ceremony: *She was born in March and christened in June.*

christening /'krɪsənɪŋ/ *noun*
a ceremony in which members of a church welcome a baby and it is officially given its name: *I cried at my granddaughter's christening.*

Christian /'krɪstʃən/ *noun*
someone who believes in Jesus Christ, and follows what he taught ● **Christian** *adjective* the Christian Church

Christianity /ˌkrɪsti'ænɪti/ *uncountable noun*
a religion that believes in Jesus Christ and follows what he taught

Christmas /'krɪsməs/ *noun* (**Christmases**)
the period around the 25th December, when Christians celebrate the birth of Jesus Christ: *'Merry Christmas!'* □ *We're staying at home for the Christmas holidays.*

chromosome /'krəʊməˌsəʊm/ *noun*
the part of a cell in an animal or a plant that controls characteristics such as hair and eye colour: *Each cell of our bodies contains 46 chromosomes.*

chubby /'tʃʌbi/ *adjective* (**chubbier, chubbiest**)
slightly fat: *Do you think I'm too chubby?*

chuckle /'tʃʌkəl/ *verb* (**chuckles, chuckling, chuckled**)
to laugh quietly: *He chuckled and said 'Of course not.'* ● **chuckle** *noun* *He gave a little chuckle.*

chunk /tʃʌŋk/ *noun*
a thick, solid piece of something: *Large chunks of ice floated past us.*

chunky /'tʃʌŋki/ *adjective* (**chunkier,
chunkiest**)
large and heavy: *She was wearing a chunky
gold necklace.*

church /tʃɜːtʃ/ *noun* (**churches**)
a building where Christians go to pray:
*We got married in Coburn United Methodist
Church.* □ *The family has gone to church.*

cider /'saɪdə/ *uncountable noun*
an alcoholic drink made from apples: *He
ordered a glass of cider.*

cigar /sɪ'gɑː/ *noun*
a brown roll of dried tobacco leaves that
some people smoke

cigarette /ˌsɪgə'ret/ *noun*
a small tube of paper containing tobacco
that some people smoke

cinema /'sɪnɪmɑː/ *noun* (*American*: **movie
theater**)
a building where people go to watch films:
*There is a shopping arcade with a multiplex
cinema (= a cinema with several screens).*
the cinema (*American*: **the movies**) films
in general

cinnamon /'sɪnəmən/ *uncountable noun*
a sweet spice used for adding flavour to
food

circle /'sɜːkəl/ *noun*
a round shape: *The Japanese flag is white,
with a red circle in the centre.* □ *She drew a
mouth, a nose and two circles for eyes.*

circuit /'sɜːkɪt/ *noun*
1 a track that cars race around: *the grand
prix circuit*
2 a complete path that electricity can
flow around: *The electrical circuit was
broken.*

circular /'sɜːkjʊlə/ *adjective*
shaped like a circle: *The circular walk around
the castle can be done in 20 minutes.*

circulate /'sɜːkjʊˌleɪt/ *verb* (**circulates,
circulating, circulated**)
to move easily and freely in a place: *The
blood circulates through the body.*
▶ **circulation** *uncountable noun* the
circulation of air

circulation /ˌsɜːkjʊ'leɪʃən/ *uncountable
noun*
the movement of blood through your
body: *Regular exercise is good for the circulation.*

circumference /sə'kʌmfrəns/
uncountable noun
the distance around the edge of a circle:
*Think of a way to calculate the Earth's
circumference.*

circumstance /'sɜːkəmstæns/ *noun*
a fact about a particular situation: *You're
doing really well, considering the circumstances.*
□ *Under normal circumstances, this trip would
only take about 20 minutes.*

circus /'sɜːkəs/ *noun* (**circuses**)
a group of people and animals that travels
around to different places and performs
shows in a big tent: *I always wanted to work
as a clown in a circus.*

citizen /'sɪtɪzən/ *noun*
1 a person who legally belongs to a
particular country: *We are proud to be
American citizens.*
2 the people who live in a town or city:
*He travelled to Argentina to meet the citizens of
Buenos Aires.*

citrus /'sɪtrəs/ *adjective*
from a family of juicy fruits with a sharp
taste such as an orange or a lemon: *Citrus
fruits are a good source of vitamin C.*

city /'sɪti/ *noun* (**cities**)
a large town: *We visited the city of
Los Angeles.*

civil /'sɪvəl/ *adjective*
1 used for talking about the people of a
country and their activities: *The American
Civil War is also called the War Between the
States.* □ *civil rights*
2 used for talking about people or things
that are connected with the state, and not
the army or the church: *We had a civil
wedding in the town hall.*
3 polite, although not very friendly
(*formal*): *Please try to be a little more civil to
people.*

civilian /sɪ'vɪliən/ *noun*
a person who is not a member of the
armed forces: *The soldiers were not shooting at
civilians.* • **civilian** *adjective* *The men were
wearing civilian clothes.*

civilization /ˌsɪvɪlaɪ'zeɪʃən/ *noun*
a group of people with their own social
organization and culture: *We learned about
the ancient civilizations of Greece.*

civilized /'sɪvɪlaɪzd/ *adjective*
1 with a high level of social organization
and cultural development: *Boxing should be
illegal in a civilized society.*

2 polite and reasonable: *She was very civilized about it.*

civil 'rights *plural noun*
the legal rights that all people have to fair treatment: *She never stopped fighting for civil rights.*

civil 'war *noun*
a war between different groups of people who live in the same country: *When did the American Civil War begin?*

claim¹ /kleɪm/ *verb* (**claims, claiming, claimed**)
1 to say that something is true: *She claimed that she was not responsible for the mistake.* □ *The man claimed to be very rich.*
2 to say that something belongs to you: *If nobody claims the money, you can keep it.*

claim² /kleɪm/ *noun*
1 something that someone says, which may or may not be true: *Most people just don't believe their claims.*
2 something that you ask for because you think you should have it: *an insurance claim*

clam /klæm/ *noun*
a type of shellfish

clamp /klæmp/ *noun*
a piece of equipment that holds two things together ● **clamp** *verb* (**clamps, clamping, clamped**)
Clamp the microphone to the stand.

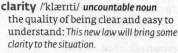

clamp

clap /klæp/ *verb* (**claps, clapping, clapped**)
to hit your hands together, usually to show that you like something: *The men danced and the women clapped.* □ *Margaret clapped her hands.*

clarify /'klærɪfaɪ/ *verb* (**clarifies, clarifying, clarified**)
to make something easier to understand, usually by explaining it (*formal*): *I would like to clarify those remarks I made.*

clarinet /ˌklærɪ'net/ *noun*
a musical instrument that you blow. It is a long black wooden tube with keys on it that you press, and a single reed (= small flat part that moves and makes a sound when you blow).

clarity /'klærɪti/ *uncountable noun*
the quality of being clear and easy to understand: *This new law will bring some clarity to the situation.*

clash /klæʃ/ *verb* (**clashes, clashing, clashed**)
1 to fight or argue with someone else: *He often clashed with his staff.* ● **clash** *noun* (**clashes**) *There have been a number of clashes between police and students.*
2 to look horrible with another thing: *His pink shirt clashed with his red hair.*

clasp¹ /klɑːsp/ *verb* (**clasps, clasping, clasped**)
to hold someone or something tightly: *She clasped the children to her.*

clasp² /klɑːsp/ *noun*
a small object that fastens something: *Kathryn undid the metal clasp of her handbag.*

class /klɑːs/ *noun* (**classes**)
1 a group of students who learn at school together: *He spent six months in a class with younger students.*
2 a time when you learn something at school: *Classes start at 9 o'clock.* □ *We do lots of reading in class.*
3 a group of things that are the same in some way: *These vegetables all belong to the same class of plants.*
4 a group of people with the same economic and social position in a society: *These programs only help the middle class.*

classic¹ /'klæsɪk/ *adjective*
of very good quality, and popular for a long time: *Fleming directed the classic film 'The Wizard of Oz'.*

classic² /'klæsɪk/ *noun*
something that is of very good quality, and has been popular for a long time: *'Jailhouse Rock' is one of the classics of modern popular music.*

classical /'klæsɪkəl/ *adjective*
traditional in form, style or content: *I like listening to classical music and reading.*

classics /'klæsɪks/ *plural noun*
the study of the languages, literature and cultures of ancient Greece and Rome: *She studied Classics at Cambridge University.*

classify /'klæsɪfaɪ/ *verb* (**classifies, classifying, classified**)
to divide things into groups or types: *Vitamins can be classified into two categories.*

classmate /ˈklɑːsmeɪt/ *noun*
a student who is in the same class as someone at school

classroom /ˈklɑːsruːm/ *noun*
a room in a school where lessons take place

clause /klɔːz/ *noun*
a group of words that contains a verb

claw /klɔː/ *noun*
the thin, hard, pointed part at the end of the foot of a bird or an animal: *Lions have very sharp claws and teeth.*

clay /kleɪ/ *uncountable noun*
a type of earth that is soft when it is wet and hard when it is dry. Clay is used for making things such as pots and bricks: *a clay pot*

clean¹ /kliːn/ *adjective* (**cleaner, cleanest**)
not dirty: *Make sure the children's hands are clean before they eat.* □ *This floor is easy to keep clean.*

clean² /kliːn/ *verb* (**cleans, cleaning, cleaned**)
to remove the dirt from something: *He fell from a ladder while he was cleaning the windows.*
clean something up to clean a place completely: *Hundreds of workers are cleaning up the beaches.* □ *Who is going to clean up this mess?*

cleaner /ˈkliːnə/ *noun*
a person whose job is to clean the rooms and furniture inside a building: *This is the hospital where Sid worked as a cleaner.*

clear¹ /klɪə/ *adjective* (**clearer, clearest**)
1 easy to understand, see or hear: *The instructions are clear and readable.* □ *It is clear that things will have to change.* □ *This camera takes very clear pictures.*
▸ **clearly** *adverb* *Clearly, the police cannot break the law.*
2 used for describing a substance that has no colour, and that you can see through: *a clear plastic bag*
3 without anything blocking the way: *The runway is clear — you can land.*
4 with no clouds: *It was a beautiful day with a clear blue sky.*

clear² /klɪə/ *verb* (**clears, clearing, cleared**)
1 to remove things from a place because you do not want or need them there: *Can someone clear the table, please?*

2 when the sky clears, it stops raining: *The sky cleared and the sun came out.*
clear something away to put the things that you have been using back in their proper place: *The waitress cleared away the plates.* □ *He helped to clear away after dinner.*
clear something out to tidy a cupboard or a place, and to throw away the things in it that you no longer want: *I cleared out my desk before I left.*
clear up to make a place tidy: *The children played while I cleared up in the kitchen.*

clerk /klɑːk/ *noun*
1 a person whose job is to work with numbers or documents in an office: *She works as a clerk in a travel agency.*
2 (*American*) → see **shop assistant**

clever /ˈklevə/ *adjective* (**cleverer, cleverest**)
intelligent and able to think and understand quickly: *He's a very clever man.*
▸ **cleverly** *adverb* *The garden has been cleverly designed.*

click /klɪk/ *verb* (**clicks, clicking, clicked**)
1 to make or cause something to make a short, sharp sound: *Hundreds of cameras clicked as she stepped out of the car.* □ *She clicked the switch on and off.* ● **click** *noun* *I heard a click and then her recorded voice.*
2 to press one of the buttons on the mouse of a computer in order to make something happen on a part of a computer screen: *I clicked on a link.* ● **click** *noun* *You can check your email with a click of your mouse.*

client /ˈklaɪənt/ *noun*
a person who pays someone for a service: *A lawyer and his client were sitting at the next table.*

> **LANGUAGE HELP**
> See note at **customer**.

cliff /klɪf/ *noun*
a high area of land with a very steep side next to the sea: *The car rolled over the edge of a cliff.*

climate /ˈklaɪmət/ *uncountable noun*
the normal weather in a place: *She loves the hot and humid climate of Florida.*

climax /ˈklaɪmæks/ *noun* (**climaxes**)
the most exciting or important moment,

near the end of something: *The climax of the story is when Romeo and Juliet die.*

climb /klaɪm/ *verb* (**climbs, climbing, climbed**)

1 to move towards the top of something: *It took half an hour to climb the hill.* □ *Climb up the steps onto the bridge.* ● **climb** *noun It was a hard climb to the top of the mountain.*

2 to move into or out of a small space: *The girls climbed into the car and drove off.* □ *He climbed out of his bed.*

3 to increase in value or amount: *The price of petrol has been climbing steadily.*

climber /ˈklaɪmə/ *noun*
a person who climbs rocks or mountains: *A climber was rescued yesterday after falling 300 metres.*

climbing /ˈklaɪmɪŋ/ *uncountable noun*
the activity of climbing rocks or mountains

cling /klɪŋ/ *verb* (**clings, clinging, clung**)
to hold someone or something tightly: *The man was rescued as he clung to the boat.*

clinic /ˈklɪnɪk/ *noun*
a place where people receive medical advice or treatment

clinical /ˈklɪnɪkəl/ *adjective*
involving medical treatment or testing people for illnesses: *She received her clinical training in Chicago.*

clip¹ /klɪp/ *noun*
1 a small object for holding things together: *She took the clip out of her hair.*
2 a short piece of a film that is shown separately: *They showed a film clip of the Apollo moon landing.*

clip² /klɪp/ *verb* (**clips, clipping, clipped**)
to fasten things together using a clip: *Clip the rope onto the ring.*

cloakroom /ˈkləʊkruːm/ *noun* (**cloakrooms**)
a room in a building where you can leave your coat

clock /klɒk/ *noun*
a device that shows you what time it is: *He could hear a clock ticking.*

around the clock all day and all night without stopping: *Firemen have been working around the clock.*

clockwise /ˈklɒkwaɪz/ *adjective, adverb*
moving in a circle in the same direction as the hands on a clock: *Move your right arm*

around in a clockwise direction. □ *The children started moving clockwise around the room.*

close¹ /kləʊz/ *verb* (**closes, closing, closed**)

1 to shut a door or a window: *If you are cold, close the window.* □ *David closed the door quietly.*

2 to stop being open, so that people cannot come and buy things: *The shop closes on Sundays and public holidays.*

close down or **close something down** to stop all work in a place, usually for ever: *That shop closed down years ago.*

close² /kləʊs/ *adjective* (**closer, closest**)

1 near to something else: *The apartment is close to the beach.* □ *The man moved closer.*
▶ **closely** *adverb They crowded closely around the fire.*

2 liking each other very much and knowing each other well: *She was close to her sister, Gail.* □ *We were close friends at school.*

3 careful and complete: *Let's have a closer look.*

4 won by only a small amount: *It was a close contest for a Senate seat.*

closed /kləʊzd/ *adjective*
not open so that people cannot buy or do anything there: *The supermarket was closed when we got there.*

closet /ˈklɒzɪt/ *noun*
(*American*) → see **wardrobe**

cloth /klɒθ/ *noun*
1 *uncountable* material that is used for making clothing: *You need two metres of cloth.*
2 a piece of cloth that you use for cleaning, drying or protecting things: *Clean the surface with a damp cloth.*

clothes /kləʊðz/ *plural noun*
the things that people wear, such as shirts, coats, trousers and dresses: *Milly went upstairs to change her clothes.*

> **LANGUAGE HELP**
>
> **Clothes** is always plural. For a single shirt, dress or skirt, for example, use a **piece of clothing** or an **item of clothing**.

clothing /ˈkləʊðɪŋ/ *uncountable noun*
the things that people wear: *She works in a women's clothing shop.*

cloud /klaʊd/ *noun*
1 a white or grey thing in the sky that is

made of drops of water: *Clouds began to form in the sky.*

2 an amount of smoke or dust floating in the air: *A cloud of black smoke spread across the sky.*

cloudy /'klaʊdi/ *adjective* (**cloudier, cloudiest**)
with a lot of clouds in the sky: *It was a windy, cloudy day.*

clown /klaʊn/ *noun*
a performer who wears funny clothes and does silly things to make people laugh

club /klʌb/ *noun*
1 an organization for people who all like doing a particular activity: *He joined the local golf club.*
2 a place where the members of a club meet: *I stopped at the club for a drink.*
3 → see **nightclub**: *The streets are full of bars, clubs and restaurants.*
4 a long, thin, metal stick that you use to hit the ball in the game of golf
5 a thick, heavy stick that can be used as a weapon: *The men were carrying knives and clubs.*

clue /klu:/ *noun*
information that helps you to find an answer: *I'll give you a clue; the answer begins with the letter 'p'.*

clumsy /'klʌmzi/ *adjective* (**clumsier, clumsiest**)
not moving in a very easy way and often breaking things: *As a child she was very clumsy.* □ *Dad was rather clumsy on his skates.*
▶ **clumsily** /'klʌmzili/ *adverb* *He fell clumsily onto the bed.*

clung /klʌŋ/ → see **cling**

cluster /'klʌstə/ *noun*
a small group of people or things close together: *There was a cluster of houses near the river.*

clutch¹ /klʌtʃ/ *verb* (**clutches, clutching, clutched**)
to hold something very tightly: *Michelle clutched my arm.*

clutch² /klʌtʃ/ *noun* (**clutches**)
the part of a vehicle that you press with your foot before you move the gear stick (= the part that changes the engine speed)

clutter /'klʌtə/ *uncountable noun*
a lot of things that you do not need in a

messy state: *I'm a very tidy person, and I hate clutter.* ● **clutter** *verb* (**clutters, cluttering, cluttered**) *Empty cans clutter the desks.*

cm
short for **centimetre** or **centimetres**

coach¹ /kəʊtʃ/ *noun* (**coaches**)
1 a comfortable bus that travels between cities or takes people on long journeys
2 a **carriage** on a train
3 someone who is in charge of teaching a person or a sports team: *She's the women's football coach at Durham University.*
4 a vehicle with four wheels that is pulled by horses

coach² /kəʊtʃ/ *verb* (**coaches, coaching, coached**)
to help someone to become better at a particular sport or skill: *She coached a golf team in San José.*

coal /kəʊl/ *uncountable noun*
a hard black substance that comes from under the ground and is burned to give heat: *Put some more coal on the fire.*

coarse /kɔːs/ *adjective* (**coarser, coarsest**)
feeling dry and rough: *His skin was coarse and dry.*

coast /kəʊst/ *noun*
the land that is next to the sea: *We stayed at a camp site on the coast.*
▶ **coastal** /'kəʊstəl/ *adjective* *Coastal areas have been flooded.*

coastline /'kəʊstlaɪn/ *noun*
the edge of a country's coast

coat¹ /kəʊt/ *noun*
1 a piece of clothing with long sleeves that you wear over other clothes when you go outside: *He put on his coat and walked out.*
2 an animal's fur or hair
3 a thin layer of paint: *The front door needs a new coat of paint.*

coat² /kəʊt/ *verb* (**coats, coating, coated**)
to cover something with a thin layer of a substance: *Coat the fish with flour.*

cobweb /'kɒbweb/ *noun*
the fine net that a spider makes for catching insects: *The windows are cracked and covered in cobwebs.*

cockpit /'kɒkpɪt/ *noun*
the part of an aeroplane or a racing car where the pilot or driver sits

cockroach /ˈkɒkrəʊtʃ/ *noun*
(**cockroaches**)
a large brown insect that likes to live in
places where food is kept

cocoa /ˈkəʊkəʊ/ *uncountable noun*
1 a brown powder used for making
chocolate
2 a hot drink made from cocoa powder
and milk or water: *Let's have a cup of cocoa.*

coconut /ˈkəʊkəˌnʌt/ *noun*
1 a very large nut with a hairy shell that
grows on trees in warm countries
2 *uncountable* the white flesh of a
coconut: *Add two cups of grated coconut.*

cocoon /kəˈkuːn/ *noun*
a case that some insects make around
themselves before they grow into adults:
The butterfly slowly breaks out of its cocoon.

cod /kɒd/ *noun* (**cod**)
1 a large sea fish with white flesh
2 *uncountable* this fish eaten as food:
We had cod and chips for dinner.

code /kəʊd/ *noun*
1 a set of rules for people to follow: *We keep
a strict dress code (= people must wear particular
clothes).*
2 a secret way to replace the words in a
message with other words or symbols, so
that some people will not understand the
message: *They sent messages using codes.*
3 *uncountable* a set of instructions that
a computer can understand: *a few lines of
simple computer code*
4 a group of numbers or letters that gives
information about something: *The dialling
code for Oxford is 01865.*

coffee /ˈkɒfi/ *noun*
1 the beans (= seeds) of the coffee plant,
made into a powder: *The island produces
plenty of coffee.*
2 *uncountable* a drink made from boiling
water and coffee beans: *Would you like some
coffee?*
3 a cup of this drink: *I'd like three coffees and
a tea, please.*
→ Look at picture on P3

coffin /ˈkɒfɪn/ *noun*
a box that you put a dead person in when
you bury them

coil /kɔɪl/ *noun*
a piece of rope or wire that forms a series
of rings: *He was carrying a coil of rope.*

coin /kɔɪn/ *noun*
a small round piece of metal money: *She
put the coins in her pocket.*

coin

coincidence /kəʊˈɪnsɪdəns/ *noun*
when similar or related events happen
at the same time without planning: *It is
a coincidence that they arrived at the same
time.* □ *We met by coincidence several years
later.*

cold¹ /kəʊld/ *adjective* (**colder, coldest**)
1 feeling uncomfortable because you are
not warm enough: *I was freezing cold.* □ *Put
on a jumper if you're cold.*
2 without any warmth: *He washed his face
with cold water.* □ *We went out into the cold,
dark night.*

> **LANGUAGE HELP**
> If something is very cold, you can say
> that it is **freezing**.

3 not showing emotion and not friendly:
Her mother was an angry, cold woman.

cold² /kəʊld/ *noun*
an illness that makes liquid flow from
your nose, and makes you cough: *I have
a bad cold.*
catch cold/catch a cold to become ill
with a cold: *Dry your hair so you don't catch
cold.*

Cold ˈWar *noun*
the difficult relationship between the
Soviet Union and the Western powers
after the Second World War: *This was the
first major crisis of the post-Cold War era.*

coleslaw /ˈkəʊlslɔː/ *uncountable noun*
a salad made from pieces of raw carrot
and cabbage (= a round vegetable with
white or green leaves), mixed with a
special sauce (= mayonnaise)

collage /ˈkɒlɑːʒ/ *noun*
a picture that you make by sticking pieces of paper or cloth on a surface: *The children made a collage of words and pictures from magazines.*

collapse /kəˈlæps/ *verb* (**collapses, collapsing, collapsed**)
to fall very suddenly: *The bridge collapsed last October.* □ *He collapsed at his home last night.*

collar /ˈkɒlə/ *noun*
1 the part of a shirt or coat that goes around someone's neck: *He pulled up his jacket collar in the cold wind.*
2 a band of leather or plastic that you put around the neck of a pet dog or cat

collarbone /ˈkɒlə,bəʊn/ *noun*
one of the two long bones between your throat and your shoulders: *Harold had a broken collarbone.*

colleague /ˈkɒliːg/ *noun*
a person someone works with: *She's busy talking to a colleague.*

collect /kəˈlekt/ *verb* (**collects, collecting, collected**)
1 to bring things together from several places or people: *Two young girls collected wood for the fire.*
▶ **collection** *uncountable noun* *Computers can help with the collection of information.*
2 to go and get someone or something from a place where they are waiting for you: *She babysits for us and collects the children from school.*
3 to get things and save them over a period of time because you like them: *I collect stamps.*

collection /kəˈlekʃən/ *noun*
a group of similar or related things: *He has a large collection of paintings.*

collector /kəˈlektə/ *noun*
someone who collects things that they like, such as stamps or old furniture: *Her parents were both art collectors.*

college /ˈkɒlɪdʒ/ *noun*
a place where students study after they leave secondary school: *I have one son in college.* □ *Joan is attending a local college.*

collide /kəˈlaɪd/ *verb* (**collides, colliding, collided**)
to crash into another person or vehicle: *The two cars collided.* □ *He ran up the stairs and collided with Susan.*

collie /ˈkɒli/ *noun* (*also* **collie dog**)
a dog with long hair and a long, narrow nose

collision /kəˈlɪʒən/ *noun*
when two moving objects hit each other: *Many passengers were killed in the collision.*

colon /ˈkəʊlən/ *noun*
1 a mark (:) that you can use to join parts of a sentence
2 the lower part of the tube that takes waste out of your body: *colon cancer*

colony /ˈkɒləni/ *noun* (**colonies**)
an area or a group of people that is controlled by another country: *Massachusetts was a British colony.*

colour¹ /ˈkʌlə/ *noun*
the way that something looks in the light. Red, blue and green are colours: *'What colour is the car?' — 'It's red.'* □ *Judy's favourite colour is pink.*

colour² /ˈkʌlə/ *adjective*
used for describing a television or photograph that shows things in all their colours, and not just in black, white and grey: *The book is illustrated with colour photos.*

colour³ /ˈkʌlə/ *verb* (**colours, colouring, coloured**)
colour something/colour something in to use pens or pencils to add colour to a picture: *The children coloured in their pictures.*

coloured /ˈkʌləd/ *adjective*
having a particular colour or colours: *They wore brightly coloured hats.*

colourful /ˈkʌləfʊl/ *adjective*
having bright colours or a lot of different colours: *The people wore colourful clothes.*

column /ˈkɒləm/ *noun*
1 a tall, solid structure that supports part

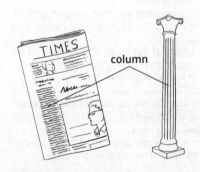

column

of a building: *The house has six white columns across the front.*

2 a narrow section of writing on one side or part of a page, for example in a newspaper: *The left column contains a list of names.*

coma /'kəʊmə/ *noun*
when someone is not conscious for a long time: *She was in a coma for seven weeks.*

comb /kəʊm/ *noun*
a thin piece of plastic or metal with teeth (= narrow, pointed parts). You use a comb to make your hair tidy. • **comb** *verb* (**combs, combing, combed**) *He combed his hair carefully.*

combat[1] /'kɒmbæt/ *uncountable noun*
fighting during a war: *More than 16 million men died in combat.*

combat[2] /'kɒmbæt/ *verb* (**combats, combating** or **combatting, combated** or **combatted**)
to try to stop something from happening: *They've introduced new laws to combat crime.*

combination /ˌkɒmbɪˈneɪʃən/ *noun*
a mixture of things: *That is an interesting combination of colours.*

combine /kəmˈbaɪn/ *verb* (**combines, combining, combined**)
1 to join two or more things together: *Combine the flour with 3 tablespoons of water.*
2 to exist together: *Disease and hunger combine to kill thousands of people.*

come /kʌm/ *verb* (**comes, coming, came, come**)
1 used for saying that someone or something arrives somewhere, or moves toward you: *Two police officers came into the hall.* □ *He came to a door.* □ *Eleanor came to see her.* □ *Come here, Tom.*
2 to happen: *The announcement came after a meeting at the White House.*
3 used for talking about the particular position of someone or something: *I came last in the race.*

come across someone/something
to find something or someone, or meet them by chance: *I came across a photo of my grandparents when I was looking for my diary.*

come back to return to a place: *He wants to come back to London.*

come down
1 to fall to the ground: *The rain came down*

for hours.
2 to become less than before: *Interest rates should come down.*

come from something used for saying that someone or something started in a particular place: *Nearly half the students come from other countries.* □ *Most of Germany's oil comes from the North Sea.*

come in to enter a place: *Come in and sit down.*

come off to be removed: *This lid won't come off.*

come on used for encouraging someone to do something or to be quicker: *Come on, or we'll be late.*

come out when the sun comes out, it appears in the sky because the clouds have moved away: *Oh, look! The sun's coming out!*

come to something to add up to a particular amount: *Lunch came to £80.*

come true used when something that you wish for or dream actually happens: *My life-long dream has just come true.*

come up
1 to be mentioned in a conversation: *The subject came up at work.*
2 when the sun comes up, it rises: *It will be so great watching the sun come up.*

comedian /kəˈmiːdiən/ *noun*
a person whose job is to make people laugh: *Who is your favourite comedian?*

comedy /'kɒmədi/ *noun* (**comedies**)
a play, film or television programme that is intended to make people laugh: *The film is a romantic comedy.*

comet /'kɒmɪt/ *noun*
a bright object that has a long tail and travels around the sun

comfort[1] /'kʌmfət/ *uncountable noun*
being relaxed, and having no pain or worry: *You can sit in comfort while you are watching the show.*

in comfort having a pleasant life in which you have everything you need: *He lived in comfort for the rest of his life.*

comfort[2] /'kʌmfət/ *verb* (**comforts, comforting, comforted**)
to make someone feel less worried or unhappy: *Ned tried to comfort her.*

comfortable /'kʌmftəbəl/ *adjective*
1 making you feel physically relaxed: *This is a really comfortable chair.* □ *A home*

should be comfortable and warm.
2 feeling physically relaxed: *Lie down on
your bed and make yourself comfortable.*
▶ **comfortably** *adverb* *Are you sitting
comfortably?*

comic ¹ /'kɒmɪk/ *adjective*
funny: *It is one of the greatest comic films.*

comic ² /'kɒmɪk/ *noun*
a magazine that contains stories told in
pictures

comical /'kɒmɪkəl/ *adjective*
funny or silly, and making you want to
laugh: *They had slightly comical smiles on
their faces.*

comma /'kɒmə/ *noun*
the punctuation mark (,)

command ¹ /kə'mɑːnd/ *noun*
1 an official instruction to do something:
He shouted a command at his soldiers.
◻ *He obeyed the command.*
2 an instruction that you give to a
computer: *The keyboard command 'Ctrl+S'
saves your document.*

command ² /kə'mɑːnd/ *verb* (**commands,
commanding, commanded**)
to tell someone that they must do
something: *He commanded his soldiers to
attack.*

commence /kə'mens/ *verb* (**commences,
commencing, commenced**)
to begin, or begin something (*formal*): *The
school year commences in the autumn.* ◻ *The
company commenced production in August.*

comment /'kɒment/ *verb* (**comments,
commenting, commented**)
to give your opinion or say something
about something: *Mr Cooke has not
commented on these reports.* ● **comment
noun** *It is difficult to make a comment about the
situation.*

commerce /'kɒmɜːs/ *uncountable noun*
the buying and selling of large amounts
of things: *There are rules for international
commerce.*

commercial ¹ /kə'mɜːʃəl/ *adjective*
relating to the buying and selling of
things: *New York is a centre of commercial
activity.*

commercial ² /kə'mɜːʃəl/ *noun*
an advertisement on television or radio:
*There are too many commercials on TV these
days.*

commit /kə'mɪt/ *verb* (**commits,
committing, committed**)
to do something illegal: *I have never
committed a crime.*

commitment /kə'mɪtmənt/ *noun*
1 *uncountable* when you work hard at
something that you think is important:
They praised him for his commitment to peace.
2 a promise to do something: *We made
a commitment to work together.*

committee /kə'mɪti/ *noun*
a group of people who meet to make
decisions or plans for a larger group: *I was
on the tennis club committee for 20 years.*

common /'kɒmən/ *adjective*
1 found in large numbers or happening
often: *Hansen is a common name in Norway.*
◻ *What is the most common cause of road
accidents?*
▶ **commonly** *adverb* *Parsley is a commonly
used herb.*
2 shared by two or more people or groups:
*The United States and Canada share a common
language.*
in common with similar qualities or
interests: *He had nothing in common with
his sister.*

common 'sense also **commonsense**
uncountable noun
the ability to make good judgements and
to be sensible: *Use common sense: don't leave
valuable items in your car.*

communicate /kə'mjuːnɪkeɪt/ *verb*
(**communicates, communicating,
communicated**)
to share information with other people,
for example by speaking or writing:
*They communicate with their friends by mobile
phone.* ◻ *They use email to communicate with
each other.*
▶ **communication** /kə,mjuːnɪ'keɪʃən/
uncountable noun *Good communication is
important in business.*

communications /kə,mjuːnɪ'keɪʃənz/
plural noun
a way of sending or receiving
information: *a communications satellite*

communism /'kɒmjʊ,nɪzəm/ also
Communism *uncountable noun*
the political idea that people should not
own private property and workers should
control how things are produced: *Walesa*

campaigned to end communism in his homeland, Poland.

communist /'kɒmjʊnɪst/ also **Communist** *noun*
someone who supports the ideas of communism: *He was a committed communist and an economics student at the University of Gdansk.* • **communist** *adjective She is a member of the Communist Party.*

community /kə'mjuːnɪti/ *noun* (**communities**)
1 a group of people who live in a particular area: *When you live in a small community, everyone knows you.*
2 a group of people who are similar in some way, or have similar interests: *These results are of great interest to the scientific community.*

commute /kə'mjuːt/ *verb* (**commutes, commuting, commuted**)
to travel to work or school: *Mike commutes to Miami every day.*
▶ **commuter** *noun In Tokyo, most commuters travel to work on trains.*

compact /kəm'pækt/ *adjective*
small, or taking up very little space: *The garden is compact and easy to manage.*

compact disc /ˌkɒmpækt 'dɪsk/ *noun*
a small shiny disc that contains music or information. The short form **CD** is also used.

companion /kəm'pænjən/ *noun*
someone who you spend time with or travel with: *Her travelling companion was her father.*

company /'kʌmpəni/ *noun* (**companies**)
1 a business that sells goods or services: *Her mother works for an insurance company.*
2 *uncountable* having another person or other people with you: *I always enjoy Nick's company.*
keep someone company to spend time with someone and stop them from feeling lonely or bored: *I'll stay here and keep Emma company.*

comparable /'kɒmpərəbəl/ *adjective*
similar: *House prices here are comparable to prices in Paris and Tokyo.*

comparative /kəm'pærətɪv/ *noun*
the form of an adjective or adverb that shows that one thing has more of a particular quality than something else has. For example, 'bigger' is the comparative form of 'big'. Compare with **superlative**.

compare /kəm'peə/ *verb* (**compares, comparing, compared**)
to consider how things are different and how they are similar: *I use the Internet to compare prices.*

comparison /kəm'pærɪsən/ *noun*
a study of the differences between two things: *The information helps parents to make comparisons between schools.*

compartment /kəm'pɑːtmənt/ *noun*
1 a separate part inside a box or a bag where you keep things: *The case has a separate compartment for camera accessories.*
2 one of the separate spaces in a railway carriage (= section of a train): *The family always sat in the first-class compartment.*

compass /'kʌmpəs/ *noun* (**compasses**)
a thing that people use for finding directions (north, south, east and west), with a needle that always points north: *You'll need a map and a compass.*

compass

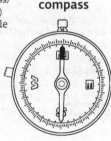

compasses /'kʌmpəsɪz/ *plural noun*
a piece of equipment that you use for drawing circles. It is made of two long thin parts, joined together at the top in the shape of the letter V.

compatible /kəm'pætɪbəl/ *adjective*
1 able to work well together: *Is your MP3 player compatible with your computer?*
2 having a good relationship with someone because you have similar opinions and interests: *Hannah and I are very compatible.*

compete /kəm'piːt/ *verb* (**competes, competing, competed**)
to participate in a contest or a game: *He will compete in the 10km road race again this year.*

competence /'kɒmpɪtəns/ *uncountable noun*
the ability to do something well: *No one doubts his competence.*

competent /'kɒmpɪtənt/ *adjective*
able to do something well: *He is a confident, competent driver.*

competition /,kɒmpɪ'tɪʃən/ *noun*
an event in which people try to show that they are best at an activity: *The two boys entered a surfing competition.*

competitive /kəm'petɪtɪv/ *adjective*
wanting to be more successful than other people: *He has always been very competitive.*

competitor /kəm'petɪtə/ *noun*
a person who takes part in a competition: *The oldest competitor won the silver medal.*

complain /kəm'pleɪn/ *verb* (complains, complaining, complained)
to say that you are not satisfied with someone or something: *Voters complained about the election result.* □ *I shouldn't complain; I've got a good job.* □ *'Someone should do something about it,' he complained.*
complain of something to say that you have a pain or an illness: *He went to the hospital, complaining of a sore neck.*

complaint /kəm'pleɪnt/ *noun*
when you say that you are not satisfied: *The police received several complaints about the noise.*

complete ¹ /kəm'pli:t/ *adjective*
1 in every way: *His birthday party was a complete surprise.*
▸ **completely** *adverb* *Thousands of homes have been completely destroyed.*
2 finished: *The project is not yet complete.*

complete ² /kəm'pli:t/ *verb* (completes, completing, completed)
1 to finish a task: *We hope to complete the project by January.*
2 to write the necessary information on a form: *Complete the first part of the application form.*

complex ¹ /'kɒmpleks/ *adjective*
having many parts and difficult to understand: *Crime is a complex problem.*

complex ² /'kɒmpleks/ *noun* (complexes)
a group of buildings used for a particular purpose: *a large industrial complex*

complexion /kəm'plekʃən/ *noun*
the natural colour of the skin on someone's face: *She had a pale complexion.*

complicate /'kɒmplɪ,keɪt/ *verb* (complicates, complicating, complicated)
to make something more difficult to understand or deal with: *Please don't complicate the situation.*

complicated /'kɒmplɪ,keɪtɪd/ *adjective*
having many parts, and difficult to understand: *The situation is very complicated.*

complication /,kɒmplɪ'keɪʃən/ *noun*
a problem or difficulty: *There were a number of complications.*

compliment /'kɒmplɪmənt/ *noun*
something nice that you say to someone, for example about their appearance: *He was very nice to me and paid me several compliments.* ● **compliment** /'kɒmplɪ,ment/ *verb* (compliments, complimenting, complimented) *They complimented me on the way I looked.*

compose /kəm'pəʊz/ *verb* (composes, composing, composed)
to write a piece of music, a speech or a letter: *Vivaldi composed a large number of concertos.*
be composed of something to be made or formed from different parts or members: *Water is composed of oxygen and hydrogen.*

composer /kəm'pəʊzə/ *noun*
a person who writes music: *Mozart and Beethoven were great composers.*

composition /,kɒmpə'zɪʃən/ *noun*
1 a piece of music or writing
2 *uncountable* the parts or members of something: *They study the chemical composition of the food we eat.*

compound /'kɒmpaʊnd/ *noun*
1 a substance that is made from two or more elements: *Dioxins are chemical compounds that are produced when material is burned.*
2 a word that is made from two or more other words, for example 'fire engine'
● **compound** *adjective* *a compound noun*

comprehend /,kɒmprɪ'hend/ *verb* (comprehends, comprehending, comprehended)
to understand something (*formal*): *I don't think you fully comprehend what's happening.*

comprehension /,kɒmprɪ'henʃən/ *uncountable noun*

the ability to understand something
(*formal*): *a reading comprehension test*

comprehensive school /ˌkɒmprɪˈhensɪv
ˌskuːl/ *noun*
in the UK, a school for students aged 11-18

compromise /ˈkɒmprəˌmaɪz/ *noun*
a situation in which people accept
something slightly different from what
they really want: *Try to reach a compromise
between the demands of work and family life.*

compulsory /kəmˈpʌlsəri/ *adjective*
used for saying that you must do
something: *In Australia, voting is compulsory.*

computer /kəmˈpjuːtə/ *noun*
an electronic machine that can store and
deal with large amounts of information:
*He watched the concert on his computer through
the Internet.* □ *The company installed a
£650,000 computer system.*

computer

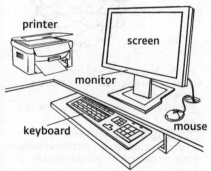

printer
screen
monitor
keyboard
mouse

computing /kəmˈpjuːtɪŋ/ *uncountable
noun*
the activity of using a computer and
writing programs for it: *They offer a course in
business and computing.*

conceal /kənˈsiːl/ *verb* (**conceals,
concealing, concealed**)
to hide something or keep it secret: *The hat
concealed her hair.* □ *Robert could not conceal
his happiness.*

conceive /kənˈsiːv/ *verb* (**conceives,
conceiving, conceived**)
1 to be able to imagine something or
believe it: *I can't even conceive of that amount
of money.*
2 used for describing the moment when
a woman becomes pregnant: *They have
been trying to conceive for three years now.*

□ *The baby was conceived naturally, and is due in
October.*

concentrate /ˈkɒnsənˌtreɪt/ *verb*
(**concentrates, concentrating,
concentrated**)
to give something all your attention: *He
should concentrate on his studies.* □ *She had to
concentrate hard to win the race.*

concentration /ˌkɒnsənˈtreɪʃən/
uncountable noun
giving something all your attention: *At
first there is greater concentration on speaking
skills.*

concept /ˈkɒnsept/ *noun*
an idea about something: *Our laws are
based on the concept of fairness.*

concern /kənˈsɜːn/ *verb* (**concerns,
concerning, concerned**)
1 to worry someone: *It concerns me that she
hasn't telephoned.* ● **concern** *uncountable
noun* *She expressed concern about my
grandfather's health.*
2 to be about a particular subject: *The book
concerns Sandy's two children.*

concerned /kənˈsɜːnd/ *adjective*
worried: *I've been concerned about you recently.*
be concerned with something to be
about something: *Randolph's work is
concerned with the effects of pollution.*

concerning /kənˈsɜːnɪŋ/ *preposition*
about something or someone (*formal*):
*Contact Mr Coldwell for more information
concerning the class.*

concert /ˈkɒnsət/ *noun*
a performance of music: *We attended a
concert by the great jazz pianist Harold Maburn.*
□ *The weekend began with an outdoor rock
concert.*

conclude /kənˈkluːd/ *verb* (**concludes,
concluding, concluded**)
1 to make a decision after thinking about
something carefully: *We've concluded that
it's best to tell her the truth.* □ *So what can we
conclude from this experiment?*
2 to end (*formal*): *The evening concluded with
dinner and speeches.*

conclusion /kənˈkluːʒən/ *noun*
1 a decision that you make after thinking
carefully about something: *I've come to the
conclusion that she's a great musician.*
2 the ending of a story: *What do you
understand from the conclusion of the story?*

concrete /'kɒŋkri:t/ *uncountable noun*
a hard substance made by mixing a grey
powder (= cement) with sand and water.
Concrete is used for building: *The hotel is
constructed from steel and concrete.* □ *We sat on
the concrete floor.*

condemn /kən'dem/ *verb* (**condemns,
condemning, condemned**)
1 to say that something is not acceptable:
Police condemned the recent violence.
2 to give someone a severe punishment:
He was condemned to life in prison.

condition /kən'dɪʃən/ *noun*
1 the state that someone or something is
in: *Doctors expect his condition to improve.*
□ *The old house is in terrible condition.*
2 *plural* the things that affect people's
comfort and safety: *People are living in
terrible conditions with little food or water.*
3 a medical problem: *Doctors think he may
have a heart condition.*

conditional /kən'dɪʃənəl/ *noun*
the verb form used for talking about a
situation that may exist or happen. Most
conditional sentences begin with 'if'.
For example 'If you work hard, you'll
pass your exams'.

conduct [1] /kən'dʌkt/ *verb* (**conducts,
conducting, conducted**)
1 to organize and do an activity or a task:
I decided to conduct an experiment.
2 to allow heat or electricity to pass
through: *Clay conducts electricity very well.*
3 to stand in front of musicians and
direct their performance: *The new musical
was composed and conducted by Bernstein.*
conduct yourself to behave in a
particular way: *The way he conducts himself
embarrasses the family.*

conduct [2] /'kɒndʌkt/ *uncountable noun*
the way someone behaves (*formal*): *She won
a prize for good conduct in school.*

conductor /kən'dʌktə/ *noun*
1 a person who stands in front of a group
of musicians and directs their
performance
2 a person on a train whose job is to help
passengers and check tickets

cone /kəʊn/ *noun*
1 a solid shape with one flat round end
and one pointed end: *Orange traffic cones
stop people from parking on the bridge.*

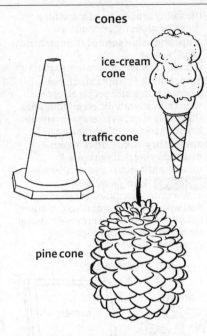

cones

ice-cream
cone

traffic cone

pine cone

2 a thin biscuit in the shape of a cone
that you put ice cream into and eat: *an
ice-cream cone*
3 the fruit of a tree such as a pine or fir:
a pine cone

conference /'kɒnfrəns/ *noun*
a long meeting about a particular subject:
*We attended a conference on education last
month.*

confess /kən'fes/ *verb* (**confesses,
confessing, confessed**)
to admit that you did something wrong:
He confessed to seventeen murders. □ *Ed
confessed that he broke the window.*

confession /kən'feʃən/ *noun*
when you admit that you have done
something wrong: *I have a confession to
make. I lied about my age.*

confidence /'kɒnfɪdəns/ *uncountable
noun*
1 the feeling that you can trust someone:
I have great confidence in you.
2 the feeling of being sure about your
own abilities and ideas: *The team is full of
confidence.*
in confidence told as a secret: *We told you
all these things in confidence.*

confident /ˈkɒnfɪdənt/ *adjective*
1 certain that the result of something will be good: *I am confident that I'll get the job.*
2 feeling sure about your own abilities and ideas: *In time he became more confident and relaxed.*

▶ **confidently** *adverb* *She walked confidently into the boss's office.*

confidential /ˌkɒnfɪˈdenʃəl/ *adjective*
used for describing information that must be kept secret: *After her death, some newspapers printed confidential information about her private life.*

▶ **confidentially** *adverb* *Any information they give will be treated confidentially.*

confine /kənˈfaɪn/ *verb* (**confines, confining, confined**)
to keep a person or an animal in a particular place so that they cannot leave it: *The animals are confined in tiny cages.*

▶ **confinement** /kənˈfaɪnmənt/ *uncountable noun* *He read a lot during his two-year confinement in prison.*

confirm /kənˈfɜːm/ *verb* (**confirms, confirming, confirmed**)
1 to say that something is true: *The doctor confirmed that my nose was broken.*
2 to say that a meeting or an arrangement will definitely happen: *He called at seven to confirm our appointment.*

▶ **confirmation** *uncountable noun* *You will receive confirmation of your order by email.*

conflict¹ /ˈkɒnflɪkt/ *noun*
a fight or an argument between people or countries: *The military conflict lasted many years.*

conflict² /kənˈflɪkt/ *verb* (**conflicts, conflicting, conflicted**)
to be very different from: *His opinions usually conflicted with mine.*

conform /kənˈfɔːm/ *verb* (**conforms, conforming, conformed**)
1 to follow a rule or a law: *The lamp conforms to new safety standards.*
2 to behave in a way that most people think is correct or normal: *At her age, it is important to conform.*

confuse /kənˈfjuːz/ *verb* (**confuses, confusing, confused**)
1 to think that one thing or person is another thing or person: *I always confuse my left with my right.*

▶ **confusion** /kənˈfjuːʒən/ *uncountable noun* *Use different colours to avoid confusion.*
2 to make it difficult for someone to understand something: *My words confused him.*

confused /kənˈfjuːzd/ *adjective*
not understanding what is happening, or not knowing what to do: *People are confused about what's going to happen.*

confusing /kənˈfjuːzɪŋ/ *adjective*
difficult to understand, making it difficult for people to know what to do: *The directions are really confusing.*

confusion /kənˈfjuːʒən/ *uncountable noun*
1 a situation in which the facts about something are not clear: *There's still confusion about the number of students.*
2 a situation in which a lot of things are happening in a badly organized way: *People were pushing and shouting, and there was confusion everywhere.*

congratulate /kənˈɡrætʃʊˌleɪt/ *verb* (**congratulates, congratulating, congratulated**)
to express pleasure about something good that has happened to someone: *She congratulated him on the birth of his son.*

▶ **congratulation** /kənˌɡrætʃʊˈleɪʃən/ *uncountable noun* *We received several letters of congratulation.*

congratulations /kənˌɡrætʃʊˈleɪʃənz/ *plural noun*
used for congratulating someone: *Congratulations on your new job.*

conjunction /kənˈdʒʌŋkʃən/ *noun*
a word that joins together parts of sentences. For example, 'and' and 'or' are conjunctions.

connect /kəˈnekt/ *verb* (**connects, connecting, connected**)
to join one thing to another: *Next, connect the printer to your computer.*

connected /kəˈnektɪd/ *adjective*
used for describing a relationship between things: *She described the problems connected with a high-fat diet.*

connection /kəˈnekʃən/ *noun*
1 a relationship between two things, people or groups: *I felt a strong connection between us.* □ *Children need to understand the connection between energy and the environment.*

2 a way of communicating using the telephone or a computer: *You'll need a fast Internet connection to view this site.*

3 a train, a bus or a plane that leaves after another one arrives and allows you continue your journey by changing from one to the other: *My flight was late and I missed the connection.*

conquer /'kɒŋkə/ *verb* (**conquers, conquering, conquered**)
1 to take complete control of the land of another country or group of people: *Germany conquered France in 1940.*
2 to manage to deal with a problem: *I've conquered my fear of spiders.*

conscience /'kɒnʃəns/ *noun*
the part of your mind that tells you if what you are doing is wrong: *My conscience is clear about everything I have done (= I do not feel that I have done anything wrong).*
have a guilty conscience to feel bad because you know you did something wrong: *They have no guilty conscience about downloading music from the Internet without paying.*

conscientious /ˌkɒnʃi'enʃəs/ *adjective*
careful to follow rules and do things correctly: *She is very conscientious about doing her homework.*
▶ **conscientiously** *adverb* *He conscientiously exercised every night.*

conscious /'kɒnʃəs/ *adjective*
awake, and not asleep or unconscious: *She was fully conscious soon after the operation.*
conscious of something
1 noticing something: *She was conscious of Nick watching her across the room.*
2 thinking about something a lot because you think it is important: *I'm very conscious of my weight.*

consent /kən'sent/ *verb* (**consents, consenting, consented**)
to agree to do something or to allow it to happen (*formal*): *She consented to marry him.*
● **consent** *uncountable noun* *Pollard finally gave his consent to the police search.*

consequence /'kɒnsɪkwens/ *noun*
a result or effect of something that has happened: *She understood the consequences of her actions.*

consequently /'kɒnsɪkwəntli/ *adverb*
as a result (*formal*): *He worked all night, and consequently he slept during the day.*

conservation /ˌkɒnsə'veɪʃən/ *uncountable noun*
the activity of taking care of the environment: *wildlife conservation*

conservative /kən'sɜːvətɪv/ *adjective*
not liking changes and new ideas: *People often become more conservative as they get older.*

Conservative /kən'sɜːvətɪv/ *adjective*
belonging to or voting for the Conservative Party in the UK and in some other countries: *Conservative MPs*
● **Conservative** *noun* *The Conservatives won the election.*

Con'servative ,Party *noun*
one of the three main political parties in the UK

conserve /kən'sɜːv/ *verb* (**conserves, conserving, conserved**)
1 to use energy or water carefully so that it lasts for a long time: *The factories have closed for the weekend to conserve energy.*
2 to take care of the environment: *World leaders agreed to work together to conserve forests.*

consider /kən'sɪdə/ *verb* (**considers, considering, considered**)
1 to have a particular opinion of a person or thing: *The police consider him to be dangerous.*
2 to think about something carefully: *The president says he's still considering the situation.* □ *You should consider the feelings of other people.*
▶ **consideration** *uncountable noun* *After careful consideration, we've decided that a change is necessary.*

considerable /kən'sɪdərəbəl/ *adjective*
great or large (*formal*): *The land cost a considerable amount of money.*
▶ **considerably** *adverb* *The king's wife was considerably taller and larger than he was.*

considerate /kən'sɪdərət/ *adjective*
thinking and caring about the feelings of other people: *He's the most considerate man I know.*

consideration /kənˌsɪdə'reɪʃən/ *uncountable noun*
when you think about and care about the feelings of other people: *Show consideration for your neighbours.*

consist /kən'sɪst/ *verb* (**consists, consisting, consisted**)
consist of something to be made up of

particular things or people: *My diet consisted of biscuits and milk.*

consistent /kən'sɪstənt/ *adjective*
always behaving in the same way: *Oakley is one of the team's most consistent players.*
▶ **consistency** *uncountable noun* *She scores goals with great consistency.*
▶ **consistently** *adverb* *The airline consistently wins awards for its service.*

console [1] /kən'səʊl/ *verb* (**consoles, consoling, consoled**)
to try to make someone who is unhappy feel more cheerful: *She started to cry and I tried to console her.*

console

console [2] /'kɒnsəʊl/ *noun*
a part of a machine that has many switches and lights. You use these switches to operate the machine, for example to play a computer game: *A light flashed on the console.*

consonant /'kɒnsənənt/ *noun*
one of the letters of the alphabet that is not a, e, i, o or u: *The word 'book' contains two consonants and two vowels.*

constant /'kɒnstənt/ *adjective*
happening all the time or always there: *Doctors say she is in constant pain.*
▶ **constantly** *adverb* *The direction of the wind is constantly changing.*

constituency /kən'stɪtʃʊənsi/ *noun* (**constituencies**)
an area, and the people who live in it. At an election, the people in the constituency choose one person for the government: *The two MPs represent very different constituencies.*

constitution /ˌkɒnstɪ'tjuːʃən/ *noun*
the laws of a country or an organization: *The government has to write a new constitution.*

construct /kən'strʌkt/ *verb* (**constructs, constructing, constructed**)
to build something: *His company constructed an office building in Nottingham.*

construction /kən'strʌkʃən/ *noun*
1 *uncountable* the process of building something: *He has started construction on a swimming pool.*
2 something that has been built: *The new theatre is an impressive steel construction.*

consult /kən'sʌlt/ *verb* (**consults, consulting, consulted**)
to ask someone for their advice: *Perhaps you should consult a lawyer.*
▶ **consultation** *noun* *I had a consultation with a doctor.*

consultant /kən'sʌltənt/ *noun*
someone who gives expert advice on a subject: *Alex is a young management consultant from Glasgow.*

consume /kən'sjuːm/ *verb* (**consumes, consuming, consumed**)
1 to eat or drink something (*formal*): *Martha consumed a box of biscuits every day.*
2 to use fuel, energy or time: *Airlines consume huge amounts of fuel every day.*

consumer /kən'sjuːmə/ *noun*
a person who buys something or uses a service: *What are my consumer rights?*

contact [1] /'kɒntækt/ *uncountable noun*
meeting or communicating with someone: *I don't have much contact with teenagers.* □ *Anita has not been in contact with us since last year.*

contact [2] /'kɒntækt/ *verb* (**contacts, contacting, contacted**)
to telephone someone or send them a message or letter: *We contacted the police.*

'contact lens *noun* (**contact lenses**)
a small, very thin piece of plastic that you put on your eyes to help you see better

contactless /'kɒntæktləs/ *adjective*
not needing you to put a card in a machine when paying: *contactless payment* □ *a contactless card*

contagious /kən'teɪdʒəs/ *adjective*
used for describing a disease that passes easily from one person to another when they touch. Compare with **infectious**: *The disease is highly contagious.*

contain /kən'teɪn/ *verb* (**contains, containing, contained**) to have other things inside: *The envelope contained a Christmas card.*

container /kən'teɪnə/ *noun*
a box that is used for holding or storing things: *Store the food in a plastic container.*

contemporary[1] /kən'tempərəri/ *adjective*
existing now, or at the same time as someone or something else: *contemporary art*

contemporary[2] /kən'tempərəri/ *noun*
(**contemporaries**)
a person who is, or was, alive at the same time as someone else

content /kən'tent/ *adjective*
happy or satisfied: *He says his daughter is quite content.*

contents /'kɒntents/ *plural noun*
1 the things inside a container: *Empty the contents of the can into a bowl.*
2 the different chapters and sections of a book: *There is no table of contents.*

contented /kən'tentɪd/ *adjective*
happy and satisfied: *Richard was a very contented baby.*

contest /'kɒntest/ *noun*
a competition or a game: *It was an exciting contest.*

contestant /kən'testənt/ *noun*
a person who takes part in a competition or a game: *Contestants on the TV show have to answer six questions correctly.*

context /'kɒntekst/ *noun*
1 the situation in which an event happens: *Don't use this sort of language in a business context.*
2 the words and sentences that come before and after a particular word or sentence, that help you to understand its meaning

continent /'kɒntɪnənt/ *noun*
a very large area of land, such as Africa or Asia
▸ **continental** /ˌkɒntɪ'nentəl/ *adjective*
Pikes Peak is the highest mountain in continental United States.

continual /kən'tɪnjʊəl/ *adjective*
happening without stopping, or happening very often: *The team has had almost continual success since last year.*
▸ **continually** *adverb Gemma cried almost*

continually when she was a baby. □ *Malcolm was continually changing his mind.*

continuation /kənˌtɪnjʊ'eɪʃən/ *uncountable noun*
the fact that something continues to happen or to exist: *We do not support the continuation of the war.*

continue /kən'tɪnjuː/ *verb* (**continues, continuing, continued**)
1 to not stop: *The war continued for another four years.*
2 to not stop doing something: *They continue to fight for justice.*
3 to start again: *The trial continues today.*
4 to start doing something again: *She looked up for a minute and then continued drawing.*
5 to keep going in a particular direction: *He continued rapidly up the path.*

continuous /kən'tɪnjʊəs/ *adjective*
1 happening over a long time without stopping: *They heard continuous gunfire.*
▸ **continuously** *adverb The police are working continuously on the case.*
2 with no spaces: *There was a continuous queue of cars outside in the street.*
3 used for describing a form of the verb that is made using the auxiliary 'be' and the present participle, as in 'I'm going on holiday'.

contract /'kɒntrækt/ *noun*
an official agreement between two companies or two people: *He signed a contract to play for the team for two years.*

contraction /kən'trækʃən/ *noun*
a short form of a word or words: *'It's' (with an apostrophe) can be used as a contraction for 'it is'.*

contradict /ˌkɒntrə'dɪkt/ *verb*
(**contradicts, contradicting, contradicted**)
to say that what someone has just said is wrong: *She looked surprised, but she did not contradict him.*

contrary /'kɒntrəri/ *adjective*
completely different from something else: *Contrary to what people think, light exercise makes you less hungry.*

on the contrary used when you disagree with something and you are going to say that the opposite is true: *'People just don't do things like that.' — 'On the contrary, they do them all the time.'*

contrast [1] /'kɒntrɑːst/ *noun*
a clear difference between two or more people or things: *There is a clear contrast between the two men.*

contrast [2] /kən'trɑːst/ *verb* (**contrasts, contrasting, contrasted**)
to show the differences between things: *In this section we contrast four different ideas.*

contribute /kən'trɪbjuːt/ *verb*
(**contributes, contributing, contributed**)
to help to pay for something: *The U.S. is contributing $4 billion to the project.* ▢ *If you are buying her a present, you must let me contribute.*
▶ **contributor** /kən'trɪbjətə/ *noun The financial services industry is a major contributor to the economy.*

contribution /ˌkɒntrɪ'bjuːʃən/ *noun*
money that someone gives to help to pay for something: *He made a £5,000 contribution to the charity.*

control [1] /kən'trəʊl/ *noun*
1 *uncountable* the power to make all the important decisions about something: *He took control of every situation.*
2 *uncountable* the ability to make a person or machine do what you want them to do: *He lost control of his car.*
3 a switch you use in order to operate a machine: *You operate the controls without looking at them.*
in control having the power to make all the important decisions about something: *She feels that she's in control of her life again.*
out of control used for describing something that people cannot deal with: *The fire was out of control.*
under control used for describing something that people can deal with: *The situation is under control.*

control [2] /kən'trəʊl/ *verb* (**controls, controlling, controlled**)
1 to have the power to make all the important decisions about something: *He controls the largest company in California.*
2 to make a person or machine do what you want them to do: *There was a computer system to control the gates.* ▢ *My parents couldn't control me.*

controversial /ˌkɒntrə'vɜːʃəl/ *adjective*
used for describing people or things that people argue about or disagree with: *In*

business, I try to stay away from controversial subjects.*

controversy /'kɒntrəvɜːsi, kən'trɒvəsi/ *uncountable noun*
when people argue about something, or disapprove of it: *The TV show caused controversy when it was shown last year.*

convenience /kən'viːniəns/ *noun*
a piece of equipment designed to make your life easier: *This flat includes all the modern conveniences.*
for your convenience done in a way that is helpful for you: *We include an envelope for your convenience.*

convenient /kən'viːniənt/ *adjective*
1 useful for a particular purpose: *This is a convenient place to get coffee before work.*
▶ **convenience** *uncountable noun They may use a credit card for convenience.*
▶ **conveniently** *adverb The house is conveniently located close to the railway station.*
2 used for describing a time when you are available to do something: *She will try to arrange a convenient time.*

conventional /kən'venʃənəl/ *adjective*
1 behaving in a way that is considered to be normal by most people: *I've always been quite conventional; I work hard and behave properly.*
2 used for describing a method or product that is usually used: *In a conventional oven, bake at 200 °C for 30 minutes.*

conversation /ˌkɒnvə'seɪʃən/ *noun*
an occasion when you talk to someone about something: *I had an interesting conversation with him.*

convert /kən'vɜːt/ *verb* (**converts, converting, converted**)
to change something into a different form: *The signal will be converted into electronic form.* ▢ *He wants to convert the building into a hotel.*

convict /kən'vɪkt/ *verb* (**convicts, convicting, convicted**)
to find someone guilty of a crime in a court of law: *He was convicted of murder.*

convince /kən'vɪns/ *verb* (**convinces, convincing, convinced**)
1 to persuade someone to do something: *He convinced her to marry Tom.*
2 to make someone believe that

something is true or that it exists: *The new players have convinced me of their ability.*

▶ **convinced** /kən'vɪnst/ *adjective She was convinced that the diamonds were real.*

cook¹ /kʊk/ *verb* (cooks, cooking, cooked)
to prepare and heat food: *I have to go and cook dinner.* □ *Let the vegetables cook for about 10 minutes.*

> **LANGUAGE HELP**
> Cooking verbs: You **roast** meat in an oven. You **bake** bread and cakes. You can **boil** vegetables in hot water. You can **fry** meat and vegetables in oil. You can also **grill** meat directly under or over a flame.

cook² /kʊk/ *noun*
a person who prepares and cooks food: *I'm a terrible cook.*

cookbook /'kʊkbʊk/ *noun*
a book that tells you how to prepare different meals

cooker /'kʊkə/ *noun*
a piece of kitchen equipment that is used for cooking food

cookie /'kʊki/ *noun* (American)
→ see **biscuit**

cooking /'kʊkɪŋ/ *uncountable noun*
1 the activity of preparing food: *He did the cooking and cleaning.*
2 food that is cooked in a particular way: *The restaurant specializes in Italian cooking.*

cool¹ /kuːl/ *adjective* (cooler, coolest)
1 having a low temperature, but not cold: *I felt the cool air on my neck.* □ *The water was cool.*
2 calm: *You have to remain cool in very difficult situations.*
3 fashionable and interesting (*informal*): *I met some really cool people last night.* □ *She had really cool boots.*

cool² /kuːl/ *verb* (cools, cooling, cooled)
to become lower in temperature: *Drain the meat and allow it to cool.*

cool down
1 same meaning as to **cool**: *Once it cools down, you'll be able to touch it.*
2 to become less angry: *He has had time to cool down.*

cooperate /kəʊ'ɒpə,reɪθ/ *verb*
(cooperates, cooperating, cooperated)
to work with or help someone: *He finally agreed to cooperate with the police.*

▶ **cooperative** /kəʊ'ɒpərətɪv/ *adjective*
I made an effort to be cooperative.

▶ **cooperation** /kəʊ,ɒpə'reɪʃən/
uncountable noun Thank you for your cooperation.

coordinate /kəʊ'ɔːdɪ,neɪt/ *verb*
(coordinates, coordinating, coordinated)
1 to organize an activity: *She coordinates the weekend activities.*
2 to make the parts of your body work together efficiently: *You need to coordinate legs, arms and breathing.*

▶ **coordination** *uncountable noun You need great hand-eye coordination to hit the ball.*

cop /kɒp/ *noun*
a policeman or policewoman (*informal*): *The cops know where to find him.*

cope /kəʊp/ *verb* (copes, coping, coped)
to deal with a problem or task in a successful way: *The group has helped her cope with a serious illness.*

copper /'kɒpə/ *uncountable noun*
a soft reddish-brown metal: *Chile produces much of the world's copper.*

copy¹ /'kɒpi/ *noun* (copies)
1 something that is produced that looks exactly like another thing: *I made a copy of Steve's letter.*
2 one of many books or newspapers that are exactly the same: *Did you get a copy of 'The Guardian'?*

copy² /'kɒpi/ *verb* (copies, copying, copied)
1 to make or write something that is exactly like another thing: *Copy files from your old computer to your new one.*
2 to try to do what another person does: *Children try to copy the behaviour of people they admire.*

coral /'kɒrəl/ *uncountable noun*
a hard substance formed from the bones of very small sea animals: *She was wearing a coral necklace.*

cord /kɔːd/ *uncountable noun*
strong, thick string: *She was carrying a package tied with heavy cord.*

core /kɔː/ *noun*
1 the central part of a fruit that contains the seeds: *Annie put her apple core in the bin.*
2 the central part of The Earth: *What is the temperature in the Earth's core?*

cork /kɔːk/ *noun*
an object that you push into the top of a bottle to close it: *He took the cork out of the bottle.*

corkscrew /ˈkɔːkskruː/ *noun*
a tool for pulling corks out of bottles

corn /kɔːn/ *uncountable noun*
crops such as wheat or barley, or their seeds: *grinding corn and baking bread*

corner /ˈkɔːnə/ *noun*
a point where two sides of something meet, or where a road meets another road: *There was a table in the corner of the room.* □ *He stood on the street corner, waiting for a taxi.*

corner

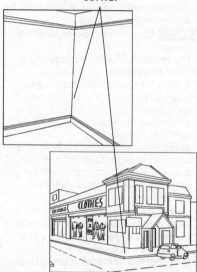

cornflakes /ˈkɔːnfleɪks/ *plural noun*
a type of dried food that people eat with milk for breakfast: *a bowl of cornflakes*

corporate /ˈkɔːprət/ *adjective*
relating to large companies: *Our city flats are popular with private and corporate customers.*

corporation /ˌkɔːpəˈreɪʃən/ *noun*
(American)
a large business or company: *Her father works for a big corporation.*

corpse /kɔːps/ *noun*
a dead body: *Police found the corpse in a nearby river.*

correct¹ /kəˈrekt/ *adjective*
right or true: *The correct answers can be found on page 8.*
▸ **correctly** *adverb* *Did I pronounce your name correctly?*

correct² /kəˈrekt/ *verb* (**corrects, corrected**)
to make a problem or a mistake right: *There is another way you can correct the problem.* □ *Students are given a chance to correct mistakes.*
▸ **correction** /kəˈrekʃən/ *noun* *You may make corrections to your final test.*

correspond /ˌkɒrɪˈspɒnd/ *verb*
(**corresponds, corresponding, corresponded**)
1 to be very similar to something or closely connected with something: *The rise in food prices corresponds closely to rises in oil prices.* □ *The two maps correspond closely.*
2 to write letters or emails to someone: *She still corresponds with her American friends.* □ *We corresponded regularly.*

correspondence /ˌkɒrɪˈspɒndəns/ *uncountable noun*
the letters or emails that someone receives or sends: *The website contains copies of Einstein's personal correspondence.*

correspondent /ˌkɒrɪˈspɒndənt/ *noun*
a person who writes news reports: *He's the White House correspondent for The Times.*

corridor /ˈkɒrɪdɔː/ *noun*
a long passage in a building: *There were doors on both sides of the corridor.*

corrupt¹ /kəˈrʌpt/ *adjective*
behaving in a dishonest way in order to gain money or power: *We know that there are some officials who are corrupt.*

corrupt² /kəˈrʌpt/ *verb* (**corrupts, corrupting, corrupted**)
to cause a computer file or program to stop working properly, so that it may not be safe to use: *The files were corrupted by a virus.*

cosmetics /kɒzˈmetɪks/ *plural noun*
products that you put on your face to make yourself look more beautiful: *She wears nail polish and cosmetics.*

cost¹ /kɒst/ *noun*
the amount of money you need in order to buy, do or make something: *The cost of*

a loaf of bread has gone up. □ *There will be an increase in the cost of posting a letter.*

cost² /kɒst/ *verb* (**costs, costing, cost**)
to have as a price: *This course costs £150 per person.* □ *It will cost us over £100,000 to buy new lorries.*

costly /'kɒstli/ *adjective* (**costlier, costliest**)
very expensive: *We must try to avoid such costly mistakes.*

costume /'kɒstjuːm/ *noun*
a set of clothes that someone wears in a performance: *The costumes and scenery were designed by Robert Rauschenberg.*

cosy /'kəʊzi/ *adjective* (**cosier, cosiest**)
comfortable and warm: *Hotel guests can relax in the cosy lounge.*

cot /kɒt/ (*American:* **crib**) *noun*
a bed for a baby
→ Look at picture on P5

cottage /'kɒtɪdʒ/ *noun*
a small house, usually in the country: *She lived in a little white cottage in the woods.*

cotton /'kɒtən/ *uncountable noun*
1 cloth or thread that is made from the cotton plant: *He's wearing a cotton shirt.*
□ *a reel of cotton*
2 a plant that is used for making cloth: *They own a large cotton plantation in Tennessee.*
3 → see **cotton wool** (*American*)

cotton wool (*American:* **cotton**) *uncountable noun*
soft cotton material used for cleaning your skin or putting cream on it: *cotton wool balls*

couch /kaʊtʃ/ *noun* (**couches**)
a long, comfortable seat for two or three people

cough¹ /kɒf/ *verb* (**coughs, coughing, coughed**)
to suddenly force air out of your throat with a noise: *James began to cough violently.*

cough² /kɒf/ *noun*
1 when you suddenly force air out of your throat with a noise: *Do you have any medicine for a cough?*
2 an illness that makes you cough: *I had a cough for over a month.*

could /kəd, STRONG kʊd/ *modal verb*
1 used for saying that you were able to do something: *I could see that something was*

wrong. □ *It was so dark that I couldn't see where I was going.*
2 used for showing that something is possibly true, or that it may possibly happen: *It could snow again tonight.*
□ *'Where's Jack?' — 'I'm not sure; he could be in the toilet.'*
3 used in questions to make polite requests: *Could I stay tonight?* □ *He asked if he could have a cup of coffee.*

couldn't /'kʊdənt/
short for 'could not'

could've /kʊdəv/
short for 'could have'

council /'kaʊnsəl/ *noun*
a group of people who are chosen to control a particular area: *The city council has decided to build a new school.*

count¹ /kaʊnt/ *verb* (**counts, counting, counted**)
1 to say all the numbers in order: *Nancy counted slowly to five.*
2 to see how many there are in a group: *I counted the £5 notes.* □ *I counted 34 sheep on the hillside.*
3 to be important: *Every penny counts if you want to be a millionaire.*

count on someone/something to feel sure that someone or something will help you: *You can count on us to keep your secret.* □ *Can we count on your support for Ms Ryan?*

count² /kaʊnt/ *noun*
keep count of something to know how many things there are: *Keep count of the number of hours you work.*
lose count of something to not know how many things there are: *I lost count of the number of times she called.*

countable noun /ˌkaʊntəbəl 'naʊn/ *noun*
a noun such as 'bird', 'chair' or 'year' that has a singular and a plural form

counter /'kaʊntə/ *noun*
1 a long flat surface in a shop or café where customers are served: *That man works behind the counter at the DVD rental shop.*
2 a very small object that you use in board games: *Move your counter one square for each spot on the dice.*

counterfeit /'kaʊntəfɪt/ *adjective*
used for describing money, goods or documents that are not real, but look

exactly like real ones: *He admitted using counterfeit notes.*

country /'kʌntri/ *noun* (**countries**)
1 an area of the world with its own government and people: *This is the greatest country in the world.* □ *We crossed the border between the two countries.*
2 land that is away from cities and towns: *You can live a healthy life in the country.* □ *She was cycling along a country road.* □ *She lived alone in a small house in the country.*
3 *uncountable* a style of popular music from the southern United States: *I always wanted to play country music.*

countryside /'kʌntri,saɪd/ *uncountable noun*
land that is away from cities and towns: *I've always loved the English countryside.*

> **LANGUAGE HELP**
> **countryside** or **nature**? **Countryside** is land that is away from towns and cities. **Nature** is used for talking about animals and plants.

county /'kaʊnti/ *noun* (**counties**)
a part of a state or country: *Maidstone is an English town in the county of Kent.*

couple /'kʌpəl/ *noun*
two people who are married or having a romantic relationship: *The couple have no children.*
a couple two or around two people or things: *There are a couple of police officers outside.* □ *Things should get better in a couple of days.*

coupon /'kuːpɒn/ *noun*
a piece of paper that allows you to pay less money than usual for a product, or to get it free: *Cut out the coupon on page 2 and take it to your local supermarket.*

courage /'kʌrɪdʒ/ *uncountable noun*
the quality someone shows when they are not afraid: *The girl had the courage to tell the police.*

courageous /kə'reɪdʒəs/ *adjective*
showing courage: *The courageous girl saved her baby sister from a house fire.*

courgette /kʊə'ʒet/ (*American:* **zucchini**) *noun*
a long, thin vegetable with a dark green skin

course /kɔːs/ *noun*
1 a series of lessons on a particular subject: *I'm taking a course in business administration.*
2 one part of a meal: *Lunch was excellent, especially the first course.*
3 an area of land for racing or for playing golf: *The hotel complex has a swimming pool, tennis courts and a golf course*
4 *uncountable* the direction in which someone or something is going: *The pilot changed course to land in Chicago.*

court /kɔːt/ *noun*
1 a place where a judge and a group of people (= a jury) decide if someone has done something wrong: *The man will appear in court later this month.*
2 an area for playing a game such as tennis or basketball: *The hotel has several tennis courts.*

courteous /'kɜːtiəs/ *adjective*
polite: *He was a kind and courteous man.*
▶ **courteously** *adverb* *He nodded courteously to me.*

courtesy /'kɜːtɪsi/ *uncountable noun*
polite behaviour and consideration for other people (*formal*): *Showing courtesy to other drivers costs nothing.*

courtyard /'kɔːtjɑːd/ *noun*
an open area that is surrounded by buildings or walls: *The second bedroom overlooked the courtyard.*

cousin /'kʌzən/ *noun*
the child of your uncle or your aunt: *Do you know my cousin Alex?*
→ Look at picture on P8

cover¹ /'kʌvə/ *verb* (**covers, covering, covered**)
1 to put something over something else to protect it: *Cover the dish with a heavy lid.*
2 to form a layer over the surface of something else: *Snow covered the city.* □ *The desk was covered with papers.*

cover² /'kʌvə/ *noun*
1 something that is put over an object to protect it: *Keep a plastic cover on your computer when you are not using it.*
2 the outside part of a book or a magazine: *She appeared on the cover of last week's 'Zoo' magazine.*

cow /kaʊ/ *noun*
a large female animal that is kept on

farms for its milk: *Dad went out to milk the cows.*

coward /'kaʊəd/ *noun*
someone who has no courage: *They called him a coward because he refused to fight.*

cowardly /'kaʊədli/ *adjective*
not brave and easily frightened: *I was too cowardly to complain.*

cowboy /'kaʊbɔɪ/ *noun*
a man who rides a horse and takes care of cows in North America

crab /kræb/ *noun*
1 a sea animal with a shell and ten legs. Crabs usually move sideways.
2 *uncountable* the meat of this animal: *I'll have the crab salad, please.*

crack[1] /kræk/ *verb* (**cracks, cracking, cracked**)
to become slightly broken, with lines on the surface, but not in separate pieces: *The plane's windscreen cracked.* □ *a cracked mirror*

crack[2] /kræk/ *noun*
1 a very narrow gap between two things: *Kathryn saw him through a crack in the curtains.*
2 a line that appears on the surface of something when it is slightly broken: *The plate had a crack in it.*
3 a sharp sound, like the sound of a piece of wood breaking: *Suddenly there was a loud crack.*

cracker /'krækə/ *noun*
a thin, hard piece of baked bread that people sometimes eat with cheese

crackle /'krækəl/ *verb* (**crackles, crackling, crackled**)
to make a lot of short, sharp noises: *The radio crackled again.*

cradle /'kreɪdəl/ *noun*
a baby's bed that you can move from side to side

craft /krɑːft/ *noun*
an activity that involves making things skilfully with your hands: *We want to teach our children about native crafts and culture.*

crafty /'krɑːfti/ *adjective* (**craftier, craftiest**)
getting what you want in a clever way, perhaps by being dishonest: *She was so crafty, nobody ever suspected her.*

cramp /kræmp/ *noun*
a sudden strong pain in a muscle: *Mike was complaining of stomach cramps.*

crane /kreɪn/ *noun*
a large machine with a long arm that can lift very heavy things

crash[1] /kræʃ/ *noun* (**crashes**)
1 an accident in which a vehicle hits something: *His son was killed in a car crash.*
2 a sudden loud noise: *People said they heard a loud crash at about 1.30 a.m.*

crash[2] /kræʃ/ *verb* (**crashes, crashing, crashed**)
1 to hit something: *Her car crashed into the back of a lorry.*
2 used for saying that a computer or a computer program suddenly stops working: *My computer crashed for the second time that day.*

crate /kreɪt/ *noun*
a large box for moving or storing things: *The pictures are packed in wooden crates.*

crater /'kreɪtə/ *noun*
a very large hole in the top of a volcano (= a mountain that forces hot gas and rocks into the air): *Rocks shot up three miles from the volcano's crater.*

crawl[1] /krɔːl/
verb (**crawls, crawling, crawled**)
to move on your hands and knees: *I began to crawl toward the door.*

crawl

crawl[2] /krɔːl/ *uncountable noun*
a way of swimming in which you lie on your front and move one arm over your head and then the other, while kicking your legs: *Neil is learning to swim the crawl.*

crayon /'kreɪɒn/ *noun*
a stick of coloured wax that you use for drawing

crazy /'kreɪzi/ *adjective* (**crazier, craziest**)
very strange or not at all sensible (*informal*): *People obviously thought we were crazy.*
▶ **crazily** *adverb* *He ran crazily around in circles.*
be crazy about someone/something
to like someone or something very much (*informal*): *He's still crazy about his job.* □ *We're crazy about each other.*

go crazy to be extremely bored or upset, or feel that you cannot wait for something any longer (*informal*): *Annie thought she might go crazy if she didn't find out soon.*

creak /kriːk/ *verb* (**creaks, creaking, creaked**)
to make a short, high sound when moved: *The stairs creaked under his feet.* □ *The door creaked open.* • **creak** *noun The door opened with a creak.*

cream¹ /kriːm/ *noun*
1 *uncountable* a thick liquid that is made from milk: *She went to the shop to buy some cream.*
2 a substance that you rub into your skin: *hand cream*
3 yellowish-white in colour: *Many women say they can't wear cream.*

cream² /kriːm/ *adjective*
of a yellowish-white colour: *She wore a cream silk shirt.*

creamy /'kriːmi/ *adjective* (**creamier, creamiest**)
1 with a lot of cream or milk: *I like rich, creamy coffee.*
2 soft and smooth: *We had pasta in a rich, creamy sauce.*

crease¹ /kriːs/ *noun*
a line that appears in cloth or paper when it has been folded: *Dad always wears trousers with sharp creases.*

crease² /kriːs/ *verb* (**creases, creasing, creased**)
to form lines when pressed or folded: *Most clothes crease a bit when you are travelling.*
▶ **creased** *adjective His clothes were terribly creased.*

create /kri'eɪt/ *verb* (**creates, creating, created**)
to make something happen or exist: *It's great for a group of schoolchildren to create a show like this.* □ *Could this solution create problems for us in the future?*
▶ **creator** /kri'eɪtə/ *noun Matt Groening, creator of The Simpsons*

creation /kri'eɪʃən/ *noun*
something that someone has made: *The new bathroom is my own creation.*

creative /kri'eɪtɪv/ *adjective*
1 good at having new ideas: *When you don't have much money, you have to be creative.*

2 using something in a new way: *He is famous for his creative use of words.*

creature /'kriːtʃə/ *noun*
a living thing that is not a plant: *Like all living creatures, birds need plenty of water.*

credit /'kredɪt/ *noun*
1 *uncountable* an arrangement that allows someone to buy something and pay for it later: *We buy everything on credit.*
2 *uncountable* praise that people give you because they think that you are responsible for something good that has happened: *I can't take all the credit myself.*
3 *plural* the list of all the people who made a film or a television programme: *It was great to see my name in the credits.*

credit card *noun*
a plastic card that you use to buy something and pay for it later: *Call this number to order by credit card.*

creep /kriːp/ *verb* (**creeps, creeping, crept**)
to move somewhere quietly and slowly: *He crept up the stairs.*

creepy /'kriːpi/ *adjective* (**creepier, creepiest**)
making you feel nervous or frightened (*informal*): *This place is really creepy at night.*

crept /krept/ → see **creep**

crescent /'kresənt, 'krez-/ *noun*
a curved shape like the shape of a new moon

crew /kruː/ *noun*
the people who work on a ship or aircraft: *He was new on the crew of the space shuttle.* □ *These ships carry small crews of about twenty men.*

crib /krɪb/ *noun* (*American*)
→ see **cot**

cricket /'krɪkɪt/ *uncountable noun*
an outdoor game played by two teams who try to score runs (= points) by hitting a ball with a wooden bat: *During the summer term we played cricket.*

crime /kraɪm/ *noun*
an illegal act: *The police are searching the scene of the crime.*

criminal /'krɪmɪnəl/ *noun*
a person who does something illegal: *We want to protect ourselves against dangerous criminals.*

cripple /ˈkrɪpəl/ *verb* (**cripples, crippling, crippled**)
to stop someone from ever moving their body normally again: *Mr Easton was crippled in an accident.*

crisis /ˈkraɪsɪs/ *noun* (**crises** /ˈkraɪsiːz/)
a situation that is very serious or dangerous: *This is a worldwide crisis that affects us all.*

crisp ¹ /krɪsp/ *adjective* (**crisper, crispest**)
pleasantly hard: *Bake the potatoes for 15 minutes, until they're nice and crisp.* □ *crisp bacon*

crisp ² /krɪsp/ *noun* (*American:* **potato chip**)
a very thin slice of potato, which is cooked in oil and eaten as a snack: *a bag of crisps*
→ Look at picture on P3

critic /ˈkrɪtɪk/ *noun*
a person who writes and gives their opinion about books, films, music or art: *Mather was a film critic for many years.*

critical /ˈkrɪtɪkəl/ *adjective*
1 very serious and dangerous: *The economic situation may soon become critical.*
▶ **critically** *adverb* *Food supplies are critically low.*
2 saying that a person or thing is wrong or bad: *His report is critical of the judges.*
▶ **critically** *adverb* *She spoke critically about Lara.*

criticism /ˈkrɪtɪˌsɪzəm/ *noun*
1 **uncountable** when someone expresses disapproval of someone or something: *The president faced strong criticism for his remarks.*
2 a statement that expresses disapproval: *Teachers should say something positive before making a criticism.*

criticize /ˈkrɪtɪˌsaɪz/ *verb* (**criticizes, criticizing, criticized**)
to express your disapproval of someone or something: *His mother rarely criticized him.*

crocodile /ˈkrɒkəˌdaɪl/ *noun*
a large animal with a long body, a long mouth and sharp teeth. Crocodiles live in rivers in hot countries.

crooked /ˈkrʊkɪd/ *adjective*
not straight: *I looked at his crooked broken nose.*

crop /krɒp/ *noun*
a plant that people grow for food: *Rice farmers here still plant their crops by hand.*

cross ¹ /krɒs/ *verb* (**crosses, crossing, crossed**)
1 to move to the other side of a place: *She crossed the road without looking.*
2 to put one of your arms, legs or fingers on top of the other: *Jill crossed her legs.*
cross something out to draw a line through words: *He crossed out her name and added his own.*

cross ² /krɒs/ *noun* (**crosses**)
1 the act of hitting or kicking the ball from one side of a sports field to a person on the other side
2 a shape like ✝ It is the most important Christian symbol: *She wore a cross around her neck.*
3 a written mark in the shape of an X: *Put a cross next to those activities you like.*

cross ³ /krɒs/ *adjective* (**crosser, crossest**)
angry: *I'm terribly cross with him.*
▶ **crossly** *adverb* *'No, no, no,' Morris said crossly.*

crossroads /ˈkrɒsrəʊdz/ *noun*
a place where two roads cross each other: *Turn right at the first crossroads.*

crosswalk /ˈkrɒswɔːk/ *noun* (*American*)
→ see **pedestrian crossing**

crossword /ˈkrɒswɜːd/ *noun* (*also* **crossword puzzle**)
a printed word game that consists of a pattern of black and white squares. You write the answers down or across on the white squares: *He could do the New York Times crossword puzzle in 15 minutes.*

crouch /kraʊtʃ/ *verb* (**crouches, crouching, crouched**)
to bend your legs so that you are close to the ground: *We crouched in the bushes to hide.*

crouch

crow¹ /krəʊ/ *noun*
a large black bird that makes a loud noise

crow² /krəʊ/ *verb* (**crows, crowing, crowed**)
to make the loud sound of a cock (= male chicken), often early in the morning: *We had to get up when the cock crowed.*

crowd¹ /kraʊd/ *noun*
a large group of people who have gathered together: *A huge crowd gathered in the town square.*

crowd² /kraʊd/ *verb* (**crowds, crowding, crowded**)
to move closely together around someone or something: *The children crowded around him.*
crowd into something to enter a place so that it becomes very full: *Thousands of people crowded into the city centre to see the president.*

crowded /'kraʊdɪd/ *adjective*
full of people: *He looked slowly around the small crowded room.* □ *This is a crowded city of 2 million.*

crown¹ /kraʊn/ *noun*
a gold or silver circle that a king or queen wears on their head

crown² /kraʊn/ *verb* (**crowns, crowning, crowned**)
to put a crown put on a person's head as a sign that they have officially become a new king or queen: *Two days later, Juan Carlos was crowned king.*

crude /kruːd/ *adjective* (**cruder, crudest**)
1 simple and rough: *We sat on crude wooden boxes.*
▶ **crudely** *adverb* *Someone has crudely painted over the original sign.*
2 rude or offensive: *The boys sang loudly and told crude jokes.* □ *Please don't be so crude.*
▶ **crudely** *adverb* *He hated it when she spoke so crudely.*

cruel /'kruːəl/ *adjective* (**crueller, cruellest**)
deliberately making people suffer: *Children can be very cruel.*
▶ **cruelly** *adverb* *Douglas was often treated cruelly by his sisters.*
▶ **cruelty** /'kruːəlti/ *uncountable noun* *There are laws against cruelty to animals.*

cruise¹ /kruːz/ *noun*
a holiday that you spend on a ship or boat: *He and his wife went on a world cruise.*

cruise² /kruːz/ *verb* (**cruises, cruising, cruised**)
to move at a steady comfortable speed: *A black and white police car cruised past.*

crumb /krʌm/ *noun*
a small piece that falls from bread when someone breaks it: *I stood up, brushing crumbs from my trousers.*

crumble /'krʌmbəl/ *verb* (**crumbles, crumbling, crumbled**)
1 to have pieces breaking off it: *The stone wall was crumbling away in places.*
2 to break something into a lot of small pieces: *Crumble the goat's cheese into a salad bowl.*

crumple /'krʌmpəl/ *verb* (**crumples, crumpling, crumpled**) (*also* **crumple something up**)
to press paper or cloth, making a lot of lines and folds in it: *She crumpled the paper in her hand.* □ *She crumpled up the note.*
▶ **crumpled** *adjective* *His uniform was crumpled and dirty.*

crunch /krʌntʃ/ *verb* (**crunches, crunching, crunched**)
1 used for describing the noise that a lot of small stones make when someone walks or drives over them: *The gravel crunched under his boots.* ● **crunch** *noun* (**crunches**) *We heard the crunch of tyres on the road up to the house.*
2 to noisily break something into small pieces between your teeth: *She crunched an ice cube loudly.*

crunchy /'krʌntʃi/ *adjective* (**crunchier, crunchiest**)
pleasantly hard, and making a noise when eaten: *We enjoyed the fresh, crunchy vegetables.*

crush /krʌʃ/ *verb* (**crushes, crushing, crushed**)
to press something very hard so that it breaks or loses its shape: *Andrew crushed his empty can.* □ *The drinks were full of crushed ice.*

crust /krʌst/ *noun*
1 the hard outer part on a loaf of bread: *Cut the crusts off the bread.*
2 the outer layer of the Earth: *Earthquakes damage the Earth's crust.*

crutch /krʌtʃ/ *noun* (**crutches**)
a long stick that you put under your arm to help you to walk if you have hurt your leg or your foot: *I can walk without crutches now.*

cry¹ /kraɪ/ *verb* (**cries, crying, cried**)
1 to have tears coming from your eyes:

I hung up the phone and started to cry.

2 (*also* **cry out**) to say something very loudly: *'Nancy Drew,' she cried, 'you're under arrest!'* □ *'You're wrong, you're all wrong!' Henry cried out.*

cry out same meaning as **cry 2**

cry² /kraɪ/ *noun* (**cries**)

1 a loud, high sound that you make when you feel a strong emotion: *She saw the spider and let out a cry of horror.*

2 the loud, high sound that a bird or an animal makes: *The cry of a strange bird sounded like a whistle.*

crystal /'krɪstəl/ *noun*

1 a small, hard piece of a natural substance: *salt crystals* □ *ice crystals*

2 *uncountable* a transparent rock used in jewellery: *Liza wore a crystal necklace at her wedding.*

3 *uncountable* high-quality glass: *Their drinking glasses were made from crystal.*

cub /kʌb/ *noun*

a young wild animal such as a bear: *young lion cubs*

cube /kju:b/ *noun*

1 a solid object with six square surfaces: *She took a tray of ice cubes from the freezer.* □ *He dropped two sugar cubes into his coffee.*

2 the number that you get if you multiply a number by itself twice: *The cube of 2 is 8.*

cubic /'kju:bɪk/ *adjective*

used for talking about units of volume. For example, a cubic metre is a space that is one metre long on each side: *They moved 3 billion cubic metres of earth.*

cucumber /'kju:kʌmbə/ *noun*

a long dark-green vegetable that you eat raw: *We had cheese and cucumber sandwiches for lunch.*

→ Look at picture on P2

cuddle /'kʌdəl/ *verb* (**cuddles, cuddling, cuddled**)

to put your arms around someone and hold them close: *Everybody wanted to cuddle the baby.* • **cuddle** *noun* *I just wanted to give him a cuddle.*

cuddly /'kʌdəli/ *adjective* (**cuddlier, cuddliest**)

looking soft and pleasant, and making you want to put your arms around them: *a big, cuddly teddy bear*

cue /kju:/ *noun*

1 an action or a statement that tells someone that they should do something: *The church bell struck eleven. That was my cue to leave.*

2 a long, thin wooden stick that you use to hit the ball across the table in some games: *a snooker cue*

cuff /kʌf/ *noun*

the end of the sleeve of a shirt: *He was wearing a blue shirt with a white collar and white cuffs.*

cultivate /'kʌltɪˌveɪt/ *verb* (**cultivates, cultivating, cultivated**)

to grow plants on a piece of land: *She cultivated a small garden of her own.*

cultural /'kʌltʃərəl/ *adjective*

relating to the arts: *We've organized a range of sports and cultural events.*

culture /'kʌltʃə/ *noun*

1 *uncountable* activities such as art, music, literature and theatre: *Films are part of our popular culture.*

2 the way of life, the traditions and beliefs of a particular group of people: *I live in the city among people from different cultures.*

cunning /'kʌnɪŋ/ *adjective*

clever and possibly dishonest: *Police described the man as cunning and dangerous.*

cup /kʌp/ *noun*

1 a small round container that you drink from: *Let's have a cup of coffee.*

2 a large round metal container that is given as a prize to the winner of a competition: *I think New Zealand will win the cup.*

3 used in the names of some competitions that have a cup as a prize: *the Ryder Cup*

cupboard /'kʌbəd/ *noun*

a piece of furniture with doors and shelves for storing things like food or dishes: *The kitchen cupboard was full of cans of soup.*

→ Look at picture on P4

cure /kjʊə/ *verb* (**cures, curing, cured**)

to make someone become well again: *The new medicine cured her headaches.* □ *Almost overnight I was cured.* • **cure** *noun* *There is still no cure for a cold.*

cups

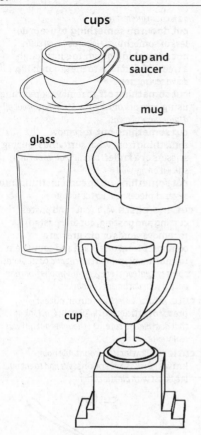

cup and saucer

mug

glass

cup

curiosity /ˌkjʊəri'ɒsɪti/ *uncountable noun*
a desire to know about something: *The children show a lot of curiosity about the past.*

curious /'kjʊəriəs/ *adjective*
wanting to know more about something: *Steve was curious about the place I came from.*
▶ **curiously** *adverb* *The woman in the shop looked at them curiously.*

curl¹ /kɜːl/ *noun*
a piece of hair shaped in curves: *She was talking to a little girl with blonde curls.*

curl² /kɜːl/ *verb* (**curls, curling, curled**)
to form curved shapes: *Her hair curled around her shoulders.* □ *Maria curled her hair for the party.*
curl up *She curled up next to him.*

curly /'kɜːli/ *adjective* (**curlier, curliest**)
shaped in curves: *I've got naturally curly hair.*

currency /'kʌrənsi/ *noun* (**currencies**)
the money that is used in a particular country: *The plans were for a single European currency.*

current¹ /'kʌrənt/ *noun*
a steady flow of water, air or energy: *The fish move with the currents of the sea.* □ *I felt a current of cool air.* □ *The wires carry a powerful electric current.*

current² /'kʌrənt/ *adjective*
happening now: *The current situation is different from the one in 1990.*
▶ **currently** *adverb* *He is currently unmarried.*

current ac'count (*American:* **checking account**) *noun*
a personal bank account that you can take money from at any time

curriculum /kə'rɪkjʊləm/ *noun*
(**curriculums** or **curricula**) /kə'rɪkjʊlə/
all the subjects that students learn about in a school or college: *Business skills should be part of the school curriculum.*

curriculum vitae /kəˌrɪkjʊləm 'viːtaɪ/ *noun*
→ see **CV**

curry /'kʌri/ *noun* (**curries**)
a dish, originally from Asia, that is cooked with hot spices: *Our favourite dish is the vegetable curry.* □ *Shall we go for a curry tonight?*

curse¹ /kɜːs/ *verb* (**curses, cursing, cursed**)
to use very impolite or offensive language (*formal*): *Jake nodded, but he was cursing silently.*

curse² /kɜːs/ *noun*
1 something very impolite or offensive that someone says: *Shouts and curses came from all directions.*
2 a strange power that seems to cause unpleasant things to happen to someone: *He believes that an evil spirit has put a curse on his business.*

cursor /'kɜːsə/ *noun*
a small line on a computer screen that shows where you are working: *He moved the cursor and clicked the mouse.*

curtain /'kɜːtən/ *noun*
1 a piece of material that hangs from the top of a window to cover it at night: *She closed her bedroom curtains.*
→ Look at picture on P5

2 the large piece of material that hangs at the front of the stage in a theatre until a performance begins: *The curtain fell, and the audience stood and clapped.*

curve ¹ /kɜːv/ *noun*
a smooth, bent line: *She carefully drew the curve of his lips.*

curve ² /kɜːv/ *verb* (**curves, curving, curved**)
to have the shape of a curve or move in a curve: *Her spine curved forward.* □ *The ball curved through the air.*
▶ **curved** *adjective* *curved lines*

cushion /'kʊʃən/ *noun*
a bag of soft material that you put on a seat to make it more comfortable: *The baby lay on a velvet cushion.*
→ Look at picture on P5

custard /'kʌstəd/ *uncountable noun*
a sweet yellow sauce made of milk, eggs and sugar: *We had apple pie and custard for dessert.*

custom /'kʌstəm/ *noun*
something that is usual or traditional among a particular group of people: *This is an ancient Japanese custom.* □ *It was the custom to give presents.*

customer /'kʌstəmə/ *noun*
someone who buys something from a shop or a website: *I was a very satisfied customer.*

> **LANGUAGE HELP**
> When you buy something from a shop, you are a **customer**. When you use a service you are a **client**.

customs /'kʌstəmz/ *uncountable noun*
the place at an airport, for example, where people have to show certain goods that they have bought abroad: *He walked through customs.*

cut /kʌt/ *verb* (**cuts, cutting, cut**)
1 to use something sharp to remove part of something, or to break it: *Mrs Haines cut the ribbon.* □ *Cut the tomatoes in half.* □ *You've had your hair cut, it looks great.* ● **cut** *noun* *Carefully make a cut in the fabric.*
2 to accidentally injure yourself on a sharp object so that you bleed: *I started to cry because I cut my finger.* □ *He cut himself shaving.* ● **cut** *noun* *He had a cut on his left eyebrow.*
3 to reduce something: *We need to cut costs.*
● **cut** *noun* *The government announced*

a 2% cut in interest rates.

cut down on something to use or do less of something: *He cut down on coffee.*

cut something down to cut through a tree so that it falls to the ground: *They cut down several trees.*

cut something off to remove something using scissors or a knife: *Mrs Johnson cut off a large piece of meat.*

cut something out to remove something from what surrounds it using scissors or a knife: *I cut the picture out and stuck it on my wall.*

cut something up to cut something into several pieces: *Cut up the tomatoes.*

cut and 'paste *verb* (**cuts and pastes, cutting and pasting, cut and pasted**)
to remove words or pictures on a computer from one place and copy them to another place: *You can cut and paste words, phrases, sentences or even paragraphs from one part of your document to another.*

cute /kjuːt/ *adjective* (**cuter, cutest**)
pretty or attractive (*informal*): *Oh, look at that dog! He's so cute.* □ *I thought that girl was really cute.*

cutlery /'kʌtləri/ *uncountable noun*
knives, forks and spoons: *We had to eat our breakfast with plastic cutlery.*

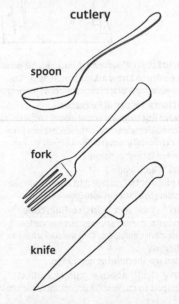

cutlery

spoon

fork

knife

CV /ˌsiː ˈviː/ *noun* (**CVs**) (*American*: **résumé**)
a written list of your education and work experience that you send when you are trying to get a new job. **CV** is short for **curriculum vitae**: *Please send your CV to the following address.*

cyberspace /ˈsaɪbəˌspeɪs/ *uncountable noun*
the imaginary place where electronic communications take place: *Our cyberspace communications started in an Internet chat room.*

cycle [1] /ˈsaɪkəl/ *noun*
1 → see **bicycle**: *a cycle ride*
2 a process that is repeated again and again: *We are studying the life cycle of the plant.*

cycle [2] /ˈsaɪkəl/ *verb* (**cycles, cycling, cycled**)
to ride a bicycle: *He cycles to school every day.*

▸ **cycling** *uncountable noun* The quiet country roads are ideal for cycling.
→ Look at picture on P6

cyclist /ˈsaɪklɪst/ *noun*
someone who rides a bicycle: *We must have better protection for cyclists.*

cylinder /ˈsɪlɪndə/ *noun*
a shape or container with circular ends and long straight sides: *Never store or change gas cylinders near a flame.*

cymbal /ˈsɪmbəl/ *noun*
a flat, round, metal musical instrument that makes a loud noise when you hit it, or when you hit two of them together

cynical /ˈsɪnɪkəl/ *adjective*
believing that people are usually bad or dishonest: *He has a cynical view of the world.*
▸ **cynically** *adverb* He laughed cynically.

Dd

dad /dæd/ *noun*
father (*informal*): *Don't tell my mum and dad about this!*

daddy /'dædi/ *noun* (**daddies**)
father (used mainly by young children) (*informal*): *Look at me, Daddy!* □ *My daddy always reads me stories and helps me with my homework.*

daffodil /'dæfədɪl/ *noun*
a yellow flower with a long stem that appears in spring

daily /'deɪli/ *adjective, adverb*
appearing or happening every day: *the French daily newspaper 'Le Monde'* □ *The students use this dictionary almost daily.*

dainty /'deɪnti/ *adjective* (**daintier, daintiest**)
small, delicate and pretty: *Did you walk here in those dainty little shoes?*
▶ **daintily** *adverb* *She walked daintily down the steps.*

dairy /'deəri/ *adjective*
used for talking about foods such as butter and cheese that are made from milk: *He can't eat dairy products.*

daisy /'deɪzi/ *noun* (**daisies**)
a small wild flower with a yellow centre and white petals

dam /dæm/ *noun*
a wall that is built across a river in order to hold back water: *Before the dam was built, the Campbell River often flooded.*

damage¹ /'dæmɪdʒ/ *verb* (**damages, damaging, damaged**)
to break or harm something: *He damaged a car with a baseball bat.* □ *The new tax will badly damage Australian industries.*
▶ **damaging** *adjective* *We can see the damaging effects of pollution in cities.*

damage² /'dæmɪdʒ/ *uncountable noun*
physical harm that happens to an object: *The explosion caused a lot of damage to the house.*

damp /dæmp/ *adjective* (**damper, dampest**)
slightly wet: *Her hair was still damp.* □ *We went out into the damp, cold air.*

dance¹ /dɑːns/ *verb* (**dances, dancing, danced**)
to move your body to music: *She turned on the radio and danced around the room.* □ *Shall we dance?*
▶ **dancing** *uncountable noun* *Let's go dancing tonight.*

dance² /dɑːns/ *noun*
1 a particular series of movements that you usually do in time to music: *a traditional Scottish dance*
2 a party where people dance with each other: *At the school dance he talked to her all evening.*

dancer /'dɑːnsə/ *noun*
a person who earns money by dancing, or a person who is dancing: *She's a dancer with Ballet Rambert.*

dandelion /'dændɪ,laɪən/ *noun*
a wild plant with yellow flowers that turn into balls of soft white seeds

danger /'deɪndʒə/ *noun*
1 *uncountable* the possibility that something unpleasant will happen, or that you may be harmed or killed: *I'm worried. I think Mary's in danger.*
2 something or someone that can hurt or harm you: *They warned us about the dangers of driving too fast.*

dangerous /'deɪndʒərəs/ *adjective*
able or likely to harm you: *We are in a very dangerous situation.* □ *He owns a dangerous dog.*
▶ **dangerously** *adverb* *He is dangerously ill.*

dare /deə/ *verb* (**dares, daring, dared**)
to be brave enough to do something: *Most people don't dare to disagree with Harry.* □ *I didn't dare open the door.* ● **dare** *modal verb* *She dare not leave the house.*

dare someone to do something to ask someone to do something dangerous in order to prove that they are brave enough to do it: *They dared me to jump into the water but I refused.*

how dare you used for showing that you are very angry about something that someone has done: *How dare you say that about my mother!*

LANGUAGE HELP
You can leave out the word **to** after **dare**. *Nobody dared complain.*

daring /'deərɪŋ/ *adjective*
willing to do dangerous things: *He made a daring escape from the island in a small boat.*

dark¹ /dɑːk/ *adjective* (**darker, darkest**)
1 with no light, or very little light: *It was too dark to see much.*
▶ **darkness** *uncountable noun* *The light went out, and we were in total darkness.*
▶ **darkly** *adverb* *a darkly lit hall*
2 having the colour black or a colour close to black: *He wore a dark suit.* □ *a dark blue dress*
▶ **darkly** *adverb* *His skin was darkly tanned.*
3 with brown or black hair, eyes, or skin: *He had dark, curly hair.*
get dark to become night: *We shut the curtains when it got dark.*

dark² /dɑːk/ *uncountable noun*
the dark the lack of light in a place: *Children are often afraid of the dark.*

darling /'dɑːlɪŋ/ *noun*
a name that you call someone that you love very much: *Thank you, darling.*

dart¹ /dɑːt/ *verb* (**darts, darting, darted**)
to move suddenly and quickly: *Ingrid darted across the street.*

dart² /dɑːt/ *noun*
a small, narrow object with a sharp point that you can throw or shoot

darts /dɑːts/ *uncountable noun*
a game in which you throw darts (= small pointed objects) at a round board that has numbers on it: *I enjoy playing darts.*

dash¹ /dæʃ/ *verb* (**dashes, dashing, dashed**)
to go somewhere quickly and suddenly: *She dashed downstairs when the doorbell rang.*

dash² /dæʃ/ *noun*
make a dash for something to go somewhere quickly and suddenly: *She screamed and made a dash for the door.*

dash³ /dæʃ/ *noun* (**dashes**)
a short, straight, horizontal line that you use in writing: *Sometimes people use a dash (—) where they could use a colon (:).*

dashboard /'dæʃbɔːd/ *noun*
the part of a car in front of the driver, where most of the controls are: *The clock on the dashboard showed two o'clock.*

data /'deɪtə/ *noun*
1 *plural* information, especially when it is in the form of facts or numbers: *Government data shows that unemployment is going up.*
2 *uncountable* information that can be used by a computer program: *A CD-ROM can hold huge amounts of data.*

database /'deɪtə,beɪs/ *noun*
a collection of information on a computer that is stored in such a way that you can use it and add to it easily: *Searching the database is quick and simple.*

date¹ /deɪt/ *noun*
1 a particular day and month or a particular year: *'What's the date today?' — '23rd July.'*
2 an arrangement to meet a boyfriend or a girlfriend: *I have a date with Bob tonight.*
3 a small, dark-brown, sticky fruit with a stone inside

date² /deɪt/ *verb* (**dates, dating, dated**)
to go out with someone regularly because you are having a romantic relationship with them: *They've been dating for three months.* □ *I once dated a woman who was a teacher.*

daughter /'dɔːtə/ *noun*
a person's female child: *We met Flora and her daughter Catherine.* □ *She's the daughter of a university professor.*
→ Look at picture on P8

daughter-in-law *noun* (**daughters-in-law**)
the wife of a person's son

dawn /dɔːn/ *noun*
the time when the sky becomes light in the morning: *Nancy woke at dawn.*

day /deɪ/ *noun*
1 a period of twenty-four hours from one midnight to the next midnight: *They'll be back in three days.* □ *It snowed every day last week.* □ *'What day is it today?' — 'It's Thursday.'*

2 the time when it is light outside: *We spent the day watching tennis.* □ *The streets are busy during the day.*

one day

1 at some time in the future: *Steven and I both dream of living in Australia one day.* □ *I hope one day you will find someone who will make you happy.*

2 at some time in the past: *One day, he came home from work, and she wasn't there.*

the other day a few days ago: *I saw Fiona in town the other day.*

these days at this time; not in the past: *These days, I have enough money to do everything I want.*

daydream /'deɪdriːm/ *verb* (**daydreams, daydreaming, daydreamed**)
to think about pleasant things for a period of time: *I was daydreaming about a job in France.* ● **daydream** *noun She was looking out the window in a daydream.*

daylight /'deɪlaɪt/ *uncountable noun*
the natural light that there is during the day: *A little daylight came through a crack in the wall.*

daytime /'deɪtaɪm/ *noun*
the part of a day between the time when it gets light and the time when it gets dark: *He rarely went anywhere in the daytime; he was always out at night.*

dazzling /'dæzlɪŋ/ *adjective*
1 extremely beautiful and impressive: *She had a dazzling smile.*
2 extremely bright and making you unable to see for a short time: *a dazzling light*

dead /ded/ *adjective*
1 not alive: *She had already told me her husband was dead.* □ *They put the dead body into the ambulance.*
2 not working: *I answered the phone but the line was dead.*

the dead people who have died: *Two soldiers were among the dead.*

deadline /'dedlaɪn/ *noun*
a particular time or date before which you must do or finish something: *We missed the deadline because of several problems.*

deadly /'dedli/ *adjective* (**deadlier, deadliest**)
able or likely to kill a person or an animal: *This deadly disease killed 70 people in Malaysia last year.*

deaf /def/ *adjective* (**deafer, deafest**)
unable to hear anything or unable to hear very well: *She is now totally deaf.* □ *He is deaf in his left ear.*

the deaf people who are deaf: *Marianne works as a part-time teacher for the deaf.*

deafen /'defən/ *verb* (**deafens, deafening, deafened**)
to make someone unable to hear anything else because of a very loud noise: *The noise of the engines deafened her.*

deafening /'defənɪŋ/ *adjective*
very loud: *All we could hear was the deafening sound of gunfire.*

deal¹ /diːl/ *verb* (**deals, dealing, dealt**)
(*also* **deal something out**)
to give playing cards to the players in a game of cards: *Natalie dealt each player a card.* □ *Dalton dealt out five cards to each player.*

deal in something to buy or sell a particular type of goods: *They deal in antiques.*
▶ **dealer** *noun an antique dealer* □ *car dealers*

deal something out same meaning as **deal**

deal with someone/something to give your attention to someone or something: *Could you deal with this customer, please?* □ *She often has to deal with complaints from customers.*

deal² /diːl/ *noun*
a business agreement: *They made a deal to share the money between them.*

a great/good deal of something a lot of a particular thing: *You can earn a great deal of money in this job.*

dear¹ /dɪə/ *adjective* (**dearer, dearest**)
1 used for describing someone that you love: *Mrs Cavendish is a very dear friend of mine.*
2 used at the beginning of a letter or an email before the name of the person you are writing to: *Dear Peter, How are you?* □ *Dear Sir or Madam...*

dear² /dɪə/ *exclamation*
oh dear used for showing that you are surprised or upset: *Oh dear! Poor Max.*

death /deθ/ *noun*
the end of a person's or an animal's life:

1.5 million people are in danger of death from hunger. □ It's the thirtieth anniversary of her death.

debate /dɪ'beɪt/ *noun*
a long discussion or argument: *The debate will continue until they vote on Thursday.* □ *There has been a lot of debate among teachers about this subject.* ● **debate** *verb* (**debates, debating, debated**) *The committee will debate the issue today.* □ *They were debating which team would win.*

debit card /'debɪt ˌkɑːd/ *noun*
a bank card that you can use to pay for things

debris /'deɪbriː, 'debriː/ *uncountable noun*
pieces from something that has been destroyed: *Debris from the plane was found over an area the size of a football pitch.*

debt /det/ *noun*
an amount of money that you owe someone: *He is still paying off his debts.*
be in debt/get into debt to owe money: *Many students get into debt.*

decade /'dekeɪd/ *noun*
a period of ten years: *She spent a decade studying in London.*

decay /dɪ'keɪ/ *verb* (**decays, decaying, decayed**)
to gradually be destroyed by a natural process; to become bad: *The bodies slowly decayed.* □ *Brush your teeth every day so that they don't decay.* ● **decay** *uncountable noun* *Eating too many sweets causes tooth decay.*

deceive /dɪ'siːv/ *verb* (**deceives, deceiving, deceived**)
to deliberately make someone believe something that is not true: *She accused the government of trying to deceive the public.*

December /dɪ'sembə/ *noun*
the twelfth and last month of the year: *I arrived on a bright morning in December.*

decent /'diːsənt/ *adjective*
1 acceptable or good enough: *Without decent housing, poor health and poverty will not be defeated.* □ *If the weather is decent, we'll have a barbecue at the weekend.*
▶ **decently** *adverb* *They treated their prisoners decently.*
2 morally right or polite: *He's a really nice, decent guy.* □ *It was very decent of him to ring and explain.*

deception /dɪ'sepʃən/ *uncountable noun*
when someone deliberately makes you

believe something that is not true: *Lies and deception are not a good way to start a marriage.*

deceptive /dɪ'septɪv/ *adjective*
making you believe something that is not true: *The sea looked warm, but appearances can be deceptive: it was absolutely freezing!*
▶ **deceptively** *adverb* *The atmosphere in the hall was deceptively peaceful.*

decide /dɪ'saɪd/ *verb* (**decides, deciding, decided**)
1 to choose to do something after thinking about it for some time: *She decided to take a course in philosophy.* □ *Think about it very carefully before you decide.*
2 to choose how something should happen or be done: *Schools need to decide the best way of testing students.*
3 to form your opinion about something: *He decided Franklin was lying to him.*

decimal¹ /'desɪməl/ *noun*
part of a number that is written in the form of a dot followed by one or more numbers: *The interest rate is shown as a decimal, such as 0.10, which means 10%.*

decimal² /'desɪməl/ *adjective*
using a system that counts in units of ten: *The mathematics of ancient Egypt used a decimal system.*

decimal point *noun*
the dot that you use when you write a number as a decimal: *A waiter forgot to put the decimal point in the £45.00 bill and they were charged £4500.*

decision /dɪ'sɪʒən/ *noun*
the act of choosing what to do: *I don't want to make the wrong decision and regret it later.*

deck /dek/ *noun*
1 one of the floors of a bus or a ship: *We went on a luxury ship with five passenger decks.*
2 a flat wooden area attached to a house, where people can sit: *A deck leads into the main room of the home.*
3 a complete set of playing cards: *Matt picked up the cards and shuffled the deck.*

declaration /ˌdeklə'reɪʃən/ *noun*
an official statement: *We consider these attacks to be a declaration of war.*

declare /dɪ'kleə/ *verb* (**declares, declaring, declared**)
1 to say that something is true in a firm,

clear way: *Melinda declared that she was leaving home.*

2 to officially state that something is the case: *The president finally declared an end to the war.* □ *The judges declared Mr Stevens innocent.*

3 to say what you have bought during a visit to another country, so that you can pay tax on it in your own country: *Please declare all food, plants and animal products.* □ *At the airport, the customs officer searched my bag and asked me if I had anything to declare.*

decline /dɪˈklaɪn/ *verb* (**declines, declining, declined**)

1 to become less in amount, importance or strength: *The local population is declining.*

2 to politely refuse to accept something (*formal*): *He declined their invitation.* □ *She offered me a cup of tea, but I declined.*

decorate /ˈdekəreɪt/ *verb* (**decorates, decorating, decorated**)

1 to make something look more attractive by adding things to it: *He decorated his room with pictures of sports stars.*

2 to put new paint or paper on the walls and ceiling of a room: *They were decorating Jemma's bedroom.* □ *She loves decorating.*

▶ **decorating** *uncountable noun* *I did a lot of the decorating myself.*

decoration /ˌdekəˈreɪʃən/ *noun*

1 an object that you use to make something look more attractive: *Colourful paper decorations were hanging from the ceiling.*

2 *uncountable* the furniture and the paint or paper on the walls of a room: *The decoration was practical for a family home.*

decorative /ˈdekərətɪv/ *adjective*

intended to look pretty or attractive: *The curtains are only decorative — they do not open or close.*

decrease [1] /dɪˈkriːs/ *verb* (**decreases, decreasing, decreased**)

to become less in amount, size or strength: *Last year the average price of property in this area decreased from £134,000 to £126,000.* □ *Property may start to decrease in value.*

decrease [2] /ˈdiːkriːs/ *noun*

the process of growing less in amount, size or strength: *There has been a decrease in the number of people without a job.*

dedicate /ˈdedɪˌkeɪt/ *verb* (**dedicates, dedicating, dedicated**)

to say on the first page of a book, a play or

a piece of music that you have written it for a particular person: *She dedicated her first book to her sons.*

▶ **dedication** *noun* *I read the dedication at the beginning of the book.*

deduct /dɪˈdʌkt/ *verb* (**deducts, deducting, deducted**)

to take away a particular amount from a total: *The company deducted £50 from his wages.*

deed /diːd/ *noun*

something that is done, especially something that is very good or very bad: *The people who did this evil deed must be punished.*

deep /diːp/ *adjective, adverb* (**deeper, deepest**)

1 going down a long way: *The water is very deep.* □ *The kids dug a deep hole in the middle of the garden.* □ *She put her hands deep into her pockets.*

2 used for emphasizing the seriousness or strength of something: *He expressed his deep sympathy to the family.*

▶ **deeply** *adverb* *He loved his brother deeply.*

3 having a low, usually strong, sound: *He spoke in a deep, warm voice.*

4 strong and dark in colour: *The sky was deep blue and starry.*

5 if you are in a deep sleep, you are sleeping so soundly that it is difficult for someone to wake you: *Una fell into a deep sleep.*

▶ **deeply** *adverb* *She slept deeply, but woke early.*

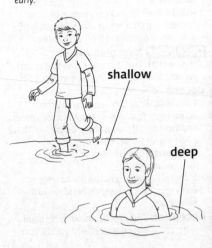

shallow

deep

take a deep breath to breathe in so that your lungs are completely filled with air: *Cal took a long, deep breath, as he tried to control his emotions.*

deepen /'di:pən/ *verb* (**deepens, deepening, deepened**)
to become stronger: *These friendships will probably deepen in your teenage years.*

deer /dɪə/ *noun* (**deer**)
a large wild animal that eats grass and leaves, the male of which usually has large horns that look like branches

default /dɪ'fɔ:lt/ *uncountable noun*
the way that something will be done if you do not give any other instruction: *The default setting on the printer is for colour.*

defeat /dɪ'fi:t/ *verb* (**defeats, defeating, defeated**)
to beat someone in a battle, a game or a competition: *They defeated the French army in 1954.* • **defeat** *noun* *He was prime minister until his party's defeat in the general election this summer.* □ *The team suffered a 2–1 defeat in the semi-finals.*

defective /dɪ'fektɪv/ *adjective*
not working properly: *If the product is defective, you can demand your money back.*

defence /dɪ'fens/ *noun*
1 *uncountable* action to protect someone or something against attack: *The land was flat, which made defence difficult.*
2 *uncountable* the organization of a country's armies and weapons, and their use to protect the country: *Twenty-eight per cent of the country's money is spent on defence.*
3 in games such as football or hockey, the group of players in a team who try to stop the opposing players from scoring a goal or a point: *Their defence was weak and allowed in 12 goals.*

defend /dɪ'fend/ *verb* (**defends, defending, defended**)
1 to take action in order to protect someone or something: *The army must be able to defend its own country against attack.*
2 in sports, to try to stop the other team from getting points: *The team scored three excellent goals and defended superbly.*
3 to argue in support of a decision: *The president defended his decision to go to war.*
4 to argue, in a law court, that a person is not guilty of a particular crime: *He has*
hired a lawyer to defend him in court.

defender /dɪ'fendə/ *noun*
a sports player whose main task is to try and stop the other side from scoring: *Lewis was the team's top defender.*

defiant /dɪ'faɪənt/ *adjective*
refusing to obey someone: *She stood looking at her father with a defiant expression on her face.*
▶ **defiantly** *adverb* *They defiantly refused to accept the plan.*

deficit /'defəsɪt/ *noun*
the amount by which something is less than the amount that is needed: *The budget showed a deficit of five billion pounds.*

define /dɪ'faɪn/ *verb* (**defines, defining, defined**)
to say clearly what something is and what it means: *The government defines a household as 'a group of people who live in the same house'.*

definite /'defɪnɪt/ *adjective*
1 firm and clear, and unlikely to change: *I need a definite answer soon.* □ *I want to make some definite plans for the future.*
2 true, rather than just being an opinion or a guess: *We didn't have any definite proof.*

definite 'article *noun*
the word 'the': *Place names often have a definite article, as in 'The Alps'.*

definitely /'defɪnɪtli/ *adverb*
certainly; without any doubt: *I'll definitely come to your birthday party.* □ *The extra money will definitely help.*

definition /ˌdefɪ'nɪʃən/ *noun*
the meaning of a word or an expression that you find in a dictionary: *What is the definition of 'an adult'?*

deform /dɪ'fɔ:m/ *verb* (**deforms, deforming, deformed**)
to cause a person's body to have an unnatural shape: *The disease deforms the arms and the legs.*
▶ **deformed** *adjective* *He had a deformed right leg.*

defy /dɪ'faɪ/ *verb* (**defies, defying, defied**)
to refuse to obey someone or something: *This was the first time I defied my mother.*

degree /dɪ'gri:/ *noun*
1 a unit for measuring temperatures that is often written as °: *It's over 35° outside.*
□ *Bake the cake at 180 degrees Celsius for 25 minutes or until light brown.*

2 a unit for measuring angles that is often written as °: *It was pointing outward at an angle of 45 degrees.* □ *Angles smaller than a right angle (less than 90°) are called acute angles.*
3 a qualification that you receive when you have successfully completed a course of study at a university or a college: *He has an engineering degree.* □ *She has a degree in Russian.*

delay /dɪ'leɪ/ *verb* (**delays, delaying, delayed**)
1 to not do something immediately or at the planned time, but to do it later: *Many women delay motherhood because they want to have a career.*
2 to make someone or something late: *Passengers were delayed at the airport for five hours.* □ *Our flight was delayed for three hours.*
● **delay** *noun* *He apologized for the delay.*

delegate /'delɪgət/ *noun*
a person who represents a group of other people at a meeting, for example: *About 750 delegates attended the conference.*

delete /dɪ'liːt/ *verb* (**deletes, deleting, deleted**)
to delete or put a line through something that has been written down or stored in a computer: *He deleted files from the computer.*

deliberate /dɪ'lɪbərət/ *adjective*
planned and not done by accident: *They told deliberate lies in order to sell newspapers.*
▶ **deliberately** *adverb* *He started the fire deliberately. It wasn't an accident.*

delicate /'delɪkət/ *adjective*
1 easily broken or damaged: *The machine even washes delicate glassware.* □ *Do not rub the delicate skin around the eyes.*
2 pleasant and light in colour, taste or smell: *The beans have a delicate flavour.* □ *The sheets were a delicate shade of pink.*

delicatessen /ˌdelɪkə'tesən/ *noun*
a shop that sells food such as cold meats and cheeses

delicious /dɪ'lɪʃəs/ *adjective*
very good to eat: *There was a wide choice of delicious meals.*
▶ **deliciously** *adverb* *This yogurt has a deliciously creamy flavour.*

delight /dɪ'laɪt/ *uncountable noun*
a feeling of great pleasure: *He expressed delight at the news.* □ *Andrew laughed with delight.*

delighted /dɪ'laɪtɪd/ *adjective*
extremely pleased: *Frank was delighted to see her.*

deliver /dɪ'lɪvə/ *verb* (**delivers, delivering, delivered**)
to take something to a particular place: *Only 90% of first-class post is delivered on time.* □ *The Canadians plan to deliver more food to Somalia.*

delivery /dɪ'lɪvəri/ *noun* (**deliveries**)
1 *uncountable* when someone brings letters, packages or other goods to a particular place: *Please allow 28 days for delivery of your order.*
2 the goods that are delivered: *I got a delivery of fresh eggs this morning.*

deluxe /dɪ'lʌks/ *adjective*
very high quality and expensive: *She only stays in deluxe hotel suites.*

demand¹ /dɪ'mɑːnd/ *verb* (**demands, demanding, demanded**)
to ask for something in a very firm way: *The victim's family is demanding an investigation into the shooting.* □ *He demanded that I give him an answer.*

demand² /dɪ'mɑːnd/ *noun*
a firm request for something: *There were demands for better services.*
in (great) demand very popular and wanted by a lot of people: *Maths teachers are always in demand.*

democracy /dɪ'mɒkrəsi/ *uncountable noun*
a system of government in which people choose their leaders by voting for them in elections: *We're studying democracy in Eastern Europe.*

democrat /'deməkræt/ *noun*
a person who believes in and wants democracy: *This is the time for democrats and not dictators.*

democratic /ˌdemə'krætɪk/ *adjective*
1 having or relating to a political system in which the leaders are elected by the people that they govern: *Bolivia returned to democratic rule in 1982.*
2 based on the idea that everyone has equal rights and should be involved in making important decisions: *Education is the basis of a democratic society.*

demolish /dɪ'mɒlɪʃ/ *verb* (**demolishes, demolishing, demolished**)
to destroy something completely: *The*

storm demolished buildings and flooded streets.
▶ **demolition** /ˌdemə'lɪʃən/ *uncountable*
noun *The bomb caused the total demolition of
the old bridge.*

demonstrate /'demənˌstreɪt/ *verb*
(**demonstrates, demonstrating,
demonstrated**)
1 to show people how something works
or how to do something: *Several companies
were demonstrating their new products.*
▶ **demonstration** *noun* *We watched a
cooking demonstration.*
2 to march or gather somewhere to show
that you oppose or support something: *Ten
thousand people demonstrated against the war.*
▶ **demonstration** *noun* *Soldiers broke up an
anti-government demonstration.*
▶ **demonstrator** *noun* *Police were dealing
with a crowd of demonstrators.*

den /den/ *noun*
the home of some types of wild animal

denial /dɪ'naɪəl/ *noun*
when you say that something is not true
or that it does not exist: *There have been
many official denials of the government's
involvement.*

denim /'denɪm/ *uncountable noun*
a thick cotton cloth, usually blue, which
is used for making clothes: *a denim jacket*

dense /dens/ *adjective* (**denser, densest**)
1 with a lot of things or people in a small
area: *The road runs through a dense forest.*
▶ **densely** *adverb* *Java is a densely populated
island.*
2 very thick and difficult to see through:
The planes came close to each other in dense fog.
3 having great weight in relation to size:
Ice is less dense than water, and so it floats.

density /'densɪti/ *noun* (**densities**)
how heavy a substance or an object is in
relation to its size: *Jupiter's moon Io has a
density of 3.5 grams per cubic centimetre.*

dent /dent/ *verb* (**dents, denting, dented**)
to make a hollow area in the surface of
something by hitting it or pressing it too
hard: *The stone dented the car door.* ● **dent**
noun *There was a dent in the side of the car.*

dental /'dentəl/ *adjective*
relating to teeth: *Regular dental care is
important.*

dentist /'dentɪst/ *noun*
1 a person whose job is to examine and

dent

treat people's teeth: *Visit your dentist twice
a year for a checkup.*
2 (*also* **dentist's**) the place where a dentist
works: *I'm going to the dentist's after school.*
→ Look at picture on P7

deny /dɪ'naɪ/ *verb* (**denies, denying,
denied**)
to say that something is not true: *Robby
denied stealing the bike.* ☐ *He denied that he was
involved in the crime.*

deodorant /di'əʊdərənt/ *noun*
a substance that you can put on your skin
to hide or prevent bad smells

depart /dɪ'pɑːt/ *verb* (**departs, departing,
departed**)
to leave: *Flight 43 will depart from Newcastle at
11.45 a.m.* ☐ *In the morning, Mr McDonald
departed for Sydney.*

department /dɪ'pɑːtmənt/ *noun*
1 one of the sections in an organization
such as a government, a business or a
university: *She works for the Department of
Health.*
2 one of the sections in a large shop:
He works in the shoe department.

de'partment store *noun*
a large shop that sells many different
types of goods

departure /dɪ'pɑːtʃə/ *noun*
the act of going away from somewhere:
*Illness delayed the president's departure for
Helsinki.*

dep'artures /dɪ'pɑːtʃəz/ *noun*
the place in an airport where passengers
wait before they get onto their plane

depend /dɪ'pend/ *verb* (**depends,
depending, depended**)
can depend on someone/something
to know that someone or something will

support you or help you when you need them: 'You can depend on me,' I assured him.

depend on someone/something to need someone or something in order to do something: I'm depending on you to protect me. ☐ He depended on his writing for his income.

depend on something to be decided by something: The cooking time depends on the size of the potato.

it/that depends used for showing that you cannot give an answer to a question because you need more information: 'How long can you stay?' — 'I don't know. It depends.'

dependable /dɪ'pendəbəl/ **adjective**
helpful and sensible: He was a dependable friend.

dependent /dɪ'pendənt/ **adjective**
needing someone or something in order to succeed or to be able to survive: The young gorillas are completely dependent on their mothers.

▸ **dependence** **uncountable noun** We discussed the city's dependence on tourism.

deposit /dɪ'pɒzɪt/ **noun**
1 a sum of money that is part of the full price of something, and that you pay when you agree to buy it: He paid a £500 deposit for the car.
2 an amount of a substance that has been left somewhere as a result of a chemical or geological process: underground deposits of gold
3 an amount of money that you put into a bank account: I made a deposit every week.

depot /'depəʊ/ **noun**
a place where goods or vehicles are kept until they are needed: The food is stored in a depot at the airport. ☐ a bus depot

depress /dɪ'pres/ **verb** (depresses, depressing, depressed)
to make you feel sad: This time of year always depresses me.

depressed /dɪ'prest/ **adjective**
feeling very sad and unable to enjoy anything for a long time: She was very depressed after her husband died.

depressing /dɪ'presɪŋ/ **adjective**
making you feel sad: The view from the window was grey and depressing.

depression /dɪ'preʃən/ **uncountable noun**
a state of mind in which you are very sad and you feel that you cannot enjoy

anything: Mr Thomas was suffering from depression.

deprive /dɪ'praɪv/ **verb** (deprives, depriving, deprived)
to take something away from someone, or prevent them from having something: They were deprived of fuel to heat their homes.
▸ **deprived** **adjective** These are some of the most deprived children in the country.

depth /depθ/ **noun**
how deep something is; the distance from the top to the bottom of something: The average depth of the sea is 4000 metres.

in depth in a very detailed way: We will discuss these three areas in depth.

deputy /'depjʊti/ **noun** (deputies)
the second most important person in an organization: Dr Amin is the museum's deputy director.

descend /dɪ'send/ **verb** (descends, descending, descended)
to move down from a higher level to a lower level (formal): We descended to the basement.

describe /dɪ'skraɪb/ **verb** (describes, describing, described)
to say what something is like: She described what she did in her spare time. ☐ The poem describes their life together.

description /dɪ'skrɪpʃən/ **noun**
an explanation of what someone looks like, or what something is: Police have given a description of the man. ☐ He gave a detailed description of how the new system will work.

desert [1] /'dezət/ **noun**
a large area of land where there is almost no water, trees or plants: They travelled through the Sahara Desert.

desert [2] /dɪ'zɜːt/ **verb** (deserts, deserting, deserted)
1 to leave a place so that it becomes empty: Poor farmers are deserting their fields and coming to the cities to find jobs.
▸ **deserted** **adjective** She led them into a deserted street.
2 to leave or abandon someone who needs your help or support: Sadly, most of her friends have deserted her.

deserve /dɪ'zɜːv/ **verb** (deserves, deserving, deserved)
to be worthy of something because of your actions or qualities: These people

deserve to get more money. □ *This is a serious crime, and it deserves a severe punishment.*

design¹ /dɪˈzaɪn/ *verb* (**designs, designing, designed**)
to make a detailed plan or drawing to show how something should be made: *They wanted to design a machine that was both attractive and practical.*

design² /dɪˈzaɪn/ *noun*
1 *uncountable* the process of planning and drawing things: *He had a talent for design.*
2 a drawing that shows how something should be built or made: *They drew the design for the house.*
3 a pattern of lines or shapes that is used for decorating something: *The table cloths come in three different designs.*

designer /dɪˈzaɪnə/ *noun*
a person whose job is to design things by making drawings of them: *Caroline is a fashion designer.*

desirable /dɪˈzaɪərəbəl/ *adjective*
so useful or attractive that everyone wants to have it: *The house is in a desirable neighbourhood, close to schools.*

desire¹ /dɪˈzaɪə/ *noun*
a strong wish to do or have something: *I had a strong desire to help people.*

desire² /dɪˈzaɪə/ *verb* (**desires, desiring, desired**)
to want something very much (*formal*): *This house is ideal for someone who desires a bit of peace.*
▶ **desired** *adjective* *This will produce the desired effect.*

desk /desk/ *noun*
1 a table that you sit at to write or work
2 a place in a public building where you can get information: *They asked for Miss Minton at the reception desk.*

desktop¹ /ˈdesktɒp/ *adjective*
of a convenient size for using on a desk or a table: *A $1,000 desktop personal computer can perform about 450 calculations per second.*

desktop² /ˈdesktɒp/ also **desk-top** *noun*
the images that you see on a computer screen when the computer is ready to use: *You can rearrange the icons on the desktop.*

despair /dɪˈspeə/ *uncountable noun*
the feeling that everything is wrong and that nothing will improve: *I looked at my wife in despair.* ● **despair** *verb* (**despairs, despairing, despaired**) *'Oh, I despair sometimes,' she said, looking at the mess.*

desperate /ˈdespərət/ *adjective*
1 willing to try anything to change your situation: *He was desperate to get back to the city.* □ *There were hundreds of patients desperate for his help.*
▶ **desperately** *adverb* *Thousands of people are desperately trying to leave the country.*
2 very difficult, serious or dangerous: *The situation in the area is desperate — there is no food.*

desperation /ˌdespəˈreɪʃən/ *uncountable noun*
the feeling that you have when you are in such a bad situation that you will try anything to change it: *There was a look of desperation in her eyes.*

despise /dɪˈspaɪz/ *verb* (**despises, despising, despised**)
to dislike someone or something very much: *She despises dishonesty, and she hated lying to Dave.*

despite /dɪˈspaɪt/ *preposition*
used for introducing a fact that makes something surprising: *The barbecue was a success, despite the rain.*

dessert /dɪˈzɜːt/ *noun*
something sweet that you eat at the end of a meal: *We had ice cream for dessert.*

dessertspoon /dɪˈzɜːtspuːn/ *noun*
a spoon that you use for eating desserts

destination /ˌdestɪˈneɪʃən/ *noun*
the place you are going to: *He wanted to arrive at his destination before dark.*

destiny /ˈdestɪni/ *noun* (**destinies**)
everything that happens to you during your life, including what will happen in the future: *Do we control our own destiny?*

destroy /dɪˈstrɔɪ/ *verb* (**destroys, destroying, destroyed**)
to cause so much damage to something that it cannot be used any longer, or does not exist any longer: *The original house was destroyed by fire.*
▶ **destruction** /dɪˈstrʌkʃən/ *uncountable noun* *We must stop the destruction of our forests.*

destructive /dɪˈstrʌktɪv/ *adjective*
causing great damage: *a destructive storm*

detach /dɪˈtætʃ/ *verb* (**detaches, detaching, detached**)
to remove something from another thing

to which it was attached (*formal*): *Detach the card and post it to this address.*

detached /dɪ'tætʃt/ *adjective*
not joined to any other building: *We have a house with a detached garage.*

detail /'diːteɪl/ *noun*
one of the small, individual parts of something: *We discussed the details of the letter.*
in detail in a way that considers all the different facts or parts of something: *Examine the contract in detail before signing it.*

detailed /'diːteɪld/ *adjective*
containing a lot of details: *She gave us a detailed description of the man.*

details /'diːteɪlz/ *plural noun*
the facts about someone or something: *See the bottom of this page for details of how to apply for this offer.*

detect /dɪ'tekt/ *verb* (**detects, detecting, detected**)
to find or notice something: *One of the hotel guests detected the smell of smoke.* □ *Arnold could detect sadness in the old man's face.*
▶ **detection** *uncountable noun* *The process is used in the detection of cancer.*

detective /dɪ'tektɪv/ *noun*
someone whose job is to discover what has happened in a crime, and to find the people who did the crime: *Detectives are still searching for the four men.*

detergent /dɪ'tɜːdʒənt/ *noun*
a chemical substance that you use for washing things such as clothes or dishes: *Hand-wash the gloves in warm water, using a mild detergent.*

deteriorate /dɪ'tɪəriəˌreɪt/ *verb* (**deteriorates, deteriorating, deteriorated**)
to get worse: *Her eyesight is rapidly deteriorating.*
▶ **deterioration** /dɪˌtɪəriə'reɪʃən/ *noun* *Too little sleep can cause a deterioration in your health.*

determination /dɪˌtɜːmɪ'neɪʃən/ *uncountable noun*
the feeling you have when you have firmly decided to do something: *Everyone behaved with courage and determination.*

determine /dɪ'tɜːmɪn/ *verb* (**determines, determining, determined**)
1 to control what will happen (*formal*): *The size of the chicken pieces will determine the cooking time.*
2 to discover something (*formal*): *The*

investigation will determine what really happened.

determined /dɪ'tɜːmɪnd/ *adjective*
certain that you want to do something, no matter how difficult it is: *He is determined to win gold at the Olympics.*

detest /dɪ'test/ *verb* (**detests, detesting, detested**)
to dislike someone or something very much: *You are probably aware that I detest smoking.*

devastate /'devəˌsteɪt/ *verb* (**devastates, devastating, devastated**)
to damage an area or a place very badly, or to destroy it completely: *The earthquake devastated parts of Indonesia.*
▶ **devastation** /ˌdevə'steɪʃən/ *uncountable noun* *The war brought massive devastation to the area.*

develop /dɪ'veləp/ *verb* (**develops, developing, developed**)
1 to grow or change over a period of time: *Children need time to develop.* □ *By 1992, their friendship had developed into love.*
▶ **developed** *adjective* *Their bodies were well developed and very fit.*
2 to begin to occur: *A problem developed aboard the space shuttle.*
3 to design and produce a new product: *Scientists have developed a car paint that changes colour.*

development /dɪ'veləpmənt/ *noun*
1 *uncountable* change or growth over a period of time: *We've been studying the development of language.*
2 the process of creating a new product: *The company is spending £850 million on research and development.*
3 an event or an incident that has recently happened and has an effect on an existing situation: *Police say this is an important development in the investigation.*

device /dɪ'vaɪs/ *noun*
something that has been invented for a particular purpose: *He used an electronic device to measure the rooms.*

devil /'devəl/ *noun*
an evil spirit who, according to some people, makes bad things happen

devise /dɪ'vaɪz/ *verb* (**devises, devising, devised**)
to invent a plan: *We devised a plan to help him.*

devote /dɪ'vəʊt/ *verb* (**devotes, devoting, devoted**)

devote yourself to something to spend all or most of your time or energy on something: *He devoted the rest of his life to science.*

devoted /dɪ'vəʊtɪd/ *adjective*
feeling deep love for someone: *He was devoted to his wife.*

dew /dju:/ *uncountable noun*
small drops of water that form on the ground during the night: *The dew formed on the leaves.*

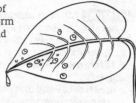

dew

diagnose /'daɪəgnəʊz/ *verb* (**diagnoses, diagnosing, diagnosed**)
to find out what is wrong with someone who is ill: *His wife was diagnosed with diabetes.* □ *Her GP has diagnosed pneumonia.*

diagnosis /ˌdaɪəg'nəʊsɪs/ *noun* (**diagnoses**)
when a doctor finds out what is wrong with someone who is ill: *I had a second test to confirm the diagnosis.*

diagonal /daɪ'ægənəl/ *adjective*
going from one corner of a square across to the opposite corner: *The screen showed a pattern of diagonal lines.*
▶ **diagonally** *adverb He ran diagonally across the field.*

diagram /'daɪəˌgræm/ *noun*
a simple drawing of lines used, for example, to explain how a machine works: *He showed us a diagram of the inside of a computer.*

dial¹ /'daɪəl/ *noun*
1 the part of a machine or a piece of equipment that shows you the time or a measurement: *The dial on the clock showed five minutes to seven.*
2 a small wheel on a piece of equipment that you can move in order to control the way it works: *He turned the dial on the radio.*

dial² /'daɪəl/ *verb* (**dials, dialling, dialled**)
to press the buttons on a telephone in order to call someone: *Dial the number, followed by the hash (= #) sign.*

dialect /'daɪəˌlekt/ *noun*
a form of a language that people speak in a particular area: *They were speaking in the local dialect.*

dialogue /'daɪəlɒg/ *noun*
a conversation between two people in a book, a film or a play: *He writes great dialogues.* □ *The film contains some very funny dialogue.*

dialogue box /'daɪəlɒg ˌbɒks/ also **dialog box** *noun*
a small area that appears on a computer screen, containing information or questions: *Clicking here brings up another dialogue box.*

'dial-up *adjective*
using a normal telephone line to connect to the Internet: *This website takes a few minutes to load over a dial-up connection.*

diameter /daɪ'æmɪtə/ *noun*
the length of a straight line that can be drawn across a round object, passing through the middle of it: *The tube is much smaller than the diameter of a human hair.*

diamond /'daɪəmənd/ *noun*
1 a hard, clear stone that is very expensive, and is used for making jewellery: *a pair of diamond earrings*
2 the shape ◆: *A baseball field is in the shape of a diamond.*

diaper /'daɪəpə/ *noun* (American)
→ see **nappy**: *She fed the baby and changed its diaper.*

diarrhoea /ˌdaɪə'ri:ə/ *uncountable noun*
an illness that makes all the waste products come out of your body as liquid: *Many team members suffered from diarrhoea.*

diary /'daɪəri/ *noun* (**diaries**)
a book with a separate space for each day of the year that you use to write down things that you plan to do, or to record what happens in your life: *I read the entry in his diary for July 10, 1940.*

dice /daɪs/ *noun* (**dice**)
a small block of wood or plastic with spots on its sides, used for playing games: *I threw both dice and got a double 6.*

dice

d

d

dictate /dɪk'teɪt/ *verb* (**dictates, dictating, dictated**)
to say or record something onto a machine, so that someone else can write it down for you: *He dictated his life story into a tape recorder while he was in prison.*

dictation /dɪk'teɪʃən/ *uncountable noun*
when one person speaks and someone else writes down what they are saying: *She was taking dictation from her boss.*

dictator /dɪk'teɪtə/ *noun*
a ruler who has complete power in a country: *The country was ruled by a dictator for more than twenty years.*

dictionary /'dɪkʃənri/ *noun* (**dictionaries**)
a book in which the words and phrases of a language are listed, together with their meanings: *We checked the spelling in the dictionary.*

did /dɪd/ → see **do**

didn't /'dɪdənt/
short for 'did not'

die /daɪ/ *verb* (**dies, dying, died**)
1 to stop living: *My dog died last week.* □ *Sadly, my mother died of cancer.*
2 to gradually becomes weaker and then stop: *My love for you will never die.*
be dying for something to want something very much (*informal*): *I'm dying for some fresh air.*
be dying to do something to want to do something very much (*informal*): *I was dying to get home and relax.*

diesel /'diːzəl/ *uncountable noun*
a fuel that is used in the engines of some vehicles instead of petrol

diet /'daɪət/ *noun*
the type of food that you regularly eat: *It's never too late to improve your diet.*
be on a diet to eat special types of food, or eat less food than usual: *Have you been on a diet? You've lost a lot of weight.* • **diet** *verb* (**diets, dieting, dieted**) *I've been dieting since the birth of my child.*

differ /'dɪfə/ *verb* (**differs, differing, differed**)
to be different from another thing: *The story he told police differed from the one he told his mother.*

difference /'dɪfrəns/ *noun*
1 the way in which two things are different from each other: *The main difference between the two computers is the price.*
2 the amount by which one quantity is more or less than another quantity: *The difference between 8532 and 8522 is 10.*
make a difference to have an important effect on you: *Where you live makes a difference to the way you feel.*
make no difference to have no effect on what you are doing; to have no importance: *It makes no difference to me what you do.*

different /'dɪfrənt/ *adjective*
1 not alike: *Although they are twins, they are so different!* □ *London was different from most European capital cities.*
▶ **differently** *adverb* *Every person learns differently.*
2 used for showing that you are talking about two or more separate things of the same type: *Different countries export different products.*
3 unusual: *Her taste in clothes is interesting and different.*

difficult /'dɪfɪkəlt/ *adjective*
1 not easy to do, understand or deal with: *The homework was too difficult for us.* □ *It was a very difficult decision to make.*
2 behaving in a way that is not reasonable or helpful: *My son is 10 years old and a very difficult child.*

difficulty /'dɪfɪkəlti/ *noun* (**difficulties**)
a problem: *There's always the difficulty of getting information.*
have difficulty doing something to be unable to do something easily: *Do you have difficulty walking?*

dig /dɪg/ *verb* (**digs, digging, dug**)
to make a hole in the ground: *I took the shovel and started digging.* □ *First, dig a large hole in the ground.*

dig

digest /daɪ'dʒest/ *verb* (**digests, digesting, digested**)
to process food in your stomach, so that your body can use it for energy: *Rice is easy to digest.* □ *Do not swim for an hour after a meal to allow time to digest your food.*

▶ **digestion** /daɪ'dʒestʃən/ *uncountable noun* Peppermint helps digestion.

digit /'dɪdʒɪt/ *noun*
a written symbol for any of the ten numbers from 0 to 9: Her telephone number differs from mine by one digit.

digital /'dɪdʒɪtəl/ *adjective*
1 using information in the form of thousands of very small signals: Most people now have digital television.
2 giving information in the form of numbers. Compare with **analogue**: I've got a new digital watch.

dignified /'dɪgnɪˌfaɪd/ *adjective*
calm, serious, and deserving respect: He was a very dignified and charming man.

dignity /'dɪgnɪti/ *uncountable noun*
serious, calm and controlled behaviour: She received the news with quiet dignity.

dilemma /daɪ'lemə/ *noun*
a difficult situation in which you have to make a choice between two things: He was facing a dilemma: should he return to his country or stay in Europe?

diligent /'dɪlɪdʒənt/ *adjective*
hard-working, in a careful and thorough way: She's a diligent student.
▶ **diligence** /'dɪlɪdʒəns/ *uncountable noun* He performed his duties with diligence.
▶ **diligently** *adverb* He was diligently searching the house.

dilute /daɪ'luːt/ *verb* (**dilutes, diluting, diluted**)
to add water to another liquid: This juice is quite strong, but you can dilute it with water.
□ The liquid is then diluted.

dim¹ /dɪm/ *adjective* (**dimmer, dimmest**)
not bright: She waited in the dim light.
▶ **dimly** *adverb* Two lamps burned dimly.

dim² /dɪm/ *verb* (**dims, dimming, dimmed**)
to become less bright: The theatre lights dimmed and the orchestra started to play.
□ Could someone dim the lights, please?

dimensions /daɪ'menʃənz/ *plural noun*
the measurements of something: We do not yet know the exact dimensions of the room.

dine /daɪn/ *verb* (**dines, dining, dined**)
to have dinner (formal): He drives a nice car and dines at the best restaurants.

'dining room *noun*
a room where people eat their meals

dinner /'dɪnə/ *noun*
1 the main meal of the day, usually served in the evening: She invited us for dinner.
□ Would you like to stay and have dinner?
2 a formal social event in the evening at which a meal is served: a series of official dinners

dinnertime /'dɪnətaɪm/ also **dinner time** *uncountable noun*
the time of the day when most people have their dinner: The telephone call came just before dinnertime.

dinosaur /'daɪnəˌsɔː/ *noun*
a large animal that lived millions of years ago

dinosaur

dip¹ /dɪp/ *verb* (**dips, dipping, dipped**)
to put something in a liquid and then quickly take it out again: Dip each apple in the syrup.

dip² /dɪp/ *noun*
a thick sauce that you dip pieces of food into before eating them: We sat and watched TV with a huge plate of crisps and dips.

diploma /dɪ'pləumə/ *noun*
a qualification that a student who has completed a course of study may receive: He was awarded a diploma in social work.

diplomacy /dɪ'pləuməsi/ *uncountable noun*
the activity or profession of managing relations between the governments of different countries: If diplomacy fails, there could be a war.

diplomat /'dɪpləˌmæt/ *noun*
a senior official whose job is to discuss international affairs with officials from other countries: Sir Harold is a Western diplomat with experience in Asia.

diplomatic /ˌdɪplə'mætɪk/ *adjective*
1 relating to diplomacy and diplomats: The two countries enjoy good diplomatic relations.

2 careful to say or do things without offending people: *She is very direct, but I prefer a more diplomatic approach.*

▶ **diplomatically** *adverb* 'Of course,' agreed Sloan diplomatically.

direct¹ /daɪˈrekt, dɪˈrekt/ *adjective, adverb*

1 toward a place or an object, without changing direction and without stopping: *They took a direct flight to Athens.* □ *You can fly direct from New York to London.*

▶ **directly** *adverb* She rushed home and went directly to her room.

2 with nothing or no-one else in between: *Protect your plants from direct sunlight.* □ *More farms are selling direct to consumers.*

▶ **directly** *adverb* Never look directly at the sun.

3 honest and open, and saying exactly what you mean: *He avoided giving a direct answer.*

▶ **directly** *adverb* Explain simply and directly what you hope to achieve.

direct² /daɪˈrekt, dɪˈrekt/ *verb* (**directs, directing, directed**)

1 to be responsible for organizing a project or a group of people: *Christopher will direct everyday operations.*

▶ **direction** /daɪˈrekʃən, dɪr-/ *uncountable noun* Organizations need clear direction.

▶ **director** *noun* The company has a new director.

2 to be responsible for the way in which a film, play or television programme is performed: *Branagh himself will direct the movie.*

direction /daɪˈrekʃən, dɪr-/ *noun*
the general line that someone or something is moving or pointing in: *The nearest town was ten miles in the opposite direction.* □ *He started walking in the direction of Larry's shop.*

directions /daɪˈrekʃənz, dɪr-/ *plural noun*
instructions that tell you what to do, how to do something, or how to get somewhere: *She stopped the car to ask for directions.*

directly /daɪˈrektli, dɪr-/ *adverb*
with nothing else separating you from something that is above, below or in front of you: *They live in the flat directly above us.*

di`rect `object *noun*
the person or thing that is affected by or involved in the action carried out by the subject. Compare with **indirect object**.

director /daɪˈrektə, dɪr-/ *noun*

1 one of the people who control a company or an organization: *We wrote to the directors of the bank.*

2 the person who tells the actors and technical staff of a play, a film or a television programme what to do

directory /daɪˈrektəri, dɪr-/ *noun* (**directories**)
a book containing lists of people's names, addresses and telephone numbers: *You'll find our number in the telephone directory.*

dirt /dɜːt/ *uncountable noun*

1 dust or mud: *I started to clean the dirt off my hands.*

2 the earth on the ground: *They all sat on the dirt under a tree.*

dirty /ˈdɜːti/ *adjective* (**dirtier, dirtiest**)
not clean: *She collected the dirty plates from the table.*

disability /ˌdɪsəˈbɪliti/ *noun* (**disabilities**)
a permanent injury or condition that makes it difficult for you to work or live normally: *We're building a new classroom for people with disabilities.*

disabled /dɪˈseɪbəld/ *adjective*
having an injury or a condition that makes it difficult for you to move around: *parents of disabled children*

disadvantage /ˌdɪsədˈvɑːntɪdʒ/ *noun*
something that makes things more difficult for you: *The big disadvantage of this computer is its size.*

be at a disadvantage to have a difficulty that many other people do not have: *Children from poor families were at a disadvantage.*

disagree /ˌdɪsəˈɡriː/ *verb* (**disagrees, disagreeing, disagreed**)

1 to have a different opinion from someone else: *I really have to disagree with you here.* □ *O'Brien disagreed with the suggestion that his team played badly.* □ *They always disagreed about politics.*

2 to disapprove of an action or a decision: *I respect the president but I disagree with his decision.*

disagreement /ˌdɪsəˈɡriːmənt/ *noun*
when people do not agree with something or with each other: *Mum and Dad had a disagreement about money.* □ *Britain and France have expressed disagreement with the plan.*

disappear /ˌdɪsəˈpɪə/ *verb* (**disappears, disappearing, disappeared**)
to go away: *The sun disappeared and it started raining again.* □ *His daughter disappeared thirteen years ago.*

▸ **disappearance** *noun* *Investigators suspect a thunderstorm in the area may have had something to do with the plane's disappearance.*

disappoint /ˌdɪsəˈpɔɪnt/ *verb* (**disappoints, disappointing, disappointed**)
to make you feel sad because something that you wanted did not happen, or was not as good as you hoped: *He apologized to fans left disappointed by the cancellation of last week's concerts.*

▸ **disappointing** *adjective* *The restaurant looked great, but the food was disappointing.*

disappointed /ˌdɪsəˈpɔɪntɪd/ *adjective*
sad because something has not happened or because something is not as good as you hoped: *I was disappointed that John was not there.*

disappointment /ˌdɪsəˈpɔɪntmənt/ *noun*
1 *uncountable* the feeling you have when you are disappointed: *She couldn't hide the disappointment in her voice.*
2 something or someone that is not as good as you hoped: *Their team's defeat was a huge disappointment for the fans.*

disapproval /ˌdɪsəˈpruːvəl/ *uncountable noun*
when you show that you think that someone or something is bad or wrong: *He stared at Marina with disapproval.*

disapprove /ˌdɪsəˈpruːv/ *verb* (**disapproves, disapproving, disapproved**)
to think that someone or something is bad or wrong: *Most people disapprove of violence.*

disaster /dɪˈzɑːstə/ *noun*
1 a very bad accident or event that may hurt many people: *It was the second air disaster (= plane crash) that month.*
2 something that is not at all successful: *The party was a total disaster — everyone went home early.*

disastrous /dɪˈzɑːstrəs/ *adjective*
causing a lot of problems for many people: *The country suffered a disastrous earthquake in July.*

disbelief /ˌdɪsbɪˈliːf/ *uncountable noun*
when you do not believe that something

is true or real: *She looked at him in disbelief.*

disc /dɪsk/ *noun*
a flat, circular object: *The food processor has three slicing discs.* □ *The earrings are made of silver discs.*

discard /dɪsˈkɑːd/ *verb* (**discards, discarding, discarded**)
to get rid of something: *Do not discard your receipt.*

discipline /ˈdɪsɪplɪn/ *uncountable noun*
1 the practice of making people obey rules: *Children need discipline in order to feel secure and safe.*
2 the quality of being able to obey particular rules and standards: *He was impressed by the team's speed and discipline.*

disc jockey /ˈdɪsk ˌdʒɒki/ *noun*
someone whose job is to play music and talk on the radio

disclose /dɪsˈkləʊz/ *verb* (**discloses, disclosing, disclosed**)
to tell people about something: *They refused to disclose details of the deal.*

disco /ˈdɪskəʊ/ *noun*
a place or an event where people dance to pop music: *Fridays and Saturdays are regular disco nights.*

discomfort /dɪsˈkʌmfət/ *uncountable noun*
an unpleasant feeling in part of your body: *Steve had some discomfort, but no real pain.*

disconnect /ˌdɪskəˈnekt/ *verb* (**disconnects, disconnecting, disconnected**)
to stop electricity, gas or water from going into a piece of equipment or a building: *If you don't pay your phone bill, the phone company will disconnect your phone.*

discount /ˈdɪskaʊnt/ *noun*
a reduction in the usual price of something: *All staff get a 20% discount.*

discourage /dɪsˈkʌrɪdʒ/ *verb* (**discourages, discouraging, discouraged**)
to make you feel less keen or confident about something: *Learning a language may be difficult at first. Don't let this discourage you.*

▸ **discouraged** *adjective* *He felt discouraged by his lack of progress.*

discover /dɪsˈkʌvə/ *verb* (**discovers, discovering, discovered**)
1 to become aware of something that you did not know about before: *After a short*

d

conversation, she discovered the reason for his unhappiness.

2 to find something: *The car was discovered on a roadside outside the city.*

3 to be the first person to find or use a new place, substance or method: *Who was the first European to discover America?*

discovery /dɪs'kʌvəri/ *noun* (**discoveries**)
when you become aware of something that you did not know about before: *The man was arrested after the discovery of stolen paintings in a garage in Queensland last week.*
make a discovery to be the first person to find or become aware of something that no one knew about before: *In that year, two important scientific discoveries were made.*

discreet /dɪs'kriːt/ *adjective*
polite and careful in what you do or say: *He was a real gentleman, and he was always very discreet.*

discriminate /dɪs'krɪmɪˌneɪt/ *verb* (**discriminates, discriminating, discriminated**)
to treat a person or a group of people unfairly: *They believe the law discriminates against women.*

discrimination /dɪsˌkrɪmɪ'neɪʃən/ *uncountable noun*
the practice of treating one person or group unfairly: *Many companies are breaking age discrimination laws.*

discus /'dɪskəs/ *noun*
the sport of throwing a heavy round object: *He won the discus at the Montreal Olympics.*

discuss /dɪs'kʌs/ *verb* (**discusses, discussing, discussed**)
to talk about something: *We are meeting next week to discuss plans for the future.*

LANGUAGE HELP
You **cannot** say *discuss about* something. Instead, you can say that you **discuss** something **with** someone. *I discussed the problem with my parents.*

discussion /dɪs'kʌʃən/ *noun*
a conversation about a subject: *Managers are having informal discussions later today.*

disease /dɪ'ziːz/ *noun*
an illness that affects people, animals or plants: *There are no drugs available to treat this disease.* □ *heart disease*

disgrace /dɪs'ɡreɪs/ *noun*
something that is very bad or wrong: *His behaviour was a disgrace.*

disgraceful /dɪs'ɡreɪsfʊl/ *adjective*
very bad or wrong: *The way they treated him was disgraceful.*
▶ **disgracefully** *adverb* *His brother behaved disgracefully.*

disguise [1] /dɪs'ɡaɪz/ *noun*
in disguise to have changed the way you look so that people will not recognize you: *He travelled in disguise, dressed as an old man.*

disguise [2] /dɪs'ɡaɪz/ *verb* (**disguises, disguising, disguised**)
to hide something or make it appear different so that people will not recognize it: *I tried to disguise the fact that I was ill.*
▶ **disguised** *adjective* *The robber was disguised as a medical worker.*

disgust /dɪs'ɡʌst/ *uncountable noun*
a very strong feeling of not liking or not approving of something: *At first I felt sorry for Mr Hart, but now I feel disgust for him.*

disgusted /dɪs'ɡʌstɪd/ *adjective*
feeling strongly that you do not like or do not approve of something: *I'm disgusted by the way that he was treated by his employers.*

disgusting /dɪs'ɡʌstɪŋ/ *adjective*
extremely unpleasant or unacceptable: *The food tasted disgusting.*

dish /dɪʃ/ *noun* (**dishes**)
1 a shallow container for cooking or serving food: *Pour the mixture into a square glass dish.*
2 food that is prepared in a particular way: *There were plenty of delicious dishes to choose from at the party.*

dishonest /dɪs'ɒnɪst/ *adjective*
not honest and unable to be trusted: *I admit that I was dishonest with him.*
▶ **dishonesty** *uncountable noun*
dishonest behaviour: *She accused the government of dishonesty.*

dishwasher /'dɪʃwɒʃə/ *noun*
a machine that washes and dries dishes → Look at picture on P4

disinfect /ˌdɪsɪn'fekt/ *verb* (**disinfects, disinfecting, disinfected**)
to clean something using a substance that kills bacteria: *Chlorine is used for disinfecting water.*

disinfectant /ˌdɪsɪnˈfektənt/ *noun*
a substance that kills bacteria: *They washed their hands with disinfectant.*

disk /dɪsk/ also **disc** *noun*
the part of a computer where information is stored: *The program uses 2.5 megabytes of disk space.*

'disk drive *noun*
the part of a computer that holds a disk

dislike /dɪsˈlaɪk/ *verb* (**dislikes, disliking, disliked**)
to not like someone or something: *Many children dislike the taste of green vegetables.*
• **dislike** *noun Make a list of your likes and dislikes about your job.*

dismay /dɪsˈmeɪ/ *uncountable noun*
a strong feeling of fear, worry or sadness (*formal*): *Local people reacted with dismay.*
▸ **dismayed** *adjective Glen was shocked and dismayed at her reaction.*

dismiss /dɪsˈmɪs/ *verb* (**dismisses, dismissing, dismissed**)
1 to say that something is not important enough for you to consider: *Perry dismissed the suggestion as nonsense.*
2 to tell someone junior to you that they can leave: *The teacher dismissed us early, and I hurried to my locker.*

disobey /ˌdɪsəˈbeɪ/ *verb* (**disobeys, disobeying, disobeyed**)
to not do what you have been told to do: *He often disobeyed his mother and father.*

disorganized /dɪsˈɔːɡəˌnaɪzd/ *adjective*
1 badly arranged, planned or managed: *He walked into the large, disorganized office.*
2 very bad at organizing things in your life: *My boss is completely disorganized.*

dispenser /dɪsˈpensə/ *noun*
a machine or a container from which you can get something: *a soap dispenser*

display[1] /dɪsˈpleɪ/ *verb* (**displays, displaying, displayed**)
to put something in a place where people can see it: *Old soldiers proudly displayed their medals.*

display[2] /dɪsˈpleɪ/ *noun*
an arrangement of things that have been put in a particular place, so that people can see them easily: *In the second gallery, there was a display of World War II aircraft.*
on display in a public place for people to see: *The artist's work is on display in New York next month.*

disposable /dɪsˈpəʊzəbəl/ *adjective*
designed to be thrown away after use: *disposable nappies □ a disposable razor*

disposal /dɪsˈpəʊzəl/ *uncountable noun*
when you get rid of something that you no longer want or need: *waste disposal*

dispose /dɪsˈpəʊz/ *verb* (**disposes, disposing, disposed**)
dispose of something to get rid of something: *How do they dispose of nuclear waste?*

dispute /dɪsˈpjuːt/ *noun*
when two people or groups cannot agree about something: *The government had to do something to end the dispute.*

disqualify /dɪsˈkwɒlɪfaɪ/ *verb* (**disqualifies, disqualifying, disqualified**)
to stop someone from taking part in a competition: *Thomson was disqualified from the race.*

disrupt /dɪsˈrʌpt/ *verb* (**disrupts, disrupting, disrupted**)
to cause difficulties that prevent an event from continuing: *A fire broke out last night, disrupting preparations for tonight's pop concert.*
▸ **disruption** *uncountable noun The bad weather caused disruption at many airports.*

disruptive /dɪsˈrʌptɪv/ *adjective*
preventing something from continuing in a normal way: *We have a lot of difficult, disruptive children.*

dissatisfied /dɪsˈsætɪsˌfaɪd/ *adjective*
not happy about something: *Thousands of dissatisfied customers called the company to complain.*

dissect /daɪˈsekt, dɪ-/ *verb* (**dissects, dissecting, dissected**)
to cut open a dead body in order to examine it: *We dissected a frog in our biology class.*
▸ **dissection** /daɪˈsekʃən, dɪ-/ *uncountable noun The dissection of the tiny insect took place under a microscope.*

dissolve

dissolve /dɪˈzɒlv/ *verb* (**dissolves, dissolving, dissolved**)
to become completely mixed with a liquid: *Heat the mixture gently until the sugar dissolves.*

distance /'dɪstəns/ *noun*
the amount of space between two places: *Measure the distance between the wall and the table.*

from a distance from a long way away: *From a distance, the lake looked beautiful.*

in the distance a long way away from you: *We had a beautiful view of the countryside with the mountains in the distance.*

distant /'dɪstənt/ *adjective*
1 very far away: *The mountains were on the distant horizon.*
2 not closely related to you: *I received a letter from a distant cousin.*

distinct /dɪ'stɪŋkt/ *adjective*
with an individual sound, appearance or taste: *Each vegetable has its own distinct flavour.*

distinct from something quite different from another thing: *Quebec is quite distinct from the rest of Canada.*

distinction /dɪ'stɪŋkʃən/ *noun*
draw/make a distinction to say clearly that two things are different: *He makes a distinction between art and culture.*

distinguish /dɪ'stɪŋgwɪʃ/ *verb* (distinguishes, distinguishing, distinguished)
to be able to see or understand how two things are different: *When do babies learn to distinguish between men and women?*

distinguished /dɪ'stɪŋgwɪʃt/ *adjective*
very successful and with a good reputation: *He came from a distinguished academic family.*

distract /dɪ'strækt/ *verb* (distracts, distracting, distracted)
to take your attention away from what you are doing: *I'm easily distracted by noise.*

distraction /dɪ'strækʃən/ *noun*
something that turns your attention away from something else that you want to concentrate on: *Mobile phones in cars are a dangerous distraction for drivers.*

distress /dɪ'stres/ *uncountable noun*
a strong feeling of sadness or pain: *The condition can cause great distress in young people.*
▶ **distressing** *adjective* It is very distressing when your baby is ill.

distribute /dɪ'strɪbju:t/ *verb* (distributes, distributing, distributed)
to give things to a number of people: *They distributed free tickets to young people.*
▶ **distribution** /,dɪstrɪ'bju:ʃən/ *uncountable noun* They are trying to stop the illegal distribution of music over the Internet.

district /'dɪstrɪkt/ *noun*
a particular area of a city or a country: *I drove around the business district.*

disturb /dɪ'stɜ:b/ *verb* (disturbs, disturbing, disturbed)
1 to interrupt someone or something by talking to them or making a noise: *Sorry, am I disturbing you?* □ *Only the occasional passing car disturbed the silence.*
2 to make someone feel upset or worried: *He was disturbed by the news of the attack.*

disturbance /dɪ'stɜ:bəns/ *noun*
an event in which people behave violently in public: *During the disturbance, three men were hurt.*

disturbing /dɪ'stɜ:bɪŋ/ *adjective*
making you feel worried or upset: *We've received some disturbing news.*

disused /,dɪs'ju:zd/ *adjective*
empty and no longer used: *a disused petrol station*

ditch /dɪtʃ/ *noun* (ditches)
a deep, long, narrow hole that carries water away from a road or a field: *Both vehicles landed in a ditch.*

dive /daɪv/ *verb* (dives, diving, dived, dived)
1 to jump into water with your arms and your head going in first: *Ben dived into the water.* ● **dive** *noun* Pam walked out and did another perfect dive.

dive

deep-sea diver

Ben dived into the water.

▸ **diving** *uncountable noun* *Shaun won medals in diving and swimming.*
2 to go under the surface of the sea or a lake, using special equipment for breathing: *We were diving to look at fish.*
• **dive** *noun* *He is already planning the next dive.*
▸ **diver** *noun* *a deep-sea diver*
▸ **diving** *uncountable noun* *equipment for diving*

diverse /daɪˈvɜːs/ *adjective*
made up of many different people or things: *We have a very diverse group of students this year.*

diversion /daɪˈvɜːʃən/ *noun*
an activity that takes your attention away from what you are doing: *The trip was a welcome diversion from their troubles at home.*

divert /daɪˈvɜːt/ *verb* (**diverts, diverting, diverted**)
to make vehicles or people use a different route: *The plane was diverted to Edinburgh Airport.*

divide /dɪˈvaɪd/ *verb* (**divides, dividing, divided**)
1 to separate into smaller parts: *Divide the pastry in half.* □ *The class was divided into two groups of six.* □ *Half a mile upstream, the river divides.*
2 to find out how many times one number can fit into another bigger number: *Measure the floor area and divide it by six.*
3 to separate two areas: *A 1969-mile border divides Mexico from the United States.*
4 to cause disagreement between people: *Several major issues divided the country.*
divide something up to separate something into smaller groups: *They divided the country up into four areas.*

'diving board *noun*
a board at the edge of a swimming pool from which people can jump into the water

division /dɪˈvɪʒən/ *noun*
1 *uncountable* when someone or something separates something into parts: *the division of land after the war*
2 *uncountable* the process of dividing one number by another smaller number: *I taught my daughter how to do division.*
3 a group of departments in a large organization: *She manages the bank's Latin American division.*

divorce /dɪˈvɔːs/ *noun*
the legal ending of a marriage: *Many marriages end in divorce.* • **divorce** *verb* (**divorces, divorcing, divorced**) *Jack and Lillian got divorced in 2006.* □ *He divorced me and married my friend.*

divorced /dɪˈvɔːst/ *adjective*
no longer legally married to your former husband or wife: *He is divorced, with a young son.*

DIY /ˌdiː aɪ ˈwaɪ/ *uncountable noun*
the activity of making or repairing things yourself, especially in your home. **DIY** is short for 'do-it-yourself': *a DIY project*

dizzy /ˈdɪzi/ *adjective* (**dizzier, dizziest**)
having the feeling that you are losing your balance and that you are about to fall: *Her head hurt, and she felt slightly dizzy.*
▸ **dizziness** *uncountable noun* *His head injury caused dizziness.*

DJ /ˌdiː ˈdʒeɪ/ also **D.J., dj** *noun*
→ see **disc jockey**

do¹ /də, STRONG duː/ *auxiliary verb* (**does, doing, did, done**)

> **LANGUAGE HELP**
> When you are speaking, you can use the negative short forms **don't** for **do not** and **didn't** for **did not**.

1 used with 'not' to form the negative of main verbs: *They don't work very hard.* □ *I did not know Jamie had a car.*
2 used with another verb to form questions: *Do you like music?* □ *What did he say?*
3 used instead of repeating a verb when you are answering a question: *'Do you think he is telling the truth?' — 'Yes, I do.'*

do² /də, STRONG duː/ *verb* (**does, doing, did, done**)
1 to take some action or perform an activity or task: *I was trying to do some work.* □ *After lunch Elizabeth and I did the dishes.*
2 used when you are asking someone what their job is: *'What does your father do?' — 'He's a doctor.'*
3 to be good enough: *It doesn't matter what you wear — anything warm will do.*
could do with someone/something to want or need something: *I could do with a rest.*
do something up to fasten something: *Mari did up the buttons on her jacket.*
do without something to be able to continue, although you do not have

d

something: *We can do without their help. We'll manage.*

have/be to do with someone/ something to be connected with someone or something: *Clarke insists all this has nothing to do with him.*

dock /dɒk/ *noun*
an area of water beside land where ships go so that people can get on or off them
● **dock** *verb* (**docks, docking, docked**) *The ferry docked and the passengers disembarked onto the island.*

doctor /'dɒktə/ *noun*
1 a person whose job is to treat people who are ill or injured: *Be sure to speak to your doctor before planning your trip.*
→ Look at picture on P7
2 (*also* **doctor's**) the place where a doctor works: *I went to the doctor today.*
3 someone who has been awarded the highest academic degree by a university: *He is a doctor of philosophy.*

document /'dɒkjəmənt/ *noun*
1 an official piece of paper with important information on it: *Always read legal documents carefully before you sign them.*
2 a piece of text that is stored on a computer: *Remember to save your document before you send it.*

documentary /ˌdɒkjə'mentri/ *noun* (**documentaries**)
a television programme or a film that provides information about a particular subject: *Did you see that documentary on TV last night?*

dodge /dɒdʒ/ *verb* (**dodges, dodging, dodged**)
1 to move suddenly, especially to avoid something: *I dodged back behind the tree and waited.*
2 to avoid something by moving: *He dodged a speeding car.*

does /dəz, STRONG dʌz/ → see **do**

doesn't /'dʌzənt/
short for 'does not'

dog /dɒg/ *noun*
an animal that is sometimes kept by people as a pet, or used to guard buildings: *He was walking his dog.*

doll /dɒl/ *noun*
a child's toy that looks like a small person or a baby

dollar /'dɒlə/ *noun*
the unit of money ($) that is used in the U.S., Canada, and some other countries. There are 100 cents in a dollar: *She earns seven dollars an hour.*

dolphin /'dɒlfɪn/
noun
a large, grey or black-and-white intelligent animal that lives in the sea

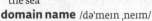
dolphin

domain name /də'meɪn ˌneɪm/
noun
the main part of a website address that tells you who the website belongs to: *I've just bought the domain name 'adamwilson.com'.*

dome /dəʊm/ *noun*
a round roof: *Kiev is known as 'the city of golden domes'.*

domestic /də'mestɪk/ *adjective*
1 happening or existing within one particular country: *The airline offers over 100 domestic flights a day.*
2 relating to the home and family: *In our family we all share the domestic chores.*

dominate /'dɒmɪˌneɪt/ *verb* (**dominates, dominating, dominated**)
to have power over another country or person: *Women are no longer dominated by men.*

dominoes /'dɒmɪnəʊz/ *uncountable noun*
a game that uses small rectangular blocks, called dominoes, that are marked with spots

donate /dəʊ'neɪt/ *verb* (**donates, donating, donated**)
1 to give something to an organization: *He often donates large amounts of money to charity.*
▶ **donation** /dəʊ'neɪʃən/ *noun Employees make regular donations to charity.*
2 to allow doctors to use some of your blood or a part of your body to help someone who is ill: *If you are able to donate blood, you should do it.*

done /dʌn/ → see **do**

donkey /'dɒŋki/ *noun*
an animal like a small horse with long ears

donor /'dəʊnə/ *noun*
a person who gives a part of their body or some of their blood so that doctors can use them to help someone who is ill: *a blood donor*

don't /dəʊnt/ short for 'do not'

door /dɔː/ *noun*

door

1 a piece of wood, glass or metal that fills an entrance: *I knocked at the front door, but there was no answer.*
2 the space in a wall when a door is open: *She looked through the door of the kitchen.*

answer the door to open a door because someone has knocked on it or rung the bell: *Carol answered the door as soon as I knocked.*

go door to door to go along a street stopping at each house, for example to sell something or to collect money for charity: *They are going from door to door collecting money.*

next door in the next room or building: *Who lives next door?*

doorbell /'dɔːbel/ *noun*
a bell next to a door that you can ring to tell the people inside that you are there

doorknob /'dɔːnɒb/ *noun*
a round handle on a door that you use to open and close it

doorstep /'dɔːstep/ *noun*
a step in front of a door outside a building: *I went and sat on the doorstep.*

doorway /'dɔːweɪ/ *noun*
a space in a wall where a door opens and closes: *David was standing in the doorway.*

dorm /dɔːm/ *noun* (informal)
→ see **dormitory**

dormitory /'dɔːmɪtri/ *noun* (**dormitories**)
a large bedroom where several people sleep

dose /dəʊs/ *noun*
the particular amount of a medicine or a drug that you take at one time: *You can treat the infection with one big dose of antibiotics.* □ *Do not exceed the stated dose.*

dot /dɒt/ *noun*
a very small round mark, like the one on the letter 'i' or in the names of websites: *He makes paintings with little tiny dots of colour.*

dot com /ˌdɒt 'kɒm/
used when you are saying someone's email or website address. For the address 'katiegreen@harpercollins.com', you say 'Katie Green at harpercollins dot com'.

dotted /'dɒtɪd/ *adjective*
made up of a row of dots: *Cut along the dotted line.*

double¹ /'dʌbəl/ *adjective*
1 with two parts: *This room has double doors opening on to a balcony.*
2 twice the normal size: *I gave him a double portion of ice cream.*
3 intended for two people: *The hotel charges £180 for a double room.* □ *One of the bedrooms has a double bed.*

double² /'dʌbəl/ *verb* (**doubles, doubling, doubled**)
to become twice as big: *The number of students has doubled from 50 to 100.*

double bass /ˌdʌbəl 'beɪs/ *noun* (**double basses**)
a very big wooden musical instrument with four strings
→ Look at picture on P11

double-'click *verb* (**double-clicks, double-clicking, double-clicked**)
to press one of the buttons on a computer mouse (= the part that you move around with your hand) twice quickly in order to make something happen: *Double-click on a file to start the application.*

doubt¹ /daʊt/ *noun*
the feeling of not being certain about something: *Rendell had doubts about the plan.* □ *There is no doubt that the Earth's climate is changing.*

in doubt not certain: *If you are in doubt about anything, please get in touch with us.*

no doubt used for showing that you feel certain about something: *She will no doubt be here soon.*

doubt² /daʊt/ *verb* (**doubts, doubting, doubted**)
1 to think that something is probably not true or will probably not happen: *I doubt if I'll learn anything new from this lesson.* □ *I doubt he will come to the party.*

d

d

2 to think that someone may be saying something that is not true: *No one doubted him.*

doubtful /'daʊtfʊl/ *adjective*
1 not likely: *It is doubtful that he will marry again.*
2 not certain: *Sophie sounded doubtful about the idea.*

dough /dəʊ/ *uncountable noun*
a mixture of flour, water and other things that can be cooked to make bread and cakes: *Leave the dough in a cool place overnight.*

doughnut /'dəʊnʌt/ *noun*
a sweet round cake with a hole in the middle

dove /dʌv/ *noun*
a bird that is used as a symbol of peace

down¹ /daʊn/ *preposition*
1 toward a lower level or in a lower place: *A man came down the stairs to meet them.* □ *He was halfway down the hill.* □ *She went down to the kitchen.*
2 along a road or a river: *They walked quickly down the street.*

down² /daʊn/ *adverb*
onto a surface: *Danny put down his glass.*

down³ /daʊn/ *adjective*
1 unhappy or depressed (*informal*): *You sound really down. What's wrong?*
2 not working: *The computer's down again.*

downhill /ˌdaʊn'hɪl/ *adjective, adverb*
down, towards the bottom of a slope: *downhill ski runs* □ *He walked downhill toward the river.*

download /ˌdaʊn'ləʊd/ *verb* (**downloads, downloading, downloaded**)
to copy a file, a program or other information from a bigger computer, a network or the Internet to your own computer: *You can download the software from the Internet.* ● **download** *noun* *The file is available as a free download.*

downloadable /daʊn'ləʊdəbl/ *adjective*
able to be copied onto your computer: *More information is available in the downloadable files below.*

downpour /'daʊnpɔː/ *noun*
a sudden heavy fall of rain: *The heavy downpours caused problems for motorists last night.*

downstairs /ˌdaʊn'steəz/ *adjective, adverb*
1 to a lower floor of a building: *Denise went downstairs and made some tea.*

2 on a lower floor of a building: *She painted the downstairs rooms.* □ *She went downstairs to the kitchen.*

downtown /ˌdaʊn'taʊn/ (*American*) *adjective, adverb*
belonging to the part of a city where the large shops and businesses are: *He works in an office in downtown Chicago.* □ *He worked downtown for an insurance firm.*

downward /'daʊnwəd/ *adjective*
moving or looking down: *John waved his hand in a downward motion.*

downwards /'daʊnwədz/ *adverb*
towards the ground or a lower level: *Ben pointed downwards with his stick.*

doze /dəʊz/ *verb* (**dozes, dozing, dozed**)
to sleep lightly or for a short period: *She dozed for a while in the cabin.*
doze off to fall into a light sleep: *I closed my eyes and dozed off.*

dozen /'dʌzən/

> **LANGUAGE HELP**
> The plural form is **dozen** after a number.

twelve: *Will you buy me a loaf of bread and a dozen eggs please?*
dozens of a lot of: *The storm destroyed dozens of buildings.*

Dr short for **Doctor**

drab /dræb/ *adjective* (**drabber, drabbest**)
dull and boring: *He was living in a small, drab apartment in Tokyo.*

draft /drɑːft/ *noun*
a piece of writing that you have not finished working on: *I emailed a first draft of the article to him.*

drag /dræg/ *verb* (**drags, dragging, dragged**)
1 to pull something along the ground: *He dragged his chair toward the table.*
2 to use a computer mouse (= the part that you move around with your hand) to move an image on the screen: *Simply drag and drop the file into the desired folder.*
3 to seem to last a long time: *The minutes dragged past while I waited for him to arrive.*

drag and 'drop *verb* (**drags and drops, dragging and dropping, dragged and dropped**) also **drag-and-drop**
to move computer files or images from one place to another on a computer screen: *Drag and drop the folder to the hard drive.*

dragon /'drægən/ *noun*
in stories, an animal with rough skin that has wings and breathes out fire

dragonfly /'drægən,flaɪ/ *noun* (**dragonflies**)
an insect that flies near water, with a long thin body and four wings

drain¹ /dreɪn/ *verb* (**drains, draining, drained**)
1 to remove a liquid by making it flow somewhere else: *They built the tunnel to drain water out of the mines.*
2 to remove the liquid surrounding food: *Drain the pasta well.* □ *Drain the potatoes and add them to the pan.*

drain² /dreɪn/ *noun*
an opening that carries a liquid away from a place: *A piece of soap was clogging the drain.*

drainage /'dreɪnɪdʒ/ *uncountable noun*
the system by which water or other liquids are removed from a place

drama /'drɑːmə/ *noun*
1 a serious play or film: *The film is a drama about a woman searching for her children.* □ *a radio/television drama*
2 a real situation that is exciting: *This novel is full of drama.*
3 *uncountable* the study of plays and acting: *drama classes*

dramatic /drə'mætɪk/ *adjective*
happening suddenly: *There's been a dramatic change in the way we shop.* □ *The world is experiencing a dramatic increase in population.*
▶ **dramatically** /drə'mætɪkli/ *adverb*
The climate has changed dramatically. □ *The cost of living has increased dramatically.*

dramatist /'dræmətɪst/ *noun*
a person who writes plays: *a famous English dramatist*

drank /dræŋk/ → see **drink**

drape /dreɪp/ *verb* (**drapes, draping, draped**)
to put a piece of cloth somewhere so that it hangs down: *He draped the damp towel over a chair.*

drastic /'dræstɪk/ *adjective*
having a very big effect: *Drastic measures are needed to improve the situation.*

draught /drɑːft/ *noun*
a stream of cold air that comes into a

room: *Block draughts around doors and windows.*

draw¹ /drɔː/ *verb* (**draws, drawing, drew, drawn**)
1 to use a pencil or a pen to make a picture: *She was drawing with a pencil.* □ *I've drawn a picture of you.*
▶ **drawing** *uncountable noun* *I like dancing, singing, and drawing.*
2 to move somewhere: *The taxi was drawing away.* □ *The train was drawing into the station.*
3 to move someone or something somewhere: *He drew his chair nearer the fire.* □ *He drew Caroline close to him.* □ *He drew an envelope from his pocket.*
4 to finish a game with the same number of points as the other player or team: *We drew 2-2 last weekend.*
5 to take money out of a bank account, so that you can use it: *A few months ago he drew out nearly all his savings.*

draw something up to write or type a list or a plan: *They drew up a formal agreement.*

draw the curtains to pull the curtains across a window: *He went to the window and drew the curtains.*

draw² /drɔː/ *noun*
the result of a game when both players or teams score the same number of points: *The match ended in a draw.*

drawback /'drɔːbæk/ *noun*
a part of something that makes it less useful than you would like: *The flat's only drawback was that it was too small.* □ *The only drawback of the plan is how long it will take.*

drawer /'drɔːə/ *noun*
the part of a desk, for example, that you can pull out and put things in: *She opened her desk drawer and took out the book.* □ *I found this old letter in his drawer.*

drawing /'drɔːɪŋ/ *noun*
a picture made with a pencil or a pen: *She did a drawing of me.* □ *There were a few children's drawings on the wall.*

drawn /drɔːn/ → see **draw**

dread /dred/ *verb* (**dreads, dreading, dreaded**)
to feel very anxious about something because you think that it will be

unpleasant or upsetting: *I've been dreading this moment for a long time.*

dreadful /ˈdredfʊl/ *adjective*
very unpleasant or very poor in quality: *They told us the dreadful news.* □ *I didn't enjoy the film; the acting was dreadful.*

dream¹ /driːm/ *noun*
1 a series of events that you see in your mind while you are asleep: *He had a dream about Claire.*
2 something that you often think about because you would like it to happen: *After all these years, my dream has finally come true.*

dream² /driːm/ *verb* (**dreams, dreaming, dreamed** or **dreamt**)
1 to see events in your mind while you are asleep: *Richard dreamed that he was on a bus.* □ *She dreamed about her baby.*
2 to often think about something that you would like to do or to be: *She dreamed of becoming an actress.*

dress¹ /dres/ *noun* (**dresses**)
1 a piece of clothing that covers the body and part of the legs of a woman or a girl: *She was wearing a short black dress.*
2 *uncountable* a particular type of clothing: *He wore formal evening dress to the dinner.*

dress² /dres/ *verb* (**dresses, dressing, dressed**)
1 (*also* **get dressed**) to put clothes on yourself: *Sarah got dressed quickly.*
2 to put clothes on another person: *I washed and dressed the children.*

dress up
1 to put on formal clothes: *You do not need to dress up for dinner.*
2 to put on clothes that make you look like someone else, for fun: *He dressed up like a cowboy for the fancy dress party.*

dressed /drest/ *adjective*
wearing clothes: *He threw her into a swimming pool, fully dressed.* □ *Are you dressed yet?*

dresser /ˈdresə/ *noun*
a piece of furniture with cupboards or drawers in the lower part and shelves in the upper part, used for storing plates and dishes

dressing gown /ˈdresɪŋ ˌɡaʊn/ *noun*
a long, loose garment that you wear over your night clothes when you are not in bed

drew /druː/ → see **draw**

dribble /ˈdrɪbəl/ *verb* (**dribbles, dribbling, dribbled**)
1 to flow in a thin stream: *Blood dribbled down Harry's face.*
2 in a game or sport, to keep the ball moving by using your hand or foot: *Owen dribbled the ball toward Ferris.*

dried /draɪd/ *adjective*
with all the water removed: *dried herbs*

drift /drɪft/ *verb* (**drifts, drifting, drifted**)
to be carried by the wind or by water: *We drifted up the river.*
drift off to gradually fall asleep: *He finally drifted off to sleep.*

drill /drɪl/ *noun*
a tool for making holes: *an electric drill*
● **drill** *verb* (**drills, drilling, drilled**) *You'll need to drill a hole in the wall.*

drink¹ /drɪŋk/ *verb* (**drinks, drinking, drank, drunk**)
1 to take liquid into your mouth and swallow it: *He drank his cup of coffee.*
2 to drink alcohol: *He drinks too much.*
▶ **drinker** *noun* *I'm not a heavy drinker.*

drink² /drɪŋk/ *noun*
an amount of a liquid that you drink: *I'll get you a drink of water.*
→ Look at pictures on P2–3

drip /drɪp/ *verb* (**drips, dripping, dripped**)
1 to fall in small drops: *The rain dripped down my face.*
2 to produce small drops of liquid: *The kitchen tap was dripping.*

drive¹ /draɪv/ *verb* (**drives, driving, drove, driven**)
1 to control the movement and direction of a car or another vehicle: *I drove into town.* □ *She has never learned to drive.* □ *We drove the car to Bristol.*
▶ **driving** *uncountable noun* *a driving instructor*
2 to take someone somewhere in a car: *She drove him to the station.*

drive² /draɪv/ *noun*
1 a trip in a car: *Let's go for a drive in the country on Sunday.*
2 the part of a computer that reads and stores information: *Save your work on drive C.*

driven /ˈdrɪvən/ → see **drive**

driver /'draɪvə/ *noun*
a person who drives a bus, a car or a train, for example: *The driver got out of his truck.* □ *a taxi driver*

driveway /'draɪvweɪ/ *noun*
a small road that leads from the street to the front of a building: *There is a driveway and a garage at the front of the house.*

'driving licence *noun*
a document that shows that you have passed a driving test and that you are allowed to drive

droop /druːp/ *verb* (**droops, drooping, drooped**)
to hang or lean downward: *His eyelids drooped and he yawned.*

drop¹ /drɒp/ *verb* (**drops, dropping, dropped**)
1 to quickly become less in level or amount: *Temperatures can drop to freezing at night.* ● **drop** *noun There was a sudden drop in the number of visitors to the site.*
2 to let something fall: *I dropped my glasses and broke them.*
3 (*also* **drop someone off**) to take someone somewhere in a car and leave them there: *He dropped me outside the hotel.* □ *Dad dropped me off at school on his way to work.*

drop by to visit someone informally: *She will drop by later.*

drop in to visit someone informally: *Why not drop in for a chat?*

drop off to go to sleep (*informal*): *Jimmy dropped off and started to snore.* □ *I lay on the bed and dropped off to sleep.*

drop out to stop attending school, or taking part in a race, before you have completed your studies or the race: *He dropped out of high school at the age of 16.*

drop someone off same meaning as **drop 3**

drop² /drɒp/ *noun*
a very small amount of liquid that is shaped like a little ball: *a drop of water*

'drop-down ˌmenu *noun*
a list of choices on a computer screen that appears when you click on an arrow or a piece of text: *If you click on the search box, a drop-down menu appears.*

drought /draʊt/ *noun*
a long period of time with no rain: *The drought has killed all their crops.*

drove /drəʊv/ → see **drive**

drown /draʊn/ *verb* (**drowns, drowning, drowned**)
to die under water because you cannot breathe: *A child can drown in only a few inches of water.*

drowsy /'draʊzi/ *adjective* (**drowsier, drowsiest**)
tired and unable to think clearly: *He felt pleasantly drowsy.*

drug /drʌg/ *noun*
1 a chemical that is used as a medicine: *The new drug is too expensive for most countries.*
2 a type of illegal substance that some people take because they enjoy its effects: *She was sure Leo was taking drugs.*

'drug ˌaddict *noun*
someone who cannot stop using illegal drugs

drum /drʌm/ *noun*
a simple musical instrument that you hit with sticks or with your hands
▶ **drummer** *noun He was a drummer in a band.*

drunk¹ /drʌŋk/ → see **drink**

drunk² /drʌŋk/ *adjective*
having drunk too much alcohol: *He got drunk and fell down the stairs.*

dry¹ /draɪ/ *adjective* (**drier, driest**)
1 having no water or any other liquid in it or on it: *Clean the metal with a soft dry cloth.*
2 without any rain: *The Sahara is one of the driest places in Africa.*

dry² /draɪ/ *verb* (**dries, drying, dried**)
1 to become dry: *Let your hair dry naturally if possible.*
2 to remove the water from something: *Mrs Mason picked up a towel and began drying dishes.*

dry up to become completely dry: *The river dried up.*

dry-'clean *verb* (**dry-cleans, dry-cleaning, dry-cleaned**)
to clean clothes with a special chemical rather than with water: *The suit must be dry-cleaned.*

dry 'cleaner (*also* **dry cleaner's**)
a shop where things can be dry-cleaned

dryer /'draɪə/ *also* **drier** *noun*
a machine for drying things: *Put the clothes in the dryer for a few minutes.*

duck /dʌk/ *noun*
a bird that lives near water: *A few ducks were swimming around in the shallow water.*

duck

due /djuː/ *adjective*
1 expected to happen or arrive at a particular time: *The results are due at the end of the month.* □ *Her second baby is due in six weeks.*
2 needing to be paid: *When is the next payment due?*
due to something as a result of something; because of something: *She couldn't do the job, due to pain in her hands.*

duet /djuːˈet/ *noun*
a piece of music performed by two people: *She sang a duet with Maurice Gibb.*

dug /dʌg/ → see **dig**

duke /djuːk/ *noun*
a man with a very high social rank in some countries: *the Duke of Edinburgh*

dull /dʌl/ *adjective* (**duller, dullest**)
1 not interesting or exciting: *I thought he was boring and dull.*
2 not bright in colour: *the dull grey sky of London*

dumb /dʌm/ *adjective* (**dumber, dumbest**)
1 completely unable to speak: *He was born deaf and dumb.*
2 (*American, informal*) stupid: *He's so clever that he makes me feel really dumb.*
3 (*American, informal*) silly and annoying: *He had this dumb idea.*

dummy /ˈdʌmi/ *noun*
1 a model of a person, often used in safety tests: *a crash-test dummy*
2 an object that you put in a baby's mouth to stop it from crying

dump¹ /dʌmp/ *verb* (**dumps, dumping, dumped**)
1 to leave something somewhere quickly and carelessly (*informal*): *We dumped our bags at the hotel and went to the market.*
2 to put or leave something somewhere because you no longer want it (*informal*): *The robbers' car was dumped near the motorway.*
3 to end a relationship with a boyfriend or girlfriend (*informal*): *My boyfriend dumped me last night.*

dump² /dʌmp/ *noun*
1 a place where you can take things that you no longer want: *I've got to take the garden waste to the dump.*
2 an ugly and unpleasant place (*informal*): *'What a dump!' Amy said, looking at the house.*

dune /djuːn/ *noun*
a hill of sand near the sea or in a desert: *Behind the beach is an area of sand dunes and grass.*

duo /ˈdjuːəʊ/ *noun*
a pair of musicians, singers or other performers: *a famous singing duo*

during /ˈdjʊərɪŋ/ *preposition*
between the beginning and the end of a period of time: *Storms are common during the winter.* □ *I fell asleep during the performance.*

> **LANGUAGE HELP**
> If you want to say how long something lasts, use **for**. *I went to Wales for two weeks.*

dusk /dʌsk/ *uncountable noun*
the time just before night when it is not completely dark: *We arrived home at dusk.*

dust¹ /dʌst/ *uncountable noun*
a fine powder of dry earth or dirt: *I could see a thick layer of dust on the furniture.*

dust² /dʌst/ *verb* (**dusts, dusting, dusted**)
to remove dust from furniture with a cloth: *I dusted and polished the furniture in the living room.* □ *I was dusting in his study.*

dustbin /ˈdʌstbɪn/ *noun*
a large container for rubbish that you keep outside

duster /ˈdʌstə/ *noun*
a cloth that you use for removing dust from furniture

dustman /ˈdʌstmən/ *noun* (**dustmen**)
a person whose job is to take away rubbish from outside people's houses

dusty /ˈdʌsti/ *adjective* (**dustier, dustiest**)
covered with dust: *a dusty room*

duty /ˈdjuːti/ *noun* (**duties**)
1 work that you have to do: *I did my duties without complaining.*
2 something that you feel that you have to do: *I consider it my duty to warn you of the dangers.*

off duty not working: *The two police officers were off duty when the accident happened.*

on duty working: *How many nurses were on duty last night?*

ˌduty-ˈfree *adjective*
sold at airports or on airplanes or ships at a cheaper price than usual because no tax has to be paid: *duty-free perfume*

duvet /'duːveɪ/ *noun*
a thick warm cover for a bed

DVD /ˌdiː viː 'diː/ *noun*
short for 'digital video disk': a disk on which a film or music is recorded

DVD burner /ˌdiː viː 'diː ˌbɜːnə/ or **DVD writer** *noun*
a piece of computer equipment that you use for putting information onto a DVD

DVD player *noun*
a machine for showing films that are stored on a DVD
→ Look at picture on P5

dwarf /dwɔːf/ *noun* (**dwarves, dwarfs**)
1 a person, animal or plant that is much smaller than usual
2 in children's stories, a small man who sometimes has magical powers

dye /daɪ/ *verb* (**dyes, dyeing, dyed**)
to change the colour of something by putting it in a special liquid: *The actor had to dye his hair for the film.* ● **dye** *uncountable noun a bottle of hair dye*

dynamic /daɪ'næmɪk/ *adjective*
full of energy and always having new and exciting ideas: *He was a dynamic and energetic leader.*

d

Ee

each /iːtʃ/ *adjective*
every: *Each book is beautifully illustrated.* □ *The library buys 2,000 new books each year.*
● **each** *pronoun We each have different needs and interests.* ● **each** *adverb Tickets are six dollars each.*

each of every one of: *He gave each of them a book.* □ *Each of these exercises takes one or two minutes to do.*

each other used for showing that each member of a group does something to or for the other members: *We looked at each other in silence.*

We looked at each other in silence.

eager /ˈiːgə/ *adjective*
wanting to do something very much: *The children are all very eager to learn.*
▶ **eagerly** *adverb 'So what do you think will happen?' he asked eagerly.*

eagle /ˈiːgəl/ *noun*
a large bird that eats small animals

ear /ɪə/ *noun*
one of the two parts of your body that you hear sounds with: *He whispered something in her ear.*
→ Look at picture on P1

earache /ˈɪəreɪk/ *uncountable noun*
a pain inside your ear: *I woke up in the morning with terrible earache.*

eardrum /ˈɪədrʌm/ also **ear drum** *noun*
the part inside your ear that reacts when sound waves reach it: *The explosion burst Ollie Williams' eardrum.*

early /ˈɜːli/ *adverb* (**earlier, earliest**)
before the usual time: *I had to get up early this morning.* □ *She arrived early to get a place at the front.* ● **early** *adjective I want to get an early start in the morning.*

earn /ɜːn/ *verb* (**earns, earning, earned**)
1 to receive money for work that you do: *She earns £27,000 a year.*
2 to get something because you deserve it: *A good manager earns the respect of his team.*

earphones /ˈɪəfəʊnz/ *plural noun*
things that you wear in your ears so that you can listen to music or the radio without anyone else hearing

earring /ˈɪərɪŋ/ *noun*
a piece of jewellery that you wear on your ear: *The woman wore large, gold earrings.*

earth /ɜːθ/ *noun*
1 the planet that we live on: *The space shuttle returned safely to Earth today.* □ *The Earth travels round the sun.*
2 the substance in which plants grow: *a huge pile of earth*

on earth used in questions that begin with 'how', 'why', 'what' or 'where', to show that you are very surprised: *How on earth did that happen?*

earthquake /ˈɜːθkweɪk/ *noun*
a sudden strong movement of the Earth's surface: *the San Francisco earthquake of 1906*

ease /iːz/ *uncountable noun*
at ease confident and relaxed: *It is important that you feel at ease with your doctor.*
with ease without difficulty or effort: *Anne passed her exams with ease.*

easel /ˈiːzəl/ *noun*
a stand that supports a picture while an artist is working on it

east¹ /iːst/ also **East** *uncountable noun*
the direction that is in front of you when you look at the sun in the morning: *The city lies to the east of the river.* ● **east** *adjective There is a line of hills along the east coast.*

the East the southern and eastern part of Asia, including India, China and Japan

east² /iːst/ also **East** *adjective, adverb*
1 towards the east: *Go east on Route 9.*
2 coming from the east: *a cold east wind*

Easter /ˈiːstə/ *noun*
a Christian festival in March or April when people celebrate Jesus Christ's return to life

easterly /ˈiːstəli/ *adjective*
1 to the east or towards the east: *We sailed in an easterly direction.*
2 blowing from the east: *It was a beautiful September day, with cool easterly winds.*

eastern /ˈiːstən/ *adjective*
1 in or from the east of a place: *Eastern Europe*
2 used for describing things or ideas that come from the countries of the East, such as India, China or Japan: *Exports to Eastern countries have gone down.*

easy /ˈiːzi/ *adjective* (**easier, easiest**)
not difficult to do: *Losing weight is not easy.* □ *The software is easy to use.*
▶ **easily** *adverb* *Most students found jobs easily at the end of the course.*
take it easy to relax and not worry (*informal*): *Take it easy for a week or two.*

eat /iːt/ *verb* (**eats, eating, ate, eaten**)
to put something into your mouth and swallow it: *What did you eat last night?* □ *I ate slowly and without speaking.*

e-book /ˈiː-bʊk/ *noun*
a digital book that you can read on a screen

echo /ˈekəʊ/ *noun* (**echoes**)
a sound that you hear again because it hits a surface and then comes back: *I heard the echo of someone laughing across the hall.*
● **echo** *verb* (**echoes, echoing, echoed**) *His feet echoed on the stone floor.*

eclipse /ɪˈklɪps/ *noun*
an occasion when the light from the sun or the moon is blocked for a short time because of the position of the sun, the moon and the Earth: *a total solar eclipse*

ˈeco-ˈfriendly *adjective*
less harmful to the environment than other similar products or services: *eco-friendly washing powder*

ecology /ɪˈkɒlədʒi/ *uncountable noun*
the study of the relationships between living things and their environment: *He is professor of ecology at the university.*
▶ **ecologist** *noun* *Ecologists are concerned that these chemicals will pollute lakes.*
▶ **ecological** /ˌiːkəˈlɒdʒɪkəl/ *adjective* *How can we save the Earth from ecological disaster?*

economic /ˌiːkəˈnɒmɪk, ˌek-/ *adjective*
connected with the organization of the money and industry of a country: *The economic situation is very bad.*

economical /ˌiːkəˈnɒmɪkəl, ˌek-/ *adjective*
not needing a lot of money or other things in order to work well: *People are driving smaller and more economical cars.*
▶ **economically** *adverb* *Services need to operate more economically.*

economics /ˌiːkəˈnɒmɪks, ˌek-/ *uncountable noun*
the study of the way in which money and industry are organized in a society: *His sister is studying economics.*

economist /ɪˈkɒnəmɪst/ *noun*
a person who studies economics

economy /ɪˈkɒnəmi/ *noun* (**economies**)
the system for organizing the money and industry of the world, a country or local government: *The Indian economy is changing fast.*

ecosystem /ˈiːkəʊˌsɪstəm/ *noun*
the relationship between all the living things in a particular area together: *These industries are destroying whole ecosystems.*

edge /edʒ/ *noun*
1 the part of something that is farthest from the middle: *We lived in a block of flats on the edge of town.* □ *She was standing at the water's edge.*

edge

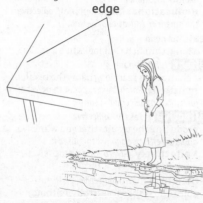

2 the sharp side of a knife: *His hand touched the edge of the sword.*

edible /'edɪbəl/ *adjective*
safe to eat: *The flowers are edible, and they look wonderful in salads.*

edit /'edɪt/ *verb* (**edits, editing, edited**)
to check a text and correct the mistakes in it: *She helped him edit his essay.*

edition /ɪ'dɪʃən/ *noun*
one of a number of books, magazines or newspapers that is printed at one time: *The second edition was published in Canada.*

editor /'edɪtə/ *noun*
a person who checks and corrects texts: *He works as an editor of children's books.*

educate /'edʒʊ,keɪt/ *verb* (**educates, educating, educated**)
1 to teach someone at a school or college: *He was educated at Yale and Stanford.*
2 to teach people better ways of doing something: *We want to educate people about healthy eating.*

> **LANGUAGE HELP**
> If you want to talk about the way parents look after their children and teach them about the world, use the verb **bring up**. *His parents brought him up very strictly.*

educated /'edʒʊ,keɪtɪd/ *adjective*
having a lot of knowledge: *He was an educated and honest man.*

education /,edʒʊ'keɪʃən/ *uncountable noun*
teaching and learning: *My children's education is important to me.* □ *We need better health education.*
▸ **educational** /,edʒʊ'keɪʃənəl/ *adjective* *the American educational system*

eel /iːl/ *noun*
a long, thin fish that looks like a snake

effect /ɪ'fekt/ *noun*
a change or a reaction that is the result of something: *Parents worry about the effect of junk food on their child's health.*

effective /ɪ'fektɪv/ *adjective*
producing the results that you want: *No drugs are effective against this disease.*
▸ **effectively** *adverb* *We need to use water more effectively.*

efficient /ɪ'fɪʃənt/ *adjective*
able to do tasks successfully, without wasting time or energy: *The engine is efficient and powerful.*
▸ **efficiency** /ɪ'fɪʃənsi/ *uncountable noun* *We must think of ways to improve efficiency.*
▸ **efficiently** *adverb* *We want people to use energy more efficiently.*

effort /'efət/ *noun*
when you try very hard to do something: *You should make an effort to speak the local language when you go abroad.*

e.g. /,iː 'dʒiː/
for example: *We need professionals of all types, e.g. teachers.*

egg /eg/ *noun*
1 a round object that contains a baby bird, insect, snake or fish
2 a hen's egg, that people eat as food in many countries: *Break the eggs into a bowl.* □ *Brush the top with egg.*
→ Look at picture on P3

eggplant /'egplɑːnt/ *noun* (American)
→ see **aubergine**

eight /eɪt/
the number 8

eighteen /,eɪ'tiːn/
the number 18
▸ **eighteenth** /,eɪ'tiːnθ/ *adjective, adverb* *I had a big party for my eighteenth birthday.*

eighth¹ /eɪtθ/ *adjective, adverb*
the item in a series that you count as number eight: *Shekhar was the eighth prime minister of India.*

eighth² /eɪtθ/ *noun*
one of eight equal parts of something ($\frac{1}{8}$): *We walked for an eighth of a mile.*

eighty /'eɪti/
the number 80
▸ **eightieth** /'eɪtiəθ/ *adjective, adverb* *Mr Stevens recently celebrated his eightieth birthday.*

either¹ /'aɪðə, 'iːðə/ *adjective*
1 each: *He couldn't remember either man's name.* □ *There are no simple answers to either of those questions.*
2 one of two things or people: *You can choose either date.* ● **either** *pronoun* *She wants a husband and children. I don't want either.*

either² /'aɪðə, 'iːðə/ *adverb*
used in negative sentences to mean also: *He said nothing, and she did not speak either.*
either...or... used for showing that there

are two possibilities to choose from: *I will either walk or take the bus.* □ *You can contact him either by phone or by email.*

eject /ɪ'dʒekt/ *verb* (**ejects, ejecting, ejected**)
to remove something or push it out: *You can eject the disc from the camera and put it into a DVD player.*

elastic /ɪ'læstɪk/ *uncountable noun*
a rubber material that stretches when you pull it, and then returns to its original size and shape: *The hat has a piece of elastic that goes under the chin.*

elbow /'elbəʊ/ *noun*
the part in the middle of your arm where it bends: *She leaned forward, with her elbows on the table.*
→ Look at picture on P1

elderly /'eldəli/ *adjective*
used as a polite way of saying that someone is old: *An elderly couple lived in the house next door.*
the elderly people who are old: *Children and the elderly are most at risk from this disease.*

elect /ɪ'lekt/ *verb* (**elects, electing, elected**)
to choose a person to do a particular job by voting for them: *The people have elected a new president.*

election /ɪ'lekʃən/ *noun*
a process in which people vote to choose a person who will hold an official position: *She won her first election in 2000.*

electric /ɪ'lektrɪk/ *adjective*
1 working using electricity: *Kelly loves to play the electric guitar.*
2 carrying electricity: *It is not safe to play near electric power lines.*

electrical /ɪ'lektrɪkəl/ *adjective*
using or relating to electricity: *an electrical appliance*

electrician /ɪlek'trɪʃən, ,elek-/ *noun*
a person whose job is to repair electrical equipment
→ Look at picture on P7

electricity /ɪlek'trɪsɪti, ,elek-/ *uncountable noun*
energy that is used for producing heat and light, and to provide power for machines

e,lectric 'shock *noun*
the sudden painful feeling that someone

gets when electricity goes through their body

electronic /ɪlek'trɒnɪk, ,elek-/ *adjective*
using electricity and small electrical parts: *Please do not use electronic equipment on the plane.*
▶ **electronically** *adverb* *The gates are operated electronically.*

elegant /'elɪgənt/ *adjective*
beautiful in a simple way: *Our room was elegant, with high ceilings and tall, narrow windows.*

element /'elɪmənt/ *noun*
1 one of the different parts of something: *Good health is an important element in our lives.*
2 a basic chemical substance such as gold, oxygen or carbon

elementary /,elɪ'mentri/ *adjective*
very easy and basic: *It's a simple system that uses elementary mathematics.*

elephant /'elɪfənt/ *noun*
a very large grey animal with a long nose called a trunk

elevator /'elɪveɪtə/ *noun* (*American*)
→ see **lift**

eleven /ɪ'levən/
the number 11

elf /elf/ *noun* (**elves**)
a very small person with pointed ears and magic powers in children's stories

eligible /'elɪdʒɪbəl/ *adjective*
allowed to do something: *Almost half the population are eligible to vote.*

eliminate /ɪ'lɪmɪ,neɪt/ *verb* (**eliminates, eliminating, eliminated**)
to remove something completely (*formal*): *The touch screen eliminates the need for a keyboard.*

else /els/ *adverb*
1 more; extra: *What else did you get for your birthday?*
2 different: *If you don't like this, try something else.*
or else used for saying what will happen if someone does not do something: *Do as I say, or else I won't help you.*

elsewhere /,el'sweə/ *adverb*
in other places or to another place: *80 per cent of the city's residents were born elsewhere.*

email /'iːmeɪl/ also **e-mail** *noun*
a system of sending written messages from one computer to another. **Email** is

short for 'electronic mail'. ● **email** *verb*
(**emails, emailing, emailed**) *Jamie emailed
me to say he couldn't come.*

embarrass /ɪmˈbærəs/ *verb*
(**embarrasses, embarrassing,
embarrassed**)
to make someone feel shy or ashamed: *His
mother's behaviour embarrassed him.*
▸ **embarrassing** *adjective* *He always found
Judith a bit embarrassing.*

embarrassed /ɪmˈbærəst/ *adjective*
feeling shy, ashamed or guilty about
something: *He looked a bit embarrassed when
he noticed his mistake.*

embarrassment /ɪmˈbærəsmənt/
uncountable noun
the feeling you have when you are
embarrassed: *I feel no embarrassment at
making mistakes.*

embrace /ɪmˈbreɪs/ *verb* (**embraces,
embracing, embraced**)
to put your arms around someone to
show that you love or like them: *Pam
embraced her sister.* □ *People were crying with
joy and embracing.*

embroider /ɪmˈbrɔɪdə/ *verb* (**embroiders,
embroidering, embroidered**)
to sew a pattern of threads onto clothing
or cloth: *The dress was embroidered with small
red flowers.*

embroidery /ɪmˈbrɔɪdəri/ *uncountable
noun*
a pattern of threads that is sewn onto
cloth for decoration: *The shorts had blue
embroidery over the pockets.*

embryo /ˈembriəʊ/ *noun*
an animal or a human that is starting to
grow, before it is born

emerald /ˈemərəld/ *noun*
a bright green stone that is used in
jewellery

emerge /ɪˈmɜːdʒ/ *verb* (**emerges,
emerging, emerged**)
to come out from a place: *Richard was
waiting when she emerged from her house.*

emergency [1] /ɪˈmɜːdʒənsi/ *noun*
(**emergencies**)
a serious situation, such as an accident,
when people need help quickly: *Come
quickly. This is an emergency!*

emergency [2] /ɪˈmɜːdʒənsi/ *adjective*
done or arranged quickly, because an

emergency has happened: *The board held an
emergency meeting.*

emigrate /ˈemɪˌɡreɪt/ *verb* (**emigrates,
emigrating, emigrated**)
to leave your own country and go to live
in another country: *His parents emigrated to
the U.S. in 1954.*

emotion /ɪˈməʊʃən/ *noun*
a feeling such as joy or love: *Andrew never
shows his emotions in public.* □ *Jill's voice was
full of emotion.*

emotional /ɪˈməʊʃənəl/ *adjective*
1 concerned with feelings: *After my wife's
death, I needed some emotional support.*
▸ **emotionally** *adverb* *By the end of the
show, I was physically and emotionally
exhausted.*
2 often showing your feelings, especially
when you are upset: *He is a very emotional man.*

emperor /ˈempərə/ *noun*
a man who rules a group of countries
(= an empire): *the emperor of Japan*

emphasis /ˈemfəsɪs/ *noun* (**emphases**
/ˈemfəsiːz/)
1 special importance that is given to
something: *Schools should place more
emphasis on health education.*
2 extra force that you put on a word or
part of a word when you are speaking:
*The emphasis is on the first syllable of the word
'elephant'.*

emphasize /ˈemfəˌsaɪz/ *verb*
(**emphasizes, emphasizing, emphasized**)
to show that something is especially
important: *He emphasizes the importance of
reading to young children.*

empire /ˈempaɪə/ *noun*
a number of separate nations that are all
controlled by the ruler of one particular
country: *the Roman Empire*

employ /ɪmˈplɔɪ/ *verb* (**employs,
employing, employed**)
to pay someone to work for a person or
a company: *The company employs 18 workers.*

employee /ɪmˈplɔɪiː/ *noun*
a person who is paid to work for another
person or a company: *The police believe that
airport employees were involved.*

employer /ɪmˈplɔɪə/ *noun*
the person or the company that you work
for: *Your employer should agree to pay you for
this work.*

employment /ɪmˈplɔɪmənt/ *uncountable noun*
work that you are paid for: *She was unable to find employment.*

empty ¹ /ˈempti/ *adjective* (**emptier, emptiest**)
used for describing a place or container that has no people or things in it: *The room was cold and empty.* □ *There were empty cans all over the floor.*

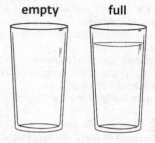

empty   full

empty ² /ˈempti/ *verb* (**empties, emptying, emptied**)
to remove the contents of a container: *I emptied the rubbish bin.* □ *Empty the noodles into a bowl.*

enable /ɪnˈeɪbəl/ *verb* (**enables, enabling, enabled**)
to make it possible for someone to do something: *The new test will enable doctors to treat the disease early.*

enclose /ɪnˈkləʊz/ *verb* (**encloses, enclosing, enclosed**)
1 to completely surround a place or an object: *The park is enclosed by a wooden fence.*
2 to put something in the same envelope as a letter: *I have enclosed a cheque for £100.*

encourage /ɪnˈkʌrɪdʒ/ *verb* (**encourages, encouraging, encouraged**)
1 to give someone hope or confidence: *When things aren't going well, he encourages me.*
2 to try to persuade someone to do something: *We want to encourage people to take more exercise.*

encouragement /ɪnˈkʌrɪdʒmənt/ *noun*
the act of encouraging someone: *Friends gave me a lot of encouragement.*

encouraging /ɪnˈkʌrɪdʒɪŋ/ *adjective*
giving people hope or confidence: *The results have been encouraging.*

encyclopedia /ɪnˌsaɪkləˈpiːdiə/ *noun*
a book or a CD-ROM containing facts about many different subjects

end ¹ /end/ *noun*
1 the final point in a period of time or a story: *Work will start before the end of the year.* □ *Don't tell me the end of the story!*
2 the furthest part of a long object: *Both ends of the tunnel were blocked.*
for hours/days/weeks on end for a long time: *We can talk for hours on end.*
make ends meet to have enough money for the things you need: *With Betty's salary they couldn't make ends meet.*

end ² /end/ *verb* (**ends, ending, ended**)
to reach the final point and stop: *The meeting quickly ended.*
end up to be in a particular place or situation after a series of events: *We ended up back at the house again.*

endangered species /ɪnˈdeɪndʒəd ˈspiːʃiz/ *noun* (**endangered species**)
a type of animal that may soon disappear from the world: *These African beetles are on the list of endangered species.*

ending /ˈendɪŋ/ *noun*
the last part of a book or a film: *The film has a happy ending.*

endless /ˈendləs/ *adjective*
lasting for a very long time: *The morning classes seemed endless.*
▶ **endlessly** *adverb* *They talk about it endlessly.*

endurance /ɪnˈdjʊərəns/ *uncountable noun*
the ability to continue with a difficult activity over a long period of time: *The exercise will improve strength and endurance.*

endure /ɪnˈdjʊə/ *verb* (**endures, enduring, endured**)
to experience a difficult situation: *She endured great pain in her life.*

enemy /ˈenəmi/ *noun* (**enemies**)
1 someone who hates a person, and wants to harm them: *His enemies hated and feared him.*
2 an army that is fighting against you in a war: *We are going to attack the enemy tomorrow morning.*

energetic /ˌenəˈdʒetɪk/ *adjective*
having a lot of energy: *Young children are very energetic.*

energy /ˈenədʒi/ *uncountable noun*
1 the ability and strength to do active physical things: *He's saving his energy for next week's race.*

2 the power from electricity or the sun, for example, that makes machines work or provides heat: *These machines are powered with energy from the sun.*

engaged /ɪnˈɡeɪdʒd/ *adjective*
if two people are engaged, they have agreed to marry each other: *We got engaged on my 26th birthday.*

engagement /ɪnˈɡeɪdʒmənt/ *noun*
an agreement to get married to somebody: *We announced our engagement in November.*

engine /ˈendʒɪn/ *noun*
1 the part of a car that produces the power to make it move: *He got into the driving seat and started the engine.*
2 the front part of a train that pulls the rest of it: *In 1941, trains were pulled by steam engines.*

engineer /ˌendʒɪˈnɪə/ *noun*
1 a person who designs, builds and repairs machines, or structures such as roads, railways and bridges
2 a person who repairs mechanical or electrical machines: *They sent an engineer to fix the computer.*

engineering /ˌendʒɪˈnɪərɪŋ/ *uncountable noun*
the work of designing and constructing machines or structures such as roads and bridges: *She studies science and engineering at college.*

English¹ /ˈɪŋɡlɪʃ/ *uncountable noun*
the language spoken by people who live in Great Britain and Ireland, the United States, Canada, Australia and many other countries: *Do you speak English?*
the English the people who come from or live in England

English² /ˈɪŋɡlɪʃ/ *adjective*
belonging to or relating to England: *He began to enjoy the English way of life.*

enhance /ɪnˈhɑːns/ *verb* (**enhances, enhancing, enhanced**)
to improve the quality of something: *A little sugar enhances the flavour of the peas.*

enjoy /ɪnˈdʒɔɪ/ *verb* (**enjoys, enjoying, enjoyed**)
to like doing something: *I enjoyed playing basketball.*
enjoy yourself to have a good time doing something: *I am really enjoying myself at the moment.*

enjoyable /ɪnˈdʒɔɪəbəl/ *adjective*
giving you pleasure: *The film was much more enjoyable than I expected.*

enjoyment /ɪnˈdʒɔɪmənt/ *uncountable noun*
the feeling of pleasure that you have when you do something that you like: *We get a lot of enjoyment from our garden.*

enlarge /ɪnˈlɑːdʒ/ *verb* (**enlarges, enlarging, enlarged**)
to make something bigger: *You can enlarge these photographs.*

enormous /ɪˈnɔːməs/ *adjective*
extremely large in size or amount: *The main bedroom is enormous.*
▶ **enormously** *adverb* *I admired him enormously.*

enough /ɪˈnʌf/ *adjective*
as much as you need: *They had enough cash for a one-way ticket.* ● **enough** *adverb* *I was old enough to work and earn money.* ● **enough** *pronoun* *They are not doing enough.*

enquire /ɪnˈkwaɪə/ *verb* (**enquires, enquiring, enquired**) also **inquire**
to ask for information about something: *He called them to enquire about the job.*

enquiry /ɪnˈkwaɪəri/ *noun* (**enquiries**) also **inquiry**
a question you ask in order to get some information about something: *He made some inquiries and discovered she had gone to Canada.*

enrol /ɪnˈrəʊl/ *verb* (**enrols, enrolling, enrolled**)
to officially join a class: *He has already enrolled at medical college.* □ *Already, 46 students are enrolled in the two classes.*

ensure /ɪnˈʃʊə/ *verb* (**ensures, ensuring, ensured**)
to make sure that something happens (*formal*): *The school ensures the safety of all students.* □ *We will work hard to ensure that this doesn't happen again.*

enter /ˈentə/ *verb* (**enters, entering, entered**)
1 to go into a place such as a room or building (*formal*): *He entered the room and stood near the door.*
2 to state that you will be a part of a competition, a race or an exam: *To enter the*

competition, go to our website and fill in the details.

3 to write or type information in a form or a book, or into a computer: *They enter the addresses into the computer.*

enterprise /'entə,praɪz/ *noun*
a company or a business: *We provide help for small and medium-sized enterprises.*

entertain /,entə'teɪn/ *verb* (**entertains, entertaining, entertained**)
1 to do something that amuses or interests people: *They were entertained by singers and dancers.*
▶ **entertaining** *adjective* *His show is entertaining, intelligent and funny.*
2 to invite guests to your home and give them food and drink: *This is the season for entertaining outdoors.*

entertainer /,entə'teɪnə/ *noun*
a person whose job is to entertain audiences, for example, by telling jokes, singing or dancing: *Chaplin was possibly the greatest entertainer of the twentieth century.*

entertainment /,entə'teɪnmənt/ *uncountable noun*
performances of plays and films, and activities such as reading and watching television, that give people pleasure: *At the party, there was children's entertainment and a swimming competition.*

enthusiasm /ɪn'θjuːzi,æzəm/ *uncountable noun*
a feeling that you have when you really enjoy something or want to do something: *Does your girlfriend share your enthusiasm for sports?*

enthusiastic /ɪn,θjuːzi'æstɪk/ *adjective*
showing how much you like or enjoy something: *Tom was not very enthusiastic about the idea.*

entire /ɪn'taɪə/ *adjective*
whole or complete: *He spent his entire life in China.*

entirely /ɪn'taɪəli/ *adverb*
completely and not just partly: *I agree entirely.* □ *I'm not entirely sure what to do.*

entitle /ɪn'taɪtəl/ *verb* (**entitles, entitling, entitled**)
be entitled to something to be allowed to have or do something: *They are entitled to first class travel.*

entrance /'entrəns/ *noun*
1 the door or gate where you go into a place: *He came out of a side entrance.*
2 the moment when someone arrives in a room: *She didn't notice her father's entrance.*
3 *uncountable* permission to go into a place: *We tried to go in, but we were refused entrance.*

entry /'entri/ *uncountable noun*
when you go into a particular place: *Entry to the museum is free.*
no entry used on signs to show that you are not allowed to go into a particular area

envelope /'envələʊp/ *noun*

envelope

the paper cover in which you put a letter before you send it to someone: *She put the letter back into the envelope and gave it to me.*

envious /'enviəs/ *adjective*
wanting something that someone else has: *I'm not envious of your success.*
▶ **enviously** *adverb* *People talked enviously about his good luck.*

environment /ɪn'vaɪərənmənt/ *noun*
1 the conditions in which someone lives or works: *The children are taught in a safe and happy environment.*
2 *uncountable* the natural world of land, the seas, the air, plants and animals: *Please respect the environment by recycling.*
▶ **environmental** /ɪn,vaɪərən'mentəl/ *adjective* *Environmental groups protested loudly during the conference.*
▶ **environmentally** *adverb* *environmentally friendly cleaning products*

envy /'envi/ *verb* (**envies, envying, envied**)
to wish that you had the same things that someone else has: *I don't envy young people these days.* ● **envy** *uncountable noun* *She was full of envy when she heard their news.*

epic /'epɪk/ *noun*
a long book, poem or film about important events: *We read Homer's epics about the Trojan war.* ● **epic** *adjective* *This is an epic story of love and war.*

epidemic /,epɪ'demɪk/ *noun*
when a particular disease affects a large number of people: *a flu epidemic*

epilogue /'epɪˌlɒg/ *noun*
an extra part that is added at the end of a piece of writing

episode /'epɪsəʊd/ *noun*
one of the parts of a story on television or radio: *The final episode will be shown next Sunday.*

equal ¹ /'iːkwəl/ *adjective*
1 the same in size, number or value: *There are equal numbers of men and women.*
▶ **equally** *adverb* *The money will be divided equally among his three children.*
2 used for saying that different groups of people have the same rights or are treated in the same way: *We want equal rights at work.*
▶ **equally** *adverb* *The system should treat everyone equally.*

equal ² /'iːkwəl/ *noun*
someone who has the same ability or rights as someone else: *You and I are equals.*

equal ³ /'iːkwəl/ *verb* (**equals, equalling, equalled**)
to be the same as a particular number or amount: *9 minus 7 equals 2.*

equality /ɪ'kwɒlɪti/ *uncountable noun*
the fair treatment of all the people in a group: *Few people really believed in racial equality in the 1800s.*

'equals sign *noun*
the sign =, which is used in mathematics to show that two numbers are equal

equation /ɪ'kweɪʒən/ *noun*
a mathematical statement that two amounts or values are the same

equator
/ɪ'kweɪtə/
noun
a line that is shown on maps around the middle of the world

equatorial
/ˌekwə'tɔːriəl/
adjective
at or near the equator
(= the imaginary line around the middle of the Earth): *The cassava plant grows in most equatorial regions.*

equator

equip /ɪ'kwɪp/ *verb*
be equipped with something to have the things that you need to do a particular job: *The army is equipped with 5,000 tanks.* □ *The phone is equipped with a camera.*

equipment /ɪ'kwɪpmənt/ *uncountable noun*
all the things that are used for a particular purpose: *tractors and other farm equipment*

equivalent /ɪ'kwɪvələnt/ *noun*
something that is the same as another thing, or used in the same way: *The Internet has become the modern equivalent of the phone.* ● **equivalent** *adjective* an equivalent amount

era /'ɪərə/ *noun*
a period of time that is considered as a single unit: *Their leader promised them a new era of peace.*

erase /ɪ'reɪz/ *verb* (**erases, erasing, erased**)
to remove something such as writing or a mark: *She erased his name from her address book.*

eraser /ɪ'reɪzə/ *noun* (American)
→ see **rubber**

erect ¹ /ɪ'rekt/ *verb* (**erects, erecting, erected**)
to build something such as a building or a bridge (formal): *The building was erected in 1900.*

erect ² /ɪ'rekt/ *adjective*
straight and upright: *Stand erect, with your arms hanging naturally.*

erode /ɪ'rəʊd/ *verb* (**erodes, eroding, eroded**)
if the wind or sea erodes land, it gradually destroys it: *The sea is gradually eroding the coastline.*
▶ **erosion** /ɪ'rəʊʒən/ *uncountable noun* *The storms caused soil erosion and flooding.*

errand /'erənd/ *noun*
a short trip to do a job or to buy something: *We ran errands and took her meals when she was sick.*

error /'erə/ *noun*
a mistake: *You should check your work for errors in grammar or spelling.*

erupt /ɪ'rʌpt/ *verb* (**erupts, erupting, erupted**)
when a volcano erupts, it throws out hot, melted rock (= lava): *Krakatoa erupted in 1883.*

▶ **eruption** /ɪˈrʌpʃən/ *noun* The country's last volcanic eruption was 600 years ago.

escalate /ˈeskəˌleɪt/ *verb* (**escalates, escalating, escalated**)
to become worse: *Nobody wants the situation to escalate.*

escalator /ˈeskəˌleɪtə/ *noun*
a set of moving stairs: *Take the escalator to the third floor.*

escalator

escape /ɪˈskeɪp/ *verb* (**escapes, escaping, escaped**)
1 to manage to get away from a place: *A prisoner has escaped from a jail in northern Texas.* • **escape** *noun* He made his escape at night.
2 to avoid an accident: *The two officers escaped serious injury.* • **escape** *noun* I had a narrow escape on the bridge.

especially /ɪˈspeʃəli/ *adverb*
used for showing that something is more important or true: *Millions of wild flowers grow in the valleys, especially in April and May.*

essay /ˈeseɪ/ *noun*
a short piece of writing on a subject: *We asked Jason to write an essay about his home town.*

essential /ɪˈsenʃəl/ *adjective*
necessary: *Play is an essential part of a child's development.*

establish /ɪˈstæblɪʃ/ *verb* (**establishes, establishing, established**)
to create an organization: *He established the business in 1990.*

establishment /ɪˈstæblɪʃmənt/ *noun*
1 an organization in a building in a particular place (*formal*): *an educational establishment*
2 the people who have power in a country: *the American establishment*

estate /ɪˈsteɪt/ *noun*
a large house in a large area of land in the country, owned by a person or an organization: *He spent the holidays at his aunt's 300-acre estate.*

eˈstate ˌagent *noun*
a person whose job is to sell buildings or land

estimate /ˈestɪˌmeɪt/ *verb* (**estimates, estimating, estimated**)
to say how much you think there is of something: *It's difficult to estimate how much money he has.* • **estimate** /ˈestɪmət/ *noun* She made an estimate of the lorry's speed.

estuary /ˈestʃʊri/ *noun* (**estuaries**)
the wide part of a river where it meets the sea

etc. /etˈsetrə/
used at the end of a list to show that there are other things that you have not mentioned. **Etc.** is short for 'etcetera'.

etcetera /etˈsetrə/ also **et cetera**
→ see **etc.**

eternal /ɪˈtɜːnəl/ *adjective*
lasting forever: *What's the secret of eternal happiness?*

ethical /ˈeθɪkəl/ *adjective*
1 relating to beliefs about right and wrong: *Heather is now a vegetarian for ethical reasons.*
2 morally right or morally acceptable: *ethical business practices*

ethnic /ˈeθnɪk/ *adjective*
relating to groups of people that have the same culture or belong to the same race: *Most of their friends come from other ethnic groups.*

euro /ˈjʊərəʊ/ *noun*
a unit of money that is used by many countries in the European Union (= an organization that encourages trade)

European /ˌjʊərəˈpiːən/ *adjective*
belonging to or coming from Europe: *European countries* • **European** *noun* When did Europeans first arrive in America?

evacuate /ɪˈvækjuˌeɪt/ *verb* (**evacuates, evacuating, evacuated**)
to move people out of a place because it is dangerous: *Families were evacuated from the area because of the fighting.*

evaluate /ɪˈvæljuˌeɪt/ *verb* (**evaluates, evaluating, evaluated**)
to consider something or someone in

order to decide how good or bad they are: *We need to evaluate the situation very carefully.*

▶ **evaluation** /ɪˌvæljʊˈeɪʃən/ *noun* The programme includes an evaluation of students' writing skills.

evaporate /ɪˈvæpəˌreɪt/ *verb* (**evaporates, evaporating, evaporated**)

to change from a liquid into a gas: *Boil the sauce until most of the liquid evaporates.*

eve /iːv/ *noun*

the day before a particular event or occasion: *The story begins on the eve of her birthday.*

even[1] /ˈiːvən/ *adjective*

1 used for describing numbers that can be divided exactly by two, for example 4, 8 and 24

2 smooth and flat: *You will need a table with an even surface.*

3 equally balanced between two sides: *It was an even game.*

even[2] /ˈiːvən/ *adverb*

1 used for saying that something is rather surprising: *Rob still seems happy, even after the bad news.*

2 used for making another word stronger: *Our car is big, but theirs is even bigger.*

even if used for showing that a particular fact does not change anything: *I'm going to the party, even if you won't come.*

even so used for adding a surprising fact: *The bus was nearly empty. Even so, the man sat down next to her.*

even though although, despite the fact that: *She wasn't embarrassed, even though she made a mistake.*

evening /ˈiːvnɪŋ/ *noun*

the part of each day between the end of the afternoon and midnight: *That evening he went to see a movie.* □ *We usually have dinner at seven in the evening.*

event /ɪˈvent/ *noun*

1 something that happens: *This terrible event caused death and injury to many.*

2 an organized activity or celebration: *Several sports events were cancelled.*

eventually /ɪˈventʃʊəli/ *adverb*

at some later time, especially after a lot of delays or problems: *They eventually married in 1996.* □ *Eventually your child will leave home.*

ever /ˈevə/ *adverb*

at any time. Ever is usually used in

questions and negative sentences: *I don't think I'll ever trust people again.* □ *Have you ever seen anything like it?* □ *Japan is more powerful than ever before.*

every /ˈevri/ *adjective*

1 used for showing that you are talking about all the members of a group: *Every room has a window facing the sea.* □ *Every child gets a free piece of fruit.*

2 used for saying how often something happens: *We had to attend meetings every day.* □ *He saw his family once every two weeks.*

every other day/every second day etc. happening one day, then not happening the next day, and continuing in this way: *I called my mother every other day.*

everybody /ˈevriˌbɒdi/ *pronoun*

→ see **everyone**

everyday /ˈevriˌdeɪ/ *adjective*

ordinary, a regular part of your life: *They were doing everyday activities around the house.* □ *Computers are a central part of everyday life.*

everyone /ˈevriˌwʌn/ *pronoun*

all people, or all the people in a particular group: *Everyone on the street was shocked when they heard the news.* □ *Not everyone thinks that the government is acting fairly.*

everything /ˈevriˌθɪŋ/ *pronoun*

used when you are talking about all the objects, actions or facts in a situation: *Everything in his life has changed.* □ *Susan and I do everything together.* □ *Is everything all right?*

everywhere /ˈevriˌweə/ *adverb*

used when you are talking about a whole area or all the places in a particular area: *People everywhere want the same things.* □ *We went everywhere together.*

evidence /ˈevɪdəns/ *uncountable noun*

an object or a piece of information that makes you believe that something is true or has really happened: *There is no evidence that he stole the money.* □ *Evidence shows that most of us are happy with our lives.*

evident /ˈevɪdənt/ *adjective*

easy to notice or understand: *Changes are evident across the country.* □ *It was evident that she was not feeling well.*

evidently /ˈevɪdəntli/ *adverb*

clearly: *The two men evidently knew each other.*

evil /ˈiːvəl/ *adjective*

morally very bad: *Who's the most evil person in all of history?*

evolution /ˌiːvəˈluːʃən, ˌev-/ *uncountable noun*

a process in which animals or plants slowly change over many years: *The evolution of mammals involved many changes in the body.*

evolve /ɪˈvɒlv/ *verb* (evolves, evolving, evolved)

to gradually develop over a period of time into something different: *Popular music evolved from folk songs.* ☐ *The theory is that humans evolved from apes.*

exact /ɪgˈzækt/ *adjective*

correct and complete in every way: *I don't remember the exact words.* ☐ *Can you tell me the exact date of the incident?*

exactly /ɪgˈzæktli/ *adverb*

1 correctly and completely: *The tower was exactly a hundred metres in height.*

2 in every way, or with all the details: *Both drugs will be exactly the same.*

3 said when you are agreeing with someone: *Eve nodded. 'Exactly.'*

exaggerate /ɪgˈzædʒəˌreɪt/ *verb* (exaggerates, exaggerating, exaggerated)

to say that something is bigger, worse or more important than it really is: *He thinks I'm exaggerating.* ☐ *Try not to exaggerate the risks of travelling alone.*

▶ **exaggeration** /ɪgˌzædʒəˈreɪʃən/ *noun* *It's not an exaggeration, it's a fact.*

exam /ɪgˈzæm/ *noun*

a formal test that you take to show your knowledge of a subject: *I don't want to take any more exams.*

> **LANGUAGE HELP**
> If you do an exam, you can say that you **take** an exam or **sit** an exam. If you do not pass an exam, you **fail** it.

examination /ɪgˌzæmɪˈneɪʃən/ *noun*

1 (*formal*) → see **exam**

2 an occasion when a doctor looks at your body in order to check how healthy you are: *She is waiting for the results of a medical examination.*

examine /ɪgˈzæmɪn/ *verb* (examines, examining, examined)

to look at something or someone carefully: *He examined her documents.* ☐ *A doctor examined her and could find nothing wrong.*

examine

A doctor examined her and could find nothing wrong.

▶ **examination** /ɪgˌzæmɪˈneɪʃən/ *noun* *The government said the plan needed careful examination.*

example /ɪgˈzɑːmpəl/ *noun*

something that shows what other things in a particular group are like: *The building is a fine example of 19th-century architecture.*

for example used for introducing an example of something: *The technique can be used for treating diseases like cancer, for example.*

exceed /ɪkˈsiːd/ *verb* (exceeds, exceeding, exceeded)

to be greater than a particular amount (*formal*): *The cost of a new boat exceeded £100,000.*

excellence /ˈeksələns/ *uncountable noun*

the quality of being extremely good in some way: *She won an award for excellence in teaching.*

excellent /ˈeksələnt/ *adjective*

extremely good: *The printing quality is excellent.*

except /ɪkˈsept/ *preposition*

used for showing that you are not including a particular thing or person: *The shops are open every day except Sunday.* ☐ *The room was empty except for a television.*

● **except** *conjunction* *I'm much better now, except that I still have a headache.*

exception /ɪkˈsepʃən/ *noun*

a particular thing, person or situation that is not included in what you say: *Not many musicians can sing well and play well, but Eddie is an exception.*

exceptional /ɪkˈsepʃənəl/ *adjective*

used for describing someone or something that is better than others in some way: *He is a player with exceptional ability.*

e

▶ **exceptionally** *adverb* She's an exceptionally talented dancer.

excess /'ıkses/ *adjective*
more than is usual or necessary: After cooking the fish, pour out any excess fat.

excessive /ık'sesıv/ *adjective*
more than is necessary: Their spending on clothes is excessive.

exchange /ıks'tʃeındʒ/ *verb* (exchanges, exchanging, exchanged)
1 to give something to someone at the same time as they give something to you: We exchanged addresses. ●**exchange** *noun* There will be a meal, followed by the exchange of gifts.
2 to take something back to a shop and get a different thing: If you are unhappy with the product, we will exchange it.

ex'change rate *noun*
the amount of another country's money that you can buy with a country's money: The exchange rate is around 3.7 pesos to the dollar.

excited /ık'saıtıd/ *adjective*
very happy or enthusiastic: I was excited about playing football again.

excitement /ık'saıtmənt/ *noun*
the feeling you have when you are excited: He shouted with excitement.

exciting /ık'saıtıŋ/ *adjective*
making you feel very happy or enthusiastic: The film is exciting, and also very scary.

exclaim /ıks'kleım/ *verb* (exclaims, exclaiming, exclaimed)
to speak suddenly or loudly, often because you are excited or shocked: 'Fantastic!' Jackson exclaimed delightedly.

exclamation /,eksklə'meıʃən/ *noun*
something that you say suddenly and loudly, showing that you are excited or angry: Sue gave an exclamation when she saw the house.

excla'mation mark *noun*
a mark (!) used in writing for showing surprise or excitement

exclude /ıks'klu:d/ *verb* (excludes, excluding, excluded)
1 to prevent someone from entering a place or doing an activity: The public was excluded from both meetings.
2 to not use or consider something: The price excludes taxes.

exclusive /ık'sklu:sıv/ *adjective*
available only to people who are rich or powerful: It was a private, exclusive club.

exclusively /ık'sklu:sıvli/ *adverb*
involving only the place or thing mentioned, and nothing else: This perfume is available exclusively from selected David Jones stores.

excuse [1] /ık'skju:s/ *noun*
a reason that you give in order to explain why you did something: They are trying to find excuses for their failure.

excuse [2] /ık'skju:z/ *verb* (excuses, excusing, excused)
to forgive someone for doing something: I'm not excusing him for what he did.

excuse me used for politely getting someone's attention: Excuse me, but are you Mr Hess?

executive /ıg'zekjʊtıv/ *noun*
someone who has an important job at a company: She loved her job as an advertising executive.

exempt /ıg'zempt/ *adjective*
not having to obey a rule or perform a duty: Men in college were exempt from military service.

exercise [1] /'eksə,saız/ *noun*
1 a movement that you do in order to stay healthy and strong: I do special neck and shoulder exercises every morning.
2 an activity that you do in order to practise a skill: Dennis said that the writing exercise was very useful.

exercise [2] /'eksə,saız/ *verb* (exercises, exercising, exercised)
to move your body in order to stay healthy and strong: You should exercise at least two or three times a week. ●**exercise** *uncountable noun* Lack of exercise can cause sleep problems.

'exercise book *noun*
a book that you use at school for writing in

exhaust [1] /ıg'zɔːst/ *verb* (exhausts, exhausting, exhausted)
to make someone very tired: We were worried that the trip would exhaust him.
▶ **exhausted** *adjective* She was too exhausted to talk.
▶ **exhausting** *adjective* It was an exhausting climb to the top of the hill.
▶ **exhaustion** /ıg'zɔːstʃən/ *uncountable*

noun *He fainted from exhaustion.*

exhaust² /ɪgˈzɔːst/ *uncountable noun*
the gas or steam that the engine of a vehicle produces: *The vehicle's exhaust fumes began to fill the garage.*

exˈhaust pipe *noun*
a pipe that carries gases or steam out of a car's engine

exhibit /ɪgˈzɪbɪt/ *verb* (**exhibits, exhibiting, exhibited**)
to put an object in a public place such as a museum so that people can come to look at it: *The paintings were exhibited in Paris in 1874.*

exhibition /ˌeksɪˈbɪʃən/ *noun*
a public event where art or interesting objects are shown: *The Museum of the City of New York has an exhibition of photographs.*

exist /ɪgˈzɪst/ *verb* (**exists, existing, existed**)
to be a real thing or situation: *It is clear that a serious problem exists.*

existence /ɪgˈzɪstəns/ *uncountable noun*
the fact that something is a real thing or situation: *We can understand the existence of stars and planets.* □ *The club is still in existence.*

existing /ɪgˈzɪstɪŋ/ *adjective*
in this world or available now: *There is a need to improve existing products.*

exit /ˈeksɪt/ *noun*
the door that you use to leave a public building: *He walked towards the exit.*

exotic /ɪgˈzɒtɪk/ *adjective*
unusual and interesting, usually because it comes from another country: *The house has a garden with exotic plants.*

expand /ɪkˈspænd/ *verb* (**expands, expanding, expanded**)
to become larger: *The industry expanded in the 19th century.* □ *We want to expand children's*

knowledge of the world.

▸ **expansion** /ɪkˈspænʃən/ *uncountable noun* *Local people are against the expansion of the airport.*

expect /ɪkˈspekt/ *verb* (**expects, expecting, expected**)
to believe that something will happen: *He expects to lose his job.* □ *We expect the price of bananas to rise.*

be expecting to have a baby growing inside you: *She announced that she was expecting another child.*

be expecting something/someone to believe that something or someone will arrive soon: *I wasn't expecting a visitor.*

expect someone to do something to believe that it is someone's duty to do something: *I expect you to help around the house.*

I expect used for showing that you think something is true or will probably happen: *I expect you're hungry.* □ *I expect she'll be here soon.*

expectation /ˌekspekˈteɪʃən/ *noun*
a belief someone has about how something should happen: *Young people have high expectations for the future.*

expel /ɪkˈspel/ *verb* (**expels, expelling, expelled**)
to officially tell someone to leave a school or an organization: *Two students were expelled for cheating.*

expense /ɪkˈspens/ *noun*
1 the cost or price of something: *He bought a big television at great expense.*
2 *plural* amounts of money that you spend on things: *Her hotel expenses were paid by the company.*

expensive /ɪkˈspensɪv/ *adjective*
costing a lot of money: *People thought that healthy food was more expensive than fast food.*

experience¹ /ɪkˈspɪəriəns/ *noun*
1 *uncountable* knowledge or skill in a job or activity that you have done for a long time: *No teaching experience is necessary.*
▸ **experienced** *adjective* *He is an experienced pilot.*
2 something important that happens to you: *What has been your most enjoyable experience?*

experience² /ɪkˈspɪəriəns/ *verb* (**experiences, experiencing, experienced**)
to have something happen to you: *I have never experienced true love.*

experiment [1] /ɪk'sperɪmənt/ *noun*

1 a scientific test that you do in order to discover what happens to something: *Laboratory experiments show that vitamin D slows cancer growth.*

2 when you test a new idea or method: *They started the magazine as an experiment.*

experiment [2] /ɪk'sperɪmənt/ *verb* (**experiments, experimenting, experimented**)

1 to do a scientific test on something: *The scientists have experimented on mice.*

2 to test a new idea or method: *I like cooking, and I have the time to experiment.*

experimental /ɪkˌsperɪ'mentəl/ *adjective*
new, or using new ideas or methods: *an experimental musician*

expert /'ekspɜːt/ *noun*
a person who knows a lot about a particular subject: *His brother is a computer expert.*

expertise /ˌekspɜː'tiːz/ *uncountable noun*
special skill or knowledge: *We're looking for someone with expertise in foreign languages.*

expire /ɪk'spaɪə/ *verb* (**expires, expiring, expired**)
to not be able to be used any more: *My contract expires in July.*

explain /ɪk'spleɪn/ *verb* (**explains, explaining, explained**)

1 to describe something to someone so that they can understand it: *He explained the law in simple language.* □ *Professor Griffiths explained how the drug works.*

2 to give reasons for something that happened: *She left a note explaining her actions.* □ *Can you explain why you didn't telephone?*

explanation /ˌeksplə'neɪʃən/ *noun*
information that you give someone to help them to understand something: *There was no explanation for the car accident.*

explicit /ɪk'splɪsɪt/ *adjective*
expressed or shown clearly, without hiding anything: *Many parents worry about explicit violence on television.*

explode /ɪk'spləʊd/ *verb* (**explodes, exploding, exploded**)
to burst with great force: *A second bomb exploded in the capital yesterday.*

exploit /ɪk'splɔɪt/ *verb* (**exploits, exploiting, exploited**)
to treat someone unfairly by using their work or ideas: *They said that he*
exploited other musicians.

explore /ɪk'splɔː/ *verb* (**explores, exploring, explored**)
to travel around a place to find out what it is like: *The best way to explore the area is in a boat.*

▶ **exploration** /ˌeksplə'reɪʃən/ *noun He led the first English exploration of North America.*

▶ **explorer** *noun Who was the US explorer who discovered the Titanic shipwreck?*

explosion /ɪk'spləʊʒən/ *noun*
when something suddenly bursts with a loud sound: *Six soldiers were injured in the explosion.*

explosive /ɪk'spləʊsɪv/ *noun*
a substance or an object that can cause an explosion: *The explosives were packaged in yellow bags.* ● **explosive** *adjective No explosive device was found.*

export [1] /ɪk'spɔːt/ *verb* (**exports, exporting, exported**)
to sell products to another country: *They also export beef.* □ *The company now exports to Japan.*
● **export** /'ekspɔːt/ *uncountable noun A lot of our land is used for growing crops for export.*

▶ **exporter** /'ekspɔːtə/ *noun Brazil is a big exporter of coffee.*

export [2] /'ekspɔːt/ *noun*
a product that one country sells to another country: *Spain's main export is oil.*

expose /ɪk'spəʊz/ *verb* (**exposes, exposing, exposed**)
to show something so that people can see it: *Vitamin D is made when the skin is exposed to sunlight.*

express [1] /ɪk'spres/ *verb* (**expresses, expressing, expressed**)
to show what you think or feel: *Only one company expressed an interest in his plan.*

express [2] /ɪk'spres/ *adjective*
used for describing a service that sends or receives things faster than usual: *An express postal service is available.*

expression /ɪk'spreʃən/ *noun*

1 the way that your face looks at a particular moment: *There was an expression of sadness on his face.*

2 a word or phrase: *Try to learn a few words and expressions in the language.*

expressive /ɪk'spresɪv/ *adjective*
clearly showing a person's feelings: *He has a very expressive face, so you always know what he's thinking.*

extend /ɪk'stend/ *verb* (**extends, extending, extended**)
to make something longer: *These treatments have extended the lives of people with cancer.*

extension /ɪk'stenʃən/ *noun*
1 an extra period of time for which something lasts: *He was given a six-month extension to his visa.*
2 a telephone that connects to the main telephone line in a building: *She can talk to me on extension 308.*
3 an extra part that is added to a building to make it bigger: *Mr Patel has built an extension to his home.*

extensive /ɪk'stensɪv/ *adjective*
covering a wide area: *It is a four-bedroom house with extensive gardens.*

extent /ɪk'stent/ *noun*
how important or serious a situation is: *The government has information on the extent of industrial pollution.* ☐ *He soon discovered the extent of the damage.*

exterior¹ /ɪk'stɪəriə/ *noun*
the outside surface of something: *They are going to paint the exterior of the building.*

exterior² /ɪk'stɪəriə/ *adjective*
used for talking about the outside parts of something: *exterior walls*

external /ɪk'stɜːnəl/ *adjective*
on or relating to the outside of a place, person or area: *You lose a lot of heat through external walls.*

extinct /ɪk'stɪŋkt/ *adjective*
not existing any more: *Many animals could become extinct in less than 10 years.*

extinction /ɪk'stɪŋkʃən/ *uncountable noun*
the death of all the living members of a species of animal or plant: *We are trying to save these animals from extinction.*

extinguish /ɪk'stɪŋgwɪʃ/ *verb* (**extinguishes, extinguishing, extinguished**)
to stop a fire from burning (*formal*): *It took about 50 minutes to extinguish the fire.*

extra /'ekstrə/ *adjective*
more than the normal amount: *He used the extra time to check his work.* ● **extra** *adverb* *You may be charged £10 extra for this service.*

extract /ɪk'strækt/ *verb* (**extracts, extracting, extracted**)

to take or pull something out: *A dentist may decide to extract the tooth.*

extraordinary /ɪk'strɔːdənri/ *adjective*
1 extremely good or special: *He's an extraordinary musician.*
2 very unusual or surprising: *An extraordinary thing just happened.*

extravagant /ɪk'strævəgənt/ *adjective*
1 spending too much money: *He was extravagant in all things – his clothing and his partying.*
2 costing too much money: *He came home with extravagant gifts for everyone.*

extreme /ɪk'striːm/ *adjective*
very great in degree: *You should use any drug with extreme care.*
▶ **extremely** *adverb* *My mobile phone is extremely useful.*

eye /aɪ/ *noun*
one of the two parts of your body with which you see: *I opened my eyes and looked.* ☐ *Mrs Brooke was a tall lady with dark brown eyes.*
→ Look at picture on P1

catch someone's eye
1 to attract someone's attention: *A movement across the garden caught her eye.*
2 to make someone notice you, so that you can speak to them: *He tried to catch Annie's eye.*

have your eye on something to want to have something (*informal*): *I've had my eye on that dress for a while now.*

eye

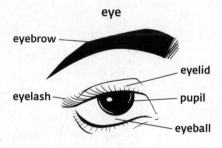

eyebrow

eyelid

eyelash

pupil

eyeball

eyeball /'aɪbɔːl/ *noun*
one of the two parts of your eyes that are like white balls

eyebrow /'aɪbraʊ/ *noun*
one of the two lines of hair that grow above your eyes
→ Look at picture on P1

eyeglasses /'aɪglɑːsiz/ *plural noun* (*American*)
→ see **glasses**

eyelash /'aɪlæʃ/ *noun* (**eyelashes**)
one of the hairs that grow on the edges of
your eyelids
→ Look at picture on P1

eyelid /'aɪlɪd/ *noun*
one of the pieces of skin that cover your
eyes when they are closed

eyesight /'aɪsaɪt/ *uncountable noun*
your ability to see: *He cannot get a driving
licence because he has poor eyesight.*

Ff

fable /ˈfeɪbəl/ *noun*
a type of story, usually about animals, that teaches people a lesson: *Here is a children's fable about love and honesty.*

fabric /ˈfæbrɪk/ *noun*
cloth that you use for making things like clothes and bags: *The shirt is made from beautiful soft fabric.*

fabulous /ˈfæbjʊləs/ *adjective*
very good (*informal*): *The flat offers fabulous views of the city.*

face¹ /feɪs/ *noun*
1 the front part of your head: *She had a beautiful face.*
2 the front or a vertical side of something: *the south face of Mount Everest* □ *a clock face*
face to face looking at someone directly: *I got off the bus and came face to face with my teacher.*
to make/pull a face to change your face into an ugly expression: *She made a face at the horrible smell.*

face² /feɪs/ *verb* (**faces, facing, faced**)
1 to look in a particular direction: *They stood facing each other.* □ *Our house faces south.*
2 to have to deal with something unpleasant: *Williams faces life in prison.* □ *I can't face telling my girlfriend.*

facilities /fəˈsɪlɪtiz/ *plural noun*
something such as rooms, buildings or pieces of equipment that are used for a particular purpose: *The hotel has excellent sports facilities, including a golf course.*

fact /fækt/ *noun*
something that you know is true: *He doesn't hide the fact that he wants to win.*
in fact used when you are giving more information about something that you have just said: *I don't watch television; in fact, I no longer own a TV.*

factor /ˈfæktə/ *noun*
something that helps to produce a result:

Exercise is an important factor in a healthy lifestyle.

factory /ˈfæktri/ *noun* (**factories**)
a large building where people use machines to make goods

fade /feɪd/ *verb* (**fades, fading, faded**)
to become lighter in colour: *The colour suddenly faded from her cheeks.* □ *Sunlight has faded the carpets and curtains.*
▶ **faded** *adjective* *Michael was wearing faded jeans and a green cotton shirt.*

Fahrenheit /ˈfærənˌhaɪt/ *adjective*
used for describing a way of measuring how hot something is. It is shown by the symbol ˚F. Water freezes at 32˚F (0˚C) and boils at 212˚F (100˚C): *The temperature was above 100˚F.*

fail /feɪl/ *verb* (**fails, failing, failed**)
1 not to pass an exam or a test: *75 per cent of secondary school students failed the exam.*
2 not to succeed when you try to do something: *The Republicans failed to get the 60 votes they needed.*
without fail always: *Andrew attended every board meeting without fail.*

failure /ˈfeɪljə/ *noun*
1 *uncountable* when you do not succeed in doing something: *Brian was depressed after the failure of his marriage.* □ *The project ended in failure in late 2001.*
2 something which is not a success: *His first novel was a failure.*

faint¹ /feɪnt/ *adjective* (**fainter, faintest**)
1 not strong or clear: *I could hear the faint sound of traffic in the distance.* □ *There was still the faint hope that Kimberly might return.*
▶ **faintly** *adverb* *The room smelled faintly of paint.*
2 feeling that you are going to fall, usually because you are ill or very tired: *Ryan was unsteady on his feet and felt faint.*

faint² /feɪnt/ *verb* (**faints, fainting, fainted**)
to become unconscious for a short time: *She suddenly fell forward and fainted.*

f

fair¹ /feə/ *adjective* (**fairer, fairest**)
1 treating everyone in the same way: *It's not fair; she's got more than me!* □ *I wanted everyone to get fair treatment.*
▸ **fairly** *adverb* *We solved the problem quickly and fairly.*
▸ **fairness** *uncountable noun* *There were concerns about the fairness of the election campaign.*
2 having light-coloured hair or skin: *My mother is very fair.* □ *Eric had thick fair hair.*
3 not bad, but not very good: *'What did you think of the film?' — 'Hmm. Fair.'*

fair² /feə/ *noun*
1 a place where you can play games to win prizes, and you can ride on special, big machines for fun
2 an event where people show, buy and sell goods, or share information: *US Airways is organizing a job fair to hire new workers.*

fairly /'feəli/ *adverb*
quite: *The team have been playing fairly well lately.* □ *She's fairly good at maths and science.*

fairy /'feəri/ *noun* (**fairies**)
a very small person with wings, who can do magic. Fairies appear in children's stories, and they are not real.

'fairy tale *noun*
a story for children about magic and fairies

faith /feɪθ/ *noun*
1 **uncountable** the belief that someone or something is good or honest, or that a thing works: *I have faith in the honesty of my employees.*
2 a particular religion: *The children will learn about a variety of faiths such as Islam and Judaism.*

faithful /'feɪθfʊl/ *adjective*
always supporting your family and friends: *Help your brothers and sisters, and be faithful to your friends.*

faithfully /'feɪθfʊli/ *adverb*
Yours faithfully words you write at the end of a formal letter, before your name, when you start the letter with the words 'Dear Sir' or 'Dear Madam'

fake¹ /feɪk/ *adjective*
used for describing a copy of something, especially something that is valuable: *The men used fake passports to get into the country.*

fake² /feɪk/ *noun*
something that is a copy of something, especially something valuable: *Art experts think that the painting is a fake.*

fall¹ /fɔːl/ *verb* (**falls, falling, fell, fallen**)
1 to move quickly towards the ground by accident: *Tyler fell from his horse and broke his arm.* □ *Jacob lost his balance and fell backwards.* □ *There was a huge crash as a large painting fell off the wall.*
2 when rain or snow falls, it comes down from the sky: *More than 30 inches of rain fell in 6 days.*
3 to become less or lower: *Unemployment fell to 4.6 per cent in May.* □ *Here, temperatures at night can fall below freezing.*

fall apart to break into pieces: *Gradually, the old building fell apart.*
fall asleep to start to sleep: *He fell asleep in front of the fire.*
fall behind to fail to make progress or move forward as fast as other people: *Some of the students fell behind in their work and lost marks.*
fall down to fall to the ground: *The wind hit Chris so hard, he fell down.*
fall ill to become ill: *Emily suddenly fell ill and was rushed to hospital.*
fall off something to come away from the thing it was fixed to: *An engine fell off the wing of the aeroplane.*
fall out
1 to come out: *His first tooth fell out when he was six.* □ *My hair is starting to fall out.*
2 to have an argument with someone and stop being friendly with them: *Ashley has fallen out with her boyfriend.*

fall² /fɔːl/ *noun*
1 when you fall to the ground: *Grandpa broke his right leg in a bad fall.*
2 when something becomes less or lower: *There has been a sharp fall in the value of the dollar.*
3 (**American**) → see **autumn**

fallen /'fɔːlən/ → see **fall**

false /fɔːls/ *adjective*
1 wrong or not true: *The president received false information from his advisers.*
▸ **falsely** *adverb* *She was falsely accused of stealing.*
2 not real or not natural: *My grandma has false teeth.*

fame /feɪm/ *uncountable noun*
when you are very well known by a lot of

people: *Connery gained fame as Agent 007 in the Bond films.*

familiar /fə'mɪliə/ *adjective*
used for describing someone or something that you have seen or heard before: *That boy's face looks familiar.* □ *Her name sounds familiar to me.*

family /'fæmɪli/ *noun* (**families**)
a group of people who are related to each other, usually parents and their children: *William and his family live in Hawaii.* □ *A ticket for a family of four costs £68.*
→ Look at pictures on P8

famine /'fæmɪn/ *noun*
a time when there is not enough food for people to eat, and many people die: *Their country is suffering from famine and war.*

famous /'feɪməs/ *adjective*
very well known: *Edvard Munch's painting 'The Scream' is one of the world's most famous paintings.*

fan¹ /fæn/ *noun*
1 someone who likes someone or something very much: *If you're a Johnny Depp fan, you'll love this film.*
2 a piece of equipment that moves the air around a room to make you cooler
3 a flat object that you move backwards and forwards in front of your face to make you cooler

fan² /fæn/ *verb* (**fans, fanning, fanned**)
to move a fan or another flat object around in front of yourself, to make yourself feel cooler: *Jessica fanned herself with a newspaper.*

fanatic /fə'nætɪk/ *noun*
someone whose behaviour or opinions are very extreme: *I am not a religious fanatic but I am a Christian.*

fancy¹ /'fænsi/ *adjective* (**fancier, fanciest**)
not simple or ordinary: *fancy jewellery*

fancy² /'fænsi/ *verb* (**fancies, fancying, fancied**)
to want to have something or do something (*informal*): *I fancied a piece of chocolate cake.* □ *Do you fancy going to the cinema tonight?*

fantastic /fæn'tæstɪk/ *adjective*
very good (*informal*): *Sarah has a fantastic social life — she's always out.*

fantasy /'fæntəsi/ *noun* (**fantasies**)
an imaginary story or thought that is very different from real life: *Everyone has had a fantasy about winning the lottery.*
□ *a fantasy novel*

FAQ /ˌef eɪ 'kjuː/ *noun* (**FAQs**)
often written on websites to mean 'frequently asked questions'

far /fɑː/ *adverb* (**farther** or **further, farthest** or **furthest**)
1 a long way from somewhere: *We've gone too far to go back now.* □ *My sister moved even farther away from home.*
2 used in questions and statements about distances: *How far is it to San Francisco?*
3 used for saying 'very much' when you are comparing things: *Your essay is far better than mine.*

by far used for saying that someone or something is the biggest, the best or the most important: *Unemployment is by far the most important issue.*

far from not at all: *What they said was far from the truth.*

so far up until now: *So far, they have failed.*

LANGUAGE HELP
Use **far** in negative sentences and questions about distance, and after 'too'. In positive sentences, you can say that a place is **a long way away,** or that it is **a long way from** another place. *Anna was still a long way away. Dubai is a long way from London.*

---

fare /feə/ *noun*
the money that you pay for a trip in a bus, a train, an aeroplane or a taxi: *The fare is £11 one way.*

farewell /ˌfeə'wel/ *noun*
goodbye: *We said our farewells and got in the car.* □ *He said farewell to us at the station.*
● **farewell** *adjective* *Before she left, she organized a farewell party for family and friends.*

farm /fɑːm/ *noun*
an area of land and buildings where people grow crops and keep animals: *Both boys like to work on the farm.*

farmer /'fɑːmə/ *noun*
a person who owns or works on a farm
→ Look at picture on P7

farmhouse /'fɑːmhaʊs/ *noun*
the house on a farm where the farmer lives

f

farming /'fɑːmɪŋ/ *uncountable noun*
the job of growing crops or keeping
animals on a farm

farther /'fɑːðə/ → see **far**

farthest /'fɑːðɪst/ → see **far**

fascinate /'fæsɪneɪt/ *verb* (**fascinates,
fascinating, fascinated**)
to interest someone very much: *American
history fascinates me.*

fascinated /'fæsɪˌneɪtɪd/ *adjective*
thinking that something is very
interesting: *My brother is fascinated by
racing cars.*

fascinating /'fæsɪˌneɪtɪŋ/ *adjective*
very interesting: *Madagascar is a fascinating
place.*

fashion /'fæʃən/ *noun*
1 *uncountable* the activity or business that
involves styles of clothing and
appearance: *The magazine contains 20
full-colour pages of fashion.*
2 a style of clothing that is popular at a
particular time: *Long dresses were the fashion
when I was a child.*
in/out of fashion popular or not popular
at a particular time: *short skirts were in
fashion back then.*

fashionable /'fæʃənəbəl/ *adjective*
1 popular at a particular time: *Long dresses
will be very fashionable this year.*
2 wearing fashionable clothes
▶ **fashionably** *adverb Katie is always
fashionably dressed.*

fast¹ /fɑːst/ *adjective, adverb* (**faster, fastest**)
1 quick: *Jane has always loved fast cars.* □ *I'm a
fast reader.* □ *The underground is the fastest way
to get around London.*
2 showing a time that is later than the
real time: *That clock is an hour fast.*
3 quickly: *James drives too fast.* □ *Can't you
run any faster?*
4 without any delay: *You need to see a doctor
— fast!*
fast asleep deeply asleep: *Anna climbed
into bed and five minutes later she was fast asleep.*

fast² /fɑːst/ *verb* (**fasts, fasting, fasted**)
to not eat any food for a period of time
● **fast** *noun The fast ends at sunset.*

fasten /'fɑːsən/ *verb* (**fastens, fastening,
fastened**)
1 to join the two sides of something
together so that it is closed: *Heather got*

fasten

quickly into her car and fastened the seat-belt.
2 to attach one thing to another: *There was
a notice fastened to the gate.*

fast food *uncountable noun*
hot food that is served quickly in a
restaurant: *He likes fast food like hamburgers,
pizzas and hot dogs.*

fat¹ /fæt/ *adjective* (**fatter, fattest**)
1 weighing too much: *I ate too much and I
began to get fat.*
2 very thick or wide: *Emily picked up a fat
book and handed it to me.*

fat² /fæt/ *uncountable noun*
1 a substance containing oil that is found
in some foods: *Cream contains a lot of fat.*
2 the soft substance that people and
animals have under their skin.

fatal /'feɪtəl/ *adjective*
1 having very bad results: *Justin made the
fatal mistake of lending her some money.*
2 causing someone's death: *The TV star was
attacked in a fatal stabbing.*
▶ **fatally** *adverb The soldier was fatally
wounded in the chest.*

fatality /fə'tælɪti/ *noun* (**fatalities**)
a death that is caused by an accident or by
violence (*formal*): *Yesterday's fatality is the
36th this year.*

fate /feɪt/ *noun*
1 *uncountable* a power that some people
believe controls everything that happens
in the world: *I think it was fate that Andy and
I met.*
2 what happens to someone or
something: *Frank was never seen again, and
we never knew his fate.*

father /'fɑːðə/ *noun*
your male parent: *His father was an artist.*
→ Look at picture on P8

'father-in-law noun (fathers-in-law)
the father of your husband or wife

fatigue /fə'tiːg/ uncountable noun
a feeling of being extremely tired: He was taken to hospital suffering from extreme fatigue.

faucet /'fɔːsɪt/ noun (American)
→ see tap

fault /fɔːlt/ noun
1 if something bad is your fault, you made it happen: The accident was my fault.
2 a weakness in someone or something: Gavin's worst fault is his temper.

faulty /'fɔːlti/ adjective
not working well: The car had worn tyres and faulty brakes.

favour /'feɪvə/ noun
something that you do to help someone: Please would you do me a favour and give David a message for me?

in favour thinking that something is a good thing: I'm in favour of income tax cuts.

favourable /'feɪvərəbəl/ adjective
right or good: The president's speech received favourable reviews. □ We hope that the weather will be favourable.

favourite /'feɪvərɪt/ adjective
used for describing the thing or person that you like more than all the others: What is your favourite film? ● **favourite** noun Of all the seasons, autumn is my favourite.

fax /fæks/ noun (faxes)
1 (also **fax machine**) a special machine that is joined to a telephone line. You use a fax to send and receive documents.
2 a copy of a document that you send or receive using a fax machine: I sent Daniel a long fax this morning. ● **fax** verb (faxes, faxing, faxed) I faxed a copy of the letter to my boss.

fear /fɪə/ noun
1 uncountable the unpleasant feeling you have when you think that you are in danger: My whole body was shaking with fear.
2 a thought that something unpleasant might happen: Sara has a fear of spiders.
● **fear** verb (fears, fearing, feared) Many people fear flying.

fearful /'fɪəfʊl/ adjective
afraid of something (formal): They were all fearful of losing their jobs.

fearless /'fɪələs/ adjective
not afraid of anything: He was a brave and

fearless man — a true hero.

feast /fiːst/ noun
a large and special meal for a lot of people: On Friday night, they had a wedding feast for 1,000 guests.

feat /fiːt/ noun
a very brave or difficult act: The men performed feats of physical bravery.

feather /'feðə/ noun
one of the light soft things that cover a bird's body: peacock feathers

feather

feature /'fiːtʃə/ noun
1 an important part of something: The house has many attractive features, including a swimming pool.
2 a special story in a newspaper or magazine: There was a feature on Tom Cruise in the New York Times.
3 your eyes, your nose, your mouth or any other part of your face: Emily's best feature is her dark eyes.

February /'febjʊəri/ noun
the second month of the year: The band's U.S. tour starts on February 7.

fed /fed/ → see feed

fed 'up adjective
unhappy or bored (informal): My brother soon became fed up with city life.

fee /fiː/ noun
1 the money that you pay to be allowed to do something: We paid the small entrance fee and drove inside.
2 the money that you pay a person or an organization for advice or for a service: We had to pay the lawyer's fees ourselves.

feeble /'fiːbəl/ adjective (feebler, feeblest)
weak: My uncle was old and feeble, and was not able to walk far.
▶ **feebly** adverb Her left hand moved feebly at her side.

feed /fiːd/ verb (feeds, feeding, fed)
to give food to a person or an animal: It's time to feed the baby. □ It's usually best to feed a small dog twice a day.

feedback /'fiːdbæk/ uncountable noun
a situation when someone tells you how well or badly you are doing: Ask your teacher for feedback on your work.

feel /fiːl/ *verb* (**feels, feeling, felt**)

1 to experience a particular emotion or physical feeling: *I am feeling really happy today.* □ *I felt a sharp pain in my shoulder.* □ *How do you feel?* □ *She felt guilty about spending so much money on clothes.*

2 used for describing the way that something seems when you touch it or experience it: *The blanket feels soft.* □ *The sun felt hot on my back.* □ *The room felt rather cold.*

3 to touch something with your hand, so that you can find out what it is like: *The doctor felt my pulse.* □ *Feel how soft this leather is.*

4 to be aware of something because you touch it or it touches you: *Anna felt something touching her face.*

5 to have an opinion about something: *We feel that this decision is fair.*

feel for someone to have sympathy for someone: *Nicole was crying, and I really felt for her.*

feel like doing something to want to do something: *'I just don't feel like going out tonight', Rose said quietly.*

feeling /'fiːlɪŋ/ *noun*

1 something that you feel in your mind or your body: *I had feelings of sadness and loneliness.*

2 when you think that something is probably going to happen: *I have a feeling that everything will be all right.*

3 *plural* what you think and feel about something: *They have strong feelings about politics.*

4 *uncountable* the ability to feel things in part of your body: *After the accident, Jason had no feeling in his legs.*

hurt someone's feelings to say or do something that makes someone upset: *I'm really sorry if I hurt your feelings.*

feet /fiːt/

the plural of **foot**

fell /fel/ → see **fall**

fellow /'feləʊ/ *adjective*

used for describing people who are like you or from the same place as you: *Richard was just 18 when he married fellow student Barbara.*

felt¹ /felt/ → see **feel**

felt² /felt/ *uncountable noun*

a type of soft thick cloth: *Amy was wearing an old felt hat.*

'felt-'tip *noun* (*also* **felt-tip pen**)

a pen with a soft point: *a pack of felt-tip pens*
→ Look at picture on P13

female /'fiːmeɪl/ *noun*

1 any animal, including humans, that can give birth to babies or lay eggs: *Each female will lay just one egg.* ●**female** *adjective* *female gorillas*

2 a woman or a girl: *This disease affects males more than females.* ●**female** *adjective* *Who is your favourite female singer?*

feminine /'femɪnɪn/ *adjective*

1 considered to be typical of women: *I love feminine clothes, so I wear skirts a lot.* □ *His voice was strangely feminine.*

2 used for describing a noun, pronoun or adjective that has a different form from other forms (such as 'masculine' forms) in some languages. Compare with **masculine**.

feminism /'femɪˌnɪzəm/ *uncountable noun*

the belief that women should have the same rights and opportunities as men

feminist /'femɪnɪst/ *noun*

a person who believes in feminism: *Feminists argue that women should not have to choose between children and a career.*
●**feminist** *adjective* *feminist writer Simone de Beauvoir*

fence /fens/ *noun*

a wooden or metal wall around a piece of land

fern /fɜːn/ *noun*

a plant that has long stems with leaves that look like feathers

ferry /'feri/ *noun* (**ferries**)

a boat that regularly takes people or things a short distance across water: *They crossed the River Gambia by ferry.*

fertile /'fɜːtaɪl/ *adjective*

1 used for describing land or soil where plants grow very well

2 able to have babies
▶ **fertility** *uncountable noun Smoking and drinking alcohol affect fertility.*

fertilizer /'fɜːtɪˌlaɪzə/ *also* **fertiliser** *uncountable noun*

a substance that you put on soil to make plants grow better

festival /'festɪvəl/ *noun*
1 a series of special events such as concerts or plays: *The actress was in Rome for the city's film festival.*
2 a time when people celebrate a special event: *Shavuot is a two-day festival for Jews.*

fetch /fetʃ/ *verb* (**fetches, fetching, fetched**)
to go somewhere and bring something or someone back: *Sylvia fetched a towel from the bathroom.* □ *Please could you fetch me a glass of water?*

fever /'fi:və/ *noun*
when your body is too hot because you are ill: *Jim had a high fever.*

feverish /'fi:vərɪʃ/ *adjective*
having a fever: *Joshua was feverish and wouldn't eat anything.*

few /fju:/ *adjective* (**fewer, fewest**)
not many: *She had few friends.*
a few some, but not many: *I'm having a dinner party for a few close friends.* □ *Here are a few ideas that might help you.* □ *Most were Americans but a few were British.*
a few of some, but not many: *I met a few of her friends at the party.*
few of not many: *Few of the houses still had lights on.*

> **LANGUAGE HELP**
> If you say *I have a few friends*, you mean that you have some friends. If you say *I have few friends*, you mean that you do not have many friends.

fiancé /fi'ɒnseɪ/ *noun*
the man that a woman is going to marry

fiancée /fi'ɒnseɪ/ *noun*
the woman that a man is going to marry

fibre /'faɪbə/ *noun*
1 a thin thread that is used for making cloth or rope: *We only sell clothing made from natural fibres.*
2 *uncountable* the part of a fruit or vegetable that helps all the food you eat to move through your body: *Most vegetables contain fibre.*

fiction /'fɪkʃən/ *uncountable noun*
books and stories about people and events that are not real
> **fictional** *adjective Harry Potter, the fictional hero of J.K. Rowling's books*

fidget /'fɪdʒɪt/ *verb* (**fidgets, fidgeting, fidgeted**)
to keep moving slightly, because you are nervous or bored: *Brenda fidgeted in her seat.*

field /fi:ld/ *noun*
1 a piece of land where crops are grown, or where animals are kept: *We drove past fields of sunflowers.*
2 a piece of land where sports are played: *a football field*
3 a subject that someone knows a lot about: *Professor Greenwood is an expert in the field of international law.*

fielder /'fi:ldə/ *noun*
a player in some sports who has to pick up or catch the ball after a player from the other team has hit it: *He hit 10 home runs and he's also a good fielder.*

fierce /fɪəs/ *adjective* (**fiercer, fiercest**)
1 very angry and likely to attack
> **fiercely** *adverb* '*Go away!' she said fiercely.*
2 very strong or enthusiastic: *There's fierce competition for places in the team.*

fifteen /ˌfɪf'ti:n/
the number 15
> **fifteenth** /ˌfɪf'ti:nθ/ *adjective, adverb the fifteenth century*

fifth¹ /fɪfθ/ *adjective, adverb*
the item in a series that you count as number five: *This is his fifth trip to Australia.*

fifth² /fɪfθ/ *noun*
one of five equal parts of something ($\frac{1}{5}$): *The machine allows us to do the job in a fifth of the usual time.*

fifty /'fɪfti/
the number 50
> **fiftieth** /'fɪftiəθ/ *adjective, adverb He's just celebrated his fiftieth birthday.*

fig /fɪg/ *noun*
a soft sweet fruit full of tiny seeds. Figs grow on trees in hot countries.

fig

fight¹ /faɪt/ *verb* (**fights, fighting, fought**)
1 to try to hurt someone with words or by using physical force: '*Stop fighting!' Mum shouted.* □ *Susan fought a lot with her younger sister.*
2 to take part in a war: *He fought in the war and was taken prisoner.*
3 to try very hard to stop something

unpleasant: *It is very hard to fight forest fires.*
4 to try very hard to get something: *Lee had to fight hard for his place on the team.*
5 to argue (*informal*): *Robert's parents fight all the time.*

fight² /faɪt/ *noun*
a situation in which people try to hurt each other with words or by using physical force: *I had a fight with Simon at the party last night.*

fighter /'faɪtə/ *noun*
a person who fights another person, especially as a sport: *He was a professional fighter for 17 years.*

figure /'fɪɡə/ *noun*
1 one of the symbols from 0 to 9 that you use to write numbers: *They've put the figures in the wrong column.* □ *John earns a six-figure salary — £100,000 at least.*
2 an amount or a price expressed as a number: *Can I see your latest sales figures?*
3 the shape of a person you cannot see clearly: *Two figures moved behind the thin curtain.*
4 the shape of someone's body: *Lauren has a very good figure.*

file¹ /faɪl/ *noun*
1 a box or a type of envelope that you keep papers in: *The file contained letters and reports.*
2 a collection of information that you keep on your computer: *I deleted the files by mistake.*
3 a tool that you use for rubbing rough objects to make them smooth: *a nail file*
in single file walking or standing in a line, one behind the other: *We walked past him in single file.*

file² /faɪl/ *verb* (**files, filing, filed**)
1 to put a document in the correct place: *The letters are all filed alphabetically.*
2 to make something smooth using a special tool (= a file): *Mum was filing her nails.*
3 to walk somewhere in a line, one behind the other: *More than 10,000 people filed past the dead woman's coffin.*

filename /'faɪlneɪm/ *noun*
the name that you give to a particular computer file

'file-sharing also **file sharing** *uncountable noun*

a way of sharing computer files among a large number of users

fill /fɪl/ *verb* (**fills, filling, filled**)
1 (*also* **fill up**) to cause a container to become full of something: *Rachel went to the bathroom and filled a glass with water.* □ *The bath was filling up quickly.*
2 (*also* **fill up**) to cause a space to be full of something: *Rows of desks filled the office.* □ *Filling up your car's petrol tank these days is very expensive.*
▶ **filled** *adjective* *The museum is filled with historical objects.*
3 (*also* **fill in**) to put a substance into a hole to make the surface smooth again: *Fill the cracks between walls and window frames.* □ *Start by filling in any cracks.*
fill something in or **fill something out**
to write information in the spaces on a form: *When you have filled in the form, send it to your employer.*
fill up same meaning as **fill 1** and **2**

filling /'fɪlɪŋ/ *noun*
1 a small amount of metal that fills a hole in a tooth: *The dentist said I needed two fillings.*
2 what is inside a cake, a pie or a sandwich: *Next, make the pie filling.*

film¹ /fɪlm/ *noun*
1 (*American:* **movie**) a story that is told using moving pictures on the television or at a cinema: *I'm going to see a film tonight.*
2 the roll of plastic that is used for taking photographs in some older cameras: *Emily put a new roll of film into the camera.*

film² /fɪlm/ *verb* (**films, filming, filmed**)
to use a camera to take moving pictures of something: *He filmed her life story.*

filter /'fɪltə/ *noun*
an object that only allows liquid or air to pass through it, and that holds back solid parts such as dirt or dust: *The water filters are available in different styles, colours and designs.*
● **filter** *verb* (**fitters, filtering, filtered**)
The device cleans and filters the air.

filthy /'fɪlθi/ *adjective* (**filthier, filthiest**)
very dirty: *He always wore a filthy old jacket.*

fin /fɪn/ *noun*
one of the flat parts like a wing that helps a fish to swim

final¹ /'faɪnəl/ *adjective*
1 last: *The team's final game of the season will be tomorrow.*

2 used for describing something that cannot be changed: *The judges' decision is final.*

final² /'faɪnəl/ *noun*
1 the last game or race in a series, that decides who is the winner: *Williams played in the final of the US Open in 1997.*
2 *plural* the exams taken by British university students at the end of their final year: *Anna took her finals in the summer.*

finalist /'faɪnəlɪst/ *noun*
someone who reaches the final of a competition: *Thompson was an Olympic finalist in 1996.*

finally /'faɪnəli/ *adverb*
1 after a long time: *The letter finally arrived at the end of last week.*
2 said before you say the last thing in a list: *Combine the flour and the cheese, and finally, add the cream.*

finance¹ /'faɪnæns/ *verb* (**finances, financing, financed**)
to provide the money to pay for something: *The government used the money to finance the war.*

finance² /'faɪnæns/ *noun*
1 *uncountable* money, or the activity of managing large amounts of money: *Professor Buckley teaches finance at Princeton University.*
2 *plural* the money that someone has: *Take control of your finances now and save thousands of pounds.*

financial /faɪ'nænʃəl, fɪ-/ *adjective*
relating to money: *The company is in financial difficulties.*

find /faɪnd/ *verb* (**finds, finding, found**)
1 to see something after you have been looking for it: *The police searched the house and found a gun.* □ *David has finally found a job.*
2 to see or discover something by chance: *If you find my purse, can you let me know?*
3 used for expressing your opinion about something: *I find his behaviour extremely rude.* □ *We all found the film very funny.*

find someone guilty/not guilty to say that someone is guilty or not guilty of a crime: *The woman was found guilty of murdering her husband.*

find something out to learn the facts about something: *I'll watch the next episode to find out what happens.*

find your way to get somewhere by choosing the right way to go: *We lost our dog, but he found his way home.*

fine¹ /faɪn/ *adjective* (**finer, finest**)
1 very good: *There is a fine view of the countryside.*
2 well or happy: *Linda is fine and sends you her love.*
3 satisfactory or acceptable: *Everything is going to be just fine.*
4 very thin: *fine hairs*
5 used for describing the weather when the sun is shining

fine² /faɪn/ *noun*
money that someone has to pay because they have done something wrong ● **fine** *verb* (**fines, fining, fined**) *She was fined £300 for driving dangerously.*

fine 'art *uncountable noun*
the paintings and objects that artists produce for other people's pleasure, rather than for a particular use: *the Museum of Fine Arts*

finger /'fɪŋgə/ *noun*
one of the long thin parts at the end of each hand: *Amber had a huge diamond ring on her finger.*
→ Look at picture on P1

cross your fingers/keep your fingers crossed to put one finger on top of another and hope for good luck

fingernail /'fɪŋgə,neɪl/ *noun*
one of the thin hard parts at the end of each of your fingers

fingerprint /'fɪŋgə,prɪnt/ *noun*
the mark that your finger makes when it touches something: *His fingerprints were found on the gun.*

fingertip /'fɪŋgə,tɪp/ also **finger-tip** *noun*
the end of your finger: *He plays the drum very lightly with his fingertips.*

finish¹ /'fɪnɪʃ/ *verb* (**finishes, finishing, finished**)
1 to stop doing something: *Dad finished eating, and left the room.*
2 to end: *The concert finished just after midnight.*

finish² /'fɪnɪʃ/ *noun*
the end of something or the last part of it: *There was an exciting finish to the women's 800-metre race.*

finished /ˈfɪnɪʃt/ *adjective*
no longer using something: *When you have finished with the book, please give it back to your teacher.*

fir /fɜː/ or **fir tree** *noun*
a tall tree with thin leaves (= needles) that do not fall in winter

fire¹ /faɪə/ *noun*
1 **uncountable** the hot, bright flames that come from things that are burning: *We learned how to make fire and hunt for fish.*
2 flames that destroy buildings or forests: *87 people died in a fire at the theatre.* □ *a forest fire*
3 a burning pile of wood or coal that you make: *There was a fire in the fireplace.*
catch fire to start burning: *Several buildings caught fire in the explosion.*
on fire burning and being damaged by a fire: *Quick! My car's on fire!*
set fire to something, set something on fire to make something start to burn

fire

bonfire

fireplace

fire

fire² /faɪə/ *verb* (**fires, firing, fired**)
1 to shoot a gun or a bullet: *Have you ever fired a gun before?*
2 to tell someone to leave their job: *She was fired from that job in August.*

'fire a,larm *noun*
a piece of equipment that makes a loud noise to warn people when there is a fire

firearm /ˈfaɪərɑːm/ *noun*
a gun (*formal*): *The guards were carrying firearms.*

fire brigade /ˈfaɪə brɪˌɡeɪd/ *noun*
an organization that has the job of putting out fires

'fire ,engine *noun*
a large vehicle that carries people and equipment for putting out fires

fire extinguisher /ˈfaɪə ɪkˌstɪŋɡwɪʃə/ *noun*
a metal container with water or chemicals inside for stopping fires

firefighter /ˈfaɪəfaɪtə/ *noun*
a person whose job is to put out fires
→ Look at picture on P7

fireman /ˈfaɪəmən/ *noun* (**firemen**)
a person whose job is to put out fires

fireplace /ˈfaɪəˌpleɪs/ *noun*
the place in a room made out of brick or stone where you can light a fire
→ Look at picture on P5

firework /ˈfaɪəˌwɜːk/ *noun*
a thing that flies up into the air and explodes, making bright colours in the sky: *We watched the fireworks from the balcony.*

firm¹ /fɜːm/ *noun*
a group of people who work together: *Kevin works for a Chicago law firm.*

firm² /fɜːm/ *adjective* (**firmer, firmest**)
1 not soft: *When you buy fruit, make sure it is firm.*
2 strong: *His handshake was firm.*
▶ **firmly** *adverb* *She held me firmly by the elbow.*
3 not changing your mind: *She was firm with him. 'I don't want to see you again.'*
▶ **firmly** *adverb* *'You must go to bed now, kids', he said firmly.*

first /fɜːst/ *adjective, adverb*
1 coming before all the others: *January is the first month of the year.* □ *Who came first in the race?*
2 before doing anything else: *First I went to the police and told them what had happened.*
3 before anyone else: *The people who lived nearby arrived first.*
at first used for talking about what happened at the beginning of an event: *At first, he seemed surprised by my questions.*
first/first of all used for introducing the

first thing that you want to say: *First of all, I'd like to thank you for coming.*

first 'aid *uncountable noun*
simple medical treatment that you give to an ill or injured person: *Each group leader must do a course in basic first aid.*

'first-'class also **first class** *adjective, adverb*
1 of the highest standard: *The Altea is a newly-built first-class hotel.*
2 used for describing the best and most expensive seats on a train or an aeroplane: *He won two first-class tickets to fly to Dublin.* □ *We never fly first class.*
3 used for describing the fastest and most expensive way of sending letters: *a first-class letter* □ *I sent the letter first-class, but it hasn't arrived.*

first 'floor *noun*
1 the floor of a building just above the floor that is level with the street
2 (American) → see **ground floor**

firstly /'fɜːstli/ *adverb*
used when you mention the first thing in a list: *Firstly, you're late, and secondly, you've forgotten your homework.*

first 'name *noun*
the name that comes before your family name: *'What's Dr Wright's first name?' 'It's Emma. Emma Wright.'*

fish¹ /fɪʃ/ *noun* (**fish** or **fishes**)
an animal that lives and swims in water, that people eat as food: *Dave caught a huge fish this morning.* □ *This fish is delicious.*

fish² /fɪʃ/ *verb* (**fishes, fishing, fished**)
to try to catch fish: *Brian learned to fish in the Colorado River.*

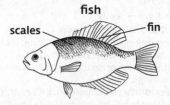

fish

scales — fin

fisherman /'fɪʃəmən/ *noun* (**fishermen**)
a person who catches fish as a job or for sport

fishing /'fɪʃɪŋ/ *uncountable noun*
the sport or business of catching fish

'fishing rod *noun*
a long thin stick with a thread and a hook, that is used for catching fish

fist /fɪst/ *noun*
your hand with your fingers closed tightly together: *Steve stood up and shook an angry fist at Patrick.*

fit¹ /fɪt/ *verb* (**fits, fitting, fitted**)
1 to be the right size for someone or something: *The costume fitted the child perfectly.* □ *The game is small enough to fit into your pocket.*
2 to attach something somewhere: *He fits locks on the doors.*
fit someone/something in to find time or space for someone or something: *The dentist can fit you in just after lunch.* □ *We can't fit any more children in the car.*

fit² /fɪt/ *adjective* (**fitter, fittest**)
1 healthy and strong: *You're looking very fit. I can tell you exercise regularly.*
▸ **fitness** *uncountable noun* *Sophie is a fitness instructor.*
2 good enough for a particular purpose: *Only two of the bicycles were fit for the road.*

fit³ /fɪt/ *noun*
1 when someone suddenly starts coughing or laughing: *I suddenly had a fit of coughing.*
2 when someone suddenly becomes unconscious and their body makes violent movements

five /faɪv/
the number 5

fix /fɪks/ *verb* (**fixes, fixing, fixed**)
1 to repair something: *This morning, a man came to fix my washing machine.*
2 to attach something firmly or securely to a particular place: *The clock is fixed to the wall.*

fizzy /'fɪzi/ *adjective* (**fizzier, fizziest**)
containing small bubbles: *fizzy water*

flag /flæg/ *noun*
a piece of coloured cloth with a pattern on it that is used as a symbol for a country or an organization: *The crowd was shouting and waving American flags.*

flake¹ /fleɪk/ *noun*
a small thin piece of something: *Large flakes of snow began to fall.*

flake² /fleɪk/ *verb* (**flakes, flaking, flaked**)
(also **flake off**)
when paint flakes, small thin pieces of it come off: *The paint was flaking off the walls.*

f

flame /fleɪm/ *noun*
the bright burning gas that comes from a fire: *The flames almost burned her fingers.*
burst into flames to suddenly start burning strongly: *The plane crashed and burst into flames.*
in flames burning: *When we arrived, the house was in flames.*

flammable /'flæməbəl/ *adjective*
burning easily: *Always store paint and flammable liquids away from the house.*

flap¹ /flæp/ *verb* (**flaps, flapping, flapped**)
1 to move quickly up and down or from side to side: *Sheets flapped on the clothes line.*
2 when a bird flaps its wings, it moves them up and down quickly: *The birds flapped their wings and flew across the lake.*

flap² /flæp/ *noun*
a flat piece of something that can move up and down or from side to side: *I opened the flap of the envelope and took out the letter.*

flash¹ /flæʃ/ *noun* (**flashes**)
a sudden bright light: *There was a flash of lightning.*

flash² /flæʃ/ *verb* (**flashes, flashing, flashed**)
to shine on and off very quickly: *They could see a lighthouse flashing through the fog.*

'flash drive *noun*
a small object for storing computer information that you can carry with you and use in different computers

flat¹ /flæt/ *adjective* (**flatter, flattest**)
1 level or smooth: *Tiles can be fixed to any flat surface.* □ *a flat roof*
2 used for describing a tyre or ball that does not have enough air in it
3 used for describing a note that is slightly lower than another note. Compare with **sharp**: *This is how to sing a B flat.*

flat² /flæt/ (American: **apartment**) *noun*
a set of rooms for living in, usually on one floor and part of a larger building

flatten /'flætən/ *verb* (**flattens, flattening, flattened**)
to make something flat: *Flatten the bread dough with your hands.*

flatter /'flætə/ *verb* (**flatters, flattering, flattered**)
to say nice things to someone because you want them to like you: *Everyone likes to be flattered, to be told that they're beautiful.*

flattering /'flætərɪŋ/ *adjective*
making someone look or seem attractive or important: *It was a very flattering photograph — he looked like a film star.*

flavour /'fleɪvə/ *noun*
the taste of a food or drink: *I added some pepper for extra flavour.* ● **flavour** *verb* (**flavours, flavouring, flavoured**) *Flavour your favourite dishes with herbs and spices.*

flaw /flɔː/ *noun*
something that is wrong with something: *There are a number of flaws in his theory.*

flea /fliː/ *noun*
a very small insect that jumps. Fleas live on the bodies of humans or animals, and drink their blood as food: *Our dog has fleas.*

fled /fled/ → see **flee**

flee /fliː/ *verb* (**flees, fleeing, fled**)
to run away from something or someone (formal): *He slammed the door behind him and fled.*

fleece /fliːs/ *noun*
1 the coat of wool that covers a sheep
2 a jacket or a jumper made from a soft warm cloth: *He was wearing tracksuit trousers and a dark blue fleece.*

fleet /fliːt/ *noun*
a large group of boats, aircraft or cars: *The fleet sailed out to sea.*

flesh /fleʃ/ *uncountable noun*
1 the soft part of your body that is between your bones and your skin: *The bullet went straight through the flesh of his arm.*
2 the soft part that is inside a fruit or vegetable

flew /fluː/ → see **fly**

flexible /'fleksɪbəl/ *adjective*
1 bending easily without breaking: *These children's books have flexible plastic covers.*
2 able to change easily: *I'm very lucky to have flexible working hours.*
▶ **flexibility** *uncountable noun* *It's possible to go there by bus, but a car gives more flexibility.*

flick /flɪk/ *noun*
a quick, sharp movement: *The pony gave a quick flick of its tail.* ● **flick** *verb* (**flicks, flicking, flicked**) *He shook his head to flick hair out of his eyes.*

flicker /'flɪkə/ *verb* (**flickers, flickering, flickered**)
to shine in a way that is not steady:

The lights flickered, and suddenly it was dark.

● **flicker** *noun* *He could see the flicker of flames.*

flight /flaɪt/ *noun*

1 a trip in an aircraft: *The flight to New York will take four hours.* □ *Our flight was two hours late.*

2 a set of stairs that go from one level to another: *Ashley walked up the short flight of steps.*

3 *uncountable* the action of flying: *The photograph showed an eagle in flight.*

fling /flɪŋ/ *verb* (**flings, flinging, flung**)
to throw something somewhere using a lot of force: *She flung down the magazine and ran from the room.*

flip /flɪp/ *verb* (**flips, flipping, flipped**)
to turn over quickly: *The car flipped over and burst into flames.*

flip through something to turn the pages of a book quickly: *He was flipping through a magazine in the living room.*

flipper /ˈflɪpə/ *noun*
a long, flat rubber shoe that you wear to help you to swim faster

flirt ¹ /flɜːt/ *verb* (**flirts, flirting, flirted**)
to behave towards someone in a way that shows that you think they are attractive: *My brother was flirting with all the girls.*

flirt ² /flɜːt/ *noun*
a person who likes to flirt a lot: *I'm not a flirt. I'm only interested in my boyfriend.*

float ¹ /fləʊt/ *verb* (**floats, floating, floated**)

float

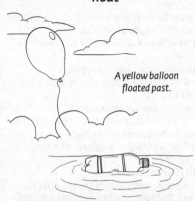

A yellow balloon floated past.

A plastic bottle was floating in the water.

1 to stay on the surface of a liquid, and not sink: *A plastic bottle was floating in the water.*

2 to move slowly and gently through the air: *A yellow balloon floated past.*

float ² /fləʊt/ *noun*
an object that stays on the surface of the water and supports your body while you are learning to swim

flock /flɒk/ *noun*
a group of birds, sheep or goats: *A flock of birds flew overhead.*

flood ¹ /flʌd/ *noun*
an occasion when a lot of water covers land that is usually dry: *More than 70 people died in the floods.*

in floods of tears crying a lot

flood ² /flʌd/ *verb* (**floods, flooding, flooded**)
to fill an area with water: *The water tank burst and flooded the house.*

▶ **flooding** *uncountable noun* *The flooding is the worst in sixty-five years.*

floodlight /ˈflʌdlaɪt/ *noun*
a very powerful light that is used outside for lighting public buildings and sports grounds at night

floor /flɔː/ *noun*

1 the part of a room that you walk on: *There were no seats, so we sat on the floor.*

2 all the rooms that are on a particular level of a building: *The café was on the seventh floor.*

> **LANGUAGE HELP**
>
> In British English, the **ground floor** of a building is the floor that is level with the street. The floor on the next level is called the **first floor**. In American English, the **first floor** is the floor that is level with the street, and the next floor up is the **second floor**.

flop /flɒp/ *verb* (**flops, flopping, flopped**)
to sit down suddenly and heavily because you are so tired: *Ben flopped down on to the bed and fell asleep at once.*

floppy /ˈflɒpi/ *adjective* (**floppier, floppiest**)
loose, and hanging down: *Stephanie was wearing a blue floppy hat.*

florist /ˈflɒrɪst/ *noun*

1 a person who works in a shop that sells flowers

2 (*also* **florist's**) a shop where you can buy flowers

flour /'flaʊə/ *uncountable noun*
a fine powder that is used for making bread, cakes and pastry

flourish /'flʌrɪʃ/ *verb* (**flourishes, flourishing, flourished**)
to grow or develop very well: *This plant flourishes in warm climates.* □ *Heckart's career really flourished in the 1950s.*

flow /fləʊ/ *verb* (**flows, flowing, flowed**)
to move somewhere in a steady and continuous way: *A stream flowed gently down into the valley.* ● **flow** *uncountable noun* *Vicky tried to stop the flow of blood.* □ *The new tunnel will speed up traffic flow.*

flower¹ /'flaʊə/ *noun*
the brightly coloured part of a plant: *Dad gave Mum a huge bunch of flowers.*

flower² /'flaʊə/ *verb* (**flowers, flowering, flowered**)
to produce flowers: *These plants will flower soon.*

flown /fləʊn/ → see **fly**

flu /fluː/ *uncountable noun*
an illness that is like a very bad cold; short for 'influenza'

fluent /'fluːənt/ *adjective*
able to speak a particular language easily and correctly: *Jose is fluent in Spanish and English.*
▶ **fluently** *adverb* *He spoke three languages fluently.*

fluffy /'flʌfi/ *adjective* (**fluffier, fluffiest**)
very soft: *I dried myself with a big fluffy towel.*

fluid /'fluːɪd/ *noun*
a liquid (*formal*): *Make sure that you drink plenty of fluids.*

flung /flʌŋ/ → see **fling**

flush /flʌʃ/ *verb* (**flushes, flushing, flushed**)
1 to clean a toilet with water by pressing or pulling a handle: *I heard someone flushing the toilet.*
2 if you flush, your face becomes red because you are hot, ill, embarrassed or angry: *Amanda flushed with embarrassment.*
▶ **flushed** *adjective* *Her face was flushed with anger.*

flute /fluːt/ *noun*
a musical instrument that you play by

blowing. You hold it sideways to your mouth.

flutter /'flʌtə/ *verb* (**flutters, fluttering, fluttered**)
to make a lot of quick, light movements: *The butterfly fluttered its wings.*

fly¹ /flaɪ/ *noun*
a small insect with two wings

fly² /flaɪ/ *verb* (**flies, flying, flew, flown**)
1 to move through the air: *The planes flew through the clouds.*
2 to travel somewhere in an aircraft: *Jerry flew to Los Angeles this morning.*
3 to make an aircraft move through the air: *He flew a small plane to Cuba.* □ *I learnt to fly in Vietnam.*

flyer /'flaɪə/ *also* **flier** *noun*
a small printed notice that advertises something: *A tall girl gave us a flyer for the concert.*

foam /fəʊm/ *uncountable noun*
the mass of small bubbles that you sometimes see on the surface of a liquid: *He drank his coffee, and wiped the foam off his moustache.*

focus¹ /'fəʊkəs/ *verb* (**focuses, focusing, focused**)
1 to give all your attention to something: *Voters are now focusing on the war.*
2 to make changes to a camera so that you can see clearly through it: *The camera was focused on his terrified face.*

focus² /'fəʊkəs/ *noun*
the person or thing that everyone is looking at: *Wherever she goes, she's the focus of attention.*

in focus clear and sharp: *Make sure that the subject of the photo is in focus.*

out of focus unclear: *The photo was out of focus.*

foetus /'fiːtəs/ *noun* (**foetuses**)
an animal or a human being before it is born

fog /fɒg/ *uncountable noun*
thick cloud that is close to the ground: *The car crash happened in thick fog.*
▶ **foggy** (**foggier, foggiest**) *adjective* *a foggy day*

foil /fɔɪl/ *uncountable noun*
very thin metal sheets that you use for covering food: *Cover the turkey with foil and cook it for another 20 minutes.*

fold /fəʊld/ *verb* (**folds, folding, folded**)
to bend a piece of paper or cloth so that one part covers another **fold your arms** part: *He folded the paper carefully.* ▢ *I folded the towels and put them in the cupboard.* ● **fold** *noun*
Make another fold down the middle of the paper.
fold your arms to put one arm under the other and hold them over your chest

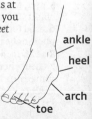

folder /'fəʊldə/ *noun*
1 a folded piece of cardboard or plastic that you keep papers in: *a work folder*
2 a group of files that are stored together on a computer: *I deleted the folder by mistake.*

folk¹ /fəʊk/ *plural noun*
1 people: *Most folk around here think she's crazy.*
2 your mother and father (*informal*): *I'll introduce you to my folks.*

folk² /fəʊk/ *adjective*
used for describing art, customs and music that belong to a particular group of people or country: *This is a collection of traditional folk music from nearly 30 countries.*

folk music /'fəʊk ˌmjuːzɪk/ *uncountable noun*
music that is traditional or typical of a particular group of people or country: *I listen to a variety of music including classical and folk music.*

follow /'fɒləʊ/ *verb* (**follows, following, followed**)
1 to move along behind someone: *We followed him up the steps.* ▢ *Please follow me, madam.* ▢ *She realized that the car was following her.*
2 to go somewhere using a path to direct you: *All we had to do was follow the road.*
3 to do something in the way that an instruction says: *Follow the instructions carefully.*
4 to understand an explanation or a film: *Can you follow the story so far?* ▢ *I'm sorry, I don't follow.*
5 to choose to receive messages that a particular person posts on a social networking site

as follows used for introducing a list or an explanation: *The winners are as follows: E. Walker; R. Foster; R. Gates.*

following /'fɒləʊɪŋ/ *adjective*
used for describing the day, week or year after the one you have just mentioned: *We had dinner together on Friday and then met for lunch the following day.*

fond /fɒnd/ *adjective* (**fonder, fondest**)
liking someone or something very much: *I am very fond of Michael.* ▢ *Dad's fond of singing.* ▢ *Mrs Johnson was very fond of cats.*

font /fɒnt/ *noun*
a set of letters of the same style and size: *You can change the font so that it's easier to read.*

food /fuːd/ *noun*
what people and animals eat: *The waitress brought our meal and said, 'Enjoy your food!'* ▢ *The people were starving — there was no food to eat.*
→ Look at pictures on P2–3

'food chain *noun*
the natural process by which one living thing is eaten by another, which is then eaten by another, and so on

fool¹ /fuːl/ *noun*
a stupid or silly person: *I didn't understand anything. I felt like a fool.*
make a fool of someone to make someone seem silly by telling people about something stupid that they have done, or by tricking them: *Your brother is making a fool of you.*

fool² /fuːl/ *verb* (**fools, fooling, fooled**)
to make someone believe something that is not true: *Harris fooled people into believing she was a doctor.*
fool around to behave in a silly way: *They fool around and get into trouble at school.*

foolish /'fuːlɪʃ/ *adjective*
stupid: *It would be foolish to ignore the risks.*
▶ **foolishly** *adverb* *He knows that he acted foolishly.*

foot /fʊt/ *noun* (**feet**)
1 the part of your body that is at the end of your leg, and that you stand on: *We danced until our feet were sore.* ▢ *He's suffering from a foot injury.*
→ Look at picture on P1
2 a unit for measuring length. A foot is equal to

foot

ankle

heel

arch

toe

30.48 centimetres. There are 12 inches in a foot. The plural form is **feet** or **foot**: *We were six thousand feet above sea level.* □ *The room is 10 foot long and 6 foot wide.*

3 the part of something that is furthest from its top: *He was waiting at the foot of the stairs.*

on foot walking: *We explored the island on foot.*

on your feet standing up: *Everyone was on their feet shouting and clapping.*

put your feet up to have a rest: *I'll do the chores, so you can put your feet up.*

football /ˈfʊtbɔːl/ *noun*
1 *uncountable* a game for two teams of eleven players. Each team tries to win points by kicking the ball into an area at the other end of the field: *Paul loves playing football.*
2 a ball that is used for playing football: *Antonio kicked the football off the pitch.*
→ Look at picture on P6

footballer /ˈfʊtbɔːlə/ *noun*
a person who plays football

footpath /ˈfʊtpɑːθ/ *noun*
a path for people to walk on, especially in the countryside

footprint /ˈfʊtprɪnt/ *noun*
the mark that your foot makes on the ground

footstep /ˈfʊtstep/ *noun*
the sound that you make each time your foot touches the ground when you are walking: *I heard footsteps outside.*

for /fə, STRONG fɔː/ *preposition*
1 used for saying who will have or use something: *These flowers are for you.*
□ *I reserved a table for two at the restaurant.*
2 used for saying which person or company employs you: *He works for a bank.*
3 done so that someone else does not have to do it: *I held the door open for the next person.*
4 used for describing a word that has the same meaning as another word: *In French, the word for 'love' is 'amour'.*
5 used for describing the purpose of an object: *This knife is for slicing bread.*
6 used for saying where a bus, train, plane or boat is going: *They took the train for Rio early the next morning.*
7 used when you are saying how long something lasts: *We talked for about half an hour.*

8 used for saying how far someone or something goes: *We continued to drive for a few miles.*
9 used for giving the price of something that you buy: *The Martins sold their house for £1.4 million.*
10 agreeing with or supporting someone or something: *Well, are you for us or against us?*
11 as part of a particular team: *Kerry plays hockey for the school team.*

forbid /fəˈbɪd/ *verb* (**forbids, forbidding, forbade, forbidden**)
to tell someone that they must not do something: *My parents have forbidden me to see my boyfriend.*

forbidden /fəˈbɪdən/ *adjective*
not allowed: *Smoking is forbidden here.*

force¹ /fɔːs/ *verb* (**forces, forcing, forced**)
1 to make someone do something when they do not want to: *They forced him to give them the money.*
2 to break the lock of a door or a window: *Police forced the door of the flat and arrested Mr Roberts.*

force² /fɔːs/ *noun*
1 *uncountable* strength used for doing something: *Police used force to break up the fight.*
2 *uncountable* the power or strength that something has: *The force of the explosion destroyed the building.*
3 a group of people, for example soldiers or police officers, who do a particular job: *Russian forces entered the region in 1994.*

forecast¹ /ˈfɔːkɑːst/ *noun*
what someone expects will happen in the future: *Did you see the weather forecast?*

forecast² /ˈfɔːkɑːst/ *verb* (**forecasts, forecasting, forecast** or **forecasted**)
to say what you think is going to happen in the future: *Economists were forecasting higher oil prices.*
▶ **forecaster** *noun* *David worked for 34 years as a weather forecaster.*

foreground /ˈfɔːɡraʊnd/ *noun*
the part of a picture that seems nearest to you. Compare with **background**: *There are five people and a dog in the foreground of the painting.*

forehead /ˈfɔːhed/ *noun*
the front part of your head between your eyebrows and your hair

foreign /'fɒrɪn/ *adjective*
coming from a country that is not your own: *It's good to learn a foreign language.*

foreigner /'fɒrɪnə/ *noun*
someone who comes from a different country

foresee /fɔː'siː/ *verb* (**foresees, foreseeing, foresaw, foreseen**)
to expect and believe that something will happen: *He did not foresee any problems.*

forest /'fɒrɪst/ *noun*
a large area where trees grow close together: *a forest fire*

forever /fə'revə/ *adverb*
used for saying that something will never change: *I think that we will live together forever.* □ *His pain was gone forever.*

foreword /'fɔːwɜːd/ *noun*
an introduction to a book: *She has written the foreword to a cookbook.*

forgave /fə'geɪv/ → see **forgive**

forge /fɔːdʒ/ *verb* (**forges, forging, forged**)
to make illegal copies of paper money, a document or a painting in order to cheat people: *He admitted to forging passports.* □ *They used forged documents to leave the country.*
▶ **forger** *noun He's an expert art forger.*

forgery /'fɔːdʒəri/ *noun* (**forgeries**)
1 something that has been forged: *The letter was a forgery.*
2 *uncountable* the crime of forging money, documents or paintings: *He was convicted of forgery.*

forget /fə'get/ *verb* (**forgets, forgetting, forgot, forgotten**)
1 to not remember something: *He never forgets his dad's birthday.* □ *I forgot to lock the door.*
2 to not bring something with you: *When we reached the airport, I realized I'd forgotten my passport.*
3 to deliberately put something out of your mind: *You will soon forget the bad experience you had today.*

> **LANGUAGE HELP**
> If you want to say that you put something somewhere and left it there, use the verb **leave**. *I left my bag on the bus.*

forgetful /fə'getfʊl/ *adjective*
often forgetting things: *My mother became very forgetful and confused when she got old.*

forgive /fə'gɪv/ *verb* (**forgives, forgiving, forgave, forgiven**)
to stop being angry with someone who has done something bad or wrong: *Hopefully Jane will understand and forgive you.* □ *Irene forgave Terry for stealing her money.*

forgot /fə'gɒt/ → see **forget**

forgotten /fə'gɒtən/ → see **forget**

fork /fɔːk/ *noun*
1 a tool with long metal points, used for eating food: *Please use your knife and fork.*
2 a place where a road, path or river divides into two parts and forms a 'Y' shape: *We arrived at a fork in the road.* ● **fork** *verb* (**forks, forking, forked**) *Jan stopped where the path forked.*

fork

form¹ /fɔːm/ *noun*
1 a type of something: *She has a rare form of the disease.* □ *I am against violence in any form.*
2 the shape of something or the way it appears: *The dress fits the form of her body exactly.*
3 a piece of paper with questions on it and spaces where you should write the answers: *Please fill in this form and sign it at the bottom.*
4 a class in a school: *He's in the sixth form of the local school.*
5 the way that a noun or a verb is spelled or spoken when it is used for talking about the plural, the past or the present, for example

form² /fɔːm/ *verb* (**forms, forming, formed**)
1 to make a particular shape: *Form a diamond shape with your legs.*
2 to make something: *These articles formed the basis of Randolph's book.*
3 to start an organization: *They tried to form a study group on human rights.*

f

formal /'fɔːməl/ *adjective*
very correct and serious rather than relaxed and friendly: *We received a very formal letter of apology.*
▸ **formally** *adverb* *He spoke formally, and without expression.*
▸ **formality** *uncountable noun* *Lilly's formality and seriousness amused him.*

format /'fɔːmæt/ *noun*
the way in which the text of a computer document is arranged: *You can change the format of your document from two columns to three.* ● **format** *verb* (**formats, formatting, formatted**) *The software can automatically format the text in a document as you type it.*

formation /fɔː'meɪʃən/ *uncountable noun*
the beginning of the existence of something: *The vitamin is essential for the formation of red blood cells.*

former ¹ /'fɔːmə/ *adjective*
used for saying that a person or thing was something in the past, but is not that thing now: *There was an interview with the former president, Richard Nixon.*

former ² /'fɔːmə/ *pronoun*
used for talking about the first of two people or things that have just been mentioned: *Both the seeds and the leaves are useful — the former for soups, and the latter for salads.*

formerly /'fɔːməli/ *adverb*
in the past, but not now: *He was formerly in the navy.*

formidable /'fɔːmɪdəbəl, fə'mɪd-/ *adjective*
making you feel slightly frightened: *We have a formidable task ahead of us.*

formula /'fɔːmjʊlə/ *noun* (**formulae** /'fɔːmjʊliː/ or **formulas**)
1 a group of letters, numbers or other symbols that represents a scientific rule: *This mathematical formula describes the distances of the planets from the Sun.*
2 a description of the chemical elements that a substance contains: *Glucose and fructose have the same chemical formula.*

fort /fɔːt/ *noun*
a strong building that is used as a military base

fortnight /'fɔːtnaɪt/ *noun*
a period of two weeks: *I'll be back in a fortnight.*

fortress /'fɔːtrɪs/ *noun* (**fortresses**)
a castle or other large strong building that is difficult for enemies to enter

fortunate /'fɔːtʃʊnɪt/ *adjective*
lucky: *He was extremely fortunate to survive.*

fortunately /'fɔːtʃʊnətli/ *adverb*
said when you start to talk about an event or a situation that is good: *Fortunately, the weather last winter was good.*

fortune /'fɔːtʃuːn/ *noun*
1 a very large amount of money: *He made a fortune buying and selling houses.*
2 *uncountable* luck: *Patrick still can't believe his good fortune.*

forty /'fɔːti/
the number 40
▸ **fortieth** /'fɔːtiəθ/ *adjective, adverb* *It was the fortieth anniversary of his death.*

forward /'fɔːwəd/ *verb* (**forwards, forwarding, forwarded**)
to send a letter or an email to someone after you have received it: *He asks each person to forward the email to 10 other people.*

forwards /'fɔːwədz/ or **forward** *adverb*
1 in a direction that is in front of you: *He came forward and asked for help.* □ *She fell forwards on to her face.*
2 in a position near the front of something: *Try to get a seat as far forwards as possible.*

forward slash *noun* (**forward slashes**)
the sloping line / that separates letters, words or numbers, for example in Internet addresses

fossil /'fɒsəl/ *noun*
the part of a plant or an animal that died a long time ago and has turned into rock

fossil fuel *noun*
a substance such as coal or oil that is found in the ground and used for producing power: *When we burn fossil fuels, we use oxygen and produce carbon dioxide.*

foster /'fɒstə/ *adjective*
used for describing someone who is paid by the government to take care of other people's children for a period of time: *living with foster parents*

fought /fɔːt/ → see **fight**

foul ¹ /faʊl/ *adjective* (**fouler, foulest**)
1 dirty, and smelling or tasting unpleasant: *foul, polluted water*
2 offensive and containing rude words: *The play was full of foul language.*

foul² /faʊl/ *noun*

a move in a game or a sport that is not allowed according to the rules: *He has committed more fouls than any other player this season.*

found¹ /faʊnd/ → see **find**

found² /faʊnd/ *verb* (**founds, founding, founded**)

to start an organization: *The charity was founded in 1892.*

▶ **founder** *noun He was one of the founders of the United Nations.*

foundation /faʊn'deɪʃən/ *noun*

1 *plural* the bricks, stones or concrete that a building is built on: *the building's foundations*

2 an organization that provides money for a special purpose: *the National Foundation for Educational Research*

fountain /'faʊntɪn/ *noun*

1 a structure in a pool or a lake where water is forced up into the air and falls down again

2 a piece of equipment that you can drink water from in a public place

four /fɔː/

the number 4

fourteen /ˌfɔː'tiːn/

the number 14

▶ **fourteenth** /ˌfɔː'tiːnθ/ *adjective, adverb The festival is now in its fourteenth year.*

fourth /fɔːθ/ *adjective, adverb*

the item in a series that you count as number four: *Last year's winner is in fourth place in today's race.*

fowl /faʊl/ *noun* (**fowl**)

a bird that can be eaten as food, such as a chicken

fox /fɒks/ *noun* (**foxes**)

a wild animal that looks like a dog, has red fur and a thick tail

fracking /'frækɪŋ/ *uncountable noun*

a method of getting oil or gas from rock by forcing liquid into the rock

fraction /'frækʃən/ *noun*

1 a part of a whole number. For example, $\frac{1}{2}$ and $\frac{1}{3}$ are both fractions.

2 a very small amount of something: *She hesitated for a fraction of a second.*

fracture¹ /'fræktʃə/ *noun*

a break in something, especially a bone: *She suffered a hip fracture.*

fracture² /'fræktʃə/ *verb* (**fractures, fracturing, fractured**)

to develop a crack or a break in a bone: *He fractured several of his ribs.*

fragile /'frædʒaɪl/ *adjective*

easily broken or damaged: *His fragile bones are the result of a bad diet.*

fragment /'frægmənt/ *noun*

a small piece of something: *We tried to pick up the tiny fragments of glass.*

fragrance /'freɪgrəns/ *noun*

a pleasant or sweet smell: *The cream is easy to apply and has a pleasant fragrance.*

frail /freɪl/ *adjective* (**frailer, frailest**)

not very strong or healthy: *He looked very frail in his hospital bed.*

frame /freɪm/ *noun*

the wood, metal or plastic around a picture: *She had a photograph of her mother in a silver frame.* ●**frame** *verb* (**frames, framing, framed**) *The picture has already been framed and hung on the wall.*

framework /'freɪmwɜːk/ *noun*

a structure that forms a support for something: *The wooden shelves sit on a steel framework.*

frank /fræŋk/ *adjective* (**franker, frankest**)

saying things in an open and honest way: *My husband has not been frank with me.*

▶ **frankly** *adverb You can talk frankly to me.*

frankly /'fræŋkli/ *adverb*

used when you are going to say something that may be surprising or direct: *Frankly, I don't care.*

frantic /'fræntɪk/ *adjective*

very frightened or worried, and not knowing what to do: *They became frantic when their 4-year-old son did not return.*

▶ **frantically** /'fræntɪkli/ *adverb Two people were waving frantically from the boat.*

fraud /frɔːd/ *noun*

the crime of getting money by not telling the truth: *He was jailed for two years for fraud.*

freak¹ /friːk/ *adjective*

very unusual: *James broke his leg in a freak accident playing golf.*

freak² /friːk/ *noun*

1 an unfriendly word for someone whose behaviour or appearance is very unusual: *I'm not a freak — I'm just like you guys.*

2 someone with a very strong interest in something (*informal*): *a health freak*

freckle /ˈfrekəl/ *noun*
a small light-brown spot on your skin, especially on your face: *He had short red hair and freckles.*

free¹ /friː/ *adjective* (**freer, freest**)
1 used for describing things that you do not have to pay for: *The classes are free, with lunch provided.*
2 not controlled by rules or other people: *They are free to bring their friends home at any time.*
▶ **freely** *adverb They all express their opinions freely in class.*
3 used for describing someone who is not a prisoner: *He walked from the court a free man.*
4 not busy: *She spent her free time shopping.*
5 not being used by anyone: *Is this seat free?*

free² /friː/ *verb* (**frees, freeing, freed**)
to help someone or something to get out of a place: *Rescue workers freed him from the car.*

freedom /ˈfriːdəm/ *uncountable noun*
the state of being able to do what you want to do: *They enjoy the freedom to spend their money as they wish.* □ *We are fighting for freedom of choice.*

freeze /friːz/ *verb* (**freezes, freezing, froze, frozen**)
1 to become solid because the temperature is low: *If the temperature drops below 0 ˚C, water freezes.* □ *The ground froze solid.*
▶ **freezing** *uncountable noun The damage was caused by freezing and thawing.*
2 to make food or drink very cold in order to preserve it
3 to stand completely still: *'Freeze', shouted the police officer.*

freezer /ˈfriːzə/ *noun*
a large container or part of a fridge used for freezing food
→ Look at picture on P4

freezing /ˈfriːzɪŋ/ *adjective*
1 very cold: *The cinema was freezing.*
2 feeling very cold: *'You must be freezing', she said.*

freight /freɪt/ *uncountable noun*
goods that are moved by lorries, trains, ships or aeroplanes: *a freight train*

French fries /ˌfrentʃ ˈfraɪz/ *plural noun*
(*American*)
→ see **chips**

French horn /ˌfrentʃ ˈhɔːn/ *noun*
a musical instrument shaped like a long round metal tube with one wide end, that is played by blowing into it

frequency /ˈfriːkwənsi/ *noun*
(**frequencies**)
1 *uncountable* the number of times an event happens: *The frequency of Kara's phone calls increased.*
2 the number of times a sound wave or a radio wave vibrates (= moves quickly up and down) within a period of time: *You can't hear waves of such a high frequency.*

frequent /ˈfriːkwənt/ *adjective*
happening often: *There are frequent trains from London to Paris.*
▶ **frequently** *adverb He was frequently unhappy.*

fresh /freʃ/ *adjective* (**fresher, freshest**)
1 picked, caught or produced recently: *We only sell fresh fish that has been caught locally.*
2 done, made or experienced recently: *There were fresh car tracks in the snow.*
▶ **freshly** *adverb We bought some freshly-baked bread.*
3 used for describing something that smells, tastes or feels clean or cool: *The air was fresh and she immediately felt better.*
4 replacing or added to an existing thing or amount: *The waiter placed a fresh glass on the table.*

Friday /ˈfraɪdeɪ, -di/ *noun*
the day after Thursday and before Saturday: *He is going home on Friday.* □ *Friday 6 November*

fridge /frɪdʒ/ or **refrigerator** *noun*
a large container that is kept cool inside, usually by electricity, so that the food and drink in it stays fresh
→ Look at picture on P4

friend /frend/ *noun*
someone who you like and know well: *She's my best friend.* □ *She was never a close friend of mine.*

be friends if you are friends with someone, you are their friend and they are yours: *I still wanted to be friends with Alison.* □ *We remained good friends.*

make friends to meet someone and become their friend: *He has made friends with the kids on the street.* □ *Dennis made friends easily.*

friendly /'frendli/ *adjective* (**friendlier, friendliest**)

behaving in a pleasant, kind way: *Godfrey was friendly to me.* □ *The man had a pleasant, friendly face.*

friendship /'frendʃɪp/ *noun*

a relationship between two or more friends: *Their friendship has lasted more than sixty years.*

fries /fraɪz/ *plural noun* (American)
→ see **chips**

fright /fraɪt/ *noun*

1 *uncountable* a sudden feeling of fear: *There was a loud noise, and Franklin jumped with fright.*

2 an experience that makes you suddenly afraid: *The snake raised its head, which gave everyone a fright.*

frighten /'fraɪtən/ *verb* (**frightens, frightening, frightened**)

to make you suddenly feel afraid, anxious or nervous: *He knew that Soli was trying to frighten him.*

frightened /'fraɪtənd/ *adjective*

anxious or afraid: *She was frightened of making a mistake.*

frightening /'fraɪtənɪŋ/ *adjective*

making you feel afraid, anxious or nervous: *It was a very frightening experience.*

frill /frɪl/ *noun*

a long narrow strip of cloth or paper with a lot of folds in it, used as a decoration: *She loves party dresses with ribbons and frills.*

fringe /frɪndʒ/ *noun*

1 (American: **bangs**) hair which is cut so that it hangs over your forehead: *She has a short fringe.*

2 a row of hanging threads that is used for decorating a piece of cloth: *The jacket had leather fringes on the sleeves.*

frog /frɒg/ *noun*

a small animal with smooth skin, big eyes and long back legs that it uses for jumping. Frogs live in or near water.

from /frəm, STRONG frɒm/ *preposition*

1 used for saying who has sent or given something to you: *I received a letter from Mary yesterday.* □ *The watch was a present from his wife.*

2 used for saying where someone lives or was born: *I come from New Zealand.*

3 leaving a place: *Everyone watched as she ran from the room.* □ *Mr Baker travelled from Washington to London for the meeting.*

4 used when you are talking about how far away something is: *The park is only a hundred yards from the centre of town.* □ *How far is the hotel from here?*

5 used for saying what was used for making something: *This bread is made from white flour.* □ *The cans are made from steel.*

6 used for saying that something stops being the first thing and becomes the second thing: *Unemployment fell from 7.5 to 7.2%.*

7 used for talking about the beginning of a period of time: *Breakfast is available from 6 a.m.* □ *She works from seven in the morning until six in the evening.*

front ¹ /frʌnt/ *noun*

the part of something that faces you, or that is nearest the direction it faces: *Stand at the front of the queue.* □ *Children under the age of three may not sit in the front of the car.*

in front

1 ahead of others in a moving group: *Don't drive too close to the car in front.*

2 winning a competition: *Richard Dunwoody is in front in the race.*

in front of someone when someone is present: *They never argued in front of their children.*

in front of something facing a particular thing, ahead of it or close to the front part of it: *She sat down in front of her mirror.* □ *A child ran in front of my car.*

front ² /frʌnt/ *adjective*

in or on the front of something: *Helen came to the front door.* □ *I've broken my front tooth.*

frontier /'frʌntɪə, -'tɪə/ *noun*

the border between two countries: *They both showed their passports at the Russian frontier.*

frost /frɒst/ *uncountable noun*

ice like white powder that forms outside when the weather is very cold: *There was frost on my windscreen this morning.*

▸ **frosty** *adjective* (**frostier, frostiest**) *a cold and frosty night*

frown /fraʊn/ *verb* (**frowns, frowning, frowned**)

to move your eyebrows together because you are annoyed, worried or confused, or because you are concentrating: *Nancy*

f

shook her head, frowning. □ He frowned at her anxiously. ● **frown** *noun* There was a deep frown on the boy's face.

froze /frəʊz/ → see **freeze**

frozen[1] /'frəʊzən/ → see **freeze**

frozen[2] /'frəʊzən/ *adjective*
1 hard because the weather is very cold: It was extremely cold and the ground was frozen hard.
2 used for describing food that has been stored at a very low temperature: Frozen fish is a healthy convenience food.
3 very cold: I'm frozen out here.

fruit /fruːt/ *noun* (**fruit**)

> **LANGUAGE HELP**
> If you are talking about different types of fruit, you can refer to these as **fruits**.

the part of a tree that contains seeds, covered with a substance that you can often eat: Fresh fruit and vegetables provide fibre and vitamins. □ We grow bananas and other tropical fruits here.

frustrate /frʌ'streɪt/ *verb* (**frustrates, frustrating, frustrated**)
to upset someone or make them angry because there is nothing they can do about a problem: His lack of ambition frustrated me.
▶ **frustrated** *adjective* Roberta felt frustrated and angry.
▶ **frustrating** *adjective* This situation is very frustrating for us.
▶ **frustration** /frʌ'streɪʃən/ *uncountable noun* The team was showing signs of frustration.

fry /fraɪ/ *verb* (**fries, frying, fried**)
to cook food in hot fat or oil: Fry the onions until they are brown.

frying pan *noun*
a flat metal pan with a long handle, in which you fry food

fuel /'fjuːəl/ *noun*
a substance such as coal or oil that is burned to provide heat or power: They bought some fuel on the motorway.

fulfil /fʊl'fɪl/ *verb* (**fulfils, fulfilling, fulfilled**)
to manage to do what you said or hoped you would do: She fulfilled her dream of starting law school.

full /fʊl/ *adjective* (**fuller, fullest**)
1 containing as much liquid or as many people or things as possible: The petrol tank was full. □ Her case was full of clothes. □ Sorry.

The bus is full. □ You'll have to get the next one.
2 feeling that you do not want any more food: You should stop eating when you're full.
3 complete, with nothing missing: For full details of the event, visit our website.
4 used when you are saying that something is as big, loud, strong, fast, etc. as possible: The car crashed into the wall at full speed.

a full moon when the moon looks like a complete circle

full name your first name, other names that you may have and your family name: 'May I have your full name?' — 'Yes, it's Patricia Mary White.'

in full completely, giving every detail: Mr Thompson signed his name in full.

full 'stop (American: **period**) *noun*
the mark (.) used in writing at the end of a sentence when it is not a question or an exclamation

'full-'time also **full time** *adjective*
for all of each normal working week: I'm looking for a full-time job. ● **full-time** *adverb* Deirdre works full time.

fully /'fʊli/ *adverb*
completely: We are fully aware of the problem. □ He promised to answer fully and truthfully.

fun[1] /fʌn/ *uncountable noun*
pleasure and enjoyment: It could be fun to watch them. □ Liz was always so much fun.

for fun as a joke, without wanting to cause any harm: Don't say such things, even for fun.

make fun of someone/something to laugh at someone or something, or make jokes about them: Don't make fun of me.

fun[2] /fʌn/ *adjective*
pleasant and enjoyable: The course is interesting and it's also fun.

function[1] /'fʌŋkʃən/ *noun*
1 the purpose of a thing or a person: One of the main functions of the skin is protection.
2 a large formal dinner or party: He attended a private function hosted by one of his students.

function[2] /'fʌŋkʃən/ *verb* (**functions, functioning, functioned**)
to work well: Your heart is functioning normally.

functional /'fʌŋkʃənəl/ *adjective*
1 useful rather than decorative: I like modern, functional furniture.

2 working properly: *We have fully functional smoke alarms on all staircases.*

fund¹ /fʌnd/ *noun*

1 *plural* amounts of money that are available to be spent: *We're having a concert to raise funds for cancer research.*
2 an amount of money that people save for a particular purpose: *There is a scholarship fund for engineering students.*

fund² /fʌnd/ *verb* (**funds, funding, funded**)
to provide money for something: *The Foundation has funded a variety of projects.*

fundamental /ˌfʌndə'mentəl/ *adjective*
very important and necessary: *We all have a fundamental right to protect ourselves.*

funding /'fʌndɪŋ/ *uncountable noun*
money that a government or organization provides for a particular purpose: *They are hoping to get government funding for the programme.*

'fund-raising also **fundraising**
uncountable noun
the activity of collecting money for a particular use

funeral /'fjuːnərəl/ *noun*
a ceremony that takes place when the body of someone who has died is buried or cremated (= burned): *The funeral will be in Edinburgh.*

fungus /'fʌŋgəs/ *noun* (**fungi** /'fʌŋgiː, 'fʌndʒaɪ/ or **funguses**)
a plant that has no flowers, leaves or green colour, and grows in wet places: *There were mushrooms and other fungi growing out of the wall.* □ *This fungus likes living in warm, wet places.*

funnel /'fʌnəl/ *noun*   **funnel**
1 a tube with a wide, round top, used for pouring liquids into a container such as a bottle
2 a tube on the top of a ship or railway engine where steam can escape

funny /'fʌni/ *adjective* (**funnier, funniest**)
1 amusing and likely to make you smile or laugh: *I'll tell you a funny story.*

2 strange, surprising or confusing: *Children get some very funny ideas sometimes!* □ *There's something funny about him.*
3 slightly ill (*informal*): *My head began to ache and my stomach felt funny.*

fur /fɜː/ *uncountable noun*
the thick hair that grows on the bodies of many animals: *This creature's fur is short and silky.*

furious /'fjʊəriəs/ *adjective*
extremely angry: *He is furious at the way he has been treated.*

furnace /'fɜːnɪs/ *noun*
a container with a very hot fire inside it, used for making glass or heating metal: *The iron bars glow in the red-hot furnace.*

furniture /'fɜːnɪtʃə/ *uncountable noun*
large objects such as tables, chairs or beds: *Each piece of furniture matched the style of the house.*

LANGUAGE HELP

Furniture is an uncountable noun. If you want to talk about a table, a chair, or a bed in general terms, you can say a **piece of furniture** or an **item of furniture**.

---

furry /'fɜːri/ *adjective* (**furrier, furriest**)
1 covered with thick, soft hair: *I love little furry animals.*
2 feeling similar to fur: *The leaves are soft and furry.*

further /'fɜːðə/ → see **far**

furthest /'fɜːðɪst/ → see **far**

fury /'fjʊəri/ *uncountable noun*
violent or very strong anger: *Her eyes were full of fury.*

fuse /fjuːz/ *noun*
a small wire in a piece of electrical equipment that stops it from working when too much electricity passes through it: *The fuse blew as he pressed the button to start the motor.*

fuss¹ /fʌs/ *noun*
anxious or excited behaviour that is not useful: *I don't know what all the fuss is about.*

fuss² /fʌs/ *verb* (**fusses, fussing, fussed**)
to worry or behave in a nervous, anxious way about things that are not important: *Carol fussed about getting me a drink.*

fuss over someone to pay someone a lot of attention and do things to make them happy or comfortable: *Aunt Laura fussed over him all afternoon.*

fussy /ˈfʌsi/ *adjective* (**fussier, fussiest**)
very difficult to please and interested in small details: *She is very fussy about her food.*

future¹ /ˈfjuːtʃə/ *noun*
1 the time that will come after now: *He was making plans for the future.*
2 what will happen to someone after the present time: *His future depends on the result of the election.*

in (the) future used when you are talking about what will happen after now: *I asked her to be more careful in the future.*

future² /ˈfjuːtʃə/ *adjective*
happening or existing after the present time: *The lives of future generations will be affected by our decisions.*

future ˈtense *noun*
the form of the verb that is used for talking about the time that will come after the present

Gg

gadget /'gædʒɪt/ *noun*
a small machine or useful object: *The shop sells computers and other electronic gadgets.*

gain /geɪn/ *verb* (gains, gaining, gained)
1 to get something: *You can gain access to the website for £14 a month.* □ *Students can gain valuable experience by working during their holidays.*
2 to have more of something: *Some women gain weight after they have a baby.* □ *The car was gaining speed as it came toward us.*

galaxy /'gæləksi/ *noun* (galaxies) also **Galaxy**
a very large group of stars and planets: *Astronomers have discovered a distant galaxy.*

gale /geɪl/ *noun*
a very strong wind: *A strong gale was blowing.*

gallery /'gæləri/ *noun* (galleries)
a place where people go to look at art: *We visited an art gallery.*

gallon /'gælən/ *noun*
a unit for measuring liquids. A gallon is equal to 4.546 litres. There are eight pints in a gallon: *The tank holds 1,000 gallons of water.*

gallop /'gæləp/ *verb* (gallops, galloping, galloped)
to run very fast: *The horses galloped away.*

gallop

gamble¹ /'gæmbəl/ *noun*
a risk that you take because you hope that something good will happen: *She took a gamble and started up her own business.*

gamble² /'gæmbəl/ *verb* (gambles, gambling, gambled)
1 to take a risk because you hope that something good will happen: *Companies sometimes have to gamble on new products.*
2 to risk money in a game or on the result of a race or competition: *John gambled heavily on horse racing.*
▸ **gambling** *uncountable noun* *The gambling laws are quite tough.*

gambler /'gæmblə/ *noun*
someone who risks money regularly, for example in card games or horse racing: *Her husband was a heavy gambler.*

game /geɪm/ *noun*
1 an activity or a sport in which you try to win: *Football is a popular game.* □ *We played a game of cards.*
2 one particular occasion when you play a game: *It was the first game of the season.*

'game ˌconsole *noun* or **games console**
a piece of electronic equipment that is used for playing computer games on a television screen: *More than half of six- to ten-year-olds have a games console.*

gang /gæŋ/ *noun*
1 a group of people, especially young people, who go around together and often deliberately cause trouble: *They had a fight with another gang.*
2 an organized group of criminals: *Police are hunting for a gang that has stolen several cars.*

gap /gæp/ *noun*
a space between two things, or a hole in something: *There was a narrow gap between the curtains.* □ *His horse escaped through a gap in the fence.*

garage /'gærɑːʒ, -rɪdʒ/ *noun*
1 a building where you keep a car: *The house has a large garage.*
2 a place where you can have your car repaired, and sometimes buy petrol and oil: *Nancy took her car to a local garage.*

garbage /'gɑːbɪdʒ/ *uncountable noun*
(*American*)
→ see **rubbish**

'**garbage can** *noun* (*American*)
→ see **dustbin**

garden¹ /'gɑːdən/ *noun*
1 (*American*: **yard**) the part of the land by your house where you grow flowers and vegetables: *She had a beautiful garden.*
2 *plural* places with plants, trees and grass, that people can visit: *The gardens are open from 10.30 a.m. until 5.00 p.m.*

garden² /'gɑːdən/ *verb* (**gardens, gardening, gardened**)
to do work in your garden: *Jim gardened at the weekends.*
▶ **gardening** *uncountable noun My favourite hobby is gardening.*

gardener /'gɑːdnə/ *noun*
a person who works in a garden: *She employed a gardener.*

garlic /'gɑːlɪk/ *uncountable noun*
a plant like a small onion with a strong flavour, which you use in cooking: *When the oil is hot, add a clove of garlic.*
→ Look at picture on P2

garment /'gɑːmənt/ *noun*
a piece of clothing: *Exports of garments to the U.S. fell by 3%.*

gas /gæs/ *noun* (**gases**)
1 any substance that is not a liquid or a solid: *Hydrogen is a gas, not a metal.*
2 *uncountable* a substance with a strong smell that is used for producing heat and for cooking: *a gas fire*
3 *uncountable* (*American*) → see **petrol**

gasoline /'gæsəliːn/ *uncountable noun*
(*American*)
→ see **petrol**

gasp /gɑːsp/ *verb* (**gasps, gasping, gasped**)
to take a short, quick breath through your mouth: *She gasped for air.* ● **gasp** *noun There was a gasp from the crowd as he scored the goal.*

gate /geɪt/ *noun*
1 a structure like a door that you use to enter a field, or the area around a building: *He opened the gate and walked up to the house.*
2 a place where passengers leave an airport and get on an aeroplane: *Please go to gate 15.*

gather /'gæðə/ *verb* (**gathers, gathering, gathered**)
1 to come together in a group: *We gathered*

around the fireplace and talked.
2 to collect things together so that you can use them: *They gathered enough firewood to make a fire.* □ *He used a hidden tape recorder to gather information.*

gathering /'gæðərɪŋ/ *noun*
an occasion when people meet together for a particular purpose: *They held a large family gathering.*

gauge¹ /geɪdʒ/ *verb* (**gauges, gauging, gauged**)
to measure or judge something: *She found it hard to gauge his mood.*

gauge² /geɪdʒ/ *noun*
a piece of equipment that measures the amount or level of something: *The temperature gauge showed that the water was boiling.*

gave /geɪv/ → see **give**

gay /geɪ/ *adjective*
attracted to people of the same sex: *The quality of life for gay men has improved.*

gaze /geɪz/ *verb* (**gazes, gazing, gazed**)
to look steadily at someone or something for a long time: *She was gazing at herself in the mirror.* □ *He gazed into the fire.*

gear /gɪə/ *noun*
1 a part of an engine that changes engine power into movement: *On a hill, use low gears.* □ *The car was in fourth gear.*
2 *uncountable* the equipment or special clothing that you use for a particular activity: *He took his fishing gear with him.* □ *camping gear*

'**gear stick** *noun*
the handle that you use to change gear in a car or other vehicle

geese /giːs/
the plural of **goose**

gel /dʒel/ *uncountable noun*
a thick substance like jelly, especially one that you use to keep your hair in a particular style or for washing your body: *shower gel*

gem /dʒem/ *noun*
a valuable stone that is used in jewellery: *precious gems*

gender /'dʒendə/ *noun*
the fact of being male or female: *We do not know the children's ages and genders.*

gene /dʒiːn/ *noun*
the part of a cell that controls a person's, an animal's or a plant's physical

characteristics, growth and development: *He carries the gene for red hair.*

general¹ /'dʒenrəl/ *adjective*
involving most people and things: *There is not enough general understanding of this problem.*

in general used for talking about something as a whole, rather than part of it: *We need to improve our educational system in general.*

general² /'dʒenrəl/ *noun*
an officer with a high rank in the army: *The troops received a visit from the general.*

general election *noun*
a time when people choose a new government

generalize /'dʒenrə,laɪz/ *verb*
(**generalizes, generalizing, generalized**)
to say something that is usually, but not always, true: *You shouldn't generalize and say that all men are the same.*

generally /'dʒenrəli/ *adverb*
1 used for describing something without giving any particular details: *He was generally a good man.*
2 used for saying that something usually happens, but not always: *It is generally true that darker fruits contain more iron.*

general practitioner /,dʒenrəl præk'tɪʃənə/ *noun*
→ see **GP**

generate /'dʒenə,reɪt/ *verb* (**generates, generating, generated**)
1 to cause something to exist: *The reforms will generate new jobs.*
2 to produce a form of energy or power: *We use oil to generate electricity.*

generation /,dʒenə'reɪʃən/ *noun*
all the people in a group or country who are of a similar age: *The current generation of teens are the richest in history.*

generator /'dʒenə,reɪtə/ *noun*
a machine that produces electricity: *The house has its own power generators.*

generous /'dʒenərəs/ *adjective*
giving you more than you expect of something: *He is generous with his money.*
▶ **generosity** /,dʒenə'rɒsɪti/ *uncountable noun* *Diana was surprised by his kindness and generosity.*
▶ **generously** *adverb* *We would like to thank everyone who generously gave their time.*

genetic /dʒə'netɪk/ *adjective*
related to genetics or genes: *a rare genetic disease*

genetically modified /dʒɪ'netɪkli 'mɒdɪ,faɪd/ *adjective*
used for describing plants and animals that have had their genetic structure (= pattern of chemicals in cells) changed in order to make them more suitable for a particular purpose. The short form **GM** is also used.

genetics /dʒɪ'netɪks/ *uncountable noun*
the study of how qualities are passed on from parents to children: *Genetics is changing our understanding of cancer.*

genius /'dʒiːniəs/ *noun* (**geniuses**)
a very skilled or intelligent person: *Chaplin was a comic genius.*

gentle /'dʒentəl/ *adjective* (**gentler, gentlest**)
1 kind, mild and calm: *My husband was a quiet and gentle man.*
▶ **gently** *adverb* *She smiled gently at him.*
2 slow or soft: *Rest and gentle exercise will make you feel better.*
▶ **gently** *adverb* *Patrick took her gently by the arm.*

gentleman /'dʒentəlmən/ *noun* (**gentlemen**)
1 a man who is polite, educated and kind to other people: *He was always such a gentleman.*
2 used for talking to men or for talking about them in a polite way: *This way, please, ladies and gentlemen.*

the gents /ðə 'dʒents/ *noun*
a public toilet for men (*informal*): *Excuse me, can you tell me where the gents is, please?*

genuine /'dʒenjʊɪn/ *adjective*
true and real: *He's a genuine American hero.* □ *We have a genuine friendship.*

genus /'dʒenəs/ *noun* (**genera** /dʒɛnərə/)
a type of animal or plant: *a genus of plants called 'Lonas'*

geography /dʒɪ'ɒgrəfi/ *uncountable noun*
the study of the countries of the world and things such as the land, seas, weather, towns, and population

geology /dʒɪ'ɒlədʒi/ *uncountable noun*
the study of the Earth's structure, surface and origins: *He was professor of geology at the University of Georgia.*

g

▶ **geologist** *noun* *Geologists have studied the way that heat flows from the Earth.*

geometry /dʒiˈɒmɪtri/ *uncountable noun*
a type of mathematics relating to lines, angles, curves and shapes.

germ /dʒɜːm/ *noun*
a very small living thing that can cause disease or illness: *This chemical is used for killing germs.*

gesture /ˈdʒestʃə/ *noun*
a movement that you make with a part of your body, especially your hands, to express emotion or information: *Sarah made a gesture with her fist.* ● **gesture** *verb* (**gestures, gesturing, gestured**) *I gestured toward the house.*

get¹ /get/ *auxiliary verb* (**gets, getting, got** or **gotten**)
used with another verb to show that something happens to someone (*informal*): *He got arrested for possession of drugs.*

get² /get/ *verb* (**gets, getting, got** or **gotten**)
1 to become: *The boys were getting bored.* □ *Don't worry. Things will get better.*
2 to make someone do something: *They got him to give them a lift in his car.*
3 to arrange for someone to do something for you: *Why don't you get your car fixed?*
4 to arrive somewhere: *He got home at 4 a.m.* □ *How do I get to your place from here?*
5 to buy or obtain something: *Dad needs to get a birthday present for Mum.* □ *I got a job at the shop.*
6 to receive something: *I'm getting a bike for my birthday.* □ *He gets a lot of letters from fans.*
7 to go and bring someone or something to a particular place: *I went downstairs to get the post.* □ *It's time to get the kids from school.*
8 to understand something: *Dad laughed, but I didn't get the joke.*
9 to become ill with an illness or a disease: *I've got flu.*
10 to leave a place on a particular train, bus, aeroplane or boat: *I got the train home at 10.45 p.m.*

get along with someone → see **get on**
get away to escape: *The thieves got away through an upstairs window.*

get away with something to not be punished for doing something wrong: *Criminals know how to steal and get away with it.*
get back to return somewhere: *I'll call you when we get back from Scotland.*

get by to have just enough of something: *We have enough money to get by.*

get down to make your body lower until you are sitting, resting on your knees, or lying on the ground: *Everybody got down on the ground and started looking for my earring.*
get in to reach a station or an airport: *Our flight got in two hours late.*
get into something to climb into a car: *We said goodbye and I got into the taxi.*
get off something to leave a bus, train, or bicycle: *He got off the train at Central Station.*

get off

He got off the train at Central Station.

get on
1 get on with someone to have a friendly relationship with someone: *He's always complaining. I can't get on with him.* □ *We all get on well.*
2 to enter a train or bus or sit on a bicycle: *She got on the train just before it left.*
3 to continue doing or start doing something: *Jane got on with her work.*
get out
1 to leave a place because you want to escape from it: *They got out of the country just in time.*
2 to leave a car: *A man got out of the van and ran away.*
get over something to become happy or well again after an unhappy experience or an illness: *It took me a long time to get over her death.*

get through something to complete a task or an amount of work: *We got through plenty of work today.*
get together to meet in order to talk about something or to spend time together: *Christmas is a time for families to get together.*

get up
1 to move your body so that you are standing: *I got up and walked over to the window.*
2 to get out of bed: *They have to get up early in the morning.*

ghetto /'getəʊ/ *noun* (**ghettos** or **ghettoes**)
a part of a city where many poor people live: *They came from the inner-city ghettos.*

ghost /gəʊst/ *noun*
the spirit of a dead person that some people believe they can see or feel: *He saw the ghost of a dead man.*

giant[1] /'dʒaɪənt/ *adjective*
very large or important: *America's giant car makers are located in Detroit.* ◻ *They watched the concert on a giant TV screen.*

giant[2] /'dʒaɪənt/ *noun*
a very big and strong man, especially one that appears in children's stories

gift /gɪft/ *noun*
1 something that you give to someone as a present: *We gave her a birthday gift.*
2 a natural ability to do something: *He had a gift for teaching.*

gigabyte /'gɪgəˌbaɪt/ *noun*
one thousand and twenty-four megabytes (= a unit for measuring the size of a computer's memory)

gigantic /dʒaɪ'gæntɪk/ *adjective*
extremely large: *There are gigantic rocks along the roadside.*

giggle /'gɪgəl/ *verb* (**giggles, giggling, giggled**)
to laugh in a silly way, like a child: *The girls began to giggle.* • **giggle** *noun He gave a little giggle.*

ginger /'dʒɪndʒə/ *uncountable noun*
the root of a plant with a sweet, spicy flavour that you use in cooking

giraffe /dʒɪ'rɑːf/ *noun*
a large African animal with a very long neck, long legs and dark spots on its body

girl /gɜːl/ *noun*
a female child: *They have two girls and a boy.*

girlfriend /'gɜːlfrend/ *noun*
1 a girl or woman who someone is having a romantic relationship with: *Does he have a girlfriend?*
2 a female friend: *I had lunch with my girlfriends.*

Girl Guide *noun*
a member of the Girl Guides (= an organization that teaches girls practical skills, and encourages them to help other people): *If you are aged between ten and fifteen, you can become a Girl Guide.*

give /gɪv/ *verb* (**gives, giving, gave, given**)
1 to let someone have something: *My parents gave me a watch for my birthday.* ◻ *They gave him the job.* ◻ *I gave him my phone number.*
2 to pass an object to someone, so that they can take it: *Give me that pencil.* ◻ *Please give me your bag to carry.*
3 used with nouns when you are talking about actions or sounds. For example, 'She gave a smile' means 'She smiled': *She gave me a big kiss.* ◻ *He gave a shout when the box fell on his foot.*

give in to agree to do something although you do not really want to do it: *After saying 'no' a hundred times, I finally gave in and said 'yes'.*

give something away to give something that you own to someone: *She likes to give away plants from her garden.*

give something back to return something to the person who gave it to you: *I gave the book back to him.* ◻ *Give me back my camera.*

give something out to give one of a number of things to each person in a group of people: *Our teacher gave out papers, pencils and calculators for the maths test.*

give something up to stop doing or having something: *We gave up hope of finding the fishermen.*

give up to decide that you cannot do something and stop trying to do it: *I give up. I'll never understand this.*

given /'gɪvən/ → see **give**

glacier /'glæsiə/ *noun*
a very large amount of ice that moves very slowly, usually down a mountain

glad /glæd/ *adjective*
happy and pleased about something: *They seemed glad to see me.* ◻ *I'm glad you like the present.*
▶ **gladly** *adverb Malcolm gladly accepted the invitation.*

glamorous /'glæmərəs/ *adjective*
very attractive, exciting or interesting: *She looked glamorous in a white dress.*

g

glance /glɑːns/ *verb* (**glances, glancing, glanced**)

to look at something or someone very quickly: *He glanced at his watch.* • **glance** *noun* *Trevor and I exchanged glances.*

glare¹ /gleə/ *verb* (**glares, glaring, glared**)

1 to look at someone with an angry expression on your face: *The old woman glared at him.*

2 to shine with a very bright light: *The sun glared down on us.*

glare² /gleə/ *noun*

1 an angry look: *She gave him a furious glare.*

2 *uncountable* very bright light that is difficult to look at: *the glare from a car's lights*

glass /glɑːs/ *noun* (**glasses**)

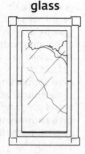

glass

1 *uncountable* a hard, transparent substance that is used for making things such as windows and bottles: *He served the salad in a glass bowl.*

2 a container made from glass, which you can drink from: *He picked up his glass and drank.* □ *I drink a glass of milk every day.*

glasses /'glɑːsɪz/ (*American*: **eyeglasses**) *plural noun*

two pieces of glass or plastic (= lenses) in a frame, that some people wear in front of their eyes to help them to see better: *He took off his glasses.*

gleam /gliːm/ *verb* (**gleams, gleaming, gleamed**)

to shine with a soft light: *His black hair gleamed in the sun.*

glide /glaɪd/ *verb* (**glides, gliding, glided**)

to move somewhere quietly and easily: *Waiters glide between the tables carrying trays.* □ *Geese glide over the lake.*

glimmer¹ /'glɪmə/ *verb* (**glimmers, glimmering, glimmered**)

to shine with a weak light: *The moon glimmered through the mist.*

glimmer² /'glɪmə/ *noun*

1 a weak light: *In the east there was a glimmer of light.*

2 a small sign of something: *The new drug offers a glimmer of hope for patients.*

glimpse /glɪmps/ *noun*

when you see someone or something for a very short amount of time: *Fans waited outside the hotel to catch a glimpse of the star.*

• **glimpse** *verb* (**glimpses, glimpsing, glimpsed**) *She glimpsed something in the water.*

glisten /'glɪsən/ *verb* (**glistens, glistening, glistened**)

to shine, often because of being wet: *The ocean glistened in the sunlight.* □ *David's face was glistening with sweat.*

glitter /'glɪtə/ *verb* (**glitters, glittering, glittered**)

to shine with small flashes of light: *The ring glittered on Andrea's finger.*

global /'gləʊbəl/ *adjective*

relating to the whole world: *American businesses compete in a global economy.*

▶ **globally** *adverb* *The company employs 5,800 people globally, including 2,000 in London.*

global e'conomy *noun*

the way in which the nations of the world work together through international trade and financial matters: *We will soon see the effect of rising oil prices on the global economy.*

globalization /'gləʊbəlaɪ'zeɪʃən/ *uncountable noun*

the idea that the world is developing a single economy as a result of modern technology and communications: *The report focuses on the globalization of business activities around the world.*

global 'warming *uncountable noun*

the gradual rise in the Earth's temperature caused by high levels of certain gases: *If we use less energy, we can help to reduce global warming.*

globe /gləʊb/ *noun*

1 an object shaped like a ball with a map of the world on it: *A large globe stood on his desk.*

2 the world: *Thousands of people across the globe took part in the survey.*

gloomy /'gluːmi/ *adjective* (**gloomier, gloomiest**)

1 almost dark so that you cannot see very well: *Inside it's gloomy after all that sunshine.*

2 sad and without much hope of success or happiness: *He is gloomy about the future of the country.* □ *The economic prospects for next year are gloomy.*

glorious /'glɔːriəs/ *adjective*

1 very beautiful; making you feel very happy: *We saw a glorious rainbow.* □ *He has glorious memories of his days as a champion.*

▶ **gloriously** *adverb It was a gloriously sunny morning.*

2 involving great fame or success: *He had a glorious career as a broadcaster and writer.*

▶ **gloriously** *adverb The mission was gloriously successful.*

glory /'glɔːri/ *uncountable noun*

the fame and admiration from other people that you get by doing something great: *He had his moment of glory when he won the cycling race.*

glossary /'glɒsəri/ *noun* (**glossaries**)

a list of difficult words that are used in a book or special subject, with explanations of their meanings

glossy /'glɒsi/ *adjective* (**glossier, glossiest**)

smooth and shiny: *She had glossy black hair.*

glove /glʌv/ *noun*

a piece of clothing that you wear on your hand, with a separate part for each finger: *He put his gloves in his pocket.*

glow /gləʊ/ *noun*

a soft, steady light, for example the light from a fire when there are no flames: *She saw the red glow of a fire.* ● **glow** *verb* (**glows, glowing, glowed**) *The lantern glowed softly in the darkness.*

glue /gluː/ *uncountable noun*

a sticky substance used for joining things together: *You will need scissors and a tube of glue.* ● **glue** *verb* (**glues, glueing** or **gluing, glued**) *She glued the pieces of newspaper together.*

GM /ˌdʒiː 'em/ *adjective*

short for **genetically modified**

go¹ /gəʊ/ *verb* (**goes, going, went, gone**)

1 to move or travel somewhere: *We went to Rome on holiday.* □ *I went home for the weekend.* □ *It took an hour to go three miles.*

2 to leave the place where you are: *It's time for me to go.*

3 to leave a place in order to do something: *We went swimming early this morning.* □ *They've gone shopping.* □ *He went for a walk.* □ *I'll go and make breakfast.*

4 to visit school, work or church

regularly: *Does your daughter go to school yet?*

5 to lead to a place: *This road goes from Blairstown to Millbrook Village.*

6 used for describing where you usually keep something: *The shoes go on the shoe shelf.*

7 to become: *I'm going crazy.* □ *The meat has gone bad.*

8 used for talking about the way that something happens: *How's your job going?* □ *Everything is going wrong.*

9 to be working: *Can you get my car going again?*

go ahead to take place: *The wedding went ahead as planned, about 14 hours after the accident.*

go away

1 to leave a place or a person: *Just go away and leave me alone!*

2 to leave a place and spend time somewhere else, especially as a holiday: *Why don't we go away this weekend?*

go back to return somewhere: *He'll be going back to college soon.*

go by to pass: *The week went by so quickly.*

go down

1 to become less: *House prices went down last month.*

2 when the sun goes down, it goes below the line between the land and the sky: *It gets cold after the sun goes down.*

go off

1 to explode: *A bomb went off, destroying the vehicle.*

2 to no longer be good to eat or drink: *This fish has gone off.*

go on

1 to continue to do something: *She just went on laughing.*

2 to be happening: *While this conversation was going on, I just listened.*

go out

1 to leave your home to do something enjoyable: *I'm going out tonight.*

2 to have a romantic relationship with someone: *I've been going out with my girlfriend for three months.*

3 to stop shining or burning: *The bedroom light went out after a moment.* □ *The fire went out and the room became cold.*

go over something to look at something or think about it very carefully: *We went over the details again.*

go through something to experience

something difficult: *He went through a difficult time when his wife died.*

go together to look or taste good together: *Cheese and tomato go together well.*

go up to become greater: *The cost of calls went up to £1.00 a minute.*

go with something to look or taste good with something else: *Those trousers would go with my blue shirt.*

go² /gəʊ/ *noun* (**goes**)
the time when someone should do something in a game or activity: *Whose go is it now?*

have a go to try to do something (*informal*): *Children should have a go at playing a musical instrument.*

goal /gəʊl/ *noun*
1 the place, in games such as football, where the players try to put the ball in order to win a point for their team: *The ball went straight into the goal.*
2 a point that is scored when the ball goes into the goal in games such as football: *He scored five goals in one game.*
3 the aim or purpose that you have when you do something: *Our goal is to make patients comfortable.*

goal

net — crossbar
goalkeeper
goalpost

goalkeeper /'gəʊlkiːpə/ *noun*
the player on a sports team whose job is to guard the goal

goalpost /'gəʊlpəʊst/ *noun*
one of the two wooden posts that form the goal in games such as football

goat /gəʊt/ *noun*
an animal that is about the size of a sheep. Goats have horns, and hairs on their chin that look like a beard.

gobble /'gɒbəl/ *verb* (**gobbles, gobbling, gobbled**) (*also* **gobble up**)
to eat food very quickly: *Don't gobble your food.* □ *Pete hungrily gobbled up the rest of the sandwiches.*

God¹ /gɒd/ *noun*
the name given to the spirit that people in many religions believe created the world: *He believes in God.*

god² /gɒd/ *noun*
a spirit that people in many religions believe has power over a particular part of the world or nature: *Poseidon was the Greek god of the sea.*

goddess /'gɒdes/ *noun* (**goddesses**)
a female god

goggles /'gɒgəlz/ *plural noun*
large glasses that fit closely to your face around your eyes to protect them: *a pair of swimming goggles*

going /'gəʊɪŋ/ *verb*
be going to
1 used for talking about something that will probably happen in the future: *I think it's going to be successful.* □ *You're going to enjoy this.*
2 used for saying that you intend to do something: *I'm going to go to bed.* □ *He announced that he's going to resign.*

gold¹ /gəʊld/ *uncountable noun*
1 a valuable, yellow-coloured metal that is used for making jewellery, ornaments and coins: *a ring made of gold* □ *The price of gold was going up.*
2 jewellery and other things that are made of gold: *We handed over all our gold and money.*

gold² /gəʊld/ *adjective*
bright yellow in colour, and often shiny: *He wore a black and gold shirt.*

golden /'gəʊldən/ *adjective*
1 bright yellow in colour: *She combed her golden hair.*
2 made of gold: *He wore a golden chain.*

goldfish /'gəʊldfɪʃ/ *noun* (**goldfish**)
a small orange fish that people often keep as a pet

gold ˈmedal *noun*
an award made of gold metal that you get as first prize in a competition: *Her dream is to win a gold medal at the Winter Olympics.*

golf /gɒlf/ *uncountable noun*
a game in which you use long sticks

(= golf clubs) to hit a small, hard ball into holes: *Do you play golf?*

▶ **golfer** *noun* *He is one of the world's best golfers.*

▶ **golfing** *uncountable noun* *You can play tennis or go golfing.*

'golf club *noun*
a long, thin metal stick with a piece of wood or metal at one end that you use to hit the ball when you play golf

'golf course *noun*
a large area of grass where people play golf

gone /gɒn/ → see **go**

good¹ /gʊd/ *adjective* (**better, best**)
1 pleasant or enjoyable: *We had a really good time.* ◻ *These people want a better life for their children.*
2 of a high quality or level: *Good food is important for your health.* ◻ *Our customers want the best possible quality at a low price.*
3 suitable for an activity: *This room is a good place for relaxing and reading.* ◻ *What would be a good time to meet?*
4 sensible: *It's a good idea to keep your desk tidy.* ◻ *There was a good reason for his strange behaviour.*
5 skilful at doing something: *I'm not very good at singing.*
6 behaving well: *The children were very good.*
7 kind and thoughtful: *You are good to me.*

good² /gʊd/ *uncountable noun*
what people consider to be morally right: *They should know the difference between good and bad, right and wrong.*

do someone good to help someone to feel better: *The fresh air will do you good.*

for good used for saying that something has disappeared and will never come back: *These forests may be gone for good.*

no good used for saying that something will not bring any success: *I asked her to repeat the question, but it was no good – I couldn't understand her.* ◻ *It's no good worrying about it now.*

good after'noon
said to someone when you see or speak to them in the afternoon (*formal*)

goodbye /ˌɡʊdˈbaɪ/ also **good-bye**
said to someone when you or they are leaving a place, or at the end of a telephone conversation

good 'evening
said the first time you see or speak to someone in the evening (*formal*)

good-'looking *adjective* (**better-looking, best-looking**)
having an attractive face: *Katy noticed him because he was good-looking.*

good 'morning
said the first time you see or speak to someone in the morning (*formal*)

goodness /ˈɡʊdnəs/ *uncountable noun*
the quality of being kind, helpful and honest: *He believes in human goodness.*

for goodness' sake used for showing that you are annoyed or worried: *For goodness' sake, do something!*

thank goodness used for showing that you are happy that something bad has not happened: *Thank goodness you're here; I've been so worried.*

good 'night
said to someone late in the evening before you go home or go to bed

goods /ɡʊdz/ *plural noun*
things that you can buy or sell: *Companies sell goods or services.*

Google /ˈɡuːɡəl/ *noun*
a computer program that you can use to search for information on the Internet (*trademark*): *Why don't you look him up on Google?* ● **Google** *verb* (**Googles, Googling, Googled**) (*trademark*): *We Googled her name, and found her website.*

goose /ɡuːs/ *noun* (**geese**)
a large bird like a duck with a long neck: *The Canada Goose is a beautiful bird.*

gorgeous /ˈɡɔːdʒəs/ *adjective*
very pleasant or attractive (*informal*): *It's a gorgeous day.* ◻ *You look gorgeous.*

gorilla /ɡəˈrɪlə/ *noun*
a very large animal like a monkey with long arms, black fur and a black face

gossip /ˈɡɒsɪp/ *uncountable noun*
informal conversation about other people: *There has been gossip about the reasons for his absence.* ● **gossip** *verb* (**gossips, gossiping, gossiped**) *They sat at the kitchen table gossiping about Jenny.*

gotten /ˈɡɒtən/ (*American*) → see **get**

govern /ˈɡʌvən/ *verb* (**governs, governing, governed**)
to officially control and organize a

country: *The people choose who they want to govern their country.*

government /'ɡʌvənmənt/ *noun*
the group of people who control and organize a country, a state or a city: *The government has decided to make changes.*
▸ **governmental** /ˌɡʌvən'mentəl/ *adjective*
relating to a particular government: *She works for a governmental agency.*

LANGUAGE HELP
In Britain, the head of the government is the **Prime Minister**.

gown /ɡaʊn/ *noun*
1 a long dress that women wear on formal occasions: *She was wearing a ball gown.*
2 a loose black piece of clothing that students wear at their graduation ceremony (= the ceremony where they receive their degree): *He was wearing a university graduation gown.*

GP /ˌdʒiː'piː/ *noun* (**GPs**)
a general doctor who treats all types of illnesses and does not work in a hospital. GP is short for **general practitioner**.

grab /ɡræb/ *verb* (**grabs, grabbing, grabbed**)
to take something suddenly and roughly: *I grabbed her hand.*

graceful /'ɡreɪsfʊl/ *adjective*
moving in a smooth and attractive way: *His movements were smooth and graceful.*
▸ **gracefully** *adverb* *She stepped gracefully onto the stage.*

grade¹ /ɡreɪd/ *noun*
1 the mark that a teacher gives you to show how good your work is: *The best grade you can get is an A.*
2 the level of quality of a product: *The price of all grades of petrol has gone up.*

grade² /ɡreɪd/ *verb* (**grades, grading, graded**)
to judge the quality of something: *Teachers grade the students' work from A to F.*

gradual /'ɡrædʒʊəl/ *adjective*
happening slowly, over a long period of time: *Losing weight is a gradual process.*
▸ **gradually** /'ɡrædʒəli/ *adverb* *We are gradually learning to use the new computer system.*

graduate¹ /'ɡrædʒʊət/ *noun*
a student who has completed a course at a college or university: *His parents are both*

college graduates. They studied at Cornell.

graduate² /'ɡrædʒʊeɪt/ *verb* (**graduates, graduating, graduated**)
to complete your studies at college or university: *Her son has just graduated from Oxford.*

graduation /ˌɡrædʒʊ'eɪʃən/ *noun*
a special ceremony for students when they have completed their studies at a university or college: *Her parents came to her graduation.*

graffiti /ɡrə'fiːti/ *uncountable noun*
words or pictures that people write or draw on walls or in public places: *There was graffiti all over the walls.*

grain /ɡreɪn/ *noun*
1 a single seed from a particular crop: *He was grateful for every single grain of rice.*
2 a tiny, hard piece of something such as sand or salt: *How many grains of sand are there in the desert?*

gram /ɡræm/ also **gramme** *noun*
a unit of weight. There are one thousand grams in a kilogram: *A football weighs about 400 grams.*

grammar /'ɡræmə/ *uncountable noun*
a set of rules for a language that describes how words go together to form sentences: *You need to know the basic rules of grammar.*

grammatical /ɡrə'mætɪkəl/ *adjective*
1 relating to grammar: *He studied a book of grammatical rules.*
2 correct, obeying the rules of grammar: *We want to see if students can write grammatical English.*

gran /ɡræn/ *noun* (informal)
→ see **grandmother**

grand /ɡrænd/ *adjective* (**grander, grandest**)
very impressive in size or appearance: *The town hall is a grand building in the centre of town.*

grandad /'ɡrændæd/ also **granddad** *noun* (informal)
→ see **grandfather**

grandchild /'ɡræntʃaɪld/ *noun* (**grandchildren**)
the child of your son or daughter: *You're grandma's favourite grandchild.*

granddaughter /'ɡrændɔːtə/ *noun*
the daughter of your son or daughter: *This is my granddaughter, Amelia.*

grandfather /'grænfɑːðə/ *noun*
the father of your father or mother: *His grandfather was a professor.*
→ Look at picture on P8

grandma /'grænmɑː/ *noun* (*informal*)
→ see **grandmother**: *Grandma was from Scotland.*

grandmother /'grænmʌðə/ *noun*
the mother of your father or mother: *My grandmothers were both teachers.*
→ Look at picture on P8

grandpa /'grænpɑː/ *noun* (*informal*)
→ see **grandfather**: *Grandpa was sitting in the garden.*

grandparent /'grænpeərənt/ *noun*
the parents of your father or mother: *Tammy lives with her grandparents.*

grandson /'grænsʌn/ *noun*
the son of your son or daughter: *My grandson's birthday was on Tuesday.*

granny /'græni/ *noun* (**grannies**) (*informal*)
→ see **grandmother**: *I hugged my granny.*

grant ¹ /grɑːnt/ *noun*
an amount of money that a government gives to a person or to an organization for a special purpose: *They got a grant to research the disease.*

grant ² /grɑːnt/ *verb* (**grants, granting, granted**)
to allow someone to have something (*formal*): *France granted him political asylum.*
take someone for granted to not show that you are grateful for anything that someone does: *She feels that her family take her for granted.*

grape /greɪp/ *noun*
a small green or purple fruit that grows in bunches and is used to make wine: *I bought six oranges and a small bunch of grapes.*
→ Look at picture on P2

grapefruit /'greɪpfruːt/ *noun* (**grapefruit**)

> **LANGUAGE HELP**
> The plural can also be **grapefruits**.

a large, round, yellow fruit that has a slightly sour taste
→ Look at picture on P2

graph /grɑːf/ *noun*
a picture that shows information about sets of numbers or measurements: *The graph shows that prices went up about 20 per cent last year.*

graphs

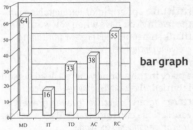

bar graph

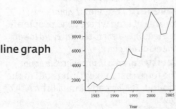

line graph

graphics /'græfɪks/ *plural noun*
drawings, pictures or symbols, especially when they are produced by a computer: *The game's graphics are very good, so you can see things clearly.*

grasp ¹ /grɑːsp/ *verb* (**grasps, grasping, grasped**)
1 to take something in your hand and hold it very firmly: *He grasped both my hands.*
2 to understand something that is complicated: *I don't think you have grasped how serious this problem is.*

grasp ² /grɑːsp/ *noun*
1 a very firm hold or grip: *He took her hand in a firm grasp.*
2 an understanding of a subject: *She has a good grasp of geometry.*

grass /grɑːs/ *uncountable noun*
a plant with thin, green leaves that cover the surface of the ground: *We sat on the grass and ate our picnic.*

grasshopper /'grɑːshɒpə/ *noun*
an insect that jumps high into the air and makes a sound with its long back legs

grassy /'grɑːsi/ *adjective* (**grassier, grassiest**)
covered in grass: *a grassy hillside*

grateful /'greɪtfʊl/ *adjective*
wanting to thank someone for something that they give you or do for you: *She was grateful to him for being so helpful.*

g

▶ **gratefully** *adverb* He said that any help would be gratefully received.

gratitude /'grætɪˌtjuːd/ *uncountable noun*
the feeling you have when you want to thank someone: He expressed gratitude to everyone for their help.

grave [1] /greɪv/ *noun*
a place in the ground where a dead person is buried: They visit her grave twice a year.

grave [2] /greɪv/ *adjective* (graver, gravest)
very serious and important: These weapons are a grave danger to the world.

graveyard /'greɪvjɑːd/ *noun*
an area of land where dead people are buried: They went to the graveyard to put flowers on her grave.

gravity /'grævɪti/ *uncountable noun*
the force that makes things fall to the ground: The force of gravity pulls everything down.

gravy /'greɪvi/ *uncountable noun*
a sauce made from the juices that come from meat when it cooks

grease /griːs/ *uncountable noun*
1 a thick substance like oil: His hands were covered in grease.
2 animal fat that is produced when you cook meat: The plates were all covered in grease.

greasy /'griːsi/ *adjective* (greasier, greasiest)
used for describing something that has grease on it or in it: greasy hair

great [1] /greɪt/ *adjective* (greater, greatest)
1 very large: She had a great big smile on her face.
2 large in amount or degree: She lived to a great age.
▶ **greatly** *adverb* (formal): He will be greatly missed.
3 important, famous or exciting: They made great scientific discoveries. □ He has the ability to be a great player.
▶ **greatness** *uncountable noun* She dreamed of achieving greatness.
4 very good (informal): We had a great time. □ It's great to meet you!

great [2] /greɪt/ *exclamation*
very good: Oh great! You made a cake.

greed /griːd/ *uncountable noun*
the feeling that you want to have more of something than you need: People say that the world economy is based on greed.

greedy /'griːdi/ *adjective* (greedier, greediest)
wanting to have more of something than you need: They still want more money? I think that's a bit greedy.
▶ **greedily** *adverb* He raised the bottle to his lips and drank greedily.

green /griːn/ *adjective* (greener, greenest)
1 having the colour of grass or leaves: She wore a green dress. ● **green** *noun* I've never looked good in green.
2 relating to the protection of the environment: the Green Party

greenhouse /'griːnhaʊs/ *noun*
a glass building where you grow plants to protect them from bad weather

greenhouse effect *noun*
the problem of the Earth's temperature getting higher because of the gases that go into the air: Carbon dioxide is one of the gases that contribute to the greenhouse effect.

greenhouse gas *noun* (greenhouse gases)
the gases that cause a gradual rise in the Earth's temperature. The main greenhouse gas is carbon dioxide: They signed an international agreement to limit greenhouse gases.

greet /griːt/ *verb* (greets, greeting, greeted)
to say 'Hello' or shake hands with someone: She greeted him when he came in from school.

greeting /'griːtɪŋ/ *noun*
something friendly that you say or do when you meet someone: We exchanged friendly greetings.

grew /gruː/ → see grow

grey /greɪ/ *adjective* (greyer, greyest)
having the colour of ashes or clouds on a rainy day: a grey suit ● **grey** *noun* She was dressed in grey.

grid /grɪd/ *noun*
a pattern of straight lines that cross over each other to make squares. On maps, you can use the grid to help you find a particular thing or place: The number puzzle uses a grid of nine squares.

grief /griːf/ *uncountable noun*
a feeling of great sadness: We all experience grief at some point in our lives.

grieve /griːv/ *verb* (**grieves, grieving, grieved**)

to feel very sad about something, especially someone's death: *He's grieving over his dead wife.*

grill¹ /grɪl/ *noun*

1 part of a cooker that cooks food placed under it using strong heat: *Put the meat under a grill until it is brown.*

2 a flat frame of metal bars that you can use to cook food over a fire: *We cooked the fish on a grill over the fire.*

grill² /grɪl/ *verb* (**grills, grilling, grilled**)

to cook food on metal bars above a fire or barbecue or under a grill: *Grill the steaks for about 5 minutes each side.* □ *grilled fish*

grin /grɪn/ *verb* (**grins, grinning, grinned**)

to have a big smile on your face: *He grinned with pleasure.* □ *Phillip grinned at her.* ● **grin** *noun* *She had a big grin on her face.*

grind /graɪnd/ *verb* (**grinds, grinding, ground**)

to rub a substance against something hard until it becomes a fine powder: *Grind some pepper into the sauce.*

grip /grɪp/ *verb* (**grips, gripping, gripped**)

to take something with your hand and hold it firmly: *She gripped the rope.* ● **grip** *noun* *Keep a tight grip on your purse.*

groan /grəʊn/ *verb* (**groans, groaning, groaned**)

to make a long, low sound because you are feeling pain, or because you are unhappy about something: *He began to groan with pain.* □ *The man on the floor was groaning.* ● **groan** *noun* *I heard a groan from the crowd.*

groceries /ˈgrəʊsəriz/ *plural noun*

the things that you buy at a grocery or at a supermarket: *a small bag of groceries*

groom¹ /gruːm/ *noun*

1 a person whose job is to look after horses

2 a man on the day of his wedding

groom² /gruːm/ *verb* (**grooms, grooming, groomed**)

to clean an animal's fur, usually by brushing it: *She groomed the horses regularly.*

groove /gruːv/ *noun*

a deep line that is cut into a surface: *He used a knife to cut a groove in the stick.*

grope /grəʊp/ *verb* (**gropes, groping, groped**)

to use your hands to try to find something that you cannot see: *He groped for the door handle in the dark.*

gross national product /ˌgrəʊs næʃənəl ˈprɒdʌkt/ *noun*

the total value of all of a country's income in a particular year

ground¹ /graʊnd/ → see **grind**

ground² /graʊnd/ *noun*

1 the surface of the Earth or the floor of a room: *He fell to the ground.*

2 an area of land that is used for a particular activity: *a sports ground*

3 *plural* the garden or area of land around a large or important building: *the palace grounds*

ground floor (American: **first floor**) *noun*

the part of a building that is at the same level as the ground: *His office is on the ground floor.*

group /gruːp/ *noun*

1 a number of people or things that are together: *A small group of people stood on the street corner.*

2 a number of people who play music together: *He played guitar in a rock group.*

grow /grəʊ/ *verb* (**grows, growing, grew, grown**)

1 to gradually become bigger: *All children grow at different rates.*

2 used for saying that a plant or a tree lives in a particular place: *There were roses growing by the side of the door.*

3 to put seeds or young plants in the ground and take care of them: *I always grow a few red onions.*

▸ **grower** *noun* *apple growers*

4 to gradually become longer: *My hair grows really fast.*

5 to gradually change: *He's growing old.*

grow out of something

1 to stop behaving in a particular way as you get older: *Most children who bite their nails grow out of it.*

2 to become too big to wear a piece of clothing: *You've grown out of your shoes again.*

grow up to gradually change from being a child into being an adult: *She grew up in Tokyo.*

growl /graʊl/ *verb* (**growls, growling, growled**)

to make a low noise in the throat, usually because of anger: *The dog was growling and showing its teeth.* ● **growl** *noun The animal gave a growl.*

gr'own-'up also **grownup** *noun*
a child's word for an adult: *Archie's almost a grown-up now.* ● **grown-up** *adjective She has two grown-up children who both live nearby.*

growth /grəʊθ/ *uncountable noun*
1 development: *The city's population growth slowed to 1.6% last year.* ☐ *The government expects strong economic growth.*
2 the process of a person, an animal or a plant getting bigger: *Milk is important for a baby's growth and development.*

grudge /grʌdʒ/ *noun*
a feeling of anger with someone because of something they did in the past: *He seems to have a grudge against me.*

grumble /'grʌmbəl/ *verb* (**grumbles, grumbling, grumbled**)
to complain about something: *They grumble about how hard they have to work.* ☐ *Dad grumbled that we never cleaned our rooms.* ● **grumble** *noun The high prices have brought grumbles from some customers.*

grumpy /'grʌmpi/ *adjective* (**grumpier, grumpiest**)
a little angry: *He's getting grumpy and depressed.*
▶ **grumpily** *adverb* '*Go away, I'm busy', said Ken grumpily.*

grunt /grʌnt/ *verb* (**grunts, grunting, grunted**)
to make a low sound, especially because you are annoyed or not interested in something: *When I said hello he just grunted.* ☐ '*Huh', he grunted.* ● **grunt** *noun Barbara replied with a grunt.*

guarantee [1] /ˌgærən'tiː/ *verb*
(**guarantees, guaranteeing, guaranteed**)
1 to promise that something will happen: *We guarantee the safety of our products.* ☐ *I guarantee that you will enjoy this film.*
2 to provide a written promise that the product will be repaired or the customer will be given a new one if it has anything wrong with it: *All our computers are guaranteed for 12 months.*

guarantee [2] /ˌgærən'tiː/ *noun*
1 a promise: *He gave me a guarantee he would finish the job.*
2 a written promise by a company to repair a product or give you a new one if it has anything wrong with it: *Keep the*

guarantee in case something goes wrong.

guard [1] /gɑːd/ *verb* (**guards, guarding, guarded**)
1 to stand near a place, person or object to watch and protect them: *Armed police guarded the court.*
2 to watch someone and keep them in a particular place to stop them from escaping: *Marines with rifles guarded them.*

guard [2] /gɑːd/ *noun*
someone such as a soldier or a police officer, who is guarding a particular place or person: *The prisoners attacked their guards.*

guardian /'gɑːdiən/ *noun*
someone who is legally responsible for another person, often a child: *Diana's grandmother was her legal guardian.*

guerrilla /gə'rɪlə/ also **guerilla** *noun*
a person who fights for a military group that does not form part of the regular army: *Five soldiers were killed in a guerrilla attack.*

guess /ges/ *verb* (**guesses, guessing, guessed**)
to give an answer or provide an opinion when you do not know if it is true: *Yvonne guessed that he was around 40 years old.* ☐ *Guess what I just did!* ● **guess** *noun* (**guesses**) *He made a guess at her age.* ☐ *If you don't know, just have a guess.*

guest /gest/ *noun*
1 someone who you invite to your home or to an event: *She was a guest at the wedding.*
2 someone who is staying in a hotel: *A few guests were having breakfast.*

'guest house *noun*
a small hotel

guidance /'gaɪdəns/ *uncountable noun*
help and advice: *My tennis game improved under his guidance.*

guide [1] /gaɪd/ *noun*
1 a book or a website that gives you information to help you to do or understand something: *He found a step-by-step guide to building your own home.*
2 a book or a website that gives tourists information about a town, an area, or a country: *The guide to Paris lists hotel rooms for as little as £25 a night.*
3 someone who shows tourists around places such as museums or cities: *A guide will take you on a tour of the city.*

guide² /gaɪd/ *verb* (**guides, guiding, guided**)

to go somewhere with someone to show them the way: *He took her by the arm and guided her toward the door.*

Guide³ /gaɪd/ *noun*

→ see **Girl Guide**

guidebook /ˈgaɪdbʊk/ *noun* (*also* **guide**)

a book for tourists that gives information about a town, an area or a country

guilt /gɪlt/ *uncountable noun*

1 an unhappy feeling that you have when you think that you have done something wrong: *She felt a lot of guilt about her children's unhappiness.*

2 the fact that you have done something wrong or illegal: *There is not enough evidence to prove his guilt.*

guilty /ˈgɪlti/ *adjective* (**guiltier, guiltiest**)

1 feeling unhappy because you think that you have done something wrong: *I feel so guilty, leaving all this work to you.*

2 having committed a crime or an offence: *The jury found them guilty of murder.*

guinea pig /ˈgɪni ˌpɪg/ *noun*

1 a person who is used in an experiment: *The doctor used himself as a guinea pig in his research.*

2 a small animal with fur and no tail. People often keep guinea pigs as pets.

guitar /gɪˈtɑː/ *noun*

a musical instrument with strings

guitarist /gɪˈtɑːrɪst/ *noun*

a person who plays the guitar: *He's one of the world's best jazz guitarists.*

gulf /gʌlf/ *noun*

a large area of sea that has land almost all the way around it: *A storm is crossing the Gulf of Mexico.*

gulp /gʌlp/ *verb* (**gulps, gulping, gulped**)

to eat or drink something very quickly: *She gulped her orange juice.* ● **gulp** *noun* *She took a gulp of fresh air.*

gum /gʌm/ *noun*

1 *uncountable* a sweet sticky substance that you keep in your mouth for a long time but do not swallow: *I do not chew gum in public.*

2 one of the areas of firm, pink flesh inside your mouth, where your teeth grow: *Gently brush your teeth and gums.*

gun /gʌn/ *noun*

a weapon that shoots bullets: *He pointed the gun at the police officer.*

gunman /ˈgʌnmən/ *noun* (**gunmen**)

a criminal who uses a gun: *A gunman fired at police.*

gush /gʌʃ/ *verb* (**gushes, gushing, gushed**)

to flow very quickly and strongly: *Gallons of water gushed out of the tank.* ● **gush** *noun* *I heard a gush of water.*

gust /gʌst/ *noun*

a short, strong, sudden rush of wind: *A gust of wind came down the valley.*

gut /gʌt/ *noun*

the tube inside the body of a person or an animal that food passes through after it has been in the stomach: *The food then passes into the gut.*

have the guts to do something to have the courage to do something that is difficult or unpleasant (*informal*): *She has the guts to say what she thinks.*

gutter /ˈgʌtə/ *noun*

1 the edge of a road, where water collects and flows away when it rains: *His hat fell into the gutter.*

2 a pipe under the edge of a roof that carries water away when it rains: *We need to fix the gutters.*

gutter

guy /gaɪ/ *noun*

a man (*informal*): *I was working with a guy from Birmingham.*

gym /dʒɪm/ *noun*

a club, building or large room with equipment for doing physical exercises: *I go to the gym twice a week.*

gymnasium /dʒɪmˈneɪziəm/ *noun* (**gymnasiums** or **gymnasia** /dʒɪmˈneɪziə/) (*formal*)

→ see **gym**

gymnastics /dʒɪmˈnæstɪks/ *uncountable noun*

a sport that consists of physical exercises that develop your strength and your ability to move easily: *The women's gymnastics team won a silver medal.*

→ Look at picture on P6

Hh

ha /hɑː/ *exclamation*
used for showing that you are surprised, annoyed or pleased: *'Ha!' said James. 'Did you really believe me?'*

habit /ˈhæbɪt/ *noun*
something bad that you do often or regularly: *He has many bad habits, such as biting his nails.*
in the habit of used for saying that someone does something regularly: *They were in the habit of watching TV every night.*

habitat /ˈhæbɪtæt/ *noun*
the environment in which an animal or a plant lives or grows: *In its natural habitat, the plant will grow up to 25 feet.*

had /hæd/ → see **have**

hadn't /ˈhædənt/
short for 'had not'

ha ˈha *exclamation*
used in writing to show the sound that people make when they laugh: *'Ha ha!' he laughed.*

hail /heɪl/ *uncountable noun*
small balls of ice that fall like rain from the sky: *There will be storms with heavy rain and hail.*

hair /heə/ *noun*
1 *uncountable* the fine threads that grow on your head: *I wash my hair every night.*
2 the short threads that grow on the bodies of humans and animals: *Most men have hair on their chest.* □ *There were dog hairs all over the sofa.*

haircut /ˈheəkʌt/ *noun*
an occasion when someone cuts your hair for you: *You need a haircut.*

hairdresser /ˈheədresə/ *noun*
1 a person whose job is to cut and style people's hair: *She works as a hairdresser.*
2 (*also* **hairdresser's**) a place where you go to have your hair cut
→ Look at picture on P7

hairdryer /ˈheədraɪə/ *noun*
a machine that you use to dry your hair

hairstyle /ˈheəstaɪl/ *noun*
the style in which your hair has been cut or arranged: *I think her new hairstyle looks great.*

hairy /ˈheəri/ *adjective* (**hairier, hairiest**)
covered with hairs: *He was wearing shorts that showed his hairy legs.*

halal /həˈlɑːl/ *adjective*
used for describing meat from animals that have been killed according to Muslim law: *a halal butcher's shop*

half ¹ /hɑːf/ *noun* (**halves** /hɑːvz/)
one of two equal parts of a number, an amount or an object: *More than half of all U.S. houses are heated with gas.* □ *We sat and talked for half an hour.* □ *They only received half the money.* ● **half** *adjective I'll stay with you for the first half hour.*

half ² /hɑːf/ *adverb*
used for saying that something is only partly in the state that you are describing: *The glass was half empty.*

ˈhalf-ˈterm *uncountable noun* also **half term**
a short holiday in the middle of a school term (= a three-month period of school): *the half-term holidays*

halftime /ˌhɑːfˈtaɪm/ *uncountable noun*
the period between the two parts of a sports event, when the players take a short rest: *We bought something to eat during halftime.*

halfway /ˌhɑːfˈweɪ/ *adverb*
1 in the middle of a place or between two points: *He was halfway up the ladder.*
2 in the middle of an event or period of time: *We were more than halfway through our tour.*

hall /hɔːl/ *noun*
1 the area that connects one room in a house or a flat to another: *The hall leads to a large living room.*

2 a large room or building that is used for public events such as concerts and meetings: *We went into the dance hall.*

Halloween /ˌhæləʊwˈiːn/ also **Hallowe'en** *uncountable noun*
the night of 31st October when children wear special clothes, and walk from house to house asking for sweets

hallway /ˈhɔːlweɪ/ *noun*
an area in a building with doors that lead into other rooms: *They walked along the quiet hallway.*

halt¹ /hɔːlt/ *verb* (**halts, halting, halted**)
to stop something: *Officials halted the race at 5.30 p.m. yesterday.*

halt² /hɔːlt/ *noun*
come to a halt to stop moving: *The lift came to a halt at the first floor.*

halves /hɑːvz/
the plural of **half**

ham /hæm/ *uncountable noun*
meat from a pig that has been prepared with salt and spices

hamburger /ˈhæmbɜːɡə/ *noun*
a type of food made from small pieces of meat that have been shaped into a flat circle. Hamburgers are fried or grilled and are often eaten in a round piece of bread (= a roll).

hammer /ˈhæmə/ **hammer**
noun
a tool that is made from a heavy piece of metal attached to the end of a handle. It is used for hitting nails into wood: *She got a hammer and a nail and two pieces of wood.*
• **hammer** *verb* (**hammers, hammering, hammered**) *She hammered a nail into the window frame.*

hamper /ˈhæmpə/ *verb* (**hampers, hampering, hampered**)
to make it difficult for someone to do what they are trying to do: *The bad weather hampered the rescue operation.*

hamster /ˈhæmstə/ *noun*
a small animal that is similar to a mouse, that is often kept as a pet

hand¹ /hænd/ *noun*
1 the part of your body at the end of your arm that you use for holding things: *I put*

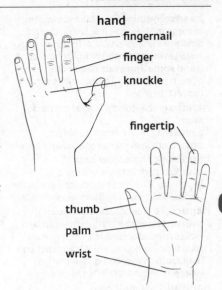

hand

- fingernail
- finger
- knuckle
- fingertip
- thumb
- palm
- wrist

my hand into my pocket and took out the letter.
→ Look at picture on P1
2 one of the long thin parts on a clock or a watch that move to show the time
by hand done or made using your hands rather than a machine: *The dress was made by hand.*

give someone a hand to help someone: *Come and give me a hand in the kitchen.*

hand in hand holding each other by the hand: *They go everywhere hand in hand.*

on hand near and ready to be used: *There are experts on hand to give you all the help you need.*

on the one hand used for talking about the first of two different ways of looking at something: *On the one hand, the body cannot survive without fat. On the other hand, if the body has too much fat, our health starts to suffer.*

on the other hand used for talking about the second of two different ways of looking at something: *The film lost money. Reviews, on the other hand, were mostly favourable.*

out of hand no longer able to be controlled: *The argument got out of hand when her boyfriend hit her.*

hand² /hænd/ *verb* (**hands, handing, handed**)
to put something into someone's hand: *He handed me a piece of paper.*

hand something in to take something to someone and give it to them: *I need to hand in my homework today.* □ *They found £7,500 in cash on the street and handed it in to police.*

hand something out to give one thing to each person in a group: *My job was to hand out the prizes.*

handbag /ˈhændbæg/ (*American*: **purse**) *noun*
a small bag that a woman uses for carrying things such as money and keys

handbook /ˈhændbʊk/ *noun*
a book that gives you advice and instructions about a particular subject: *The staff handbook says we get two weeks of holiday.*

handcuffs /ˈhændkʌfs/ *plural noun*
two connected metal rings that can be locked around someone's wrists: *He was taken to prison in handcuffs.* ● **handcuff** *verb* (**handcuffs, handcuffing, handcuffed**) *Police tried to handcuff him but he ran away.*

handful /ˈhændfʊl/ *noun*
1 a small number of people or things: *Only a handful of people knew his secret.*
2 the amount of something that you can hold in your hand: *She threw a handful of sand into the water.*

handkerchief /ˈhæŋkəˌtʃɪf/ *noun*
a small square piece of cloth that you use for blowing your nose

handle¹ /ˈhændəl/ *noun*
1 an object that is attached to a door or drawer, used for opening and closing it: *I turned the handle and the door opened.*
2 the part of a tool, a bag or a cup that you hold: *I held the knife handle tightly.*

handle² /ˈhændəl/ *verb* (**handles, handling, handled**)
1 to deal with a situation: *I think I handled the meeting very badly.*
2 to hold something or move it with your hands: *Wash your hands before handling food.*

handmade /ˌhændˈmeɪd/ also **hand-made** *adjective*
made by someone without using machines: *The shop sells beautiful handmade jewellery.*

handout /ˈhændaʊt/ *noun*
a piece of paper containing information that is given to people in a meeting or a class: *The instructions are all written in the handout.*

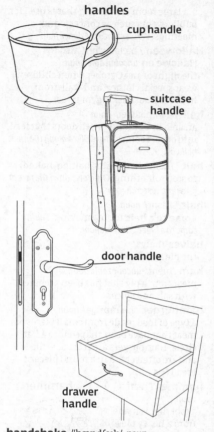

handles

cup handle

suitcase handle

door handle

drawer handle

handshake /ˈhændʃeɪk/ *noun*
when you take someone's right hand with your own right hand and move it up and down as a way of greeting them or showing that you have agreed about something: *He has a strong handshake.*

handsome /ˈhænsəm/ *adjective*
having an attractive face: *The photo showed a tall, handsome soldier.*

handwriting /ˈhændraɪtɪŋ/ *uncountable noun*
your style of writing with a pen or a pencil: *The address was in Anna's handwriting.*

handy /ˈhændi/ *adjective* (**handier, handiest**)
1 useful: *The book gives handy ideas on growing plants.*
2 nearby and easy to reach: *Make sure you have a pencil and paper handy.*

hang /hæŋ/ *verb* (hangs, hanging, hung or hanged)

> **LANGUAGE HELP**
> Use **hangs, hanging, hanged** for the sense **be hanged**.

1 to be attached somewhere without touching the ground: *Flags hang at every entrance.*
2 to attach something somewhere so that it does not touch the ground: *She hung her clothes outside to dry.*
be hanged to be killed by having a rope tied around your neck: *The five men were hanged on Tuesday.*
hang on
1 to wait (*informal*): *Can you hang on for a minute?*
2 to hold something very tightly: *He hung on to the rail as he went downstairs.*
hang out to spend a lot of time somewhere (*informal*): *I often hang out at the shopping arcade.*
hang up to end a phone call: *Don't hang up on me!*

happen /'hæpən/ *verb* (happens, happening, happened)
1 to take place without being planned: *We don't know what will happen.*
2 to take place and affect someone: *What's the worst thing that has ever happened to you?*
happen to do something to do something by chance: *I happened to be at the library at the same time as Jim.*

happily /'hæpɪli/ *adverb*
added to something you say in order to show that you are glad that something happened: *Happily, this situation will soon get much easier.*

happy /'hæpi/ *adjective* (happier, happiest)
1 feeling pleased and satisfied: *Marina was a happy child.*
▸ **happily** *adverb* *The children played happily together all day.*
▸ **happiness** *uncountable noun* *I think she was looking for happiness.*
2 full of happy feelings and pleasant experiences: *She had a very happy childhood.* □ *Grandma's house was always a happy place.*
3 used in some expressions to say that you hope someone will enjoy a special occasion: *Happy Birthday!*

happy to do something very willing to do something: *I'm happy to answer any questions.*

harbour /'ha:bə/ *noun*
an area of water next to the land where boats can safely stay: *The fishing boats left the harbour and went out to sea.*

hard /ha:d/ *adjective, adverb* (harder, hardest)
1 feeling very firm, and not easily bent, cut or broken: *The glass hit the hard wooden floor.*
2 very difficult to do or deal with: *That's a very hard question.* □ *She's had a hard life.*
3 with a lot of effort: *I admire him because he's a hard worker.* □ *If I work hard, I'll finish the job tomorrow.*

'hard disk *noun*
the part inside a computer where information and programs are stored

'hard drive *noun*
the part of a computer that contains the computer's hard disk: *You can download music to your hard drive.*

hardly /'ha:dli/ *adverb*
1 used for saying that something is almost, or only just true: *I hardly know you.* □ *I've hardly slept for three days.*
2 used in expressions such as **hardly ever** and **hardly any** to mean almost never or almost none: *We hardly ever eat fish.* □ *They hire young workers with hardly any experience.*

hardware /'ha:dweə/ *uncountable noun*
1 things in computer systems such as the computer, the keyboard and the screen, rather than the software programs that tell the computer what to do. Compare with **software**: *The hardware costs about £200.*
2 tools and equipment that are used in the home and garden: *He bought a hammer and some nails at a hardware shop.*

harm /ha:m/ *verb* (harms, harming, harmed)
to injure or damage someone or something: *The boys didn't mean to harm anyone.* □ *This product may harm the environment.* ● **harm** *uncountable noun* *Don't worry. He won't do you any harm.*

harmful /'ha:mfʊl/ *adjective*
having a bad effect on someone or something: *People should know about the harmful effects of the sun.*

h

harmless /'hɑːmləs/ *adjective*
not having any bad effects: *These insects are harmless.*

harmony /'hɑːməni/ *noun* (**harmonies**)
1 *uncountable* when people are living together without harming anyone or anything: *People have lived in harmony with nature for centuries.*
2 the pleasant combination of different notes of music played at the same time: *The children were singing in harmony.*

harp /hɑːp/ *noun*
a large musical instrument that has strings stretched from the top to the bottom of a frame. You play the harp with your fingers.

harsh /hɑːʃ/ *adjective* (**harsher, harshest**)
1 hard and unpleasant: *a harsh winter*
2 unkind: *She said many harsh things about her brother.*
▶ **harshly** *adverb* *He was harshly treated in prison.*
3 unpleasant because of being too hard, bright or rough: *The leaves can burn badly in harsh sunlight.*

harvest /'hɑːvɪst/ *noun*
the gathering of a farm crop: *Wheat harvests were poor in both Europe and America last year.* • **harvest** *verb* (**harvests, harvesting, harvested**) *Farmers here still plant and harvest their crops by hand.*

has /həz, STRONG hæz/ → see **have**

hashtag /'hæʃˌtæg/ *noun*
a word or phrase with a hash (#) in front of it, to show that it is the topic of a message on the Twitter website

hasn't /'hæzənt/
short for 'has not'

haste /heɪst/ *noun*
when you do things too quickly: *He almost fell in his haste to get to the phone.*

hasty /'heɪsti/ *adjective* (**hastier, hastiest**)
done suddenly or quickly: *Perhaps I was too hasty when I said she couldn't come.*
▶ **hastily** /'heɪstɪli/ *adverb* *A meeting was hastily arranged to discuss the problem.*

hat /hæt/ *noun*
a thing that you wear on your head: *Look for a woman in a red hat.*

hatch /hætʃ/ *verb* (**hatches, hatching, hatched**)
when a baby bird, insect or other animal hatches, it comes out of its egg. You can also say that an egg hatches: *The young birds died soon after they hatched.* ◻ *The eggs hatch after a week.*

hate /heɪt/ *verb* (**hates, hating, hated**)
to have a strong feeling of dislike for someone or something: *She thinks that everyone hates her.* ◻ *He hates losing.* • **hate** *uncountable noun* *He spoke of the hate that he felt for some people.*

haul /hɔːl/ *verb* (**hauls, hauling, hauled**)
to move something somewhere using a lot of effort: *They hauled the car out of the water.*

haunted /'hɔːntɪd/ *adjective*
used for describing a building where people believe ghosts (= spirits of dead people) appear: *a haunted house*

have¹ /həv, STRONG hæv/ *auxiliary verb* (**has, having, had**)

> **LANGUAGE HELP**
> When you are speaking, you can use the short forms **I've** for **I have** and **hasn't** for **has not**.

used with another verb to form perfect tenses: *Alex hasn't left yet.* ◻ *What have you found?* ◻ *Frankie hasn't been feeling well today.*

have² /həv, STRONG hæv/ *verb* (**has, having, had**)
1 used with a noun to talk about an action or an event: *Come and have a look at this!* ◻ *We had a long talk.* ◻ *Let's have dinner tonight.* ◻ *We are having a meeting to decide what to do.* ◻ *I had an accident.*
2 (*also* **have got**) used for saying that someone or something owns something: *Billy has a new bicycle.* ◻ *Have we got enough chairs?*
3 used for talking about people's relationships: *Do you have any brothers or sisters?*
4 (*also* **have got**) used when you are talking about a person's appearance or character: *You have beautiful eyes.* ◻ *George has a terrible temper.*
5 used for saying that something is in a particular position or state: *Mary had her eyes closed.*

have something done used for saying that someone does something for you: *He had his hair cut yesterday.*

have to do something/have got to do

something used when you are saying that someone must do something, or that something must happen. If you do not have to do something, it is not necessary for you to do it: *I have to go home soon.* □ *You've got to tell me the truth.* □ *'You don't have to explain.'*

haven't /'hævənt/
short for 'have not'

hawk /hɔːk/ *noun*
a large bird that catches and eats small birds and animals

hay /heɪ/ *uncountable noun*
grass that has been cut and dried so that it can be used for feeding animals

hazard /'hæzəd/ *noun*
something that could be dangerous: *Too much salt may be a health hazard.*

HDTV /,eɪtʃ diː tiː 'viː/ *uncountable noun*
a television system that provides a very clear image. **HDTV** is short for 'high-definition television': *The quality of digital TV is better, especially HDTV.*

he /hi, STRONG hiː/ *pronoun*
used for talking about a man, a boy or a male animal: *John was my boss, but he couldn't remember my name.*

head¹ /hed/ *noun*
1 the top part of your body that has your eyes, mouth and brain in it: *The ball came down and hit him on the head.*
→ Look at picture on P1
2 your mind: *I just said the first thing that came into my head.*
3 the person who is in charge of a company or an organization: *I spoke to the head of the department.*
4 the top, the start or the most important end of something: *She sat at the head of the table.*
a/per head used for describing the cost or amount for one person: *This simple meal costs less than £4 a head.*

head² /hed/ *verb* (**heads, heading, headed**)
to be the person who is in charge of a department, a company or an organization: *Michael Williams heads the department's Office of Civil Rights.*
be heading for to be going towards a particular place: *We're heading back to London tomorrow.*

headache /'hedeɪk/ *noun*
a pain in your head: *I have a terrible headache.*

headfirst /,hed'fɜːst/ also **head-first**
adverb
with your head in front of your body when you are moving: *Chee dived headfirst into the water.*

headfirst

heading /'hedɪŋ/ *noun*
a title that is written at the top of a page: *When you read the book, notice the chapter headings.*

headlight /'hedlaɪt/ *noun*
one of the large lights at the front of a vehicle: *He turned on the car's headlights when the rain started.*

headline /'hedlaɪn/ *noun*
1 the title of a newspaper story, printed in large letters: *The headline said: 'New Government Plans'.*
2 *plural* the important parts of the news that you hear first on radio or television news reports: *Claudia Polley read the news headlines.*

headphones /'hedfəʊnz/ *plural noun*
things that you wear on your ears so that you can listen to music or the radio without anyone else hearing: *I listened to the programme on headphones.*

headphones

headquarters /'hedkwɔːtəz/ *noun*
the main offices of an organization: *The news broadcast came from Chicago's police headquarters.*

head 'teacher *noun*
a teacher who is in charge of a school

heal /hiːl/ *verb* (**heals, healing, healed**)
to become healthy again: *It took six months for her injuries to heal.*

health /helθ/ *uncountable noun*
the condition of a person's body: *Too much fatty food is bad for your health.*

'health care also **healthcare** *uncountable noun*
services for preventing and treating illnesses and injuries: *Nobody wants to pay more money for health care.*

healthy /'helθi/ *adjective* (**healthier, healthiest**)
1 well, and not often ill: *People need to exercise to be healthy.*
2 good for your health: *Try to eat a healthy diet.*

heap /hiːp/ *noun*
a messy pile of things: *There was a heap of clothes in the corner of the room.* ● **heap** *verb* (**heaps, heaping, heaped**) *His mother heaped more carrots onto Michael's plate.*

hear /hɪə/ *verb* (**hears, hearing, heard** /hɜːd/)
1 to become aware of a sound through your ears: *She could hear music in the distance.* □ *I heard him say, 'Thanks.'*
2 to find out about something by someone telling you, or from the radio or television: *My mother heard about the school from Karen.* □ *I hear that Bruce Springsteen is playing at Madison Square Garden tomorrow evening.*
3 to know about something or someone: *I've heard of him, but I've never met him.*
hear from someone to receive a letter, an email or a telephone call from someone: *It's always great to hear from you.*

LANGUAGE HELP
hear or **listen**? Use **hear** to talk about sounds that you notice when they reach your ears. *I heard a noise downstairs.* Use **listen** when you are paying attention to something you can hear. *He turned on the radio and listened to the news.*

hearing /'hɪərɪŋ/ *uncountable noun*
the sense that makes it possible for you to be aware of sounds: *His hearing was excellent.*

'hearing aid *noun*
a small piece of equipment that people wear in their ear to help them to hear better

heart /hɑːt/ *noun*
1 the part inside your chest that makes the blood move around your body: *His heart was beating fast.*
2 your deep feelings: *Anne's words filled her heart with joy.*
3 the middle part of a place: *They own a busy hotel in the heart of the city.*
4 the shape ♥

heart

break someone's heart to make someone very unhappy: *I fell in love on holiday but the girl broke my heart.*
by heart used for saying that you can remember every word of a poem or a song: *Mike knew this song by heart.*

'heart at,tack *noun*
when someone suddenly has a lot of pain in their chest and their heart stops working: *He died of a heart attack.*

heartbeat /'hɑːtbiːt/ *noun*
the regular movement of your heart as it pushes blood through your body: *The doctor listened to her heartbeat.*

heat /hiːt/ *uncountable noun*
when something is hot: *Our clothes dried quickly in the heat of the sun.* ● **heat** *verb* (**heats, heating, heated**) *Heat the tomatoes and oil in a pan.*

heater /'hiːtə/ *noun*
a piece of equipment that is used for making a room warm: *There's an electric heater in the bedroom.*

heating /'hiːtɪŋ/ *noun*
the equipment that is used for keeping a building warm: *She turned on the heating.*

heaven /'hevən/ *noun*
the place where some people believe good people go when they die: *I believe that when I die I will go to heaven.*

heavy /'hevi/ *adjective* (**heavier, heaviest**)
1 weighing a lot: *This bag is very heavy. What's in it?*
2 used for asking about how much someone or something weighs: *How heavy is your suitcase?*
3 great in amount: *We drove through heavy traffic for two hours.*
▶ **heavily** *adverb It rained heavily all day.*

hectic /'hektɪk/ *adjective*
very busy and involving a lot of activity: *Ben had a hectic work schedule.*

he'd /hɪd, STRONG hiːd/
1 short for 'he had'
2 short for 'he would'

hedge /hedʒ/ *noun*
a row of small trees growing close together around a garden or a field

hedgehog /'hedʒhɒg/ *noun*
a small brown animal with sharp points covering its back

heel /hiːl/ *noun*
1 the back part of your foot, just below your ankle: *I have a big blister on my heel.*
2 the raised part on the bottom at the back of a shoe: *She always wears shoes with high heels.*

height /haɪt/ *noun*
1 the size of a person or thing from the bottom to the top: *Her weight is normal for her height.* □ *I am five feet six inches in height.*
2 the distance that something is above the ground: *You can change the height of the seat.*

heir /eə/ *noun*
someone who will receive a person's money or property when that person dies: *Elizabeth was her father's heir.*

held /held/ → see **hold**

helicopter /'helikɒptə/ *noun*
an aircraft with long blades on top that go around very fast. It is able to stay still in the air and to move straight upwards or downwards as well as forwards and backwards.

hell /hel/ *noun*
the place where some people believe bad people go when they die: *My mother says I'll go to hell if I lie.*

he'll /hɪl, STRONG hiːl/
short for 'he will'

hello /he'ləʊ/ also **hallo**
1 said to someone when you meet them: *Hello, Trish. How are you?*
2 said when you answer the phone: *Cohen picked up the phone and said 'Hello?'*

helmet /'helmɪt/ *noun*
a hat made of a hard material, which you wear to protect your head

help /help/ *verb* (**helps, helping, helped**)
1 to make it easier for someone to do something: *Can somebody help me, please?* □ *You can help by giving them some money.* ● **help** *uncountable noun Thanks very much for your help.*
2 to improve a situation: *Thanks for your advice. That helps.*

can't help something to be unable to stop the way you feel or behave: *I couldn't help laughing when I saw her face.*

help yourself to take what you want of something: *There's bread on the table. Help yourself.*

helpful /'helpfʊl/ *adjective*
helping you by being useful or willing to work for you: *The staff in the hotel are very helpful.*

helpless /'helpləs/ *adjective*
not having the strength or ability to do anything useful: *Parents often feel helpless when their children are ill.*
▶ **helplessly** *adverb They watched helplessly as the house burned to the ground.*

hemisphere /'hemɪˌsfɪə/ *noun*
1 one half of the Earth: *These animals live in the northern hemisphere.*
2 one half of a sphere (= an object that is shaped like a ball)

hen /hen/ *noun*
a female chicken

her¹ /hə, STRONG hɜː/ *pronoun*
used for talking about a woman, a girl or a female animal: *I told her that dinner was ready.*

her² /hə, STRONG hɜː/ *adjective*
used for showing that something belongs to or relates to a girl or a woman: *She took her coat off and sat down.* □ *She travelled around the world with her husband.*

herb /hɜːb/ *noun*
a plant whose leaves are used in cooking to add flavour to food, or as a medicine: *Fry the mushrooms in a little olive oil and add the chopped herbs.*

h

▶ **herbal** *adjective* Do you know any herbal remedies for colds?

herbivore /ˈhɜːbɪvɔː/ *noun*
an animal that eats only plants. Compare **carnivore** and **omnivore**.

herd /hɜːd/ *noun*
a large group of one type of animal that lives together: Herds of elephants crossed the river each day.

here /hɪə/ *adverb*
1 used when you are talking about the place where you are: I can't stay here all day. □ Come and sit here. □ Sophie was in here a couple of minutes ago.
2 used when you are offering or giving something to someone: Here's your coffee. □ Here's the letter for you to sign.

here's /hɪəz/
short for 'here is'

hero /ˈhɪərəʊ/ *noun* (**heroes**)
1 the main male character of a story: The actor Daniel Radcliffe plays the hero in the Harry Potter films.
2 someone who has done something brave or good: Mr Mandela is a hero who has inspired millions.

heroic /hɪˈrəʊɪk/ *adjective*
used for saying that you admire a person or their actions because they have been very brave: He made a heroic effort to save the boy from the fire.

heroin /ˈherəʊɪn/ *uncountable noun*
a strong illegal drug

heroine /ˈherəʊɪn/ *noun*
1 the main female character of a story: The heroine of the book is a young doctor.
2 a woman who has done something brave or good: China's first gold medal winner became a national heroine.

hers /hɜːz/ *pronoun*
used for showing that something belongs to a woman, girl or female animal: She admitted that the bag was hers. □ Wasn't Rachel a good friend of hers?

herself /həˈself/ *pronoun*
1 used for talking about a woman, girl or female animal that you have just mentioned: She looked at herself in the mirror. □ If she's not careful, she'll hurt herself.
2 used for saying that something is done by a woman or girl, and not by anyone else: She doesn't go to the hairdresser's.

She cuts her hair herself.

he's /hɪz, STRONG hiːz/
short for 'he is' or 'he has'

hesitate /ˈhezɪˌteɪt/ *verb* (**hesitates, hesitating, hesitated**)
to not act quickly, usually because you are not sure about what to say or do: Catherine hesitated before answering.
▶ **hesitation** /ˌhezɪˈteɪʃən/ *noun* After some hesitation, Annabel replied, 'I'll have to think about that.'

hexagon /ˈheksəgən/ *noun*
a shape with six straight sides

hey /heɪ/
1 used in informal situations to attract someone's attention: 'Hey! Be careful!' shouted Patty.
2 used in informal situations to greet someone: He smiled and said 'Hey, Kate, how are you doing?'

hi /haɪ/
used in informal situations to greet someone: 'Hi, Liz,' she said.

hibernation /ˌhaɪbəˈneɪʃən/ *uncountable noun*
the time when some animals sleep through the winter: The animals consume three times more calories to prepare for hibernation.

hiccup /ˈhɪkʌp/ *noun*
a sudden short sound in your throat that often happens because you have been eating or drinking too quickly: Do you know how to cure hiccups? □ Babies can get hiccups in the womb. ● **hiccup** *verb* (**hiccups, hiccuping** or **hiccupping, hiccuped** or **hiccupped**) He laughed so hard he started hiccuping.

hid /hɪd/ → see **hide**

hidden¹ /ˈhɪdən/ → see **hide**

hidden² /ˈhɪdən/ *adjective*
not easy to see or know about: There are hidden dangers on the beach. □ These are the hidden costs of buying a house.

hide /haɪd/ *verb* (**hides, hiding, hid, hidden**)
1 to put something or someone in a place where they cannot easily be seen or found: He hid the bicycle behind the wall.
2 to go somewhere where people cannot easily find you: The little boy hid in the wardrobe.

3 to cover something so that people cannot see it: *She hid her face in her hands.*

4 to not let people know what you feel or know: *Lee tried to hide his excitement.*

hideous /'hɪdiəs/ *adjective*
very ugly or unpleasant: *She saw a hideous face at the window.* □ *He was injured in a hideous knife attack.*

▶ **hideously** *adverb* *I was convinced that I was hideously ugly.*

high /haɪ/ *adjective, adverb* (**higher, highest**)

1 extending a long way from the bottom to the top: *They lived in a house with a high wall around it.* □ *Mount Everest is the highest mountain in the world.*

2 used for talking or asking about how much something measures from the bottom to the top: *The grass in the garden was a foot high.*

3 a long way above the ground: *I looked down from the high window.* □ *The sun was high in the sky.* □ *She can jump higher than other people.*

4 great in amount or strength: *High winds destroyed many trees and buildings.*

5 not deep: *She spoke in a high voice.*

> **LANGUAGE HELP**
> When you are describing people, use **tall**. *She was a tall woman.*

'high jump *noun*
a sports event that involves jumping over a bar that can be raised higher after each jump

highlight¹ /'haɪlaɪt/ *verb* (**highlights, highlighting, highlighted**)
to show that a point or problem is important: *Her talk highlighted the problems of homeless people.*

highlight² /'haɪlaɪt/ *noun*
one of the most interesting parts of an event: *That tennis game was one of the highlights of the tournament.*

highly /'haɪli/ *adverb*

1 used before some adjectives to mean 'very': *Mr Singh was a highly successful salesman.*

2 used for saying that you think something or someone is very good: *Michael thought highly of the school.*

high-tech /ˌhaɪ'tek/ also **high tech, hi tech** *adjective*

using modern methods and computers: *high-tech camera equipment*

hijack /'haɪdʒæk/ *verb* (**hijacks, hijacking, hijacked**)
to illegally take control of a plane or other vehicle while it is travelling from one place to another: *Two men hijacked the plane.*

hike¹ /haɪk/ *noun*
a long walk, especially in the countryside: *We went for a hike in the Campsie Hills.*

hike² /haɪk/ *verb* (**hikes, hiking, hiked**)
to go for a long walk: *We hiked to the top of the mountain.*

▶ **hiker** *noun* *The hikers spent the night in the mountains.*

▶ **hiking** *uncountable noun* *I love hiking in the mountains.*

→ Look at picture on P6

hilarious /hɪ'leəriəs/ *adjective*
very funny: *He told me a hilarious story.*

hill /hɪl/ *noun*
an area of land that is higher than the land around it: *The castle is on a hill above the old town.*

hillside /'hɪlsaɪd/ *noun*
the slope of a hill

hilly /'hɪli/ *adjective* (**hillier, hilliest**)
with a lot of hills: *The countryside in this area is quite hilly.*

him /hɪm/ *pronoun*
used for talking about a man, a boy or a male animal: *Elaine met him at the railway station.* □ *Is Sam there? Let me talk to him.*

himself /hɪm'self/ *pronoun*

1 used for talking about a man, a boy or a male animal that you have just mentioned: *He poured himself a cup of coffee.* □ *He was talking to himself.*

2 used for saying that something is done by a man or a boy, and not by anyone else: *He made your card himself.* □ *He'll probably tell you about it himself.*

Hindu /'hɪndu:, hɪn'du:/ *noun*
a person who believes in Hinduism

● **Hindu** *adjective* *We visited a Hindu temple.*

Hinduism /'hɪndu:ɪzəm/ *uncountable noun*
an Indian religion that has many gods and teaches that people have another life on earth after they die

hinge /hɪndʒ/ *noun*
a piece of metal that is used for joining two pieces of wood together so that they

h

open and shut: *The hinge is broken and the door won't shut.*

hint[1] /hɪnt/ *noun*
1 a suggestion that is not made directly: *Has he given you any hints about what he wants for his birthday?*
2 a helpful piece of advice: *Here are some helpful hints to make your trip easier.*

hint[2] /hɪnt/ *verb* (**hints, hinting, hinted**)
to suggest something in a way that is not direct: *She has hinted at the possibility of having a baby.*

hip /hɪp/ *noun*
one of the two areas or bones at the sides of your body between the tops of your legs and your waist: *Tracey put her hands on her hips and laughed.*
→ Look at picture on P1

'hip-hop *uncountable noun*
a type of music and dance that developed among African-American people in the United States in the 1970s and 1980s

hippo /'hɪpəʊ/ *noun*
a hippopotamus (*informal*)

hippopotamus /ˌhɪpə'pɒtəməs/ *noun* (**hippopotamuses**)
a very large animal with short legs and thick skin that lives in and near rivers

hire /haɪə/ *verb* (**hires, hiring, hired**)
to pay someone to do a job for you: *He just hired a new secretary.*

his /hɪz/ *adjective*
used for showing that something belongs or relates to a man, a boy or a male animal: *He spent part of his career in Hollywood.*
◻ *He went to the party with his girlfriend.*
● **his** *pronoun Henry said the decision was his.*

hiss /hɪs/ *verb* (**hisses, hissing, hissed**)
to make a sound like a long 's': *My cat hisses when I step on its tail.* ● **hiss** *noun* (**hisses**) *The hiss of steam came from the kitchen.*

history /'hɪstəri/ *uncountable noun*
1 events that happened in the past: *The film showed great moments in football history.*
2 the study of events that happened in the past: *He studied history at Indiana University.*

hit[1] /hɪt/ *verb* (**hits, hitting, hit**)
1 to touch someone or something with a lot of force: *She hit the ball hard.* ◻ *The car hit a traffic sign.*
2 to affect a person, place or thing very badly: *The earthquake hit northern Peru.*

hit[2] /hɪt/ *noun*
1 a CD, film or play that is very popular and successful: *The song was a big hit in Japan.*
2 a single visit to a web page: *The company has had 78,000 hits on its website.*
3 when someone finds a website that contains the information they are looking for

hitchhike /'hɪtʃhaɪk/ *verb* (**hitchhikes, hitchhiking, hitchhiked**)
to travel by getting rides from passing vehicles without paying: *Neil hitchhiked to Scotland during his holiday.*
▶ **hitchhiker** *noun On my way to Newcastle I picked up a hitchhiker.*

HIV /ˌeɪtʃ aɪ 'viː/ *uncountable noun*
a virus (= a harmful thing that can make you ill) that reduces the ability of people's bodies to fight illness and that can cause AIDS
HIV negative not infected with the HIV virus
HIV positive infected with the HIV virus

hive /haɪv/ *noun*
a structure in which bees live

hoax /həʊks/ *noun* (**hoaxes**)
an occasion when someone says that something bad is going to happen, when this is not true: *Police say that the bomb alert was a hoax.*

hob /hɒb/ *noun*
the top part of a cooker (= a piece of equipment that you use for cooking food) where you put pans
→ Look at picture on P4

hobby /'hɒbi/ *noun* (**hobbies**)
an activity that you enjoy doing in your free time: *My hobbies are music and tennis.*

hockey /'hɒki/ *uncountable noun*
a sport for two teams of eleven players, in which players use long curved sticks to hit a small hard ball
→ Look at picture on P6

'hockey stick *noun*
a long curved stick that is used for hitting a small ball in the game of hockey

hold[1] /həʊld/ *verb* (**holds, holding, held**)
1 to have something in your hands or your arms: *She held his hand tightly.* ◻ *I held the baby in my arms.*
2 to put something into a particular

position and keep it there: *Hold your hands up.* □ *Try to hold the camera steady.*

3 to be able to contain a particular amount of something: *One CD-ROM disk can hold over 100,000 pages of text.*

4 used with nouns such as 'party' and 'meeting' to talk about particular activities that people are organizing: *The country will hold elections within a year.*

5 (*also* **hold the line**) to wait for a short time when you are making a telephone call: *Please can you hold, sir?*

hold on or **hold onto something** to keep your hand on or around something: *The thief pulled me to the ground but I held onto my handbag.* □ *You must hold on tightly. Don't fall!*

hold someone up to make someone late: *I won't hold you up — I just have one quick question.*

hold something/someone back to stop something or someone from moving forwards or from doing something: *The police held back the crowd.*

hold² /həʊld/ *noun*

1 when you have something in your hands or your arms: *Cooper took hold of the rope and pulled on it.*

2 the place in a ship or an aeroplane where goods or luggage are stored

get hold of someone to succeed in speaking to someone: *I've called him several times but I can't get hold of him.*

get hold of something to find something, usually after some difficulty: *It is hard to get hold of medicines in some areas of the country.*

holdup /'həʊldʌp/ *also* **hold-up** *noun* when someone uses a weapon to make someone give them money or other valuable things: *Police are looking for a man after a hold-up in a local bank.*

hole /həʊl/ *noun*

an opening or an empty space in something: *He dug a hole 45 feet wide and 15 feet deep.* □ *I've got a hole in my jeans.*

hole

holiday /'hɒlɪˌdeɪ/ (*American*: **vacation**) *noun*

1 a time when you do not go to work or school: *I can't wait for the summer holidays.*

2 a time when you go somewhere away from home and stay there for a while: *We're going on holiday in July.*

hollow /'hɒləʊ/ *adjective* having an empty space inside: *a hollow tree*

holly /'hɒli/ *noun* (**hollies**) a plant that has hard, shiny leaves with sharp points, and red berries (= small round fruit) in winter

holocaust /'hɒləkɔːst/ *noun* **the Holocaust** the organized killing by the Nazis of millions of Jews during the Second World War

holy /'həʊli/ *adjective* (**holier, holiest**) connected with God or a particular religion: *This is a holy place.*

home /həʊm/ *noun*

1 the house or flat where someone lives: *He died from a fall at his home in London.* □ *Hi, Mum, I'm home!* ● **home** *adverb She wasn't feeling well and she wanted to go home.*
→ Look at pictures on P4–5

2 the town or country where someone lives or was born: *I'm going home to Scotland for the holidays.*

3 a building where people who cannot care for themselves live and are cared for: *It's a home for elderly people.*

at home

1 in the place where you live: *She stayed at home, waiting for him to call.*

2 used for saying that a sports team is playing on its own ground. Compare with away: *Manchester United are playing at home tonight.* ● **home** *adjective Nolan may return for Saturday's home game against the New York Rangers.*

homeless /'həʊmləs/ *adjective* having nowhere to live: *There are a lot of homeless families in the city.*

the homeless homeless people: *We're collecting money for the homeless.*

homemade /'həʊmmeɪd, həʊm'meɪd/ *adjective* made in someone's home, rather than in a shop or factory: *I miss my mother's homemade bread.*

h

'home page *noun*
the main page of a person's or an organization's website: *The company offers a number of services on its home page.*

homesick /'həʊmsɪk/ *adjective*
feeling unhappy because you are away from home and missing your family and friends: *He was homesick for his family.*

homework /'həʊmwɜːk/ *uncountable noun*
school work that teachers give to students to do at home in the evening or at the weekend: *Have you done your homework, Gemma?*

homosexual /ˌhɒməʊˈsekʃʊəl, ˌhəʊ-/ *adjective*
attracted to people of the same sex: *The study found that 4 to 10 per cent of American men are homosexual.* ● **homosexual** *noun* *The organization wants equal treatment for homosexuals.*

honest /'ɒnɪst/ *adjective, adverb*
1 always telling the truth and not stealing or cheating: *She's honest, and I trust her.*
▶ **honestly** *adverb* *Please try to answer these questions honestly.*
2 used before or after a statement to show that you want people to believe you (*informal*): *I'm not sure, honest.*
▶ **honestly** *adverb* *Honestly, I don't know anything about it.*

honesty /'ɒnɪsti/ *uncountable noun*
the quality of being honest: *I admire his courage and honesty.*

honey /'hʌni/ *noun*
1 a sweet, sticky food that is made by bees (= black-and-yellow insects)
2 a name you call someone as a sign of affection: *Honey, I don't think that's a good idea.*

honeymoon /'hʌniˌmuːn/ *noun*
a holiday taken by a man and a woman who have just got married: *We went to Florida on our honeymoon.*

honour [1] /'ɒnə/ *noun*
a special award that is given to someone: *He won many honours — among them an award for his film performance.*

honour [2] /'ɒnə/ *verb* (**honours, honouring, honoured**)
to give someone public praise for something they have done: *Maradona was honoured with an award from Argentina's football association.*

hood /hʊd/ *noun*
the part of a coat that you can pull up to cover your head: *Put up your hood — it's starting to rain.*

hoof /huːf/ *noun* (**hoofs** or **hooves**)
one of the hard parts of the feet of horses, cows and some other animals: *He heard the sound of horses' hooves behind him.*

hook /hʊk/ *noun*
1 a curved piece of metal or plastic that you use for hanging things on: *His jacket hung from a hook.*
2 a curved piece of metal with a sharp point that you tie to the end of a fishing line to catch fish with: *Mr Kruger removed the hook from the fish's mouth.*

hoop /huːp/ *noun*
1 a ring made of wood, metal or plastic: *Jessica was wearing jeans, trainers and gold hoop earrings.*
2 the ring that players try to throw the ball into in basketball in order to score points for their team

hoot /huːt/ *verb* (**hoots, hooting, hooted**)
to make the loud noise of an owl: *An owl hooted in the distance.* ● **hoot** *noun* *Suddenly, he heard the loud hoot of a train.*

hooves /huːvz/
a plural of **hoof**

hop /hɒp/ *verb* (**hops, hopping, hopped**)
1 to move by jumping on one foot
2 used when birds and animals move by jumping on both of their feet or all four of their feet together: *A small brown bird hopped in front of them.*
3 to move somewhere quickly or suddenly (*informal*): *We hopped on the train.*

hope [1] /həʊp/ *verb* (**hopes, hoping, hoped**)
to want something to be true or to happen: *The team are hoping to win a medal at the Olympic Games.* ☐ *I hope that you get better soon.* ☐ *We're all hoping for some good weather.* ☐ *'I hope we'll meet again soon.' — 'I hope so, too.'*

hope [2] /həʊp/ *noun*
the feeling of wanting something good to happen, and believing that it will happen: *What are your hopes for the future?* ☐ *This medicine will give new hope to millions of people around the world.* ☐ *As time passes, the police are losing hope of finding the men alive.*

hopeful /'həʊpfʊl/ *adjective*
thinking that something that you want

will probably happen: *The doctors are hopeful that Grandma will get better soon.*

hopefully /'həʊpfʊli/ *adverb*
1 said when you are talking about something that you hope will happen: *Hopefully, you won't have any more problems.*
2 hoping that something good will happen: *David looked hopefully at the coffee pot.*

hopeless /'həʊpləs/ *adjective*
1 having no chance of success: *I don't believe the situation is hopeless.*
2 very bad: *I'm hopeless at sport.*
▸ **hopelessly** *adverb Harry realized that he was hopelessly lost.*

horizon /hə'raɪzən/ *noun*
the line that appears between the sky and the land or the sea: *A small boat appeared on the horizon.*

horizontal /ˌhɒrɪ'zɒntəl/ *adjective*
flat and level with the ground: *She was wearing a grey sweater with black horizontal stripes.*

hormone /'hɔːməʊn/ *noun*
a chemical substance in your body that affects the way your body works: *This hormone is present in both sexes.*

horn /hɔːn/ *noun*
1 one of the hard pointed things that grow from an animal's head
2 an object in a car or another vehicle that makes a loud noise, and that you use as a warning of danger: *I could hear the sound of a car horn outside.*
3 a musical instrument with a long metal tube that you play by blowing into it: *Joshua started playing the horn when he was eight.*

horoscope /'hɒrəˌskəʊp/ *noun*
what some people believe will happen to you in the future, using the position of the stars when you were born: *I always read my horoscope in the newspaper.*

horrible /'hɒrɪbəl/ *adjective*
very unpleasant (*informal*): *The smell was horrible.* □ *It was a horrible experience.* □ *Stop being horrible to me!*
▸ **horribly** /'hɒrɪbli/ *adverb Sam was feeling horribly ill.*

horrify /'hɒrɪfaɪ/ *verb* (**horrifies, horrifying, horrified**)
to shock someone greatly: *His family was horrified by the news.*

▸ **horrifying** *adjective It was a horrifying sight.*

horror[1] /'hɒrə/ *uncountable noun*
a feeling of great shock and fear when you see or experience something very unpleasant: *I felt sick with horror.*

horror[2] /'hɒrə/ *adjective*
used about a film that is very frightening that you watch for entertainment: *I'm not a fan of horror films.*

horse /hɔːs/ *noun*
a large animal that people can ride: *Have you ever ridden a horse?*

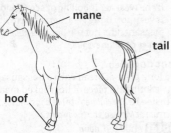

horse racing *uncountable noun*
a sport in which people ride horses in races

horse riding *uncountable noun*
the sport or activity of riding a horse
→ Look at picture on P6

horseshoe /'hɔːsʃuː/ *noun*
a piece of metal in the shape of a U, that is fixed to a horse's foot

hose /həʊz/ *noun*
a long rubber or plastic pipe that you use to put water on plants or on a fire

hospital /'hɒspɪtəl/ *noun*
a place where doctors and nurses care for people who are ill or injured: *The two men were taken to hospital after the car crash.*

host /həʊst/ *noun*
the person at a party who has invited the guests: *I didn't know anyone at the party, except the host.*

hostage /'hɒstɪdʒ/ *noun*
someone who is kept as a prisoner by people until the people get what they want: *The two hostages were freed yesterday.*

hostess /'həʊstɪs/ *noun* (**hostesses**)
the woman at a party who has invited the guests: *She's the perfect hostess, making sure that all her guests are relaxed and happy.*

h

hostile /'hɒstaɪl, AM -təl/ *adjective*
very unfriendly: *A large, hostile crowd surrounded him.*

hot /hɒt/ *adjective* (**hotter, hottest**)
1 having a high temperature: *When the oil is hot, add the sliced onion.* □ *Have some hot coffee. That will warm you up.* □ *I was too hot and tired to eat.*
2 describing the weather when the temperature is high: *It's too hot to play tennis.*
3 having a strong, burning taste: *I love eating hot curries.*

> **LANGUAGE HELP**
> If the weather is **boiling** or **scorching**, it is very hot. If the weather is **warm**, it is pleasant, and not too hot. *We sat in the garden on warm evenings.*

'hot dog *noun*
a long piece of bread with a hot sausage (= a long thin piece of hot cooked meat) inside it: *The children ate hot dogs and ice cream at Melissa's birthday party.*

hotel /ˌhəʊ'tel/ *noun*
a building where people pay to sleep and eat meals: *Janet stayed the night in a small hotel near the harbour.*

hour /aʊə/ *noun*
a period of sixty minutes: *They waited for about two hours.* □ *I only slept about half an hour last night.*

hourly /'aʊəli/ *adjective, adverb*
happening once every hour: *He listened to the hourly news programme on the radio.* □ *The buses run hourly between the two cities.*

house /haʊs/ *noun*
a building where people live: *Amy's invited me to her house for dinner.* □ *Grandma has moved to a small house in the country.*
→ Look at pictures on P4–5

household /'haʊshəʊld/ *noun*
all the people who live together in a house: *I grew up in a large household, with three brothers and three sisters.*

housewife /'haʊswaɪf/ *noun*
(**housewives**)
a woman who does not have a paid job, but spends most of her time looking after her house and family: *Sarah's a housewife and mother of four children.*

housework /'haʊswɜːk/ *uncountable noun*
the work that you do to keep a house
clean and tidy: *Men are doing more housework nowadays.*

hover /'hɒvə/ *verb* (**hovers, hovering, hovered**)
to stay in one place in the air, and not move forwards or backwards: *Helicopters hovered over the scene of the accident.*

how /haʊ/ *adverb*
1 used for asking about the way that something happens or is done: *How do you spell his name?* □ *'How do you get to work?' 'By bus.'* □ *How does a mobile phone work?*
2 used for asking questions about time, or the amount or age of something: *How much money do you have?* □ *How many people will be at the dinner?* □ *How long will you stay?* □ *How old is your son?*
3 used when you are asking someone whether something was good: *How was your trip to Orlando?*
4 used for asking if someone is well: *Hi! How are you doing?* □ *How's Rosie?*
how about... said when you are suggesting something to someone: *How about a cup of coffee?* □ *How about meeting tonight?*
How do you do? used in order to be polite when you meet someone for the first time. The other person answers by saying 'How do you do?' also.

> **LANGUAGE HELP**
> If you ask '**How is Susan?**', you are asking about her health. If you want to know about her appearance, ask '**What does Susan look like?**'. If you want to know about her personality, ask '**What is Susan like?**'.

however¹ /haʊ'evə/ *adverb*
used when you are saying something that is not expected because of what you have just said: *The flat is rather small. It is, however, much nicer than our old flat.*

however² /haʊ'evə/ *conjunction*
used when you want to say that it makes no difference how something is done: *Wear your hair however you want.*

howl /haʊl/ *verb* (**howls, howling, howled**)
to make a long, loud, crying sound: *A dog suddenly howled.* □ *Daniel fell to the ground, howling with pain.* ● **howl** *noun* *The dog gave a long howl.*

HTML /ˌeɪtʃ ti: em 'el/ *uncountable noun*
the standard way of preparing documents so that people can read them on the Internet. **HTML** is short for 'hypertext markup language'.

hub /hʌb/ *noun*
a very important centre for a particular activity: *They say that New York is the hub of the art world.*

hug /hʌg/ *verb* (**hugs, hugging, hugged**)
to put your arms around someone and hold them tightly, to show your love or friendship: *Crystal hugged him and invited him to dinner the next day.* ● **hug** *noun She gave him a hug and said 'Well done.'*

huge /hju:dʒ/ *adjective* (**huger, hugest**)
very large: *Emily was wearing huge dark sunglasses.*
▶ **hugely** *adverb This hotel is hugely popular.*

hum /hʌm/ *verb* (**hums, humming, hummed**)
1 to make a low continuous noise: *The birds sang and the bees hummed.* ● **hum** *noun I could hear the distant hum of traffic.*
2 to sing a tune with your lips closed: *Barbara began humming a song.*

human /'hju:mən/ *adjective*
relating to people, and not animals or machines: *What is the smallest bone in the human body?* ● **human** *noun Humans are capable of some wonderful achievements.*

human being *noun*
a man, a woman or a child: *Every human being has the right to freedom.*

humanity /hju:'mænɪti/ *uncountable noun*
1 all the people in the world: *Can humanity survive the future?*
2 the quality of being kind and thoughtful: *Her speech showed great humanity.*

human nature *uncountable noun*
the way that most people behave: *It is human nature to worry about your children.*

human race *noun*
all the people living in the world: *Some people believe that the human race is destroying the Earth.*

human rights *plural noun*
basic rights that all people should have: *Both armies promised to respect human rights.*

humble /'hʌmbəl/ *adjective* (**humbler, humblest**)
1 not believing that you are better than other people: *He remains humble about his achievements.*
2 ordinary and not special in any way: *Ms Cruz comes from a humble background.*

humid /'hju:mɪd/ *adjective*
wet and warm: *Tomorrow, we can expect hot and humid conditions.*

humidity /hju:'mɪdɪti/ *uncountable noun*
the amount of water in the air: *The humidity is relatively low at the moment.*

humorous /'hju:mərəs/ *adjective*
making you laugh or smile: *He usually likes to write humorous poems.*
▶ **humorously** *adverb Mr Stevenson smiled humorously.*

humour /'hju:mə/ *uncountable noun*
the quality of being funny: *I laughed when I saw the humour of the situation.*

hump /hʌmp/ *noun*
1 a small hill or raised area
2 the large lump on a camel's back: *Camels store water in their hump.*

hump

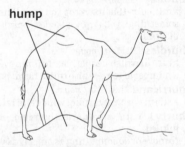

hundred /'hʌndrəd/ (*also* **one hundred**)

LANGUAGE HELP
The plural form is **hundred** after a number.

the number 100: *More than a hundred people were there.*
▶ **hundredth** /'hʌndrədθ/ *adjective, adverb The bank's hundredth anniversary is in December.*
hundreds of something a lot of things or people: *He received hundreds of letters.*

hung /hʌŋ/ → see **hang**

hunger /'hʌŋgə/ *uncountable noun*
the feeling that you get when you need something to eat: *Hunger is the body's signal that you need to eat.*

hungry /'hʌŋgri/ *adjective* (**hungrier, hungriest**)

wanting to eat: *My friend was hungry, so we drove to a supermarket to get some food.*

▸ **hungrily** /'hʌŋgrɪli/ *adverb* *James ate hungrily.*

hunt /hʌnt/ *verb* (**hunts, hunting, hunted**)

1 to chase and kill wild animals for food or as a sport: *I learned to hunt and fish when I was a child.* ● **hunt** *noun* *Dad went on a fox hunt last year.*

▸ **hunting** *uncountable noun* *He went deer hunting with his cousins.*

2 to try to find something or someone by searching carefully: *Police are still hunting for clues at the victim's flat* ● **hunt** *noun Many people helped in the hunt for the missing children.*

▸ **hunting** *uncountable noun Job hunting is not easy.*

hunter /'hʌntə/ *noun*

a person who hunts wild animals for food or as a sport: *Hundreds of deer hunters will visit the area this season.*

hurdle /'hɜːdəl/ *noun*

a difficulty that may stop you from doing something: *Writing a CV is the first hurdle in a job search.*

hurdles /'hɜːdəlz/ *noun*

a race in which people have to jump over a number of fences (also called hurdles)

hurricane /'hʌrɪkən/ *noun*

a storm with very strong winds and rain

hurry¹ /'hʌri/ *verb* (**hurries, hurrying, hurried**)

to move or do something as quickly as you can: *Claire hurried along the road.* □ *Everyone hurried to find a seat.*

hurry up to do something more quickly: *Hurry up and get ready, or you'll miss the school bus!*

hurry² /'hʌri/ *noun*

in a hurry needing or wanting to do something quickly: *I'm sorry, I'm in a hurry and I have to go!*

hurt /hɜːt/ *verb* (**hurts, hurting, hurt**)

1 to make someone or something feel pain: *Yasin hurt himself while he was playing football.* □ *I fell over and hurt my leg yesterday.*

● **hurt** *adjective How badly are you hurt?*

2 used for saying that you feel pain in a part of your body: *His arm hurt.*

3 to say or do something that makes someone unhappy: *I'm really sorry if I hurt your feelings.* ● **hurt** *adjective She was deeply hurt by what Smith said.*

husband /'hʌzbənd/ *noun*

the man a woman is married to: *Eva married her husband in 1957.*

→ Look at picture on P8

hush¹ /hʌʃ/

used when you are telling someone to be quiet: *Hush! The teacher's talking.*

hush² /hʌʃ/ *noun*

when everything is quiet in a place: *There was a sudden hush in the room.*

hut /hʌt/ *noun*

a small simple building, especially one made of wood

hygiene /'haɪdʒiːn/ *uncountable noun*

the practice of keeping yourself and the things you use clean: *The key to good hygiene is washing your hands before touching food.*

▸ **hygienic** /haɪ'dʒiːnɪk/ *adjective This kitchen is easy to keep clean and hygienic.*

hymn /hɪm/ *noun*

a religious song that Christians (= people who believe in Jesus Christ) sing in church: *I like singing hymns.*

hyperlink /'haɪpəlɪŋk/ *noun*

a link to another part of a document on a computer or to another document: *Web pages are full of hyperlinks.*

hyphen /'haɪfən/ *noun*

the punctuation sign (-) that you use to join two words together, as in 'left-handed'. You also use a hyphen to show that a word continues on the next line.

hypnosis /hɪp'nəʊsɪs/ *uncountable noun*

when someone is in a sort of deep sleep, but they can still see, hear and speak: *Ms Chorley uses hypnosis to help her clients relax.*

I i

I /aɪ/ *pronoun*
used for talking about yourself as the subject of a verb: *I live in Arizona.* □ *Jim and I are getting married.*

ice /aɪs/ *uncountable noun*
frozen water: *The ground was covered with ice.* □ *Do you want ice in your drink?*

iceberg /'aɪsbɜːg/ *noun*
a very large piece of ice that floats in the sea

ice 'cream *noun*
1 a very cold sweet food that is made from frozen cream: *Serve the pie warm with vanilla ice cream.*
2 a portion of ice cream: *Do you want an ice cream?*
→ Look at picture on P3

'ice cube *noun*
a small block of ice that you put into a drink to make it cold

'ice ,hockey *uncountable noun*
a game that is played on ice by two teams. They use long curved sticks to try to hit a small rubber disc (= a puck) into a goal.

'ice-skate also **ice skate** *noun*
a boot with a thin metal bar underneath that people wear to move quickly on ice

'ice-,skating *noun*
the activity or sport of moving about on ice wearing ice-skates: *I love watching ice-skating on television.*

icicle /'aɪsɪkəl/ *noun*
a long pointed piece of ice that hangs down from a surface

icicle

icing /'aɪsɪŋ/
uncountable noun
a sweet substance that you use for decorating cakes

icon /'aɪkɒn/ *noun*
a picture on a computer screen that you can choose, in order to open a particular program: *Kate clicked on the mail icon on her computer screen.*

icy /'aɪsi/ *adjective* (**icier**, **iciest**)
1 extremely cold: *An icy wind was blowing.*
2 covered in ice: *an icy road*

ID /ˌaɪ 'diː/ *uncountable noun*
a document that shows who you are: *I had no ID so I couldn't prove that it was my car.*

I'd /aɪd/
1 short for 'I had': *I was sure I'd seen her before.*
2 short for 'I would': *There are some questions I'd like to ask.*

idea /aɪ'diːə/ *noun*
1 a thought, especially a new one: *These people have a lot of great ideas.* □ *'Let's have something to eat.' — 'Good idea.'*
2 how much you know or understand about something: *We had no idea what was happening.*
3 the aim or purpose of something: *The idea is to have fun.*

ideal¹ /aɪ'diːəl/ *adjective*
1 best possible: *You are the ideal person to do the job.*
2 perfect: *Imagine for a moment that you're living in an ideal world.*

ideal² /aɪ'diːəl/ *noun*
a principle or idea that people try to achieve: *We must defend the ideals of liberty and freedom.*

identical /aɪ'dentɪkəl/ *adjective*
exactly the same: *The houses were almost identical.*

identification /aɪˌdentɪfɪ'keɪʃən/
uncountable noun
a document that proves who you are: *The police asked him to show some identification.*

identify /aɪ'dentɪfaɪ/ *verb* (**identifies**, **identifying**, **identified**) to be able to say who or what a person or thing is: *Now we have identified the problem, we must decide how to fix it.* □ *The handbook tells you how to identify the different birds.*

▶ **identification** /aɪ,dentɪfɪˈkeɪʃən/ **uncountable noun** *Early identification of the disease is important.*

identity /aɪˈdentɪti/ **noun** (**identities**)
who you are: *He uses the name Abu to hide his identity.*

idiom /ˈɪdiəm/ **noun**
a group of words that have a particular meaning when you use them together. For example, 'to hit the roof' is an idiom that means to become very angry.

idiot /ˈɪdiət/ **noun**
someone who is very stupid: *I felt like an idiot.*

idol /ˈaɪdəl/ **noun**
a famous person who is greatly admired or loved: *The crowd cheered when their idol waved to the cameras.*

if /ɪf/ **conjunction**
1 used for talking about things that might happen: *You can go if you want.* □ *He might win — if he's lucky.*
2 used when you are talking about a question that someone has asked: *He asked if I wanted some water.*

as if used for comparing one thing with another: *He moved his hand as if he was writing something.*

if only used for expressing a strong wish: *If only I had a car.*

ignorant /ˈɪgnərənt/ **adjective**
not knowing things: *People don't want to appear ignorant.* □ *Most people are ignorant of these facts.*

▶ **ignorance** /ˈɪgnərəns/ **uncountable noun** *I feel embarrassed by my ignorance of world history.*

ignore /ɪgˈnɔː/ **verb** (**ignores, ignoring, ignored**)
to not pay any attention to someone or

ignore

He completely ignored the 'No Parking' sign.

something: *He completely ignored the 'No Parking' sign.*

ill /ɪl/ **adjective**
not in good health: *He is seriously ill with cancer.*

I'll /aɪl/
short for 'I will' or 'I shall'

illegal /ɪˈliːgəl/ **adjective**
not allowed by law: *It is illegal for the interviewer to ask your age.* □ *I have done nothing illegal.*

▶ **illegally** **adverb** *He received a fine for parking illegally.*

illness /ˈɪlnəs/ **noun** (**illnesses**)
1 a particular disease or a period of bad health: *She is recovering from a serious illness.*
2 **uncountable** the fact or experience of being ill: *He was away from school because of illness.*

illusion /ɪˈluːʒən/ **noun**
1 a false idea or belief: *He's under the illusion that money makes people happy.*
2 something that seems to exist: *Large windows can give the illusion of more space.*

illustrate /ˈɪləstreɪt/ **verb** (**illustrates, illustrating, illustrated**)
to put pictures into a book: *She illustrates children's books.*

▶ **illustration** **noun** *It's a book with beautiful illustrations.*

IM /,aɪ ˈem/ **noun**
short for **instant messaging**: *The device lets you chat via IM.*

I'm /aɪm/
short for 'I am'

image /ˈɪmɪdʒ/ **noun**
1 a picture of someone or something (*formal*): *The image on screen changes every 10 seconds.*
2 a picture or idea of someone or something in your mind: *If you talk about California, people have an image of sunny blue skies.*
3 the way that a person, group or organization appears to other people: *The government does not have a good public image.*

imaginary /ɪˈmædʒɪnəri/ **adjective**
existing only in your mind or in a story, and not in real life: *Lots of children have imaginary friends.*

imagination /ɪ,mædʒɪˈneɪʃən/ **noun**
your ability to invent pictures or ideas in your mind: *You must use your imagination to*

find an answer to this problem.

imagine /ɪˈmædʒɪn/ *verb* (**imagines, imagining, imagined**)

1 to form a picture or idea of something in your mind: *He could not imagine a more peaceful scene.*

2 to think that you have seen, heard or experienced something, when in fact you have not: *I realize that I imagined the whole thing.*

imitate /ˈɪmɪˌteɪt/ *verb* (**imitates, imitating, imitated**)

to copy what someone does or produces: *I didn't like the way he imitated my voice.*

imitation [1] /ˌɪmɪˈteɪʃən/ *noun*

a copy of something: *He tried to do an imitation of an English accent.* ▢ *Make sure you get the real thing — don't buy an imitation.*

imitation [2] /ˌɪmɪˈteɪʃən/ *adjective*

made to look like another, more expensive product: *The books are covered in imitation leather.*

immature /ˌɪməˈtjʊə/ *adjective*

behaving in a silly way that is more typical of young people: *He's too immature to get married.*

immediate /ɪˈmiːdiət/ *adjective*

happening next or very soon: *There is no immediate solution to the problem.*

immediately /ɪˈmiːdiətli/ *adverb*

happening without any delay: *'Call the police immediately!' she shouted.*

immense /ɪˈmens/ *adjective*

extremely large: *We still need to do an immense amount of work.*

immensely /ɪˈmensli/ *adverb*

very much: *I enjoyed the film immensely.*

immigrant /ˈɪmɪɡrənt/ *noun*

a person who comes to live in a country from another country: *The company employs several immigrants.*

immigration /ˌɪmɪˈɡreɪʃən/ *uncountable noun*

when people come into a country to live and work there: *The government is changing the immigration laws.*

immoral /ɪˈmɒrəl/ *adjective*

bad or wrong: *Some people think that it's immoral to earn a lot of money.*

immortal /ɪˈmɔːtəl/ *adjective*

living or lasting forever: *They prayed to their immortal gods.* ▢ *When you're young, you think you're immortal.*

immune /ɪˈmjuːn/ *adjective*

safe from being affected by a particular disease: *Some people are naturally immune to measles.*

impact /ˈɪmpækt/ *noun*

1 having a strong effect: *The experience had a huge impact on her.*

2 the action of one object hitting another: *The impact of the crash turned the lorry over.*

impatient /ɪmˈpeɪʃənt/ *adjective*

1 annoyed because you have to wait too long for something: *People are impatient for the war to be over.*

▸ **impatiently** *adverb* *She waited impatiently for the post to arrive.*

2 becoming annoyed very quickly: *Try not to be impatient with your kids.*

▸ **impatience** *uncountable noun* *She tried to hide her growing impatience with him.*

imperative /ɪmˈperətɪv/ *noun*

the base form of a verb, usually without a subject. The imperative is used for telling someone to do something. Examples are 'Go away' and 'Please be careful.'

imperfect /ɪmˈpɜːfɪkt/ *adjective*

having faults (*formal*): *We live in an imperfect world.*

imperialism /ɪmˈpɪəriəlɪzəm/ *uncountable noun*

a system in which a powerful country controls other countries: *These nations are victims of imperialism.*

▸ **imperialist** *noun* *She accused me of being a Western imperialist.*

import [1] /ɪmˈpɔːt/ *verb* (**imports, importing, imported**)

to buy goods from another country for use in your own country: *The U.S. imports over half of its oil.*

▸ **importer** *noun* *The UK is the world's biggest importer of champagne.*

import [2] /ˈɪmpɔːt/ *noun*

a product bought from another country for use in your own country: *Cheap imports are adding to the problems of our farmers.*

important /ɪmˈpɔːtənt/ *adjective*

1 that you feel you must do, have or think about: *The most important thing in my life is my career.* ▢ *It's important to answer her questions honestly.*

▸ **importance** *uncountable noun* *The teacher stressed the importance of doing our homework.*

▶ **importantly** *adverb* I was hungry and, more importantly, my children were hungry.
2 having influence or power: She's an important person in the world of television.

impossible /ɪmˈpɒsɪbəl/ *adjective*
unable to be done or to happen: It is impossible for me to get another job at my age. □ The snow made it impossible to play the game.

impractical /ɪmˈpræktɪkəl/ *adjective*
not sensible or realistic: She was wearing impractical high-heeled shoes.

impress /ɪmˈpres/ *verb* (**impresses, impressing, impressed**)
to make you feel great admiration: Their speed impressed everyone.
▶ **impressed** *adjective* I was very impressed by his lecture.

impression /ɪmˈpreʃən/ *noun*
what you feel or think about someone or something: What were your first impressions of college?
make an impression have a strong effect: It's her first day at work and she has already made an impression.
under the impression believing that something is true: I was under the impression that you were moving to New York.

impressive /ɪmˈpresɪv/ *adjective*
making you feel strong admiration: They collected an impressive amount of cash: $390.8 million.

improve /ɪmˈpruːv/ *verb* (**improves, improving, improved**)
to get better: Your general health will improve if you drink more water. □ Their French improved during their trip to Paris. □ We are trying to improve our services to customers.
▶ **improvement** /ɪmˈpruːvmənt/ *noun* There have been some great improvements in technology in recent years.

impulse /ˈɪmpʌls/ *noun*
a sudden feeling that you must do something: I felt a sudden impulse to tell her that I loved her.
on impulse suddenly deciding to do something: Sean usually acts on impulse.

impulsive /ɪmˈpʌlsɪv/ *adjective*
doing things suddenly, without thinking about them carefully first: He is too impulsive to be a good leader.

in ¹ /ɪn/ *preposition*
1 used when you are saying where someone

or something is: My brother was playing in the garden. □ Mark now lives in Singapore. □ Are you still in bed? It's almost lunchtime!
2 used for saying that you are wearing a particular piece of clothing: Who is the woman in the red dress?
3 used for talking about the job that someone does: John's son is in the navy. □ Dad works in the music industry.
4 used for talking about a particular period of time: He was born in 1996. □ Sales improved in April.
5 used for talking about how long something takes: He walked two hundred miles in eight days.
6 used for talking about a state or situation: Dave was in a hurry to get back to work. □ The kitchen's in a mess.
7 used for talking about the way that something is done or said: Please do not write in pencil — use a pen. □ The men were speaking in Russian. □ She always talks in a loud voice.

in ² /ɪn/ *adjective, adverb*
1 to a place, from outside: I knocked on the door, and went in.
2 at your home: Maria isn't in just now.
3 inside the area of play in games such as tennis or basketball. Compare with **out**: The line judge signalled that the ball was in.

inability /ˌɪnəˈbɪlɪti/ *uncountable noun*
the fact that someone cannot do something: Her inability to concentrate could cause an accident.

inaccurate /ɪnˈækjʊrət/ *adjective*
not completely correct: Her comments are inaccurate and untrue.

inappropriate /ˌɪnəˈprəʊpriət/ *adjective*
wrong or bad in a particular situation: The film is inappropriate for young children.

inbox /ˈɪnbɒks/ *noun* (**inboxes**) also **in-box**
the place where your computer stores emails that have arrived for you: I went home and checked my inbox.

incapable /ɪnˈkeɪpəbəl/ *adjective*
unable to do something: She is incapable of making sensible decisions.

incentive /ɪnˈsentɪv/ *noun*
something that makes you want to do something: We want to give our employees an incentive to work hard.

inch /ɪntʃ/ *noun* (**inches**)
a unit for measuring length. There are

2.54 centimetres in an inch. There are twelve inches in a foot: *Dig a hole 18 inches deep.*

incident /'ɪnsɪdənt/ *noun*
something unpleasant that happens (*formal*): *The incident happened in the early hours of Sunday morning.*

inclined /ɪn'klaɪnd/ *adjective*
having a particular opinion, but without feeling strongly about it: *I am inclined to agree with Alan.*

include /ɪn'kluːd/ *verb* (**includes, including, included**)
to have something as one part: *The trip will include a day at the beach.*

including /ɪn'kluːdɪŋ/ *preposition*
part of a particular group of people or things: *Thousands were killed, including many women and children.*

income /'ɪnkʌm/ *noun*
the money that a person earns or receives: *Many of the families here are on low incomes.*

'income tax *noun* (**income taxes**)
a part of your income that you have to pay regularly to the government: *You pay income tax every month.*

incompetent /ɪn'kɒmpɪtənt/ *adjective*
unable to do a job properly: *He always fires incompetent employees.*

incomplete /ˌɪnkəm'pliːt/ *adjective*
not yet finished, or not having all the parts that are needed: *The data we have is incomplete.*

inconsiderate /ˌɪnkən'sɪdərət/ *adjective*
not thinking enough about how your behaviour will affect other people: *It was inconsiderate of her to come without calling.*

inconvenient /ˌɪnkən'viːniənt/ *adjective*
causing difficulties for someone: *I know it's inconvenient, but I have to see you now.*

incorrect /ˌɪnkə'rekt/ *adjective*
wrong or untrue: *The answer he gave was incorrect.*
▸ **incorrectly** *adverb* *The article suggested, incorrectly, that he was sick.*

increase /ɪn'kriːs/ *verb* (**increases, increasing, increased**)
to get bigger in some way: *The population continues to increase.* □ *Japanese exports increased by 2% last year.* ● **increase** /'ɪnkriːs/ *noun* *There was a sudden increase in the cost of oil.*

increasingly /ɪn'kriːsɪŋli/ *adverb*
more and more: *He was finding it increasingly difficult to make decisions.*

incredible /ɪn'kredɪbəl/ *adjective*
1 used for saying how good something is, or to make what you are saying stronger: *The food was incredible.* □ *I work an incredible number of hours.*
▸ **incredibly** *adverb* *It was incredibly hard work.*
2 used for saying that you cannot believe that something is really true: *It seems incredible that nobody saw the danger.*

indeed /ɪn'diːd/ *adverb*
1 used for making something you have said stronger: *He admitted that he had indeed paid him.*
2 used for making the word 'very' stronger: *The results were very strange indeed.*

indefinite /ɪn'defɪnɪt/ *adjective*
without a fixed finishing time: *He was sent to jail for an indefinite period.*
▸ **indefinitely** *adverb* *We cannot allow this situation to continue indefinitely.*

in,definite 'article *noun*
the words 'a' and 'an'

independence /ˌɪndɪ'pendəns/ *uncountable noun*
1 when one country is not ruled by another country: *In 1816, Argentina declared its independence from Spain.*
2 the fact that a person does not need help from other people: *He was afraid of losing his independence.*

independent /ˌɪndɪ'pendənt/ *adjective*
1 not affected by, or not needing help from other people: *We need an independent review.*
▸ **independently** *adverb* *We have groups of people working independently in different parts of the world.*
2 able to take care of yourself without needing help or money from anyone else: *Children become more independent as they grow.*
▸ **independently** *adverb* *We want to help disabled students to live independently.*
3 not ruled by other countries, but having a separate government: *Papua New Guinea became independent from Australia in 1975.*

index /'ɪndeks/ *noun* (**indices** or **indexes**)
a list printed at the back of a book that tells you what is included in it and on

which pages you can find each item: *There's a subject index at the back of the book.*

indicate /'ɪndɪˌkeɪt/ *verb* (**indicates, indicating, indicated**)
1 to show that something is true: *The report indicates that most people agree.*
2 to show someone where something is (*formal*): *He indicated a chair. 'Sit down.'*

indication /ˌɪndɪ'keɪʃən/ *noun*
a sign that suggests something: *This statement is a strong indication that the government is changing its mind.*

indicator /'ɪndɪˌkeɪtə/ *noun*
a flashing light on a car that tells you when the car is going to turn left or right

indifferent /ɪn'dɪfərənt/ *adjective*
not at all interested in something: *We have become indifferent to the suffering of other people.*

indigestion /ˌɪndɪ'dʒestʃən/ *uncountable noun*
pains in your stomach because of something that you have eaten

indirect /ˌɪndaɪ'rekt, -dɪr-/ *adjective*
1 not caused directly by the person or thing mentioned, but happening because of them: *Millions could die of hunger as an indirect result of the war.*
▶ **indirectly** *adverb The government is indirectly responsible for the violence.*
2 not the shortest route between two places: *He took an indirect route back home.*
3 suggesting something, without stating it clearly: *It was an indirect criticism of the president.*
▶ **indirectly** *adverb She indirectly suggested that he should leave.*

indirect 'object *noun*
the thing or person that something is done to in a sentence. For example, in 'She gave him her address', 'him' is the indirect object. Compare with **direct object**.

individual¹ /ˌɪndɪ'vɪdʒʊəl/ *adjective*
relating to one person or thing, rather than to a large group: *We ask each individual customer for suggestions.*
▶ **individually** *adverb You can remove each seat individually.*

individual² /ˌɪndɪ'vɪdʒʊəl/ *noun*
a person: *We want to reward individuals who do good things.*

indoor /'ɪndɔː/ *adjective*
done or used inside a building: *The hotel has an indoor pool.*

indoors /ˌɪn'dɔːz/ *adverb*
in or to the inside of a building: *They warned us to close the windows and stay indoors.*

industrial /ɪn'dʌstriəl/ *adjective*
1 describing things that relate to industry: *The company sells industrial machinery and equipment.*
2 used for describing a city or a country in which industry is very important: *Western industrial countries*

industry /'ɪndəstri/ *noun* (**industries**)
1 *uncountable* the work of making things in factories: *The meeting was for leaders in banking and industry.*
2 all the people and activities involved in making a particular product or providing a particular service: *The country depends on its tourism industry.*

inefficient /ˌɪnɪ'fɪʃənt/ *adjective*
not using time or energy in the best way: *inefficient work methods*

inequality /ˌɪnɪ'kwɒlɪti/ *uncountable noun*
when people do not have the same social position, wealth or chances: *Now there is even greater inequality between the rich and the poor.*

inevitable /ɪn'evɪtəbəl/ *adjective*
impossible to prevent or avoid: *Suffering is an inevitable part of life.*
▶ **inevitably** /ɪn'evɪtəbli/ *adverb Advances in technology will inevitably lead to unemployment.*

inexperienced /ˌɪnɪk'spɪəriənst/ *adjective*
having little knowledge or experience of a particular subject: *She was treated by an inexperienced young doctor.*

infant /'ɪnfənt/ *noun*
a baby or very young child (*formal*): *He held the infant in his arms.*

infect /ɪn'fekt/ *verb* (**infects, infecting, infected**)
to give a person or an animal a disease or an illness: *A single mosquito can infect a large number of people.*
▶ **infection** /ɪn'fekʃən/ *uncountable noun Even a small cut can lead to infection.*

infection /ɪn'fekʃən/ *noun*
an illness that is caused by bacteria: *Ear infections are common in young children.*

infectious /ɪnˈfekʃəs/ *adjective*
passed easily from one person to another.
Compare with **contagious**: *The disease is
highly infectious.*

inferior /ɪnˈfɪəriə/ *adjective*
not as good as something else: *If you buy it
somewhere else, you'll get an inferior product.*

infertile /ɪnˈfɜːtaɪl/ *adjective*
1 unable to produce babies: *Ten per cent of
couples are infertile.*
2 used for describing soil that is of poor
quality: *Nothing grew on the land, which was
poor and infertile.*

infinite /ˈɪnfɪnɪt/ *adjective*
having no limit, end or edge: *There is an
infinite number of stars.*

infinitive /ɪnˈfɪnɪtɪv/ *noun*
the basic form of a verb, for example, 'do',
'be', 'take' and 'eat'. The infinitive is often
used with 'to' in front of it.

inflatable /ɪnˈfleɪtəbəl/ *adjective*
needing to be filled with air before being
used: *He played on the inflatable castle.*

inflate /ɪnˈfleɪt/ *verb* (**inflates, inflating,
inflated**)
to fill something with air: *You should inflate
tyres to the level recommended by the manufacturer.*

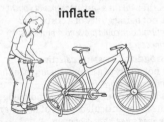

inflate

inflation /ɪnˈfleɪʃən/ *uncountable noun*
a general increase in the prices of goods
and services in a country: *The whole world is
suffering from rising inflation.*

influence¹ /ˈɪnfluəns/ *uncountable noun*
the power to make other people agree
with you or do what you want: *He used his
influence to get his son into medical school.*
**have an influence on someone/
something** to affect what someone does
or what happens: *Alan had a big influence on
my career.*

influence² /ˈɪnfluəns/ *verb* (**influences,
influencing, influenced**)
to use your power to make someone agree

with you or do what you want: *The
newspapers tried to influence public opinion.*

influential /ˌɪnfluˈenʃəl/ *adjective*
having a lot of influence over people or
events: *He was influential in changing the law.*

info /ˈɪnfəʊ/ *uncountable noun* (*informal*)
short for **information**

inform /ɪnˈfɔːm/ *verb* (**informs, informing,
informed**)
to tell someone about something: *We will
inform you of any changes.* □ *My daughter
informed me that she was leaving home.*

informal /ɪnˈfɔːməl/ *adjective*
relaxed and friendly, rather than serious
or official: *Her style of writing is very informal.*
□ *The house has an informal atmosphere.*
▶ **informally** *adverb* *She was chatting
informally to the children.*

information /ˌɪnfəˈmeɪʃən/ *uncountable
noun*
facts about someone or something: *Pat did
not give her any information about Sarah.* □ *We
can provide information on training.*

> **LANGUAGE HELP**
> **Information** is an uncountable noun.
> You can say a **piece of information**
> when you are talking about a
> particular fact.

infor·mation tech·nology *uncountable
noun*
the study and practice of using computers.
The short form **I.T.** is often used: *He works
in the information technology industry.*

informative /ɪnˈfɔːmətɪv/ *adjective*
giving you useful information: *The meeting
was friendly and informative.*

ingredient /ɪnˈɡriːdiənt/ *noun*
one of the things that you use to make
something, especially when you are
cooking: *Mix together all the ingredients.*

inhabit /ɪnˈhæbɪt/ *verb* (**inhabits,
inhabiting, inhabited**)
to live in a particular place: *The people who
inhabit these islands do not use money.*

inhabitant /ɪnˈhæbɪtənt/ *noun*
the people who live in a particular place:
*The inhabitants of the town wrote a letter to the
president.*

inhale /ɪnˈheɪl/ *verb* (**inhales, inhaling,
inhaled**)
to breathe in: *He took a long slow breath,*

inhaling deeply. □ The men inhaled the poisonous gas and began to feel sick.

inherit /ɪnˈherɪt/ *verb* (**inherits, inheriting, inherited**)
1 to receive money or property from someone who has died: *He has no child to inherit his house.*
2 to be born with a personal quality because other members of your family had it: *Her children have inherited her love of sports.*

inheritance /ɪnˈherɪtəns/ *noun*
money or property that you receive from someone who has died: *She used her inheritance to buy a house.*

initial ¹ /ɪˈnɪʃəl/ *adjective*
happening at the beginning of a process: *The initial reaction has been excellent.*

initial ² /ɪˈnɪʃəl/ *noun*
the capital letter that begins a name: *She drove a silver car with her initials on the side.*

initially /ɪˈnɪʃəli/ *adverb*
near the beginning of a process or situation: *The list initially included 11 players.*

inject /ɪnˈdʒekt/ *verb* (**injects, injecting, injected**)
to put a substance into someone's body using a special type of needle: *The drug was injected into patients four times a week.*

injection
/ɪnˈdʒekʃən/
noun
medicine that someone puts into your body using a special type of needle: *They gave me an injection to help me sleep.*

injection

injure /ˈɪndʒə/ *verb* (**injures, injuring, injured**)
to damage part of someone's body: *The bomb seriously injured five people.*

injured /ˈɪndʒəd/ *adjective*
having suffered damage to part of the body: *Nurses helped the injured man.*
the injured *Army helicopters moved the injured (= injured people).*

injury /ˈɪndʒəri/ *noun* (**injuries**)
damage to a person's or an animal's body: *He was suffering from serious head injuries.*

injustice /ɪnˈdʒʌstɪs/ *uncountable noun*
when a situation is not fair or right: *They have fought injustice all their lives.*

ink /ɪŋk/ *noun*
the coloured liquid that you use for writing or printing: *The letter was written in blue ink.*

inland /ɪnˈlænd, ˈɪnlænd/ *adjective, adverb*
not beside the sea, but in or near the middle of a country: *inland lakes* □ *Most of the population lives inland.*

'in-laws *plural noun*
the parents of your husband or wife: *At Christmas, we had lunch with my in-laws.*

inner /ˈɪnə/ *adjective*
used for describing the parts inside something, or the parts closest to its centre: *James has an infection of the inner ear.*

ˌinner ˈcity *noun* (**inner cities**)
the poor areas near the centre of a big city: *Samuel grew up in an inner-city neighbourhood in Houston.*

innocence /ˈɪnəsəns/ *uncountable noun*
1 the quality of having no experience or knowledge of the more difficult aspects of life: *Ah! The sweet innocence of youth!*
2 not being guilty of a crime: *This information could prove your brother's innocence.*

innocent /ˈɪnəsənt/ *adjective*
1 not guilty of a crime: *The jury found him innocent of murder.*
2 having no experience or knowledge of the more difficult aspects of life: *They seemed so young and innocent.*

innovation /ˌɪnəˈveɪʃən/ *noun*
a new thing or a new way of doing something: *They showed us some of their latest technological innovations.*

innovative /ˈɪnəvətɪv, -veɪtɪv/ *adjective*
1 new and different: *The company produces innovative car designs.*
2 having new ideas and doing different things: *He is one of America's most innovative film-makers.*

input /ˈɪnpʊt/ *noun*
1 the help, information or advice that one person gives to another person: *There has been a lot of hard work and input from the public.*
2 *uncountable* information that you type

into a computer: *Who is responsible for data input here?* • **input** *verb* (**inputs, inputting, input**) *We need more staff to input the data.*

inquisitive /ɪn'kwɪzɪtɪv/ *adjective*
wanting to find out about things: *Amy was very inquisitive, always wanting to know how things worked.*

insane /ɪn'seɪn/ *adjective*
1 seriously mentally ill: *For a while, I thought I was going insane.*
2 very foolish: *I thought the idea was completely insane.*

insect /'ɪnsekt/ *noun*
a very small animal that has six legs. Most insects have wings.

insecure /ˌɪnsɪ'kjʊə/ *adjective*
1 thinking that you are not good enough: *Most people are a little insecure about their looks.*
▶ **insecurity** /ˌɪnsɪ'kjʊərɪti/ *uncountable noun* *Both men and women can have feelings of shyness and insecurity.*
2 not firm or steady: *Don't take risks with an insecure ladder.*

insensitive /ɪn'sensɪtɪv/ *adjective*
not thinking about or caring about other people's feelings: *My husband is very insensitive to my problem.*
▶ **insensitivity** /ɪnˌsensɪ'tɪvɪti/ *uncountable noun* *I'm sorry about my insensitivity towards her.*

insert /ɪn's3ːt/ *verb* (**inserts, inserting, inserted**)
to put an object inside something: *Mike took a key from his pocket and inserted it into the lock.*

insert

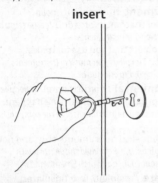

inside¹ /ɪn'saɪd/ *preposition*
used for showing that one thing is in another: *Inside the envelope was a photograph.* □ *There's a telephone inside the entrance hall.*

• **inside** *adjective Josh took his mobile phone from the inside pocket of his jacket.*

inside² /ˌɪn'saɪd/ *adverb*
into a building: *The couple chatted on the doorstep before going inside.*

inside³ /ˌɪn'saɪd/ *noun*
the inner part of something: *I've painted the inside of the house.*

inside out with the part that is normally inside on the outside: *I didn't realize that my T-shirt was inside out.*

insight /'ɪnsaɪt/ *noun*
a good understanding of something: *This book provides fascinating insights into the way the mind works.*

insignificant /ˌɪnsɪg'nɪfɪkənt/ *adjective*
not important: *In 1949, Bonn was a small, insignificant city.*

insist /ɪn'sɪst/ *verb* (**insists, insisting, insisted**)
1 to say firmly that something must happen: *Rob insisted on driving them to the station.* □ *Paul and Esther insisted that I stay for dinner.*
2 to say very firmly that something is true: *Clarke insisted that he was telling the truth.*

insomnia /ɪn'sɒmniə/ *uncountable noun*
a condition in which someone finds it difficult to sleep: *My mother has always suffered from insomnia.*

inspect /ɪn'spekt/ *verb* (**inspects, inspecting, inspected**)
to look at something very carefully: *Dad inspected the car carefully before he bought it.*
▶ **inspection** /ɪn'spekʃən/ *noun Dixon still makes weekly inspections of all his shops.*

inspector /ɪn'spektə/ *noun*
1 a person whose job is to check that people do things correctly: *a fire inspector*
2 an officer in the police: *Police Inspector John Taylor*

inspiration /ˌɪnspɪ'reɪʃən/ *uncountable noun*
a feeling of enthusiasm and new ideas that you get from someone or something: *My inspiration as a writer comes from poets like Walt Whitman.*

inspire /ɪn'spaɪə/ *verb* (**inspires, inspiring, inspired**)
1 to give you new ideas and a strong feeling of enthusiasm: *Singer and songwriter Bob Dylan inspired a generation of young people.*

▶ **inspiring** *adjective* She was one of the most inspiring people I ever met.

2 to make someone feel a particular way: A teacher has to inspire confidence in the students.

install /ɪnˈstɔːl/ *verb* (**installs, installing, installed**)

to put something somewhere so that it is ready to be used: They installed a new telephone line in the flat.

▶ **installation** *uncountable noun* The installation of smoke alarms could save hundreds of lives.

instalment /ɪnˈstɔːlmənt/ *noun*

1 one of several small regular payments that you make over a period of time: She is repaying the loan in monthly instalments of £30.

2 one part of a story in a magazine, or on TV or radio: Charles Dickens' novel, The Old Curiosity Shop, was published in weekly instalments.

instance /ˈɪnstəns/ *noun*

for instance used for giving an example of what you are talking about: I want to talk about environmental issues, for instance, global warming.

instant¹ /ˈɪnstənt/ *noun*

a very short period of time: For an instant, I wanted to cry.

instant² /ˈɪnstənt/ *adjective*

1 immediate: Her book was an instant success.

▶ **instantly** *adverb* The man was killed instantly.

2 prepared very quickly and easily: He stirred instant coffee into a mug of hot water.

instant messaging *uncountable noun*

the activity of sending written messages from one computer to another. The message appears immediately on the screen of the computer you send it to if this computer is also using the service: Instant messaging is my favourite way to communicate with friends.

instead /ɪnˈsted/ *adverb, preposition*

in the place of someone or something: Robert didn't want to go bowling. He went to the cinema instead.

instead of someone/something in the place of someone or something: Why don't you walk to work, instead of driving?

instinct /ˈɪnstɪŋkt/ *noun*

the natural way that a person or an animal behaves or reacts: My first instinct was to laugh.

instinctive /ɪnˈstɪŋktɪv/ *adjective*

felt or done without consideration: Smiling is instinctive to all human beings.

▶ **instinctively** *adverb* When the phone rang, Jane instinctively knew something was wrong.

institute /ˈɪnstɪtjuːt/ *noun*

an organization or a place where people study a particular subject in detail in order to discover new facts: My uncle works at the National Cancer Institute.

institution /ˌɪnstɪˈtjuːʃən/ *noun*

a large organization such as a school, a bank or a church: Most financial institutions offer interest-only loans for home-buyers.

instruct /ɪnˈstrʌkt/ *verb* (**instructs, instructing, instructed**)

1 to formally tell someone to do something (formal): Grandpa's doctor instructed him to get more fresh air.

2 to teach someone a particular subject: Our teachers instruct the children in music, dance and physical education.

instruction /ɪnˈstrʌkʃən/ *noun*

1 something that someone tells you to do: We had instructions from our teacher not to leave the building.

2 *plural* information on how to do something: The cookbook uses simple instructions and photographs.

instructor /ɪnˈstrʌktə/ *noun*

someone whose job is to teach a skill or an activity: Rachel is a swimming instructor.

instrument /ˈɪnstrəmənt/ *noun*

1 a tool that you use for doing a particular job: scientific instruments

2 an object that you use for making music: Tim plays four musical instruments, including piano and guitar.

instrumental /ˌɪnstrəˈmentəl/ *adjective*

1 helping to make something happen: Mr Johnson was instrumental in the company's success.

2 for musical instruments only, and not for voices: We welcomed the visitors with traditional dance and instrumental music.

insulate /ˈɪnsjʊleɪt/ *verb* (**insulates, insulating, insulated**)

to cover something with rubber or plastic to prevent electricity from passing through: insulated wire

insult [1] /ɪn'sʌlt/ *verb* (**insults, insulting, insulted**)

to say or do something to someone that is rude or offensive: *I'm sorry. I didn't mean to insult you.*

▶ **insulted** *adjective* *I was really insulted by the way he spoke to me.*

▶ **insulting** *adjective* *Don't use insulting language.*

insult [2] /'ɪnsʌlt/ *noun*

something rude that a person says or does: *The boys shouted insults at each other.*

insurance /ɪn'ʃʊərəns/ *uncountable noun*

an agreement that you make with a company in which you pay money to them regularly, and they pay you if something bad happens to you or your property: *I pay about £40 per month for car insurance.*

insure /ɪn'ʃʊə/ *verb* (**insures, insuring, insured**)

to pay money regularly to a company so that, if you become ill, or if your property is damaged or stolen, the company will pay you an amount of money: *It costs a lot of money to insure your car.*

intellectual /ˌɪntɪ'lektʃʊəl/ *adjective*

involving a person's ability to think and to understand ideas and information: *Dr Miller is an expert on the intellectual development of children.*

intelligence /ɪn'telɪdʒəns/ *uncountable noun*

1 the ability to understand and learn things quickly and well: *Stephanie's a woman of great intelligence.*

2 information that is collected by the government or the army about other countries' activities: *There is a need for better military intelligence.*

intelligent /ɪn'telɪdʒənt/ *adjective*

able to think, understand and learn things quickly and well: *Susan's a very intelligent woman.*

▶ **intelligently** *adverb* *William can talk intelligently on many different subjects.*

intend /ɪn'tend/ *verb* (**intends, intending, intended**)

1 to plan to do something: *We're intending to stay in Philadelphia for four years.* □ *What do you intend to do when you leave college?*

2 to plan or make something for a

particular purpose: *This money is intended for schools.* □ *The big windows were intended to make the room brighter.*

intense /ɪn'tens/ *adjective*

very great or strong: *The intense heat made him sweat.*

▶ **intensely** *adverb* *The fast-food business is intensely competitive.*

intensive /ɪn'tensɪv/ *adjective*

involving a lot of effort or many people: *The course begins with sixteen weeks of intensive training.*

▶ **intensively** *adverb* *Dan is working intensively on his new book.*

intention /ɪn'tenʃən/ *noun*

something that you plan to do: *It is my intention to retire later this year.* □ *Karen has no intention of getting married again.*

intentional /ɪn'tenʃənəl/ *adjective*

done on purpose, and not by mistake: *I'm sorry if I hurt him — it wasn't intentional.*

▶ **intentionally** *adverb* *He intentionally crashed his car to collect insurance money.*

interactive /ˌɪntə'ræktɪv/ *adjective*

used for describing something that allows direct communication between itself and the user: *Press the red button on your interactive TV to vote for your favourite singer.*

interactive whiteboard *noun*

an electronic board in a classroom. Teachers and students can write on it using a special pen, or by touching it with their finger.

interest [1] /'ɪntrəst, -tərest/ *noun*

1 a feeling that you want to know more about something: *There is a lot of interest in making the book into a film.* □ *She liked Jason at first, but she soon lost interest in him.*

2 something that you like doing: *'What are your interests?' 'I enjoy riding horses and I also play tennis.'*

3 *uncountable* the extra money that you pay if you have borrowed money, or the extra money that you receive if you have money in some types of bank account: *Do you earn much interest on that account?* □ *How much interest do you have to pay on the loan?*

interest [2] /'ɪntrəst, -tərest/ *verb* (**interests, interesting, interested**) to make you feel that you want to know more about something: *Fashion does not interest her.*

interested /'ɪntrestɪd/ *adjective*
wanting to know more about something: *I thought you might be interested in this article in the newspaper.*

interesting /'ɪntrestɪŋ/ *adjective*
making you want to know more about something: *It was interesting to be in a new town.*

▸ **interestingly** /'ɪntrestɪŋli/ *adverb*
Interestingly, there are no British writers on the list.

interfere /ˌɪntə'fɪə/ *verb* (**interferes, interfering, interfered**)
1 to get involved in a situation when other people do not want you to: *I wish everyone would stop interfering and just leave me alone.*

▸ **interference** /ˌɪntə'fɪərəns/ **uncountable noun** *She didn't appreciate her mother's interference in her life.*

2 to stop an activity from going well: *Mobile phones can interfere with aircraft equipment.*

interior /ɪn'tɪəriə/ *noun*
the inside part of something: *The interior of the house was dark and old-fashioned.*

● **interior** *adjective* *They painted the interior walls of the house white.*

intermediate /ˌɪntə'miːdiət/ *adjective*
in the middle level, between two other levels: *We teach beginner, intermediate and advanced level students.*

internal /ɪn'tɜːnəl/ *adjective*
existing or happening on the inside of something: *After the accident, Aaron suffered internal bleeding.*

international /ˌɪntə'næʃənəl/ *adjective*
involving different countries: *The best way to end poverty is through international trade.*

▸ **internationally** *adverb* *Bruce Lee is an internationally famous film star.*

Internet /'ɪntəˌnet/ also **internet** *noun*
the network that allows computer users to connect with computers all over the world, and that carries email: *Do you have Internet access at home?*

interpret /ɪn'tɜːprɪt/ *verb* (**interprets, interpreting, interpreted**)
1 to decide what something means: *You can interpret the data in different ways.*
2 to put the words that someone says into another language

▸ **interpreter** /ɪn'tɜːprɪtə/ *noun* *Speaking through an interpreter, he said that he was very happy to be in the UK.*

interrogate /ɪn'terəˌɡeɪt/ *verb*
(**interrogates, interrogating, interrogated**)
to ask someone questions for a long time in order to get some information from them: *Mr Wright was interrogated by police for eight hours on Thursday night.*

▸ **interrogation** /ɪnˌterə'ɡeɪʃən/ *noun* *He confessed during an interrogation by police.*

interrupt /ˌɪntə'rʌpt/ *verb* (**interrupts, interrupting, interrupted**)
1 to say or do something that causes someone to stop what they are doing: *Don't interrupt the teacher when she's speaking.* □ *I'm sorry to interrupt, but there's a phone call for you.*

▸ **interruption** /ˌɪntə'rʌpʃən/ *noun* *I can't concentrate on my work — there are too many interruptions.*

2 to cause an activity to stop for a period of time: *Rain interrupted the tennis match for two hours.*

▸ **interruption** *noun* *The meeting continued with no more interruptions.*

interval /'ɪntəvəl/ *noun*
the period of time between two events: *We met again after an interval of 12 years.*

interview ¹ /'ɪntəˌvjuː/ *noun*
a formal meeting in which someone asks you questions to find out if you are the right person for a job: *The interview went well, so I hope that I've got the job.*

interview ² /'ɪntəˌvjuː/ *verb* (**interviews, interviewing, interviewed**)
to ask someone questions to find out if they are the right person for a particular job: *Anna was interviewed for a job at The New York Times yesterday.*

▸ **interviewer** *noun* *The interviewer asked me why I wanted the job.*

intestine /ɪn'testɪn/ *noun*
the tube in your body that food passes through when it has left your stomach

intimate /'ɪntɪmət/ *adjective*
knowing someone very well and liking them a lot: *I told my intimate friends I wanted to have a baby.*

▸ **intimately** *adverb* *He knows the family fairly well, but not intimately.*

intimidate /ɪnˈtɪmɪˌdeɪt/ *verb* (**intimidates, intimidating, intimidated**)
to frighten someone in order to make them do what you want: *Many people feel intimidated by these teenage gangs.*
▸ **intimidation** /ɪnˌtɪmɪˈdeɪʃən/ **uncountable noun** *Witnesses are often afraid of intimidation.*

into /ˈɪntə, ˈɪntu, STRONG ˈɪntuː/ *preposition*
1 inside: *Put the apples into a dish.*
2 to the inside from the outside: *Mum got into the car and started the engine.*
3 against: *A train crashed into the barrier at the end of the track.*
4 used for talking about putting a different piece of clothing on: *I'm cold — I'll change into some warmer clothes.*
5 used for talking about things changing to a different form: *The book has been made into a film.*
6 used for talking about how something is divided: *I cut the cake into 12 slices.*
7 used when you are dividing one number by another number: *5 into 15 is 3.*

intolerant /ɪnˈtɒlərənt/ *adjective*
not accepting people who behave and think differently to you: *They are intolerant of the opinions of others.*
▸ **intolerance** **uncountable noun** *They worry about people's intolerance toward foreigners.*

intranet /ˈɪntrənet/ *noun*
a network of computers in a particular organization

intransitive /ɪnˈtrænsɪtɪv/ *adjective*
used for describing a verb that does not have an object

introduce /ˌɪntrəˈdjuːs/ *verb* (**introduces, introducing, introduced**)
1 to tell people each other's names so that they can get to know each other: *Tim, may I introduce you to my wife, Jennifer?*
2 to bring something new to a place; to make something exist for the first time: *The airline introduced a new direct service from Houston last month.*
▸ **introduction** /ˌɪntrəˈdʌkʃən/ **uncountable noun** *Did the introduction of the euro affect prices?*

introduce yourself to tell someone your name: *Before the meeting, we all introduced ourselves.*

introduction /ˌɪntrəˈdʌkʃən/ *noun*
the part at the beginning of a book that tells you what the book is about: *J.D. Salinger wrote the introduction to the book.*

intuition /ˌɪntjuˈɪʃən/ *noun*
an ability to know or understand something through your feelings: *My intuition told me that I could trust him.*

invade /ɪnˈveɪd/ *verb* (**invades, invading, invaded**)
to attack and enter a country: *In 1944 the Allies invaded the Italian mainland.*

invalid¹ /ˈɪnvəlɪd/ *noun*
someone who needs to be cared for by another person because they are very sick or badly injured: *Both of Mary's parents were invalids.*

invalid² /ɪnˈvælɪd/ *adjective*
used for describing a document that cannot be accepted, because it breaks an official rule: *He was trying to board a flight for the Philippines with an invalid passport.*

invasion /ɪnˈveɪʒən/ *noun*
an occasion when an army enters a country and attacks it: *Cyprus has been divided since an invasion in 1974.*

invent /ɪnˈvent/ *verb* (**invents, inventing, invented**)
1 to be the first person to think of something or to make it: *The ballpoint pen was invented by the Hungarian, Laszlo Biro.*
▸ **inventor** *noun* *Who was the inventor of the telephone?*
2 to try to make other people believe that something is true when it is not: *Heather invented an excuse not to attend Ryan's birthday party.*

invention /ɪnˈvenʃən/ *noun*
1 something that has been invented by someone: *Paper was a Chinese invention.*
2 *uncountable* when something is invented: *The invention of the telescope led to the discovery of Uranus in 1781.*

invertebrate /ɪnˈvɜːtɪˌbrət/ *noun*
an animal that does not have a spine (= bones in its back). Compare with **vertebrate.** ● **invertebrate** *adjective* *Ponds contain many invertebrate species.*

inverted commas /ɪnˈvɜːtɪd ˌkɒməz/ *plural noun*

marks that are used in writing to show what someone said. You write them as ' ' or " ".

invest /ɪn'vest/ *verb* (**invests, investing, invested**)
to put money into a business or a bank, in order to try to make a profit from it: *He invested millions of dollars in the business.*

investigate /ɪn'vestɪˌgeɪt/ *verb* (**investigates, investigating, investigated**)
to try to find out how something happened: *Police are investigating how the accident happened.*
▶ **investigation** /ɪnˌvestɪ'geɪʃən/ *noun*
We have begun an investigation into the man's death.

investigator /ɪn'vestɪˌgeɪtə/ *noun*
a person whose job is to find out about something: *Investigators have been questioning the survivors.*

investment /ɪn'vesmənt/ *noun*
1 *uncountable* the activity of investing money: *an investment advisor*
2 an amount of money that you invest, or the thing that you invest your money in: *Anthony made a $1 million investment in the company.*

invisible /ɪn'vɪzɪbəl/ *adjective*
impossible to see: *In the story, Matilda becomes invisible after eating blue sweets.*

invitation /ˌɪnvɪ'teɪʃən/ *noun*
when someone asks you to go to an event: *I accepted the invitation to Jo's party.*

invite /ɪn'vaɪt/ *verb* (**invites, inviting, invited**)
to ask someone to come to an event: *She invited him to her 26th birthday party.*

invoice /'ɪnvɔɪs/ *noun*
a document that shows how much money you must pay for goods you have ordered or the work that someone has done for you: *We sent them an invoice for £11,000 four months ago.* ● **invoice** *verb* (**invoices, invoicing, invoiced**) *You will not be invoiced for the work until January.*

involve /ɪn'vɒlv/ *verb* (**involves, involving, involved**)
1 to have something as a necessary part: *Running a household involves lots of different skills.*
2 if an activity involves someone, they take part in it: *The scandal involved a former senator.*

3 to get someone to take part in something: *We involve the children in everything we do.*

involved /ɪn'vɒlvd/ *adjective*
taking part in something: *All of their children are involved in the family business.*

involvement /ɪn'vɒlvmənt/ *uncountable noun*
when you take part in something: *Edwards has always denied any involvement in the crime.*

iPad /'aɪˌpæd/ *noun*
a small, flat computer that you use by touching the screen (*trademark*)

iPod /'aɪpɒd/ *noun*
a small piece of electronic equipment that you can carry with you. It stores music, photos and movies. (*trademark*)

iris /'aɪərɪs/ *noun* (**irises**)
the round coloured part of a person's eye

iron¹ /'aɪən/ *noun*
1 *uncountable* a hard, dark grey metal
2 a piece of electrical equipment with a flat metal base that you heat and move over clothes to make them smooth

iron² /'aɪən/ *verb* (**irons, ironing, ironed**)
to make clothes smooth using an iron: *I began to iron some shirts.*
▶ **ironing** *uncountable noun* *I was doing the ironing when she called.*

iron

ironic /aɪ'rɒnɪk/ or **ironical** /aɪ'rɒnɪkəl/ *adjective*
strange or funny; very different from what people expect: *It is ironic that we lie in the sun to make our skin look more attractive.*
▶ **ironically** /aɪ'rɒnɪkli/ *adverb* *His enormous dog is ironically called 'Tiny'.*

irony /'aɪrəni/ *uncountable noun*
a type of humour where you say the opposite of what you really mean: *'You're early!' he said, as we arrived two hours late, his voice full of irony.*

irrational /ɪˈræʃənəl/ *adjective*
not based on sensible, clear thinking:
I think hatred is often irrational.
▶ **irrationally** *adverb* *My husband is
irrationally jealous of my ex-boyfriends.*

irregular /ɪˈregjʊlə/ *adjective*
1 used for describing something that
happens at different times: *The tests
showed that his heartbeat was irregular.*
▶ **irregularly** *adverb* *He was eating
irregularly and losing weight.*
2 not following the usual rules of
grammar. For example, 'run' is an irregular
verb, because the past form is 'ran' (and
not 'runned'). Compare with **regular**.

irrelevant /ɪˈrelɪvənt/ *adjective*
not connected with what you are talking
about or doing: *Remove any irrelevant details
from your essay.*

irresponsible /ˌɪrɪˈspɒnsɪbəl/ *adjective*
not thinking about the possible results of
your actions: *There are still too many
irresponsible drivers who use their mobile phones
while driving.*

irritable /ˈɪrɪtəbəl/ *adjective*
becoming angry very easily: *After waiting for
him for over an hour, Amber was feeling irritable.*
▶ **irritably** /ˈɪrɪtəbli/ *adverb* *'Why are you
talking so loudly?' he asked irritably.*

irritate /ˈɪrɪˌteɪt/ *verb* (**irritates, irritating,
irritated**)
1 to repeatedly annoy someone: *His voice
really irritates me.*
▶ **irritated** *adjective* *He has become
increasingly irritated by questions about his
retirement.*
▶ **irritating** *adjective* *The children have an
irritating habit of leaving the door open.*
2 to make a part of your body slightly
painful: *The smoke from the fire irritated his
eyes, nose and throat.*

irritation /ˌɪrɪˈteɪʃən/ *noun*
1 *uncountable* the feeling you have when
you are annoyed: *David tried not to show his
irritation.*
2 a feeling of slight pain in a part of
your body: *These oils may cause irritation to
sensitive skins.*

is /ɪz/ → see **be**

Islam /ˈɪzlɑːm/ *uncountable noun*
the religion that was started by
Muhammed: *My oldest cousin Michael*

converted to Islam at the age of 16.
▶ **Islamic** /ɪzˈlæmɪk/ *adjective* *He's an
expert in Islamic law.*

island /ˈaɪlənd/ *noun*
a piece of land that is completely
surrounded by water: *They live on the
Caribbean island of Barbados.*

island

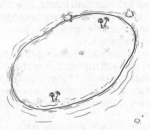

isle /aɪl/ *noun*
an island: *Ireland is sometimes called
'the Emerald Isle'.*

isn't /ˈɪzənt/
short for 'is not'

isolate /ˈaɪsəˌleɪt/ *verb* (**isolates, isolating,
isolated**)
to keep someone away from other people:
*Julie was quickly isolated from other patients in
the hospital.*

isolated /ˈaɪsəˌleɪtɪd/ *adjective*
far away from other places: *Mark and his
girlfriend have bought an isolated farmhouse in
Spain.*

ISP /ˌaɪ es ˈpiː/ *noun*
a company that provides Internet and
email services. **ISP** is short for 'Internet
service provider'.

issue¹ /ˈɪsjuː, ˈɪʃuː/ *noun*
1 an important subject that people are
talking about: *Climate change is a major
environmental issue.*
2 the copy of a magazine or newspaper
that is published in a particular month or
on a particular day: *Have you read the latest
issue of the 'Scientific American'?*

issue² /ˈɪsjuː, ˈɪʃuː/ *verb* (**issues, issuing,
issued**)
to officially say or give something: *The
government issued a warning of possible attacks.*
□ *The embassy has stopped issuing visas to
journalists.*

I.T. /ˌaɪ 'tiː/
short for **information technology**

it /ɪt/ *pronoun*

1 used when you are talking about an object, an animal, a thing or a situation that you have already mentioned: *They live in a beautiful cottage. Here's a photo of it.* □ *She has a problem but she's too embarrassed to talk about it.*

2 used before certain nouns, adjectives and verbs to talk about your feelings: *It was nice to see Steve again.* □ *It's a pity you can't come to the party, Sarah.*

3 used when you are talking about the time, the date, the weather or the distance to a place: *It's three o'clock.* □ *It was Saturday, so she was at home.* □ *It was snowing yesterday.* □ *It's ten miles to the next petrol station.*

4 used when you are saying who someone is: *'Who's that on the phone?' — 'It's Mrs Williams.'*

italic /ɪˈtælɪk/ *plural noun*
letters that slope to the right. The examples in this dictionary are printed in italics. ● **italic** *adjective italic type*

itch¹ /ɪtʃ/ *verb* (**itches, itching, itched**)
to have an unpleasant feeling on your skin that makes you want to scratch it: *Her perfume made my eyes itch.*
▶ **itchy** *adjective My eyes feel itchy and sore.*

itch² /ɪtʃ/ *noun* (**itches**)
an unpleasant feeling on your skin that makes you want to scratch it: *Can you scratch my back? I've got an itch.*

it'd /ˈɪtəd/
1 short for 'it would'
2 short for 'it had'

item /ˈaɪtəm/ *noun*

1 one thing in a list or a group of things: *The most valuable item in the sale was a Picasso drawing.*

2 a piece of news in a newspaper or a magazine, or on television or radio: *There was an item in the paper about him.*

it'll /ˈɪtəl/
short for 'it will'

its /ɪts/ *adjective*
used for showing that something belongs to or relates to a thing, a place or an animal that has just been mentioned: *He held the knife by its handle.*

> **LANGUAGE HELP**
>
> **Its** or **it's**? **Its** means 'belonging to it': *The horse raised its head.* **It's** is short for 'it is' or 'it has': *It's hot in here. It's stopped raining.*

it's /ɪts/
short for 'it is' or 'it has'

itself /ɪtˈself/ *pronoun*

1 used as the object of a verb or preposition when an animal or a thing is both the subject and the object of the verb: *The kitten washed itself, then lay down by the fire.*

2 used for making a word stronger: *There are lots of good restaurants on the road to Wilmington, and in Wilmington itself.*

by itself without any help: *The company is working on a car that can drive by itself.*

I've /aɪv/
short for 'I have'

ivy /ˈaɪvi/ *noun* (**ivies**)
a dark-green plant that grows up walls or along the ground

ivy

Jj

jacket /'dʒækɪt/ *noun*
a short coat with long sleeves: *He wore a black leather jacket.*

jackpot /'dʒækpɒt/ *noun*
a large sum of money that is the most valuable prize in a game: *She won the jackpot of £5 million.*

jagged /'dʒægɪd/ *adjective*
having a rough edge with lots of sharp points: *There were sharp jagged rocks just below the surface of the water.*

jail /dʒeɪl/ *noun*
a place where criminals have to stay as a punishment: *He went to jail for 15 years.* □ *Three prisoners escaped from a jail.*

jam ¹ /dʒæm/ *verb* (**jams, jamming, jammed**)
to push something somewhere hard: *He jammed the key in the lock.*

jam ² /dʒæm/ *noun*
1 *uncountable* a sweet food that contains soft fruit and sugar: *Kate spread the strawberry jam on her toast.*
→ Look at picture on P3
2 a situation when there are so many vehicles on a road that they cannot move: *The lorries sat in a traffic jam for ten hours.*

January /'dʒænjəri/ *noun*
the first month of the year

jar /dʒɑː/ *noun*
a glass container, with a lid, that is used for storing food: *There were several glass jars filled with sweets.*

javelin /'dʒævlɪn/ *noun*
a long pointed stick that is thrown in sports competitions

jaw /dʒɔː/ *noun*
the top and bottom bones of a person's or an animal's mouth: *Andrew broke his lower jaw.*

jazz /dʒæz/ *uncountable noun*
a style of music that has strong rhythms: *The club plays live jazz on Sundays.*

jealous /'dʒeləs/ *adjective*
1 feeling angry because you think that another person is trying to take away someone or something that you love: *He got jealous and there was a fight.*
2 feeling angry or unhappy because you do not have something that someone else has: *She was jealous of her sister's success.*
▶ **jealously** *adverb* *Gloria looked jealously at his new car.*

jealousy /'dʒeləsi/ *uncountable noun*
1 the feeling of anger that someone has when they think that another person is trying to take away someone or something that they love: *He could not control his jealousy when he saw her new husband.*
2 the feeling of anger or sadness that someone has when they want something that another person has

jeans /dʒiːnz/ *plural noun*
trousers that are made of strong cotton cloth: *We saw a young man in jeans and a T-shirt.*

Jeep /dʒiːp/ *noun*
a type of car that can travel over rough ground (*trademark*): *a U.S. Army Jeep*

jelly /'dʒeli/ *uncountable noun*
a soft sweet food made from fruit juice and sugar that moves from side to side when you touch it: *After dinner, we had jelly with ice cream.*

jellyfish /'dʒeli,fɪʃ/ *noun* (**jellyfish**)
a sea animal that has a clear soft body and that can sting you.

jerk /dʒɜːk/ *verb* (**jerks, jerking, jerked**)
to move a short distance very suddenly and quickly: *The train jerked violently from side to side.* □ *Sam jerked his head in my direction.* ●**jerk** *noun He gave a jerk of his head to the other two men.*

jerky /'dʒɜːki/ *adjective* (**jerkier, jerkiest**)
very sudden and quick: *Avoid any sudden or jerky movements.*

jersey /'dʒɜːzi/ *noun*
a piece of clothing with sleeves that you wear on the top part of your body: *The boys wore baseball caps and jerseys.*

jet /dʒet/ *noun*
1 an aircraft with jet engines: *He arrived from Key West by jet.*
2 a strong, fast, thin stream of liquid or gas: *A jet of water poured through the windows.*

Jew /dʒuː/ *noun*
a person who practises the religion of Judaism

jewel /'dʒuːəl/ *noun*
a valuable stone, such as a diamond: *The box was filled with precious jewels and gold.*

jeweller /'dʒuːələ/ *noun*
1 a person who makes, sells and repairs jewellery and watches
2 (*also* **jeweller's**) a shop where you can buy jewellery and watches: *We went to a jeweller's on Oxford Street.*

jewellery /'dʒuːəlri/ *uncountable noun*
decorations that you wear on your body, such as a ring that you wear on your finger: *She sold all her gold jewellery.*

Jewish /'dʒuːɪʃ/ *adjective*
1 belonging or relating to the religion of

jewellery

earring

necklace

bracelet

Judaism: *We celebrated the Jewish festival of Passover.*
2 believing in and practising the religion of Judaism: *She was from a traditional Jewish family.*

jigsaw /'dʒɪgsɔː/ *noun* (*also* **jigsaw puzzle**)
a picture on cardboard or wood that has been cut up into different shapes that you have to put back together again: *The children put the last pieces in the jigsaw puzzle.*

jingle /'dʒɪŋgəl/ *verb* (**jingles, jingling, jingled**)
to make a gentle sound like small bells: *Her bracelets jingled on her thin wrist.* □ *Brian put his hands in his pockets and jingled some coins.*

job /dʒɒb/ *noun*
1 the work that someone does to earn money: *I want to get a job.* □ *Terry was looking for a new job.*
→ Look at pictures on P7
2 a particular task: *I have some jobs to do in the house today.*
do a good job to do something well: *Most of our teachers are doing a good job in the classroom.*

jobless /'dʒɒbləs/ *adjective*
without a job: *The number of jobless people went up last month.*

jockey /'dʒɒki/ *noun*
someone who rides a horse in a race

jog /dʒɒg/ *verb* (**jogs, jogging, jogged**)
to run slowly, often as a form of exercise: *They went jogging every morning.* ●**jog** *noun He went for an early-morning jog.*
▶**jogger** *noun The park was full of joggers.*
▶**jogging** *uncountable noun The jogging helped him to lose weight.*
→ Look at picture on P6

join /dʒɔɪn/ *verb* (**joins, joining, joined**)
1 to become a member of an organization: *He joined the Army five years ago.*
2 to stand at the end of a queue so that you are part of it: *He joined the queue of people waiting to get on the bus.*
3 to attach or fasten two things together: *'And' is often used for joining two sentences.* □ *Join the two squares of fabric to make a bag.*

joint¹ /dʒɔɪnt/ *noun*
a part of your body, such as your elbow or your knee, where two bones meet and are able to move together: *Her joints ache if she exercises.*

joint² /dʒɔɪnt/ *adjective*
shared by two or more people: *We opened a joint bank account.*

joke /dʒəʊk/ *noun*
something that someone says to make you laugh: *He made a joke about it.* • **joke** *verb* (**jokes, joking, joked**) *She often joked about her big feet.* ▢ *I was only joking! I didn't mean it.*

jolly /'dʒɒli/ *adjective* (**jollier, jolliest**)
happy and cheerful: *She was a jolly, kind woman.*

jolt /dʒəʊlt/ *verb* (**jolts, jolting, jolted**)
to move suddenly and quite violently: *She was jolted awake by a crash of thunder.* ▢ *The train jolted again.* • **jolt** *noun* *The plane hit the runway with a jolt.*

jot /dʒɒt/ *verb* (**jots, jotting, jotted**)
jot something down to write something down quickly: *David jotted down the address on a notepad.*

journal /'dʒɜːnəl/ *noun*
1 a magazine or a newspaper that deals with a special subject: *The results were published in scientific journals.*
2 a notebook or a diary: *Sara wrote her private thoughts in her journal.*

journalist /'dʒɜːnəlɪst/ *noun*
a person whose job is to collect news stories and write about them for newspapers, magazines, television or radio: *The president spoke to an audience of two hundred journalists.*
▸ **journalism** *uncountable noun* *He began a career in journalism.*

journey /'dʒɜːni/ *noun*
an occasion when you travel from one place to another: *Their journey took them from Paris to Brussels.*

joy /dʒɔɪ/ *uncountable noun*
a feeling of great happiness: *She shouted with joy.*

joyful /'dʒɔɪfʊl/ *adjective*
causing happiness and pleasure (*formal*): *A wedding is a joyful occasion.*
▸ **joyfully** *adverb* *The children cheered joyfully.*

Judaism /'dʒuːdeɪˌɪzəm/ *uncountable noun*
the religion of the Jewish people

judge¹ /dʒʌdʒ/ *noun*
1 the person in a court of law who decides how criminals should be punished: *The judge sent him to jail for 100 days.*

2 a person who decides who will be the winner of a competition: *A panel of judges will choose the winner.*

judge² /dʒʌdʒ/ *verb* (**judges, judging, judged**)
1 to decide who is the winner of a competition: *He will judge the contest and award the prize.*
2 to form an opinion about someone or something: *People should wait, and judge the film when they see it for themselves.*

judgment /'dʒʌdʒmənt/ also **judgement** *noun*
1 *uncountable* the ability to make sensible decisions about what to do: *I respect his judgment, and I'll follow his advice.*
2 a decision made by a judge or by a court of law: *The judge has promised to deliver a full written judgment next Tuesday.*

judo /'dʒuːdəʊ/ *uncountable noun*
a sport in which two people fight without weapons: *He was also a black belt in judo.*

jug /dʒʌg/ *noun*
a container with a handle used for holding and pouring liquids

juggle /'dʒʌgəl/ *verb* (**juggles, juggling, juggled**)
to keep several objects in the air by throwing and catching them repeatedly: *She was juggling five balls.*
▸ **juggler** *noun* *He was a professional juggler.*
▸ **juggling** *uncountable noun* *It's a children's show, with juggling and comedy.*

juggle

juice /dʒuːs/ *noun*
1 *uncountable* the liquid from a fruit or a vegetable: *He had a large glass of fresh orange juice.*
→ Look at picture on P3

j

2 *plural* the liquid that comes out of a piece of meat when you cook it: *Pour the cooking juices into a pan, and add the cream.*

juicy /'dʒuːsi/ *adjective* (**juicier, juiciest**)
containing a lot of juice and very enjoyable to eat: *The waiter brought a thick, juicy steak to the table.*

July /dʒʊ'laɪ/ *noun*
the seventh month of the year: *In July 1969, Neil Armstrong walked on the moon.*

jump /dʒʌmp/ *verb* (**jumps, jumping, jumped**)
1 to bend your knees, push against the ground with your feet, and move quickly upwards into the air: *I jumped over the fence.*
●**jump** *noun She set a world record for the longest jump by a woman.*
2 to move quickly and suddenly: *Adam jumped up when he heard the doorbell.*

jump at something to accept an offer or an opportunity quickly and with enthusiasm: *She jumped at the chance to be on TV.*

make someone jump to make someone move suddenly because they are frightened or surprised: *The phone rang and made her jump.*

jumper /'dʒʌmpə/ *noun*
a warm piece of clothing that covers the top part of your body

June /dʒuːn/ *noun*
the sixth month of the year: *He spent two weeks with us in June 2006.*

jungle /'dʒʌŋgəl/ *noun*
a forest in a tropical country where large numbers of tall trees and plants grow very close together: *The trail led them deeper into the jungle.*

junior /'dʒuːniə/ *adjective*
having one of the lower positions in

an organization: *His father was a junior officer in the army.*

junk /dʒʌŋk/ *uncountable noun*
old and useless things that you do not want or need (*informal*): *What are you going to do with all that junk?*

jury /'dʒʊəri/ *noun* (**juries**)
the group of people in a court of law who listen to the facts about a crime and decide if a person is guilty or not: *The jury decided she was not guilty of murder.*

just /dʒʌst/ *adjective, adverb*
1 a very short time ago: *I just had the most awful dream.*
2 at this moment; very soon: *I'm just making some coffee.* □ *I'm just going to bed.*
3 only: *It costs just a few dollars.*
4 used to make the next thing that you say stronger: *Just stop talking and listen to me!*
5 exactly: *They are just like the rest of us.*
6 fair or right (*formal*): *I think he got his just punishment.*

just about almost: *All our money is just about gone.*

just a minute/just a moment/just a second used when you are asking someone to wait for a short time: *Just a moment. What did you say?*

justice /'dʒʌstɪs/ *uncountable noun*
the fair treatment of people: *We want freedom, justice and equality.*

justified /'dʒʌstɪ,faɪd/ *adjective*
reasonable and acceptable: *In my opinion, the decision was justified.* □ *I work very hard, so I feel justified in asking for more money.*

justify /'dʒʌstɪ,faɪ/ *verb* (**justifies, justifying, justified**)
to show that a decision or an action is reasonable or necessary: *Is there anything that can justify a war?*

Kk

kangaroo /ˌkæŋɡəˈruː/ *noun*
a large Australian animal, the female of which carries her baby in a pocket on her stomach

karate /kəˈrɑːti/ *uncountable noun*
a Japanese sport in which people fight using their hands and feet

KB or **K**
in writing, short for **kilobyte** or **kilobytes**

keen /kiːn/ *adjective* (**keener, keenest**)
1 wanting to do something or very interested in something: *Charles was keen to show his family the photos.* □ *Father was always a keen golfer.* □ *I'm not keen on TV game shows.*
2 very strong or good: *For this job, you need to have a keen sense of adventure.*
keen on someone/something liking someone or something a lot: *I'm not keen on physics and chemistry.*

keep /kiːp/ *verb* (**keeps, keeping, kept**)
1 to remain in a particular state or place: *Keep away from the doors while the train is moving.* □ *We burned wood to keep warm.* □ *'Keep still!'*
2 to make someone or something stay in a particular state or place: *The noise of the traffic kept him awake.* □ *He kept his head down, hiding his face.*
3 to continue to have something: *I want to keep these clothes, and I want to give these away.*
4 to store something in a particular place: *She kept her money under the bed.*
keep a promise to do what you said you would do: *He kept his promise to come to my birthday party.*
keep doing something to do something many times or continue to do something: *I keep forgetting the password for my computer.* □ *She kept running although she was exhausted.*
keep something up to continue to do something: *I could not keep the diet up for longer than a month.*
keep up with someone to move as fast as another person so that you are moving together: *Sam walked faster to keep up with his father.*

kennel /ˈkenəl/ *noun*
a small house for a dog: *Dad built a kennel for our dog in the garden.*

kept /kept/ → see **keep**

kerb /kɜːb/ *noun*
the edge of a pavement (= a path next to a road) that is nearest to the road: *I pulled over to the kerb.*

ketchup /ˈketʃʌp/ *noun*
a thick, red sauce made from tomatoes: *He was eating a burger with ketchup.*

kettle /ˈketəl/ *noun*
a metal container with a lid and a handle, that you use for boiling water: *I'll put the kettle on and make us some tea.*
→ Look at picture on P4

key¹ /kiː/ *noun*

key

1 a specially shaped piece of metal that opens or closes a lock: *They put the key in the door and entered.*
2 one of the buttons that you press in order to operate a computer keyboard: *Now press the 'Delete' key.*
3 one of the white and black bars that you press in order to play a piano
4 a particular scale of musical notes: *the key of A minor*

key² /kiː/ *adjective*
most important: *He's a key player on the team.*

keyboard /ˈkiːbɔːd/ *noun*
1 the set of keys that you press in order to operate a computer
2 the set of black and white keys that you press when you play a piano
3 (*also* **keyboards**) an electronic musical instrument that has a keyboard

keyhole /'ki:həʊl/ *noun*
the part of a lock where you put a key: *I looked through the keyhole, but I couldn't see anything inside.*

'key ring *noun*
a metal ring on which you keep keys: *He pulled his key ring from his pocket.*

keyword /'ki:wɜ:d/ also **key word** *noun*
a word or a phrase that you can use when you are searching for a particular document in an Internet search: *Users can search by title, by author, by subject and by keyword.*

kg
in writing, short for **kilogram** or **kilograms**

khaki /'kɑ:ki/ *adjective*
greenish-brown or yellowish-brown in colour: *He was dressed in khaki trousers.*

kHz
short for **kilohertz**

kick[1] /kɪk/ *verb* (**kicks, kicking, kicked**)
1 to hit someone or something with your foot: *He kicked the door hard.* □ *He kicked the ball away.*
2 to move your legs up and down quickly: *Abby was taken away, kicking and screaming.* □ *The baby smiled and kicked her legs.*

kick[2] /kɪk/ *noun*
1 an act of hitting someone or something with your foot: *He went over to the door and gave it a kick.*
2 a feeling of pleasure or excitement (*informal*): *I love acting. I get a big kick out of it.*

kid[1] /kɪd/ *noun*
a child (*informal*): *They have three kids.*

kid[2] /kɪd/ *verb* (**kids, kidding, kidded**)
to say something that is not really true, as a joke (*informal*): *I thought he was kidding but he was serious.* □ *I'm just kidding.*

kidnap /'kɪdnæp/ *verb* (**kidnaps, kidnapping, kidnapped**)
to take someone away by force and keep them as a prisoner, often until their friends or family pay a large amount of money: *The tourists were kidnapped by a group of men with guns.*
▶ **kidnapper** *noun His kidnappers have threatened to kill him.*
▶ **kidnapping** *noun Williams was jailed for eight years for the kidnapping.*

kidney /'kɪdni/ *noun*
one of the two organs in your body that remove waste liquid from your blood: *She urgently needs a kidney transplant.*

kill /kɪl/ *verb* (**kills, killing, killed**)
to make a person, an animal or other living thing die: *More than 1,000 people have been killed by the armed forces.* □ *Drugs can kill.*
▶ **killing** *uncountable noun The TV news reported the killing of seven people.*

killer /'kɪlə/ *noun*
1 a person who has killed someone: *The police are searching for the killer.*
2 something that causes death: *Heart disease is the biggest killer of men in some countries.*

kilo /'ki:ləʊ/ *noun*
→ see **kilogram**: *He's lost ten kilos in weight.*

kilobyte /'kɪlə,baɪt/ *noun*
a unit for measuring information in computing (1 kilobyte = 1,024 bytes)

kilogram /'kɪlə,græm/ also **kilogramme** *noun*
a unit for measuring weight (1 kilogram = 2.2 pounds; 1000 grams = 1 kilogram): *The box weighs 4.5 kilograms.*

kilohertz /'kɪlə,hɜːts/ *noun* (**kilohertz**)
a unit for measuring radio waves: *The frequency of the radio waves slowly increased to 4 kilohertz.*

kilometre /'kɪlə,mi:tə, kɪ'lɒmɪtə/ *noun*
a unit for measuring distance (1 kilometre = 0.62 miles; 1000 metres =1 kilometre): *We're now only one kilometre from the border.*

kilowatt /'kɪlə,wɒt/ *noun*
a unit of electrical power: *The system produces 25 kilowatts of power.*

kind[1] /kaɪnd/ *noun*
a type of person or thing: *What kind of car do you drive?* □ *He travels a lot, and sees all kinds of interesting things.*
kind of a little; in some way (*informal*): *I'm kind of thirsty.*

kind[2] /kaɪnd/ *adjective* (**kinder, kindest**)
friendly and helpful: *Thank you for being so kind to me.*
▶ **kindly** *adverb The woman smiled kindly at her.*
▶ **kindness** *uncountable noun I'll never forget his generosity and kindness.*

kindly /'kaɪndli/ *adjective*
kind and caring: *He gave her a kindly smile.*

king /kɪŋ/ *noun*
a man from a royal family, who is the

head of state of that country: *the king and
queen of Spain*

kingdom /'kɪŋdəm/ *noun*
a country that is ruled by a king or a
queen: *the Kingdom of Denmark*

kiosk /'ki:ɒsk/ *noun*
a small building with a window where
people can buy things like newspapers:
I was getting a newspaper at the kiosk.

kiss /kɪs/ *verb* (**kisses, kissing, kissed**)
to touch someone with your lips to show
love or to greet them: *She smiled and kissed
him on the cheek.* □ *The woman gently kissed her
baby.* □ *We kissed goodbye at the airport.* ● **kiss**
noun (**kisses**) *I put my arms around her and
gave her a kiss.*

kit /kɪt/ *noun*
1 a group of items that are kept and used
together for a particular purpose: *a first aid
kit* □ *She's just got her first drum kit.*
2 a set of parts that you can put together
in order to make something: *a model
aeroplane kit*

kitchen /'kɪtʃɪn/ *noun*
a room that is used for cooking
→ Look at picture on P4

kite /kaɪt/ *noun*
a toy that you fly in the wind at the end of
a long string: *We went to the beach to fly kites.*

kitten /'kɪtən/ *noun*
a very young cat

kiwi fruit /'ki:wi: ˌfru:t/ *noun*

> **LANGUAGE HELP**
> The plural can also be **kiwi fruits**.

a small fruit with brown skin, black
seeds, and bright green flesh

km
in writing, short for **kilometre**

knead /ni:d/ *verb* (**kneads, kneading,
kneaded**)
to press and stretch dough (= a mixture of
flour, water and other things) when you
are making bread: *Knead the dough for a few
minutes.*

knee /ni:/ *noun*
the part in the middle of your leg where it
bends: *Lie down and bring your knees up toward
your chest.*
→ Look at picture on P1

kneel /ni:l/ *verb* (**kneels, kneeling, kneeled**
or **knelt**) (*also* **kneel down**)

to bend your legs and rest with one or
both of your knees on the ground: *She knelt
by the bed and prayed.* □ *Other people were
kneeling, but she just sat.* □ *She kneeled down
beside him.*

kneel

knew /nju:/ → see **know**

knickers /'nɪkəz/ *plural noun*
a piece of underwear that girls and
women wear on the lower part of their
body

knife /naɪf/ *noun* (**knives**)
a sharp flat piece of metal with a handle,
that you can use to cut things or as a
weapon: *I stopped eating and put down my
knife and fork.*

knight /naɪt/ *noun*
in the past, a special type of soldier who
rode a horse: *King Arthur's knights*

knit /nɪt/ *verb* (**knits, knitting, knitted**)
to make a piece of clothing from wool by
using two long sticks (= needles): *I had
many hours to knit and sew.* □ *I have already
started knitting baby clothes.*
▶ **knitting** *uncountable noun My favourite
hobbies are knitting and reading.*

knives /naɪvz/
the plural of **knife**

knob /nɒb/ *noun*
a round handle or switch: *He turned the
knob and pushed the door.* □ *a volume knob*

knock /nɒk/ *verb* (**knocks, knocking,
knocked**)
1 to hit something in order to make a
noise: *She went to Simon's flat and knocked on
the door.* ● **knock** *noun They heard a knock at
the front door.*
▶ **knocking** *noun There was a loud knocking
at the door.*
2 to touch or hit something roughly:
*She accidentally knocked the glass and it fell off
the shelf.*

k

knock someone out to hit someone hard on the head so that they fall, go into a kind of deep sleep and cannot get up again: *He was knocked out in a fight.*

knock someone/something over to hit someone or something so that they fall over: *The third wave was so strong it knocked me over.* □ *She stood up suddenly, knocking over a glass of milk.*

knock something down to destroy a building or part of a building: *We're knocking down the wall between the kitchen and the dining room.*

knot /nɒt/ **verb** (**knots, knotting, knotted**) to tie two pieces of string or rope together: *He knotted the laces securely together.* ● **knot noun** *Tony wore a bright-red scarf tied in a knot around his neck.*

know /nəʊ/ **verb** (**knows, knowing, knew, known**)

1 to have a fact or an answer in your mind: *You should know the answer to that question.* □ *I don't know his name.* □ *'How old is he?' – 'I don't know.'*

2 to be familiar with a person or a place: *I've known him for nine years.* □ *I know Leeds well. I used to live there.*

3 to understand something: *I know how you feel.*

I know used when you are agreeing with what someone has just said: *'The weather is awful.' – 'I know.'*

you know used when you want someone to listen to what you are saying (*informal*): *I'm doing this for you, you know.*

knowledge /'nɒlɪdʒ/ **uncountable noun** information and understanding about a subject: *He has a wide knowledge of sports.* □ *Scientists have very little knowledge of the disease.*

knowledgeable /'nɒlɪdʒəbəl/ also **knowledgable adjective** knowing a lot about a particular subject: *Our staff are all extremely knowledgeable about our products.*

known¹ /nəʊn/ → see **know**

known² /nəʊn/ **adjective** familiar to a particular group of people: *Hawaii is known for its beautiful beaches.*

knuckle /'nʌkəl/ **noun** one of the parts of your body where your fingers join your hands, and where your fingers bend: *She tapped on the door with her knuckles.*

the Koran /ðə kɔːˈrɑːn/ **noun** the most important book in the religion of Islam

kph written after a number to show the speed of something; short for 'kilometres per hour'

kW in writing, short for **kilowatt**

Ll

lab /læb/ *noun*
→ see **laboratory**

label /'leɪbəl/ *noun*
a piece of paper or plastic that
is attached to an object to give
information about it: *Always
read the label on the bottle.*
● **label** *verb* (**labels, labelling,
labelled**) *All foods must be clearly
labelled.*

label

laboratory /lə'bɒrətri/ *noun*
(**laboratories**)
a building or a room where
scientific work is done: *He
works in a research laboratory at
Columbia University.*

labour /'leɪbə/ *uncountable noun*
1 very hard work, usually physical work:
*The punishment for refusing to fight was a year's
hard labour.*
2 the workers of a country or an industry:
Employers want cheap labour.

Labour Party *noun*
one of the three main political parties in
the UK

lace /leɪs/ *noun*
1 *uncountable* a delicate cloth with a
design made of fine threads: *She wore a blue
dress with a lace collar.*
2 one of two thin pieces of material that
are used for fastening shoes: *Barry put on
his shoes and tied the laces.* ● **lace** *verb* (**laces,
lacing, laced**) *I laced my shoes tightly.*

lack /læk/ *uncountable noun*
when there is not enough of something
or it does not exist: *I was tired from lack of
sleep.* ● **lack** *verb* (**lacks, lacking, lacked**)
The meat lacked flavour.

lad /læd/ *noun*
a young man or boy (*informal*): *When I was a
lad, we used to go to Yorkshire every summer.*

ladder /'lædə/ *noun*
a piece of equipment used for reaching
high places. It is made of two long pieces

of wood or metal with short steps
between them: *He climbed the ladder so he
could see over the wall.*

the ladies /ðə 'leɪdiːz/ *noun*
a public toilet for women (*informal*): *Excuse
me, can you tell me where the ladies is, please?*

ladle /'leɪdəl/ *noun*
a large, round, deep spoon with a long
handle, used for serving soup

lady /'leɪdi/ *noun* (**ladies**)
used when you are talking about a
woman in a polite way: *She's a very sweet
old lady.*

ladybird /'leɪdi,bɜːd/ *noun*
a small round insect that is red or yellow
with black spots

laid /leɪd/ → see **lay**

laid-'back *adjective*
behaving in a calm, relaxed way (*informal*):
Everyone here is really laid-back.

lain /leɪn/ → see **lie**

lake /leɪk/ *noun*
a large area of water with land around it:
They went fishing in the lake.

lamb /læm/ *noun*
1 a young sheep
2 *uncountable* the flesh of a lamb eaten as
food: *For supper she served lamb and vegetables.*

lame /leɪm/ *adjective* (**lamer, lamest**)
1 not able to walk very well: *The horses were
lame and the men were tired.*
2 used about an excuse that is not very
good: *He gave me some lame excuse about being
too busy to call me.*

lamp /læmp/ *noun*
a light that works using electricity or by
burning oil or gas: *She switched on the lamp
by her bed.*

land[1] /lænd/ *uncountable noun*
an area of ground, especially one that is
used for a particular purpose such as
farming or building: *There is not enough
good farm land.*

land² /lænd/ *verb* (**lands, landing, landed**)
1 to come down to the ground after moving through the air: *The ball landed 20 feet away.*
2 to arrive somewhere: *The plane landed just after 10 pm.*
▶ **landing** *noun The pilot made an emergency landing into the sea.*

landform /'lændfɔ:m/ also **land form** *noun*
a natural feature of the Earth's surface, such as a hill, a lake or a beach: *This small country has a wide variety of landforms.*

landing /'lændɪŋ/ *noun*
the flat area at the top of the stairs in a house or building

landlady /'lændleɪdi/ *noun* (**landladies**)
a woman who owns a building and allows people to live there in return for rent: *There was a note under the door from my landlady.*

landlord /'lændlɔ:d/ *noun*
a man who owns a building and allows people to live there in return for rent: *His landlord doubled the rent.*

landmark /'lændmɑ:k/ *noun*
a building or other object that helps people to know where they are: *The Empire State Building is a New York landmark.*

landscape /'lændskeɪp/ *noun*
1 everything you can see when you look across an area of land: *We travelled through the beautiful landscape of northern Scotland.*
2 a painting that shows a scene in the countryside: *She paints landscapes of hills and river valleys.*

lane /leɪn/ *noun*
1 a narrow road, especially in the countryside: *Our house was on a quiet country lane.*
2 a part of a road that is marked by a painted line: *The lorry was travelling at 20 mph in the slow lane.*

language /'læŋgwɪdʒ/ *noun*
1 a system of sounds and written symbols that people of a particular country or region use in talking or writing: *The English language has over 500,000 words.* □ *Students must learn to speak a second language.*
2 *uncountable* the use of a system of communication that has a set of sounds or written symbols: *Some children develop language more quickly than others.*

lantern /'læntən/ *noun*
a light in a metal frame with glass sides

lap¹ /læp/ *noun*
1 the flat area formed by the tops of your legs when you are sitting down: *Ravi was sitting on his dad's lap.*
2 one turn around a race course: *He was not able to run the last lap of the race.*

lap

Ravi was sitting on his dad's lap.

lap² /læp/ *verb* (**laps, lapping, lapped**)
to use short quick movements of the tongue to take liquid up into the mouth: *The cat lapped milk from a dish.*

lapel /lə'pel/ *noun*
the folds on the front of a jacket or coat: *He wore a flower in his lapel.*

laptop /'læptɒp/ *noun*
a small computer that you can carry with you: *She was working at her laptop.*

large /lɑ:dʒ/ *adjective* (**larger, largest**)
1 greater in size than most other things of the same type: *This fish lives mainly in large rivers and lakes.* □ *In the largest room a few people were sitting on the floor.*
2 more than the average amount or number: *The robbers got away with a large amount of cash.* □ *A large number of people are still looking for jobs.*

largely /'lɑ:dʒli/ *adverb*
used for saying that something is mostly true: *The project is largely paid for by taxes.* □ *The government is largely to blame for this.*

laser /'leɪzə/ *noun*
a strong light that is produced by a special machine: *Doctors are trying new laser technology to help patients.*

'laser ,printer *noun*
a computer printer that produces clear words and pictures on paper using laser beams (= strong lines of light)

last¹ /lɑ:st/ *adjective, adverb*
1 the most recent: *I got married last July.* □ *He didn't come home last night.* □ *A lot has changed since my last visit.*

2 happening or coming after all the others of the same type: *I read the last three pages of the chapter.*

3 at the end, or after everyone else: *I arrived home last.* ● **last** *pronoun Rosa was the last to go to bed.*

4 the only one that is left: *Can I have the last piece of pizza?*

at last finally; after you have been waiting for a long time: *I'm so glad that we've found you at last!*

last² /lɑ:st/ *verb* (**lasts, lasting, lasted**)

1 to continue to exist for a particular length of time: *The marriage lasted for less than two years.*

2 to be able to be used for a particular length of time: *One tube of glue lasts for a long time.*

lasting /'lɑ:stɪŋ/ *adjective*
continuing to exist for a very long time: *Everyone wants lasting peace.*

lastly /'lɑ:stli/ *adverb*
used when you want to mention a final item: *Lastly, can I ask about your future plans?*

'last name *noun*
the name of your family. In English, your **last** name comes after all your other names: *'What is your last name?' — 'Garcia.'*

latch /lætʃ/ *noun* (**latches**)
a metal bar that you use to fasten a door or a gate. You lift the bar to open the door or gate: *She lifted the latch and pushed the door open.*

late /leɪt/ *adjective, adverb* (**later, latest**)

1 near the end of a period of time: *He was in his late 20s.* □ *It was late in the afternoon.* □ *He married late in life.*

2 near the end of the day: *It was very late and the streets were empty.*

3 after the time that something should start or happen: *The train was 40 minutes late.* □ *Steve arrived late for his class.*

lately /'leɪtli/ *adverb*
used for talking about events that happened recently: *Dad's health hasn't been good lately.*

later¹ /'leɪtə/
the comparative of **late**

later² /'leɪtə/ *adverb*
used for talking about a time that is after the one that you have been talking about: *He joined the company in 1990 and left his job ten years later.*

latest /'leɪtɪst/ *adjective*

1 most recent: *I really liked her latest book.*

2 new and modern: *That shop sells only the latest fashions.*

latitude /'lætɪ,tju:d/ *noun*
the distance of a place from the equator (= the line around the middle of the Earth). Compare with **longitude**: *The evenings are already long at this northern latitude.*

latter /'lætə/ *pronoun*
the second of two things that have been mentioned. The first of them is called **the former**: *He found his cousin and uncle. The latter was sick.* ● **latter** *adjective Some people like speaking in public and some don't. Mike belongs in the latter group.*

laugh /lɑ:f/ *verb* (**laughs, laughing, laughed**)

1 to make a sound while smiling to show that you think something is funny: *When I saw what he was wearing, I started to laugh.* □ *Some of the boys laughed at his jokes.* ● **laugh** *noun Len gave a loud laugh.*

2 to make jokes about someone or something: *People used to laugh at me because I was so small.*

laughter /'lɑ:ftə/ *uncountable noun*
the sound of people laughing: *Their laughter filled the room.*

launch /lɔ:ntʃ/ *verb* (**launches, launching, launched**)

1 to send a spacecraft (= a vehicle that goes into space) away from Earth: *NASA plans to launch a new satellite.*

2 to put a ship or a boat into water: *The Titanic was launched in 1911.*

3 to start a large and important activity: *The police have launched a search for the missing girl.*

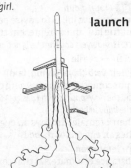

launch

launderette /ˌlɔːndəˈret/ *noun*
a place where people pay to use machines to wash and dry their clothes

laundry /ˈlɔːndri/ *noun* (**laundries**)
1 *uncountable* clothes and other things that are going to be washed: *I'll do your laundry.*
2 a business that washes and irons clothes and other things for people: *He takes his shirts to the laundry.*

lava /ˈlɑːvə/ *uncountable noun*
the very hot liquid rock that comes out of a volcano (= a mountain with a hole at the top that throws out hot substances): *Lava poured from the volcano.*

lavatory /ˈlævətri/ *noun* (**lavatories**)
a toilet

law /lɔː/ *noun*
1 a system of rules that a society or government develops to deal with things like crime: *Driving too fast is against the law.* □ *These companies are breaking the law.*
2 one of the rules in a system of law: *The government has introduced a new law to protect young people.*

lawful /ˈlɔːfʊl/ *adjective*
allowed by law (*formal*): *We want fair and lawful treatment of prisoners.*
▸ **lawfully** *adverb* *Did the police act lawfully in shooting him?*

lawn /lɔːn/ *noun*
an area of short grass around a house or other building: *They were sitting on the lawn.*

lawnmower /ˈlɔːnməʊə/ *noun*
a machine for cutting grass

lawsuit /ˈlɔːsuːt/ *noun*
a case that a court of law deals with (*formal*): *The lawsuit accuses him of theft and kidnapping.*

lawyer /ˈlɔɪə/ *noun*
a person whose job is to advise people about the law and to represent them in court: *His lawyers say that he is not guilty.*

lay¹ /leɪ/ → see **lie**

lay² /leɪ/ *verb* (**lays, laying, laid**)
1 to put something somewhere carefully: *He laid the newspaper on the desk.* □ *She gently laid the baby in her cot.*
2 when a female bird lays an egg, it pushes an egg out of its body

layer /ˈleɪə/ *noun*
a substance or a material that covers a surface, or that lies between two other things: *A fresh layer of snow covered the street.*

layout /ˈleɪaʊt/ *noun*
the way the parts of a place are arranged: *He tried to remember the layout of the farmhouse.*

lazy /ˈleɪzi/ *adjective* (**lazier, laziest**)
not wanting to work: *I'm not lazy; I like to be busy.*
▸ **laziness** *uncountable noun* *Too much TV encourages laziness.*

lb.

LANGUAGE HELP
The plural is **lbs.** or **lb.**

short for **pound**, when you are talking about weight

lead¹ /liːd/ *verb* (**leads, leading, led**)
1 to go in front of a group of people: *A jazz band led the parade.*
2 to take someone to a place: *I took his hand and led him into the house.*
3 used for describing where a road or path goes: *This path leads down to the beach.*
4 to be winning in a race or competition: *The Eagles led by three points at half-time.*
5 to be in control of a group of people: *Chris leads a large team of salespeople.*
6 used for describing someone's life: *She led a normal, happy life.*
7 to cause a particular situation: *Every time we talk about money it leads to an argument.*

lead² /liːd/ *noun*
a long thin piece of leather or a chain, that you use to control a dog: *All dogs in public places should be on a lead.*
in the lead winning in a race or competition: *Harvard were already in the lead after ten minutes.*

lead³ /led/ *noun*
1 *uncountable* a soft, grey, heavy metal: *In the past, most water pipes were made of lead.*
2 the grey part in the middle of a pencil that makes a mark on paper: *He started writing, but his pencil lead immediately broke.*

leader /ˈliːdə/ *noun*
1 the person who is in charge of a group of people or an organization: *Members today will elect a new leader.*
2 the person who is in front of all the others in a race or competition, or who is winning: *The leader came in two minutes before the other runners.*

leadership /'li:dəʃɪp/ *noun*
1 the people who are in control of a group or organization: *He attended a meeting with the Croatian leadership.*
2 **uncountable** someone's position of being in control of a group of people: *The company doubled in size under her leadership.*

leading /'li:dɪŋ/ *adjective*
1 most important or successful in a particular area: *a leading violin player*
2 used for describing the person or team that is winning a race or competition: *It always feels good to be in the leading team.*

leaf /li:f/ *noun* (**leaves**)
the parts of a tree or plant that are flat, thin, and usually green: *A brown, dry oak leaf fell into the water.*

leaflet /'li:flət/ *noun*
a piece of paper containing information about a particular subject: *My doctor gave me a leaflet about healthy eating.*

league /li:g/ *noun*
1 a group of people, clubs or countries that have joined together for a particular purpose: *The League of Nations was formed after World War I.*
2 a group of teams that play against each other: *the football league*

leak /li:k/ *verb* (**leaks, leaking, leaked**)
1 to let liquid or gas escape: *The roof leaks every time it rains.* • **leak noun** *A gas leak caused the explosion.*
2 when liquid or gas leaks, it escapes from something: *The water is leaking out from the bottom of the bucket.*

leak

The water is leaking out from the bottom of the bucket.

lean ¹ /li:n/ *verb* (**leans, leaning, leaned**)
1 to bend your body from your waist in a particular direction: *The driver leaned across and opened the passenger door.*
2 to rest on someone or something: *She was feeling tired and leaned against him.*

lean ² /li:n/ *adjective* (**leaner, leanest**)
1 used for describing meat that does not have very much fat
2 thin, but fit and healthy: *He was lean and strong.*

lean

The driver leaned across and opened the passenger door.

leap /li:p/ *verb* (**leaps, leaping, leaped** or **leapt**)
1 to jump high in the air or to jump a long distance: *He leaped in the air and waved his hands.* • **leap noun** *Powell won the long jump with a leap of 8 metres 95 centimetres.*
2 to move somewhere suddenly and quickly: *The two men leapt into the car and drove away.*

learn /lɜ:n/ *verb* (**learns, learning, learned** or **learnt**)
to get knowledge or a skill by studying, training, or through experience: *Where did you learn English?* □ *He is learning to play the piano.*
▸ **learner noun** *Clint is a quick learner; he's one of my smarter students.*

lease /li:s/ *verb* (**leases, leasing, leased**)
1 to pay someone to allow you to use their property: *He leased an apartment in Toronto.*
2 to allow someone to use your property in exchange for money: *She's going to lease the building to students.*

least /li:st/ *adjective, adverb*
a smaller amount than anyone or anything else, or the smallest amount possible: *He wants to spend the least amount of money possible on a car.* □ *He is one of the least friendly people I have ever met.* • **least pronoun** *The report found that teenage girls exercised the least.*
at least not less than a particular number or amount: *Drink at least half a pint of milk each day.*

leather /'leðə/ *noun*
animal skin that is used for making shoes, clothes, bags and furniture: *She bought a leather jacket.*

leave¹ /liːv/ *verb* (**leaves, leaving, left**)
1 to go away from a place or person: *He left the country yesterday.* □ *My flight leaves in less than an hour.*
2 to not bring something with you: *I left my bags in the car.*
3 to not use all of something: *Please leave some cake for me!*
4 to give something to someone when you die: *He left everything to his wife when he died.*
5 to forget to bring something with you: *I left my purse in the petrol station.*
leave someone alone to stop annoying someone: *Please just leave me alone!*
leave something alone to stop touching something: *Leave my purse alone!*
leave something out to not include someone or something: *Why did they leave her out of the team?*

leave² /liːv/ *uncountable noun*
a period of time when you are away from work: *Why don't you take a few days' leave?*
on leave not working at your job: *She has gone on leave for a week.*

leaves /liːvz/
1 the plural form of **leaf**
2 → see **leave¹**

lecture /'lektʃə/ *noun*
a talk that someone gives in order to teach people about a particular subject: *We attended a lecture by Professor Eric Robinson.*
● **lecture** *verb* (**lectures, lecturing, lectured**) *She invited him to Atlanta to lecture on the history of art.*

lecturer /'lektʃərə/ *noun*
a teacher at a university or college: *a lecturer in law*

led /led/ → see **lead**

ledge /ledʒ/ *noun*
1 a narrow shelf of rock on the side of a mountain
2 a narrow shelf along the bottom edge of a window: *a window ledge*

leek /liːk/ *noun*
a long, thin vegetable that is white at one end and has long green leaves
→ Look at picture on P2

left¹ /left/ → see **leave**

left² /left/ *adjective, adverb*
1 still there after everything else has gone or been used: *Is there any milk left?*

2 opposite the side that most people write with: *I've broken my left leg.* □ *Turn left at the corner.* ● **left** *noun* *The bank is on the left at the end of the road.* □ *There is a high brick wall to the left of the building.*

'left-hand *adjective*
positioned on the left of something: *The Japanese drive on the left-hand side of the road.*

'left-'handed *adjective*
using your left hand rather than your right hand for activities such as writing and sports: *A left-handed tennis player won the tournament.*

leftover /'leftəʊvə/ *adjective*
used for describing an amount of something that remains after the rest of it has been used or eaten: *If you have any leftover chicken, use it to make this delicious pie.*

leftovers /'leftəʊvəz/ *plural noun*
food that has not been eaten after a meal: *Put any leftovers in the fridge.*

'left-'wing *adjective*
supporting the ideas of the political left: *I'm not going to vote for him because he is too left-wing.*

leg /leg/ *noun*
1 one of the long parts of a person's or an animal's body that they use for walking and standing: *He broke his right leg in a motorcycle accident.*
→ Look at picture on P1
2 one of the parts of a pair of trousers that cover your legs: *Anthony dried his hands on the legs of his jeans.*
3 one of the long parts of a table or a chair that it stands on: *a broken chair leg*

legal /'liːgəl/ *adjective*
1 used for describing things that relate to the law: *He promised to take legal action.* □ *the legal system*
2 allowed by law: *My actions were completely legal.*

legalize /'liːgəˌlaɪz/ *verb* (**legalizes, legalizing, legalized**)
to pass a law to make something legal: *Divorce was legalized in 1981.*

legend /'ledʒənd/ *noun*
a very old and popular story: *The play is based on an ancient Greek legend.*

leisure /'leʒə/ *uncountable noun*
the time when you are not working, when you can relax and do things that

you enjoy: *They spend their leisure time painting or drawing.*

leisurely /'leʒəli/ *adjective*
done in a relaxed way: *Lunch was a leisurely meal.*

lemon /'lemən/ *noun*
a yellow fruit with very sour juice: *I like a slice of lemon in my tea.*
→ Look at picture on P2

lemonade /ˌleməˈneɪd/ *noun*
a drink that is made from lemons, sugar and water: *They ordered two lemonades.*

lend /lend/ *verb* (**lends, lending, lent**)
1 to give someone money that they must give back after a certain amount of time: *The government will lend you money at very good rates.*
2 to allow someone to use something of yours for a period of time: *Will you lend me your pen?*

length /leŋθ/ *noun*
1 the measurement from one end of something to the other: *The table is about a metre in length.*
2 how long an event lasts: *The average length of a patient's stay in hospital is about 48 hours.*
at length for a long time or in great detail: *They spoke at length about their families.*

lengthen /'leŋθən/ *verb* (**lengthens, lengthening, lengthened**)
to make or become longer: *The sun went down and the shadows lengthened.* ◻ *This exercise will lengthen the muscles in your legs.*

lengthy /'leŋθi/ *adjective* (**lengthier, lengthiest**)
1 lasting for a long time: *There was a lengthy meeting to decide the company's future.*
2 containing a lot of words: *The United Nations produced a lengthy report on the subject.*

lens /lenz/ *noun* (**lenses**)
a thin, curved piece of glass or plastic used in things such as cameras and glasses. A lens makes things look larger, smaller or clearer: *I bought a powerful lens for my camera.*

lent /lent/ → see **lend**

lentil /'lentɪl/ *noun*
a small, round dried seed that you use in cooking, for example to make soups

leopard /'lepəd/ *noun*
a large wild cat. Leopards have yellow fur with black spots, and live in Africa and Asia.

leotard /'liːəˌtɑːd/ *noun*
a tight piece of clothing that covers the top part of your body. People wear leotards when they practise dancing or do exercises.

lesbian /'lezbiən/ *noun*
a woman who is sexually attracted to other women: *The main character in the novel is a lesbian.* ● **lesbian** *adjective The organization supports lesbian and gay members.*

less /les/ *adjective*
a smaller amount of something: *People should eat less fat.* ◻ *He earns less money than his brother.* ◻ *The population of the country is less than 12 million.* ● **less** *pronoun He thinks people should spend less and save more.*

lessen /'lesən/ *verb* (**lessens, lessening, lessened**)
to make something smaller: *A change in diet might lessen your risk of heart disease.*

lesson /'lesən/ *noun*
a time when you learn about a particular subject: *Johanna has started taking piano lessons.*

let /let/ *verb* (**lets, letting, let**)
1 to not try to stop something from happening: *I just let him sleep.*
2 to give someone your permission to do something: *I love sweets but Mum doesn't let me eat them very often.*
3 to allow someone to enter or leave a place: *I went down and let them into the building.*
4 to allow someone to live in your property in exchange for money: *When I moved to London, I let my flat in New York.*
5 used when you are offering to do something: *Let me hang up your coat.*
let go of someone/something to stop holding a thing or a person: *She let go of Mona's hand.*
let someone know to tell someone about something: *I want to let them know that I'm safe.*
let someone off to give someone a lighter punishment than they expect or no punishment at all: *He thought that if he said he was sorry, the judge would let him off.*
let's short for 'let us'; used when you are making a suggestion

lethal /'li:θəl/ *adjective*
used for describing something that can kill people or animals: *She swallowed a lethal dose of sleeping pills.*

letter /'letə/ *noun*
1 a message that you write or type on paper and send to someone: *I received a letter from a friend.* □ *Mrs Franklin sent a letter offering me the job.*
2 a written symbol that represents a sound in a language: *The children practised writing the letters of the alphabet.*

letter box *noun* (**letter boxes**) (American: **mailbox**)
a hole in a door for putting letters through

lettering /'letərɪŋ/ *uncountable noun*
writing or printing: *On the door was a small blue sign with white lettering.*

lettuce /'letɪs/ *noun*
a plant with large green leaves that is eaten mainly in salads
→ Look at picture on P2

level¹ /'levəl/ *noun*
1 used for describing the amount or quality of something: *We have the lowest level of inflation since 1986.*
2 the height of something: *The water level was 6.5 feet below normal.*

level² /'levəl/ *adjective*
1 at the same height as another thing: *He sat down so his face was level with the boy's.*
2 completely flat: *Make sure the ground is level before you start building.*

lever /'li:və/ *noun*
1 a handle that you push or pull to operate a machine: *Push the lever to switch the machine on.*
2 a bar that you use to lift something heavy. You put one end of it under the heavy object, and then push down on the other end: *Joseph found a stick to use as a lever and lifted up the stone.*

liable /'laɪəbəl/ *adjective*
liable to very likely: *Some of this old equipment is liable to break down.*

liar /'laɪə/ *noun*
someone who tells lies: *He's a liar and a cheat.*

liberal /'lɪbərəl/ *adjective*
understanding and accepting that other people have different ideas and beliefs, and may therefore behave differently: *My parents are very liberal and relaxed.*

liberty /'lɪbəti/ *uncountable noun*
the freedom to live in the way that you want to: *We must do all we can to defend liberty and justice.*

librarian /laɪ'breərɪən/ *noun*
a person who works in a library

library /'laɪbrəri/ *noun* (**libraries**)
a place where books, newspapers, DVDs and music are kept for people to use or borrow: *I found the book I needed at the local library.*

lice /laɪs/
the plural of **louse**

licence /'laɪsəns/ *noun*
an official document that gives you permission to do, use or own something: *You need a licence to drive a car.*

lick /lɪk/ *verb* (**licks, licking, licked**)
to move your tongue across the surface of something: *She licked the stamp and pressed it onto the envelope.* ● **lick** *noun* *Can I have a lick of your ice cream?*

licorice /'lɪkərɪs/ *uncountable noun*
a firm black substance with a strong taste that is used for making a type of sweet

lid /lɪd/ *noun*
the top of a container that can be removed: *She lifted the lid of the box.*

lie¹ /laɪ/ *verb* (**lies, lying, lay, lain**)
1 to be in a flat position, and not standing or sitting: *There was a man lying on the ground.*
2 to be in a flat position on a surface: *His clothes were lying on the floor by the bed.*
3 to say something that you know is not true: *I know he's lying.* □ *Never lie to me again.*
lie down to move your body so that it is flat on something, usually when you want to rest or sleep: *Why don't you go upstairs and lie down?*

LANGUAGE HELP
lie or **lay**? **Lie** does not have an object. *Lie on the floor with your arms by your sides.* **Lay** has an object. *Lay the baby on the bed.*

lie² *noun*
something that someone says or writes that they know is not true: *You told me a lie!* □ *'How old are you?' — 'Eighteen.' — 'That's a lie.'*

lieutenant /lef'tenənt/ *noun*
an officer in the army or navy: *Lieutenant Campbell ordered the men to stop firing.*

life /laɪf/ *noun* (**lives** /laɪvz/)

1 someone's state of being alive, or the period of time when they are alive: *Your life is in danger.* □ *A nurse tried to save his life.* □ *He spent the last fourteen years of his life in France.*

2 **uncountable** the quality of being interesting and full of energy: *The town was full of life.*

lifebelt /'laɪfbelt/ *noun*

a large ring that you can hold onto to stop you from going under water

lifeboat /'laɪfbəʊt/ *noun*

a boat that is used for saving people who are in danger at sea

'life ˌcycle *noun*

the series of changes that happen to an animal or a plant from the beginning of its life until its death: *This plant completes its life cycle in a single season.*

lifeguard /'laɪfɡɑːd/ *noun*

a person who works at a beach or a swimming pool and helps people when they are in danger

'life ˌjacket *noun*

a jacket that helps you to float when you have fallen into deep water

lifestyle /'laɪfstaɪl/ also **life-style, life style** *noun*

the way someone has chosen to live and behave: *She talked about the benefits of leading a healthier lifestyle.*

lifetime /'laɪftaɪm/ *noun*

the length of time that someone is alive: *He travelled a lot during his lifetime.*

lift 1 /lɪft/ *verb* (**lifts, lifting, lifted**) (*also* **lift something up**)

to take something and move it upwards: *He lifted the bag onto his shoulder.* □ *She lifted the baby up and gave him to me.*

lift 2 /lɪft/ *noun*

1 (*American*: **elevator**) a machine that carries people or things up and down inside tall buildings: *We took the lift to the fourteenth floor.*

2 when you take someone somewhere in your car: *He often gave me a lift home.*

light 1 /laɪt/ *noun*

1 **uncountable** the energy that comes from the sun, that lets you see things: *He opened the curtains, and suddenly the room was filled with light.*

2 something such as an electric lamp

light

that produces light: *Remember to turn the lights out when you leave.*

light 2 /laɪt/ *verb* (**lights, lighting, lit** or **lighted**)

1 to produce light for a place: *The room was lit by only one light.*

2 to start something burning: *Stephen took a match and lit the candle.*

light 3 /laɪt/ *adjective* (**lighter, lightest**)

1 full of natural light during the day: *Here it gets light at about 6 a.m.*

2 not heavy; easy to lift or move: *The printer is quite light, so it's easy to move around.*

3 not very great in amount or power: *She had a light lunch of salad and fruit.* □ *There was a light wind that day.*

4 pale in colour: *He was wearing jeans and a light-blue T-shirt.*

'light bulb *noun*

the glass part that you put in an electric light to produce light

lighten /'laɪtən/ *verb* (**lightens, lightening, lightened**)

to make something less dark: *She lightened her hair with a special cream.*

lighter /'laɪtə/ *noun*

a small object that produces a flame. It is used for lighting things such as candles or fires.

lighthouse /'laɪthaʊs/ *noun*

a tower that is built near or in the sea. It has a flashing lamp that warns ships of danger.

lighting /'laɪtɪŋ/ *uncountable noun*

the way that a place is lit: *The kitchen had bright overhead lighting.*

lightning /'laɪtnɪŋ/ *uncountable noun*

the very bright flashes of light in the sky

that happen during a storm: *One man died when he was struck by lightning.* □ *A flash of lightning lit up the house.*

like¹ /laɪk/ *preposition*

1 similar to another person or thing: *He looks like my uncle.* □ *His house is just like yours.*

2 used when you are talking about how a thing or person seems to you: *What does Maria look like?* □ *'What was the party like?' – 'Great!'*

3 used for giving an example: *large cities like New York and Chicago*

like² /laɪk/ *verb* (**likes, liking, liked**)

to think a thing or a person is interesting, enjoyable or attractive: *He likes baseball.* □ *Do you like swimming?*

I'd like used for saying politely that you want something: *I'd like to ask you a few questions.* □ *I'd like a cup of tea and a cheese sandwich, please.*

if you like used when you are suggesting something to someone in an informal way: *You can stay here if you like.*

Would you like...? used for politely offering something: *Would you like some coffee?*

likeable /'laɪkəbəl/ *also* **likable** *adjective*

pleasant and easy to be with: *He was a clever and likable guy.*

likelihood /'laɪkli,hʊd/ *uncountable noun*

how probable something is: *The likelihood of getting the disease is small.*

likely /'laɪkli/ *adjective* (**likelier, likeliest**)

1 probably true in a particular situation: *A gas leak was the most likely cause of the explosion.*

2 used for saying that a person or thing will probably do something: *Eric is a bright young man who is likely to succeed in life.*

likewise /'laɪkwaɪz/ *adverb*

the same: *He gave money to charity and encouraged others to do likewise.*

liking /'laɪkɪŋ/ *noun*

to your liking used when something suits you: *London was more to his liking than Rome.*

lilac¹ /'laɪlək/ *noun*

1 a purple, pink or white flower that grows on a small tree: *Lilac grew against the garden wall.*

2 pale purple: *Would you prefer lilac or yellow for your bedroom?*

lilac² /'laɪlək/ *adjective*

pale purple in colour: *The bride wore a lilac dress.*

lily /'lɪli/ *noun* (**lilies**)

a plant with large sweet-smelling flowers

limb /lɪm/ *noun*

an arm or a leg: *She stretched out her aching limbs.*

lime /laɪm/ *noun*

a round, green fruit that tastes like a lemon: *Use fresh lime juice and fresh herbs in this recipe.*

→ Look at picture on P2

limit¹ /'lɪmɪt/ *noun*

1 the greatest amount or degree of something: *There is no limit to how much fresh fruit you should eat in a day.*

2 the largest or smallest amount of something that is allowed: *He was driving 40 miles per hour over the speed limit.*

limit² /'lɪmɪt/ *verb* (**limits, limiting, limited**)

to stop something from becoming greater than a particular amount: *Try to limit the amount of time you spend on the Internet.*

limousine /,lɪmə'ziːn/ *noun* (*also* **limo**)

a large and very comfortable car: *As the president's limousine approached, the crowd began to cheer.*

limp¹ /lɪmp/ *verb* (**limps, limping, limped**)

to walk with difficulty because you have hurt one of your legs or feet: *James limps because of a hip injury.* ● **limp** *noun* *Anne walks with a limp.*

limp² /lɪmp/ *adjective* (**limper, limpest**)

soft or weak: *Her body was limp and she was too weak to move.*

line¹ /laɪn/ *noun*

1 a long, thin mark on something: *Draw a line at the bottom of the page.*

2 a series of words written or printed in a row: *Now read the next line of the poem.*

3 a long piece of string or rope that you use for a particular purpose: *Melissa was outside, hanging the clothes on the line.*

4 a route that trains move along: *We stayed on the train to the end of the line.*

5 a very long wire for telephones or electricity: *Suddenly the telephone line went dead.*

6 a number of people or vehicles that are waiting one behind the other: *There was a*

line of people waiting to go into the cinema
stand/wait in line (*American*):
→ see **queue**: *For the homeless, standing in line for meals is part of the daily routine.*

line² /laɪn/ *verb* (**lines, lining, lined**)
1 to stand in lines along a road: *Thousands of local people lined the streets to welcome the president.*
2 to cover the inside of a container with something: *Line the box with newspaper.*

linen /'lɪnɪn/ *uncountable noun*
a type of strong cloth: *She wore a white linen suit.*

liner /'laɪnə/ *noun*
a large ship in which people travel long distances, especially on holiday: *a luxury ocean liner*

lingerie /'lænʒəri/ *uncountable noun*
women's underwear: *The shop sells expensive designer lingerie.*

lining /'laɪnɪŋ/ *noun*
a piece of cloth that is attached to the inside of a piece of clothing or a curtain: *She wore a black jacket with a red lining.*

link¹ /lɪŋk/ *noun*
1 a connection between two things, often because one of them causes the other: *Scientists believe there is a link between poor diet and cancer.*
2 an area on a computer screen that allows you to move from one web page or website to another: *The website has links to other tourism sites.*
3 one of the rings in a chain: *She was wearing a chain of heavy gold links.*

link² /lɪŋk/ *verb* (**links, linking, linked**)
to make a connection between two things, often because one of them causes the other: *Studies have linked television violence with aggressive behaviour.*

lion /'laɪən/ *noun*
a large wild cat that lives in Africa. Lions have yellow fur, and male lions have long hair on their head and neck (= a mane).

lip /lɪp/ *noun*
one of the two outer parts of the edge of your mouth: *He kissed her gently on the lips.*
→ Look at picture on P1

lipstick /'lɪpstɪk/ *noun*
a coloured substance that women sometimes put on their lips: *She was wearing red lipstick.*

liquid /'lɪkwɪd/ *noun*
a substance that is not a solid or a gas. Liquids flow and can be poured. Water and oil are liquids: *She took out a small bottle of clear liquid.* □ *Drink plenty of liquids while you are flying and after you land.*

list¹ /lɪst/ *noun*
a set of names or other things that are written or printed one below the other: *I added coffee to my shopping list.* □ *There were six names on the list.*

list² /lɪst/ *verb* (**lists, listing, listed**)
to write or say names or other things one after another: *The students listed the sports they liked best.*

listen /'lɪsən/ *verb* (**listens, listening, listened**)
1 to give your attention to a sound, or to what someone is saying: *He spends his time listening to the radio.*
2 used when you want someone to pay attention to you because you are going to say something: *Listen, there's something I should warn you about.*

LANGUAGE HELP
See note at **hear**.

listener /'lɪsnə/ *noun*
someone who is listening to a speaker: *When he finished talking, his listeners applauded loudly.*

lit /lɪt/ → see **light**

literacy /'lɪtərəsi/ *uncountable noun*
the ability to read and write: *The library's adult literacy programme helps about 2,000 people a year.*

literally /'lɪtərəli/ *adverb*
1 saying what each word means in another language: *Volkswagen literally means 'people's car'.*
2 used for emphasizing what you are saying: *The view is literally breathtaking.*

literature /'lɪtrətʃə/ *uncountable noun*
books, plays and poetry that most people consider to be of high quality: *Chris is studying English literature at Leeds University.*

litre /'liːtə/ *noun*
a unit for measuring liquid. There are 1,000 millilitres in a litre: *Adults should drink about two litres of water each day.*

litter¹ /'lɪtə/ *noun*
1 *uncountable* paper or rubbish that people

litter

leave lying on the ground in public places: *I hate it when I see people dropping litter.*
2 all the babies that are born to an animal at the same time: *Our cat has just given birth to a litter of three kittens.*

litter² /'lɪtə/ *verb* (**litters, littering, littered**)
to be lying around or over a place in a messy way: *Broken glass littered the pavement.*
▶ **littered** *adjective* *The room was littered with toys.*

little /'lɪtəl/ *adjective, adverb* (**littler, littlest**)
1 small: *We all sat at a little table.*
2 short: *Go down the road a little way and then turn left.* □ *We waited for a little while, and then we went home.*
3 not much: *I have little money and little free time.* □ *I get very little sleep these days.* • **little** *pronoun* *He ate little, and drank less.*
4 not very often or not very much: *They spoke very little.*
5 rather; to a small degree: *He was a little bit afraid of the dog.*
a little a small amount of something: *I need a little help sometimes.*

> **LANGUAGE HELP**
>
> **a little** or **little**? If you say *I have a little money*, you are saying that you have some money. If you say *I have little money*, you are saying that you do not have much money.

live¹ /lɪv/ *verb* (**lives, living, lived**)
1 to have your home in a particular place: *She lived in New York for 10 years.* □ *Where do you live?*
2 to have a particular type of life: *Pete lives a quiet life in Cornwall.*

3 to be alive: *We all need water to live.*
4 to stay alive until you are a particular age: *He lived to 103.*
live on something to eat a particular type of food: *Sheep live mainly on grass.*

live² /laɪv/ *adjective, adverb*
1 not dead: *The local market sells live animals.*
2 used for describing a television or radio programme that you watch at the same time that it happens: *They watch all the live football games on TV.* □ *The president's speech was broadcast live.*

lively /'laɪvli/ *adjective* (**livelier, liveliest**)
cheerful; having a lot of energy: *Amy is a lively, sociable little girl.*

liver /'lɪvə/ *noun*
1 the large organ in your body that cleans your blood: *liver disease*
2 the liver of some animals that you can cook and eat: *They ate lamb's liver for dinner.*

lives /laɪvz/
the plural of **life**

living¹ /'lɪvɪŋ/ *adjective*
alive, and not dead: *He is perhaps the world's most famous living artist.* □ *He has no living relatives.*

living² /'lɪvɪŋ/ *noun*
1 the way you earn money: *What does she do for a living?* □ *Scott earns a living as a lawyer.*
2 *uncountable* the way that people live: *Mum believes in healthy living.*

'living room *noun*
a room where people sit together and talk or watch television: *We were sitting in the living room watching TV.*
→ Look at picture on P5

lizard /'lɪzəd/ *noun*
a small animal with a long tail and rough skin

load¹ /ləʊd/ *verb* (**loads, loading, loaded**)
to put a large amount of things into a vehicle or a container: *The men finished loading the van.*

load² /ləʊd/ *noun*
something heavy that is being carried: *This car can take a big load.*

loaf /ləʊf/ *noun* (**loaves**)
bread that has been shaped and baked in one piece: *He bought a loaf of bread and some cheese.*

loan¹ /ləʊn/ *noun*
an amount of money that you borrow:

Right now it's very difficult to get a loan from a bank.

loan² /ləʊn/ *verb* (**loans, loaning, loaned**)
to lend something to someone: *Brandon loaned his girlfriend £6,000.*

loathe /ləʊð/ *verb* (**loathes, loathing, loathed**)
to dislike someone very much (*formal*): *The two men loathe each other.*

loaves /ləʊvz/
the plural of **loaf**

lobby /'lɒbi/ *noun* (**lobbies**)
the area inside the entrance to a big building: *I met her in the hotel lobby.*

lobster /'lɒbstə/ *noun*
a sea animal that has a hard shell and eight legs: *She sold me two live lobsters.*

local /'ləʊkəl/ *adjective*
in, or relating to, the area where you live: *Susan put an advertisement in the local paper.*
▶ **locally** *adverb* *I prefer to shop locally.*

locate /ləʊ'keɪt/ *verb* (**locates, locating, located**)
to find someone or something: *Did you manage to locate the items?*

located /ləʊ'keɪtɪd/ *adjective*
in a particular place: *The gym and beauty salon are located on the second floor.*

location /ləʊ'keɪʃən/ *noun*
the place where something is: *For dates and locations of the meetings, call this number.*

lock¹ /lɒk/ *verb* (**locks, locking, locked**)
1 to close a door or a container with a key: *Are you sure you locked the front door?*
2 to put a thing or a person somewhere and to close the door or the lid with a key: *She locked the case in the cupboard.*
lock something away to put something in a container and to close it with a key: *She cleaned her jewellery and locked it away in a case.*
lock up to lock all the windows and doors of a house or a car: *Don't forget to lock up before you leave.*

lock² /lɒk/ *noun*
the part of a door or a container that you use to keep it shut and to make sure that no-one can open it. You can open a lock with a key: *She turned the key in the lock and opened the door.*

locker /'lɒkə/ *noun*
a small cupboard with a lock, that you

keep things in at a school or at a sports club

loft /lɒft/ *noun*
the space directly under the roof of a building: *The loft was filled with boxes of old photos.*

log¹ /lɒg/ *noun*
a thick piece of wood that has been cut from a tree: *a log fire*

log² /lɒg/ *verb* (**logs, logging, logged**)
to write something down as a record of the event: *They log everything that comes in and out of the warehouse.*
log in or **log on** to type a special secret word so that you can start using a computer or a website: *She turned on her computer and logged in.*
log out or **log off** to stop using a computer or website by clicking on an instruction: *I logged off and went out for a walk.*

logic /'lɒdʒɪk/ *uncountable noun*
a way of working things out, by saying that one fact must be true if another fact is true: *The students study philosophy and logic.*

logical /'lɒdʒɪkəl/ *adjective*
reasonable or sensible: *There must be a logical explanation for his behaviour.*

logo /'ləʊgəʊ/ *noun*
the special design that an organization puts on all its products or advertisements: *The company's logo is a penguin.*

LOL
short for 'laughing out loud' or 'lots of love'; often used in email and text messages

lollipop /'lɒlɪ,pɒp/ *noun*
a hard sweet on the end of a stick: *What's your favourite flavour of lollipop?*

lonely /'ləʊnli/ *adjective* (**lonelier, loneliest**)
1 unhappy because you are alone: *Mr Garcia has been lonely since his wife died.*
▶ **loneliness** *uncountable noun* *I have a fear of loneliness.*
2 used for describing a place where very few people go: *Her car broke down on a lonely country road.*

long¹ /lɒŋ/ *adjective, adverb* (**longer** /'lɒŋgə/, **longest** /'lɒŋgɪst/)
1 a lot of time: *Cleaning up didn't take too long.* □ *Have you been waiting long?*
2 lasting for a lot of time: *We had a long meeting.* □ *She is planning a long holiday in Europe.*
□ *'How long is the film?' — 'About two hours.'*

3 measuring a great distance from one end to the other: *There was a long table in the middle of the kitchen.* □ *Lucy had long dark hair.*
4 used for describing a great distance: *The long trip made him tired.*

as long as/so long as if: *They can do what they want as long as they are not breaking the law.*

no longer/not any longer used when something was true in the past, but is not true now: *Ben and I are no longer in the same class.*

long² /lɒŋ/ *verb* (**longs, longing, longed**)
to want something very much: *I'm longing to meet her.*

long-'distance *adjective*
used for talking about travel or communication between places that are a long way from each other: *Long-distance travel can be very tiring.* □ *Stacey makes a lot of long-distance calls on her mobile phone.*

longitude /'lɒndʒɪˌtjuːd/ *noun*
how far a place is to the west or east of an imaginary line that goes from the North Pole to the South Pole. Compare with **latitude**.

'long jump *noun*
a sports event that involves jumping as far as you can

loo /luː/ *noun*
a toilet (*informal*): *I asked if I could go to the loo.*

look¹ /lʊk/ *verb* (**looks, looking, looked**)
1 to turn your eyes in a particular direction so that you can see what is there: *I looked out of the window.* □ *If you look over there, you'll see a lake.* □ *Look at me!*
2 to try to find someone or something: *I'm looking for a child.* □ *I looked everywhere for my purse.*
3 seem: *'You look lovely, Marcia!'* □ *Sheila was looking sad.*
4 used when you want someone to pay attention to you: *Look, I'm sorry. I didn't mean it.*

look after someone to take care of someone: *Maria looks after the kids while I'm at work.*

look forward to something to want something to happen because you think you will enjoy it: *She's looking forward to her holiday in Hawaii.*

look out used when you are warning someone that they are in danger: *'Look out!' somebody shouted, as the lorry started to move towards us.*

look out for something to pay attention so that you see something if it happens: *Officers are looking out for the stolen vehicle.*

look something up to find a fact or piece of information by looking in a book or on a computer: *I looked up your number in my address book.*

LANGUAGE HELP

look or **watch**? You **look at** something that is not moving. *I asked him to look at the picture.* You **watch** something that is moving or changing. *He watched the children playing outside.*

---

look² /lʊk/ *noun*
1 when you turn your eyes in a particular direction so that you can see what is there: *Lucille took a last look in the mirror.*
2 a particular appearance or expression: *He saw the look of surprise on her face.* □ *Be very careful. I don't like the look of those guys.*

loom /luːm/ *noun*
a machine that is used for making cloth

loop /luːp/ *noun*
a shape like a circle in a piece of string or rope: *On the ground beside them was a loop of rope.*

loose /luːs/ *adjective* (**looser, loosest**)
1 not firmly fixed to something else: *One of Hannah's top front teeth is loose.*
▶ **loosely** *adverb* *He held the gun loosely in his hand.*
2 used when a person or an animal escapes from the place where they are held: *Our dog got loose and ran away yesterday.*
3 not fitting closely: *Wear loose, comfortable clothing when exercising.*
▶ **loosely** *adverb* *A scarf hung loosely around his neck.*

loosen /'luːsən/ *verb* (**loosens, loosening, loosened**)
to make something less tight: *He loosened his tie around his neck.*

lord /lɔːd/ *noun*
1 a man with a high position in society: *Kathleen Kennedy married Lord Cavendish in 1944.*
2 God or Jesus Christ: *She prayed now. 'Lord, help me to find courage.'*

lorry /'lɒri/ *noun* (**lorries**) (*American*: **truck**)
a large vehicle that is used for transporting goods by road

The body

head
wrist
shoulder
chest
arm
calf
stomach
hip
thigh
foot
leg
knee
bottom
waist
back
eyebrow
head
elbow
hand
eyelash
eye
nose
ear
mouth
lip
tooth
neck

Food and drink

Fruit

apple   banana   cherries   grapes   mango   pineapple

peach   pear   melon   plum   raspberry

strawberry   grapefruit   lemon   lime   orange

Vegetables

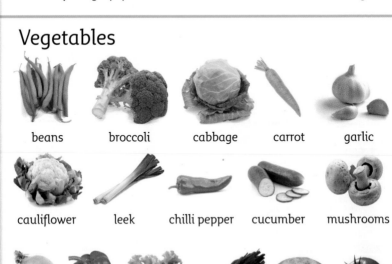

beans   broccoli   cabbage   carrot   garlic

cauliflower   leek   chilli pepper   cucumber   mushrooms

onion   pepper   lettuce   spring onions   potato   tomato

Other Foods

biscuit cheese crisps chips egg

ice cream jam pasta salt and pepper

cake salad sandwich soup

rice cereal yoghurt butter bread

Drinks

coffee orange juice milk tea

House and Home

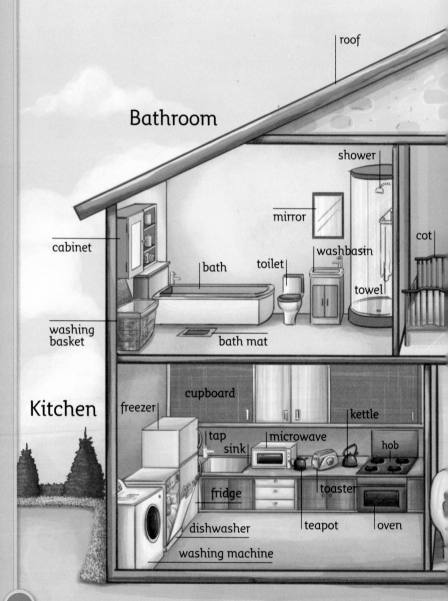

roof

Bathroom

shower

mirror

cabinet

bath

toilet

washbasin

cot

towel

washing basket

bath mat

Kitchen

freezer

cupboard

kettle

tap

microwave

sink

hob

fridge

toaster

dishwasher

teapot

oven

washing machine

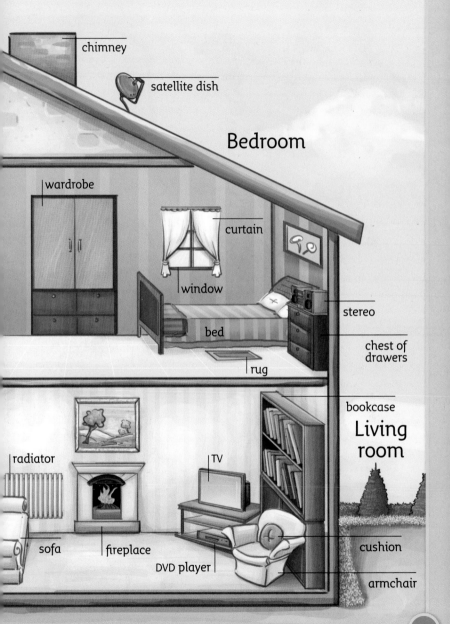

chimney

satellite dish

Bedroom

wardrobe

curtain

window

stereo

bed

chest of
drawers

rug

bookcase

Living
room

radiator

TV

sofa

fireplace

cushion

DVD player

armchair

Sports

rugby

football/soccer

basketball

hockey

cycling

skiing

swimming

gymnastics

jogging

tennis

hiking

horse riding

Jobs

actor/actress

builder

businessman/
businesswoman

carpenter

chef

dentist

doctor

electrician

farmer

firefighter

hairdresser

mechanic

nurse

pilot

plumber

police officer

shop assistant

teacher

vet

waiter/waitress

Family

Kate's grandfather

Kate's grandmother

Kate's father

Kate's mother

Kate's uncle

Kate's aunt

Kate's cousin

Kate   **Rob**

Rob's wife

Kate's husband

Kate's sister

Kate's brother-in-law

Kate's sister-in-law

Kate's brother

Kate's niece

Kate's son

Kate's daughter

Kate's nephew

lose /luːz/ *verb* (**loses, losing, lost**)
1 to not win a game: *Our team lost the game by one point.* □ *No one likes to lose.*
2 to not know where something is: *I've lost my keys.*
3 to not have something any more because someone has taken it away from you: *I lost my job when the company shut down.*
lose money used when a business earns less money than it spends: *The company has been losing money for the last three years.*
lose weight to become less heavy: *His doctor told him to lose weight.*

loser /'luːzə/ *noun*
the person who does not win a game: *In any game, there's always a winner and a loser.*
bad loser a person who does not like losing, and complains about it
good loser a person who accepts that they have lost a game without complaining: *I try to be a good loser.*

loss /lɒs/ *noun* (**losses**)
1 when you do not have something that you used to have, or when you have less of it than before: *The first symptoms are a slight fever and a loss of appetite.*
2 *uncountable* the death of a friend or relative: *He is mourning the loss of his wife and child.*
3 when a business earns less money than it spends: *The company made a loss again last year.*

lost¹ /lɒst/ → see **lose**

lost² /lɒst/ *adjective*
1 not knowing where you are; unable to find your way: *I realized I was lost.*
2 used for talking about something that you cannot find: *We complained to the airline about our lost luggage.*

lost property *noun*
things that people have lost or accidentally left in a public place: *Lost property should be handed to the driver.*

lot¹ /lɒt/ *pronoun* (*also* **lots**)
a large amount: *I learned a lot from him.*
a lot of something (*also* **lots of**) a large amount of something: *A lot of our land is used for growing crops.* □ *He drank lots of milk.*

lot² /lɒt/ *adverb*
a lot very much or very often: *I like you a lot.* □ *Matthew goes out quite a lot.*

lotion /'ləʊʃən/ *noun*
a liquid that you use to clean or to protect your skin: *Remember to put on some suntan lotion.*

lottery /'lɒtəri/ *noun* (**lotteries**)
a type of game where people buy tickets with numbers on them. If the numbers on your ticket are chosen, you win a prize: *She has won the national lottery twice.*

loud /laʊd/ *adjective* (**louder, loudest**)
with a high level of sound: *The music was so loud that I couldn't hear what she was saying.*
▶ **loudly** *adverb* *The cat rolled onto its back, purring loudly.*
out loud so that other people can hear: *Parts of the book made me laugh out loud.*

lounge /laʊndʒ/ *noun*
1 a room in a hotel or an airport where people can sit: *an airport lounge*
2 → see **living room**

louse /laʊs/ *noun* (**lice**)
a small insect that lives on the bodies of people or animals

lousy /'laʊzi/ *adjective* (**lousier, lousiest**)
very bad (*informal*): *The weather was lousy all weekend.* □ *I was a lousy secretary.*

lovable /'lʌvəbəl/ *adjective*
easy to love: *He is a sweet, lovable dog.*

love¹ /lʌv/ *verb* (**loves, loving, loved**)
1 to care very much about someone, or to have strong romantic feelings for them: *Oh, Amy, I love you.* □ *You will love your baby from the moment she is born.*
2 to like something very much: *I love food, I love cooking and I love eating.* □ *Sophie loves to play the piano.*

love² /lʌv/ *uncountable noun*
1 the very strong warm feeling that you have when you care very much about someone, or you have strong romantic feelings for them: *In the four years since we married, our love has grown stronger.* □ *a love story*
2 used at the end of a letter to a friend or relative: *The letter ended, 'love from Anna.'*
fall in love to start to love someone in a romantic way: *Maria fell in love with Danny as soon as she met him.*

lovely /'lʌvli/ *adjective* (**lovelier, loveliest**)
beautiful, very nice or very enjoyable: *You look lovely, Marcia.* □ *Sam has a lovely voice.* □ *'Thank you for a lovely evening!'*

lover /'lʌvə/ *noun*
1 a person who has a sexual relationship,

but is not married: *Every Thursday she met her lover Leon.*

2 a person who likes something very much: *The website is for music lovers.*

loving /'lʌvɪŋ/ *adjective*
feeling or showing love for other people: *My parents had a loving relationship.*
▶ **lovingly** *adverb* *Brian looked lovingly at Mary.*

low /ləʊ/ *adjective, adverb* (**lower, lowest**)
1 close to the ground: *It was late afternoon and the sun was low in the sky.* □ *An aeroplane flew low over the beach.*
2 small in amount: *House prices are still very low.*
3 very bad: *The hospital was criticized for its low standards of care.*
4 deep and quiet: *His voice was so low she couldn't hear him.*

lower ¹ /'ləʊə/ *adjective*
used for describing something that is under another thing: *Emily bit her lower lip nervously.*

lower ² /'ləʊə/ *verb* (**lowers, lowering, lowered**)
1 to move something down: *They lowered the coffin into the grave.*
2 to make something less: *The Central Bank lowered interest rates yesterday.*

lower case *uncountable noun*
small letters, not capital letters. Compare with **upper case**: *Type your user name and password in lower case.*

loyal /'lɔɪəl/ *adjective*
keeping your friends or your beliefs, even in difficult times: *They have always stayed loyal to the Republican party.*
▶ **loyally** *adverb* *The staff loyally supported their boss.*

loyalty /'lɔɪəlti/ *uncountable noun*
when you continue to be someone's friend, or to believe in something, even in difficult times: *I believe in family loyalty.*

Ltd
a written short form of 'Limited', used after the name of a company: *Holmes Healthfoods Ltd*

luck /lʌk/ *uncountable noun*
the good things that happen to you, that have not been caused by yourself or other people: *Before the game, we shook hands and wished each other luck.*

bad luck the bad things that happen to you, that have not been caused by yourself or other people: *We had a lot of bad luck during the first half of this season.*

good luck/best of luck used for telling someone that you hope they will be successful in something they are trying to do (*informal*)

luckily /'lʌkɪli/ *adverb*
used when you want to say that it is good that something happened: *Luckily, nobody was seriously injured in the accident.*

lucky /'lʌki/ *adjective* (**luckier, luckiest**)
1 having good luck: *I am luckier than most people here. I have a job.* □ *Rob is very lucky to be alive after that accident.*
2 bringing success or good luck: *I'm wearing my lucky shirt. How can I lose?*

luggage /'lʌgɪdʒ/ *uncountable noun*
the bags that you take with you when you travel: *Do you have any luggage?*

> **LANGUAGE HELP**
> **Luggage** is an uncountable noun. If you want to talk about one bag or suitcase, use **a piece of luggage** or **some luggage**.

luggage

luggage rack *noun*
a shelf for putting luggage on in a train or a bus

lukewarm /ˌluːkˈwɔːm/ *adjective*
slightly warm: *Freddy drank the lukewarm coffee.*

lullaby /'lʌləˌbaɪ/ *noun* (**lullabies**)
a quiet song that you sing to a baby to help it to go to sleep

lump /lʌmp/ *noun*
1 a solid piece of something: *a lump of coal*

2 a small, hard part on or in your body: *I've got a painful lump in my mouth.*

lumpy /'lʌmpi/ *adjective* (**lumpier, lumpiest**)
containing lumps or covered with lumps: *I lay on the lumpy bed and listened to the noise of traffic outside.*

lunch /lʌntʃ/ *noun* (**lunches**)
the meal that you have in the middle of the day: *Are you free for lunch?* □ *Dad doesn't enjoy business lunches.*

lunchtime /'lʌntʃtaɪm/ *uncountable noun*
the time of the day when people have their lunch: *Could we meet at lunchtime?*

lung /lʌŋ/ *noun*
one of the two large organs inside your chest that you use for breathing: *Her father died of lung cancer last year.*

lush /lʌʃ/ *adjective* (**lusher, lushest**)
having a lot of very healthy grass or plants: *The lawn was lush and green.*

luxurious /lʌgˈʒʊəriəs/ *adjective*
very comfortable and expensive: *My aunt and uncle stayed in a luxurious hotel in Paris.*

luxury /'lʌkʃəri/ *noun* (**luxuries**)
1 *uncountable* when you are able to buy all the beautiful and expensive things that you want: *He leads a life of luxury.*
2 something pleasant and expensive that people want but do not really need: *Having a holiday is a luxury they can no longer afford.*

lying /'laɪɪŋ/ → see **lie**

lyrics /'lɪrɪks/ *plural noun*
the words of a song: *The music is great, and the lyrics are so funny.*

Mm

macaroni /ˌmækəˈrəʊni/ *uncountable noun*
a type of pasta made in the shape of short,
hollow tubes

machine /məˈʃiːn/ *noun*
a piece of equipment that uses electricity
or an engine to do a particular job: *I put the
coin in the coffee machine.*

machinery /məˈʃiːnəri/ *uncountable noun*
large pieces electrical equipment that do
a particular job: *We need to invest in new
machinery for our factories.*

mad /mæd/ *adjective* (**madder, maddest**)
1 having a medical condition that makes
you behave in a strange way (*informal*): *She
was afraid of going mad.*
2 very stupid (*informal*): *You're going to swim
in that water? You must be mad!*
3 not controlled: *There was a mad rush to get
out of the building.*
▶ **madly** *adverb* *People on the streets were
waving madly.*

be mad about something/someone
to like something or someone very much
(*informal*): *I'm mad about sports.* ◻ *He's mad
about you.*

drive someone mad to make someone
very angry (*informal*): *Stop asking questions!
You're driving me mad!*

go mad to become very angry (*informal*):
My mum went mad when I told her about the vase.

madam /ˈmædəm/ *also* **Madam** *noun*
1 a polite way of talking to a woman: *Good
morning, madam.*
2 a word that you use at the beginning of
a formal letter to a woman: *Dear Madam ....*

made¹ /meɪd/ → see **make**

made² /meɪd/ *adjective*
made of something used for describing
the substance that was used to make
something: *The top of the table is made of glass.*

madly /ˈmædli/ *adverb*
1 very much: *She is madly in love with him.*
2 in a wild way: *The crowd was cheering
madly.*

magazine /ˌmægəˈziːn/ *noun*
a thin book with stories and pictures that
you can buy every week or every month:
a fashion magazine

magic /ˈmædʒɪk/ *uncountable noun*
1 a special power that seems to make
impossible things happen: *Most children
believe in magic.*
2 tricks that a person performs in order
to entertain people: *His stage act combines
magic, music and humour.*

magical /ˈmædʒɪkəl/ *adjective*
seeming to use magic: *I loved the story of
a little boy who has magical powers.*

magician /məˈdʒɪʃən/ *noun*
a person who entertains people by doing
magic tricks

magnet /ˈmægnɪt/ *noun*
a piece of
special
metal that
attracts
iron
towards it: *The
children used a magnet
to find objects made of iron.*

magnet

magnetic /mægˈnetɪk/ *adjective*
1 acting like a magnet: *Because steel is made
from iron, it is magnetic.*
2 describing objects that use a magnetic
substance to hold information that can
be read by computers: *The bank sent him an
ID card with a magnetic strip.*

magnificent /mægˈnɪfɪsənt/ *adjective*
extremely good or beautiful: *They bought a
magnificent country house.*

magnify /ˈmægnɪfaɪ/ *verb* (**magnifies,
magnifying, magnified**)
to make something look larger than it
really is: *This telescope magnifies objects n times.*

'magnifying glass *noun* (**magnifying
glasses**)
a piece of glass that makes objects seem

to be bigger than they really are.

maid /meɪd/ *noun*
a woman whose job is to clean rooms in a hotel or private house: *A maid comes every morning to clean the hotel room.*

mail¹ /meɪl/ *uncountable noun*
the letters and packages or email that you receive: *There was no mail this morning.*
□ *With web-based email, you can check your mail from anywhere.*

mail² /meɪl/ *verb* (**mails, mailing, mailed**) (*American*)
→ see **post**: *I'll mail it to you on Friday.*

mailbox /ˈmeɪlbɒks/ *noun* (**mailboxes**)
1 (*American*) → see **letter box**
2 (*American*) → see **postbox**
3 the file on a computer where your email is stored: *There were 30 new messages in his mailbox.*

mail order *uncountable noun*
a system of buying goods, in which you order things from a website or a special book (called a catalogue), and the company sends them to you by post: *The toys are available by mail order.*

main /meɪn/ *adjective*
most important: *The main reason I came today was to say sorry.*

main clause *noun*
a part of a sentence that can stand alone as a complete sentence

mainland /ˈmeɪnlænd/ *noun*
the largest piece of land in a country, not including any smaller islands: *The island's teenagers go to school on the mainland.*

mainly /ˈmeɪnli/ *adverb*
used for saying that a statement is mostly true: *The African people living here are mainly from Senegal.*

maintain /meɪnˈteɪn/ *verb* (**maintains, maintaining, maintained**)
1 to make something continue at the same level: *The army is trying to maintain order in the country.*
2 to keep a road, building, vehicle or machine in good condition: *The house costs a lot to maintain.*

maintenance /ˈmeɪntɪnəns/ *uncountable noun*
the process of keeping something in good condition: *Maintenance work on the building starts at the beginning of next week.*

majestic /məˈdʒestɪk/ *adjective*
very beautiful and grand: *We will miss the majestic mountains and the emerald green sea.*

majesty /ˈmædʒɪsti/ *uncountable noun*
the quality of being beautiful and grand: *The poem describes the majesty of the mountains.*
Your/His/Her Majesty used when you are talking to or about a king or a queen: *His Majesty would like to see you now.*

major¹ /ˈmeɪdʒə/ *adjective*
1 more important than other things: *Homelessness is a major problem in some cities.*
2 used for talking about a scale (= a series of musical notes) with half steps in sound between the third and fourth and the seventh and eighth notes. Compare with **minor**: *A C major scale uses only the white keys on a piano.*

major² /ˈmeɪdʒə/ *noun*
an officer of high rank in the army: *Marine Major General Wayne Rollings*

majority /məˈdʒɒriti/ *noun* (**majorities**)
more than half of the people or things in a group: *The majority of my patients are women.*

make¹ /meɪk/ *verb* (**makes, making, made**)
1 to produce, build or create something: *She makes all her own clothes.* □ *We make solid wood furniture.*
2 used with nouns to show that someone does or says something: *I'd just like to make a comment.* □ *I made a few phone calls.*
3 to cause someone to do or feel something: *The smoke made him cough.* □ *My boss's behaviour makes me so angry!*
4 to force someone to do something: *Mum made me apologize to him.*
5 to earn money: *He's good-looking, smart and makes lots of money.*
6 used for saying what two numbers add up to: *Four twos make eight.*

make something into something to change something so that it becomes a different thing: *They made their flat into a beautiful home.*

make something/someone out to be able to see, hear or understand something: *I could just make out a tall figure of a man.* □ *I couldn't make out what he was saying.*

m

make something up to invent something such as a story or excuse: *It was all lies. I made it all up.*

make up to become friends again after an argument: *You two are always fighting and then making up again.*

make² /meɪk/ *noun*
the name of the company that made something: *What make of car do you drive?*

maker /'meɪkə/ *noun*
the person or company that makes something: *Japan's two largest car makers reported increased sales last month.*

make-up /'meɪkʌp/ *uncountable noun*
the creams and powders that people put on their face to make themselves look more attractive. Actors also wear makeup: *She doesn't usually wear much makeup.*

malaria /mə'leəriə/ *uncountable noun*
a serious disease that small flying insects (= mosquitoes) carry

male¹ /meɪl/ *noun*
a person or an animal that belongs to the sex that does not have babies: *Two 17-year-old males were arrested at their school on Tuesday.*

male² /meɪl/ *adjective*
1 belonging to the sex that does not have babies: *She reported the unacceptable behaviour of her male colleagues.* □ *Two male cats were fighting in the street.*
2 relating to men rather than women: *The rate of male unemployment has gone up.*

mall /mɔːl, mæl/ *noun* (American)
→ see **shopping centre**

mammal /'mæməl/ *noun*
an animal that feeds its babies with milk

man /mæn/ *noun* (men)
1 an adult male human: *A handsome man walked into the room.* □ *Both men and women will enjoy this film.*
2 used for talking about all humans, including both males and females. Some people dislike this use, and prefer to say **human beings** or **people**: *Man first arrived in the Americas thousands of years ago.*

manage /'mænɪdʒ/ *verb* (manages, managing, managed)
1 to control a business: *Two years after starting the job, he was managing the shop.*
2 to succeed in doing something, especially something difficult: *Three girls managed to escape the fire.*

management /'mænɪdʒmənt/ *noun*
1 *uncountable* the control of a business or other organization: *The zoo needed better management, not more money.*
2 the people who control a business or other organization: *The management is trying hard to keep employees happy.*

manager /'mænɪdʒə/ *noun*
a person who controls all or part of a business or organization: *Each department manager is responsible for staff training.*

mane /meɪn/ *noun*
the long, thick hair that grows from the neck of some animals: *You can wash the horse's mane at the same time as its body.*

mango /'mæŋɡəʊ/ *noun* (mangoes or mangos)
a large, sweet, yellow or red fruit that grows on trees in hot countries
→ Look at picture on P2

manicure /'mænɪˌkjʊə/ *verb* (manicures, manicuring, manicured)
to care for your hands or nails by rubbing cream into your skin and cleaning and cutting your nails: *She carefully manicured her long nails.* ● **manicure** *noun I have an appointment for a manicure this afternoon.*

manipulate /mə'nɪpjʊˌleɪt/ *verb* (manipulates, manipulating, manipulated)
to control people or events for your own benefit: *The government is trying to manipulate public opinion.*

mankind /ˌmæn'kaɪnd/ *uncountable noun*
used for talking about all humans when you are considering them as a group. Some people dislike this use: *We hope for a better future for all mankind.*

man-ˈmade also **manmade** *adjective*
made by people: *Some of the world's problems are man-made.* □ *When the dam was built, three man-made lakes were created.*

manner /'mænə/ *noun*
1 the way that you do something: *She smiled in a friendly manner.*
2 *plural* how polite you are when you are with other people: *He dressed well and had perfect manners.* □ *Is it bad manners to talk on a mobile phone on the train?*

manoeuvre /mə'nuːvə/ *verb* (manoeuvres, manoeuvring, manoeuvred) to skilfully move something into or out of a difficult position: *He manoeuvred the car through the narrow gate.* ● **manoeuvre** *noun* *The aeroplanes performed some difficult manoeuvres.*

mansion /ˈmænʃən/ *noun*
a very large, expensive house: *He bought an eighteenth-century mansion in Berkshire.*

mantelpiece /ˈmæntəlˌpiːs/ *noun*
a shelf above the place where a fire is in a room

manual¹ /ˈmænjʊəl/ *adjective*
1 used for describing work in which you use your hands or your physical strength: *He began his career as a manual worker.*
2 operated by hand, rather than by electricity or a motor: *We used a manual pump to get the water out of the hole.*

manual² /ˈmænjʊəl/ *noun*
a book that tells you how to do something: *He advised me to read the instruction manual first.*

manufacture /ˌmænjʊˈfæktʃə/ *verb*
(**manufactures, manufacturing, manufactured**)
to make something in a factory: *The company manufactures plastics.*
● **manufacture** *uncountable noun* *Coal is used in the manufacture of steel.*

manufacturer /ˌmænjʊˈfæktʃərə/ *noun*
a company that makes large amounts of things: *He works for the world's largest doll manufacturer.*

manufacturing /ˌmænjʊˈfæktʃərɪŋ/ *uncountable noun*
the business of making things in factories: *During the 1980s, 300,000 workers in the manufacturing industry lost their jobs.*

many /ˈmeni/ *adjective, adverb*
1 used for talking about a large number of people or things: *Many people would disagree with that opinion.* □ *Not many shops are open on Sunday.* ● **many** *pronoun* *He made a list of his friends. There weren't many.*
2 used when you are asking or replying to questions about numbers of things or people: *'How many of their songs were hits?' — 'Not very many.'*

many of used for talking about a large number of people or things: *Why do many of us feel that we need to get married?*

map /mæp/ *noun*
a drawing of a particular area such as a city or a country, that shows things like mountains, rivers and roads: *The detailed map helps tourists find their way around the city.*

map

marathon /ˈmærəθən/ *noun*
a race in which people run a distance of 26 miles (= about 42 km): *He is running in his first marathon next weekend.*

marble /ˈmɑːbəl/ *uncountable noun*
a type of very hard rock that people use to make parts of buildings or statues (= models of people)
marbles a children's game that you play with small balls made of coloured glass (called marbles): *Two boys were playing marbles.*

march¹ /mɑːtʃ/ *verb* (**marches, marching, marched**)
1 to walk somewhere with regular steps, as a group: *Some soldiers were marching down the street.* ● **march** *noun* (**marches**) *After a short march, the soldiers entered the village.*
2 to walk through the streets in a large group of people in order to show that you disagree with something: *Thousands of people marched through the city to protest against the war.* ● **march** *noun* (**marches**) *Organizers expect 300,000 protesters to join the march.*

m

3 to walk somewhere quickly, often because you are angry.: *He marched into the kitchen without knocking.*

March² /mɑːtʃ/ *noun*
the third month of the year: *I flew to Milwaukee in March.* □ *She was born on 6th March, 1920.*

margarine /ˌmɑːdʒəˈriːn/ *noun*
a yellow substance that is made from vegetable oil, and is similar to butter

margin /ˈmɑːdʒɪn/ *noun*
1 the difference between two amounts: *The team won with a 5-point margin.*
2 the empty space down the side of a page: *She wrote comments in the margin.*

marine /məˈriːn/ *adjective*
relating to the sea: *The film shows the colourful marine life in the Indian Ocean.*

marital /ˈmærɪtəl/ *adjective*
relating to marriage: *When I was thirteen, my parents started having marital problems.*

mark¹ /mɑːk/ *noun*
1 a small area of something such as dirt that has accidentally got onto a surface or piece of clothing: *There was a red paint mark on the wall.*
2 a written or printed symbol: *a question mark*

mark² /mɑːk/ *verb* (**marks, marking, marked**)
1 to write a particular word on something: *She marked the bill 'paid'.*
2 to write a number or letter on a student's work to show how good it is: *The teacher was marking essays after class.*
3 to show where a particular thing is: *A big hole in the road marks the place where the bomb landed.*

market¹ /ˈmɑːkɪt/ *noun*
1 a place where people buy and sell products: *They usually buy their fruit and vegetables at the market.*
2 the people who want to buy a particular product: *The market for organic wines is growing.*

market² /ˈmɑːkɪt/ *verb* (**markets, marketing, marketed**)
to advertise and sell a product: *The products were marketed under a different brand name in Europe.*
▸ **marketing** *uncountable noun* *She works in the marketing department of a large company.*

marmalade /ˈmɑːməleɪd/ *uncountable noun*
a food like jam that is usually made from oranges

marriage /ˈmærɪdʒ/ *noun*
1 the relationship between a husband and a wife: *In a good marriage, both husband and wife are happy.*
2 the time when two people get married: *a marriage ceremony*

married /ˈmærɪd/ *adjective*
having a husband or wife: *We have been married for 14 years.* □ *She is married to an Englishman.*

marry /ˈmæri/ *verb* (**marries, marrying, married**)
to legally become husband and wife in a special ceremony: *I thought he would change after we got married.* □ *They married a month after they met.* □ *He wants to marry her.*

marsh /mɑːʃ/ *noun* (**marshes**)
a soft, wet area of land

marshmallow /ˈmɑːʃˌmæləʊ/ *noun*
a soft pink or white sweet

marvellous /ˈmɑːvələs/ *adjective*
very good: *It's a marvellous piece of music.*

masculine /ˈmæskjʊlɪn/ *adjective*
1 typical of men: *She has a deep, rather masculine voice.*
2 used for describing a noun, pronoun or adjective that has a different form from other forms (such as 'feminine' forms) in some languages. Compare with **feminine**.

mash /mæʃ/ *verb* (**mashes, mashing, mashed**)
to press food to make it soft: *Mash the bananas with a fork.*

mask /mɑːsk/ *noun*
something that you wear over your face to protect it or to hide it: *A man wearing a mask entered the restaurant at about 1.40 p.m. and took out a gun.* □ *Wear a mask to protect yourself from the smoke.*

masked /mɑːskt/ *adjective*
wearing a mask: *Two masked men came through the doors carrying guns.*

mass /mæs/ *noun* (**masses**)
1 a large amount of something: *She had a mass of black hair.*
2 a Christian church ceremony, especially in a Roman Catholic church: *She went to Mass each day.*
3 *uncountable* the amount of physical

matter that something contains: *Pluto and Triton have nearly the same size, mass and density.*

masses of something a large amount of something (*informal*): *I have masses of work to do.*

massacre /'mæsəkə/ *noun*
an occasion when a large number of people are killed at the same time in a violent and cruel way: *Her mother died in the massacre.* ● **massacre** *verb* (**massacres, massacring, massacred**) *Three hundred people were massacred by the soldiers.*

massage /'mæsɑːʒ/ *noun*
the activity of rubbing someone's body to make them relax or to reduce their pain: *Alex asked me if I wanted a massage.*
● **massage** *verb* (**massages, massaging, massaged**) *She was massaging her right foot.*

massive /'mæsɪv/ *adjective*
very large: *They borrowed massive amounts of money.*

mast /mɑːst/ *noun*
one of the tall poles that support the sails of a boat

master¹ /'mɑːstə/ *noun*
1 the person who controls another person or an animal: *The dog was listening to its master's voice.*
2 someone who is extremely skilled at a particular activity: *She was a master of the English language.*

master² /'mɑːstə/ *verb* (**masters, mastering, mastered**)
to learn how to do something well: *David soon mastered the skills of baseball.*

masterpiece /'mɑːstəpiːs/ *noun*
an extremely good painting, novel, film or other work of art: *His book is a masterpiece.*

'master's de,gree *noun*
a university qualification that is of a higher level than an ordinary degree

mat /mæt/ *noun*
1 a small piece of cloth, wood or plastic that you put on a table to protect it: *a set of red and white checked place mats*
2 a small piece of thick material that you put on the floor: *There was a letter on the door mat.*

match¹ /mætʃ/ *noun* (**matches**)
1 a small wooden or paper stick that produces a flame when you move it along a rough surface: *Kate lit a match and*

held it up to the candle.
2 a sports game between two people or teams: *He was watching a tennis match.*
□ *Are you playing in the football match tomorrow?*

match

match² /mætʃ/ *verb* (**matches, matching, matched**)
to have the same colour or design as another thing, or to look good with it: *Do these shoes match my dress?*
▶ **matching** *adjective She wore a hat and a matching scarf.*

mate¹ /meɪt/ *noun*
1 the sexual partner of an animal: *The male bird shows its brightly coloured feathers to attract a mate.*
2 a friend (*informal*): *A mate of mine used to play football for Liverpool.*

mate² /meɪt/ *verb* (**mates, mating, mated**)
when male and female animals mate, they have sex in order to produce babies: *After mating, the female does not eat.*

material /mə'tɪəriəl/ *noun*
1 cloth: *The thick material of her skirt was too warm for summer.*
2 *plural* the things that you need for a particular activity: *building materials*

maternal /mə'tɜːnəl/ *adjective*
typical of a mother towards her child: *No love is stronger than maternal love.*

mathematical /ˌmæθə'mætɪkəl/ *adjective*
involving numbers and calculating: *He made some quick mathematical calculations.*

mathematics /ˌmæθə'mætɪks/ *uncountable noun*
the study of numbers, quantities or shapes: *Dr Lewis is a lecturer in mathematics at Leeds university.*

maths /mæθs/ *uncountable noun*
→ see **mathematics**

matinee /'mætɪneɪ/ *noun*
a performance of a play or a showing of a film in the afternoon

m

matter¹ /'mætə/ *noun*

1 something that you must talk about or do: *She wanted to discuss a private matter with me.*

2 *plural* a situation that someone is involved in: *If it would make matters easier, I will come to New York.*

3 a type of substance: *There was a strong smell of rotting vegetable matter.*

what's the matter? used when you think that someone has a problem and you want to know what it is: *Carol, what's the matter? You don't seem happy.*

matter² /'mætə/ *verb* (**matters, mattering, mattered**)

to be important to someone: *A lot of the food goes on the floor but that doesn't matter.*

mattress /'mætrəs/ *noun* (**mattresses**)

the thick, soft part of a bed that you lie on

mature¹ /mə'tjʊə/ *adjective* (**maturer, maturest**)

1 fully grown

2 behaving in a responsible and sensible way: *Fiona was mature for her age.*

▶ **maturity** *uncountable noun Her speech showed great maturity.*

mature² /mə'tjʊə/ *verb* (**matures, maturing, matured**)

to become an adult: *The children will face many challenges as they mature into adulthood.*

maximum /'mæksɪməm/ *adjective*

used for describing the largest amount possible: *Today's maximum temperature in the city will be 80 degrees.* ● **maximum** *noun Brett faces a maximum of two years in prison.*

may¹ /meɪ/ *modal verb*

1 used for showing that there is a possibility that something will happen or is true: *We may have some rain today.* □ *I may be back next year.*

2 used for saying that someone is allowed to do something: *You may send a cheque or pay by credit card.* □ *May we come in?*

May² /meɪ/ *noun*

the fifth month of the year: *We went on holiday in May.*

maybe /'meɪbi/ *adverb*

1 used when you are uncertain about something: *Maybe she is in love.* □ *I do think about having children, maybe when I'm 40.*

2 used when you are making suggestions or giving advice: *Maybe we can go to the*

cinema or something. □ *Maybe you should see a doctor.*

mayonnaise /ˌmeɪə'neɪz/ *uncountable noun*

a cold, thick sauce made from eggs and oil

mayor /meə/ *noun*

the person who is responsible for the government of a city or a town: *The mayor of New York made a speech.*

maze /meɪz/ *noun*

a place that is difficult to find your way through: *Only the local people know their way through the town's maze of streets.*

me /mi, STRONG miː/ *pronoun*

used when you are talking about yourself: *He asked me to go to California with him.*

meadow /'medəʊ/ *noun*

a field that has grass and flowers growing in it

meal /miːl/ *noun*

1 an occasion when people sit down and eat: *She sat next to him during the meal.*

2 the food you eat during a meal: *Logan finished his meal in silence.*

mean¹ /miːn/ *verb* (**means, meaning, meant**)

1 to have a particular meaning: *'Unable' means 'not able'.* □ *What does 'software' mean?*

2 used for saying that a second thing will happen because of a first thing: *The new factory means more jobs for people.*

3 to be serious about what you are saying: *He said he loves her, and I think he meant it.*

mean a lot to someone to be very important to someone: *Be careful with the photos. They mean a lot to me.*

mean to do something to do something deliberately: *I'm so sorry. I didn't mean to hurt you.*

mean² /miːn/ *adjective* (**meaner, meanest**)

unkind or cruel: *Don't be mean to your brother!*

mean³ /miːn/ *noun*

the amount that you get if you add a set of numbers together and divide them by the number of things that you originally added together. For example, the mean of 1, 3, 5 and 7 is 4 (1+3+5+7=16; 16÷4=4).

meaning /'miːnɪŋ/ *noun*

the idea that a word or an expression represents: *Do you know the meaning of the words you're singing?*

meaningless /'mi:nɪŋləs/ *adjective*
having no meaning or purpose: *After her death, he felt that his life was meaningless.*

means /mi:nz/ *noun*
a means of doing something a way to do something: *He searched for a door or some other means of escape.*

meant¹ /ment/ → see **mean**

meant² /ment/ *verb*
meant to intended to be or do a particular thing: *I can't say any more, it's meant to be a big secret.* □ *He was meant to arrive an hour ago.*

meantime /'mi:ntaɪm/ *noun*
in the meantime used for talking about the period of time between two events: *Elizabeth wants to go to college but in the meantime she has to work.*

meanwhile /'mi:nwaɪl/ *adverb*
used for talking about the period of time between two events or what happens while another thing is happening: *I'll be ready to meet them tomorrow. Meanwhile, I'm going to talk to Karen.* □ *We stayed up late into the night. Meanwhile, the snow was still falling outside.*

measles /'mi:zəlz/ *uncountable noun*
an illness that gives you a high fever and red spots on your skin

measure¹ /'meʒə/ *verb* (**measures, measuring, measured**)
1 to find out the size of something: *Measure the length of the table.*
2 used for describing the size of something as a particular length or amount: *The football pitch measures 400 feet.*

measure² /'meʒə/ *noun*
a way of trying to achieve something (*formal*): *The police are taking measures to deal with the problem.*

measurement /'meʒəmənt/ *noun*
the number that you get when you measure something: *You'll need to take the measurements of the room when you go to buy the furniture.*

meat /mi:t/ *noun*
the part of an animal that people cook and eat: *I don't eat meat or fish.*

mechanic /mɪˈkænɪk/ *noun*
a person whose job is to repair machines and engines, especially car engines: *Your mechanic should check the brakes on your car at least once a year.*
→ Look at picture on P7

mechanical /mɪˈkænɪkəl/ *adjective*
used for describing an object that has parts that move when it is working: *a mechanical clock*

mechanism /'mekənɪzəm/ *noun*
a part of a machine: *The locking mechanism on the car door was broken.*

medal /'medəl/ *noun*
a small metal disc that you receive as a prize for doing something very good: *He won the Olympic gold medal.*

medal

media¹ /'mi:diə/ *noun*
television, radio, newspapers and magazines: *A lot of people in the media have asked me that question.* □ *They told their story to the news media.*

media² /'mi:diə/
a plural of **medium²**

median /'mi:diən/ *noun*
the number that is in the middle of a set of numbers when they are arranged in order. For example, in the numbers 1, 2, 3, 4, 5, the median is 3.

medical /'medɪkəl/ *adjective*
relating to illness and injuries and how to treat or prevent them: *Several police officers received medical treatment for their injuries.*

medication /ˌmedɪˈkeɪʃən/ *uncountable noun*
medicine that is used for treating and curing illness: *Are you taking any medication?*

medicine /'medsən/ *noun*
1 *uncountable* the treatment of illness and injuries by doctors and nurses: *He decided on a career in medicine.*
2 a substance that you use to treat or cure an illness: *The medicine saved his life.*

medieval /ˌmediˈi:vəl/ *adjective*
relating to the period of European history between A.D. 476 and about A.D. 1500: *On our trip we visited a medieval castle.*

m

medium¹ /'mi:diəm/ *adjective*
neither large nor small: *Mix the cream and eggs in a medium bowl.* □ *For this recipe, you will need one medium-sized onion.*

medium² /'mi:diəm/ *noun* (**mediums** or **media**)
a substance or material such as paint, wood or stone that an artist uses: *Hyatt uses the medium of oil paint.*

meet /mi:t/ *verb* (**meets, meeting, met**)
1 to see someone who you know by chance and speak to them: *I met Shona in town today.*
2 to see someone who you do not know and speak to them for the first time: *I have just met an amazing man.*
3 to go somewhere with someone because you have planned to be there together: *We could meet for a game of tennis after work.*
4 to go to a place and wait for someone to arrive: *Mum met me at the station.*
5 to join together: *This is the point where the two rivers meet.*

meeting /'mi:tɪŋ/ *noun*
an event in which a group of people come together to discuss things or make decisions: *Can we have a meeting to discuss that?*

megabyte /'megəˌbaɪt/ *noun*
a unit for measuring information in computing. There are one million bytes in a megabyte: *The hard drive has 256 megabytes of memory.*

melody /'melədi/ *noun* (**melodies**)
a group of musical notes that sound pleasant together: *He could sing a melody before he could talk.*

melon /'melən/ *noun*
a large fruit with soft, sweet flesh and a hard green or yellow skin: *For dessert, there were grapes and juicy slices of melon.*
→ Look at picture on P2

melt /melt/ *verb* (**melts, melting, melted**)
to change from a solid substance to a liquid because of heat: *The snow melted.* □ *Melt the chocolate in a bowl.*

'melting point *noun*
the temperature at which a substance melts when you heat it.

member /'membə/ *noun*
someone or something that belongs to a group or an organization: *Joe is a member of the Democratic party.* □ *A member of the team saw the accident.*

Member of 'Parliament *noun*
a person who has been chosen by the people in a particular area to represent them in a country's parliament. The short form 'MP' is also used.

membership /'membəʃɪp/ *noun*
1 *uncountable* being a member of an organization: *Employees have free membership at the gym.*
2 the people who belong to an organization: *By 2008, the organization had a membership of 409,000.*

memo /'meməʊ/ *noun*
a short note that you send to a person who works with you: *He sent a memo to everyone in his department.*

memorable /'memərəbəl/ *adjective*
easy to remember because of being special or very enjoyable: *Our wedding was a very memorable day.*

memorize /'meməˌraɪz/ *verb* (**memorizes, memorizing, memorized**)
to learn something so that you can remember it exactly: *He tried to memorize the way to Rose's street.*

memory /'meməri/ *noun* (**memories**)
1 your ability to remember things: *All the details of the meeting are clear in my memory.* □ *He has a good memory for faces.*
2 something that you remember from the past: *She has happy memories of her childhood.*
3 the part of a computer where it stores information: *The data is stored in the computer's memory.*

'memory card *noun*
a small part that stores information inside a piece of electronic equipment such as a camera

'memory stick *noun*
a small object for storing computer information that you can carry with you and use in different computers

men /men/
plural of **man**

mend /mend/ *verb* (**mends, mending, mended**)
to repair something: *He earns money by mending bicycles.*

menswear /'menzweə/ *uncountable noun*
clothing for men: *Charlton bought the menswear shop in 2005.*

mental /'mentəl/ *adjective*
relating to the mind: *mental illness*
▶ **mentally** *adverb* *The exam made him mentally tired.*

mention /'menʃən/ *verb* (**mentions, mentioning, mentioned**)
to say something about someone or something, without giving much information: *She mentioned her mother but not her father.* □ *I mentioned that I didn't really like pop music.*

menu /'menjuː/ *noun*
1 a list of the food and drink that you can have in a restaurant: *A waiter offered him the menu.*
2 a list of choices on a computer screen, showing things that you can do using a particular program: *Press F7 to show the print menu.*

merchandise /'mɜːtʃənˌdaɪz, -ˌdaɪs/ *uncountable noun*
products that you can buy (*formal*): *The company's annual football merchandise sales are about £1.5 billion.*

mercury /'mɜːkjʊri/ *uncountable noun*
a silver-coloured liquid metal that is used in thermometers

mercy /'mɜːsi/ *uncountable noun*
when someone chooses not to harm or punish someone: *His life was now at the mercy of a judge.*

mere /mɪə/ *adjective* (**merest**)
used for saying that something is small or not important: *A mere five per cent of school headteachers are women.*

merely /'mɪəli/ *adverb*
only: *She said this was merely her own opinion.*
□ *Dieter merely looked at him, saying nothing.*

merge /mɜːdʒ/ *verb* (**merges, merging, merged**)
to join together to make one new thing: *His company has merged with the advertising firm Saatchi & Saatchi.*

merit /'merɪt/ *noun*
1 *uncountable* good qualities: *The drawings have great artistic merit.*
2 *plural* the good points of something: *We will consider the merits of all candidates before making our decision.*

mermaid /'mɜːmeɪd/ *noun*
a woman in stories who has a fish's tail and lives in the sea

merry /'meri/ *adjective* (**merrier, merriest**)
happy and cheerful: *She sang a merry little tune.* □ *Merry Christmas, everyone!*

mess [1] /mes/ *noun*
1 when a place is not tidy: *After the party, the house was a mess.*
2 a situation that is full of problems: *I've made such a mess of my life.* □ *Those are the reasons why the economy is in such a mess.*

mess [2] /mes/ *verb* (**messes, messing, messed**)
mess about/around to spend time doing things for fun, or for no particular reason: *We were just messing around playing with paint.*
mess something up
1 to make something go wrong (*informal*): *This has messed up our plans.*
2 to make a place or a thing dirty or not tidy (*informal*): *He didn't want to mess up his tidy hair.*

message /'mesɪdʒ/ *noun*
a piece of information that you send to someone: *I'm getting emails and messages from friends all over the world.*

'message board *noun*
a system that allows users to send and receive messages on the Internet

messy /'mesi/ *adjective* (**messier, messiest**)
1 not tidy: *His writing is rather messy.*
2 making things dirty or not tidy: *She's a terribly messy cook.*

messy

She's a terribly messy cook.

met /met/ → see **meet**

metal /'metəl/ *noun*
a hard substance such as iron, steel or gold: *All of the houses had metal roofs.*

m

metaphor /'metə,fɔːr/ *noun*
a way of describing someone or something by showing their similarity with something else. For example, the metaphor 'a shining light' describes a person who is very skilful or intelligent: *She uses a lot of religious metaphors in her writing.*

meteor /'miːtɪə/ *noun*
a piece of rock from space that burns very brightly when it falls to Earth

meter /'miːtə/ *noun*
1 an instrument that measures and records something: *A man came to read the electricity meter.*
2 (American) → see **metre**

method /'meθəd/ *noun*
a way of doing something: *Teachers are allowed to try out different teaching methods.*

metre /'miːtə/ (American: **meter**) *noun*
a unit for measuring length. There are 100 centimetres in a metre: *She's running the 1,500 metre race.*

metric /'metrɪk/ *adjective*
expressed in metres, grams or litres: *A gram is a unit of weight in the metric system.*

metric ton *noun*
1,000 kilograms: *The Wall Street Journal uses 220,000 metric tons of paper each year.*

mg
short for **milligram** or **milligrams**

miaow /mɪ'aʊ, mjaʊ/ *noun*
the sound that a cat makes: *We could hear the miaow of a cat.* ● **miaow** *verb* (**miaows, miaowing, miaowed**) *I could hear a cat miaowing outside.*

mice /maɪs/
the plural of **mouse**

microbe /'maɪkrəʊb/ *noun*
a very small living thing that you cannot see without special equipment: *We have to kill the microbes that cause food poisoning.*

microchip
/'maɪkrəʊ,tʃɪp/
noun
a very small part
inside a computer
that makes it work

microphone
/'maɪkrə,fəʊn/ *noun*
a piece of electronic
equipment that you use

microphone

to make sounds louder or to record them onto a machine

microscope /'maɪkrə,skəʊp/ *noun*
a scientific instrument that makes very small objects look bigger

microwave /'maɪkrəʊ,weɪv/ *noun* (*also* **microwave oven**)
an oven that cooks food very quickly using electric waves
→ Look at picture on P4

midday /,mɪd'deɪ/ *uncountable noun*
twelve o'clock in the middle of the day: *At midday everyone had lunch.*

middle¹ /'mɪdəl/ *noun*
1 the part of something that is furthest from the edges: *Howard stood in the middle of the room.*
2 the part between the beginning and the end of a period of time: *I woke up in the middle of the night and heard a noise outside.*
in the middle of doing something busy doing something: *I'm in the middle of cooking dinner.*

middle² /'mɪdəl/ *adjective*
having an equal number of objects on each side: *The middle button of his uniform jacket was missing.*

middle age *uncountable noun*
the time in your life when you are between the ages of about 40 and 65: *Men often gain weight in middle age.*

middle-aged *adjective*
between the ages of about 40 and 65: *Most of the men were middle-aged married businessmen.*

Middle Ages *plural noun*
the period of time in European history between the end of the Roman Empire in 476 AD and about 1500 AD

middle class *noun* (**middle classes**) (*also* **middle classes**)
the people in a society who are not very rich and not very poor, for example business people, doctors and teachers: *Most writers come from the middle class.*
● **middle class** *adjective* *They live in a very middle class area.*

midnight /'mɪdnaɪt/ *uncountable noun*
twelve o'clock in the middle of the night: *It was well after midnight.*

midway /,mɪd'weɪ/ *adverb*
the same distance from each of two

places: *The studio is midway between his office and his home.*

might [1] /maɪt/ *modal verb*
used when something is possible: *I might go to study in England.* □ *They still hope that he might be alive.*

might [2] /maɪt/ *uncountable noun*
power or strength: *I pulled with all my might.*

mightn't /'maɪtənt/
short for 'might not'

might've /'maɪtəv/
short for 'might have'

mighty /'maɪti/ *adjective* (**mightier, mightiest**)
very large or powerful: *There was a mighty roar from the crowd as the band came on stage.*

migraine /'mi:greɪn/ *noun*
a severe pain in your head that makes you feel very ill: *Her mother suffered from migraines.*

migrant /'maɪgrənt/ *noun*
a person who moves from one place to another, especially in order to find work: *Most of his workers were migrants from the South.*

migrate /maɪ'greɪt/ *verb* (**migrates, migrating, migrated**)
1 to move from one place to another, usually in order to find work: *People migrate to cities like Jakarta searching for work.*
▶ **migration** /maɪ'greɪʃ°n/ *uncountable noun*
There was a large migration of people to the city.
2 to move from one part of the world to another at the same time every year: *Most birds have to fly long distances to migrate.*
▶ **migration** *uncountable noun Scientists are tracking the migration of bears.*

mild /maɪld/ *adjective* (**milder, mildest**)
1 not very strong: *This cheese has a soft, mild flavour.*
2 not too hot and not too cold: *We like the area because it has very mild winters.*

mile /maɪl/ *noun*
a unit for measuring distance. A mile is equal to 1.6 kilometres. There are 5,280 feet in a mile: *They drove 600 miles across the desert.*

mileage /'maɪlɪdʒ/ *noun*
the distance that a vehicle has travelled, measured in miles: *The car has a low mileage.*

military /'mɪlɪtri/ *adjective*
relating to the armed forces of a country: *Military action may become necessary.* □ *The president attended a meeting of military leaders.*

milk [1] /mɪlk/ *uncountable noun*
1 the white liquid that cows and some other animals produce, which people drink: *He went out to buy a pint of milk.*
→ Look at picture on P3
2 the white liquid that a mother makes in her body to feed her baby: *Milk from the mother's breast is a perfect food for the human baby.*

milk [2] /mɪlk/ *verb* (**milks, milking, milked**)
to take milk from a cow or another animal: *Farm workers milks the cows in the morning.*

milky /'mɪlki/ *adjective* (**milkier, milkiest**)
containing a lot of milk: *I want a big cup of milky coffee.*

mill /mɪl/ *noun*
1 a building in which flour is made from grain: *The old mill is now a restaurant.*
2 a factory where materials such as steel, wool or cotton are made: *He started work in a cotton mill at the age of ten.*

milligram /'mɪlɪˌgræm/ also **milligramme** *noun*
a unit for measuring weight. There are one thousand milligrams in a gram: *He added 0.5 milligrams of sodium.*

millilitre /'mɪlɪˌli:tə/ *noun*
a unit for measuring volume for liquids and gases. There are one thousand millilitres in a litre: *The nurse measured 100 millilitres of blood.*

millimetre /'mɪlɪˌmi:tə/ *noun*
a unit for measuring length. There are ten millimetres in a centimetre: *The creature is tiny, just 10 millimetres long.*

million /'mɪliən/

LANGUAGE HELP
The plural form is **million** after a number.

(*also* **a million, one million**)
the number 1,000,000: *A million people visit the county each year.*
millions of something a very large number of people or things: *The programme was watched on television in millions of homes.*

millionaire /ˌmɪliə'neə/ *noun*
a person who has more than a million pounds: *By the time he died, he was a millionaire.*

mime [1] /maɪm/ *noun*
a way of telling a story using your face, hands and body, but without using

m

speech: *The story is told through music and mime.*

mime ² /maɪm/ *verb* (**mimes, miming, mimed**)

to describe something using movements rather than speech: *He mimed the act of hammering a nail into a piece of wood.*

mimic /'mɪmɪk/ *verb* (**mimics, mimicking, mimicked**)

to copy someone in an amusing way: *He could mimic anybody, and often made Olivia laugh.*

mince /mɪns/ *uncountable noun*

meat that has been cut into very small pieces using a machine: *Fry the mince in a frying pan.*

mind ¹ /maɪnd/ *noun*

all your thoughts and the way that you think about things: *She is a bit deaf, but her mind is still sharp.*

change your mind to change a decision or an opinion: *I was going to vote for him, but I changed my mind.*

make up your mind to decide something: *He made up his mind to call Kathy.*

on your mind used for describing something that you are worried about and think about a lot: *I don't sleep well. I've got a lot on my mind.*

out of your mind crazy (*informal*): *What are you doing? Are you out of your mind?*

take your mind off something to help you to stop thinking about a problem for a while: *A film might take your mind off your problems.*

mind ² /maɪnd/ *verb* (**minds, minding, minded**)

to feel annoyed or angry about something: *Mr Hernandez, would you mind waiting here a moment?* □ *It was hard work but she didn't mind.*

I don't mind used when you are happy to do or have either of two choices: *'Would you rather play tennis or baseball?' – 'I don't mind.'*

I wouldn't mind something/doing something used for saying that someone would like something: *I wouldn't mind a cup of coffee.*

mind out! used for telling someone to be careful

never mind used when something is not important: *'He's not coming.' – 'Oh, never mind, we'll start eating without him.'*

mine ¹ /maɪn/ *pronoun*

belonging to me: *Her right hand was close to mine.* □ *That isn't your bag, it's mine.*

mine ² /maɪn/ *noun*

1 a deep hole in the ground from which people dig coal, diamonds or gold: *The company owns gold and silver mines.*

2 a bomb that is hidden under the ground

mine ³ /maɪn/ *verb* (**mines, mining, mined**)

to dig deep holes and tunnels into the ground to remove coal, diamonds or gold: *Diamonds are mined in South Africa.*

▶ **miner** *noun My father was a miner.*

mineral /'mɪnərəl/ *noun*

a natural substance such as gold, salt or coal that comes from the ground

'mineral ,water *uncountable noun*

water that comes from the ground that contains substances that are good for your health

miniature /'mɪnɪtʃə/ *adjective*

very small, or much smaller than usual: *The toy house was filled with miniature chairs and tables.*

minimal /'mɪnɪməl/ *adjective*

very small: *The health risk is minimal, so there's no need to worry.*

minimize /'mɪnɪˌmaɪz/ *verb* (**minimizes, minimizing, minimized**)

to make something as small as possible: *We have done everything possible to minimize the risk of accidents.*

minimum /'mɪnɪməm/ *adjective*

used for talking about the smallest amount that is possible: *Pupils remain at school at least until the minimum age of 16.* □ *Many people in the country are still working for less than the minimum wage.* ● **minimum** *noun Dr Rayman runs a minimum of three miles every day.*

minister /'mɪnɪstə/ *noun*

1 a religious leader in some types of church: *Thirty priests, ministers and rabbis attended the meeting.*

2 a senior person in a government in some countries: *Clark became finance minister in 1991.*

ministry /'mɪnɪstri/ *noun* (**ministries**)

a government department that deals with one particular thing: *He has worked for both the ministry of education and the ministry of the interior.*

minor /'maɪnə/ *adjective*

1 not very important or serious: *The soldier suffered only minor injuries.* □ *They both have minor roles in the film.*

2 used in music for talking about a scale (= a series of musical notes) in which the third note is one half step lower that the related major scale. Compare with **major**: *an A minor scale*

minority /mɪ'nɒrɪti, AM -'nɔːr-/ *noun* (**minorities**)

fewer than half the amount of people or things: *Only a minority of mothers in this neighbourhood go out to work.*

mint /mɪnt/ *noun*

1 *uncountable* a plant that has leaves with a fresh, strong taste and smell: *The waiter brought us two glasses of mint tea.*

2 a sweet with this flavour: *Sam offered me a mint.*

minus¹ /'maɪnəs/ *conjunction*

used when you are taking one number away from another number: *One minus one is zero.*

minus² /'maɪnəs/ *adjective*

used before a number or an amount to show that it is less than zero: *The temperature dropped to minus 20 degrees F.*

minute¹ /'mɪnɪt/ *noun*

a unit for measuring time. There are sixty seconds in one minute, and there are sixty minutes in one hour: *The pizza will take twenty minutes to cook.*

in a minute very soon: *The doctor will be with you in a minute.*

just a minute/wait a minute said when you want someone to wait for a short period of time: *Wait a minute, something is wrong here.*

this minute immediately: *You come back here this minute!*

minute² /maɪ'njuːt/ *adjective*

very small: *You only need to use a minute amount of glue.*

miracle /'mɪrəkəl/ *noun*

a surprising and lucky event that you cannot explain: *It's a miracle that Chris survived the accident.*

mirror /'mɪrə/ *noun*

a flat piece of special glass that you can see yourself in

→ Look at picture on P4

mirror

Dan looked at himself in the mirror.

misbehaviour /ˌmɪsbɪ'heɪvjə/ *uncountable noun*

bad behaviour (*formal*): *Our teachers will not tolerate misbehaviour.*

mischief /'mɪstʃɪf/ *uncountable noun*

bad or silly behaviour that is annoying but not too serious: *Jacob's a typical little boy — full of mischief.*

mischievous /'mɪstʃɪvəs/ *adjective*

liking to play tricks on people and behaving in a silly, but not very bad way: *Megan gave me a mischievous smile.*

▶ **mischievously** *adverb* *Thomas grinned mischievously at Anna.*

miserable /'mɪzərəbəl/ *adjective*

1 very unhappy: *My job was making me miserable.*

▶ **miserably** /'mɪzərəbli/ *adverb* *'I feel so guilty', Diane said miserably.*

2 making you feel unhappy: *It was a grey, wet, miserable day.*

misery /'mɪzəri/ *noun* (**miseries**)

great unhappiness: *People never forget the misery of war.*

misfortune /ˌmɪs'fɔːtʃuːn/ *noun*

something unpleasant or unlucky that happens to you: *She seems to enjoy other people's misfortunes.*

mislead /ˌmɪs'liːd/ *verb* (**misleads, misleading, misled**)

to make someone believe something that is not true: *The administration has misled the public about this issue.*

misleading /ˌmɪs'liːdɪŋ/ *adjective*

making you believe something that is not true: *Companies must make sure that their advertisements are not misleading.*

m

misled /ˌmɪsˈled/ → see **mislead**

miss¹ /mɪs/ **verb** (**misses, missing, missed**)

1 to not manage to hit or catch something: *His first shot missed the goal completely.* □ *Morrison just missed the ball.*

2 to not notice something: *What did he say? I missed it.*

3 to feel sad that someone is not there: *I miss my family terribly.*

4 to feel sad because you no longer have something: *I love my flat, but I miss my garden.*

5 to arrive too late to get on an aeroplane or a train: *He missed the last bus home.*

6 to not take part in a meeting or an activity: *He missed the party because he had to work.*

miss out on something to not have the chance take part in something: *You missed out on all the fun yesterday.*

Miss² /mɪs/ **noun** (**Misses**)
used in front of the name of a girl or a woman who is not married (*formal*): *It was nice talking to you, Miss Ellis.*

missile /ˈmɪsaɪl/ **noun**

1 a weapon that flies through the air and explodes when it hits something: *The army fired missiles at the building.*

2 anything that you can throw as a weapon: *The youths were throwing missiles at the police.*

missing /ˈmɪsɪŋ/ **adjective**
used for describing someone or something that is not in its usual place, and that you cannot find: *I discovered that my mobile phone was missing.* □ *Police are hunting for the missing girl.*

mission /ˈmɪʃən/ **noun**
an important job that someone has to do, especially one that involves travelling: *His government sent him on a mission to North America.*

misspell /ˌmɪsˈspel/ **verb** (**misspells, misspelling, misspelled**)
to not spell a word correctly: *Sorry I misspelled your last name.*

mist /mɪst/ **uncountable noun**
a lot of tiny drops of water in the air, that make it difficult to see: *The mist did not lift until midday.*

▶ **misty** **adjective** *Charlie looked across the misty valley.*

mistake¹ /mɪˈsteɪk/ **noun**
something that is not correct: *Tony made three spelling mistakes in the letter.*

by mistake accidentally: *I was in a hurry and called the wrong number by mistake.*

mistake² /mɪˈsteɪk/ **verb** (**mistakes, mistaking, mistook, mistaken**)
to wrongly think that one person is another person: *People are always mistaking Lauren for her sister because they are so alike.*

mistaken /mɪˈsteɪkən/ **adjective**
wrong about something: *I think that you must be mistaken — Jackie wouldn't do a thing like that.*

▶ **mistakenly** **adverb** *The thieves mistakenly believed there was no one in the house.*

mistook /mɪˈstʊk/ → see **mistake**

mistrust /ˌmɪsˈtrʌst/ **verb** (**mistrusts, mistrusting, mistrusted**)
to not trust someone: *He mistrusts all journalists.* ● **mistrust uncountable noun** *There is a deep mistrust of the police around here.*

misunderstand /ˌmɪsʌndəˈstænd/ **verb** (**misunderstands, misunderstanding, misunderstood**)
to not understand someone or something correctly: *I think you've misunderstood me.*

misunderstanding /ˌmɪsʌndəˈstændɪŋ/ **noun**
a situation where someone does not understand something correctly: *Make your plans clear to avoid misunderstandings.*

misunderstood /ˌmɪsʌndəˈstʊd/ → see **misunderstand**

mitten /ˈmɪtən/ **noun**
a glove that has one part that covers your thumb and another part that covers your four fingers together: *a pair of mittens*

mix /mɪks/ **verb** (**mixes, mixing, mixed**)

1 to put different things together so that they make something new: *Mix the sugar with the butter.*

mix

2 to join together and make something new: *Oil and water don't mix.*

mix someone/ something up
to think that one of two things

or people is the other one: *People often mix me up with my brother.* □ *Children often mix up their words.*

mixed /mɪkst/ *adjective*
including different types of things or people: *There was a very mixed group of people at the party.* □ *For lunch we had pasta and a mixed salad.*

mixer /'mɪksə/ *noun*
a machine that you use for mixing things together: *Beat the egg yolks and sugar with an electric mixer.*

mixture /'mɪkstʃə/ *noun*
a substance that you make by mixing different substances together: *The sauce is a mixture of chocolate and cream.*

ml
short for **millilitre** or **millilitres**

mm
short for **millimetre** or **millimetres**

moan /məʊn/ *verb* (**moans, moaning, moaned**)
1 to make a low sound because you are unhappy or in pain: *The wounded soldier was moaning in pain.* ● **moan** *noun* *She gave a soft moan of discomfort.*
2 to complain, or speak in a way which shows that you are unhappy: *They're always moaning about the weather.*

mobile /'məʊbaɪl/ *adjective*
that can easily move or be moved from place to place: *The family live in a three-bedroom mobile home near Las Cruces in New Mexico.* □ *Grandpa's eighty but he's still very mobile.*

mobile 'phone (*American:* **cellphone**) *noun* (*also* **mobile**)
a telephone that you can carry wherever you go: *The woman called the police on her mobile phone.*

mock /mɒk/ *verb* (**mocks, mocking, mocked**)
to laugh at someone and try to make them feel foolish: *My friends mocked me because I didn't have a girlfriend.*

modal /'məʊdəl/ *noun* (*also* **modal auxiliary**)
used, in grammar for describing a word such as 'can' or 'would' that you use with another verb to express ideas such as possibility, intention or necessity

model¹ /'mɒdəl/ *noun*
1 a small copy of something: *At school, the*

children are making a model of the solar system. □ *I made the model using paper and glue.*
● **model** *adjective* *I spent my childhood building model aircraft.*
2 a particular design of a vehicle or a machine: *You don't need an expensive computer, just a basic model.*
3 a person who sits or stands in front of an artist so that they can draw or paint them: *The model for his painting was his sister.*
4 a person whose job is to wear and show new clothes in photographs and at fashion shows, so that people can see them and buy them: *Kim dreams of becoming a fashion model.*

model² /'mɒdəl/ *verb* (**models, modelling, modelled**)
to wear clothes as a model: *Nicole began modelling at age 15.*

modem /'məʊdem/ *noun*
a piece of equipment that uses a telephone line to connect computers: *a mobile phone with a built-in modem*

moderate /'mɒdərət/ *adjective*
not too much or too little: *Temperatures are moderate between October and March.*
▶ **moderately** *adverb* *Heat the oil until it is moderately hot.*

modern /'mɒdən/ *adjective*
new, or relating to the present time: *I like antiques, but my husband prefers modern furniture.* □ *modern society*

modernize /'mɒdə,naɪz/ *verb* (**modernizes, modernizing, modernized**)
to change something such as a system or a factory by introducing new equipment, methods or ideas: *We need to modernize our schools.*

modest /'mɒdɪst/ *adjective*
not talking much about your abilities, skills or successes: *He's modest, as well as being a great player.*
▶ **modestly** *adverb* *'I was just lucky', Hughes said modestly.*

modesty /'mɒdɪsti/ *uncountable noun*
the quality of not talking much about your abilities, skills or successes: *His humour and gentle modesty won affection and friendships everywhere.*

modify /'mɒdɪfaɪ/ *verb* (**modifies, modifying, modified**)
to change something slightly, usually in

order to improve it: *Helen and her husband modified the design of the house to suit their family's needs.*

▶ **modification** /ˌmɒdɪfɪ'keɪʃən/ *noun*
They made a few small modifications to the plan.

moist /mɔɪst/ *adjective* (**moister, moistest**)
slightly wet: *The soil was moist after the rain.*

moisture /'mɔɪstʃə/ *uncountable noun*
small drops of water in the air, on a surface, or in the ground: *Keep the food covered so that it doesn't lose moisture.*

mole /məʊl/ *noun*
1 a natural dark spot on your skin: *Rebecca has a mole on the side of her nose.*
2 a small animal with black fur that lives under the ground

mole

molecule /'mɒlɪˌkjuːl/ *noun*
the smallest amount of a chemical substance that can exist by itself: *When hydrogen and oxygen molecules combine, the reaction produces heat and water.*

mom /mɒm/ *noun* (American, informal)
→ see **mum**

moment /'məʊmənt/ *noun*
1 a very short period of time: *In a moment he was gone.*
2 the time when something happens: *At that moment a car stopped at the house.*
at the/this moment at or around the time when you are speaking: *At the moment, the team is playing very well.*
for the moment now, but not in the future: *For the moment, everything is fine.*
in a moment very soon: *'Please take a seat. Mr Garcia will see you in a moment.'*

monarchy /'mɒnəki/ *noun* (**monarchies**)
a system in which a country has a king or queen: *Greece abolished the monarchy in 1974.*

Monday /'mʌndeɪ, -di/ *noun*
the day after Sunday and before Tuesday: *I went back to work on Monday.* □ *The first meeting was last Monday.*

money /'mʌni/ *uncountable noun*
the coins or notes that you use to buy things: *Cars cost a lot of money.* □ *She spends too much money on clothes and shoes.*

monitor /'mɒnɪtə/ *verb* (**monitors, monitoring, monitored**)
to watch how something develops or progresses over a period of time: *Doctors closely monitored her progress.*

monk /mʌŋk/ *noun*
a member of a group of religious men who live together in a special building

monkey /'mʌŋki/ *noun*
an animal that has a long tail and can climb trees

monopoly /mə'nɒpəli/ *noun*
1 a situation where a company or a person has complete control over something: *The East India Company had a monopoly on all trade to Britain from the East.*
2 the only company that provides a particular product: *The company is a state-owned monopoly.*

monotonous /mə'nɒtənəs/ *adjective*
very boring; never changing: *It's monotonous work, like most factory jobs.*

monsoon /mɒn'suːn/ *noun*
the season in Southern Asia when there is a lot of very heavy rain: *The monsoon season lasts for about four months each year.*

monster /'mɒnstə/ *noun*
a big, ugly and frightening creature in stories: *The film is about a monster in the wardrobe.*

month /mʌnθ/ *noun*
one of the twelve parts that a year is divided into: *September is the ninth month of the year.* □ *We go on holiday next month.*

monthly /'mʌnθli/ *adjective, adverb*
happening every month: *The monthly rent for his flat is £1,000.* □ *The magazine is published monthly.*

monument /'mɒnjʊmənt/ *noun*
something that you build to help people remember an important event or person: *This monument was built in memory of the soldiers who died in the war.*

moo /muː/ *verb* (**moos, mooing, mooed**)
to make the long, low sound of a cow: *We could hear the cows mooing.*

mood /muːd/ *noun*
the way you are feeling at a particular time: *Dad is in a very good mood today.* □ *I had an argument with my girlfriend, so I was in a bad mood.*

moody /'muːdi/ *adjective* (**moodier, moodiest**)

often becoming sad or angry without any warning: *David's mother is very moody.*

moon /muːn/ *noun*
the large object that shines in the sky at night: *The first man on the moon was an American, Neil Armstrong.*

moonlight /'muːnlaɪt/ *uncountable noun*
the light that comes from the moon at night: *They walked along the road in the moonlight.*

moose /muːs/ *noun* (**moose**)
the largest member of the deer family. (A deer is a large wild animal with horns that are like branches): *In the autumn, they hunt moose and deer.*

mop /mɒp/ *noun*
a long stick with a lot of thick pieces of string at one end. You use it for washing floors. • **mop** *verb* (**mops, mopping, mopped**) *I could see a woman mopping the stairs.*

mop

moral¹ /'mɒrəl/ *noun*
1 *plural* your ideas and beliefs about right and wrong behaviour: *Amy has strong morals and high standards.*
2 what you learn from a story or event about how you should or should not behave: *The moral of this sad story is 'do not trust anyone'.*

moral² /'mɒrəl/ *adjective*
relating to people's beliefs about what is right or wrong: *We all have a moral duty to stop racism.*
▸ **morally** *adverb* *It is morally wrong to kill a person.*

more /mɔː/ *adjective, adverb*
1 used for talking about a greater amount of something: *More people are surviving heart attacks than ever before.* ▫ *I need more time to*

think about what to do. • **more** *pronoun* *As they worked harder, they ate more.* ▫ *We should do more to help these people.*
2 used for showing that something continues to happen: *You should talk about your problems more.*

more and more used for showing that something is becoming greater all the time: *She began eating more and more.*

more of something a greater amount of something than before, or than usual: *They're doing more of their own work.*

more than something used for talking about a greater amount of something than the amount mentioned: *The airport had been closed for more than a year.*

moreover /mɔːˈrəʊvə/ *adverb*
used when you are adding more information about something (*formal*): *She saw that there was a man behind her. Moreover, he was staring at her.*

morning /'mɔːnɪŋ/ *noun*
the part of each day between the time that people usually wake up and noon: *Tomorrow morning we will take a walk around the city.* ▫ *On Sunday morning the telephone woke Bill.*

in the morning during the morning of the following day: *I'm flying to St. Louis in the morning.*

mortgage /'mɔːɡɪdʒ/ *noun*
a loan of money that you get from a bank in order to buy a house: *I had to sell my home because I couldn't afford the mortgage payments.*

mosaic /məʊˈzeɪɪk/ *noun*
a surface that is made of small pieces of coloured glass or stone: *a Roman house with a beautiful mosaic floor*

Moslem /'mɒzləm, 'mʊzlɪm/ → see **Muslim**

mosque /mɒsk/ *noun*
a building where Muslims go to pray

mosquito /mɒ'skiːtəʊ/ *noun* (**mosquitoes** or **mosquitos**)
a small flying insect that bites people and animals

moss /mɒs/ *noun* (**mosses**)
a very small, soft, green plant that grows on wet soil, or on wood or stone: *The ground was covered with moss.*

most /məʊst/ *adjective, adverb*
1 used for talking about the largest amount of people or things: *Most people*

m

think he is a great actor. ● **most** *pronoun*
Seventeen people were hurt. Most were students.
2 used for showing that something is
true or happens more than anything else:
What do you like most about your job?

make the most of something to use
something in the best possible way: You
should make the most of what you have if you
want to be happy.

most of used for talking about the
largest quantity of people or things: Most
of the houses here are very old. □ I was away
from home most of the time.

mostly /'məʊstli/ *adverb*
almost always: My friends are mostly
students. □ Cars are made mostly of metal.

motel /məʊ'tel/ *noun*
a hotel for people who are travelling by
car

moth /mɒθ/ *noun*
an insect that has large wings and is
attracted by lights at night

mother /'mʌðə/ *noun*
your female parent: She's a mother of two
children.
→ Look at picture on P8

motherhood /'mʌðə,hʊd/ *uncountable
noun*
the state of being a mother: I love
motherhood. It's just the most extraordinary
thing.

'mother-in-law *noun* (**mothers-in-law**)
the mother of your husband or wife

motion /'məʊʃən/ *uncountable noun*
movement: The doors will not open when the
lift is in motion.

motionless /'məʊʃənləs/ *adjective*
not moving at all: They stood motionless,
staring at each other.

motivate /'məʊtɪ,veɪt/ *verb* (**motivates,
motivating, motivated**)
to make someone feel determined to do
something: How do you motivate people to
work hard?
▶ **motivated** *adjective* We are looking for a
highly motivated and hard-working professional.
▶ **motivation** /,məʊtɪ'veɪʃən/ *uncountable
noun* His poor performance is caused by lack of
motivation.

motive /'məʊtɪv/ *noun*
your reason for doing something: Police do
not think robbery was a motive for the killing.

motor /'məʊtə/ *noun*
the part of a machine that makes it move
or work: She got in the boat and started the
motor.

motorbike /'məʊtə,baɪk/ *noun*
a vehicle with two wheels and an engine

motorist /'məʊtərɪst/ *noun*
a person who drives a car: Motorists should
take extra care on the roads when it is raining.

motorway /'məʊtə,weɪ/ *noun*
a wide road that allows cars to travel very
fast over a long distance: the M1 motorway

motto /'mɒtəʊ/ *noun* (**mottoes** or **mottos**)
a short sentence or phrase that gives a
rule for sensible behaviour: My motto is
'Don't start what you can't finish'.

mould[1] /məʊld/ *noun*
1 a hollow container that you pour liquid
into. When the liquid becomes solid,
it takes the same shape as the mould:
Pour the mixture into moulds and place them in
the fridge.
2 *uncountable* a soft grey, green or blue
substance that grows on old food or on
damp surfaces: Hannah discovered mould
growing in her bedroom cupboard.

mould[2] /məʊld/ *verb* (**moulds, moulding,
moulded**)
to make a soft substance into a
particular shape: The mixture is heated then
moulded.

mound /maʊnd/ *noun*
a large, round pile of something: huge
mounds of soil

mountain /'maʊntɪn/ *noun*
a very high area of land with steep sides:
Mt. McKinley is the highest mountain in North
America.

**mountains of something/a mountain
of something** a very large amount of
something (informal): He has a mountain of
homework.

'mountain ,bike *noun*
a bicycle with a strong frame and thick
tyres

mountaineer /,maʊntɪn'ɪə/ *noun*
a person who is skilful at climbing the
steep sides of mountains

mountainous /'maʊntɪnəs/ *adjective*
having a lot of mountains: There were some
beautiful photos of the country's mountainous
landscape.

mourn /mɔːn/ *verb* (**mourns, mourning, mourned**)

to show your deep sadness about someone who has died in the way that you behave: *He mourned for his dead son.*

▸ **mourning** *uncountable noun* *He is still in mourning for his fiancée.*

mourner /'mɔːnə/ *noun*

a person who goes to a funeral: *Crowds of mourners gathered outside the church.*

mouse /maʊs/ *noun* (**mice**)

1 a small animal with a long tail
2 an object that you use to do things on a computer without using the keyboard: *I clicked the mouse and the message appeared on the screen.*

mouse

'**mouse mat** *noun*

a flat piece of soft material that you move the mouse on when you use a computer

mousse /muːs/ *uncountable noun*

a sweet, light food made from eggs and cream: *His favourite dessert is chocolate mousse.*

moustache /mə'stɑːʃ/

the hair that grows on a man's upper lip: *He was short and bald, and he had a moustache.*

mouth /maʊθ/ *noun*

1 the part of your face that you use for eating or speaking: *When you cough, please cover your mouth.*
→ Look at picture on P1
2 the entrance or opening of a cave or a bottle: *He stopped at the mouth of the tunnel.*
3 the place where a river goes into the sea

mouthful /'maʊθfʊl/ *noun*

the amount of drink or food that you can put in your mouth at one time: *She drank a mouthful of coffee.*

move¹ /muːv/ *verb* (**moves, moving, moved**)

1 to put something in a different place: *A police officer asked him to move his car.*
2 to change position or go to a different place: *The train began to move.* □ *She waited for him to get up, but he didn't move.*
3 to go to live in a different place: *She's moving to Cornwall next month.*
4 to make someone have strong feelings, especially of sadness, pity or sympathy: *The story surprised and moved me.*

▸ **moved** *adjective* *We felt quite moved when we heard his story.*

move in to begin to live somewhere: *A new family has moved in next door.*

move out to stop living in a particular place: *I wasn't happy living there, so I decided to move out.*

move² /muːv/ *noun*

1 when you change position or go to a different place: *The doctor made a move towards the door.*
2 when you go to live in a different place: *After his move to Liverpool, he got a job as an actor.*
3 something you do in order to achieve something: *Leaving my job was a good move.*

movement /'muːvmənt/ *noun*

1 when you change position, or go from one place to another: *Brian was injured and now has limited movement in his left arm.*
2 a group of people who have the same beliefs or ideas: *It was one of the biggest political movements in the country.*

mover /'muːvə/ *noun*

a person whose job is to move furniture or equipment from one building to another: *furniture movers*

movie /'muːvi/ *noun*

(*American*) → see **film**

the movies (*American*) → see **the cinema**

moving /'muːvɪŋ/ *adjective*

making you feel a strong emotion such as sadness, pity or sympathy: *This is a moving story of the love between a master and his loyal dog.*

mow /məʊ/ *verb* (**mows, mowing, mowed, mown**)

to cut an area of grass using a machine

(called a mower): *Connor was in the garden, mowing the lawn.*

mozzarella /ˌmɒtsəˈrelə/ *uncountable noun*
a type of white Italian cheese: *Maria made a delicious pizza topped with tomato and mozzarella.*

MP /ˌem ˈpiː/ *noun* (**MPs**)
In Britain, a person who has been elected to represent the people from a particular area in the government. MP is short for 'Member of Parliament'.

MP3 /ˌem piː ˈθriː/ *noun* (**MP3s**)
a type of computer file that contains music

MP3 player *noun*
a small machine for listening to music that is stored on computer files

mph also **m.p.h.**
used for showing the speed of a vehicle. Mph is short for 'miles per hour'.

Mr /ˈmɪstə/ *noun*
used before a man's name when you want to be polite or formal: *Could I please speak to Mr Johnson?* □ *Our teacher this term is called Mr Becker.*

Mrs /ˈmɪsɪz/ *noun*
used before the name of a married woman when you want to be polite or formal: *Hello, Mrs Morley. How are you?* □ *Excuse me, does Mrs Anne Pritchard live here?*

Ms /məz, mɪz/ *noun*
used, especially in written English, before a woman's name, instead of **Mrs** or **Miss**: *Ms Kennedy refused to speak to reporters after the meeting.*

much /mʌtʃ/ *adjective, adverb*
1 used for talking about the large amount of something: *I ate too much food.* □ *These plants do not need much water.* □ *I don't have much free time these days.* • **much** *pronoun* *I ate too much.*
2 a lot: *His car is much bigger than mine.* □ *Thank you very much.* □ *He doesn't like jazz much.*
how much used to ask questions about amounts: *How much money can I spend?*
not...much not very often: *Gwen did not see her father very much.*

LANGUAGE HELP
See note at **many**.

mud /mʌd/ *uncountable noun*
a sticky mixture of earth and water: *Andy's clothes were covered with mud.*

muddle¹ /ˈmʌdəl/ *noun*
in a muddle confused: *My thoughts are all in a muddle.*

muddle² /ˈmʌdəl/ *verb* (**muddles, muddling, muddled**) (also **muddle someone or something up**)
to think that someone or something is another person or thing: *People often muddle up the two names.*

muddled /ˈmʌdəld/ *adjective*
confused: *I'm a bit muddled. I'm not sure where to begin.*

muddy /ˈmʌdi/ *adjective* (**muddier, muddiest**)
covered with mud: *Philip left his muddy boots at the kitchen door.*

muffin /ˈmʌfɪn/ *noun*
a small, round, sweet cake that often has fruit inside: *a blueberry muffin*

mug¹ /mʌg/ *noun*
a deep cup with straight sides: *He poured tea into the mugs.*

mugs

mug² /mʌg/ *verb* (**mugs, mugging, mugged**)
to attack someone and steal their money: *I was walking to my car when this guy tried to mug me.*
▶ **mugger** *noun* *When the mugger grabbed her handbag, Ms Jones fell to the ground.*

multicoloured /ˌmʌltiˈkʌləd/ *adjective*
having many different colours: *Diego was wearing a new, multicoloured shirt.*

multimedia /ˌmʌltiˈmiːdiə/ *uncountable noun*
used for describing computer programs that have sound, pictures and film, as well as text: *Most of his teachers use multimedia in the classroom.*

multinational /ˌmʌltiˈnæʃənəl/ *adjective*
1 having offices or businesses in many different countries: *multinational companies*
• **multinational** *noun* *Large multinationals control the industry.*
2 involving people from several different countries: *The U.S. troops would be part of a multinational force.*

multiple /'mʌltɪpəl/ *adjective*
consisting of many parts, involving many
people or having many uses: *He died of
multiple injuries.*

multiply /'mʌltɪˌplaɪ/ *verb* (**multiplies,
multiplying, multiplied**)
to add a number to itself a certain
number of times: *What do you get if you
multiply six by nine?*
▸ **multiplication** *uncountable noun* *a
multiplication sum*

multistorey /ˌmʌltiˈstɔːri/ *adjective*
with several floors at different levels
above the ground: *The shop is in a big
multistorey building.*

mum /mʌm/ *noun* (American: **mom**)
your mother (*informal*): *We waited for my
mum and dad to get home.* □ *Bye, Mum.
Love you.*

mumble /'mʌmbəl/ *verb* (**mumbles,
mumbling, mumbled**)
to speak quietly and not clearly: *The boy
blushed and mumbled a few words.*

mummy /'mʌmi/ *noun* (**mummies**)
1 a young child's word for their mother
(*informal*): *Please can I have a biscuit, Mummy?*
□ *I want my mummy.*
2 a dead body that was preserved long ago
by being rubbed with special oils and
wrapped in cloth: *an Ancient Egyptian
mummy*

murder¹ /'mɜːdə/ *noun*
the crime of deliberately killing a person:
The jury found him guilty of murder. □ *The
detective has worked on hundreds of murder
cases.*

murder² /'mɜːdə/ *verb* (**murders,
murdering, murdered**)
to commit the crime of killing someone
deliberately: *The film is about a woman who
murders her husband.*
▸ **murderer** /'mɜːdərə/ *noun* *One of these
men is the murderer.*

murmur /'mɜːmə/ *verb* (**murmurs,
murmuring, murmured**)
to say something very quietly: *He turned
and murmured something to Karen.* □ *'It's
lovely', she murmured.* ● **murmur** *noun* *They
spoke in low murmurs.*

muscle /'mʌsəl/ *noun*
one of the parts inside your body that

connect your bones, and that help you to
move: *Exercise helps to keep your muscles strong.*

muscular /'mʌskjʊlə/ *adjective*
having strong, firm muscles: *Jordan was
tall and muscular.*

museum /mjuːˈziːəm/ *noun*
a building where you can look at
interesting and valuable objects: *Hundreds
of people came to the museum to see the
exhibition.*

mushroom
/'mʌʃruːm/ *noun*
a plant with a short
stem and a round
top that you can eat:
*There are many types of
wild mushroom, and
some of them are
poisonous.*
→ Look at picture on P2

mushroom

music /'mjuːzɪk/
uncountable noun
1 the pleasant sound that you make when
you sing or play instruments: *Diane is
studying classical music.* □ *What's your
favourite type of music?*
2 the symbols that you write on paper to
tell people what to sing or play: *He can't
read music.*

musical¹ /'mjuːzɪkəl/ *adjective*
1 relating to playing or studying music:
Many of the kids have real musical talent.
2 having a natural ability and interest in
music: *I come from a musical family.*

musical² /'mjuːzɪkəl/ *noun*
a play or a film that uses singing and
dancing in the story: *Have you seen the
musical, 'Miss Saigon'?*

ˌmusical ˈinstrument *noun*
an object such as a piano, guitar or violin
that you play in order to produce music:
*The drum is one of the oldest musical
instruments.*

musician /mjuːˈzɪʃən/ *noun*
a person who plays a musical instrument
as their job or hobby: *Michael is a brilliant
musician.*

Muslim /'mʊzlɪm/ *noun*
someone who believes in the religion
of Islam and lives according to its rules
● **Muslim** *adjective* *an ancient Muslim
mosque*

m

must /məst, STRONG mʌst/ *modal verb*
1 used for showing that you think something is very important or necessary: *Your clothes must fit well.* ☐ *You must tell me everything you know.*
2 used for showing that you are almost sure that something is true: *Claire's car isn't there, so she must be at work.*

mustard /'mʌstəd/ *noun*
a spicy yellow or brown sauce that you eat with meat: *I had a chicken and mustard sandwich for lunch.*

must-have *noun* (**must-haves**)
something that many people want to have: *The mobile phone is now a must-have for children.* ● **must-have** *adjective It's this season's must-have bag.*

mustn't /'mʌsənt/
short for 'must not'

must've /'mʌstəv/
short for 'must have'

mutter /'mʌtə/ *verb* (**mutters, muttering, muttered**)
to speak in a very quiet voice that is difficult to hear, often when you are angry about something: *'He's crazy', she muttered.*

mutual /'mjuːtʃuəl/ *adjective*
felt or done by two people or groups: *It was a mutual decision by Dean and me.* ☐ *Nick didn't like me, and the feeling was mutual.*

my /maɪ/ *adjective*
belonging or relating to yourself: *We can eat at my house tonight.* ☐ *I love my sister.*

myself /maɪ'self/ *pronoun*
1 used when the person speaking or writing is both the subject and the object of the verb: *I asked myself what I should do.*
2 used for saying that you do something alone without help from anyone else: *'Where did you get that dress?' – 'I made it myself.'*

mysterious /mɪ'stɪəriəs/ *adjective*
strange, and not known about or understood: *A mysterious illness made him sick.*
▶ **mysteriously** *adverb The evidence mysteriously disappeared.*

mystery /'mɪstəri/ *noun* (**mysteries**)
1 something that you cannot explain or understand: *Why he behaved in this way is a mystery.*
2 a story or a film about a crime or strange events that are only explained at the end: *I was alone at home watching a murder mystery on TV.*

myth /mɪθ/ *noun*
1 an ancient story about gods and magic: *the famous Greek myth of Medusa, the snake-haired monster*
2 a belief or an explanation that is not true: *This story is a myth.*

Nn

nag /næg/ *verb* (**nags, nagging, nagged**)
to keep asking someone to do something:
*My mum's always nagging me about getting
a good job.*

nail¹ /neɪl/ *noun*
1 a thin piece of metal with one pointed
end and one flat end that you hit with a
hammer in order to fix things together:
A mirror hung on a nail above the sink.
2 the thin hard part that grows at the end
of each of your fingers and toes: *Try to keep
your nails short.*

nail

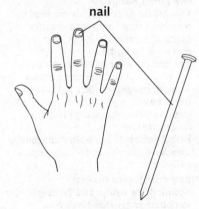

nail² /neɪl/ *verb* (**nails, nailing, nailed**)
to fasten something in a particular
position using one or more nails: *The sign
was nailed to a tree.*

naive /naɪˈiːv/ also **naïve** *adjective*
without much experience of life;
expecting things to be easy: *I was naive to
think they would agree.*

naked /ˈneɪkɪd/ *adjective*
not wearing any clothes: *She held the naked
baby in her arms.*

name¹ /neɪm/ *noun*
1 the word or words that you use to talk to
a particular person, or to talk about them:
'What's his name?' — 'Peter.'

2 the word or words that you use to talk
about a particular place or thing: *What is
the name of this street?* □ *Can you tell me the
name of this plant?*

name² /neɪm/ *verb* (**names, naming,
named**)
to give someone or something a name:
*He named his first child Christopher after his
brother.*
call someone names to say unpleasant
things to someone: *It's cruel to call people
names.*

nanny /ˈnæni/ *noun* (**nannies**)
a person whose job is to take care of
children in a family

nap /næp/ *noun*
a short sleep, usually during the day: *We
had a nap after lunch.*

napkin /ˈnæpkɪn/ *noun*
a square of cloth or paper that you use
when you are eating to protect your
clothes, or to wipe your mouth or hands

nappy /ˈnæpɪn/ *noun* (**nappies**)
(*American*: **diaper**)
a piece of cloth or strong paper that a baby
wears around its bottom and between its
legs: *I need to change the baby's nappy.*

narrator /nəˈreɪtə/ *noun*
the person who tells the story in a book or
a film: *The story's narrator is a famous actress.*

narrow /ˈnærəʊ/ *adjective* (**narrower,
narrowest**)
small in distance from one side to the
other: *We walked through the town's narrow
streets.*

nasty /ˈnɑːsti/ *adjective* (**nastier, nastiest**)
1 very unpleasant: *This medicine has a very
nasty taste.* □ *The tax increase was a nasty
surprise for businesses.*
2 unkind: *If anyone is nasty to you, you should
tell the teacher.*

nation /ˈneɪʃən/ *noun*
an individual country, its people and its

n

social and political structures: *the United States and other nations*

national /ˈnæʃənəl/ *adjective*

1 relating to the whole of a country or nation: *He's the manager of the French national football team.* ▫ *The ad appeared in the national newspapers.*

2 typical of the people or traditions of a particular country or nation: *When you travel abroad, you must respect national traditions.* ▫ *The national dress of Scotland is the kilt.*

national anthem /ˌnæʃənəl ˈænθəm/ *noun*

the official song of a country: *The national anthem was played while the winners received their medals.*

nationality /ˌnæʃəˈnælɪti/ *noun* (**nationalities**)

the state of being a legal citizen of a particular country: *I'm not sure of her nationality, but I think she's Canadian.*

nationwide /ˌneɪʃənˈwaɪd/ *adjective, adverb*

happening or existing in all parts of a country: *Car crime is a nationwide problem.* ▫ *Unemployment fell nationwide last month.*

native [1] /ˈneɪtɪv/ *adjective*

relating to the particular country, region or town where you were born: *It was his first visit to his native country since 1948.* ▫ *The garden features Australian native plants.*

  native language the first language that you learned to speak when you were a child: *Her native language was Swedish.*

native [2] /ˈneɪtɪv/ *noun*

someone who was born in a particular country, region or town: *The owner of the restaurant is a native of Hong Kong.*

natural /ˈnætʃərəl/ *adjective*

1 normal: *It is natural for young people to want excitement.*

2 existing in nature and not created by people: *I love the natural beauty of the landscape.*

▸ **naturally** *adverb* *Allow your hair to dry naturally in the sun.*

naturally /ˈnætʃərəli/ *adverb*

used for showing that something is very obvious and not surprising: *When things go wrong, we naturally feel disappointed.*

nature /ˈneɪtʃə/ *noun*

1 *uncountable* all the animals, plants and things that happen in the world that are not made or caused by people: *The essay discusses the relationship between humans and nature.*

> **LANGUAGE HELP**
> See note at **countryside**.

2 a person's character, which they show by the way they behave: *People called her 'Sunny' because of her friendly nature.*

naughty /ˈnɔːti/ *adjective* (**naughtier, naughtiest**)

badly behaved; not doing what someone tells you to do: *When I'm very naughty, my mum sends me to bed early.*

nausea /ˈnɔːziə/ *uncountable noun*

a feeling that you are going to vomit: *The symptoms include headaches and nausea.*

naval /ˈneɪvəl/ *adjective*

relating to a country's navy: *He was a senior naval officer.*

navigate /ˈnævɪˌɡeɪt/ *verb* (**navigates, navigating, navigated**)

1 to find the direction that you need to travel in, using a map or the sun, for example: *We navigated using the sun by day and the stars by night.*

2 to find the information that you need in a website by clicking on particular words or images (= links) that take you from one web page to another: *A home page gives users information and helps them to navigate the site.*

▸ **navigation** /ˌnævɪˈɡeɪʃən/ *uncountable noun* *Navigation through the site is simple and quick.*

navy /ˈneɪvi/ *noun* (**navies**)

a country's warships and the people who work in them: *Her son is in the navy.*

navy blue *adjective*

very dark blue in colour: *I wore navy blue trousers and a white shirt.* ● **navy blue** *noun* *She was dressed in navy blue.*

near /nɪə/ *preposition*

only a short distance away; close to someone or something: *Don't come near me!* ▫ *The café is near the station in Edmonton.*

● **near** *adjective* (**nearer, nearest**) *Excuse me, where's the nearest post office?*

  in the near future very soon: *I hope I'll be able to meet her in the near future.*

nearby /ˌnɪəˈbaɪ/ *adjective, adverb*

only a short distance away; close: *He sat at a nearby table.* ▫ *Her sister lives nearby.*

nearly /'nɪəli/ *adverb*
1 almost a particular amount: *He has worked for the company for nearly 20 years.*
2 almost a particular time or state: *'What time is it?' — 'Nearly five o'clock.'* □ *I've nearly finished.*

neat /ni:t/ *adjective* (**neater, neatest**)
with everything in the correct place: *She's got very neat handwriting.*
▶ **neatly** *adverb* *He folded his newspaper neatly and put it in his bag.*

necessary /'nesɪsəri/ *adjective*
needed in order to do something, have something or make something happen: *Exercise is necessary if you want to lose weight.* □ *I'm sure I've got the necessary skills for this job.*

necessity /nɪ'sesɪti/ *noun* (**necessities**)
something that you must have to live: *The price of food and other necessities has increased.*

neck /nek/ *noun*
1 the part of your body between your head and the rest of your body: *He was wearing a red scarf around his neck.*
→ Look at picture on P1
2 the part of a shirt or dress that surrounds your neck: *She wore a dress with a high neck.*

necklace /'neklɪs/ *noun*
a piece of jewellery that you wear around your neck: *She was wearing a diamond necklace.*

necklace

nectarine /'nektəri:n, -rɪn/ *noun*
a red-and-yellow fruit with a smooth skin

need¹ /ni:d/ *verb* (**needs, needing, needed**)
1 to require something: *He desperately needed money.*
2 to have to do something because it is necessary: *I need to make a phone call.*

need² /ni:d/ *noun*
1 a situation in which you must have or do something: *There is a need for more schools in the area.* □ *There is a need to recruit more doctors and nurses in this country.*
2 *plural* things that you want or must have: *Parents have to look after their child's physical and emotional needs.*

needle /'ni:dəl/ *noun*
1 a small, thin metal tool with a sharp point that you use for sewing: *If you get me a needle and thread, I'll sew the button on.*
2 a thin hollow metal tube with a sharp point that is used for putting a drug into someone's body: *Dirty needles spread disease.*
3 the long strip of metal or plastic on an instrument that shows a measurement of, for example, speed or weight: *The needle on the boiler is pointing to 200 degrees.*
4 one of the thin, hard, pointed parts of some trees that stay green all year: *There was a thick layer of pine needles on the ground.*

needless /'ni:dləs/ *adjective*
not necessary; able to be avoided: *His death was so needless.*
▶ **needlessly** *adverb* *Children are dying needlessly.*

needn't /'ni:dənt/
short for 'need not'

needy /'ni:di/ *adjective* (**needier, neediest**)
without enough food, medicine or clothing: *They provide housing for needy families.*

negative¹ /'negətɪv/ *adjective*
1 unpleasant or harmful: *Patients talked about their negative childhood experiences.*
2 considering only the bad aspects of a situation: *When someone asks for your opinion, don't be negative.*
▶ **negatively** *adverb* *Why do so many people think negatively?*
3 saying or meaning 'no': *Dr Robertson gave a negative response.*
▶ **negatively** *adverb* *Sixty percent of people answered negatively.*
4 less than zero. Compare with **positive**: *a negative number such as minus 5*

negative² /'negətɪv/ *noun*
in grammar, a form that is used for saying 'no' or 'not', such as 'don't' and 'haven't'

neglect /nɪ'glekt/ *verb* (**neglects, neglecting, neglected**)
to not take care of someone or something:

The neighbours claim that she is neglecting her children. ● **neglect** *uncountable noun The house is being repaired after years of neglect.*

▶ **neglected** *adjective a neglected child*

negligence /'neglɪdʒəns/ *uncountable noun*

when someone does not do something that they should do: *His negligence caused the accident.*

▶ **negligent** *adjective The jury decided that the airline was negligent.*

▶ **negligently** *adverb I believe that the doctor acted negligently.*

negotiate /nɪ'ɡəʊʃieɪt/ *verb* (**negotiates, negotiating, negotiated**)

to talk about a problem or a situation in order to reach an agreement: *The unions are negotiating with the Japanese car firm.*

negotiations /nɪˌɡəʊʃi'eɪʃənz/ *plural noun*

discussions between people, during which they try to reach an agreement: *The negotiations were successful.*

neigh /neɪ/ *verb* (**neighs, neighing, neighed**)

when a horse neighs, it makes its typical loud sound: *The horse neighed and disappeared amongst the trees.* ● **neigh** *noun The horse gave a loud neigh.*

neighbour /'neɪbə/ *noun*

someone who lives near you: *Sometimes we invite the neighbours over for dinner.*

neighbourhood /'neɪbəˌhʊd/ *noun*

one of the parts of a town where people live: *Their house is in a quiet, residential neighbourhood.*

neither /'naɪðə, 'niːðə/ *adjective, adverb*

1 not one or the other: *At first, neither man could speak.* □ *Neither of us felt like going out.*

2 also not: *I never learned to swim and neither did they.*

neither ... nor used when you are talking about two or more things that are not true or do not happen: *Professor Hisamatsu spoke neither English nor German.*

neon /'niːɒn/ *adjective*

filled with a special gas (= neon) that produces a bright electric light: *In the city streets the neon lights flashed.*

nephew /'nefjuː, 'nev-/ *noun*

the son of your sister or brother: *I am planning a birthday party for my nephew.*

→ Look at picture on P8

nerve /nɜːv/ *noun*

1 one of the long thin threads in your body that send messages between your brain and other parts of your body: *pain from a damaged nerve*

2 *uncountable* the courage that you need to do something difficult or dangerous: *I don't know why he lost his nerve.*

get on someone's nerves to annoy someone (*informal*): *The children's noisy games were getting on his nerves.*

nerves /nɜːvz/ *plural noun*

feelings of worry or fear: *He plays the piano to calm his nerves and relax.*

nervous /'nɜːvəs/ *adjective*

frightened or worried: *I was very nervous during the job interview.*

▶ **nervously** *adverb Beth stood up nervously when the teacher came into the room.*

▶ **nervousness** *uncountable noun I smiled warmly so he wouldn't see my nervousness.*

nest¹ /nest/ *noun*

the place where a bird, a small animal or an insect keeps its eggs or its babies: *The cuckoo leaves its eggs in the nests of other birds.*

nest² /nest/ *verb* (**nests, nesting, nested**)

to build a nest and lay eggs there: *There are birds nesting on the cliffs.*

net /net/ *noun*

1 *uncountable* a material made of threads or wire with spaces in between: *There were net curtains in the windows.*

2 a piece of net that you use for a particular purpose, often in sports: *a fishing net* □ *Torres headed the ball into the net.*

the Net → see **Internet**: *We've been on the Net since 1993.*

netball /'netbɔːl/ *noun*

a game where two teams of seven players, usually women, try to score goals by throwing a ball through a high net

network /'netwɜːk/ *noun*

a large number of people or things that have a connection with each other and that work together: *She has a strong network of friends and family to help her.* □ *Their computers are connected on a wireless network.*

neutral /'njuːtrəl/ *adjective*

1 not supporting either side in an argument or a war: *Switzerland remained neutral during World War II.*

n

2 not showing what you are thinking or feeling: *Isabel said in a neutral voice, 'You're very late, darling.'*

never /'nevə/ *adverb*
at no time in the past, the present or the future: *I have never been abroad.* □ *That was a mistake. I'll never do it again.* □ *Never look directly at the sun.*

nevertheless /ˌnevəðə'les/ *adverb*
however; in spite of that (*formal*): *Leon had problems, but nevertheless managed to finish his most famous painting.*

new /njuː/ *adjective* (**newer, newest**)
1 recently created or invented: *They've just opened a new hotel.* □ *These ideas are not new.*
2 not used or owned by anyone before you: *That afternoon she went out and bought a new dress.* □ *There are many boats, new and used, for sale.*
3 different from before: *I had to find somewhere new to live.* □ *Rachel has a new boyfriend.*

newborn /'njuːbɔːn/ *adjective*
having just been born: *a mother and her newborn child*

newcomer /'njuːkʌmə/ *noun*
a person who has recently arrived in a place: *She's a newcomer to London.*

newly /'njuːli/ *adverb*
used for showing that an action or a situation is very recent: *She was young at the time, and newly married.*

news /njuːz/ *uncountable noun*
1 information about recent events: *We waited and waited for news of him.* □ *I've just had some bad news — I failed my exam.*
2 information about recent events that is reported in newspapers, or on the radio, television or Internet: *Here are some of the top stories in the news.*
3 a television or radio programme that gives information about recent events: *I heard all about the bombs on the news.*

> **LANGUAGE HELP**
>
> **News** is an uncountable noun. When you are talking about a particular fact or message, you can say a **piece of news**. You call an individual story or report a **news item**.

newsagent /'njuːzeɪdʒənt/ *noun*
1 a person who sells things like

newspapers, cigarettes and sweets
2 (*also* **newsagent's**) a shop that sells things like newspapers, cigarettes and sweets

newsletter /'njuːzletə/ *noun*
a report giving information about an organization that is sent regularly to its members: *All members receive a free monthly newsletter.*

newspaper /'njuːspeɪpə/ *noun*
a number of large sheets of folded paper, with news, advertisements and other information printed on them: *They read about it in the newspaper.*

New Year's 'Day *uncountable noun*
1st January, the time when people celebrate the start of a year

next /nekst/ *adjective, adverb*
1 coming immediately after this one or after the previous one: *I got up early the next morning.* □ *I took the next available flight.* □ *Who will be the next mayor?*
2 used for talking about the first day, week or year that comes after this one or the previous one: *Let's go to see a film next week.* □ *He retires next January.*
3 nearest: *There was a party going on in the next room.* □ *He married a girl from the next village.*
4 immediately after this time or a time in the past: *I don't know what to do next.* □ *What happened next?*

next to someone/something beside: *She sat down next to him on the sofa.*

nibble /'nɪbəl/ *verb* (**nibbles, nibbling, nibbled**)
to eat something by biting very small pieces of it: *He was nibbling a biscuit.* □ *She nibbled at a piece of bread.*

nice /naɪs/ *adjective* (**nicer, nicest**)
1 attractive, pleasant or enjoyable: *The chocolate cake was very nice.* □ *It's nice to be here together again.*
▸ **nicely** *adverb* *The book is nicely illustrated.*
2 friendly and pleasant: *I've met your father and he's very nice.* □ *They were extremely nice to me.*
▸ **nicely** *adverb* *He treated you nicely.*

nickname /'nɪkneɪm/ *noun*
an informal name for someone or something: *His nickname is 'Red' because of his red hair.* ● **nickname** *verb* (**nicknames,**

nicknaming, nicknamed) *The children nicknamed him 'The Giraffe' because he was so tall.*

niece /niːs/ *noun*
the daughter of your sister or brother: *He bought a present for his niece.*
→ Look at picture on P8

night /naɪt/ *noun*
1 the time when it is dark outside, and most people sleep: *The rain continued all night.* □ *It was a dark, cold night.* □ *It's eleven o'clock at night in Moscow.*
2 the period of time between the end of the afternoon and the time that you go to bed: *Did you go to Kelly's party last night?*

nightclub /ˈnaɪtklʌb/ *noun*
a place where people go late in the evening to drink and dance

nightdress /ˈnaɪtdres/ *noun* (**nightdresses**)
a loose dress that a woman or girl wears in bed

nightly /ˈnaɪtli/ *adjective, adverb*
happening every night: *We watched the nightly news.* □ *She appears nightly on the television news.*

nightmare /ˈnaɪtmeə/ *noun*
1 a very frightening dream: *She had nightmares for weeks after seeing that film.*
2 something that is very unpleasant: *New York traffic is a nightmare.*

'night-time *noun*
the period of time between the time when it gets dark and the time when it gets light: *The pain is often worse at night-time.*

nil /nɪl/
zero; often used in scores of sports games: *They lost two nil to Italy.*

nine /naɪn/
the number 9

nineteen /ˌnaɪnˈtiːn/
the number 19

ninety /ˈnaɪnti/
the number 90

ninth¹ /naɪnθ/ *adjective, adverb*
counted as number nine in a series: *January the ninth* □ *He came ninth in the race.*

ninth² /naɪnθ/ *noun*
one of nine equal parts of something (¹⁄₉): *The area covers one ninth of the Earth's surface.*

no¹ /nəʊ/ *exclamation*
1 used for giving a negative response to a question: *'Are you having any problems?' — 'No, I'm OK.'* □ *'Would you like a coffee?' — 'No, thank you, I've had one already.'* □ *'Can I have another biscuit, mum?' — 'No; you've had enough.'*
2 used when you are shocked or disappointed about something: *Oh no! I've forgotten to do my maths homework.*

no² /nəʊ/ *adjective*
1 not any or not one person or thing: *I have no idea what you are talking about.* □ *In this game, there are no rules.*
2 used in notices to say that something is not allowed: *No parking.* □ *NO ENTRY.*

No. (**Nos**)
short for **number**

nobody /ˈnəʊbɒdi/ *pronoun*
not a single person: *For a long time nobody spoke.*

nod /nɒd/ *verb* (**nods, nodding, nodded**)
to move your head downwards and upwards to show that you are answering 'yes' to a question, or to show that you agree with something: *'Are you okay?' I asked. She nodded and smiled.* ● **nod** *noun* *She gave a nod and said, 'I see.'*

noise /nɔɪz/ *noun*
1 *uncountable* a loud or unpleasant sound: *Don't make so much noise!* □ *I'll never forget the noise from the crowd at the end of the game.*
2 a sound that someone or something makes: *Suddenly there was a noise like thunder.*

noisy /ˈnɔɪzi/ *adjective* (**noisier, noisiest**)
1 making a lot of loud or unpleasant noise: *It was a car with a particularly noisy engine.*
▸ **noisily** *adverb* *The students cheered noisily.*
2 full of a lot of loud or unpleasant noise: *The airport was crowded and noisy.*

nominate /ˈnɒmɪˌneɪt/ *verb* (**nominates, nominating, nominated**)
to formally suggest someone's name for a job, a position or a prize: *The Australian actor was nominated for an Oscar.*
▸ **nomination** /ˌnɒmɪˈneɪʃən/ *noun* *He'll probably get a nomination for best actor.*

none /nʌn/
not one or not any of a group of people or things: *None of us knew her.*

nonetheless /ˌnʌnðəˈles/ *adverb*
however; in spite of this *(formal)*: *There is*

still a long way to go. Nonetheless, some progress has been made.

nonfiction /nɒn'fɪkʃən/ *uncountable noun*
writing that is about real people and events rather than imaginary ones: *The school library contains both fiction and nonfiction.*

nonsense /'nɒnsəns/ *uncountable noun*
something that is not true or that is silly: *Most doctors say that this idea is complete nonsense.* □ *Peter said I was talking nonsense.*

non-stop /,nɒn'stɒp/ *adjective, adverb*
continuing without stopping: *A non-stop flight from London takes you straight to Antigua.* □ *We drove non-stop from New York to Miami.*

noodles /'nu:dəlz/ *plural noun*
long, thin strips of pasta (= a type of food made from eggs, flour and water) used especially in Chinese and Italian cooking

noodles

noon /nu:n/
uncountable noun
twelve o'clock in the middle of the day: *The meeting started at noon.*

'no one *pronoun*
not a single person, or not a single member of a particular group or set: *We asked everyone in the room, but no one wanted to help.*

nor /nɔ:/ *conjunction*
used after 'neither' to introduce the second of two negative things: *Neither his friends nor his family knew how old he was.*

the norm /ðə 'nɔ:m/ *noun*
the usual, expected situation: *Families of six or seven are the norm here.*

normal /'nɔ:məl/ *adjective*
usual and ordinary: *Her height and weight are normal for her age.*

normally /'nɔ:məli/ *adverb*
1 used for saying what usually happens: *Normally the bill is less than £30 a month.* □ *I normally get up at 7 a.m. for work.*
2 in the usual or ordinary way: *She's getting better and beginning to eat normally again.*

north /nɔ:θ/ also **North** *uncountable noun*
the direction that is on your left when you

are looking at the sun in the morning: *In the north, snow and ice cover the ground.* □ *He lives in the north of Canada.* ●**north** *adjective, adverb* North America □ *A cold north wind was blowing.* □ *Anita drove north up the M1 motorway.*
▶ **northern** /'nɔ:ðən/ *adjective* Northern Ireland

north-east *uncountable noun*
the direction that is between north and east: *They live in Jerusalem, more than 250 miles to the north-east.* ●**north-east** *adjective* northeast Louisiana
▶ **north-eastern** *adjective* Ian comes from northeastern Canada.

northerly /'nɔ:ðəli/ *adjective*
1 moving to the north or towards the north: *The storm is moving in a northerly direction.*
2 coming from the north: *a cold northerly wind*

north-west /,nɔ:θ'west/ *uncountable noun*
the direction that is between north and west: *My home town is in the north-west.*
●**north-west** *adjective* I live in north-west London.
▶ **north-western** /,nɔ:θ'westən/ *adjective* We visited a resort in north-western Australia.

nose /nəʊz/ *noun*
the part of your face above your mouth, that you use for smelling and breathing: *She wiped her nose with a tissue.*
→ Look at picture on P1

nostril /'nɒstrɪl/ *noun*
one of the two holes at the end of your nose: *Keeping your mouth closed, breathe in through your nostrils.*

not /nɒt/ *adverb*

LANGUAGE HELP
Use the short form **n't** when you are speaking English. For example, 'didn't' is short for 'did not'.

used for forming negative sentences: *Their plan was not working.*
not at all used as a strong way of saying 'No' or of agreeing that the answer to a question is 'No': *'Sorry, am I bothering you?'* — *'No. Not at all.'*

note[1] /nəʊt/ *noun*
1 a short letter: *Steven wrote her a note and*

left it on the table where she would find it.

2 something that you write down to remind yourself of something: *She didn't take notes on the lecture.*

3 a short piece of extra information in a book or an article: *See Note 16 on p.223.*

4 a piece of paper money: *He paid the taxi driver with a £20 note.*

5 one particular sound, or a symbol that represents this sound: *She has a deep voice and can't sing high notes.*

note² /nəʊt/ *verb* (**notes, noting, noted**)
(*also* **note something down**)
to write something down: *The police officer noted the number.* ▫ *She noted down his phone number.*

notebook /'nəʊtbʊk/ *noun*
1 a small book for writing notes in: *He took a notebook and pen from his pocket.*
2 a small personal computer that you can carry with you: *She watched the DVD on her notebook.*

notepaper /'nəʊtpeɪpə/ *noun*
paper that you use for writing letters on

nothing /'nʌθɪŋ/ *pronoun*
not a single thing, or not a single part of something: *There is nothing wrong with the car.* ▫ *There was nothing in the fridge except some butter.*

for nothing
1 without a successful result: *I've done all this work for nothing!*
2 for no money; free: *I'm giving all my CDs away for nothing.*

nothing like not at all like: *You're nothing like your brother.*

notice¹ /'nəʊtɪs/ *verb* (**notices, noticing, noticed**)
to become aware of someone or something: *Did you notice anything unusual about him?* ▫ *She noticed he was acting strangely.*

notice² /'nəʊtɪs/ *noun*
1 a piece of writing in a place where everyone can read it: *The notice said 'Please close the door.'*
2 *uncountable* a warning in advance that something is going to happen: *They moved her to a different office without notice.* ▫ *You must give 30 days' notice if you want to cancel the contract.*

take no notice/not take any notice
to pay no attention to someone or

something: *I tried to warn them, but they didn't take any notice.*

noticeable /'nəʊtɪsəbəl/ *adjective*
easy to see, hear or recognize: *The improvement in the quality of the food here is noticeable.*

noticeboard /'nəʊtɪsˌbɔːd/ *noun*
a board on a wall for notices giving information: *Her telephone number was pinned to the noticeboard.*

notify /'nəʊtɪfaɪ/ *verb* (**notifies, notifying, notified**)
to officially tell someone about something (*formal*): *We have notified the police.*

nought /nɔːt/
the number 0

noun /naʊn/ *noun*
a word such as 'car', 'love' or 'Anne' that is used for talking about a person or a thing

nourish /'nʌrɪʃ/ *verb* (**nourishes, nourishing, nourished**)
to give a person, an animal or a plant the food that they need to live, grow and be healthy: *The food you eat nourishes both you and your baby.*
▸ **nourishing** *adjective* nourishing home-cooked food
▸ **nourishment** *uncountable noun* These drinks will provide sick children with the nourishment they need to recover.

novel¹ /'nɒvəl/ *noun*
a long written story about imaginary people and events: *He's reading a novel by Herman Hesse.*

novel² /'nɒvəl/ *adjective*
new or different from anything else: *Here's a novel way to entertain a group of friends.*

novelist /'nɒvəlɪst/ *noun*
a person who writes novels (= long written stories about imaginary people and events): *Archer was a best-selling novelist.*

novelty /'nɒvəlti/ *noun* (**novelties**)
something that is new and interesting: *Tourists are still a novelty on the island.*

November /nəʊ'vembə/ *noun*
the eleventh month of the year: *He came to New York in November 1939.*

now¹ /naʊ/ *adverb*
used for talking about the present time:

I must go now. □ *She should know that by now.*

● **now** *pronoun Now is your chance to talk to him.*

now and then sometimes but not very often or regularly: *Now and then they heard the sound of traffic outside.* □ *My daughter comes home to visit every now and again.*

now² /naʊ/ *conjunction*

used for showing that something has happened, and as a result something else will happen: *Now that our children are older, I am returning to full-time work.*

nowadays /'naʊəˌdeɪz/ *adverb*

now generally, and not in the past: *Nowadays almost all children spend some time playing electronic and computer games.*

nowhere /'nəʊweə/ *adverb*

not in any place, or not to any place: *I have nowhere else to go.*

nuclear /'nju:klɪə/ *adjective*

1 relating to the energy that is released when the central parts (= nuclei) of atoms are split or combined: *We're building a nuclear power station.* □ *They don't have any nuclear weapons.*

2 used for describing the central part of an atom or cell (= nucleus): *He is studying nuclear physics.*

nucleus /'nju:klɪəs/ *noun* (**nuclei** /'nju:klɪˌaɪ/)

the central part of an atom or a cell

nude¹ /nju:d/ *adjective*

not wearing any clothes: *She came into the room, almost completely nude.*

nude² /nju:d/ *noun*

a painting or a piece of art that shows someone who is not wearing any clothes

nudge /nʌdʒ/ *verb* (**nudges, nudging, nudged**)

to push someone gently, usually with your elbow: *I nudged Stan and pointed again.*

● **nudge** *noun She gave him a nudge.*

nuisance /'nju:səns/ *noun*

someone or something that annoys you: *He can be a bit of a nuisance sometimes.*

numb /nʌm/ *adjective* (**number, numbest**)

unable to feel anything: *It was so cold that his fingers were numb.*

number¹ /'nʌmbə/ *noun*

1 a word such as 'two', 'nine' or 'twelve' or a symbol such as 1, 3 or 47 that is used in counting: *I don't know my room number.*

□ *What's your phone number?*

2 used with words such as 'large' or 'small' to say approximately how many things or people there are: *I received a large number of emails on the subject.*

number² /'nʌmbə/ *verb* (**numbers, numbering, numbered**)

to mark something with a number, usually starting at 1: *He cut the paper up into tiny squares, and he numbered each one.*

'number plate *noun*

a metal sign on the back and front of a vehicle, with numbers and letters on it: *a car with foreign number plates*

numeral /'nju:mərəl/ *noun*

a written symbol that represents a number: *The Roman numeral for 7 is VII.*

numerous /'nju:mərəs/ *adjective*

many: *He made numerous attempts to lose weight.*

nun /nʌn/ *noun*

a member of a group of religious women who often live together in a special building: *When I was seventeen, I decided to become a nun.*

nurse /nɜ:s/ *noun*

a person whose job is to care for people who are ill or injured: *She thanked the nurses who cared for her.* ● **nurse** *verb* (**nurses, nursing, nursed**) *My mother has nursed him for the last ten years.*

→ Look at picture on P7

nursery /'nɜ:səri/ *noun* (**nurseries**)

1 a place where small children and babies are cared for while their parents are at work: *My daughter goes to nursery in the mornings.*

2 a room in a family home in which the young children of the family sleep or play: *We painted bright pictures on the walls in the children's nursery.*

3 a place where people grow and sell plants: *Buy your plants at the local nursery.*

'nursery rhyme *noun*

a poem or a song for young children

'nursing home *noun*

a residence for old or ill people: *He died in a nursing home in Florida at the age of 87.*

nut /nʌt/ *noun*

1 a dry fruit with a hard shell: *Nuts and seeds are very good for you.*

2 a thick metal ring that you put onto

n

nuts

brazil nut

almond

peanut

walnut

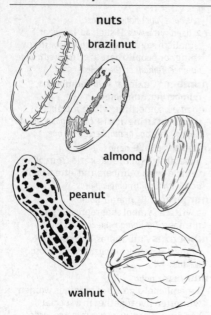

a bolt (= a long piece of metal), that is used for holding heavy things together: *If you want to repair the wheels, you must remove the four nuts.*

nutrient /ˈnjuːtriənt/ *noun*
a substance that helps plants and animals to grow and stay healthy: *The juice contains vitamins, minerals and other essential nutrients.*

nutritious /njuːˈtrɪʃəs/ *adjective*
containing things that help your body to be healthy: *It is important to eat nutritious foods.*

nylon /ˈnaɪlɒn/ *uncountable noun*
a strong, artificial substance that is used for making cloth and plastic: *I packed a sleeping bag, a pocket knife and some strong nylon rope.*

Oo

oak /əʊk/ *noun*
a type of large tree ● oak *uncountable noun*
He sat down at the oak table.

oar /ɔː/ *noun*
a long pole with one flat end that you use
for rowing a boat

oasis /əʊˈeɪsɪs/ *noun* (**oases** /əʊˈeɪsiːz/)
a small area in a desert where you find
water and plants

oasis

oatmeal /ˈəʊtmiːl/ *uncountable noun*
a hot, thick food that people eat for
breakfast. It is made from oats cooked in
water or milk.

oats /əʊts/ *plural noun*
a type of grain that is used in foods

obedient /əʊˈbiːdiənt/ *adjective*
doing what you are told to do: *As a child,
Charlotte was an obedient daughter.*
▶ **obedience** /əʊˈbiːdiəns/ *uncountable
noun* *He expected complete obedience from
his sons.*
▶ **obediently** *adverb* *The dog sat beside him
obediently.*

obese /əʊˈbiːs/ *adjective*
very fat, in a way that is not healthy:
*Obese people often have more health problems
than thinner people.*

obey /əʊˈbeɪ/ *verb* (**obeys, obeying,
obeyed**)
to do what you are told to do: *Most people
obey the law.*

object ¹ /ˈɒbdʒɪkt/ *noun*
1 a thing that has a shape, and that is not
alive: *I have to wear glasses because I can't see
distant objects clearly.* □ *We could hear someone
throwing small, hard objects on to the roof.*
2 the purpose of what someone is doing:
The object of the event is to raise money.
3 the person or thing that is affected by
the action of a verb

object ² /əbˈdʒekt/ *verb* (**objects,
objecting, objected**)
to say that you do not agree with
something, or that you do not like it: *A lot
of people objected to the book.*

objection /əbˈdʒekʃən/ *noun*
a reason for not liking or agreeing with
something: *I don't have any objection to people
making money.*

objective /əbˈdʒektɪv/ *noun*
the thing that you are trying to achieve:
Our main objective was to find the child.

obligation /ˌɒblɪˈɡeɪʃən/ *noun*
something that you should do: *The judge
has an obligation to find out the truth.*

obligatory /əˈblɪɡətri/ *adjective*
something that you must do because of
a rule or a law: *These medical tests are not
obligatory.*

oblige /əˈblaɪdʒ/ *verb* (**obliges, obliging,
obliged**)
be obliged to do something to have to
do something because a situation or a law
makes it necessary for you to do it: *My
family needed the money so I was obliged to work.*

oblong /ˈɒblɒŋ/
a shape that has two long sides and two
short sides: *a pattern of oblongs* □ *'What do
you call this shape?' — 'It's an oblong.'* ● **oblong**
adjective *Ten people sat around a large oblong
table.*

oboe /ˈəʊbəʊ/ *noun*
a musical instrument that you blow. It is
a long black wooden tube with keys on it

o

that you press, and a double reed (= small flat part that moves and makes a sound when you blow).

observe /əb'zɜːv/ *verb* (**observes, observing, observed**)
to watch people or things carefully in order to learn something about them: *Olson observed the behaviour of babies and their parents.*

obsession /əb'seʃən/ *noun*
a person or thing that someone spends too much time thinking about: *She tried to forget her obsession with Christopher.*

obstacle /'ɒbstəkəl/ *noun*
something that makes it difficult for you to do what you want to do: *We had to overcome two major obstacles.* □ *The main obstacle to progress is a lack of money.*

obstinate /'ɒbstɪnət/ *adjective*
determined to do what you want to do: *When Rebecca says 'no', nothing can make her change her mind, and she can be very obstinate.*

obstruct /əb'strʌkt/ *verb* (**obstructs, obstructing, obstructed**)
to stop someone from passing: *A group of cars obstructed the road.*

obstruction /əb'strʌkʃən/ *noun*
something that blocks a road or a path: *The cars outside his house were causing an obstruction.*

obtain /əb'teɪn/ *verb* (**obtains, obtaining, obtained**)
to get something (*formal*): *Evans tried to obtain a false passport.*

obvious /'ɒbviəs/ *adjective*
easy to see or understand: *It's obvious that he's worried about us.*

obviously /'ɒbviəsli/ *adverb*
used for saying that something is easily noticed, seen or recognized: *He obviously likes you very much.*

occasion /ə'keɪʒən/ *noun*
1 a time when something happens: *I gave her money on several occasions.* □ *I've asked for help on three separate occasions.*
2 an important event, ceremony or celebration: *The wedding was a happy occasion.*

occasional /ə'keɪʒənəl/ *adjective*
happening sometimes, but not often: *I get occasional headaches.*

▶ **occasionally** *adverb He misbehaves occasionally.*

occupant /'ɒkjʊpənt/ *noun*
the person who lives or works in a building or a room: *Most of the occupants left the building before the fire spread.*

occupation /ˌɒkjʊ'peɪʃən/ *noun*
1 someone's job: *Please write down your name and occupation.*
2 something that you spend time doing, either for fun or because it needs to be done: *Cooking was his favourite occupation.*
3 *uncountable* when a foreign army enters and controls a country: *She lived in France during Nazi Germany's occupation.*

occupied /'ɒkjʊ‚paɪd/ *adjective*
1 being used: *The chair was occupied by his wife.*
2 busy: *Don't get bored. Keep your brain occupied.*

occupy /'ɒkjʊpaɪ/ *verb* (**occupies, occupying, occupied**)
1 to live or work in a place: *The company occupies the top floor of the building.*
2 to move into a place and use force to control it: *U.S. forces occupy a part of the country.*
3 to be busy doing something or thinking about it: *Her career occupies all of her time.*

occur /ə'kɜː/ *verb* (**occurs, occurring, occurred**)
to happen: *The car crash occurred at night.*
occur to someone to suddenly come into somebody's mind: *Suddenly it occurred to her that the door might be open.*

occurrence /ə'kʌrəns/ *noun*
something that happens (*formal*): *Complaints against the company were an everyday occurrence.*

ocean /'əʊʃən/ *noun*
one of the five very large areas of salt water on the Earth's surface: *the Pacific Ocean*

o'clock /ə'klɒk/ *adverb*
used after numbers from one to twelve to say what time it is: *I went to bed at ten o'clock last night.*

octave /'ɒktɪv/ *noun*
a series of eight notes in music, or the difference between the first and last notes in the series

October /ɒkˈtəʊbə/ *noun*
the tenth month of the year: *We went away in early October.* □ *They left on October 2.*

octopus /ˈɒktəpəs/
noun
(**octopuses**)
a soft sea
animal
with eight
long arms

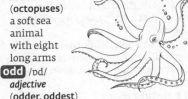
octopus

odd /ɒd/
adjective
(**odder, oddest**)
1 strange or
unusual: *His behaviour was odd.*
▸ **oddly** *adverb* *He dresses rather oddly.*
2 used for describing numbers such as 3 and 17, that cannot be divided exactly by the number two
3 not belonging to the same set or pair: *I'm wearing odd socks.*

odds /ɒdz/ *plural noun*
how likely it is that something will happen: *What are the odds of finding a parking space right outside the door?*

odour /ˈəʊdə/ *noun*
a smell: *A bad egg will have an unpleasant odour when you break open the shell.*

of /əv, STRONG ɒv/ *preposition*
1 used for saying what someone or something is connected with: *Police searched the homes of the criminals.* □ *the mayor of Los Angeles*
2 used for saying what something relates to: *He was trying to hide his feelings of anger.*
3 used for talking about someone or something else who is involved in an action: *He was dreaming of her.*
4 used for showing that someone or something is part of a larger group: *She is the youngest child of three.*
5 used for talking about amounts or contents: *The boy was drinking a glass of milk.*
6 used for saying what caused a person's or an animal's death: *He died of a heart attack.*
7 used for describing someone's behaviour: *It's very kind of you to help.* □ *It was rude of him to interrupt you.*

of course *adverb*
1 used for suggesting that something is not surprising: *Of course there were lots of interesting things to see.*

2 used as a polite way of giving permission: *'Can I ask you something?' — 'Yes, of course.'*

off¹ /ɒf/ *preposition*
1 used for saying that something is no longer on another thing: *He took his feet off the desk.* ● **off** *adverb* *I broke off a piece of chocolate and ate it.*
2 out of a bus, a train or a plane: *Don't get off a moving train!* ● **off** *adverb* *At the next station, the man got off.*
3 away from a place: *The police told visitors to keep off the beach.*

off² /ɒf/ *adverb*
1 away: *He was just about to drive off.*
2 away from work or school: *She took the day off.*
3 away in time: *An agreement is still a long way off.*
4 not being used: *Her bedroom light was off.*

offence /əˈfens/ *noun*
1 a crime that breaks a law: *There is a fine of $1,000 for a first offence.*
2 *uncountable* when someone is upset by another person's behaviour: *He didn't mean to cause offence.*
take offence to be upset by something that someone says or does: *Many people took offence at his sexist jokes.*

offend /əˈfend/ *verb* (**offends, offending, offended**)
to say or do something that upsets someone: *I'm sorry if I offended you.*

offensive /əˈfensɪv/ *adjective*
rude or insulting; upsetting people: *an offensive remark*

offer¹ /ˈɒfə/ *verb* (**offers, offering, offered**)
1 to ask someone if they would like to have something: *He offered his seat to the young woman.* □ *She offered him a cup of coffee.*
2 to say that you are willing to do something: *Peter offered to teach me to drive.*

offer² /ˈɒfə/ *noun*
something that someone says they will give you or do for you: *I hope you will accept my offer of help.*

office /ˈɒfɪs/ *noun*
1 a place where people work sitting at a desk: *I work in an office with about 25 people.*
2 a department of an organization, especially the government: *the Foreign Office*
3 a small building or room where people

o

can go for information or tickets: *a tourist office*

4 *uncountable* an important job in a government: *The events marked the president's four years in office.*

officer /'ɒfɪsə/ *noun*

1 a person who is in charge of other people in the armed forces: *Her son is an officer in the army.*

2 a member of the police force: *The officer saw no sign of a robbery.* □ *Officer Montoya was the first on the scene.*

3 a person who has a responsible position in an organization: *She's the chief executive officer of the company.*

official¹ /ə'fɪʃəl/ *adjective*

1 approved by the government or by someone in power: *They destroyed all the official documents.*

▶ **officially** *adverb* *The results have not been officially announced.*

2 carried out by a person in power as part of their job: *The president is in Brazil for an official visit.*

official² /ə'fɪʃəl/ *noun*

a person who holds a position of power in an organization: *Government officials said that they discussed the matter this morning.*

offline /ˌɒf'laɪn/ *adjective, adverb*

not connected to the Internet. Compare with **online**: *Test your website offline before you put it on the Web.* □ *Your computer is currently offline.*

often /'ɒfən/ *adverb*

happening many times or much of the time: *They often spend the weekend together.* □ *That doesn't happen very often.*

every so often happening sometimes, but not very often: *She visited her aunt in Scotland every so often.*

how often? used for asking questions about frequency: *How often do you brush your teeth?*

LANGUAGE HELP

If you want to talk about something that happens several times within a short period of time, you say, for example, *I phoned her several times yesterday.*

oh /əʊ/ *exclamation*

used for expressing a feeling such as surprise, pain, annoyance or happiness: *'Oh!' Kenny said. 'Has everyone gone?'*

oil¹ /ɔɪl/ *noun*

1 a smooth, thick liquid that is used for making machines work. Oil is found underground: *The company buys and sells 600,000 barrels of oil a day.*

2 a smooth, thick liquid made from plants, that is often used for cooking: *olive oil*

oil² /ɔɪl/ *verb* (**oils, oiling, oiled**)

to put oil onto or into something to make it work smoothly or to protect it: *He oiled the lock on the door.*

'oil ,painting *noun*

a picture that is painted using oil paints

oily /'ɔɪli/ *adjective* (**oilier, oiliest**)

looking, feeling or tasting like oil: *He wiped his hands on an oily rag.* □ *Paul thought the sauce was too oily.*

ointment /'ɔɪntmənt/ *noun*

a smooth, thick substance that you put on sore or damaged skin: *Ointments are available for the treatment of skin problems.*

okay /ˌəʊ'keɪ/ also **OK, O.K., ok** *adjective*

1 acceptable (*informal*): *Is it okay if I go by myself?*

2 safe and well (*informal*): *Check that the baby's okay.*

3 used for showing that you agree to something (*informal*): *'Just tell him I would like to talk to him.' — 'OK.'*

4 used for checking whether the person you are talking to understands what you have said and accepts it (*informal*): *We'll meet next week, OK?*

old /əʊld/ *adjective* (**older, oldest**)

1 having lived for many years; not young: *Mr Kaufmann was a small old man with a beard.*

2 used for talking or asking about the age of someone or something: *He is three months old.* □ *Her car is less than three years old.*

3 having existed for a long time: *We live in a beautiful old house.* □ *These books look very old.*

4 used for talking about something that used to be part of your life: *I still remember my old school.*

5 an old friend is someone who has been your friend for a long time: *I called my old friend John Horner.*

'old 'age *uncountable noun*

the part of your life when you are old: *They didn't have much money in their old age.*

ˌold-ˈfashioned *adjective*
no longer used, done or believed by most people: *The kitchen was old-fashioned and in bad condition.*

olive /ˈɒlɪv/ *noun*
a small green or black fruit with a bitter taste

ˈolive oil *uncountable noun*
a type of oil that is used in cooking

Olympic Games /əˌlɪmpɪk ˈɡeɪmz/ *noun*
an international sports competition that takes place every four years, each time in a different country

omelette /ˈɒmlət/ *also* **omelet** *noun*
a type of food made by beating eggs and cooking them in a frying pan: *She made a cheese omelette.*

OMG
short for 'oh my God' in an email or text message

omit /əˈmɪt/ *verb* (omits, omitting, omitted)
to not include something: *Omit the salt in this recipe.*

omnivore /ˈɒmnɪˌvɔː/ *noun*
an animal that eats both meat and plants. Compare with **carnivore** and **herbivore**.

on¹ /ɒn/ *preposition*
1 supported by or touching a surface: *He was sitting on the sofa.* □ *There was a large box on the table.*
2 attached to a surface: *We hung some paintings on the walls.* □ *You've got dirt on your face.*
3 into a bus, train or plane: *We got on the plane.*
4 travelling in a bus, train or plane: *I'm on the train at the moment.*
5 used for showing the instrument or equipment that is used to do something: *I played these songs on the piano.* □ *My dad called me on my mobile phone.*
6 used for showing the piece of equipment that is used to do something: *She spends most of the day on the computer.* □ *Let's look it up on the Internet.*
7 being broadcast: *What's on TV tonight?*
8 used for showing a day or a date: *This year's event will be on June 19th.* □ *We'll see you on Tuesday.*
9 used for saying what something is about: *He wrote a book on the history of Russian ballet.*

on² /ɒn/ *adverb*
1 used for showing that someone is wearing a piece of clothing: *He put his coat on.* □ *I can't go out. I don't have any shoes on.*
2 used for saying that someone is continuing to do something: *They walked on for a while.*
3 being used: *You left the light on.*

once¹ /wʌns/ *adverb*
1 happening one time only: *I met Miquela once, at a party.* □ *The baby hasn't once slept through the night.*
2 true at some time in the past, but no longer true: *Her parents once owned a shop.*
at once immediately: *I have to go at once.*
for once happening on this particular occasion only: *For once, Dad is right.*

once² /wʌns/ *conjunction*
happening immediately after another thing has happened: *The decision was easy once he read the letter.*

one¹ /wʌn/ *pronoun*
1 used instead of the name of a person or a thing: *'Which dress do you prefer?' — 'I like the red one.'* □ *Cut up the large potatoes, but leave the small ones, please.*
2 people in general (*formal*): *One can get very tired on these long flights.*
one or two a few: *We made one or two changes.*

one² /wʌn/
the number 1: *They have one daughter.*

one³ /wʌn/ *adjective*
used for talking about a time in the past or in the future: *Would you like to go out one night?* □ *One day, she called me at my office.*

one's¹ /wʌnz/ *adjective*
used for showing that something belongs to or relates to people in general (*formal*): *It is natural to want to care for one's family and children.*

one's² /wʌnz/
a spoken form of 'one is' or 'one has': *No one's going to hurt you.* □ *This one's been broken too.*

oneself /wʌnˈself/ *pronoun*
used by speakers or writers to make statements about themselves and people in general (*formal*): *To think, one must have time to oneself.*
by oneself alone (*formal*): *Travelling by oneself can be an enjoyable experience.*

o

onesie /'wʌnzi/ *noun*
a piece of clothing consisting of a top and trousers joined together, that you wear to sleep or relax in

one-'way *adjective*
1 with traffic moving in one direction
2 from one place to another, but not back again: *a one-way ticket to New Zealand*

onion /'ʌnjən/ *noun*
a round vegetable with many layers. It has a strong, sharp smell and taste.
→ Look at picture on P2

online /ˌɒn'laɪn/ *adjective, adverb*
1 using the Internet to sell goods: *an online bookshop*
2 connected to the Internet. Compare with **offline**: *You can chat to other people who are online.* □ *I buy most of my clothes online.*

onlooker /'ɒnlʊkə/ *noun*
someone who watches an event but does not take part in it: *A group of onlookers stood and watched the fight.*

only¹ /'əʊnli/ *adjective, adverb*
1 and nobody or nothing else: *Only one person replied.* □ *We have only twelve students.*
2 one person or thing of a particular type: *She's the only girl in the class.*
3 used for describing a child who has no brothers or sisters: *I'm an only child, and I like it.*
4 used for saying how small or short something is: *Their house is only a few miles from here.*
only just used for saying that something happened a very short time ago: *She's only just arrived.*

only² /'əʊnli/ *conjunction*
but (*informal*): *It's like my house, only it's nicer.*

onto /'ɒntu:/ *preposition*
1 to a position on a surface: *The cat climbed onto her lap.*
2 into a bus, train or plane: *He got onto the plane.*

ooh /u:/ also **oo** *exclamation*
used for showing that you are surprised or excited, or when you think something is pleasant or unpleasant (*informal*): *Ooh, that hurts.*

oops /ʊps/ *exclamation*
used when a small mistake or accident has happened: *Oops! Sorry. Are you all right?*

ooze /u:z/ *verb* (**oozes, oozing, oozed**)
to flow out of something slowly and in

small amounts: *They drank the liquid that oozed from the fruit.*

open¹ /'əʊpən/ *verb* (**opens, opening, opened**)
1 to move something so that it is no longer covered or closed: *He opened the window.*
□ *After a few seconds, I opened my eyes.* ● **open** *adjective His eyes were open and he was smiling.*

open

He opened the window.

2 to remove part of a container so that you can take out what is inside: *Nicole opened the silver box on the table.*
3 to move the covers of a book so that you can see the pages inside: *He opened the book and started to read.*
4 to give a computer an instruction to show a file on the screen: *To open a file, go to the File menu.*
5 when a shop, office or public building opens, people can go into it: *The banks will open again on Monday morning.* ● **open** *adjective The shop is open Monday to Friday, 9 a.m. to 6 p.m.*

open² /'əʊpən/ *adjective*
1 honest about your thoughts and feelings: *He was always open with her.*
2 willing to accept suggestions or ideas: *We are always open to suggestions.*

'open-'air *adjective*
outside; not in a building: *an open-air concert*

opener /'əʊpənə/ *noun*
a tool that is used for opening cans or bottles: *a tin opener*

opening¹ /'əʊpənɪŋ/ *adjective*
used for describing the first one in a series: *The team lost the opening game.*

opening² /'əʊpənɪŋ/ *noun*
a hole or an empty space that things or

people can pass through: *He managed to get through a narrow opening in the fence.*

open-'minded *adjective*
willing to listen to other people's ideas: *He says that he is open-minded about tomorrow's talks.*

opera /'ɒpərə/ *noun*
a play with music in which all the words are sung: *an opera singer*
▶ **operatic** /ˌɒpə'rætɪk/ *adjective* He was famous for his operatic voice.

operate /'ɒpəˌreɪt/ *verb* (**operates, operating, operated**)
1 when an organization operates, it does the work it is supposed to: *The organization has been operating in the area for some time.*
2 to make a machine work: *Weston showed him how to operate the machine.*
3 to cut open a patient's body in order to remove or repair a part: *Surgeons operated on Max to remove a brain tumour.*

'operating ˌsystem *noun*
the main program of a computer that controls all the other programs: *Which operating system do you use?*

operation /ˌɒpə'reɪʃən/ *noun*
1 an organized activity that involves many people doing different things: *The rescue operation began on Friday.*
2 when a doctor cuts open a patient's body in order to remove, replace or repair a part: *Charles had an operation on his arm.*

operator /'ɒpəˌreɪtə/ *noun*
1 a person who connects telephone calls in a place such as an office or a hotel: *He called the operator.*
2 a person whose job is to operate or control a machine: *a crane operator*
3 a person or a company that operates a business: *Several tour operators offer day trips to lakes and castles around the city.*

opinion /ə'pɪnjən/ *noun*
1 what someone thinks about something: *I didn't ask for your opinion.*
2 what you think about someone's character or ability: *I don't have a very high opinion of Thomas.*

opponent /ə'pəʊnənt/ *noun*
the person who is against you in a sports competition: *She'll face six opponents in today's race.*

opportunity /ˌɒpə'tju:nɪti/ *noun* (**opportunities**)
a situation in which it is possible for you to do something that you want to do: *I had an opportunity to go to New York and study.*

oppose /ə'pəʊz/ *verb* (**opposes, opposing, opposed**)
to disagree with what someone wants to do, and to try to stop them from doing it: *He said that he would oppose any tax increase.*

opposed /ə'pəʊzd/ *adjective*
disagreeing with something: *I am opposed to any form of terrorism.*

opposite¹ /'ɒpəzɪt/ *preposition*
across from: *Jennie sat opposite Sam at breakfast.* ●**opposite** *adverb* He looked at the buildings opposite.

opposite² /'ɒpəzɪt/ *adjective*
used for describing similar things that are completely different in a particular way: *We watched the cars driving in the opposite direction.* ●**opposite** *noun* Whatever he says, he's probably thinking the opposite.

opposition /ˌɒpə'zɪʃən/ *uncountable noun*
strong disagreement: *There is strong opposition to the plan from local people.*

optician /ɒp'tɪʃən/ *noun*
a person whose job is to make and sell glasses

optimism /'ɒptɪˌmɪzəm/ *uncountable noun*
a feeling of hope about the success of something: *There is optimism about the possibility of peace.*
▶ **optimist** *noun* He is an optimist about the country's future.

optimistic /ˌɒptɪ'mɪstɪk/ *adjective*
hopeful about the success of something: *She is optimistic that they can reach an agreement.*

option /'ɒpʃən/ *noun*
a choice between two or more things: *We will consider all options before making a decision.*

optional /'ɒpʃənəl/ *adjective*
if something is optional, you can choose whether or not you do it or have it: *All students have to study maths, but history and geography are optional.*

or /ə, STRONG ɔ:/ *conjunction*
1 used for showing choices or possibilities: *'Do you want tea or coffee?' John asked.* □ *Either you change your behaviour, or you will have to leave.*

o

2 used between two numbers to show that you are giving an approximate amount: *You should only drink one or two cups of coffee a day.*

3 used for introducing a warning that something bad could happen: *She has to have the operation, or she will die.*

oral /'ɔːrəl/ *adjective*

1 spoken rather than written: *The English test includes written and oral examinations.*

2 relating to your mouth: *good oral hygiene*

orange¹ /'ɒrɪndʒ/ *adjective*
of a colour between red and yellow

orange² /'ɒrɪndʒ/ *noun*

1 a round, juicy fruit with a thick, orange-coloured skin
→ Look at picture on P2

2 a colour between red and yellow: *His supporters were dressed in orange.*

orbit /'ɔːbɪt/ *noun*
the curved path of an object that goes around a planet, a moon or the sun: *The Earth has an orbit that changes.* ● **orbit** *verb* (**orbits, orbiting, orbited**) *The moon orbits the Earth.*

orbit

orchard /'ɔːtʃəd/ *noun*
an area of land where fruit trees grow

orchestra /'ɔːkɪstrə/ *noun*
a large group of musicians who play different instruments together: *The orchestra began to play.*

ordeal /ɔːˈdiːl/ *noun*
a difficult and very unpleasant experience: *The attack was a terrifying ordeal for both victims.*

order¹ /'ɔːdə/ *verb* (**orders, ordering, ordered**)

1 to tell someone to do something: *Williams ordered him to leave.*

2 to ask for something to be sent to you from a company: *They ordered a new washing machine on the Internet.*

3 to ask for food and drinks to be brought

to you in a restaurant: *The waitress asked, 'Are you ready to order?'*

order² /'ɔːdə/ *noun*

1 the words that someone says when they tell you to do something: *The commander gave his men orders to move out of the camp.*

2 the thing that someone has asked for: *He's just placed an order for a new car.* □ *The waiter returned with their order.*

3 *uncountable* an arrangement where one thing is first, another thing is second, another thing is third, and so on: *The books are all arranged in alphabetical order.*

4 *uncountable* the situation that exists when everything is in the correct place, or happens at the correct time: *Everything on the desk is in order.*

5 *uncountable* the situation that exists when people obey the law and do not fight: *The army went to the islands to restore order.*

in order to so that you can achieve something: *The operation was necessary in order to save the baby's life.*

in working order working properly: *His old car is still in perfect working order.*

out of order not working properly: *Their phone's out of order.*

ordinary /'ɔːdɪnri/ *adjective*
normal and not special or different: *These are just ordinary people living ordinary lives.*

out of the ordinary unusual or different: *The police asked people to report anything out of the ordinary.*

organ /'ɔːgən/ *noun*

1 a part of your body that has a particular purpose: *The brain is the most powerful organ in the body.*

2 a large musical instrument that is like a piano: *a church organ*

organic /ɔːˈgænɪk/ *adjective*
grown without using chemicals: *We buy only organic fruit and vegetables.*

organism /'ɔːgə,nɪzəm/ *noun*
a living thing: *We study very small organisms such as bacteria.*

organization /,ɔːgənaɪˈzeɪʃən/ *noun*

1 an official group of people such as a business or a club: *She worked for the same organization for six years.*

2 *uncountable* when you plan or arrange an activity: *I helped in the organization of the concert.*

organize /'ɔːgə,naɪz/ *verb* (**organizes, organizing, organized**)
1 to plan or arrange something: *We decided to organize a concert.*
▶ **organizer** *noun* *Organizers are hoping to raise £65,000 from the concert.*
2 to plan or arrange things in a tidy and effective way: *He began to organize his papers.*

organized /'ɔːgə,naɪzd/ *adjective*
planning your work and activities carefully: *Managers need to be very organized.*

oriental /,ɔːri'entəl/ *adjective*
used for talking about things that come from places in eastern Asia. Do not use **oriental** for talking about people: *He was an expert in oriental art.*

origin /'ɒrɪdʒɪn/ *noun*
the way something started: *Scientists study the origin of life on Earth.* □ *Americans of Hispanic origin*

original¹ /ə'rɪdʒɪnəl/ *adjective*
1 used for talking about something that existed at the beginning: *The original plan was to go by bus.*
▶ **originally** *adverb* *Wright lives in London but he is originally from Melbourne.*
2 showing that the person who did something has imagination and new ideas: *He is the most original painter of the past 100 years.*

original² /ə'rɪdʒɪnəl/ *noun*
something that is not a copy: *Make a copy of the document and send the original to your employer.*

ornament /'ɔːnəmənt/ *noun*
an attractive object that you use to decorate your home: *There were a few ornaments on the shelf.*

orphan /'ɔːfən/ *noun*
a child whose parents are dead

orphanage /'ɔːfənɪdʒ/ *noun*
a place where orphans live

OS /,əʊ 'es/ *noun* (**OS's**)
short for **operating system**

ostrich /'ɒstrɪtʃ/ *noun* (**ostriches**)
a very large bird that cannot fly

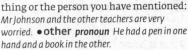
ostrich

other /'ʌðə/ *adjective*
1 used for talking about more things or people that are like the

thing or the person you have mentioned: *Mr Johnson and the other teachers are very worried.* ● **other** *pronoun* *He had a pen in one hand and a book in the other.*
2 used for talking about a thing or a person that is different from the thing or the person you have mentioned: *He will have to accept it; there is no other way.*
3 used for talking about the second of two things or people: *William was at the other end of the room.*

the other day used for talking about a day in the recent past: *I called her the other day.*

otherwise /'ʌðə,waɪz/ *adverb*
1 used for saying what the result would be if the situation was different: *I really enjoy this job, otherwise I would not be here.*
2 used when you mention a different condition or way: *He was very tired but otherwise happy.* □ *Take one pill three times a day, unless you are told otherwise by a doctor.*

ouch /aʊtʃ/ *exclamation*
used when you suddenly feel pain: *The stones cut her feet. 'Ouch, ouch!' she cried.*

ought /ɔːt/
1 used for saying that something is the right thing to do: *You ought to read this book.*
2 used for saying that you think something will be true or will happen: *'This party ought to be fun,' he told Alex.*

oughtn't /'ɔːtənt/
short for **'ought not'**

ounce /aʊns/ *noun*
a unit for measuring weight. There are sixteen ounces in a pound and one ounce is equal to 28.35 grams.

our /aʊə/ *adjective*
belonging or relating both to you and to one or more other people: *We're expecting our first baby.*

ours /aʊəz/ *pronoun*
used when you are talking about something that belongs to you and one or more other people: *That car is ours.*

ourselves /aʊə'selvz/ *pronoun*
1 used when you are talking about yourself and one or more other people: *We sat by the fire to keep ourselves warm.*
2 used for showing that you and one or more other people did something, rather than anyone else: *We built the house ourselves.*

o

out /aʊt/ *adjective, adverb*

1 away from a place: *He took out his notebook.*

2 not at home: *I called you yesterday, but you were out.*

3 no longer shining: *All the lights were out in the house.*

4 no longer burning: *Please don't let the fire go out.*

5 published and for sale: *Their new CD is out now.* ● **out** *adverb The book came out in 2006.*

6 outside the area of play in games such as tennis and basketball. Compare with **in**: *The referee agreed that the ball was out.*

7 If you go out of a place, you leave it: *She ran out of the house.*

8 If you take something out of a container, you remove it: *I took the key out of my handbag.*

out of used for talking about a smaller group that is part of a larger group: *Three out of four people say there's too much violence on TV.*

out of something

1 used for showing that something has all been used: *We're out of milk. Can you get some at the supermarket?*

2 used for saying what something has been produced from: *The house is made out of wood.*

outbreak /'aʊtbreɪk/ *noun*

a sudden start of something bad: *This is the worst ever outbreak of the disease.*

outcome /'aʊtkʌm/ *noun*

the situation that exists at the end of an activity: *It's too early to know the outcome of the election.*

outdoor /ˌaʊt'dɔː/ *adjective*

happening outside and not in a building: *If you enjoy outdoor activities, you should try rock climbing.*

outdoors /ˌaʊt'dɔːz/ *adverb*

happening outside rather than in a building: *It was warm enough to play outdoors all afternoon.*

outer /'aʊtə/ *adjective*

covering the other parts of something: *This material forms the hard outer surface of the tooth.*

outfit /'aʊtfɪt/ *noun*

a set of clothes: *I need a new outfit for the wedding.*

outing /'aʊtɪŋ/ *noun*

a short trip, usually with a group of people: *We went on an outing to the local cinema.*

outline¹ /'aʊtlaɪn/ *noun*

outline

1 a general explanation or description of something: *We are sending you an outline of the plan.*

2 the general shape of an object or a person: *He could only see the dark outline of the man.*

outline² /'aʊtlaɪn/ *verb* (**outlines, outlining, outlined**)

to give a general explanation or description of something: *The report outlined some possible changes to the rules.*

outlook /'aʊtlʊk/ *noun*

1 what will probably happen: *The economic outlook is not good.*

2 your general feeling about life: *He had a positive outlook on life.*

out of 'date also **out-of-date** *adjective*

old-fashioned and no longer useful: *The rules are out of date.* □ *They were using an out-of-date map.*

output /'aʊtpʊt/ *uncountable noun*

the amount that a person or a thing produces: *There has been a large fall in industrial output.*

outrage¹ /ˌaʊt'reɪdʒ/ *verb* (**outrages, outraging, outraged**)

to shock someone or make them very angry: *Many people were outraged by his comments.*

outrage² /'aʊtreɪdʒ/ *uncountable noun*

an intense feeling of anger and shock: *Several teachers wrote to the newspapers to express their outrage.*

outrageous /aʊt'reɪdʒəs/ *adjective*

shocking someone or making them very angry: *It was outrageous behaviour.*

outside¹ /ˌaʊt'saɪd/ *adverb*

not in a building, but very close to it: *She went outside to look for Sam.* ● **outside** *preposition She found him standing outside the classroom.*

outside² /ˌaʊt'saɪd/ *noun*

the part of something that surrounds or covers the rest of it: *The outside of the*

building was recently painted. ●**outside**
adjective The outside wall is painted white.

outskirts /'aʊtskɜ:ts/ *plural noun*
the parts of a town or a city that are
furthest away from its centre: *I live on the
outskirts of the city.*

outstanding /ˌaʊt'stændɪŋ/ *adjective*
much better than other people or things
of a similar type: *She is an outstanding
athlete.*

oval /'əʊvəl/ *adjective*
having a shape like an egg: *She had an oval
face with large, dark eyes.* ●**oval** *noun* Draw
an oval with two eyes, a nose and a mouth.

oven /'ʌvən/ *noun*
a piece of equipment for cooking that is
like a large metal box with a door
→ Look at picture on P4

over¹ /'əʊvə/ *preposition*
1 directly above or higher than another
thing: *There was a gold mirror over the fireplace.*
□ *I heard some planes flying over the house.*
2 covering part or all of something: *He lay
down and pulled the blanket over himself.* □ *Pour
the sauce over the mushrooms.*
3 across to the other side of something:
They jumped over the wall.
4 more than a particular amount: *The
house cost over £1 million.*

over² /'əʊvə/ *adjective, adverb*
1 used for talking about a short distance:
Come over here! □ *The café is just over there.*
2 in a different position so that the part
that was facing up is now facing down:
His car rolled over on an icy road.
3 completely finished: *The war is over.*
□ *I am glad it's all over.*

overcame /ˌəʊvə'keɪm/ → see **overcome**

overcast /'əʊvəˌkɑ:st/ *adjective*
completely covered with cloud: *He looked
up at the grey, overcast sky.*

overcome /ˌəʊvə'kʌm/ *verb* (**overcomes,
overcoming, overcame, overcome**)
1 to successfully deal with or control a
problem or a feeling: *Molly finally overcame
her fear of flying.*
2 if you are overcome by a feeling, you
feel it very strongly: *The night before the test
I was overcome by fear.*

overcrowded /ˌəʊvə'kraʊdɪd/ *adjective*
with too many people: *We sat on the
overcrowded beach.*

overdue /ˌəʊvə'dju:/ *adjective*
late or delayed: *Your tax payment is overdue.*
□ *Mr Giuliano said the changes were long
overdue.*

overflow /ˌəʊvə'fləʊ/ *verb* (**overflows,
overflowing, overflowed**)
1 to have liquid flowing over the edges:
The sink overflowed.
2 to flow over the edges: *During the heavy
rains, the river overflowed.*

overflow

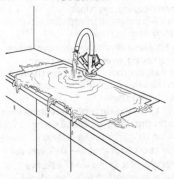

overhead *adjective, adverb*

PRONUNCIATION HELP
adjective /'əʊvəhed/, adverb /ˌəʊvə'hed/.

above you: *She turned on the overhead light.*
□ *Planes passed overhead.*

overhear /ˌəʊvə'hɪə/ *verb* (**overhears,
overhearing, overheard**)
to hear what someone says when they are
not talking to you: *I overheard two doctors
discussing me.*

overheat /ˌəʊvə'hi:t/ *verb* (**overheats,
overheating, overheated**)
to become too hot: *The car's engine was
overheating.*

overlap /ˌəʊvə'læp/ *verb* (**overlaps,
overlapping, overlapped**)
to cover a part of another thing: *The two
circles overlap.*

overlook /ˌəʊvə'lʊk/ *verb* (**overlooks,
overlooking, overlooked**)
1 to not notice something: *We cannot
overlook this important fact.*
2 if a building or window overlooks a
place, you can see the place clearly from
the building or window: *The hotel's rooms
overlook a beautiful garden.*

o

overnight /ˌəʊvəˈnaɪt/ *adjective, adverb*
happening through the whole night or at some point during the night: *He decided to take an overnight fishing trip.* □ *The decision was made overnight.*

overseas /ˌəʊvəˈsiːz/ *adjective, adverb*
used for describing things or people that are in or that come from foreign countries: *He enjoyed his overseas trip.* □ *He's now working overseas.*

oversleep /ˌəʊvəˈsliːp/ *verb* (**oversleeps, oversleeping, overslept**)
to sleep longer than you should: *I forgot to set my alarm and I overslept.*

overtake /ˌəʊvəˈteɪk/ *verb* (**overtakes, overtaking, overtook, overtaken**)
to pass another car or person that is going in the same direction: *You should never overtake on a bend.*

overtime /ˈəʊvətaɪm/ *uncountable noun*
extra time that you spend doing your job: *He worked overtime to finish the job.*

overtook /ˌəʊvəˈtʊk/ → see **overtake**

overweight /ˌəʊvəˈweɪt/ *adjective*
weighing more than is considered healthy or attractive

overwhelming /ˌəʊvəˈwelmɪŋ/ *adjective*
affecting you very strongly: *She had an overwhelming feeling of guilt.*

owe /əʊ/ *verb* (**owes, owing, owed**)
1 to have to pay money to someone: *The company owes money to more than 60 banks.* □ *Blake owed him £50.*
2 to want to do something for someone because you are grateful to them: *She thought Will owed her a favour.*

owl /aʊl/ *noun*
a bird with large eyes that is active at night

own ¹ /əʊn/ *adjective*
1 used for saying that something belongs to or is done by a particular person or thing: *I wanted to have my own business.* □ *They prefer to make their own decisions.*
● **own** *pronoun The man's face was a few inches from my own.*
2 used for saying that something is used by only one person or thing: *Jennifer wanted her own room.*

on your own
1 alone: *He lives on his own.*
2 without any help: *I work best on my own.*

own ² /əʊn/ *verb* (**owns, owning, owned**)
to have something that belongs to you: *His father owns a local computer shop.*

owner /ˈəʊnə/ *noun*
the person that something belongs to: *My brother is the owner of the shop.*

ownership /ˈəʊnəʃɪp/ *uncountable noun*
when you own something: *There has been an increase in home ownership.*

oxygen /ˈɒksɪdʒən/ *uncountable noun*
a gas in the air that is needed by all plants and animals

oyster /ˈɔɪstə/ *noun*
a small flat sea animal that has a hard shell and is eaten as food. Oysters can produce pearls (= small round white objects used for making jewellery).

oz.
short for **ounce**

the ozone layer /ði ˈəʊzəʊn ˌleɪə/ *noun*
the area high above the Earth's surface that protects living things from the harmful effects of the sun: *Scientists discovered another hole in the ozone layer last month.*

Pp

pace¹ /peɪs/ *noun*

1 the speed at which something happens: *Since her illness, she is taking life at a slower pace.*

2 the distance that you move when you take one step: *Peter walked a few paces behind me.*

pace² /peɪs/ *verb* (paces, pacing, paced)
to keep walking around in a small area because you are worried: *As they waited, Kravis paced the room nervously.*

pack¹ /pæk/ *verb* (packs, packing, packed)
to put clothes and other things into a bag, because you are going away: *When I was 17, I packed my bags and left home.* □ *I began to pack for the trip.*

pack

pack² /pæk/ *noun*

1 a collection of things that are kept together: *The club will send you an information pack.*

2 a group of wild dogs or similar animals

3 a set of 52 playing cards: *a pack of playing cards*

package /'pækɪdʒ/ *noun*
something that is wrapped in paper, or in a box or an envelope: *I tore open the package.*

packaging /'pækɪdʒɪŋ/ *uncountable noun*
the paper or plastic that something is in when you buy it: *Avoid buying food with plastic packaging.*

packed /pækt/ *adjective*
very full of people: *The shop was packed.*

packed 'lunch *noun* (packed lunches)
food that you take to work or school, and eat as your lunch

packet /'pækɪt/ *noun*
a small box, bag or envelope in which an amount of something is sold: *He bought a packet of biscuits.*

pad /pæd/ *noun*

1 a thick, flat piece of soft material, used for cleaning things or for protection: *Please wear a helmet and elbow pads.* □ *Have you tried using an oven-cleaning pad?*

2 a number of pieces of paper attached together along one side: *Have a pad ready and write down the information.*

padded /'pædɪd/ *adjective*
containing soft material that makes something softer or warmer, or that protects it: *a padded jacket* □ *a padded envelope*

padding /'pædɪŋ/ *uncountable noun*
soft material in something that makes it softer or warmer, or that protects it: *These headphones have foam rubber padding.* □ *Players must wear padding to protect them from injury.*

paddle¹ /'pædəl/ *noun*
a short pole with a wide flat part at the end, that you use to move a small boat through water

paddle² /'pædəl/ *verb* (paddles, paddling, paddled)

1 to walk or stand in shallow water, for example at the edge of the sea, for pleasure: *There is a lovely little stream that you can paddle in.* ● **paddle** *noun Let's go for a paddle in the sea.*

2 to move a small boat through water using a paddle: *He paddled a canoe across the Congo river.*

padlock /'pædlɒk/ *noun*
a metal lock that is used for fastening two things together: *They put a padlock on the door of his house.*

P

page /peɪdʒ/ *noun*

one side of a piece of paper in a book, a magazine or a newspaper: *Turn to page 4.* □ *The story was on the front page of the Times.*

paid /peɪd/ → see **pay**

pain /peɪn/ *noun*

1 the feeling that you have in a part of your body, because of illness or an injury: *I felt a sharp pain in my lower back.* □ *My legs are sore and I'm in pain all the time.*

2 *uncountable* the sadness that you feel when something upsets you: *I could see that my words caused him great pain.*

a pain/a pain in the neck very annoying (*informal*): *I like her work, but she can be a pain in the neck.*

painful /ˈpeɪnfʊl/ *adjective*

1 hurting: *Her toe was swollen and painful.*
▶ **painfully** *adverb* *Matt banged his head painfully as he climbed out of the window.*

2 making you feel sad and upset: *His unkind remarks brought back painful memories.*

painkiller /ˈpeɪnkɪlə/ *noun*

a drug that reduces or stops physical pain

painless /ˈpeɪnləs/ *adjective*

causing no physical pain: *The operation is a quick, painless procedure.*

paint¹ /peɪnt/ *uncountable noun*

a coloured liquid that you put onto a surface with a brush: *We'll need about three cans of red paint.*

paint² /peɪnt/ *verb* (**paints, painting, painted**)

1 to cover a wall or an object with paint: *They started to paint the walls.*

paint

They started to paint the walls.

2 to produce a picture of something using paint: *He is very good at painting flowers.* □ *Monet painted hundreds of pictures of water lilies.*

paintbrush /ˈpeɪntbrʌʃ/ *noun* (**paintbrushes**)

a brush that you use for painting

painter /ˈpeɪntə/ *noun*

1 an artist who paints pictures: *The film is about the Dutch painter, Vincent van Gogh.*

2 a person whose job is to paint walls, doors or other parts of buildings: *I worked as a house painter for about five years.*

painting /ˈpeɪntɪŋ/ *noun*

1 a picture that someone has painted: *She hung a large painting on the wall.*

2 *uncountable* the activity of painting pictures or covering surfaces with paint: *I really enjoy painting and gardening.*

pair /peə/ *noun*

1 two things of the same size and shape that are used together: *She wore a pair of plain black shoes.* □ *a pair of earrings*

2 an object that has two main parts of the same size and shape: *He was wearing a pair of old jeans.* □ *She took a pair of scissors out of her bag.*

3 two people who are doing something together: *a pair of teenage boys* □ *The eight children are working in pairs.*

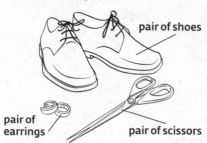

pair of shoes

pair of earrings

pair of scissors

pal /pæl/ *noun*

a friend (*informal*): *They talked like old pals.*

palace /ˈpælɪs/ *noun*

a very large impressive house where a king, a queen, or a president lives: *We visited Buckingham Palace.*

pale /peɪl/ *adjective* (**paler, palest**)

1 not strong or bright in colour: *She's wearing a pale blue dress.*

2 with a face that is a lighter colour than usual: *She looked pale and tired.*

palm /pɑːm/ *noun*

1 (also **palm tree**) a tree that grows in hot countries, with long leaves at the top, and no branches: *white sand and palm trees*

2 the inside part of your hand, between your fingers and your wrist: *Danny hit the table with the palm of his hand.*

pamphlet /'pæmflət/ *noun*
a very thin book with a paper cover that gives information about something: *They gave me a pamphlet about parenting.*

pan /pæn/ *noun*
a round metal container with a long handle, that you use for cooking things in: *Heat the butter and oil in a large pan*

pancake /'pænkeɪk/ *noun*
a thin, round food made from milk, flour and eggs, cooked in a frying pan.

panda /'pændə/ *noun*
a large animal from China with black and white fur

pane /peɪn/ *noun*
a flat sheet of glass in a window or a door: *Her mother had replaced the broken pane of glass.*

panel /'pænəl/ *noun*
1 a flat piece of wood or other material that forms part of a larger object such as a door: *There was a glass panel in the centre of the door.*
2 a board with switches and controls on it: *You can switch the lights on or off using a control panel.*
3 a small group of people who discuss something in public or who make a decision: *The government will take advice from a panel of experts.*

panic /'pænɪk/ *uncountable noun*
a strong feeling of worry or fear that makes you act without thinking carefully: *An earthquake caused panic among the population.* ●**panic** *verb* (**panics, panicking, panicked**) *Guests panicked and screamed when the bomb exploded.*

pant /pænt/ *verb* (**pants, panting, panted**)
to breathe quickly and loudly, because you have been running or because you are very hot: *Dogs lose body heat by panting and sweating.*

pants /pænts/ *plural noun*
1 a piece of underwear that covers the area between your waist and your legs
2 (*American*) → see **trousers**: *He wore brown corduroy pants and a white cotton shirt.*

paper /'peɪpə/ *noun*
1 *uncountable* a material that you write on

or wrap things with: *He wrote his name down on a piece of paper.* □ *He carried the groceries in a paper bag.*
2 a newspaper: *I might get a paper when I go into town.*
3 *plural* sheets of paper with information on them: *The briefcase contained important official papers.*

paperback /'peɪpə,bæk/ *noun*
a book with a thin cardboard or paper cover: *I'll buy the book when it comes out in paperback.*

paperboy /'peɪpə,bɔɪ/ *noun*
a boy who delivers newspapers to people's homes

paper clip *noun*
a small piece of metal that is used for holding pieces of paper together

paperwork /'peɪpə,wɜːk/ *uncountable noun*
work that involves dealing with letters, reports and records: *There will be paperwork — forms to fill in, letters to write.*

parachute /'pærəʃuːt/ *noun*
a large piece of thin material that a person attaches to their body when they jump from an aircraft to help them float safely to the ground: *They fell 41,000 feet before opening their parachutes.*

parade /pə'reɪd/ *noun*
a line of people or vehicles moving through a public place in order to celebrate an important event: *A military parade marched down Pennsylvania Avenue.*

paradise /'pærə,daɪs/ *noun*
1 in some religions, a beautiful place where good people go after they die: *After his death, he will live with God in paradise.*
2 a beautiful or perfect place: *The island really is a tropical paradise.*

paraffin /'pærə,fɪn/ *uncountable noun*
a type of oil that is used as a fuel for heating and lights

paragraph /'pærə,grɑːf/ *noun*
a section of a piece of writing that begins on a new line and contains more than one sentence: *The essay begins with a short introductory paragraph.*

parallel /'pærəlel/ *adjective*
used for describing two lines that are the same distance apart along their whole

p

length: *Remsen Street is parallel with Montague Street.*

paralyse /'pærə,laɪz/ *verb* (**paralyses, paralysing, paralysed**)

to cause someone to be unable to move all or part of their body because of an accident or an illness: *She is paralysed from the waist down.*

parcel /'pɑːsəl/ *noun*

something that is wrapped in paper so that it can be sent by post: *They sent parcels of food and clothing.*

pardon /'pɑːdən/ *exclamation*

I beg your pardon used as a way of apologizing for making a small mistake: *I beg your pardon. I thought you were someone else.*

Pardon?/I beg your pardon? used when you want someone to repeat what they have just said: *'Will you let me open it?' — 'Pardon?' — 'Can I open it?'*

parent /'peərənt/ *noun*

your mother or your father: *Children need their parents.*

parenthood /'peərənt,hʊd/ *uncountable noun*

the state of being a parent: *They had to deal with the responsibilities of parenthood.*

park¹ /pɑːk/ *noun*

a public area of land with grass and trees, usually in a town, where people go to relax and enjoy themselves: *Hyde Park* □ *I took a walk with the dog around the park.*

park² /pɑːk/ *verb* (**parks, parking, parked**)

to stop a vehicle and leave it somewhere: *They parked in the street outside the house.* □ *He found a place to park the car.*

▶ **parking** *uncountable noun Parking is allowed only on one side of the street.*

parliament /'pɑːləmənt/ also **Parliament** *noun*

the group of people who make or change the laws of some countries: *The German Parliament today approved the policy.*

parody /'pærədi/ *noun* (**parodies**)

a piece of writing, drama or music that copies something in an amusing way: *The school show was a parody of the 'StarWars' films.*

parrot /'pærət/ *noun*

a tropical bird with a curved beak and very bright or grey feathers

parsley /'pɑːsli/ *uncountable noun*

a type of plant (= a herb) with small green leaves that you use in cooking

part¹ /pɑːt/ *noun*

1 a piece of something: *This was a part of Paris he loved.* □ *Perry spent part of his childhood in Canada.*

2 a piece of a machine: *The company makes small parts for planes.*

3 one character's words and actions in a play or film: *He played the part of Hamlet.*

take part in something to do an activity together with other people: *Thousands of students took part in the demonstrations.*

part² /pɑːt/ *verb* (**parts, parting, parted**)

part with something to give or sell something that you would prefer to keep: *Think carefully before parting with money.*

partial /'pɑːʃəl/ *adjective*

not complete: *These plants prefer to grow in partial shade.*

▶ **partially** *adverb Lisa is partially blind.*

participant /pɑː'tɪsɪpənt/ *noun*

a person who takes part in an activity: *Participants in the course will learn techniques to improve their memory.*

participate /pɑː'tɪsɪ,peɪt/ *verb* (**participates, participating, participated**)

to take part in an activity: *Some of the children participated in sports or other physical activities.*

▶ **participation** /pɑː,tɪsɪ'peɪʃən/ *uncountable noun Doctors recommend exercise or participation in sport at least two times a week.*

participle /'pɑːtɪsɪpəl/ *noun*

a form of the verb that usually ends in '-ed' or '-ing'

particular /pə'tɪkjʊlə/ *adjective*

1 used for showing that you are talking about one thing or one type of thing rather than other similar ones: *Where did you hear that particular story?* □ *I have to know exactly why I'm doing a particular job.*

2 greater or stronger than usual: *We place particular importance on language training.*

3 choosing and doing things very carefully: *Ted is very particular about the clothes he wears.*

in particular especially; more than others: *Why did he notice her car in particular?*

particularly /pə'tɪkjʊləli/ *adverb*

more than usual or more than others:

Keep your office space looking good, particularly your desk. ☐ *I particularly liked the wooden chairs.*

partly /ˈpɑːtli/ *adverb*
not completely, but a little: *It's partly my fault.*

partner /ˈpɑːtnə/ *noun*
1 your husband or wife, or your boyfriend or girlfriend: *Len's partner died four years ago.*
2 the person you are playing or dancing with: *She needed a new partner for the doubles game.*
3 one of the people who own a firm or a business: *He's a partner in a Chicago law firm.*

partnership /ˈpɑːtnəʃɪp/ *noun*
a relationship in which two or more people or groups work together: *We want to develop a closer partnership between the government and the car industry.*

part of ˈspeech *noun* (parts of speech)
a particular class of word such as noun, adjective or verb

ˈpart-ˈtime *adjective, adverb*

> **LANGUAGE HELP**
> The adverb is spelled **part time**.

working for only part of each day or week: *She is trying to get a part-time job in an office.* ☐ *I want to work part time.*

party /ˈpɑːti/ *noun* (parties)
1 a social event at which people enjoy themselves doing things like eating or dancing: *The couple met at a party.* ☐ *We organized a huge birthday party.*
2 a political organization whose members have similar aims and beliefs: *He is a member of the Republican Party.*
3 a group of people doing something together: *We passed by a party of tourists.*

pass¹ /pɑːs/ *verb* (passes, passing, passed)
1 to go past someone or something: *When she passed the library door, the telephone began to ring.* ☐ *Jane stood aside to let her pass.*
2 to move in a particular direction: *He passed through the doorway into the kitchen.* ☐ *A helicopter passed overhead.*
3 to give an object to someone: *Pam passed the books to Dr Wong.*
4 to kick or throw a ball to someone: *Hawkins passed the ball to Payton.*
5 to go by: *Time passes quickly when you are enjoying yourself.*
6 to spend time in a particular way: *The*

children passed the time watching TV.
7 to succeed in an examination: *Tina passed her driving test last week.*
8 to formally agree to a new law: *The government passed a law that allowed banks to sell insurance.*

pass away to die: *She passed away last year.*
pass out to suddenly become unconscious: *He felt sick and then passed out.*
pass something on to give someone some information: *Mary Hayes passed on the news to McEvoy.*

pass² /pɑːs/ *noun* (passes)
1 a document that allows you to do something: *He used his journalist's pass to enter the White House.*
2 an act of throwing or kicking a ball to someone on your team: *Bryan Randall threw a short pass to Ernest Wilford.*

passage /ˈpæsɪdʒ/ *noun*
1 a long narrow space that connects one place or room with another: *A dark narrow passage led to the kitchen.*
2 a short part of a book: *He read a passage to her from one of Max's books.*

passenger /ˈpæsɪndʒə/ *noun*
a person who is travelling in a vehicle such as a bus, a boat or a plane, but who is not driving it: *Mr Smith was a passenger in the car when it crashed.*

passion /ˈpæʃən/ *noun*
1 *uncountable* a very strong feeling about something or a strong belief in something: *He spoke with great passion.*
2 a very strong interest in something that you like very much: *She has a passion for music.*

passionate /ˈpæʃənət/ *adjective*
having very strong feelings about something or a strong belief in it: *He is very passionate about the project.*

passive¹ /ˈpæsɪv/ *adjective*
allowing things to happen without taking action: *I disliked his passive attitude.*
▶ **passively** *adverb* *He sat there passively, waiting for me to say something.*

passive² /ˈpæsɪv/ *noun*
the form of a verb that you use to show that the subject does not perform the action but is affected by it. For example, in 'He's been murdered', the verb **murder** is in the passive. Compare with **active**.

P

passport /ˈpɑːspɔːt/ *noun*
an official document that you have to show when you enter or leave a country: *You should take your passport with you when you change your money.*

password /ˈpɑːswɜːd/ *noun*
a secret word or phrase that allows you to enter a place or to use a computer system: *Please contact us for a username and password.*

past¹ /pɑːst/ *noun*
the time before the present, and the things that happened then: *In the past, most babies with the disease died.*

past² /pɑːst/ *preposition*
1 used for talking about a time that is thirty minutes or less after a particular hour: *It's ten past eleven.*
2 from one side to the other of someone or something: *I walked past her.* ● **past** *adverb An ambulance drove past.*

past

I walked past her.

pasta /ˈpæstə/ *noun*
a type of food made from a mixture of flour, eggs and water that is made into different shapes and then boiled: *Italian pizzas and pasta are the restaurant's speciality.*
→ Look at picture on P3

paste /peɪst/ *verb* (**pastes, pasting, pasted**)
1 to put glue onto a surface and stick something onto it: *He pasted labels onto the bottles.*
2 to copy or move text or images into a computer document from another part of the document, or from another document: *The text can be copied and pasted into your email program.*

pastel¹ /ˈpæstəl/ *adjective*
pale rather than dark or bright in colour: *Mother always chooses clothes in delicate pastel shades.* ◻ *pastel pink, blue and green*

pastel² /ˈpæstəl/ *noun*
a stick of colour made of a substance like chalk, and used by artists for drawing: *This paper is ideal for use with paints, crayons and pastels.*

pastry /ˈpeɪstri/ *noun* (**pastries**)
1 *uncountable* a food made from flour, fat and water that is often used for making pies (= dishes of meat, vegetables or fruit with a cover made of pastry)
2 a small cake: *The bakery sells delicious cakes and pastries.*

past tense *noun*
the form of a verb that is used for talking about the time that came before the present. For example, the past tense of the verb 'see' is 'saw'.

pat /pæt/ *verb* (**pats, patting, patted**)
to touch something or someone lightly with your flat hand: *'Don't you worry,' she said, patting me on the knee.* ◻ *The lady patted her hair nervously.* ● **pat** *noun He gave her a friendly pat on the shoulder.*

patch /pætʃ/ *noun* (**patches**)
1 a part of a surface that is different in appearance from the area around it: *She noticed the bald patch on the top of his head.*
◻ *There was a small patch of blue in the grey clouds.*
2 a piece of material that you use to cover a hole in a piece of clothing: *Brad was wearing an old jacket with leather patches on the elbows.*

path /pɑːθ/ *noun*
a long, narrow piece of ground that people walk along: *We followed the path along the cliff.*

pathetic /pəˈθetɪk/ *adjective*
weak or not very good: *What a pathetic attempt to hide the truth.*

patience /ˈpeɪʃəns/ *uncountable noun*
the ability to stay calm and not get annoyed, for example, when something takes a long time: *He doesn't have the patience to wait.*

patient¹ /ˈpeɪʃənt/ *noun*
a person who receives medical treatment from a doctor: *The patient was suffering from heart problems.*

patient² /ˈpeɪʃənt/ *adjective*
able to stay calm and not get annoyed, for example, when something takes a long time: *Please be patient — your cheque will arrive soon.*

p

▶ **patiently** *adverb* *She waited patiently for Frances to finish talking.*

patio /ˈpætiəʊ/ *noun*
a flat area next to a house, where people can sit and relax or eat

patriotic /ˌpætriˈɒtɪk, ˌpeɪt-/ *adjective*
loving your country and feeling very loyal towards it: *They are very patriotic men who give everything for their country.*

patrol¹ /pəˈtrəʊl/ *verb* (**patrols, patrolling, patrolled**)
to move around an area to make sure that there is no trouble there: *Prison officers continued to patrol the grounds.*

patrol² /pəˈtrəʊl/ *noun*
1 when someone moves around an area to make sure that there is no trouble there: *The army is now on patrol.*
2 a group of soldiers or vehicles that move around an area in order to make sure that there is no trouble there: *The three men attacked a border patrol last night.*

pattern /ˈpætən/ *noun*
1 the repeated or regular way in which something happens or is done: *All three attacks followed the same pattern.*
2 an arrangement of lines or shapes that form a design: *The carpet had a pattern of light and dark stripes.*

pattern

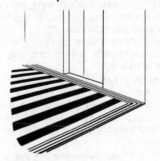

pause /pɔːz/ *verb* (**pauses, pausing, paused**)
to stop for a short time while you are doing something, and then continue: *'It's rather embarrassing,' he began, and paused.* □ *She started speaking when I paused for breath.*
● **pause** *noun* *After a pause Al said: 'I'm sorry if I upset you.'*

pavement /ˈpeɪvmənt/ (*American:* **sidewalk**) *noun*
a path with a hard surface, usually by the side of a road: *He was hurrying along the pavement.*

paw /pɔː/ *noun*
the foot of an animal such as a cat, dog or bear: *The kitten was black with white front paws.*

pay /peɪ/ *verb* (**pays, paying, paid**)
1 to give someone an amount of money for something that you are buying: *Can I pay for my ticket with a credit card?*
2 to give someone an amount of money for something such as a bill or a debt: *She paid the hotel bill before she left.* □ *The company was fined and ordered to pay court costs.*
3 to give someone money for the work that they do: *The lawyer was paid a huge salary.* □ *I get paid monthly.* ● **pay** *uncountable noun* *They complained about their pay and working conditions.*
pay someone back to give someone the money that you owe them: *He promised to pay the money back as soon as he could.*

> **LANGUAGE HELP**
> See note at **salary**.

payment /ˈpeɪmənt/ *noun*
1 an amount of money that is paid to someone: *You will receive 13 monthly payments.*
2 *uncountable* the act of paying money or of being paid: *Players now expect payment for interviews.*

PC /ˌpiːˈsiː/ *noun* (**PCs**)
a computer that people use at school, at home or in an office. **PC** is short for **personal computer**.

PDF /ˌpiːdiːˈef/ *noun* (**PDFs**)
a computer document that looks exactly like the original document. **PDF** is short for 'Portable Document Format'.

PE /ˌpiːˈiː/ *uncountable noun*
short for **physical education**

pea /piː/ *noun*
a very small, round, green vegetable

peace /piːs/ *uncountable noun*
1 a situation where there is not a war: *The new rulers brought peace to the country.* □ *The two countries signed a peace agreement.*
2 the state of being quiet and calm: *I just want some peace and quiet.*

peaceful /ˈpiːsfʊl/ *adjective*
1 not involving war or violence: *He has*

p

attempted to find a peaceful solution to the conflict.

▶ **peacefully** *adverb The governor asked the protestors to leave peacefully.*

2 quiet and calm: *The garden looked so peaceful.*

peach ¹ /piːtʃ/ *noun* (**peaches**)

1 a round fruit with a soft red-and-orange skin

→ Look at picture on P2

2 a pale colour between pink and orange: *The room was decorated in peach.*

peach ² /piːtʃ/ *adjective*

of a pale colour between pink and orange: *a peach silk blouse*

peak /piːk/ *noun*

1 the point at which a process or an activity is at its strongest: *His career was at its peak when he died.*

2 a mountain or the top of a mountain: *They could see the snowy peaks of the Canadian Rockies.*

peanut /ˈpiːnʌt/ *noun*

a small nut that you can eat

pear /peə/ *noun*

a juicy fruit that is narrow at the top and wider at the bottom. Pears have white flesh and green, yellow or brown skin.

→ Look at picture on P2

pearl /pɜːl/ *noun*

a hard, white, shiny round object that grows inside the shell of an oyster (= a water creature). Pearls are used for making jewellery: *She wore a string of pearls.*

peasant /ˈpezənt/ *noun*

a poor farmer or farm worker in a poor country: *The film describes the customs and habits of peasants in Peru.*

pebble /ˈpebəl/ *noun*

a small, smooth stone

peculiar /pɪˈkjuːliə/ *adjective*

strange or unusual: *Mr Kennet has a rather peculiar sense of humour.*

pedal ¹ /ˈpedəl/ *noun*

1 one of the two parts that you push with your feet to make a bicycle move

2 a part that you press with your foot in order to control a car or a machine: *the brake pedal*

pedal ² /ˈpedəl/ *verb* (**pedals, pedalling, pedalled**)

to push the pedals of a bicycle around

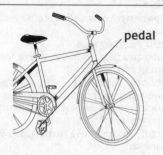

pedal

with your feet to make it move: *We pedalled slowly through the city streets.*

pedestrian /pɪˈdestriən/ *noun*

a person who is walking, especially in a town or city: *The city's pavements were busy with pedestrians.*

pedestrian crossing (American: **crosswalk**) *noun*

a place where drivers must stop to let people cross a street

peek /piːk/ *verb* (**peeks, peeking, peeked**)

to look at something or someone quickly and often secretly: *She peeked at him through a crack in the wall.* ● **peek** *noun I had a peek at his computer screen.*

peel ¹ /piːl/ *noun*

the skin of a fruit such as a lemon or an apple: *Add in the grated lemon peel.*

peel ² /piːl/ *verb* (**peels, peeling, peeled**)

1 to remove the skin of fruit or vegetables: *She began peeling potatoes.*

2 to come away from a surface: *Paint was peeling off the walls.* □ *It took me two days to peel off the labels.*

peep /piːp/ *verb* (**peeps, peeping, peeped**)

to take a quick look at something: *A small child was peeping through the window at him.*

● **peep** *noun She lifted the lid and took a quick peep inside.*

peer /pɪə/ *verb* (**peers, peering, peered**)

to look at something very closely, usually because it is difficult to see clearly: *He found her peering at a computer print-out.*

peg /peg/ *noun*

1 a small piece of wood or metal that you use for attaching one thing to another

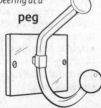

peg

thing: *He builds furniture using wooden pegs instead of nails.*

2 a small hook on a wall that you hang things on: *His jacket hung on the peg in the kitchen.*

pelvis /'pelvɪs/ *noun* (**pelvises**)
the wide, curved group of bones between your back and your legs

pen /pen/ *noun*
a long thin object that you use for writing with ink (= coloured liquid)

penalty /'penəlti/ *noun* (**penalties**)
1 a punishment for doing something that is against a law or rule: *The maximum penalty for dangerous driving is five years in prison.*
2 a punishment for the team that breaks a rule in sports such as football and hockey, and an advantage for the other team: *The referee awarded a penalty.*

pence /pens/
the plural of **penny**

pencil /'pensəl/ *noun*
a thin piece of wood with a black or coloured substance through the middle that you use to write or draw with: *She used a pencil and some blank paper to draw the picture.*

pencil sharpener /'pensəl 'ʃɑːpənə/ *noun*
an object with a blade inside, used for making pencils sharper

penetrate /'penɪˌtreɪt/ *verb* (**penetrates, penetrating, penetrated**)
to get into an object or pass through it: *X-rays can penetrate many objects.*

penguin /'peŋgwɪn/ *noun*
a black-and-white bird that lives in very cold places. Penguins can swim but they cannot fly.

peninsula /pə'nɪnsjʊlə/ *noun*
a long narrow piece of land that sticks out from a larger piece of land and is almost completely surrounded by water: *the Alaskan peninsula*

penis /'piːnɪs/ *noun* (**penises**)
the part of a man's body that he uses when he gets rid of waste liquid (= urine) and when he has sex

penknife /'pennaɪf/ *noun* (**penknives**)
a small knife with a blade that folds back into the handle

penny /'peni/ *noun* (**pennies** or **pence**)
a small British coin. There are one hundred pennies in a pound: *The price of petrol rose by more than a penny a litre.*

pension /'penʃən/ *noun*
money that you regularly receive from a business or the government after you stop working because of your age: *He gets a £35,000-a-year pension.*
▸ **pensioner** *noun She's an 83-year-old pensioner who still enjoys cycling.*

pentagon /'pentəˌgɒn/ *noun*
a shape with five straight sides

people /'piːpəl/ *plural noun*
men, women and children: *Millions of people have lost their homes.* □ *He's reading a book about the people of Angola.*

pepper /'pepə/ *noun*
1 *uncountable* a spice with a hot taste that you put on food: *Season with salt and pepper.*
→ Look at picture on P3
2 a hollow green, red or yellow vegetable with seeds inside it: *Thinly slice two red or green peppers.*
→ Look at picture on P2

peppermint /'pepəˌmɪnt/ *noun*
1 *uncountable* oil from the peppermint plant with a strong, sharp flavour
2 a sweet with a peppermint flavour

per /pɜː/ *preposition*
for each or in each. For example, if a vehicle is travelling at 40 miles per hour, it travels 40 miles in each hour: *They spend £200 per week on groceries.*

per annum /pər 'ænəm/ *adverb*
each year: *They must pay a fee of £3000 per annum.*

perceive /pə'siːv/ *verb* (**perceives, perceiving, perceived**)
1 to notice or realize something, especially when it is not obvious: *A great artist teaches us to perceive reality in a different way.*
2 to think of something in a particular way: *Stress is widely perceived as a cause of heart disease.*

per cent /pə 'sent/ *noun* (**per cent**)
used for talking about amounts as parts of a hundred. One hundred per cent (100%) is all of something, and 50 per cent (50%) is half: *Only ten per cent of our customers live in this city.*

p

percentage /pə'sentɪdʒ/ *noun*
an amount of something: *He regularly eats foods with a high percentage of protein.*

perch /pɜːtʃ/ *verb* (**perches, perching, perched**)
1 to sit on the edge of something: *He perched on the corner of the desk.*
2 to land on a branch or a wall and stand there: *Two birds perched on a nearby fence.*

percussion /pə'kʌʃən/ *uncountable noun*
musical instruments that you hit, such as drums: *This is a piece for the orchestra's powerful percussion section.*

perfect /'pɜːfɪkt/ *adjective*
as good as it could possibly be: *He spoke perfect English.* □ *Nobody is perfect.*
▶ **perfectly** *adverb The system worked perfectly.*

perfection /pə'fekʃən/ *uncountable noun*
the quality of being as good as possible: *The meat was cooked to perfection.*

perfect tense *noun*
the form of a verb that is made with 'has' or 'had' and the past participle. For example, in the sentence 'I have seen that film', the verb 'see' is in the perfect tense.

perform /pə'fɔːm/ *verb* (**performs, performing, performed**)
1 to do a task or an action: *You must perform this exercise correctly to avoid back pain.*
2 to do a play, a piece of music or a dance in front of an audience: *They will be performing works by Bach and Scarlatti.*
▶ **performer** *noun She was one of the top jazz performers in New York City.*
3 to do a piece of work: *The surgeon performed an operation on his leg.*
4 to do something well or badly: *He performed well in his exams.* □ *The industry has performed poorly this year.*

performance /pə'fɔːməns/ *noun*
1 when you entertain an audience by singing, dancing or acting: *They were giving a performance of Bizet's 'Carmen'.*
2 how successful someone or something is or how well they do something: *The study looked at the performance of 18 surgeons.* □ *He spoke about the poor performance of the economy.*

perfume /'pɜːfjuːm/ *noun*
a liquid with a pleasant smell that you put on your skin: *The hall smelled of her mother's perfume.*

perhaps /pə'hæps, præps/ *adverb*
used for showing that you are not sure whether something is true, possible or likely: *In the end they lost millions, perhaps billions.* □ *Perhaps, in time, they will understand.*

perimeter /pə'rɪmɪtə/ *noun*
the total distance around the edge of a flat shape: *To work out the perimeter of a rectangle, you need to know its length and width.*

period /'pɪəriəd/ *noun*
1 a length of time: *He couldn't work for a long period of time.*
2 (*American*) → see **full stop**
3 the time when a woman loses blood from her body each month

permanent /'pɜːmənənt/ *adjective*
continuing forever or for a very long time: *Some ear infections can cause permanent damage.* □ *He's never had a permanent job.*
▶ **permanently** *adverb His confidence has been permanently affected.*

permission /pə'mɪʃən/ *uncountable noun*
when you are allowed to do something: *He asked permission to leave the room.* □ *They cannot leave the country without permission.*

permit¹ /pə'mɪt/ *verb* (**permits, permitting, permitted**)
to allow someone to do something (*formal*): *The guards permitted me to bring my camera.*

permit² /'pɜːmɪt/ *noun*
an official document that allows you to do something: *She hasn't got a work permit.*

persevere /ˌpɜːsɪ'vɪə/ *verb* (**perseveres, persevering, persevered**)
to continue to do something difficult: *Berman ignored their criticisms, and persevered with his plan.*

person /'pɜːsən/ *noun* (**people**)
a man, a woman or a child: *At least one person died and several others were injured.* □ *They were both lovely, friendly people.*
in person in the same place as someone, and not speaking to them on the telephone or writing to them: *She saw him in person for the first time last night.*

personal /'pɜːsənəl/ *adjective*
1 relating to a particular person: *The story is based on his own personal experience.* □ *That's*

p

just my personal opinion.

2 relating to your feelings, relationships and health: Did he mention that he has any personal problems?

,personal com'puter *noun*
a computer that you use at work, school or home. The short form **PC** is also used.

personality /ˌpɜːsəˈnælɪti/ *noun* (**personalities**)
the qualities that make you different from other people: She has such a kind, friendly personality.

personally /ˈpɜːsənəli/ *adverb*
1 used for showing that you are giving your own opinion: Personally I think it's a waste of time.
2 used for showing that you do something yourself rather than letting someone else do it: He wrote to them personally to explain the situation.

personnel /ˌpɜːsəˈnel/ *plural noun*
the people who work for an organization: The president will give a speech to military personnel at the army base.

perspective /pəˈspektɪv/ *noun*
1 a particular way of thinking about something: The death of his father has given him a new perspective on life.
2 a way, in art, of making some objects or people in a picture seem further away than others

perspiration /ˌpɜːspɪˈreɪʃən/ *uncountable noun*
the liquid that appears on your skin when you are hot (formal): His hands were wet with perspiration.

persuade /pəˈsweɪd/ *verb* (**persuades, persuading, persuaded**)
to make someone do something by talking to them: My husband persuaded me to come.

persuasion /pəˈsweɪʒən/ *uncountable noun*
the process of making someone do or think something: After much persuasion from Ellis, she agreed to perform.

pessimism /ˈpesɪˌmɪzəm/ *uncountable noun*
the belief that bad things are going to happen: There was a general pessimism about the economy.

▶ **pessimist** *noun* I'm a natural pessimist, so I usually expect the worst.

▶ **pessimistic** /ˌpesɪˈmɪstɪk/ *adjective* She is so pessimistic about the future.

pest /pest/ *noun*
1 an insect or a small animal that damages crops or food: They use chemicals to fight pests and diseases.
2 someone, especially a child, who is annoying you (informal): He climbed on the table, pulled my hair, and was generally a pest.

pet /pet/ *noun*
an animal that you keep in your home: Do you have any pets?

petal /ˈpetəl/ *noun*
the thin coloured parts of a plant that form the flower: rose petals

petition /pəˈtɪʃən/ *noun*
a document that contains the signatures of a group of people who are asking a government or other official group to do a particular thing: The government received a petition signed by 4,500 people.

petrol /ˈpetrəl/ (American: **gasoline**) *uncountable noun*
the fuel which you use in cars and some other vehicles to make the engine go

petrol station *noun*
a place where you buy fuel for your car

pharmacist /ˈfɑːməsɪst/ *noun*
a person whose job is to prepare and sell medicines: Ask your pharmacist for advice.

pharmacy /ˈfɑːməsi/ *noun* (**pharmacies**)
a place where you can buy medicines: Pick up the medicine from the pharmacy.

phase /feɪz/ *noun*
a particular stage in a process: 6000 women will take part in the first phase of the project.

philosopher /fɪˈlɒsəfə/ *noun*
a person who studies or writes about philosophy: He admired the Greek philosopher Plato.

philosophy /fɪˈlɒsəfi/ *noun* (**philosophies**)
1 *uncountable* the study of ideas about the meaning of life: She is studying traditional Chinese philosophy.
▶ **philosophical** /ˌfɪləˈsɒfɪkəl/ *adjective* They often had philosophical discussions.
2 a particular theory or belief: The best philosophy is to change to a low-sugar diet.

phone¹ /fəʊn/ *noun*
a piece of equipment that you use to talk to someone else in another place: Two minutes later the phone rang.

phone² /fəʊn/ *verb* (phones, phoning, phoned)

to contact someone and speak to them by telephone: *He phoned Laura to see if she was better.* □ *'Did anybody phone?' asked Alberg.*

on the phone speaking to someone by telephone: *She's always on the phone.*

'phone book *noun*

a book that contains a list of the names, addresses, and telephone numbers of the people in a town or area

'phone call *noun*

when you use a telephone to speak to someone who is in another place: *I have to make a phone call.*

'phone ,number *noun*

the number of a particular phone: *What's your phone number?*

photo /'fəʊtəʊ/ *noun*
→ see **photograph**

photocopier /'fəʊtəʊˌkɒpiə/ *noun*

a machine that copies documents by photographing them

photocopy /'fəʊtəʊˌkɒpi/ *noun* (photocopies)

a copy of a document that you make using a special machine (= a photocopier): *He gave me a photocopy of the letter.* ● **photocopy** *verb* (photocopies, photocopying, photocopied) *He photocopied the documents before sending them off.*

photograph /'fəʊtəˌgrɑːf/ *noun*

a picture that you take with a camera: *He wants to take some photographs of the house.* ● **photograph** *verb* (photographs, photographing, photographed) (*formal*): *She photographed the children.*

photographer /fə'tɒgrəfə/ *noun*

someone who takes photographs as a job or a hobby: *He's a professional photographer.*

photography /fə'tɒgrəfi/ *uncountable noun*

the skill or process of producing photographs: *Photography is one of her hobbies.*

photosynthesis /ˌfəʊtəʊ'sɪnθəsɪs/ *uncountable noun*

the way that green plants make their food using the light of the sun

phrasal verb /ˌfreɪzəl 'vɜːb/ *noun*

a combination of a verb and an adverb or preposition, for example, 'get over' or 'give up', which together have a particular meaning

phrase /freɪz/ *noun*

a group of words that you use together as part of a sentence, for example, 'in the morning': *At the end of the book, there is a glossary of useful words and phrases.*

physical /'fɪzɪkəl/ *adjective*

connected with a person's body, rather than with their mind: *Physical activity promotes good health.*

▶ **physically** *adverb* *Kerry is physically active and in excellent health.*

,physical edu'cation *uncountable noun*

the school subject in which students do physical exercises or take part in physical games and sports

physicist /'fɪzɪsɪst/ *noun*

a person who studies physics: *He was one of the best nuclear physicists in the country.*

physics /'fɪzɪks/ *uncountable noun*

the scientific study of things such as heat, light and sound: *His favourite school subjects were chemistry and physics.*

pianist /'piːənɪst/ *noun*

a person who plays the piano: *She wants to be a concert pianist.*

piano /pi'ænəʊ/ *noun*

a large musical instrument that you play by pressing black and white bars (= keys): *I taught myself how to play the piano.*

piccolo /'pɪkələʊ/ *noun*

a musical instrument that is like a small flute (= a pipe that you put across your lips and blow)

pick /pɪk/ *verb* (picks, picking, picked)

1 to choose a particular person or thing: *Mr Nowell picked ten people to interview.*

2 to take flowers, fruit or leaves from a plant or tree: *I've picked some flowers from the garden.*

pick on someone to repeatedly criticize someone or treat them unkindly (*informal*): *Bullies often pick on younger children.*

pick someone/something out

1 to recognize someone or something when it is difficult to see them: *I had trouble picking out the words, even with my glasses on.*

2 to choose someone or something from a group of people or things: *They picked me* out to represent the whole team.

pick someone/something up to collect someone or something from a place, often in a car: *Please could you pick me up at 5pm?* □ *She went to her parents' house to pick up some clean clothes.*

pick something up

1 to lift something up: *He picked his cap up from the floor.*

2 to learn a skill or an idea over a period of time without really trying (*informal*): *Her children have picked up English really quickly.*

pickle /'pɪkəl/ *noun*

1 *uncountable* a cold, spicy sauce with pieces of vegetable and fruit in it: *a cheese and pickle sandwich*

2 *plural* a vegetable that has been kept in vinegar (= a strong, sharp liquid) for a long time: *He had a hamburger with pickles.*

picnic /'pɪknɪk/ *noun*

when you eat a meal outdoors, usually in a park or a forest, or at the beach: *We're going on a picnic tomorrow.* ● **picnic** *verb* (**picnics, picnicking, picnicked**) *Afterwards, we picnicked by the river.*

picture¹ /'pɪktʃə/ *noun*

1 a drawing or painting: *She drew a picture with coloured chalk.*

2 a photograph: *I love taking pictures of animals.*

picture² /'pɪktʃə/ *verb* (**pictures, picturing, pictured**)

to think of something and see it in your mind: *He pictured her with long black hair.*

pie /paɪ/ *noun*

a dish of fruit, meat or vegetables that is covered with pastry (= a mixture of flour, butter and water) and baked: *We each had a slice of apple pie.*

piece /piːs/ *noun*

1 a part of something: *You must only take one piece of cake.* □ *Cut the chicken into pieces.*

2 an amount of something: *That's an interesting piece of information.* □ *This is his finest piece of work yet.* □ *He has composed 1500 pieces of music for TV.*

in pieces broken: *The china vase was in pieces on the floor.*

pierce /pɪəs/ *verb* (**pierces, piercing, pierced**)

1 to make a hole in something with a sharp object: *Pierce the chicken with a sharp*

knife to check that it is cooked.

2 to make small holes through someone's ears so that they can wear earrings (= jewellery for the ears) in them: *I'm having my ears pierced on Saturday.*

piercing /'pɪəsɪŋ/ *adjective*

used for describing a sound that is high and clear in a sharp and unpleasant way: *She let out a piercing scream.*

pig /pɪg/ *noun*

1 a farm animal with a fat body and short legs, that is kept for its meat: *Children can help feed the pigs.*

2 used as a rude way of talking about someone who is unkind or who eats too much (*informal*): *You've eaten my toast, you greedy pig!*

pigeon /'pɪdʒɪn/ *noun*

a large grey bird that is often seen in cities

pigtail /'pɪgteɪl/ *noun*

a length of hair hanging loose in a bunch, or twisted and tied at the end: *Her hair was tied back in pigtails.*

pile¹ /paɪl/ *noun*

several things lying on top of each other: *We searched through the pile of boxes.* □ *There was a huge pile of shoes by the door.*

pile² /paɪl/ *verb* (**piles, piling, piled**)

to put things somewhere so that they form a pile: *He was piling clothes into the suitcase.*

pile something up to put one thing on top of another to form a pile: *They piled up rocks to build a wall.*

pill /pɪl/ *noun*

a small, solid, round piece of medicine that you swallow: *Why do I have to take all these pills?*

pillar /'pɪlə/ *noun*

a tall, solid structure that usually supports part of a building: *There were eight huge pillars supporting the roof.*

pillow /'pɪləʊ/ *noun*

a soft object that you rest your head on when you are in bed

pillowcase /'pɪləʊˌkeɪs/ *noun*

a cloth cover for a pillow

pilot /'paɪlət/ *noun*

a person who controls an aircraft: *He spent seventeen years as an airline pilot.*

→ Look at picture on P7

P

pin[1] /pɪn/ *noun*
a very small, thin piece of metal with a point at one end, used for fastening things together: *She looked in her box of needles and pins.*

pin[2] /pɪn/ *verb* (pins, pinning, pinned)
1 to fix something somewhere with a pin: *They pinned a notice to the door.*
2 to press someone against a surface so that they cannot move: *I pinned him down until the police arrived.*

pinch[1] /pɪntʃ/ *verb* (pinches, pinching, pinched)
1 to press someone's skin between your thumb and first finger: *She pinched his arm as hard as she could.*
2 to steal something (*informal*): *Alex has pinched my book.*

pinch[2] /pɪntʃ/ *noun* (pinches)
1 when you press someone's skin between your thumb and first finger: *She gave him a little pinch.*
2 the amount of salt, pepper or other powder that you can hold between your thumb and your first finger: *Add a pinch of cinnamon to the apples.*

pine /paɪn/ *noun*
1 (*also* **pine tree**) a tall tree with long, thin leaves that it keeps all year: *The high mountains are covered in pine trees.*
2 *uncountable* the wood of this tree: *There's a big pine table in the kitchen.*

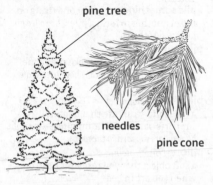

pine tree

needles

pine cone

pineapple /'paɪnæpəl/ *noun*
a large fruit with sweet, yellow flesh and thick, brown skin
→ Look at picture on P2

pink /pɪŋk/ *adjective* (pinker, pinkest)
of the colour between red and white: *She wore pink lipstick.* ● **pink** *noun I prefer pale pinks and blues.*

pint /paɪnt/ *noun*
a unit for measuring liquids that is equal to 0.57 litres: *Each carton contains a pint of milk.* □ *half a pint of beer*

pioneer /ˌpaɪəˈnɪə/ *noun*
one of the first people to be involved in a particular activity: *He was one of the leading pioneers of the Internet.*

pip /pɪp/ *noun*
one of the small, hard seeds in a fruit such as an apple or an orange

pipe /paɪp/ *noun*
1 a long tube that a liquid or a gas can flow through: *They are going to replace the old water pipes.*
2 an object that is used for smoking tobacco (= dried leaves that are used for making cigarettes): *Do you smoke a pipe?*

pirate /'paɪrət/ *noun*
a person who attacks ships and steals property from them: *The hero must find the pirates and the hidden gold.*

pistol /'pɪstəl/ *noun*
a small gun

pit /pɪt/ *noun*
1 a large hole that is dug in the ground: *Eric fell into the pit.*
2 the part of a coal mine that is under the ground

pitch /pɪtʃ/ *noun* (pitches)
1 an area of ground that is used for playing a game such as football: *a cricket pitch*
2 how high or low a sound is: *The pitch of a voice falls at the end of a sentence.*

pity[1] /'pɪti/ *verb* (pities, pitying, pitied)
to feel very sorry for someone: *I don't know whether to hate or pity him.*

pity[2] /'pɪti/ *uncountable noun*
when you feel very sorry for someone: *He felt a sudden tender pity for her.*
a pity used for saying that you feel disappointed: *It's a pity you arrived so late.*

pizza /'piːtsə/ *noun*
a flat, round piece of bread that is covered with tomatoes, cheese and sometimes other foods, and then baked in an oven: *I ordered a thin-crust pizza.*

place[1] /pleɪs/ *noun*
1 a particular building, area, town or

country: *Keep your dog on a lead in public places.* □ *Please state your time and place of birth.*

2 the right or usual position for something: *He returned the photo to its place on the shelf.*

3 a seat for one person: *This girl was sitting in my place.*

4 someone's position in a race or competition: *Victoria is in third place with 22 points.*

5 your home (*informal*): *Let's all go back to my place!*

in place in the correct position: *A wide band held her hair in place.*

in place of something/someone instead of something or someone: *Try using herbs and spices in place of salt.*

take place to happen: *The discussions took place in Paris.*

place² /pleɪs/ **verb** (**places, placing, placed**)

to put something somewhere: *Brand placed the letter in his pocket.*

plain¹ /pleɪn/ **adjective** (**plainer, plainest**)

1 all one colour, without any pattern or writing: *A plain carpet makes a room look bigger.* □ *He placed the paper in a plain envelope.*

2 very simple in style: *It was a plain, grey stone house.*

3 easy to recognize or understand: *It was plain to him what he had to do.*

4 ordinary and not at all beautiful: *She was a shy, rather plain girl.*

plain² /pleɪn/ **noun**

a large flat area of land with very few trees on it: *She stood alone on the grassy plain.*

plait /plæt/ **verb** (**plaits, plaiting, plaited**)

to put three pieces of hair or rope over and under each other to make one thick piece: *Joanna plaited her hair.* ● **plait noun** *Her hair was tied in a long plait.*

plan¹ /plæn/ **noun**

1 a method for doing something that you think about in advance: *They are meeting to discuss the peace plan.* □ *She says that everything is going according to plan.*

2 *plural* ideas about something that you are intending to do: *We have plans to build a new kitchen at the back of the house.*

3 a detailed drawing of something: *Draw a plan of the garden before you start planting.*

plan² /plæn/ **verb** (**plans, planning, planned**)

to decide in detail what you are going to do: *Plan what you're going to eat.* □ *He plans to leave Baghdad on Monday.* □ *They came together to plan for the future.*

▶ **planning uncountable noun** *The trip needs careful planning.*

plane /pleɪn/ **noun**

a vehicle with wings and engines that can fly: *He had plenty of time to catch his plane.*

planet /ˈplænɪt/ **noun**

a large, round object in space that moves around a star. The Earth is a planet: *We study the planets in the solar system.*

plant¹ /plɑːnt/ **noun**

1 a living thing that grows in the earth and has a stem, leaves and roots: *Water each plant daily.*

2 a factory, or a place where power is produced: *We visited one of Ford's car assembly plants.*

plant² /plɑːnt/ **verb** (**plants, planting, planted**)

to put something into the ground so that it will grow: *He plans to plant fruit trees.*

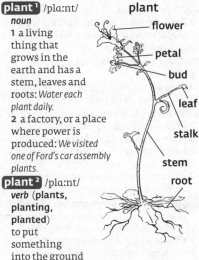

plant

flower
petal
bud
leaf
stalk
stem
root

plasma screen /ˈplæzmə skriːn/ or **plasma display noun**

a type of thin television screen or computer screen with good quality images

plaster¹ /ˈplɑːstə/ **noun**

1 a small piece of sticky material used for covering small cuts on your body: *He had cuts on his face and a plaster on his right hand.*

2 *uncountable* a substance that is used for making a smooth surface on the inside of walls and ceilings: *There were huge cracks in the plaster.*

in plaster with a hard white cover around your leg or arm to protect a broken bone: *I had my arm in plaster for two months.*

P

plaster² /ˈplɑːstə/ verb (**plasters, plastering, plastered**)
to cover a wall or a ceiling with a layer of plaster: *He has just plastered the ceiling.*

plastic /ˈplæstɪk/ noun
a light but strong material that is produced by a chemical process: *The windows are made from sheets of plastic.*
□ *a plastic bottle* □ *a plastic bag*

plastic ˈsurgery uncountable noun
an operation to repair damaged skin, or to change someone's appearance: *She had plastic surgery to change the shape of her nose.*

plate /pleɪt/ noun
a flat dish that is used for holding food: *Anita pushed her plate away.* □ *He ate a huge plate of bacon and eggs.*

plateau /ˈplætəʊ/ noun (**plateaus** or **plateaux**)
a large area of high and fairly flat land: *The house is on a wide grassy plateau.*

platform /ˈplætfɔːm/ noun
1 a flat, raised structure on which someone or something can stand: *He walked towards the platform to begin his speech.*
2 the area in a train station where you wait for a train: *a railway platform*

play¹ /pleɪ/ verb (**plays, playing, played**)
1 to spend time using toys and taking part in games: *Polly was playing with her dolls.*
2 to take part in a game or a sport: *The twins played cards.* □ *I used to play basketball.*
3 to compete against another person or team in a sport or a game: *Manchester United will play Liverpool today.*
4 to perform the part of a particular character in a play or film: *He played Mr Hyde in the film.*
5 to produce music from a musical instrument: *Nina was playing the piano.*
□ *He played for me.*
6 to put a CD into a machine and listen to it: *She played her CDs too loudly.*

play a joke/trick on someone to deceive someone or give them a surprise for fun: *She wanted to play a trick on her friends.*

play² /pleɪ/ noun
1 uncountable when someone spends time using toys and taking part in games: *Children learn mainly through play.*
2 a piece of writing performed in a theatre, on the radio or on television: *'Hamlet' is my favourite play.*

player /ˈpleɪə/ noun
1 a person who takes part in a sport or game: *She was a good tennis player.* □ *The game is for three players.*
2 a musician: *He's a professional trumpet player.*

playful /ˈpleɪfʊl/ adjective
not very serious: *She gave him a playful kiss.*

playground /ˈpleɪɡraʊnd/ noun
a piece of land where children can play: *The park has playground equipment made of wood.*

playgroup /ˈpleɪɡruːp/ also **play group** noun
an informal school for very young children

ˈplaying card noun
a thin piece of cardboard with numbers or pictures printed on it that is used for playing games: *He started to shuffle a pack of playing cards.*

ˈplaying field noun
a large area of grass where people play sports: *The town has three grass playing fields and 18 football teams.*

playtime /ˈpleɪtaɪm/ noun
the period of time between lessons at school when children can play outside: *Friends in different classes can meet up at playtime.*

playwright /ˈpleɪraɪt/ noun
a person who writes plays

plea /pliː/ noun
an emotional request for something: *Their president made a desperate plea for international help.* □ *It was an emotional plea for help.*

plead /pliːd/ verb (**pleads, pleading, pleaded**)
to ask someone in an emotional way to do something: *The lady pleaded with her daughter to come back home.*

plead guilty/not guilty to officially say in a court of law that you are guilty or not guilty of a crime: *Morris pleaded guilty to robbery.*

pleasant /ˈplezənt/ adjective (**pleasanter, pleasantest**)
1 enjoyable or attractive: *It was a very pleasant surprise to receive a free ticket.* □ *I have many pleasant memories of this place*
2 nice and friendly: *The doctor was a handsome, pleasant young man.*

please ¹ /pliːz/ *adverb*
1 used when you are politely asking someone to do something: *Can you help us, please?* □ *Please come in.* □ *Can we have the bill, please?*
2 used when you are accepting something politely: *'Tea?' — 'Yes, please.'*

please ² /pliːz/ *verb* (**pleases, pleasing, pleased**)
to make someone feel happy and satisfied: *I just want to please you.* □ *He always tried to please her.*

pleased /pliːzd/ *adjective*
happy about something or satisfied with something: *I'm so pleased that we solved the problem.* □ *I am very pleased with your work.*
pleased to meet you a polite way of saying hello to someone that you are meeting for the first time

pleasing /ˈpliːzɪŋ/ *adjective*
giving you pleasure and satisfaction: *The pleasing smell of fresh coffee came from the kitchen.*

pleasure /ˈpleʒə/ *noun*
1 *uncountable* a feeling of happiness and satisfaction: *Watching sports gave him great pleasure.* □ *Everybody takes pleasure in eating.*
2 an activity or an experience that you find enjoyable: *Watching TV is our only pleasure.* □ *It was a pleasure to see her smiling face.*
It's a pleasure/my pleasure a polite way of answering someone who thanks you for doing something: *'Thanks very much for waiting for me.' — 'It's a pleasure.'*

plectrum /ˈplektrʌm/ *noun*
a small piece of plastic that you use for playing the strings of a guitar

plenty /ˈplenti/
plenty of something a large amount of something: *Don't worry. There's still plenty of time.* □ *Most businesses face plenty of competition.* ●**plenty** *pronoun I don't like long interviews. Fifteen minutes is plenty.*

pliers /ˈplaɪəz/ *plural noun*
a tool with two handles at one end and two hard, flat, metal parts at the other that is used for holding or pulling things: *Hold the nail at its base with pliers.*

pliers

plop /plɒp/ *noun*
the soft sound of something dropping into water: *Another drop of water fell with a soft plop.* ●**plop** *verb* (**plops, plopping, plopped**) *The ice cream plopped to the ground.*

plot ¹ /plɒt/ *verb* (**plots, plotting, plotted**)
to plan secretly to do something: *They plotted to overthrow the government.*

plot ² /plɒt/ *noun*
1 a secret plan to do something: *We have uncovered a plot to kill the president.*
2 a series of events that make up the story of a film or a book: *He told me the plot of his new book.*
3 a small piece of land, especially one that is intended for a particular purpose: *I bought a small plot of land and built a house on it.*

plough /plaʊ/ *noun*
a large farming tool that is pulled across the soil to turn it over, usually before seeds are planted ●**plough** *verb* (**ploughs, ploughing, ploughed**) *They were using horses to plough their fields.*

pluck /plʌk/ *verb* (**plucks, plucking, plucked**)
to pull the strings of a musical instrument with your fingers, so that they make a sound: *Nell was plucking a harp.*

plug ¹ /plʌg/ *noun*
1 the plastic object with metal pins that connects a piece of electrical equipment to the electricity supply: *Remove the power plug when you have finished.*
2 a round object that you use to block the hole in a bath or a sink: *She put in the plug and filled the sink with cold water.*

plug

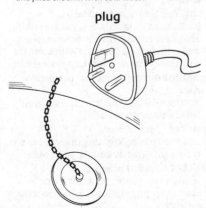

plug ² /plʌg/ *verb* (plugs, plugging, plugged)
to block a hole with something: *We are working to plug a major oil leak.*

plug something in to connect a piece of electrical equipment to the electricity supply: *I had a TV, but there was no place to plug it in.*

plum /plʌm/ *noun*
a small, sweet fruit with a smooth purple, red or yellow skin and a large seed (= a stone) in the middle
→ Look at picture on P2

plumber /'plʌmə/ *noun*
a person whose job is to put in and repair things like water and gas pipes, toilets and baths
→ Look at picture on P7

plump /plʌmp/ *adjective* (plumper, plumpest)
round and rather heavy: *Maria was small and plump.*

plunge /plʌndʒ/ *verb* (plunges, plunging, plunged)
1 to fall or jump into water: *The bus plunged into a river.*
2 to push an object violently into something: *He plunged a fork into his dinner.*

plural /'plʊərəl/ *noun*
the form of a noun that is used for talking about more than one person or thing: *'People' is the plural of 'person'.* ● **plural** *adjective* *'Men' is the plural form of 'man'.*

plus /plʌs/ *conjunction*
used for showing that one number is being added to another: *Two plus two equals four.*

p.m. /ˌpiː 'em/ also **pm** *adverb*
used after a number when you are talking about a particular time between 12 noon and 12 midnight. Compare with **a.m.**: *The pool is open from 7.00 a.m. to 9.00 p.m. every day.*

pneumonia /njuː'məʊniə/ *uncountable noun*
a serious disease that affects the lungs: *She nearly died of pneumonia.*

pocket ¹ /'pɒkɪt/ *noun*
a part of a piece of clothing that you can put things in: *He put the key in his jacket pocket.*

pocket ² /'pɒkɪt/ *adjective*
used for describing something that is small enough to fit into a pocket: *a pocket calculator*

pocket money *uncountable noun*
money that parents give to their children, usually every week: *Her parents gave her £6 pocket money a week.*

pod /pɒd/ *noun*
a seed container that grows on some plants: *We bought fresh peas in their pods.*

podcast /'pɒdkɑːst/ *noun*
a file containing a radio show or something similar, that you can listen to on a computer or an MP3 player (= a small piece of electrical equipment for listening to music): *There are thousands of new podcasts available every day.*

poem /'pəʊɪm/ *noun*
a piece of writing in which the words are chosen for their beauty and sound, and are arranged in short lines: *He read to her from a book of love poems.*

poet /'pəʊɪt/ *noun*
a person who writes poems: *He was a painter and a poet.*

poetry /'pəʊɪtri/ *uncountable noun*
the form of literature that consists of poems: *We studied Russian poetry last term.*

point ¹ /pɔɪnt/ *noun*
1 an idea or a fact: *We disagreed with every point she made.*
2 the purpose of something: *What is the point of worrying?* □ *There's no point in fighting.*
3 a particular position or time: *We're all going to die at some point.*
4 the thin, sharp end of a knife: *Griego felt the cold point of a knife against his neck.*
5 the small dot that separates whole numbers from parts of numbers: *The highest temperature today was 98.5° ('ninety-eight point five degrees').*
6 a mark that you win in a game or a sport: *Chamberlain scored 50 points.*

on the point of something about to do something: *He was on the point of answering when the phone rang.*

point of view your opinion about something: *We would like to hear your point of view.*

point ² /pɔɪnt/ *verb* (points, pointing, pointed)
1 to use your finger to show where someone or something is: *I pointed at the boy sitting near me.*
2 to hold something towards someone

point

I pointed at the boy sitting near me.

or something: *She smiled when Laura pointed a camera at her.*

point something out to tell someone about a fact or show it to them: *He pointed out the errors in the book.*

pointed /'pɔɪntɪd/ *adjective*
with a point at one end: *William was uncomfortable in his new pointed shoes.*

pointless /'pɔɪntləs/ *adjective*
with no sense or purpose: *Without an audience, the performance is pointless.*

poison¹ /'pɔɪzən/ *noun*
a substance that harms or kills people or animals if they swallow or touch it: *Poison from the factory is causing the fish to die.*

poison² /'pɔɪzən/ *verb* (**poisons, poisoning, poisoned**)
to harm someone or something by giving them poison: *They say that she poisoned her husband.*

poisonous /'pɔɪzənəs/ *adjective*
1 containing poison: *All parts of this tree are poisonous.*
2 used for describing an animal that produces a substance that will kill you or make you ill if the animal bites you: *The zoo keeps a selection of poisonous spiders and snakes.*

poke /pəʊk/ *verb* (**pokes, poking, poked**)
1 to quickly push someone or something with your finger or with a sharp object: *Lindy poked him in the arm.* ● **poke** *noun John gave Richard a playful poke.*
2 to push one thing into another: *He poked the stick into the hole.*

poker /'pəʊkə/ *uncountable noun*
a card game that is usually played in order to win money: *Len and I play poker every week.*

pole /pəʊl/ *noun*
1 a long thin piece of wood or metal, used especially for supporting things: *The car went off the road, knocking down a telephone pole.*
2 the two opposite ends of the Earth, which are its most northern and southern points: *For six months of the year, there is very little light at the poles.*

police /pə'liːs/ *plural noun*
1 the organization that is responsible for making sure that people obey the law: *The police are looking for the car.* □ *Police say they have arrested twenty people.*
2 men and women who are members of the police: *More than one hundred police are in the area.*

po'lice car *noun*
a vehicle used by the police

po'lice force *noun*
an organization that is responsible for making sure that people obey the law: *I want to join the police force.*

policeman /pə'liːsmən/ *noun* (**policemen**)
a man who is a member of the police force

po'lice officer *noun*
a member of the police force: *a senior police officer*
→ Look at picture on P7

po'lice station *noun*
the local office of the police in a particular area: *Two police officers arrested him and took him to the police station.*

policewoman /pə'liːswʊmən/ *noun* (**policewomen**)
a woman who is a member of the police force

policy /'pɒlɪsi/ *noun* (**policies**)
a set of ideas or plans about a particular subject, especially in politics, economics or business: *There will be some important changes in foreign policy.*

polish¹ /'pɒlɪʃ/ *noun* (**polishes**)
a substance that you put on a surface in order to clean it and make it shine: *Furniture polish will clean and protect your table.*

polish² /'pɒlɪʃ/ *verb* (**polishes, polishing, polished**)
to rub something to make it shine: *He polished his shoes.*

P

polish

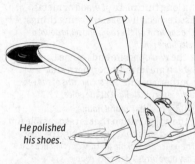

He polished his shoes.

polite /pə'laɪt/ *adjective* (**politer, politest**)
behaving with respect towards other people: *He seemed a quiet and very polite young man.*
▸ **politely** *adverb* *'Your home is beautiful,' I said politely.*
▸ **politeness** *uncountable noun* *She listened to him, but only out of politeness.*

political /pə'lɪtɪkəl/ *adjective*
relating to politics or the government: *I am not a member of any political party.*
▸ **politically** /pə'lɪtɪkli/ *adverb* *Politically, this is a very risky move.*

po,litical 'party *noun* (**political parties**)
an organization whose members share similar ideas and beliefs about politics: *Some members of the main political parties gave interviews to reporters.*

politician /,pɒlɪ'tɪʃən/ *noun*
a person who works in politics, especially a member of a government: *They have arrested a number of politicians.*

politics /'pɒlɪtɪks/ *noun*
1 *uncountable* the activities and ideas that are concerned with government: *He was involved in local politics.*
2 *plural* your beliefs about what a government should do: *His politics are extreme and often confused.*

poll /pəʊl/ *noun*
a way of discovering what people think about something by asking them questions: *The polls are showing that women are very involved in this campaign.*

pollen /'pɒlən/ *noun*
a powder that is produced by flowers: *The male bee carries the pollen from one flower to another.*

pollute /pə'luːt/ *verb* (**pollutes, polluting, polluted**)
to make water, air or land dirty: *Industry pollutes our rivers with chemicals.*
▸ **polluted** *adjective* *Fish are dying in the polluted rivers.*

pollution /pə'luːʃən/ *uncountable noun*
1 the process of making water, air or land dirty and dangerous: *The government announced plans for reducing pollution of the air, sea, rivers and soil.*
2 poisonous substances that pollute water, air or land: *The level of pollution in the river was falling.*

polyester /,pɒli'estə/ *uncountable noun*
a type of artificial material that is mainly used for making clothes: *He wore a shirt made of green polyester.*

pond /pɒnd/ *noun*
a small area of water: *We sat on a bench beside the duck pond.*

pony /'pəʊni/ *noun* (**ponies**)
a small or young horse

ponytail /'pəʊni,teɪl/ *noun*
a hairstyle in which your hair is tied up at the back of your head and hangs down like a horse's tail: *Her long, fine hair was tied back in a ponytail.*

pool /puːl/ *noun*
1 → see **swimming pool**: *Does the hotel have a heated indoor pool?*
2 a small area of liquid: *a pool of blood*
3 *uncountable* a game that is played on a special table. Players use a long stick to hit a white ball so that it knocks numbered coloured balls into six holes around the edge of the table.

poor /pʊə, pɔː/ *adjective* (**poorer, poorest**)
1 having very little money and few possessions: *'We were very poor in those days,' he says.*
2 used for showing that you are sorry for someone: *I feel sorry for that poor child.* □ *Poor Mike. Does he feel better now?*
3 bad: *The illegal copies are of very poor quality.* □ *The actors gave a poor performance.*
▸ **poorly** *adverb* *'We played poorly in the first game,' Mendez said.*

the poor people who are poor: *There are huge differences between the rich and the poor.*

pop[1] /pɒp/ *noun*
1 *uncountable* modern music that usually

has a strong rhythm and uses electronic equipment: *Their music is a combination of Caribbean rhythms and European pop.* □ *Her room is covered with posters of pop stars.*

2 a short, sharp sound: *Each piece of corn will make a loud pop when it is cooked.*

pop² /pɒp/ *verb* (**pops, popping, popped**)
1 to make a short, sharp sound: *He heard a balloon pop behind his head.*

2 to put something somewhere quickly (*informal*): *He popped some gum in his mouth.*

3 to go somewhere quickly: *Their mum popped out to post a letter.*

pop in to go to someone's house for a short time: *Wendy popped in for coffee.*

popcorn /'pɒpkɔːn/ *uncountable noun*
a type of food that consists of grains of corn that have been heated until they have burst and become large and light

pope /pəʊp/ *noun*
the leader of the Roman Catholic Church: *The pope prayed for peace.*

popular /'pɒpjʊlə/ *adjective*
1 liked by a lot of people: *He was the most popular politician in Scotland.* □ *Chocolate sauce is always popular with kids.*
▸ **popularity** /ˌpɒpjʊ'lærɪti/ *uncountable noun* *The singer's popularity grew with his successful 1999 album.*

2 believed or thought by most people: *There is a popular belief that unemployment causes crime.*

population /ˌpɒpjʊ'leɪʃən/ *noun*
all the people who live in a country or an area: *Bangladesh now has a population of about 150 million.*

porch /pɔːtʃ/ *noun* (**porches**)
a covered area with a roof and sometimes walls at the entrance to a building: *I was standing in the porch because it was raining.*

pore /pɔː/ *noun*
one of the very small holes in your skin: *Use hot water to clear blocked pores.*

pork /pɔːk/ *uncountable noun*
meat from a pig: *He said he didn't eat pork.*

porridge /'pɒrɪdʒ/ *uncountable noun*
a thick food made by cooking oats (= a type of grain) in water or milk

port /pɔːt/ *noun*
1 a town by the sea where ships arrive and leave: *We stopped at the Mediterranean port of Marseilles.*

2 a place on a computer where you can attach another piece of equipment: *The scanner plugs into the printer port of your computer.*

portable /'pɔːtəbəl/ *adjective*
designed to be carried or moved around: *The iPod can be used as a portable storage device for all types of file.*

porter /'pɔːtə/ *noun*
a person whose job is to carry things, for example, people's luggage: *Our taxi arrived at the station and a porter came to the door.*

portion /'pɔːʃən/ *noun*
1 a part of something: *Only a small portion of the castle was damaged.* □ *I have spent a large portion of my life here.*

2 the amount of food that is given to one person at a meal: *The portions were huge.*

portrait /'pɔːtrət/ *noun*
a painting, drawing or photograph of a particular person: *The wall was covered with family portraits.*

pose¹ /pəʊz/ *verb* (**poses, posing, posed**)
1 to stay in one position so that someone can photograph you or paint you: *The six foreign ministers posed for photographs.*

2 to ask a question (*formal*): *I finally posed the question, 'Why?'*

pose² /pəʊz/ *noun*
a position that you stay in when someone is photographing you or painting you: *We tried various poses.*

posh /pɒʃ/ *adjective* (**posher, poshest**)
fashionable and expensive (*informal*): *We stayed one night in a posh hotel.*

position /pə'zɪʃən/ *noun*
1 the place where someone or something is: *Measure and mark the position of the handle on the door.*

2 the way you are sitting, lying or standing: *Mr Horwood raised himself to a sitting position.*

3 a job in a company or an organization (*formal*): *He left a career in teaching to take a position with IBM.*

4 the situation you are in at a particular time: *He's going to be in a very difficult position if things go badly.* □ *The club's financial position is still uncertain.*

positive /'pɒzɪtɪv/ *adjective*
1 hopeful and confident: *Be positive about your future.*
▸ **positively** *adverb* *You really must try to start thinking positively.*

p

2 pleasant and helpful: *I want to have a positive effect on my children's lives.*

3 completely sure about something: *'Judith's never late. Are you sure she said eight?' — 'Positive.'*

4 showing that something has happened or is present in a medical or scientific test: *If the test is positive, treatment will start immediately.*

5 higher than zero. Compare with **negative**.

possess /pə'zes/ *verb* (**possesses, possessing, possessed**)
to have or own something: *They sold everything they possessed to raise the money.*

possession /pə'zeʃən/ *noun*
1 *uncountable* the state of having or owning something (*formal*): *He was found in possession of stolen goods.*
2 *plural* the things that you own or have with you at a particular time: *People have lost their homes and all their possessions.*

possessive /pə'zesɪv/ *adjective*
used for describing a word such as 'my' or 'his' that shows who or what something belongs to

possibility /ˌpɒsɪ'bɪlɪti/ *noun*
(**possibilities**)
a situation when something might happen: *There is a possibility that they jailed the wrong man.*

possible /'pɒsɪbəl/ *adjective*
1 able to be done: *If it is possible to find out where your brother is, we will.* □ *Anything is possible if you want it enough.*
2 used for describing a situation where something might be true, although you do not know for sure: *It is possible that he's telling the truth.*
as soon as possible as soon as you can: *Please make your decision as soon as possible.*

possibly /'pɒsɪbli/ *adverb*
1 used when you are not sure if something is true or if it will happen: *Exercise will possibly protect against heart attacks.*
2 used for saying that something is possible: *They've done everything they can possibly think of.* □ *I can't possibly answer that!*

post¹ /pəʊst/ *verb* (**posts, posting, posted**)
1 (*American*: **mail**) to send a letter or a parcel somewhere by post: *I posted a letter*

to Stanley. □ *I'm posting you a cheque.*
2 to put something on a wall so that everyone can see it: *Officials began posting warning notices.*
3 to put information on a website so that other people can see it: *The statement was posted on the Internet.*

post² /pəʊst/ *noun*
1 (*American*: **mail**) the system that collects and delivers letters and packages: *The cheque is in the post.* □ *The winner will be informed by post.*
2 (*American*: **mail**) *uncountable* letters and packages that you send or receive: *There has been no post for three weeks.*
3 an important job in an organization (*formal*): *She accepted the post of the director's assistant.*
4 a strong piece of wood or metal that is set into the ground: *The car went through a red light and hit a fence post.*

postage /'pəʊstɪdʒ/ *uncountable noun*
the money that you pay for sending post: *All prices include postage.*

postbox /'pəʊstbɒks/ *noun* (**postboxes**)
also **post box** (*American*: **mailbox**)
a box in the street where you put letters that you want to send

postcard /'pəʊstkɑːd/ also **post card** *noun*
a thin card, often with a picture on one side, that you can write on and post to someone without using an envelope

postcode /'pəʊstkəʊd/ also **post code**
(*American*: **zip code**) *noun*
a short series of numbers and letters at the end of an address

poster /'pəʊstə/ *noun*
a large notice or picture that you stick on a wall: *I saw a poster for the jazz festival in Monterey.*

postman /'pəʊstmən/ *noun* (**postmen**)
a man who collects and delivers letters and packages

post office *noun*
a building where you can buy stamps and send post: *She needed to get to the post office before it closed.*

postpone /pəʊs'pəʊn/ *verb* (**postpones, postponing, postponed**)
to arrange for an event to happen at a later time: *He decided to postpone the trip until the following day.*

pot /pɒt/ *noun*
1 a deep round container used for cooking food: *The shelf is full of metal cooking pots.*
2 a round container that is used for a particular purpose: *She asked him to pass the coffee pot.* □ *a pot of paint*

potato /pəˈteɪtəʊ/ *noun* (**potatoes**)
a hard, round, white vegetable with brown or red skin. Potatoes grow under the ground.
→ Look at picture on P2

po'tato chip *noun* (*American*)
→ see **crisp**

potential¹ /pəˈtenʃəl/ *adjective*
used for saying that someone or something could become a particular type of person or thing: *The company has identified 60 potential customers.* □ *We are aware of the potential problems.*
▶ **potentially** *adverb* *This is a potentially dangerous situation.*

potential² /pəˈtenʃəl/ *uncountable noun*
the possibility that someone or something could become successful or useful in the future: *The boy has great potential.*

pottery /ˈpɒtəri/ *uncountable noun*
pots, dishes and other objects made from a special type of earth (= clay): *The shop sells a fine range of pottery.*

poultry /ˈpəʊltri/ *plural noun*
birds that people keep for their eggs and meat, such as chickens

pounce /paʊns/ *verb* (**pounces, pouncing, pounced**)
to suddenly jump on someone or something: *He pounced on the photographer and knocked him to the ground.*

pound /paʊnd/ *noun*
1 a unit of weight that is used in the U.S., Britain and some other countries. One pound is equal to 0.454 kilograms: *Her weight was under ninety pounds.* □ *a pound of cheese*
2 the unit of money (£) that is used in the U.K.

pour /pɔː/ *verb* (**pours, pouring, poured**)
1 to make a liquid or other substance flow out of a container: *She poured some water into a bowl.* □ *She asked Tillie to pour her a cup of coffee.*
2 to flow somewhere quickly and in large amounts: *Blood was pouring from his broken nose.* □ *Tears poured down our faces.*

pour

3 to rain very heavily: *It was still pouring outside.*

poverty /ˈpɒvəti/ *uncountable noun*
the state of being very poor: *Many of these people are living in poverty.*

powder /ˈpaʊdə/ *uncountable noun*
a fine dry dust: *Put a small amount of the powder into a container and mix with water.* □ *cocoa powder*

power /ˈpaʊə/ *noun*
1 *uncountable* control over people: *When children are young, parents still have a lot of power.*
2 your ability to do something: *She has the power to charm anyone.*
3 the legal right to do something: *The police have the power to arrest people who carry knives.*
4 *uncountable* the physical strength of something, or the ability that it has to affect things: *This vehicle has more power and better brakes.*
5 *uncountable* energy that can be used for making electricity or for making machines work: *Nuclear power is cleaner than coal.* □ *The storm left a million homes without electrical power.*
6 used in maths for talking about the number of times that you multiply a number by itself. For example, '5 to the power of 5' means '5×5'.
in power in charge of a country or an organization: *Amin was in power for eight years.*

powerful /ˈpaʊəfʊl/ *adjective*
1 able to control people and events: *You're a powerful man — people will listen to you.* □ *Russia and India are two large, powerful countries.*
2 physically strong: *He lifts weights to maintain his powerful muscles.*

3 very strong or having a strong effect: *We need more and more powerful computer systems.* □ *There was a powerful smell of petrol in the car.*
4 loud: *Mrs Jones's powerful voice interrupted them.*

powerless /'paʊələs/ *adjective*
unable to do anything to control a situation: *If you don't have money, you're powerless.* □ *Security guards were powerless to stop the crowd.*

power line *noun*
a cable, especially above ground, along which electricity travels to an area or building

practical /'præktɪkəl/ *adjective*
1 involving real situations and events, rather than ideas and theories: *Our system is the most practical way of preventing crime.*
2 sensible and able to deal effectively with problems: *We need a practical person to take care of the details.* □ *You were always so practical, Maria.*
3 useful rather than just being fashionable or attractive: *We'll need plenty of lightweight, practical clothes.*

practically /'præktɪkəli/ *adverb*
almost: *He's known the old man practically all his life.*

practice /'præktɪs/ *noun*
1 something that people do regularly: *They campaign against the practice of using animals for experiments.*
2 *uncountable* the act of doing something regularly in order to be able to do it better: *It takes a lot of practice to become a good musician.*

practise /'præktɪs/ *verb* (**practises, practising, practised**)
to do something regularly in order to do it better: *She practised the piano in the school basement.* □ *Keep practising, and maybe next time you'll do better*

praise /preɪz/ *verb* (**praises, praising, praised**)
to say that you admire or respect someone or something for something they have done: *The passengers praised John for saving their lives.* ● **praise** *uncountable noun* *The ladies are full of praise for the staff.*

pram /præm/ *noun*
a small bed with four wheels, used for pushing a baby around when you go out

prawn /prɔːn/ (American: **shrimp**) *noun*
a small sea animal with ten legs which becomes pink when you cook it

pray /preɪ/ *verb* (**prays, praying, prayed**)
1 to speak to God or a god: *We pray that Billy's family will now find peace.*
2 to hope very much that something will happen: *I'm praying for good weather.* □ *I'm praying that someone will do something before it's too late.*

prayer /preə/ *noun*
1 the words that a person says when they speak to God or a god: *They should say a prayer for the people on both sides.*
2 *uncountable* the activity of speaking to God or a god: *The monks give their lives to prayer.*

precaution /prɪ'kɔːʃən/ *noun*
an action that is intended to prevent something bad from happening: *Just as a precaution, he should move to a safe place.*

precede /prɪ'siːd/ *verb* (**precedes, preceding, preceded**)
to happen before something else (*formal*): *In English, adjectives usually precede the noun they describe.*

precious /'preʃəs/ *adjective*
1 rare and worth a lot of money: *The company mines precious metals throughout North America.*
2 important to you; that you do not want to lose: *Her family's support is particularly precious to Josie.*

precise /prɪ'saɪs/ *adjective*
exact and accurate in all details: *I can remember the precise moment when I heard the news.*

precisely /prɪ'saɪsli/ *adverb*
accurately and exactly: *Nobody knows precisely how many people are still living there.*

precision /prɪ'sɪʒən/ *uncountable noun*
when someone does something exactly as it should be done: *He hits the ball with precision.*

predator /'predətə/ *noun*
an animal that kills and eats other animals: *With no natural predators on the island, the animals lived happily.*

predict /prɪ'dɪkt/ *verb* (**predicts, predicting, predicted**)
to say that an event will happen: *The man correctly predicted the results of fifteen matches.*

▶ **prediction** /prɪˈdɪkʃən/ *noun* My prediction is that the process will take about 5 years.

predictable /prɪˈdɪktəbəl/ *adjective*
that can be predicted: This was a predictable reaction.

preface /ˈprefɪs/ *noun*
an introduction at the beginning of a book: Have you read the preface to Kelman's novel?

prefer /prɪˈfɜː/ *verb* (**prefers, preferring, preferred**)
to like someone or something better than another person or thing: Does he prefer a particular type of music? □ I preferred books to TV. □ He would prefer to be in Philadelphia.

> **LANGUAGE HELP**
> Expressions such as **like…better** and **would rather** are used more often than **prefer**. Instead of saying I prefer football to tennis, you can say I like football better than tennis. Instead of I'd prefer an apple, you can say I'd rather have an apple. Instead of I'd prefer to walk, you can say I'd rather walk.

preferable /ˈprefrəbəl/ *adjective*
better or more suitable than something else: For me, a trip to the supermarket is preferable to buying food on the Internet.
▶ **preferably** /ˈprefrəbli/ *adverb* Get exercise, preferably in the fresh air.

preference /ˈprefərəns/ *noun*
a feeling that you would like to have or do one thing rather than something else: Customers have shown a preference for salty snacks.

prefix /ˈpriːfɪks/ *noun* (**prefixes**)
a letter or group of letters that is added to the beginning of a word in order to form a different word. For example, the prefix 'un-' is added to 'happy' to form 'unhappy'. Compare with **suffix**.

pregnant /ˈpregnənt/ *adjective*
having a baby or babies developing in your body: I'm seven months pregnant.
▶ **pregnancy** /ˈpregnənsi/ *noun* (**pregnancies**) We keep a record of your weight gain during pregnancy.

prejudice /ˈpredʒʊdɪs/ *noun*
an unreasonable dislike of a particular group of people or things: These people have always suffered from racial prejudice. □ There seems to be some prejudice against workers over 45.

prejudiced /ˈpredʒʊdɪsd/ *adjective*
having an unreasonable dislike of someone from a different group: They complained that the police were racially prejudiced.

preliminary /prɪˈlɪmɪnri/ *adjective*
taking place at the beginning of an event, often as a form of preparation: Preliminary results show the Republican Party with 11 per cent of the vote.

premature /ˌpreməˈtʃʊə/ *adjective*
1 happening earlier than people expect: Heart disease is a common cause of premature death.
2 born before the expected date: Even very young premature babies respond to their mother's presence.

preparation /ˌprepəˈreɪʃən/ *noun*
1 *uncountable* the process of getting something ready for use: Todd put the papers in his briefcase in preparation for the meeting.
2 *plural* all the arrangements that are made for a future event: We were making preparations for our wedding.

prepare /prɪˈpeə/ *verb* (**prepares, preparing, prepared**)
1 to make something ready: We will need several weeks to prepare the report for publication.
2 to get ready for an event: You should begin to prepare for the cost of your child's education.
3 to get food ready: She started preparing dinner.

prepared /prɪˈpeəd/ *adjective*
1 willing to do something if necessary: Are you prepared to help if we need you?
2 ready for something that you think is going to happen: Police are prepared for large crowds.

preposition /ˌprepəˈzɪʃən/ *noun*
a word such as 'by', 'for', 'into' or 'with' that usually comes before a noun

prescribe /prɪˈskraɪb/ *verb* (**prescribes, prescribing, prescribed**)
to tell someone what medicine or treatment to have: The doctor examines the patient and prescribes medication.

P

prepositions

across

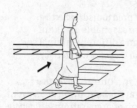

*She is walking **across** the road.*

against

*The ladder is leaning **against** the wall.*

along

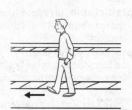

*He is walking **along** the road.*

among

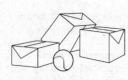

*The ball is **among** the boxes.*

behind

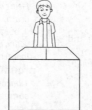

*The boy is **behind** the box.*

beside

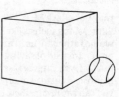

*The ball is **beside** the box.*

between

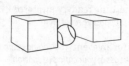

*The ball is **between** the boxes.*

down

*He is climbing **down** the ladder.*

far away

near

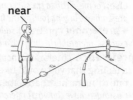

*He is **near** the road.*
*She is **far away** from him.*

from

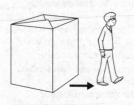

*He is walking away **from** the box.*

in front of

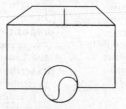

*The ball is **in front of** the box.*

inside

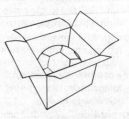

*The ball is **inside** the box.*

prepositions

into

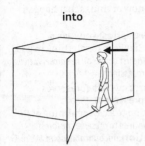

*He is walking **into** the box.*

on

*The ball is **on** the box.*

on top of

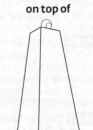

*The ball is **on top of** the box.*

opposite

*They are **opposite** each other.*

out of

*She is jumping **out of** the box.*

over

*He is jumping **over** the box.*

round

*She is running **round** the box.*

through

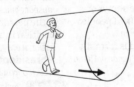

*He is walking **through** the tunnel.*

towards

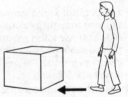

*She is walking **towards** the box.*

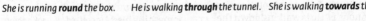

under

*She is **under** the table.*

up

*He is climbing **up** the ladder.*

p

prescription /prɪˈskrɪpʃən/ *noun*
a piece of paper on which a doctor writes
an order for medicine: *He gave me a
prescription for some cream.*

presence /ˈprezəns/ *noun*
the fact that someone is in a place: *His
presence always causes trouble.*

in someone's presence in the same
place as someone: *Children should do their
homework in the presence of their parents.*

present¹ /ˈprezənt/ *adjective*
1 at an event or in a place: *Nine people were
present at the meeting.*
2 existing now: *The present situation is very
difficult for us.*

at present now: *At present, we do not know
the cause of the disease.*

present² /ˈprezənt/ *noun*
something that you give to someone,
for example, on their birthday: *She bought
a birthday present for her mother.*

present³ /prɪˈzent/ *verb* (**presents,
presenting, presented**)
to formally give something to someone:
The mayor presented him with a gold medal.
□ *Betty will present the prizes to the winners.*

presentation /ˌprezənˈteɪʃən/ *noun*
1 an event at which someone is given an
award: *He received his award at a presentation
in Oxford.*
2 an occasion when someone shows or
explains something to a group of people:
Philip and I gave a short presentation.
3 *uncountable* when an award is formally
given to someone: *The evening began with the
presentation of awards.*

present con'tinuous *noun*
the structure that uses 'be' and the '-ing'
form of a verb. An example of the present
continuous is 'He is walking down the
road'.

present 'perfect *noun*
the form of a verb that you use to talk
about things that began in the past and
are still happening or still important in
the present. The present perfect is formed
with the verb 'have' and a past participle
(= a verb form that ends in '-ed' for
regular verbs). An example of the present
perfect is 'She has promised to come'.

present 'tense *noun*
the form of a verb that is used for talking

about things that exist, things that are
happening now or things that happen
regularly

preservative /prɪˈzɜːvətɪv/ *noun*
a chemical that keeps something in good
condition: *The list shows all the preservatives
used in food processing.*

preserve /prɪˈzɜːv/ *verb* (**preserves,
preserving, preserved**)
1 to take action to save something or
protect it: *We need to preserve the forest.*
▶ **preservation** *uncountable noun* *We're
collecting money for the preservation of our
historic buildings.*
2 to treat food in order to make it last
longer: *Use only enough sugar to preserve the
plums.*

preside /prɪˈzaɪd/ *verb* (**presides,
presiding, presided**)
to be in charge of a meeting: *He presided
over the weekly meetings of the organization.*

presidency /ˈprezɪdənsi/ *noun*
(**presidencies**)
the position of being the president of a
country or an organization: *He was offered
the presidency of the University of
Saskatchewan.*

president /ˈprezɪdənt/ *noun*
1 the person who is in charge of a country
that has no king or queen: *The president
must act quickly.*
2 the person who has the highest
position in an organization: *He is the
national president of the Screen Actors Guild.*
▶ **presidential** /ˌprezɪˈdenʃəl/ *adjective*
He is reporting on Peru's presidential election.

press¹ /pres/ *verb* (**presses, pressing,
pressed**)
1 to push something firmly against
something else: *He pressed his back against
the door.*
2 to push a button or a switch with your
finger in order to make a machine work:
David pressed a button and the door closed.
3 to push hard against something with
your foot or hand: *He pressed the accelerator
hard.*
4 to iron clothes: *Vera pressed his shirt.*

press² /pres/ *uncountable noun*
newspapers and magazines, and the
people who write for them: *She gave several
interviews to the local press.*

P

pressure /'preʃə/ *uncountable noun*
1 force that you produce when you press hard on something: *The pressure of his fingers on her arm relaxed.*
2 force produced by the gas or liquid in a place or a container: *If the pressure falls in the cabin, an oxygen mask will drop in front of you.*
3 a situation where you feel that you must do a lot of things or make an important decision in very little time: *Can you work under pressure?*

presumably /prɪ'zjuːməbli/ *adverb*
probably: *He's not going this year, presumably because of his age.*

presume /prɪ'zjuːm/ *verb* (**presumes, presuming, presumed**)
to think that something is true, although you are not sure: *I presume that you're here on business.* □ *'Has he been home all week?' — 'I presume so.'*

pretend /prɪ'tend/ *verb* (**pretends, pretending, pretended**)
1 to try to make people believe that something is true, although in fact it is not: *I pretend that things are really okay when they're not.* □ *He pretended to be asleep.*
2 to imagine that you are doing something, for example, as part of a game: *She can sunbathe and pretend she's in Cancun.*

pretty /'prɪti/ *adjective, adverb* (**prettier, prettiest**)
1 attractive and pleasant: *She's a very charming and pretty girl.* □ *We stayed in a very pretty little town.*

> **LANGUAGE HELP**
> See note at **beautiful**.

2 used before an adjective or adverb to mean 'fairly' (*informal*): *I had a pretty good idea what she was going to do.*

prevent /prɪ'vent/ *verb* (**prevents, preventing, prevented**)
to make sure that something does not happen: *The best way to prevent injury is to wear a seat belt.* □ *The disease can prevent you from walking properly.*
▶ **prevention** *uncountable noun* *Scientists are still learning about the prevention of heart disease.*

previous /'priːviəs/ *adjective*
used for describing something that happened or existed before something

else: *She has a teenage daughter from a previous marriage.*
▶ **previously** *adverb* *The railways were previously owned by private companies.*

prey /preɪ/ *uncountable noun*
the birds or other animals that an animal hunts and eats in order to live: *These animals can hunt prey in the water or in trees.*

price /praɪs/ *noun*
the amount of money that you have to pay in order to buy something: *We have seen huge changes in the price of gas.* □ *They expect house prices to rise.*

priceless /'praɪsləs/ *adjective*
1 worth a very large amount of money: *Several priceless treasures were stolen from the Palace Museum last night.*
2 extremely useful or valuable: *Our national parks are priceless treasures.*

prick /prɪk/ *verb* (**pricks, pricking, pricked**)
1 to make small holes in something with a sharp object: *Prick the potatoes and rub the skins with salt.*
2 to press into someone's skin and hurt them: *It felt like a needle pricking me in the foot.*

pride /praɪd/ *uncountable noun*
1 a feeling of satisfaction that you have because you have done something well: *We all felt the sense of pride when we finished early.* □ *We take pride in offering you the highest standards.*
2 a sense of dignity and self-respect: *His pride wouldn't allow him to ask for help.*

priest /priːst/ *noun*
a person who has religious duties in a place where people worship: *He trained to be a Catholic priest.*

primarily /'praɪmərɪli/ *adverb*
mainly: *These reports come primarily from passengers on the plane.*

primary /'praɪməri/ *adjective*
1 most important (*formal*): *Language difficulties were the primary cause of his problems.*
2 relating to the first few years of formal education for children: *Most primary students now have experience with computers.*

'primary ,colour *noun*
one of the three colours (red, yellow and blue) that can be mixed together to produce other colours: *The toys come in bright primary colours that kids will love.*

p

'primary school *noun*
a school for children between the ages of
4 or 5 and 11: *She's in her third year at Greenside
Primary School.*

prime 'minister *noun*
the leader of the government in some
countries

primitive /'prɪmɪtɪv/ *adjective*
1 belonging to a society in which people
live in a very simple way, usually without
industries or a writing system: *He has
travelled the world, visiting many primitive
societies.*
2 belonging to a very early period in the
development of an animal or a plant:
primitive man
3 very simple in style: *The conditions in the
camp are primitive.*

prince /prɪns/ *noun*
a male member of a royal family,
especially the son of the king or queen

princess /ˌprɪn'ses, 'prɪnses/ *noun*
(**princesses**)
a female member of a royal family,
usually the daughter of a king or queen or
the wife of a prince

principal¹ /'prɪnsɪpəl/ *adjective*
first in order of importance: *Money was not
the principal reason for his action.* □ *Newspapers
were the principal source of information.*

principal² /'prɪnsɪpəl/ *noun*
the person in charge of a school, college
or university: *Donald King is the principal of
Dartmouth High School.*

principle /'prɪnsɪpəl/ *noun*
1 *plural* rules or ideas that you have about
how you should behave: *It's against my
principles to be dishonest.*
2 a rule about how something works or
happens: *The first principle of democracy is that
people should have the right to vote.*

print¹ /prɪnt/ *verb* (**prints, printing, printed**)
1 to use a machine to put words or
pictures on paper: *The publishers have printed
40,000 copies of the novel.*
2 to write in letters that are not joined
together: *Please sign here, then print your name
and address.*

print something out to use a machine
to produce a copy of a computer file on
paper: *I printed out a copy of the letter and put it
on Mr Miller's desk.*

print² /prɪnt/ *uncountable noun*
all the letters and numbers in a printed
document: *I can't read this—the print is too small.*

printer /'prɪntə/ *noun*
1 a machine for printing copies of
computer documents on paper
2 a person or a company whose job is
printing things such as books: *Franklin was
a printer, a publisher and a diplomat.*

printout /'prɪntaʊt/ also **print-out** *noun*
a piece of paper with information from a
computer printed on it: *Maria gave me a
printout of the email.*

prior /'praɪə/ *adjective*
prior to something happening before a
particular time or event (*formal*): *Prior to his
trip to Japan, Steven was in New York.*

priority /praɪ'ɒrɪti/ *noun* (**priorities**)
the most important thing, that you have
to deal with before everything else: *Her
children are her first priority.* □ *The government's
priority is to build more schools.*

give priority to someone/something
to treat someone or something as more
important than anyone or anything else:
*The government should give priority to
environmental issues.*

take priority/have priority to be more
important than other things: *The needs of
the poor must take priority over the desires of the
rich.*

prison /'prɪzən/ *noun*
a building where criminals are kept as
punishment: *He was sent to prison for five years.*

prisoner /'prɪzənə/ *noun*
a person who is not free, usually because
they are in prison: *A prisoner escaped from
Holloway Prison early on Monday.* □ *More than
30,000 Australians were taken prisoner in
World War II.*

privacy /'prɪvəsi/ *uncountable noun*
the freedom to do things without people
knowing what you are doing: *We have
changed the names to protect the privacy of the
people involved.*

private /'praɪvɪt/ *adjective*
1 not owned by the government: *a private
hospital* □ *Their children go to a private school.*
2 only for one particular person or group,
and not for everyone: *It was a private
conversation, so I'm not going to talk about it to
anyone else.*

▶ **privately** *adverb* We need to talk privately.

3 concerning your personal relationships and activities, and not your job: I've always kept my private and professional life separate.

4 quiet, where you can be alone without being disturbed: It was the only private place they could find.

in private without other people being there: Mark asked to talk to his boss in private.

privilege /ˈprɪvɪlɪdʒ/ *noun*
a special advantage that only one person or group has: We are not asking for special privileges, we simply want equal opportunity.

privileged /ˈprɪvɪlɪdʒd/ *adjective*
having an advantage that most other people do not have, often because you are rich: They had a privileged childhood.

prize /praɪz/ *noun*
money or a special object that you give to the person who wins a game, a race or a competition: He won first prize in the golf tournament.

probability /ˌprɒbəˈbɪlɪti/ *noun*
(**probabilities**)
how likely something is to happen: We believe there is a high probability of success.

probable /ˈprɒbəbəl/ *adjective*
likely to be true or likely to happen: Jess is a great player, and it's highly probable that she will win.

probably /ˈprɒbəbli/ *adverb*
likely to be true or to happen, although you are not sure: I will probably go home on Tuesday. □ Van Gogh is probably the best-known painter in the world.

problem /ˈprɒbləm/ *noun*
1 something or someone that causes difficulties, or that makes you worry: Pollution is a problem in this city. □ The government has failed to solve the problem of unemployment.
2 a special type of question that you have to think hard about in order to answer: a maths problem

procedure /prəˈsiːdʒə/ *noun*
the usual or correct way of doing something: If your car is stolen, the correct procedure is to report the theft to the local police.

proceed /prəˈsiːd/ *verb* (**proceeds, proceeding, proceeded**)
1 to do something after doing something else: He picked up a book, which he proceeded to read.

2 to continue (formal): The building work is proceeding very slowly.

process /ˈprəʊses/ *noun* (**processes**)
a series of actions that have a particular result: After the war, the population began the long process of returning to normal life.

procession /prəˈseʃən/ *noun*
a line of people or vehicles that follow one another as part of a ceremony: Sam watched the procession pass him slowly on its way to the palace.

processor /ˈprəʊsesə/ *noun*
the part of a computer that performs the tasks that the user has requested

produce¹ /prəˈdjuːs/ *verb* (**produces, producing, produced**)
1 to make or grow something: The company produces about 2.3 million tons of steel a year.
▶ **producer** *noun* Saudi Arabia is the world's leading oil producer.
2 to cause something to happen: The talks failed to produce results.
3 to organize a play or a film, and decide how it should be made: The film was produced and directed by Johnny White.
▶ **producer** *noun* The film was created by producer Alison Millar.

produce² /ˈprɒdjuːs/ *uncountable noun*
food that you grow on a farm to sell: The restaurant uses as much local produce as possible.

product /ˈprɒdʌkt/ *noun*
something that you make or grow in order to sell it: This mobile phone is one of the company's most successful products.

production /prəˈdʌkʃən/ *noun*
1 *uncountable* the process of making or growing something in large amounts, or the amount of goods that you make or grow: This car went into production last year. □ The factory needs to increase production.
2 a play or other show that is performed in a theatre: Tonight our class is going to see a production of 'Othello'.

productive /prəˈdʌktɪv/ *adjective*
producing or doing a lot: Training makes workers more productive.

profession /prəˈfeʃən/ *noun*
a type of job for which you need special education or training: Ava was a doctor by profession.

professional¹ /prəˈfeʃənəl/ *adjective*
1 relating to a person's work, especially

p

work that requires special training: *Get professional advice from your accountant first.*
2 doing a particular activity as a job rather than just for enjoyment: *My parents were professional musicians.*

▶ **professionally** *adverb* *I've been singing professionally for 10 years.*

professional² /prə'feʃənəl/ *noun*
someone who does an activity as a job, rather than just for enjoyment: *The competition is open to both professionals and amateurs.*

professor /prə'fesə/ *noun*
a senior teacher at a university: *Kate is a professor of history at Oxford University.*

profile /'prəʊfaɪl/ *noun*
the shape of your face when people see it from the side: *He was slim, with black hair and a handsome profile.*

profit /'prɒfɪt/ *noun*
the amount of money that you gain when you sell something for more than you paid for it: *When he sold the house, Chris made a profit of about £50,000.*

profitable /'prɒfɪtəbəl/ *adjective*
making a profit: *The business started to be profitable in its second year.*

program¹ /'prəʊɡræm/ *noun*
a set of instructions that a computer uses to do a particular task: *Ada Lovelace wrote the world's first computer program in 1842.*

program² /'prəʊɡræm/ *verb* (**programs, programming, programmed**)
to give a computer or a machine a set of instructions so that it can do a particular task: *They can teach you how to program a computer in two weeks.*

▶ **programming** *uncountable noun* *Java is a popular programming language.*

▶ **programmer** *noun* *Greg works as a computer programmer.*

programme /'prəʊɡræm/ *noun*
1 a plan of things to do: *The art gallery's education programme includes art classes for all ages.*
2 a television or radio show: *a network television programme*
3 a small book or sheet of paper that tells you about a play or concert: *When you go to concerts, it's helpful to read the programme.*

progress¹ /'prəʊɡres/ *uncountable noun*
the process of gradually improving or

getting nearer to achieving something: *We are making progress in the fight against cancer.*

progress² /prə'ɡres/ *verb* (**progresses, progressing, progressed**)
1 to improve or become more advanced or successful: *All our students are progressing well.*
2 to continue to happen over a period of time: *As the evening progressed, Leila grew tired.*
in progress having started and still happening: *The game was already in progress when we arrived.*

prohibit /prə'hɪbɪt/ *verb* (**prohibits, prohibiting, prohibited**)
to officially say that something is illegal (*formal*): *Smoking is prohibited here.*

project /'prɒdʒekt/ *noun*
1 a plan that takes a lot of time and effort: *The charity is funding a housing project in India.*
2 a piece of work that involves a student finding out a lot of information about a subject and then writing about it: *Our class has just finished a project on ancient Greece.*

projector /prə'dʒektə/ *noun*
a machine that shows films or pictures on a screen or a wall

prologue /'prəʊlɒɡ/ *noun*
a part of a play, book or film that introduces the story: *She first appears in the prologue to the novel.*

prolong /prə'lɒŋ/ *verb* (**prolongs, prolonging, prolonged**)
to make something last longer: *I did not wish to prolong the conversation.*

prominent /'prɒmɪnənt/ *adjective*
1 important and well-known: *Michelle is married to a prominent lawyer in Portland.*
2 big; that can be seen very easily: *a prominent nose*

promise /'prɒmɪs/ *verb* (**promises, promising, promised**)
to say that you will certainly do something: *She promised to write to me soon.*
□ *I promise that I'll help you all I can.* □ *Promise me you'll come to the party.* ● **promise** *noun* *If you make a promise, you should keep it.* □ *James broke every promise he made.*

promote /prə'məʊt/ *verb* (**promotes, promoting, promoted**)
1 to help to make something successful: *There will be a new TV campaign to promote the products.*

2 to give someone a more important job in the same organization: *Richard has just been promoted to general manager.*
▶ **promotion** *noun We went out for dinner to celebrate Dad's promotion.*

prompt /'prɒmpt/ *adjective*
done quickly: *These questions require prompt answers from the government.*

promptly /'prɒmptli/ *adverb*
1 immediately: *Grandma sat down, and promptly fell asleep.*
2 at exactly a particular time: *Promptly at seven o'clock, we left the hotel.*

pronoun /'prəʊnaʊn/ *noun*
a word that you use instead of a noun when you are talking about someone or something. 'It', 'she', 'something' and 'myself' are pronouns.

pronounce /prə'naʊns/ *verb*
(pronounces, pronouncing, pronounced)
to make the sound of a word: *Have I pronounced your name correctly?*

pronunciation /prə,nʌnsi'eɪʃən/ *noun*
the way that you say a word: *We are learning about the differences between Canadian and American pronunciation.*

proof /pruːf/ *uncountable noun*
something that shows that something else is true or exists: *The scientists hope to find proof that there is water on Mars.*

propaganda /,prɒpə'gændə/ *uncountable noun*
information that a political organization uses in order to influence people: *The media began a huge propaganda campaign.*

propeller /prə'pelə/ *noun*
a part of a boat or an aircraft that turns around very fast and makes the boat or the aircraft move: *One of the ship's propellers was damaged in the accident.*

propeller

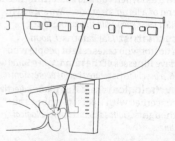

proper /'prɒpə/ *adjective*
1 real (*informal*): *He hasn't got a proper job.*
2 correct or most suitable: *The book is intended as a guide to proper behaviour.*

proper noun *noun* (*also* **proper name**)
the name of a particular person, place, organization or thing. Proper nouns begin with a capital letter.

property /'prɒpəti/ *noun* (**properties**)
1 *uncountable* anything that belongs to you (*formal*): *'That's my property. You can't just take it.'*
2 a building and the land around it (*formal*): *Get out of here — this is a private property!*

proportion /prə'pɔːʃən/ *noun*
1 a part of an amount (*formal*): *A large proportion of the fish in that area have died.*
2 the number of one type of person or thing in a group compared to the total number of people or things in the group: *The proportion of the population using mobile phones is 90-95%.*
3 *uncountable* the correct relationship between the size of objects in a piece of art: *the symmetry and proportion of classical Greek and Roman architecture*

proposal /prə'pəʊzəl/ *noun*
1 a suggestion or a plan: *The president has announced new proposals for a peace agreement.*
2 the act of asking someone to marry you: *Pam accepted Matt's proposal of marriage.*

propose /prə'pəʊz/ *verb* (**proposes, proposing, proposed**)
1 to suggest a plan or an idea: *The minister has proposed a change in the law.*
2 to ask someone to marry you: *David proposed to his girlfriend when they were on holiday in Paris.*

prose /prəʊz/ *uncountable noun*
ordinary written language, not poetry: *Hannah writes both poetry and prose.*

prosecute /'prɒsɪ,kjuːt/ *verb* (**prosecutes, prosecuting, prosecuted**)
to say formally in a law court that a person has committed a crime: *The man was prosecuted for a killing at a petrol station in Birmingham.*
▶ **prosecution** *noun This evidence led to the prosecution of the former leader.*

protect /prə'tekt/ *verb* (**protects, protecting, protected**)
to keep someone or something safe from

P

harm or damage: *Make sure you protect your children from the sun's harmful rays.*

protection /prə'tekʃən/ *noun*
something that stops you from being harmed or damaged by something unpleasant: *Long-sleeved t-shirts offer greater protection against the sun.*

protective /prə'tektɪv/ *adjective*
1 intended to protect you from injury or harm: *You should wear protective gloves when you are gardening.*
2 looking after someone and trying to keep them safe: *Ben is very protective toward his mother.*

protein /'prəʊtiːn/ *noun*
a substance that the body needs which is found in meat, eggs, fish and milk: *Fish is a major source of protein.*

protest¹ /prə'test/ *verb* (**protests, protesting, protested**)
to say or show publicly that you do not approve of something: *The students were protesting against the arrest of one of their teachers.*
▶ **protester** also **protestor** *noun* The protesters say that the government is corrupt.

protest² /'prəʊtest/ *noun*
the act of showing publicly that you do not approve of something: *I took part in a protest against the war.*

Protestant /'prɒtɪstənt/ *noun*
a Christian (= a person who believes that Jesus Christ is the son of God) who is not a Catholic (= a member of the part of the Christian church whose leader is known as the Pope)

protractor /prə'træktə/ *noun*
a flat piece of plastic or metal in the shape of a half-circle, used for measuring angles

proud /praʊd/ *adjective* (**prouder, proudest**)
1 pleased and satisfied about something good that you or other people close to you have done: *His dad was very proud of him.*
▶ **proudly** *adverb* Nick wears his police uniform proudly.
2 thinking that you are better or more important than other people: *He described his boss as 'proud and selfish'.*

prove /pruːv/ *verb* (**proves, proving, proved**)
to show that something is true: *These results prove that we were right.*

proverb /'prɒvɜːb/ *noun*
a short sentence that people often say, because it gives advice or tells you something about life: *An old Arab proverb says, 'The enemy of my enemy is my friend'.*

provide /prə'vaɪd/ *verb* (**provides, providing, provided**)
to give something to someone that they need or want: *The company's website provides lots of useful information.* □ *The refugees were provided with food and accommodation.*

provided /prə'vaɪdɪd/ *conjunction*
used for saying that something will happen only if a second thing also happens: *He can go running at his age, provided that he is sensible.*

providing /prə'vaɪdɪŋ/ *conjunction*
→ see **provided**

province /'prɒvɪns/ *noun*
a large part of a country that has its own local government: *the Canadian province of British Columbia*

provision /prə'vɪʒən/ *uncountable noun*
the act of giving something to people who need or want it: *This department is responsible for the provision of legal services.*

provisional /prə'vɪʒənəl/ *adjective*
used for describing something that has been arranged or exists now, but that may be changed in the future: *Your provisional driving licence is valid for 18 months.*
▶ **provisionally** *adverb* She provisionally accepted the job offer.

provoke /prə'vəʊk/ *verb* (**provokes, provoking, provoked**)
to deliberately annoy someone and try to make them angry: *The demonstrators did not provoke the police and everyone remained calm.*

prune /pruːn/ *noun*
a dried plum

P.S. /,piː 'es/ also **PS**
written when you add something at the end of a letter after you have signed it: *P.S. Please show your friends this letter.*

psychiatrist /saɪ'kaɪətrɪst/ *noun*
a doctor who takes care of people who have illnesses of the mind: *When Sarah was 16, a psychiatrist treated her for depression.*

psychological /,saɪkə'lɒdʒɪkəl/ *adjective*
concerned with a person's mind and thoughts: *Guilt can lead to psychological illness.*

psychology /saɪˈkɒlədʒi/ *uncountable noun*
the study of the human mind and the
reasons for people's behaviour: *Scott is
a professor of educational psychology at Sussex
University.*
▸ **psychologist** *noun Amy is seeing
a psychologist.*

pub /pʌb/ *noun*
a building where people can buy and
drink alcoholic drinks

public¹ /ˈpʌblɪk/ *noun*
the public people in general, or
everyone: *The exhibition is open to the public
from tomorrow.*

public² /ˈpʌblɪk/ *adjective*
1 relating to all the people in a country or
a community: *The government's policies still
have strong public support.*
2 for everyone to use: *The city's public library
was built in 1911.* ▢ *The government has promised
to improve public services such as schools and
post offices.* ▢ *public transport*
in public when other people are there: *He
hasn't performed in public in more than 40 years.*

publication /ˌpʌblɪˈkeɪʃən/ *noun*
1 *uncountable* the act of printing a book or
a magazine and sending it to shops to be
sold: *The shop stayed open late to celebrate the
book's publication.*
2 a book or a magazine: *My uncle has written
for several publications.*

publicity /pʌˈblɪsɪti/ *uncountable noun*
when people are provided with
information about a person or a product:
A lot of publicity was given to the talks.

publicize /ˈpʌblɪˌsaɪz/ *verb* (**publicizes,
publicizing, publicized**)
to let people know about something: *The
author appeared on television to publicize her
latest book.*

ˌpublic ˈschool *noun*
in Britain, a school for students aged
between 13 and 18 which parents have to
pay for. The students often live at the
school while they are studying.

publish /ˈpʌblɪʃ/ *verb* (**publishes,
publishing, published**)
to prepare and print copies of a book, a
magazine or a newspaper: *HarperCollins
will publish his new novel on March 4.*

publisher /ˈpʌblɪʃə/ *noun*
a person or a company that publishes

books, newspapers or magazines: *She sent
the book to a publisher and got a positive response.*

pudding /ˈpʊdɪŋ/ *noun*
1 a sweet dish that you eat at the end of
a meal: *There's fruit salad and ice cream for
pudding.*
2 a cooked sweet food like a warm cake,
made with flour, fat and eggs: *a Christmas
pudding*

puddle /ˈpʌdəl/ *noun*
a small pool of water on the ground: *Young
children love splashing in puddles.*

puddle

puff¹ /pʌf/ *noun*
a small amount of air or smoke that is
blown from somewhere: *Puffs of steam rose
into the air and vanished.*

puff² /pʌf/ *verb* (**puffs, puffing, puffed**)
to breathe loudly and quickly, usually
because you have been running: *He puffs
and pants if he has to walk up the stairs.*

pull /pʊl/ *verb* (**pulls, pulling, pulled**)
to hold something firmly and use force to
move it: *The dentist had to pull out all
Grandpa's teeth.* ▢ *I helped to pull the boy out
of the water.* ▢ *Someone pulled her hair.*
● **pull** *noun He felt a pull on the fishing line.*
pull away when a vehicle pulls away, it
starts moving forwards: *I watched the car
pull away.*
pull in to stop a vehicle somewhere: *The
bus pulled in at the side of the road.*
pull into something to move a vehicle
into a place and stop there: *David pulled into
the driveway in front of her garage.*
pull out to move a vehicle out into the road
or nearer the centre of the road: *I looked in
the rear mirror, and pulled out into the street.*
pull over to move a vehicle closer to the
side of the road and stop there: *I pulled over
to let the police car pass.*

P

pull something down to deliberately destroy a building: *They pulled the offices down, leaving a large open space.*

pull up to slow down a vehicle and stop: *The taxi pulled up and the driver jumped out.*

pull yourself together to control your feelings and be calm again: *'Now stop crying and pull yourself together!'*

pullover /'pʊləʊvə/ *noun*
a warm piece of clothing that covers the upper part of your body and your arms

pulse /pʌls/ *noun*
the regular beat of your heart that you can feel when you touch your wrist and other parts of your body: *Dr Garcia checked her pulse and breathing.*

pump¹ /pʌmp/ *noun*
a machine that makes a liquid or a gas flow in a particular direction: *A pump brings water directly from the well.* □ *There are three water pumps in the village.*

pump² /pʌmp/ *verb* (**pumps, pumping, pumped**)
to make a liquid or a gas flow in a particular direction: *The heart pumps blood around the body.*

pump something up to fill something such as a tyre with air: *Pump all the tyres up well.*

pumpkin /'pʌmpkɪn/ *noun*
a large, round, orange vegetable with a thick skin: *pumpkin pie*

pun /pʌn/ *noun*
a clever and amusing use of a word or phrase that has two meanings.

punch /pʌntʃ/ *verb* (**punches, punching, punched**)
1 to hit someone or something hard with your fist (= your hand, when your fingers are all closed tightly): *During a concert, the singer punched a photographer.* ● **punch** *noun* (**punches**) *My brother gave me a punch in the nose.*
2 to make holes in something by pushing or pressing it with something sharp: *I took a pen and punched a hole in the box.*

punctual /'pʌŋktʃʊəl/ *adjective*
arriving somewhere at the right time: *He's always very punctual.*
▶ **punctually** *adverb* *The guests all arrived punctually, at eight o'clock.*

punctuation /ˌpʌŋktʃʊ'eɪʃən/ *uncountable noun*

signs such as ( ), ! or ? that you use to divide writing into sentences and phrases: *You have to give more attention to punctuation and grammar.*

punctuation mark *noun*
a symbol such as ( ), ! or ?

puncture /'pʌŋktʃə/ *noun*
a small hole that has been made by a sharp object: *I repaired the puncture in my front tyre.* ● **puncture** *verb* (**punctures, puncturing, punctured**) *The bullet punctured his left lung.*

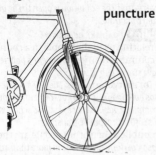

puncture

punish /'pʌnɪʃ/ *verb* (**punishes, punishing, punished**)
to make someone suffer in some way because they have done something wrong: *His parents punished him for being rude.*

punishment /'pʌnɪʃmənt/ *noun*
a particular way of punishing someone: *There will be tougher punishments for violent crimes.*

pup /pʌp/ *noun*
1 a young dog: *We've had Pongo since he was a pup.*
2 a baby of some other animals: *grey seal pups*

pupil /'pjuːpɪl/ *noun*
1 one of the children who go to a school: *Around 270 pupils attend this school.*
2 the small, round, black hole in the centre of your eye: *In low light the pupils are wide open to allow light into the eye.*

puppet /'pʌpɪt/ *noun*
a small model of a person or animal that you can move

puppy /'pʌpi/ *noun* (**puppies**)
a young dog

purchase¹ /'pɜːtʃɪs/ *verb* (**purchases, purchasing, purchased**) to buy something (*formal*): *He purchased a ticket for the concert.*

purchase² /ˈpɜːtʃɪs/ *noun*
1 *uncountable* the act of buying something (*formal*): *The Canadian company announced the purchase of 1,663 shops in the U.S.*
2 something that you buy (*formal*): *Her latest purchase is a shiny, black motorcycle.*

pure /pjʊə/ *adjective* (**purer, purest**)
1 not mixed with anything else: *I bought a carton of pure orange juice.*
2 clean and not containing any harmful substances: *The water is so pure that we drink it from the stream.*
3 complete and total: *There was a look of pure surprise on his face.*

purely /ˈpjʊəli/ *adverb*
only or completely: *This car is designed purely for speed.*

purple /ˈpɜːpəl/ *adjective*
a red-blue colour: *She wore a purple dress.*
● **purple** *noun* *I love the purples and greys of the Scottish mountains.*

purpose /ˈpɜːpəs/ *noun*
the reason why you do something: *The purpose of the occasion was to raise money for charity.*

on purpose not by accident: *I'm sure that Pedro hit me on purpose.*

purr /pɜː/ *verb* (**purrs, purring, purred**)
when a cat purrs, it makes a low sound with its throat: *The little black kitten purred and rubbed against my leg.*

purse /pɜːs/ *noun*
1 a very small bag used for carrying money, especially by women: *a brown leather purse*
2 (*American*) → see **handbag**

pursue /pəˈsjuː/ *verb* (**pursues, pursuing, pursued**)
to follow someone or something because you want to catch them (*formal*): *Police pursued the driver for two miles.*

pursuit /pəˈsjuːt/ *uncountable noun*
when you are trying to get something: *He has travelled the world in pursuit of his dream.*

push /pʊʃ/ *verb* (**pushes, pushing, pushed**)
1 to use force to make something move forward or away from you: *I pushed back my chair and stood up.* □ *The men pushed him into the car and locked the door.* □ *Justin put both hands on the door and pushed hard.* ● **push**

push

Justin put both hands on the door and pushed hard.

noun (**pushes**) *Laura gave me a sharp push and I fell to the ground.*
2 to press a button on a machine with your finger: *Christina got inside the lift and pushed the button for the third floor.*

pushchair /ˈpʊʃtʃeə/ *noun*
a small chair on wheels used for moving a young child around

put /pʊt/ *verb* (**puts, putting, put**)
1 to move something into a particular place or position: *Steven put the photograph on the desk.* □ *She put her hand on Grace's arm.* □ *Now, where did I put my purse?*
2 to cause someone or something to be in a particular state or situation: *Your carelessness put the children in danger.*

put someone through to connect someone on the telephone to the person they want to speak to: *Hold on, please. I'll just put you through.*

put something away to put something back in the place where it is usually kept: *Kyle put the milk away in the fridge.*

put something down to stop holding something and place it on a surface: *The woman put down her newspaper and looked at me.*

put something off to delay doing something: *Tony always puts off making difficult decisions.*

put something on
1 to place clothing or make-up on your body in order to wear it: *Grandma put her coat on and went out.* □ *She put on lipstick and combed her hair.*
2 to make a piece of electrical equipment start working: *Maria sat up in bed and put on the light.*

p

3 to place a CD in a CD player and listen to it

put something out to make a fire stop burning: *All day, firefighters have been trying to put out the blaze.*

put something up

1 to build a wall or a building: *The Smiths have put up electric fences on their farm.*

2 to attach a poster or a notice to a wall or board: *They're putting new street signs up.*

put up with something to accept someone or something unpleasant without complaining: *I won't put up with your bad behaviour any longer.* □ *It was a very bad injury, and he's put up with a lot of pain.*

puzzle ¹ /ˈpʌzəl/ *verb* (**puzzles, puzzling, puzzled**)

to leave you feeling confused because you do not understand something: *My sister's behaviour puzzles me.*

▸ **puzzled** /ˈpʌzəld/ *adjective* Joshua was puzzled by her reaction to the news.

▸ **puzzling** *adjective* Michael's comments are very puzzling.

puzzle ² /ˈpʌzəl/ *noun*

1 a question that is difficult to answer correctly, or a game or a toy that is difficult to put together properly: *Mum loves doing word puzzles.*

2 someone or something that is hard to understand: *The rise in the number of accidents on the motorway remains a puzzle.*

pyjamas /pəˈdʒɑːməz/ *plural noun*

loose trousers and a top that people wear in bed: *I don't usually get out of my pyjamas on Saturday mornings.*

pyramid /ˈpɪrəˌmɪd/ *noun*

a solid shape with a flat base and flat sides that form a point where they meet at the top: *the Egyptian Pyramids*

python /ˈpaɪθən/ *noun*

a type of large snake

p

Qq

quack /kwæk/ *noun*
the sound that a duck makes: *the quack of a duck* ● **quack** *verb* (**quacks, quacking, quacked**) *There were ducks quacking on the lawn.*

qualification /ˌkwɒlɪfɪˈkeɪʃən/ *noun*
an examination result or a skill that you need to be able to do something: *I believe I have all the qualifications to be a good teacher.* □ *All our workers have professional qualifications in engineering.*

qualified /ˈkwɒlɪˌfaɪd/ *adjective*
having the right skills or special training in a particular subject: *Blake is qualified in both UK and US law.*

qualify /ˈkwɒlɪfaɪ/ *verb* (**qualifies, qualifying, qualified**)
1 to be successful in one part of a competition so that you can go on to the next stage: *We qualified for the final by beating Stanford.*
2 to have the right to do or have something: *This course does not qualify you for a job in sales.*
3 to finish your training for a particular job: *I qualified, and started teaching last year.*

quality /ˈkwɒlɪti/ *noun* (**qualities**)
1 *uncountable* how good or bad something is: *The quality of the food here is excellent.*
2 a particular characteristic of a person or thing: *He has a childlike quality.*

quantity /ˈkwɒntɪti/ *noun* (**quantities**)
an amount: *Pour a small quantity of water into a pan.*

quarrel /ˈkwɒrəl/ *noun*
an angry argument between two or more people: *I had a terrible quarrel with my brother.*
● **quarrel** *verb* (**quarrels, quarrelling, quarrelled**) *Yes, we quarrelled over something silly.*

quarry /ˈkwɒri/ *noun* (**quarries**)
a place where stone or minerals are dug out of the ground

quarter /ˈkwɔːtə/ *noun*   **quarter**
1 one of four equal parts of something: *A quarter of the residents are over 55 years old.* □ *I'll be with you in a quarter of an hour.*
2 a fixed period of three months: *We will send you a bill every quarter.*
(a) quarter to/(a) quarter past used when you are telling the time to talk about the fifteen minutes before or after an hour: *We arrived at quarter to nine that night.*

quartet /kwɔːˈtet/ *noun*
1 a group of four people who play musical instruments or sing together: *a string quartet*
2 a piece of music for four instruments or four singers

quay /kiː/ *noun*
a long structure built next to water where boats can stop

queen /kwiːn/ *noun*
1 a woman from a royal family who rules a country: *Queen Elizabeth*
2 the wife of a king

query /ˈkwɪəri/ *noun* (**queries**)
a question: *If you have any queries, please do not hesitate to contact us.*

question[1] /ˈkwestʃən/ *noun*
1 something that you say or write in order to ask a person about something: *They asked a lot of questions about her health.*
2 doubt about something: *There's no question about their success.*
3 a problem or a subject that needs to be considered: *The question of nuclear energy is complex.*
4 a problem in an examination that tests your knowledge: *Please answer all six questions.*

q

out of the question completely impossible: *An expensive holiday is out of the question for him.*

question² /'kwestʃən/ *verb* (**questions, questioning, questioned**)

1 to ask someone a lot of questions about something: *The doctor questioned Jim about his parents.*

▸ **questioning** *uncountable noun* *The police want thirty-two people for questioning.*

2 to express doubts about something: *They never question the doctor's decisions.*

questionnaire /,kwestʃə'neə/ *noun*
a list of questions that a lot of people answer in order to provide information for a person or an organizaton: *Each person will fill out a five-minute questionnaire.*

'question mark *noun*
the mark (?) that is used in writing at the end of a question

queue /kju:/ (*American*: **line**) *noun*
a line of people or vehicles that are waiting for something: *She waited in the bus queue.* ● **queue** *verb* (**queues, queuing** or **queueing, queued**) (*also* **queue up**) *I had to queue for quite a while.* □ *We all had to queue up to get our tickets.*

quick /kwɪk/ *adjective* (**quicker, quickest**)

1 moving or doing things with great speed: *You'll have to be quick.*

▸ **quickly** *adverb* *Cussane worked quickly.*

2 taking or lasting only a short time: *He took a quick look around the room.*

▸ **quickly** *adverb* *You can get fit quite quickly if you exercise.*

3 happening with very little delay: *We are hoping for a quick end to the strike.*

▸ **quickly** *adverb* *We need to get the money back as quickly as possible.*

quiet /'kwaɪət/ *adjective* (**quieter, quietest**)

1 making only a small amount of noise: *The car has an extremely quiet engine.*

▸ **quietly** *adverb* *She spoke so quietly that we couldn't understand what she said.*

2 with no activity or trouble: *It's a quiet little village.*

3 not saying anything: *Be quiet and go to sleep.*

▸ **quietly** *adverb* *Amy stood quietly in the doorway.*

quilt /kwɪlt/ *noun*
a bed cover filled with soft, warm material

quit /kwɪt/ *verb* (**quits, quitting, quit**)
to choose to stop doing an activity (*informal*): *Christina quit her job last year.* □ *That's enough! I quit!*

quite /kwaɪt/ *adverb*

1 a little or a lot, but not extremely: *I felt quite bad about it at the time.* □ *I knew her mother quite well.* □ *Our house is quite a long way from the city.*

2 completely: *I haven't quite finished my project.* □ *My position is quite different.*

quite a/an used before a noun to say that a person or thing is very impressive or unusual: *He's quite a character.*

quiz /kwɪz/ *noun* (**quizzes**)
a game or a competition in which someone tests your knowledge by asking you questions: *We'll have a quiz after our visit to the museum.*

quotation /kwəʊ'teɪʃən/ *noun*
a sentence or a phrase from a book, a poem, a speech or a play: *He used quotations from Martin Luther King Jr. in his lecture.*

quo'tation mark *noun*
one of the marks that are used in writing to show where speech begins and ends. Quotation marks are usually written or printed as "...".

quote¹ /kwəʊt/ *verb* (**quotes, quoting, quoted**)
to repeat what someone has written or said: *She quoted a line from a book.*

quote² /kwəʊt/ *noun*

1 a section from a book, poem, play or speech: *He finished with a quote from one of his favourite poems.*

2 *plural* (*informal*) → see **quotation marks**: *The word 'remembered' is in quotes here.*

the Qu'ran /ðə kʊ'rɑːn/ *noun*
→ see **Koran**

Rr

rabbi /'ræbaɪ/ *noun*
a Jewish religious leader

rabbit /'ræbɪt/ *noun*
a small animal that has long ears and lives in a hole in the ground

race¹ /reɪs/ *noun*
1 a competition to see who is the fastest: *Mark easily won the race.* □ *a horse race*
2 one of the groups that humans can be divided into because they look similar, for example with the same skin colour: *The college welcomes students of all races.*

race² /reɪs/ *verb* (**races, racing, raced**)
1 to take part in a race: *Leo started racing in the early 1950s.* □ *We raced them to the top of the hill.*
2 to go somewhere as quickly as possible: *He raced across town to the hospital.*

racecourse /'reɪskɔːs/
also **race course** *noun*
a place where horses race

racial /'reɪʃəl/ *adjective*
relating to people's race: *The new law promotes racial equality.*
▶ **racially** *adverb* *a racially-mixed school*

racing /'reɪsɪŋ/ *uncountable noun*
the sport of competing in races: *a racing car*

racism /'reɪsɪzəm/ *uncountable noun*
the belief that people of some races are not as good as others: *Many of these children experienced racism in their daily lives.*

racist¹ /'reɪsɪst/ *adjective*
influenced by the belief that some people are better than others because they belong to a particular race: *We live in a racist society.*
▶ **racism** *uncountable noun* *The level of racism is increasing.*

racist² /'reɪsɪst/ *noun*
someone who is racist: *He was attacked by a gang of white racists.*

rack /ræk/ *noun*
a frame or a shelf, usually with bars, that is used for holding things: *Put all your bags in the luggage rack.*

racket /'rækɪt/ *noun*
1 (*also* **racquet**) a thing that is used for hitting the ball in some games: *I got a tennis racket for my birthday.*
2 a loud, unpleasant noise: *The children were making a racket upstairs.*

racket

radar /'reɪdɑː/ *noun*
a way of discovering the position of objects when they cannot be seen, by using radio signals: *They saw the submarine on the ship's radar screen.*

radiation /ˌreɪdi'eɪʃən/ *uncountable noun*
a type of energy that comes from some substances. Too much radiation is harmful to living things: *The gas protects the Earth against radiation from the sun.*

radiator /'reɪdiˌeɪtə/ *noun*
1 a metal object that is full of hot water or steam, and is used for heating a room
→ Look at picture on P5
2 the part of the engine of a car that is filled with water in order to cool the engine

radio /'reɪdiəʊ/ *noun*
1 a piece of equipment that you use in order to listen to radio programmes: *He turned on the radio.*
2 *uncountable* a system of sending and receiving sound using electronic signals: *They are in radio contact with the leader.*
3 a piece of equipment that is used for sending and receiving spoken messages: *The police officer called for extra help on his radio.*
● **radio** *verb* (**radios, radioing, radioed**)
The officer radioed for advice.

'radio wave *noun*
the form in which radio signals travel

radius /'reɪdiəs/ *noun* (**radii** /'reɪdiaɪ/)
the distance from the centre of a circle to its outside edge: *We offer free delivery within a 5-mile radius of our shop.*

r

raffle /'ræfəl/ *noun*
a competition in which you buy tickets with numbers on them. If your number is chosen, you win a prize: *raffle tickets*

raft /rɑːft/ *noun*
a flat boat that is made from large pieces of wood that are tied together

rag /ræg/ *noun*
1 a piece of old cloth: *He was wiping his hands on an oily rag.*
2 *plural* old torn clothes: *The streets were full of children dressed in rags.*

rage /reɪdʒ/ *noun*
strong anger that is difficult to control: *His face was red with rage.*

ragged /'rægɪd/ *adjective*
1 wearing clothes that are old and torn: *A thin ragged man sat on the park bench.*
2 old and torn: *children in ragged clothes*

raid /reɪd/ *verb* (raids, raiding, raided)
to enter a building suddenly in order to look for someone or something: *Police raided the company's offices.* ●**raid** *noun*
They were arrested after a raid on a house by police.

rail /reɪl/ *noun*
1 a horizontal bar that you hold for support: *She held the hand rail tightly.*
2 a horizontal bar that you hang things on: *a curtain rail*
3 one of the metal bars that trains run on: *The train left the rails.*
by rail on a train: *The president arrived by rail.*

railing /'reɪlɪŋ/ *noun*
a fence that is made from metal bars: *He jumped over the railing to shake hands with the fans.*

railway /'reɪlweɪ/ *noun*
a metal track between two places that trains travel along: *The road ran beside a railway.*

'railway ,station *noun*
a place where trains stop so that people can get on or off

rain /reɪn/ *uncountable noun*
water that falls from the clouds in small drops: *We got very wet in the rain.* ●**rain** *verb* (rains, raining, rained) *It was raining hard.*

rainbow /'reɪnbəʊ/ *noun*
a half circle of different colours that you can sometimes see in the sky when it rains

raincoat /'reɪnkəʊt/ *noun*
a coat that you can wear to keep dry when it rains

raindrop /'reɪndrɒp/ *noun*
a single drop of rain

rainfall /'reɪnfɔːl/ *uncountable noun*
the amount of rain that falls in a place during a particular period: *This month we have recorded below-average rainfall.*

rainforest /'reɪnfɒrɪst/ *noun*
a thick forest of tall trees that grows in tropical areas where there is a lot of rain: *We watched a programme about the destruction of the Amazon Rainforest.*

rainy /'reɪni/ *adjective* (rainier, rainiest)
raining a lot: *Here are some fun things to do on a rainy day.*

raise /reɪz/ *verb* (raises, raising, raised)
1 to move something upwards: *He raised his hand to wave.* □ *Milton raised the glass to his lips.*
2 to increase the rate or level of something: *Many shops have raised their prices.* □ *Keep calm, and don't raise your voice.*
3 to ask people for money for a particular purpose: *The event is to raise money for the school.*
4 to start to talk about a subject: *The matter will be raised at our annual meeting.*
5 to take care of children until they are grown up: *She raised four children on her own.*

LANGUAGE HELP
See note at **rise**.

raisin /'reɪzən/ *noun*
a dried grape (= a small green or purple fruit)

rake /reɪk/
noun
a garden tool with a long handle, used for collecting loose grass or leaves
●**rake** *verb* (rakes, raking, raked) *We raked the leaves into a pile.*

rake

rally /'ræli/ *noun* (rallies)
a large public meeting that is held in order to show support for something:

They organized a rally to demand better working conditions.

ram[1] /ræm/ *noun*
an adult male sheep

RAM[2] /ræm/ *uncountable noun*
the part of a computer where information is stored while you are using it. **RAM** is short for 'Random Access Memory'.

ramp /ræmp/ *noun*
a surface with a slope between two places that are at different levels: *There's a wheelchair ramp at the front entrance of the school.*

ran /ræn/ → see **run**

ranch /rɑːntʃ/ *noun* (**ranches**)
a large farm used for keeping animals: *He owns a cattle ranch in Texas.*

random /'rændəm/ *adjective*
1 used for describing a process in which all the people or things involved have an equal chance of being chosen: *The survey used a random sample of two thousand people.*
2 not following a plan or pattern: *We have seen random violence against innocent victims.*
at random happening without a plan or a pattern: *The gunman fired at random.*

rang /ræŋ/ → see **ring**

range[1] /reɪndʒ/ *noun*
1 a number of different things of the same type: *These products come in a wide range of colours.*
2 the complete group that is included between two points on a scale: *The age range is between 35 and 55.*
3 how far something can reach: *This electric car has a range of 100 miles.*
4 a group of mountains or hills: *snowy mountain ranges*

range[2] /reɪndʒ/ *verb* (**ranges, ranging, ranged**)
to be between two fixed points on a scale: *The children range in age from five to fourteen.*

rank /ræŋk/ *noun*
the position that someone has in an organization: *He holds the rank of colonel in the British Army.*

ransom /'rænsəm/ *noun*
the money that has to be paid to someone so that they will set a person free: *Her kidnapper asked for a £250,000 ransom.*

rap[1] /ræp/ *uncountable noun*
a type of modern music in which the words are spoken: *He performs with a rap group.*
▶ **rapper** *noun* *He's a singer and a talented rapper.*

rap[2] /ræp/ *verb* (**raps, rapping, rapped**)
to perform rap music: *The kids rap and also sing.*

rape[1] /reɪp/ *verb* (**rapes, raping, raped**)
to force someone to have sex when they do not want to: *Many women were raped during the war.*
▶ **rapist** *noun* *The information led to the rapist's arrest.*

rape[2] /reɪp/ *noun*
the crime of forcing someone to have sex

rapid /'ræpɪd/ *adjective*
1 happening very quickly: *This is the end of the country's rapid economic growth.*
▶ **rapidly** *adverb* *The firm continues to grow rapidly.*
2 moving very fast: *He walked at a rapid pace.*
▶ **rapidly** *adverb* *He was moving rapidly around the room.*

rare /reə/ *adjective* (**rarer, rarest**)
1 not seen or heard very often: *This is one of the rarest birds in the world.*
2 not happening very often: *They have dinner together on the rare occasions when they are both at home.*
▶ **rarely** *adverb* *I rarely take taxis.*
3 used for describing meat that is cooked very lightly so that the inside is still red: *freshly-cooked rare steak*

rash[1] /ræʃ/ *adjective*
acting without thinking carefully first: *Don't make any rash decisions.*

rash[2] /ræʃ/ *noun* (**rashes**)
an area of red spots that appears on your skin: *I always get a rash when I eat nuts.*

raspberry /'rɑːzbri/ *noun* (**raspberries**)
a small, soft, red fruit that grows on bushes
→ Look at picture on P2

rat /ræt/ *noun*
an animal that has a long tail and looks like a large mouse

rate /reɪt/ *noun*
1 how fast or how often something happens: *An adult's heart rate is about 72 beats per minute.* □ *Spain has the lowest birth rate in Europe.*

r

2 the amount of money that goods or services cost: *The hotel offers a special weekend rate.*

at any rate anyway: *His friends liked her — well, most of them at any rate.*

rather /'rɑ:ðə/ *adverb*
more than a little: *I thought the film was rather boring.*

rather than instead of, in place of: *I use the bike when I can, rather than the car.*

would rather do something would prefer to do something: *Kids would rather play than study.*

ratio /'reɪʃɪəʊ/ *noun*
a relationship between two things when it is expressed in numbers or amounts: *The adult to child ratio is one to six.*

ration [1] /'ræʃən/ *noun*
1 a small amount of something that you are allowed to have when there is not much of it: *The meat ration was 250 grams per month during the war.*
2 *plural* the food that is given to soldiers or to people who do not have enough food

ration [2] /'ræʃən/ *verb* (**rations, rationing, rationed**)
to only allow someone to have a small amount of something: *Food such as bread and rice was rationed.*

rational /'ræʃənəl/ *adjective*
based on reason rather than on emotion: *They discussed it in a rational manner.*
▶ **rationally** *adverb* *It is difficult to think rationally when you're worried.*

rattle [1] /'rætəl/ *verb* (**rattles, rattling, rattled**)
to hit against something hard and make short, sharp, knocking sounds: *The windows rattled in the wind.*

rattle [2] /'rætəl/ *noun*
a baby's toy with small, loose objects inside that make a noise when the baby shakes it

rave /reɪv/ *verb* (**raves, raving, raved**)
to speak or write about something with great enthusiasm: *Rachel raved about the film.*

raw /rɔ:/ *adjective* (**rawer, rawest**)
1 used for describing materials or substances that are in their natural state: *raw sugar*
2 not cooked: *This is a Japanese dish made of raw fish.*

ray /reɪ/ *noun*
a narrow line of light: *Protect your eyes against the sun's rays.*

razor /'reɪzə/ *noun*
a tool that people use for shaving

razor

reach /ri:tʃ/ *verb*
(**reaches, reaching, reached**)
1 to arrive at a place: *He did not stop until he reached the door.*
2 to be at a certain level or amount: *The number of unemployed could reach 3 million next year.*
3 to move your arm and hand to take or touch something: *She tried to reach the cake on the counter.*
4 to be able to touch something by stretching out your arm or leg: *Can you reach your toes with your fingertips?*
5 to contact someone, usually by telephone: *You can reach me at this phone number.*

reach

She tried to reach the cake on the counter.

react /ri'ækt/ *verb* (**reacts, reacting, reacted**)
1 to behave in a particular way because of something that has happened: *They reacted violently to the news.*
2 to combine chemically to form another substance: *Calcium reacts with water.*

reaction /ri'ækʃən/ *noun*
1 what you feel, say or do because of something: *He showed no reaction when I told him the result.*
2 a process in which two substances combine together chemically to form another substance: *a chemical reaction between oxygen and hydrogen*

r

read *verb* (**reads, reading, read**)

PRONUNCIATION HELP
When it is the present tense, **read** is
pronounced /riːd/; **read** is also the past
tense and past participle, when it is
pronounced /red/.

1 to look at written words and
understand them: *Have you read this book?*
□ *I read about it in the paper.* □ *She spends all
her time reading.*
2 to say words that you can see: *Kevin
always read a story to the twins when he got
home.*
read someone's mind/thoughts to
know exactly what someone is thinking
read something out to read something
to other people: *She asked us to read out the
answers to the exercise.*

reader /'riːdə/ *noun*
a person who reads a newspaper, a
magazine or a book: *The article gives readers
an interesting view of life in Spain.*

readily /'redɪli/ *adverb*
in a way that shows that you are very
willing to do something: *I asked her to help,
and she readily agreed.*

reading /'riːdɪŋ/ *uncountable noun*
the activity of reading books: *I love reading.*

ready /'redi/ *adjective* (**readier, readiest**)
1 completely prepared for something: *It
takes her a long time to get ready for school.*
2 prepared so that you can use it: *Go and
tell your sister that lunch is ready.*
3 willing to do something: *They were ready
to help.*

real /riːl/ *adjective*
1 actually existing: *No, it wasn't a dream.
It was real.*
2 natural, and not a copy: *I love the smell of
real leather.*
3 true: *This was the real reason for her call.*

realistic /ˌriːə'lɪstɪk/ *adjective*
1 recognizing and accepting the true
nature of a situation: *Police must be realistic
about violent crime.*
2 when the people and things in a
picture, a story or a film are like people
and things in real life

reality /riː'ælɪti/ *noun* (**realities**)
1 *uncountable* used for talking about real
things rather than imagined or invented

ideas: *Her dream ended and she had to return to
reality.*
2 the truth about a situation, especially
when it is unpleasant: *Politicians do not
understand the realities of war.*

realize /'riːəˌlaɪz/ *verb* (**realizes, realizing,
realized**)
to become aware that something is true
or to understand it: *As soon as we realized
that something was wrong, we rushed to help.*
□ *People don't realize how serious the situation is.*
▶ **realization** *noun A terrible realization
struck him.*

really /'riːəli/ *adverb*
1 used for giving a sentence a stronger
meaning: *I'm very sorry. I really am.*
2 used when you are discussing the real
facts about something: *You're not really
leaving, are you?*
really? used for expressing surprise at
what someone has said: *'I once met the
president.' — 'Really?'*

reappear /ˌriːə'pɪə/ *verb* (**reappears,
reappearing, reappeared**)
to return again after having been away or
out of sight

rear[1] /rɪə/ *noun*
the back part of something: *Mr Forbes was
sitting in the rear of the vehicle.* □ *The car hit the
rear of the lorry.* ● **rear** *adjective You must
fasten all rear seat belts.*

rear[2] /rɪə/ *verb* (**rears, rearing, reared**)
1 to take care of children until they are
old enough to take care of themselves:
I was reared in Texas.
2 to keep and take care of a young animal
until it is old enough to be used for work
or food: *She spends a lot of time rearing animals.*
3 used for saying that a horse moves the
front part of its body upwards, so that it is
standing on its back legs: *The horse reared
and threw off its rider.*

rearrange /ˌriːə'reɪndʒ/ *verb* (**rearranges,
rearranging, rearranged**)
to change the way that things are
organized: *Malcolm rearranged all the
furniture.*

reason /'riːzən/ *noun*
1 a fact or situation that explains why
something happens: *There is a reason for
every important thing that happens.*
2 *uncountable* the ability that people have

r

to think and to make sensible judgements: *He was more interested in emotion than reason.*

reasonable /ˈriːzənəbəl/ *adjective*
1 fair and sensible: *She seems to be a reasonable person.* □ *That's a perfectly reasonable decision.*
2 fairly good, but not very good: *The boy spoke reasonable French.*
▶ **reasonably** *adverb* *I can dance reasonably well.*

reassure /ˌriːəˈʃʊə/ *verb* (**reassures, reassuring, reassured**)
to say or do things to make someone stop worrying about something
▶ **reassurance** *uncountable noun* *He needed reassurance that she loved him.*

reassuring /ˌriːəˈʃʊərɪŋ/ *adjective*
making you feel less worried about something: *It was reassuring to hear Jane's voice.*

rebel¹ /ˈrebəl/ *noun*
a person who is fighting against the people who are in charge somewhere, for example the government: *There is still heavy fighting between rebels and government forces.*

rebel² /rɪˈbel/ *verb* (**rebels, rebelling, rebelled**)
to fight against the people who are in charge: *Teenagers often rebel against their parents.*

rebellion /rɪˈbeliən/ *noun*
when a large group of people fight against the people who are in charge, for example, the government: *We are awaiting the government's response to the rebellion.*

reboot /riːˈbuːt/ *verb* (**reboots, rebooting, rebooted**)
to turn off a computer and start it again: *When you reboot your computer, the software is ready to use.*

recall /rɪˈkɔːl/ *verb* (**recalls, recalling, recalled**)
to remember something: *He recalled meeting Pollard during a business trip.*

receipt /rɪˈsiːt/ *noun*
a piece of paper that shows that you have received goods or money from someone: *I gave her a receipt for the money.*

receive /rɪˈsiːv/ *verb* (**receives, receiving, received**)
to get something after someone gives it

to you or sends it to you: *They received their awards at a ceremony in San Francisco.*

receiver /rɪˈsiːvə/ *noun*
the part of a telephone that you hold near to your ear and speak into: *She picked up the receiver and started to dial.*

recent /ˈriːsənt/ *adjective*
that happened only a short time ago: *Brad broke his leg on a recent trip to Dorset.*

recently /ˈriːsəntli/ *adverb*
only a short time ago: *The bank recently opened a branch in Manchester.*

reception /rɪˈsepʃən/ *noun*
1 a formal party that is given to welcome someone, or to celebrate a special event: *We were invited to their wedding reception.*
2 *uncountable* the desk in a hotel or a large building that you go to when you first arrive: *She was waiting at reception.*

receptionist /rɪˈsepʃənɪst/ *noun*
a person in a hotel or a large building whose job is to answer the telephone and deal with visitors

recession /rɪˈseʃən/ *noun*
a period when the economy of a country is not growing: *The oil price increases sent Europe into recession.*

recipe /ˈresɪpi/ *noun*
a list of food and a set of instructions telling you how to cook something: *Do you have a recipe for chocolate cake?*

recite /rɪˈsaɪt/ *verb* (**recites, reciting, recited**)
to say a poem or other piece of writing to other people after you have learned it: *We each had to recite a poem in front of the class.*

reckless /ˈrekləs/ *adjective*
not caring about danger, or the results of your actions: *He was stopped for reckless driving.*

reckon /ˈrekən/ *verb* (**reckons, reckoning, reckoned**)
to think that something is probably true (*informal*): *I reckon it's about three o'clock.*

recognition /ˌrekəgˈnɪʃən/ *uncountable noun*
the act of knowing who a person is or what something is when you see them: *There was no sign of recognition on her face.*

recognize /ˈrekəgnaɪz/ *verb* (**recognizes, recognizing, recognized**)
to know someone or something because

you have seen or heard them before: *She recognized him immediately.*

recollection /ˌrekəˈlekʃən/ *noun*
a memory: *Pat has few recollections of the trip.*

recommend /ˌrekəˈmend/ *verb*
(**recommends, recommending, recommended**)
1 to suggest that someone would find a particular person or thing good or useful: *I recommend Barbados as a place for a holiday.* □ *I'll recommend you for the job.*
2 to suggest that something should be done: *The doctor recommended that I lose some weight.*
▶ **recommendation** *noun* *The best way of finding a dentist is to get someone else's recommendation.* □ *We listened to the committee's recommendations.*

record ¹ /ˈrekɔːd/ *noun*
1 a written account or photographs of something that can be looked at later: *Keep a record of all the payments.*
2 a round, flat piece of black plastic on which sound, especially music, is stored, that can be played on a record player (= machine for playing records)
3 the best result ever in a particular sport or activity: *He set the world record of 12.92 seconds.*

record ² /rɪˈkɔːd/ *verb* (**records, recording, recorded**)
1 to write down or photograph a piece of information or an event so that in the future people can look at it: *Her letters record the details of her life in China.*
2 to store something such as a speech or a performance in a computer file or on a disk so that it can be heard or seen again later: *Viewers can record the films.*

recorder /rɪˈkɔːdə/ *noun*
a wooden or plastic musical instrument in the shape of a pipe. You play it by blowing down one end and covering holes with your fingers.

recording /rɪˈkɔːdɪŋ/ *noun*
1 a computer file or a disk on which moving pictures and sounds are stored: *There is a video recording of his police interview.*
2 *uncountable* the process of storing moving pictures and sounds on computer files or disks: *This has been a bad time for the recording industry.*

recount /rɪˈkaʊnt/ *verb* (**recounts, recounting, recounted**)
to tell or describe a story or an event to people (*formal*): *He recounted the story of his first day at work.*

recover /rɪˈkʌvə/ *verb* (**recovers, recovering, recovered**)
1 to become well again after an illness or an injury: *He is recovering from a knee injury.*

> **LANGUAGE HELP**
> **Recover** is a fairly formal word. In conversation, you usually say that someone **gets better**.

2 to find or get back something that has been lost or stolen: *Police searched houses and recovered stolen goods.*

recovery /rɪˈkʌvəri/ *noun* (**recoveries**)
when an ill person becomes well again: *Natalie is making an excellent recovery from a serious knee injury.*

recreation /ˌrekriˈeɪʃən/ *uncountable noun*
things that you do in your spare time to relax: *Saturday afternoon is for recreation.*

recruit ¹ /rɪˈkruːt/ *verb* (**recruits, recruiting, recruited**)
to ask people to join an organization: *We need to recruit and train more teachers.*
▶ **recruitment** *uncountable noun* *There has been a drop in the recruitment of soldiers.*

recruit ² /rɪˈkruːt/ *noun*
a person who has recently joined an organization or an army: *He's a new recruit to the police force.*

rectangle /ˈrektæŋgəl/ *noun*
a shape with four straight sides and four 90° angles
▶ **rectangular** /rekˈtæŋgjʊlə/ *adjective* *The room contains a rectangular table.*

recur /rɪˈkɜː/ *verb* (**recurs, recurring, recurred**)
to happen more than once: *I have a recurring dream about being late for an important meeting.*

recycle /ˌriːˈsaɪkəl/ *verb* (**recycles, recycling, recycled**)
to put things such as paper or bottles that have already been used through a process so that they can be used again
▶ **recycled** *adjective* *recycled plastic*

red ¹ /red/ *adjective* (**redder, reddest**)
1 having the colour of blood or of a

r

tomato: *a bunch of red roses*

2 used for describing hair that is between red and brown in colour

red² /red/ *noun*

the colour of blood or a tomato

reduce /rɪ'djuːs/ *verb* (**reduces, reducing, reduced**)

to make something smaller or less: *Exercise reduces the risks of heart disease.* □ *The dress was reduced from £35 to £20.*

reduction /rɪ'dʌkʃən/ *noun*

when something is made smaller or less: *We have noticed a sudden reduction in prices.*

redundant /rɪ'dʌndənt/ *adjective*

without a job because there is not enough work or money to keep you: *My husband was made redundant last year.*

reed /riːd/ *noun*

a tall plant that grows in large groups in shallow water or on wet ground

refer /rɪ'fɜː/ *verb* (**refers, referring, referred**)

refer to something

1 to describe a particular thing: *The word 'man' refers to an adult male.*

2 to look in a book or on the Internet for information: *He referred briefly to his notebook.*

▸ **reference** /'refərəns/ *uncountable noun* Keep this book in a safe place for reference.

refer to something/someone to mention a particular subject or person: *He referred to his trip to Canada.*

▸ **reference** *noun* He made no reference to any agreement.

with/in reference to something used for saying what something is about: *I am writing in reference to your advertisement for a personal assistant.*

referee /ˌrefə'riː/ *noun*

the person who controls a sports event such as a football game or a boxing match

● **referee** *verb* (**referees, refereeing, refereed**) Vautrot refereed in two football games.

reference¹ /'refərəns/ *adjective*

used for describing books that you look at when you need information or facts about a subject

reference² /'refərəns/ *noun*

a letter that is written by someone who knows you, describing your character and your abilities: *My boss gave me a good reference.*

reflect /rɪ'flekt/ *verb* (**reflects, reflecting, reflected**)

1 to show that an opinion or a situation exists: *The report reflects the views of both students and teachers.*

2 used for saying that light or heat is sent back from a surface: *The sun reflected off the snow-covered mountains.*

3 to show the image of something in a mirror or in water: *His face was reflected in the mirror.*

reflection /rɪ'flekʃən/ *noun*

1 an image that you can see in a mirror or in glass or water: *Meg stared at her reflection in the mirror.*

2 something that shows what someone or something is like: *His drawings are a reflection of his own unhappiness.*

reflexive pronoun /rɪ'fleksɪv 'prəʊnaʊn/ *noun*

a word such as 'myself' that you use to talk about the subject of a sentence

reflexive verb /rɪ'fleksɪv 'vɜːb/ *noun*

a verb whose subject and object always refer to the same person or thing. An example is 'to enjoy yourself'.

reform¹ /rɪ'fɔːm/ *noun*

1 **uncountable** changes and improvements to a law or a social system: *We will introduce a programme of economic reform.*

2 a change that is intended to be an improvement: *The government promised tax reforms.*

reform² /rɪ'fɔːm/ *verb* (**reforms, reforming, reformed**)

1 to change or improve something such as a law or a social system: *He has plans to reform the country's economy.*

2 to start behaving well: *After his time in prison, James promised to reform.*

refresh /rɪ'freʃ/ *verb* (**refreshes, refreshing, refreshed**)

to make you feel better when you are hot, tired or thirsty: *The water refreshed them.*

▸ **refreshed** *adjective* He awoke feeling completely refreshed.

refreshing /rɪ'freʃɪŋ/ *adjective*

1 making you feel less hot, tired or thirsty: *They serve refreshing drinks at the poolside.*

r

2 unusual in a pleasant way: *It's refreshing to hear someone speaking so honestly.*

refreshments /rɪˈfreʃmənts/ *plural noun*
drinks and small amounts of food that are provided, for example, during a meeting or a trip: *Refreshments will be provided.*

refrigerator /rɪˈfrɪdʒəˌreɪtə/ *noun* (formal)
→ see **fridge**

refuge /ˈrefjuːdʒ/ *noun*
a place where you go for safety and protection: *He works in a refuge for homeless people.*
take refuge to go somewhere to try to protect yourself from harm: *They took refuge in a shelter.*

refugee /ˌrefjuˈdʒiː/ *noun*
a person who has been forced to leave their home or their country, because it is too dangerous for them there: *She grew up in a refugee camp in Pakistan.*

refund¹ /ˈriːfʌnd/ *noun*
money that is returned to you because you have paid too much, or because you have returned goods to a shop: *He took the boots back to the shop and asked for a refund.*

refund² /rɪˈfʌnd/ *verb* (**refunds, refunding, refunded**)
to return the money that someone has paid for something: *We will refund your delivery costs if the items arrive later than 12 noon.*

refusal /rɪˈfjuːzəl/ *noun*
when someone says that they will not do, allow or accept something: *The workers have repeated their refusal to take part in the programme.*

refuse /rɪˈfjuːz/ *verb* (**refuses, refusing, refused**)
1 to say that you will not do something: *He refused to comment.*
2 to say that you will not give something to someone: *The United States has refused him a visa.*
3 to not accept something that is offered to you: *The patient has the right to refuse treatment.*

regard¹ /rɪˈgɑːd/ *verb* (**regards, regarding, regarded**)
to believe that someone or something is a particular thing: *He was regarded as the most successful president of modern times.*

regard² /rɪˈgɑːd/ *noun*
1 *uncountable* a feeling of respect for someone or something: *I have a very high regard for him and his achievements.*
2 *plural* used as a way of expressing friendly feelings toward someone: *Give my regards to your family.*
in/with regard to something used for showing which subject is being talked about: *How happy are you with regard to your work?*

regarding /rɪˈgɑːdɪŋ/ *preposition*
about someone or something: *He refused to give any information regarding the man's financial situation.*

regardless /rɪˈgɑːdləs/ *adverb*
regardless of something used for saying that a first thing is not affected or influenced at all by a second thing: *The organization helps anyone regardless of their age.*

reggae /ˈregeɪ/ *uncountable noun*
a type of West Indian popular music with a very strong beat

regiment /ˈredʒɪmənt/ *noun*
a part of an army

region /ˈriːdʒən/ *noun*
an area of a country or of the world: *Do you have a map of the coastal region of Brazil?*
▶ **regional** *adjective* *French regional cooking*

register¹ /ˈredʒɪstə/ *noun*
an official list of people or things: *We'll check the register of births, deaths and marriages.*

register² /ˈredʒɪstə/ *verb* (**registers, registering, registered**)
1 to put your name on an official list, in order to be able to do a particular thing: *Thousands of people registered to vote.*
▶ **registration** /ˌredʒɪˈstreɪʃən/ *uncountable noun* *The website is free, but it asks for registration from users.*
2 to show a particular value on a scale or a measuring instrument: *The earthquake registered 5.7 on the Richter scale.*

regiˈstration ˌnumber *noun*
the numbers and letters on the front and back of a car or other road vehicle

regret¹ /rɪˈgret/ *verb* (**regrets, regretting, regretted**)
to feel sorry that you did something: *I regret my decision to leave my job.* □ *I regret breaking up with my boyfriend.*

regret² /rɪˈgret/ *noun*
a feeling of sadness or disappointment, caused by something that you have done or not done: *He had no regrets about leaving.*

r

regular /'regjʊlə/ *adjective*
1 used for describing events that have equal amounts of time between them, so that they happen, for example, at the same time each day or each week: *Get regular exercise.*
2 happening often: *We meet on a regular basis.*
▶ **regularly** *adverb* *He writes regularly for the magazine.*
3 going to a place or a shop often: *She was a regular visitor to the museum.*
4 normal or usual: *He sat at his regular table by the windows.*
5 used for describing a shape with straight or smooth edges, or where both halves are the same: *He's a man of average height with regular features.*
6 used for describing a noun or a verb that follows the usual rules of grammar. For example, 'work' is a regular verb, because the past is formed with '-ed'. Compare with **irregular**: *The past tense of English regular verbs ends in -ed.*

regulation /ˌregjʊ'leɪʃən/ *noun*
a rule for controlling the way people behave or do things: *Here are the new safety regulations.*

rehearsal /rɪ'hɜːsəl/ *noun*
a practice of a performance: *Tomorrow we start rehearsals for the concert.*

rehearse /rɪ'hɜːs/ *verb* (**rehearses, rehearsing, rehearsed**)
to practise a play, a dance or a piece of music: *The actors are rehearsing a play.*
□ *Thousands of people are rehearsing for the ceremony.*

reign /reɪn/ *verb* (**reigns, reigning, reigned**)
to rule a country as king or queen: *Henry II reigned in England from 1154 to 1189.* ● **reign** *noun* *Queen Victoria's reign*

rein /reɪn/ *plural noun*
the long thin pieces of leather that fit around a horse's neck, and that are used

reins

for controlling the horse: *She held the reins while the horse pulled.*

reindeer /'reɪndɪə/ *noun* (**reindeer**)
a big animal with large horns that lives in northern areas of Europe, Asia and America

reject /rɪ'dʒekt/ *verb* (**rejects, rejecting, rejected**)
1 to not accept or agree to something: *The president rejected the offer.*
2 to not offer a job or a course of study to someone: *He was rejected by several universities.*
▶ **rejection** *noun* *Be prepared for lots of rejections before you get a job.*

rejoice /rɪ'dʒɔɪs/ *verb* (**rejoices, rejoicing, rejoiced**)
to be very happy about something and show this in the way that you behave: *We rejoiced in the victory.*
▶ **rejoicing** *uncountable noun* *There was much rejoicing at the news.*

relate /rɪ'leɪt/ *verb* (**relates, relating, related**)
1 to be about a particular subject: *We are collecting all the information relating to the crime.*
2 used for describing the connection that exists between two things: *There is new thinking about how the two sciences relate.*

related /rɪ'leɪtɪd/ *adjective*
1 connected in some way: *Crime and poverty are closely related.*
2 belonging to the same family: *The boys have the same last name but they are not related.*

relation /rɪ'leɪʃən/ *noun*
1 the connection between two things: *He has spent years studying the relation between exercise and health.*
2 a member of your family: *We make frequent visits to friends and relations.*
3 *plural* the way in which people, groups or countries behave towards each other: *The country has good relations with Israel.*

relationship /rɪ'leɪʃənʃɪp/ *noun*
1 the way in which two people or groups feel and behave towards each other: *The ministers want to maintain the friendly relationship between the two countries.*
2 a close friendship between two people, especially involving romantic or sexual feelings: *She could not accept that their relationship was over.*

3 the way in which two things are connected: *Is there a relationship between diet and cancer?*

relative /'relətɪv/ *noun*
a member of your family: *Ask a relative to look after the children.*

relax /rɪ'læks/ *verb* (relaxes, relaxing, relaxed)
1 to feel more calm and less worried: *You should relax and stop worrying.*
▸ **relaxation** /ˌriːlæk'seɪʃən/ *uncountable noun Try learning some relaxation techniques.*
▸ **relaxed** *adjective The atmosphere at lunch was relaxed.*
▸ **relaxing** *adjective I find cooking very relaxing.*
2 to make a part of your body become less stiff or tight: *Have a massage to relax your muscles.*

relay /'riːleɪ/ *noun* (*also* **relay race**)
a race between two or more teams in which each member of the team runs or swims one section of the race: *Britain's chances of winning the relay are good.*

release¹ /rɪ'liːs/ *verb* (releases, releasing, released)
1 to allow a person or an animal to go free: *He was released from prison the next day.*
2 to stop holding someone or something (*formal*): *He released her hand.*
3 to make a new CD, DVD or film available so that people can buy it or see it: *He is releasing a CD of love songs.*

release² /rɪ'liːs/ *noun*
a CD, DVD or film that has just become available for people to buy or see: *a new release*

relevant /'reləvənt/ *adjective*
important in a situation or to a person: *They are trying to make politics more relevant to younger people.*

reliable /rɪ'laɪəbəl/ *adjective*
1 that you can trust to work well: *She was efficient and reliable.*
2 probably correct: *There is no reliable information about how many people have died.*
▸ **reliably** *adverb We are reliably informed that he is here.*
▸ **reliability** *noun We have serious doubts about the reliability of this information.*

relief /rɪ'liːf/ *uncountable noun*
1 when you feel happy because something unpleasant has not happened or is no longer happening: *I breathed a sigh of relief.*
2 when pain or worry stops: *These drugs will give relief from pain.*
3 money, food or clothing that is provided for people who suddenly need it: *Relief agencies are hoping to provide food and shelter in the flooded area.*

relieved /rɪ'liːvd/ *adjective*
feeling happy because something unpleasant has not happened or is no longer happening: *We are relieved to be back home.*

religion /rɪ'lɪdʒən/ *noun*
1 *uncountable* belief in a god or gods and the activities that are connected with this belief: *There's little interest in organized religion.*
2 a particular system of belief in a god or gods and the activities that are connected with this system: *the Christian religion*

religious /rɪ'lɪdʒəs/ *adjective*
1 connected with religion: *Religious groups are able to meet quite freely.*
2 having a strong belief in a god or gods

reluctant /rɪ'lʌktənt/ *adjective*
unwilling to do something: *Mr Phillips was reluctant to ask for help.*
▸ **reluctantly** *adverb We have reluctantly agreed to let him go.*
▸ **reluctance** *uncountable noun Frank boarded his train with great reluctance.*

rely /rɪ'laɪ/ *verb* (relies, relying, relied)
rely on someone/something
1 to need someone or something in order to live or work properly: *They relied heavily on our advice.*
2 to be able to trust someone to do something: *I know I can rely on you to deal with the problem.*

remain /rɪ'meɪn/ *verb* (remains, remaining, remained)
1 to stay in a particular state or condition: *The men remained silent.* □ *The government remained in control.*
2 to stay in a place and not move away: *Police asked people to remain in their homes.*

remainder /rɪ'meɪndə/ *uncountable noun*
the remainder the part of something that is still there after the first part has gone: *He drank the remainder of his coffee.*

remaining /rɪ'meɪnɪŋ/ *adjective*
the things or people out of a group that

r

still exist, or that are still present: *He spoke to his few remaining supporters.*

remains /rɪˈmeɪmz/ *plural noun*
the parts of something that are left after most of it has been taken away or destroyed: *They were cleaning up the remains of their picnic.*

remark¹ /rɪˈmɑːk/ *verb* (remarks, remarking, remarked)
to say something: *He remarked that it was very cold.* □ *She remarked on how tired I looked.*

remark² /rɪˈmɑːk/ *noun*
something that you say: *She made rude remarks about his weight.*

remarkable /rɪˈmɑːkəbəl/ *adjective*
very unusual or surprising in a good way: *He was a remarkable man.*
▸ **remarkably** /rɪˈmɑːkəbli/ *adverb* *The book was remarkably successful.*

remedy /ˈremədi/ *noun* (remedies)
1 something that stops a problem or a bad situation: *The government's remedy involved tax increases.*
2 something that makes you feel better when you are ill: *natural remedies for infections*

remember /rɪˈmembə/ *verb* (remembers, remembering, remembered)
1 to still have an idea of people or events from the past in your mind: *I remember the first time I met him.* □ *I remember that we went to his wedding.* □ *The weather was terrible; do you remember?*
2 to become aware of something again after a time when you did not think about it: *She remembered that she was going to the club that evening.*
3 to not forget to do something: *Please remember to post the letter.*

remind /rɪˈmaɪnd/ *verb* (reminds, reminding, reminded)
1 to say something that makes someone think about a fact or an event that they already know about: *She reminded Tim of the last time they met.*
2 to say something that makes someone remember to do something: *Can you remind me to buy some milk?*
3 to be similar to another person or thing and make someone think about them: *She reminds me of your sister.*

reminder /rɪˈmaɪndə/ *noun*
something that makes you think about

something again: *The scar on her hand was a constant reminder of the accident.*

remorse /rɪˈmɔːs/ *uncountable noun*
a strong feeling of sadness and regret about something wrong that you have done: *He was filled with remorse.*

remote /rɪˈməʊt/ *adjective* (remoter, remotest)
far away from cities and places where most people live: *They came from distant villages in remote areas.*

re,mote con'trol *noun*
the piece of equipment that you use to control a television or other piece of equipment from a distance: *Rachel picked up the remote control and turned on the television.*

remotely /rɪˈməʊtli/ *adverb*
used with a negative to mean 'in any way': *He wasn't remotely interested in her.*

removal /rɪˈmuːvəl/ *uncountable noun*
the act of removing something: *She had surgery for the removal of a tumour.*

remove /rɪˈmuːv/ *verb* (removes, removing, removed)
1 to take something away from a place (*formal*): *Remove the cake from the oven when it is cooked.*
2 to take off clothing (*formal*): *He removed his jacket.*

renew /rɪˈnjuː/ *verb* (renews, renewing, renewed)
to get something new to replace something old, or to arrange for the old thing to continue: *Larry's landlord refused to renew his lease.*

renewable /rɪˈnjuːəbəl/ *adjective*
used for describing resources that are natural and always available, such as wind, water and sunlight: *renewable energy sources*

rent /rent/ *verb* (rents, renting, rented)
1 to pay the owner of something in order to be able to use it yourself: *She rents a house with three other women.* ● **rent** *noun* *She worked hard to pay the rent on the flat.*
2 (*also* **rent something out**) to let someone have and use something in exchange for money: *She rented rooms to university students.* □ *Last summer Brian rented out his house and went camping.*

repair /rɪˈpeə/ *verb* (repairs, repairing, repaired)
to fix something that has been damaged

repair

He has repaired the roof.

or is not working properly: *He has repaired the roof.* ●**repair** *noun Repairs were made to the roof.*

repay /rɪˈpeɪ/ *verb* (**repays, repaying, repaid**)
to pay back money that you borrowed from someone: *They will have to repay the debt with interest.*

repayment /rɪˈpeɪmənt/ *noun*
1 *uncountable* the act or process of paying money back to the person you borrowed it from: *The bank will expect the repayment of the £114 million loan.*
2 money that you pay back to the person you borrowed it from: *He took a loan with small, frequent repayments.*

repeat ¹ /rɪˈpiːt/ *verb* (**repeats, repeating, repeated**)
1 to say or write something again: *She repeated her request for more money.* ☐ *He repeated that he was innocent.*
2 to say or write the same thing that someone else has said or written: *She had a habit of repeating everything I said to her.*
3 to do an action again: *Repeat this exercise five times a week.*

repeat ² /rɪˈpiːt/ *noun*
a television or radio programme that has been shown before

repeated /rɪˈpiːtɪd/ *adjective*
happening many times: *He did not return the money, despite repeated reminders.*
▶ **repeatedly** *adverb I asked him repeatedly to help me.*

repetition /ˌrepɪˈtɪʃən/ *noun*
an occasion when something happens again: *The city government wants to prevent a repetition of last year's violence.*

repetitive /rɪˈpetɪtɪv/ *adjective*
boring because it involves repeating an action many times: *They are factory workers who do repetitive jobs.*

replace /rɪˈpleɪs/ *verb* (**replaces, replacing, replaced**)
1 to do the job of another person or thing: *During the war, many women replaced male workers.*
2 to get something new in the place of something that is damaged or lost: *The shower broke so we have to replace it.*
3 to put something back where it was before: *Replace the caps on the bottles.*

replacement /rɪˈpleɪsmənt/ *noun*
a person or a thing that replaces another: *It won't be easy to find a replacement for Grace.*

replay /ˈriːpleɪ/ *noun*
1 an occasion when an action on television is broadcast again: *We watched the replay of the incident.*
2 a game which two teams play again because nobody won the first time

reply /rɪˈplaɪ/ *verb* (**replies, replying, replied**)
to say or write an answer to something that someone says or writes to you: *'That's a nice dress,' said Michael. 'Thanks,' she replied.* ☐ *He replied that this was impossible.* ☐ *He never replied to my letters.* ●**reply** *noun* (**replies**)
I called his name, but there was no reply.

report ¹ /rɪˈpɔːt/ *verb* (**reports, reporting, reported**)
1 to tell people about something that happened: *I reported the crime to the police.* ☐ *Officials reported that four people were killed.*
2 to tell an official person or organization about something wrong that someone has done: *His boss reported him to the police.*

report ² /rɪˈpɔːt/ *noun*
1 a newspaper article or a broadcast that gives information about something that happened: *According to a newspaper report, they are getting married next month.*
2 a piece of work that a student writes on a particular subject: *We had to do a book report on 'Huckleberry Finn'.*
3 a document that a teacher writes to tell parents about their children's work and progress

reporter /rɪˈpɔːtə/ *noun*
someone who writes newspaper articles or broadcasts the news: *My dad is a TV reporter.*

r

represent /ˌreprɪ'zent/ *verb* (**represents, representing, represented**)
1 to act or make decisions for a person or a group: *We vote for politicians to represent us.*
2 to mean something or be a sign of something: *The red line on the map represents a wall.*

representative /ˌreprɪ'zentətɪv/ *noun*
a person who acts or makes decisions for another person or group: *Michael is our class representative.*

reproduce /ˌri:prə'dju:s/ *verb* (**reproduces, reproducing, reproduced**)
1 to copy something: *The effect was hard to reproduce.*
2 to produce babies, eggs or seeds: *Some plants and animals reproduce in this way.*
▶ **reproduction** /ˌri:prə'dʌkʃən/ *uncountable noun* human reproduction

reptile /'reptaɪl/ *noun*
one of a group of animals that lay eggs and have cold blood. Snakes are reptiles.

reptiles

lizard

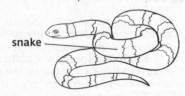
snake

republic /rɪ'pʌblɪk/ *noun*
a country with no king or queen where the people choose their government: *In 1918, Austria became a republic.*

repulsive /rɪ'pʌlsɪv/ *adjective*
used for describing a person or a thing that is so unpleasant that people do not want to see them: *Some people found the film repulsive.*

reputation /ˌrepjʊ'teɪʃən/ *noun*
the opinion that people have about someone or something: *This college has a good reputation.* □ *He has a reputation for honesty.*

request /rɪ'kwest/ *verb* (**requests, requesting, requested**)
to ask for something politely or formally (formal): *To request more information, please tick this box.* ● **request** *noun* *They agreed to his request for more money.*

require /rɪ'kwaɪə/ *verb* (**requires, requiring, required**)
1 to need something (formal): *If you require more information, please write to this address.*
2 to demand that someone does something or has something (formal): *The rules require employers to provide safety training.*

requirement /rɪ'kwaɪəmənt/ *noun*
something that you must have: *Our products meet all legal requirements.*

rescue ¹ /'reskju:/ *verb* (**rescues, rescuing, rescued**)
to save someone from a dangerous situation: *They rescued 20 people from the roof of the building.*

rescue ² /'reskju:/ *noun*
an attempt to save someone from a dangerous situation: *He helped in the rescue of a bus driver from the river.* □ *a big rescue operation*
come to someone's rescue to help someone when they are in danger: *A neighbour came to her rescue.*

research /rɪ'sɜːtʃ/ *uncountable noun*
when someone studies something and tries to discover facts about it: *My brother does scientific research.* ● **research** *verb* (**researches, researching, researched**) *She spent two years researching the subject.*

resemblance /rɪ'zembləns/ *noun*
when two people or things are similar to each other: *There was a strong resemblance between the two girls.*

resemble /rɪ'zembəl/ *verb* (**resembles, resembling, resembled**)
to look similar to another person or thing: *She resembles her mother.*

resent /rɪ'zent/ *verb* (**resents, resenting, resented**)
to feel angry about something because you think it is not fair: *Certain people resented my success.*

resentment /rɪ'zentmənt/ *noun*
anger that someone feels about something because they think it is not fair: *Too many rules can cause resentment.*

r

reservation /ˌrezəˈveɪʃən/ *noun*
a room or a seat that a hotel, a transport company or a restaurant keeps ready for you: *Have you cancelled our reservation?*

reserve¹ /rɪˈzɜːv/ *verb* (**reserves, reserving, reserved**)
to keep something for a particular person or purpose: *A room was reserved for him.*

reserve² /rɪˈzɜːv/ *noun*
a supply of something that you can use when you need it: *Saudi Arabia has the world's largest oil reserves.*
in reserve for using when you need it: *I always try to keep a little money in reserve.*

reserved /rɪˈzɜːvd/ *adjective*
hiding your feelings: *He was quiet and reserved.*

reservoir /ˈrezəˌvwɑː/ *noun*
a lake that is used for storing water before people use it: *The reservoir provides drinking water for the city of Oxford.*

residence /ˈrezɪdəns/ *noun*
a large house where an important person lives (*formal*): *the president's official residence*

resident /ˈrezɪdənt/ *noun*
a person who lives in a house or an area: *Local residents complained that the road was dangerous.*

residential /ˌrezɪˈdenʃəl/ *adjective*
containing houses rather than offices or shops: *We drove through a residential area of Birmingham.*

resign /rɪˈzaɪn/ *verb* (**resigns, resigning, resigned**)
to tell your employer that you are leaving a job: *He was forced to resign.*
resign yourself to something to accept an unpleasant situation because you cannot change it: *We resigned ourselves to another summer without a boat.*

resignation /ˌrezɪɡˈneɪʃən/ *noun*
an occasion when you tell your employer that you are leaving your job: *Barbara offered her resignation this morning.*

resist /rɪˈzɪst/ *verb* (**resists, resisting, resisted**)
1 to fight against something such as force or a change: *There are people in the organization who resist change.*
2 to stop yourself from doing something although you would like to do it: *Resist the temptation to help your child too much.*

resistance /rɪˈzɪstəns/ *uncountable noun*
when you fight against something such as force or a change: *I am aware of his resistance to anything new.* □ *The soldiers are facing strong resistance.*

resolution /ˌrezəˈluːʃən/ *noun*
when you decide to try very hard to do something: *They made a resolution to get more exercise.*

resolve /rɪˈzɒlv/ *verb* (**resolves, resolving, resolved**)
1 to find a solution to a problem, an argument or a difficulty (*formal*): *We must resolve these problems.*
2 to make a decision to do something (*formal*): *Judy resolved to be a better friend.*

resort /rɪˈzɔːt/ *noun*
a place that provides activities for people who stay there during their holiday: *The ski resorts are busy.*
as a last resort because you can find no other solution to a problem: *As a last resort, we hired an expert.*

resources /rɪˈzɔːsɪz/ *plural noun*
money and other things that a country, an organization or a person has and can use: *We must protect the country's natural resources, including water.*

respect¹ /rɪˈspekt/ *verb* (**respects, respecting, respected**)
to have a good opinion of someone: *I want people to respect me for my work.*

respect² /rɪˈspekt/ *uncountable noun*
when you have a good opinion of someone or something, and consider them to be important: *I have great respect for Tom.* □ *You should show respect for people's rights.*

respectable /rɪˈspektəbəl/ *adjective*
used for describing someone or something that people have a good opinion of, and think is morally correct: *He comes from a respectable family.*

respectful /rɪˈspektfʊl/ *adjective*
polite to people: *The children were always respectful to older people.*

respiration /ˌrespərˈeɪʃən/ *uncountable noun*
the process of breathing

respond /rɪˈspɒnd/ *verb* (**responds, responding, responded**)
to react to something that someone does

r

or says by doing or saying something: *They responded to the president's request for financial help.* □ *The army responded with bombs.*

response /rɪˈspɒns/ *noun*
a reply or a reaction to something that someone does or says: *There was no response to his remarks.*

responsibility /rɪˌspɒnsɪˈbɪlɪti/ *noun* (**responsibilities**)
1 *uncountable* to have the job of dealing with something or someone: *Each manager had responsibility for ten people.*
2 *uncountable* when you agree that something bad that happened was your fault: *No one admitted responsibility for the attacks.*
3 *plural* duties: *He is busy with work and family responsibilities.*

responsible /rɪˈspɒnsɪbəl/ *adjective*
1 having the job or duty to deal with something: *I met the people who are responsible for sales and advertising.*
2 used for saying that a particular event or situation is someone's fault: *He still felt responsible for her death.*
3 behaving in a proper and sensible way: *She's a responsible child who often helps around the house.*

rest [1] /rest/ *verb* (**rests, resting, rested**)
1 to spend some time relaxing after doing something tiring: *He's tired, and the doctor advised him to rest.*
2 to put one thing on another thing: *He rested his arms on the table.*

rest [2] /rest/ *noun*
when you spend some time relaxing after doing something tiring: *You're exhausted — go home and get some rest.*
the rest the parts of something that are left: *It was an experience I will remember for the rest of my life.* □ *I ate two cakes and saved the rest.*

restaurant /ˈrestərɒnt/ *noun*
a place where you can buy and eat a meal: *We ate at an Italian restaurant.*

restless /ˈrestləs/ *adjective*
bored or nervous, and wanting to move around: *I got restless and moved to San Francisco.* □ *My father seemed very restless and excited.*

restore /rɪˈstɔː/ *verb* (**restores, restoring, restored**)
to make something or someone good or

well again: *We will restore her to health.*
□ *They are experts in restoring old buildings.*

restrain /rɪˈstreɪn/ *verb* (**restrains, restraining, restrained**)
1 to use force to stop someone from doing something: *Wally held my arm to restrain me.*
2 to stop yourself from showing an emotion: *She was unable to restrain her anger.*

restrict /rɪˈstrɪkt/ *verb* (**restricts, restricting, restricted**)
1 to limit something: *The school is restricting the number of students it accepts this year.*
2 to prevent someone or something from acting freely: *The bandage restricts the movement in my right arm.*
▶ **restriction** /rɪˈstrɪkʃən/ *noun Are there any parking restrictions in this street?*

restroom /ˈrestrʊm/ also **rest room** *noun* (*American*)
→ see **toilets**

result [1] /rɪˈzʌlt/ *noun*
1 something that happens or exists because something else has happened: *People developed the disease as a direct result of their work.*
2 facts such as a score that you get at the end of a competition or a test: *Are you happy with the election results?*

result [2] /rɪˈzʌlt/ *verb* (**results, resulting, resulted**)
result from something to be caused by a particular event or action: *Many health problems result from a poor diet.*
result in something to cause a particular situation or event: *Half of all road accidents result in head injuries.*

resume /rɪˈzjuːm/ *verb* (**resumes, resuming, resumed**)
to begin an activity again (*formal*): *After the war he resumed his job at Wellesley College.*
□ *The talks will resume on Tuesday.*

résumé /ˈrezjʊmeɪ/ also **resume** *noun* (*American*)
→ see **CV**

retail /ˈriːteɪl/ *uncountable noun*
when a business sells goods directly to the public: *My sister works in retail, in a clothing shop.*

retailer /ˈriːteɪlə/ *noun*
a business that sells goods directly to the public: *a furniture retailer*

retain /rɪˈteɪn/ *verb* (**retains, retaining, retained**)

r

to continue to have something (*formal*): *He was looking for a way to retain control of his company.*

rethink /ˌriːˈθɪŋk/ *verb* (**rethinks, rethinking, rethought**)
to think about something such as a problem or a plan again and change it: *Both political parties are rethinking their policies.*

retire /rɪˈtaɪə/ *verb* (**retires, retiring, retired**)
to leave your job and usually stop working completely: *He planned to retire at 65.*
▶ **retired** *adjective* I am a retired teacher.

retirement /rɪˈtaɪəmənt/ *uncountable noun*
the period in someone's life after they retire: *What do you plan to do during retirement?*

retreat /rɪˈtriːt/ *verb* (**retreats, retreating, retreated**)
to move away from something or someone: *I retreated from the room.* □ *The French soldiers were forced to retreat.*

return ¹ /rɪˈtɜːn/ *verb* (**returns, returning, returned**)
1 to go back to a place: *He will return to Moscow tomorrow.*
2 to give back or put back something that you borrowed or took: *They will return the money later.*

return ² /rɪˈtɜːn/ *noun*
1 when someone arrives back at a place where they were before: *Kenny explained the reason for his return to London.*
2 (*also* **return ticket**) a ticket for a journey to a place and back again
in return done because someone did something for you: *He smiled at Alison and she smiled in return.*

reunion /riːˈjuːniən/ *noun*
a meeting between people who have not seen each other for a long time: *I am planning a family reunion.*

reunite /ˌriːjuːˈnaɪt/ *verb* (**reunites, reuniting, reunited**)
to see each other again after a long time: *She was finally reunited with her family.*

reveal /rɪˈviːl/ *verb* (**reveals, revealing, revealed**)
1 to tell people something that they do not know already: *She has refused to reveal any more details.*

2 to show something by removing the thing that was covering it: *She smiled, revealing small white teeth.*

revenge /rɪˈvendʒ/ *uncountable noun*
something bad you do to someone who has hurt or harmed you: *He wanted revenge for the way they treated his mother.*

revenue /ˈrevəˌnjuː/ *noun*
money that a company, organization or government receives from people: *The company gets 98% of its revenue from Internet advertising.*

Reverend /ˈrevərənd/ *noun*
a title used before the name of a Christian church leader: *The Reverend Jim Simons led the service.*

reverse ¹ /rɪˈvɜːs/ *verb* (**reverses, reversing, reversed**)
1 to change a decision or a situation to the opposite decision or situation: *They will not reverse the decision to increase prices.*
2 to arrange a group of things in the opposite order: *You've made a spelling mistake. You need to reverse the 'i' and the 'e'.*
3 to drive backwards in a vehicle: *A car reversed out of the driveway.*

reverse ² /rɪˈvɜːs/ *uncountable noun*
the control that makes a car ready to drive backwards: *I put the car in reverse.*

review ¹ /rɪˈvjuː/ *noun*
1 an occasion when you examine something to see if it needs changes: *The president ordered a review of the situation.*
2 a report that gives an opinion about something such as a book or a film: *The film got a good review in the magazine.*

review ² /rɪˈvjuː/ *verb* (**reviews, reviewing, reviewed**)
1 to consider something carefully to see if it needs changes: *The new plan will be reviewed by the city council.*
2 to write a report that gives your opinion of something such as a book or a film: *She reviews all the new DVDs.*
▶ **reviewer** *noun* He's a reviewer for the New York Times.

revise /rɪˈvaɪz/ *verb* (**revises, revising, revised**)
1 to change something in order to make it better or more correct: *Ask a friend to revise a paragraph that you have written.* □ *We are revising the rules.*

r

2 to study something again in order to prepare for an exam: *I have to revise for my maths exam.*
▸ **revision** /rɪ'vɪʒən/ *uncountable noun* *exam revision*

revive /rɪ'vaɪv/ *verb* (**revives, reviving, revived**)
to become conscious again or to make someone conscious again: *A doctor revived the patient.*

revolt /rɪ'vəʊlt/ *noun*
an occasion when a group of people fight against a person or an organization that has control: *It was a revolt by ordinary people against their leaders.* ● **revolt** *verb* (**revolts, revolting, revolted**) *California citizens revolted against higher taxes.*

revolting /rɪ'vəʊltɪŋ/ *adjective*
extremely unpleasant: *The smell was revolting.*

revolution /ˌrevə'luːʃən/ *noun*
1 an attempt by a group of people to change their country's government by using force: *The period since the revolution has been peaceful.*
2 an important change in a particular area of activity: *There was a revolution in ship design in the nineteenth century.*

revolutionary /ˌrevə'luːʃənri/ *adjective*
1 trying to cause a revolution: *Do you know anything about the revolutionary movement?*
2 changing the way that something is done or made: *It is a revolutionary new product.*

revolve /rɪ'vɒlv/ *verb* (**revolves, revolving, revolved**)
to move or turn in a circle: *The Earth revolves around the sun.*
revolve around something to have something as the most important part: *Her life has revolved around sports.*

revolver /rɪ'vɒlvə/ *noun*
a type of small gun

reward /rɪ'wɔːd/ *noun*
something that someone gives you because you have done something good: *The school gives rewards for good behaviour.*
● **reward** *verb* (**rewards, rewarding, rewarded**) *She was rewarded for her years of hard work.*

rewarding /rɪ'wɔːdɪŋ/ *adjective*
giving you satisfaction or bringing you

benefits: *I have a job that is very rewarding.*

rewrite /ˌriː'raɪt/ *verb* (**rewrites, rewriting, rewrote, rewritten**)
to write something in a different way in order to improve it: *She decided to rewrite her article.*

rhetorical /rɪ'tɒrɪkəl/ *adjective*
used to describe a question which is intended as a statement and which does not need an answer: *a rhetorical question*

rhinoceros /raɪ'nɒsərəs/ *noun* (**rhinoceroses**)
a large animal from Asia or Africa with a horn on its nose

rhyme ¹ /raɪm/ *verb* (**rhymes, rhyming, rhymed**)
to end with a very similar sound to another word: *'June' rhymes with 'moon'.*
□ *'June' and 'moon' rhyme.*

rhyme ² /raɪm/ *noun*
a poem that has words that rhyme at the ends of its lines: *He was teaching Helen a rhyme.*

rhythm /'rɪðəm/ *noun*
a regular pattern of sounds or movements: *Listen to the rhythms of jazz.*

rhythmic /'rɪðmɪk/ or **rhythmical** /'rɪðmɪkəl/ *adjective*
repeated in a regular pattern: *Good breathing is slow and rhythmic.*

rib /rɪb/ *noun*
one of the 12 pairs of curved bones that surround your chest: *Her heart was beating hard against her ribs.*

ribbon /'rɪbən/ *noun*
a long, narrow piece of cloth that you use to tie things together, or as a decoration: *She tied her hair with a ribbon.*

'rib cage *noun*
the structure of bones in your chest that protects your lungs and other organs

rice /raɪs/ *uncountable noun*
white or brown grains from a plant that grows in wet areas: *The meal consisted of chicken, rice and vegetables.*
→ Look at picture on P3

rich /rɪtʃ/ *adjective* (**richer, richest**)
having a lot of money or valuable possessions: *He was a very rich man.*
the rich rich people: *Only the rich can afford to live there.*

r

rid /rɪd/ *adjective*
get rid of something/someone to remove something or someone completely or make them leave: *We had to get rid of our old car because it was too small.*

ridden /'rɪdən/ → see **ride**

riddle /'rɪdəl/ *noun*
a question that seems to be nonsense, but that has a clever answer

ride¹ /raɪd/ *verb* (**rides, riding, rode, ridden**)
1 to sit on a bicycle or a horse, control it and travel on it: *Riding a bike is great exercise.* □ *We passed three men riding on motorcycles.*
2 to travel in a vehicle: *He rode in the bus to the hotel.*

ride² /raɪd/ *noun*
a trip on a horse or a bicycle, or in a vehicle: *She took some friends for a ride in the car.*

rider /'raɪdə/ *noun*
someone who rides a horse, a bicycle or a motorcycle

ridge /rɪdʒ/ *noun*
a long, narrow part of something that is higher than the rest: *It's a high road along a mountain ridge.*

ridiculous /rɪ'dɪkjʊləs/ *adjective*
very silly or not serious: *They thought it was a ridiculous idea.*

riding /'raɪdɪŋ/ *uncountable noun*
the activity or sport of riding horses: *The next morning we went riding.*

rifle /'raɪfəl/ *noun*
a long gun: *They shot him with a rifle.*

right¹ /raɪt/
1 *adjective, adverb* correct: *Ron was right about the result of the election.* □ *'C' is the right answer.* □ *If I'm going to do something, I want to do it right.*
2 *adjective* best: *You made the right choice in moving to New York.*
3 *exclamation* used for checking whether you are correct: *'You're coming to the party, right?'*
4 *adjective* morally good and acceptable: *It's not right to leave the children here alone.*
5 *adverb* to the side that is towards the east when you look north: *Turn right into the street.*
6 *adjective* on the right side of your body: *He held his right arm out in front of him.*

7 *adverb* used for saying that something happens exactly in a particular place or at a particular time: *A car appeared right in front of him.* □ *Liz arrived right on time.*

be right back to get back to a place in a very short time: *I'm going to get some water. I'll be right back.*

right away immediately (*informal*): *He wants to see you right away.*

right² /raɪt/ *noun*
1 *uncountable* used for talking about actions that are morally good and acceptable: *He knew right from wrong.*
2 the side that is towards the east when you look north: *On the right is a vegetable garden.*
3 something that you are allowed to do morally, or by law: *Make sure you know your rights.* □ *We have the right to protest.*

'right ˌangle *noun*
an angle that looks like a letter 'L' and equals 90 degrees

'right-hand *adjective*
on or near the right side of something: *There's a church on the right-hand side of the road.*

right-'handed *adjective*
using your right hand rather than your left hand for activities such as writing and sports

right-'wing *adjective*
supporting the ideas of the political right: *a right-wing politician*

rigid /'rɪdʒɪd/ *adjective*
1 that cannot be changed: *We have rigid rules about student behaviour.*
2 stiff and not bending, stretching or twisting easily: *Use rigid plastic containers.*

rim /rɪm/ *noun*
the edge of a curved object: *She looked at him over the rim of her glass.*

rind /raɪnd/ *noun*
1 the thick outside skin of a fruit such as a lemon or an orange
2 the hard outside edge of cheese that you do not eat

ring¹ /rɪŋ/ *verb* (**rings, ringing, rang, rung**)
1 to make the sound of a bell: *The school bell rang.* □ *They rang the bell but nobody came to the door.*
2 (*also* **ring someone up**) to telephone someone: *He rang me at my mother's.*

ring someone back to phone someone again: *Tell her I'll ring back in a few minutes.*

ring someone up same meaning as **ring 2**: *You can ring us up any time.*

ring² /rɪŋ/ *noun*

1 the sound of a bell: *There was a ring at the door.*

2 a small circle of metal that you wear on your finger: *She was wearing a gold wedding ring.*

3 something in the shape of a circle: *They built the fire in a ring of stones.*

to give someone a ring to make a telephone call to somebody (*informal*): *We'll give him a ring later.*

ringtone /'rɪŋtəʊn/ *noun*

the sound that your mobile phone makes when someone calls you

rink /rɪŋk/ *noun*

a large area of ice where people go to ice-skate (= move over ice in special boots): *There were hundreds of skaters on the rink.*

rinse /rɪns/ *verb* (**rinses, rinsing, rinsed**)

to wash something in order to remove dirt or soap from it: *Make sure you rinse all the shampoo out of your hair.*

riot /'raɪət/ *noun*

an occasion when a group of people behave violently in a public place: *Twelve people were injured during a riot at the prison.*

● **riot** *verb* (**riots, rioting, rioted**) *They rioted against the government.*

rip /rɪp/ *verb* (**rips, ripping, ripped**)

to tear something quickly: *I ripped my trousers when I fell.*

rip something up to tear something into small pieces: *He ripped up the letter and threw it in the fire.*

ripe /raɪp/ *adjective* (**riper, ripest**)

used for describing fruit or vegetables that are ready to eat: *Choose firm but ripe fruit.*

ripple /'rɪpəl/ *noun*

a little wave on the surface of water

● **ripple** *verb* (**ripples, rippling, rippled**) *If you throw a stone in a pool, the water ripples.*

rise /raɪz/ *verb* (**rises, rising, rose, risen**)

1 to move upwards: *We could see black smoke rising from the chimney.*

2 to stand up (*formal*): *He rose slowly from the chair.*

3 to get out of bed (*formal*): *Tony rose early.*

4 when the sun or the moon rises, it appears in the sky

5 to increase: *His income rose by £5,000.*

● **rise** *noun* *a pay rise*

> **LANGUAGE HELP**
>
> **rise** or **raise**? **Rise** does not have an object. *House prices are likely to rise.* **Raise** has an object. *The government has decided to raise taxes.*

risk¹ /rɪsk/ *noun*

1 a possibility that something bad will happen: *There is a small risk of damage.*

2 something or someone that is likely to harm you: *Being very fat is a health risk.*

at risk in a situation where something bad might happen: *Our nation is at risk from an attack.*

take a risk to do something that might have bad results: *You're taking a big risk by leaving your job.*

risk² /rɪsk/ *verb* (**risks, risking, risked**)

1 to do something knowing that something bad might happen as a result: *He risked breaking his leg when he jumped.*

2 to behave in a way that might result in something important being lost or harmed: *She risked her own life to help him.*

risky /'rɪski/ *adjective* (**riskier, riskiest**)

dangerous or likely to fail: *They encourage young people to avoid risky behaviour.*

ritual /'rɪtʃʊəl/ *noun*

a series of actions that people perform in a particular order: *Every religion has holy days and rituals such as praying.*

rival /'raɪvəl/ *noun*

someone who competes against someone else: *He was accused of spying on his political rivals.*

river /'rɪvə/ *noun*

a long line of water that flows into a sea

road /rəʊd/ *noun*

a long piece of hard ground that vehicles travel on: *There was very little traffic on the roads.*

roam /rəʊm/ *verb* (**roams, roaming, roamed**)

to move around an area without planning where exactly you are going: *Children roamed the streets in groups.*

roar /rɔː/ *verb* (roars, roaring, roared)
to make a very loud noise: *The engine roared, and the vehicle moved forward.* ● **roar** *noun*
When did you first hear the roar of a lion?

roast /rəʊst/ *verb* (roasts, roasting, roasted)
to cook meat or other food in an oven or over a fire: *He roasted the chicken.* ● **roast** *adjective* *We had roast beef.*

rob /rɒb/ *verb* (robs, robbing, robbed)
to steal money or property from someone: *She was robbed of her watch.*
▶ **robber** *noun* *a bank robber*

robbery /'rɒbəri/ *noun* (robberies)
an occasion when a person steals money or property from a place: *There have been several robberies in the area.*

robe /rəʊb/ *noun*
a special piece of clothing that an important person wears during a ceremony (*formal*): *The judge was wearing a black robe.*

robin /'rɒbɪn/ *noun*
a brown bird with a red chest

robot /'rəʊbɒt/ *noun*
a machine that can move and perform tasks automatically: *We have robots that we could send to the moon.*

rock ¹ /rɒk/ *noun*
1 *uncountable* the hard substance that is in the ground and in mountains: *We tried to dig, but the ground was solid rock.*
2 a large piece of rock: *She sat on a rock and looked out across the sea.*
3 *uncountable* (*also* **rock music**) loud music with a strong beat that you play on electric instruments: *We went to a rock concert.*

rock ² /rɒk/ *verb* (rocks, rocking, rocked)
1 to move slowly backwards and forwards: *His body rocked gently in the chair.*
2 to make something move slowly backwards and forwards: *She rocked the baby in her arms.*

rock and 'roll also **rock'n'roll** *uncountable noun*
a type of music that was popular in the 1950s: *Elvis Presley was known as the King of Rock and Roll.*

rocket /'rɒkɪt/ *noun*
1 a vehicle that people use to travel into outer space: *This is the rocket that took them to the moon.*
2 → see **missile**: *There was another rocket attack on the city.*

rocky /'rɒki/ *adjective* (rockier, rockiest)
having a lot of rocks in it: *The paths are very rocky.*

rod /rɒd/ *noun*
a long, thin, metal or wooden bar: *The roof was supported with steel rods.*

rode /rəʊd/ → see **ride**

rodent /'rəʊdənt/ *noun*
a small animal such as a mouse, with sharp front teeth

role /rəʊl/ *noun*
1 what someone or something should do in a situation: *We discussed the role of parents in raising their children.*
2 the character that an actor plays in a film or a play: *Who plays the role of the doctor?*

roll ¹ /rəʊl/ *verb* (rolls, rolling, rolled)
1 to move along a surface, turning over many times: *The pencil rolled off the desk.*
□ *I rolled a ball to the baby.*
2 to move quickly down a surface: *Tears rolled down her cheeks.*
roll something up to form something into the shape of a ball or a tube: *Steve rolled up the paper bag.*

roll ² /rəʊl/ *noun*
1 a long piece of something such as paper that you form into the shape of a tube: *There are twelve rolls of cloth here.*
2 a small piece of bread that is round or long: *He spread some butter on a roll.*

Rollerblade /'rəʊlə,bleɪd/ *noun* (trademark)
a type of roller-skate with a single line of wheels along the bottom
▶ **rollerblading** *uncountable noun*
(*trademark*): *Rollerblading is great fun for everyone.*

roller-skate /'rəʊlə,skeɪt/ *noun*
a boot with small wheels on the bottom: *a pair of roller skates*
▶ **roller-skating** *uncountable noun*
Roller-skating and swimming are my favourite hobbies.

Roman Catholic /,rəʊmən 'kæθlɪk/ *adjective* (*also* **Catholic**)
belonging to a section of the Christian Church that has the Pope as its leader: *I am a Roman Catholic priest.* ● **Roman Catholic** *noun* *Maria was a Roman Catholic.*

romance /rə'mæns, 'rəʊmæns/ *noun*
1 a relationship between two people who love each other but who are not married:

r

After a short romance they got married.
2 a book or a film about a romantic relationship: *Claire writes romances and young adult fiction.*

romantic /rəʊˈmæntɪk/ *adjective*
used when you are talking about love and romance: *He was not interested in a romantic relationship with me.* □ *It is a lovely romantic film.*

roof /ruːf/ *noun*
1 the top surface that covers a building: *The house has a red roof.*
→ Look at picture on P4
2 the top of a vehicle: *He listened to the rain on the roof of the car.*

room /ruːm, rʊm/ *noun*
1 a separate area inside a building that has its own walls: *A minute later he left the room.*
2 *uncountable* enough empty space: *There is room for 80 guests.*

root /ruːt/ *noun*
the part of a plant that grows under the ground: *She dug a hole near the roots of an apple tree.*

rope /rəʊp/ *noun*
a type of very thick string that is made by twisting together several strings or wires: *He tied the rope around his waist.*

rose¹ /rəʊz/ → see **rise**

rose² /rəʊz/ *noun*
a flower with a pleasant smell and sharp points (= thorns) on its stems

rot /rɒt/ *verb* (**rots, rotting, rotted**)
to get old and become softer, and sometimes smell bad: *The grain will start to rot after the rain.*

rotate /rəʊˈteɪt/ *verb* (**rotates, rotating, rotated**)
to turn in a circle around a central line or point: *The Earth rotates every 24 hours.*
▸ **rotation** /rəʊˈteɪʃən/ *noun* *We learned about the daily rotation of the Earth.*

rotten /ˈrɒtən/ *adjective*
1 old and soft, and sometimes smelling bad: *The smell was very strong — like rotten eggs.*
2 very unpleasant or bad (*informal*): *I think it's a rotten idea.*

rough /rʌf/ *adjective* (**rougher, roughest**)
1 not smooth or even: *His hands were rough.*
2 using too much force: *Football's a rough game.*
▸ **roughly** *adverb* *They roughly pushed past him.*

3 not exact or complete: *This is a rough guess of how much petrol we need.*
▸ **roughly** *adverb* *Cancer kills roughly half a million people a year.*

round¹ /raʊnd/ *adjective* (**rounder, roundest**)
shaped like a circle or a ball: *She has a round face.*

round² /raʊnd/ *noun*
one game or a part of a competition: *The team went through to the fifth round of the competition.* □ *On Sundays, he has a round of golf at the club.*

roundabout /ˈraʊndəˌbaʊt/ *noun*
1 a circle in the road where several roads meet, that vehicles must drive round until they reach the road they need
2 a round structure in a park, that children can sit on and turn around and around

rounded /ˈraʊndɪd/ *adjective*
curved in shape, without any points or sharp edges: *We came to a low, rounded hill.*

route /ruːt/ *noun*
a way from one place to another: *Which is the most direct route to the centre of the town?*

routine /ruːˈtiːn/ *noun*
the usual activities that you do every day: *The players changed their daily routine.*

row¹ /rəʊ/ *noun*
a line of things or people: *They drove past a row of pretty little houses.*

row² /rəʊ/ *verb* (**rows, rowing, rowed**)
to make a boat move through the water by using oars (= long pieces of wood with flat ends): *I rowed across the lake.*

row

I rowed across the lake.

row³ /raʊ/ *noun*
an argument: *She was having a row with her husband.*

royal /ˈrɔɪəl/ *adjective*
relating to a king or a queen: *We have an invitation to a royal garden party.*

r

royalty /ˈrɔɪəlti/ *uncountable noun*
used when you are talking about the
members of royal families: *He met
royalty and government leaders from around the
world.*

rub /rʌb/ *verb* (**rubs, rubbing, rubbed**)
1 to move a cloth or your fingers
backwards and forwards over
something: *He rubbed his stiff legs.* □ *She
took off her glasses and rubbed them with a
soft cloth.*
2 to spread a substance over the surface
using your hand: *He rubbed oil into my back.*
rub something out to use a rubber to
remove something you have written
on paper

rubber /ˈrʌbə/ *noun*
1 *uncountable* a strong substance used for
making tyres, boots and other products:
I can smell burning rubber.
2 (*American*: **eraser**) a small piece of rubber
that you use for removing marks you have
made with a pencil

rubber ˈband *noun*
a thin circle of rubber that you put
around things such as papers in order to
keep them together: *Her blonde hair was tied
back with a rubber band.*

rubbish /ˈrʌbɪʃ/ (*American*: **trash**)
uncountable noun
1 things you do not want any more:
I thought her note was just a bit of rubbish.
2 something that is very poor quality:
He thought her book was rubbish.

ruby /ˈruːbi/ *noun* (**rubies**)
a dark-red stone that is used in jewellery:
I want a ruby ring.

rucksack /ˈrʌksæk/ *noun*
a bag that you carry on your back

rude /ruːd/ *adjective* (**ruder, rudest**)
1 not polite: *He's so rude to her friends.*
▸ **rudely** *adverb* *Some hotel guests treat our
employees rudely.*
▸ **rudeness** *uncountable noun* *Mum was
annoyed at Cathy's rudeness.*
2 likely to embarrass or offend people:
Fred keeps telling rude jokes.

rug /rʌg/ *noun*
a piece of thick cloth that you put on
a small area of a floor: *There was a beautiful
red rug on the floor.*
→ Look at picture on P5

rugby /ˈrʌgbi/ *uncountable noun*
a game that is played by two teams who
try to get a ball past a line at the end of
the pitch
→ Look at picture on P6

ruin /ˈruːɪn/ *verb* (**ruins, ruining, ruined**)
to completely harm, damage or spoil
something: *My wife was ruining her health.*

ruins /ˈruːɪnz/ *plural noun*
the parts of a building that remain after
something destroys the rest: *Police found
two bodies in the ruins of the house.*
in ruins with only some parts remaining:
The church was in ruins.

rule¹ /ruːl/ *noun*
something that tells you what you must
do or must not do: *I need a book that explains
the rules of basketball.*

rule² /ruːl/ *verb* (**rules, ruling, ruled**)
to control the affairs of a country: *King
Hussein ruled for 46 years.*
rule something out to decide that a
course of action, an idea or a solution is
impossible or not practical

ruler /ˈruːlə/ *noun*
1 the person who rules a country: *He was
the ruler of France at that time.*
2 a long, flat object that you use for
measuring things and for drawing
straight lines

rumble /ˈrʌmbəl/ *noun*
a low, continuous noise: *We could hear the
distant rumble of traffic.* ● **rumble** *verb*
(**rumbles, rumbling, rumbled**) *Her
stomach was rumbling because she did not eat
breakfast.*

rumour /ˈruːmə/ *noun*
information that people talk about, that
may not be true: *There's a rumour that you're
leaving.*

run¹ /rʌn/ *verb* (**runs, running, ran, run**)
1 to move very quickly on your legs: *It's
very dangerous to run across the road.*
▸ **running** *uncountable noun* *He goes
running every morning.*
2 to go in a particular direction: *The road
runs east from Oxford to Cowley.*
3 to be in charge of a business or an
activity: *She runs a restaurant in San Francisco.*
4 to be switched on and working: *Sam
waited in the car, with the engine running.*
5 to take passengers between two places:

r

A bus runs between the station and the town centre.

6 to flow in a particular direction: *Tears were running down her cheeks.*

run away to leave a place because you are unhappy or afraid there: *The girl turned and ran away.*

run into someone to meet someone unexpectedly: *He ran into William in the supermarket.*

run into someone/something to hit someone or something with a vehicle: *The driver was going too fast and ran into a tree.*

run off to go away from a place when you should stay there: *Our dog is always running off.* □ *The thief ran off with her handbag.*

run out of something to have no more of something left: *We ran out of milk this morning.*

run someone over to hit someone with a vehicle so that they fall to the ground: *A police car ran her over.*

run ² /rʌn/ *noun*

1 when you move very quickly on your legs: *After a six-mile run, Jackie went home for breakfast.*

2 one point in the game of cricket or baseball: *The Blue Jays have scored 173 runs in their past 24 games.*

in the long run used for saying what you think will happen over a long period of time in the future: *Spending more on education now will save money in the long run.*

run-down /ˌrʌnˈdaʊn/ *adjective*

1 tired or slightly ill (*informal*)

2 in very bad condition: *He promised financial help for run-down areas.*

rung ¹ /rʌŋ/ → see **ring**

rung ² /rʌŋ/ *noun*
one of the steps that you climb up on a ladder

rung

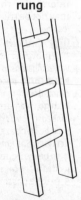

runner /ˈrʌnə/ *noun*
a person who runs, or who is running: *He is the oldest runner in the race.*

runner-'up *noun*
(**runners-up**)
the person who is in second place in a race or competition: *The runner-up will receive £500.*

runny /ˈrʌni/ *adjective* (**runnier, runniest**)
having more liquid than usual: *Warm the jelly until it is runny.*

a runny nose when a thick liquid flows from your nose, for example because you have a cold

runway /ˈrʌnweɪ/ *noun*
a long road that an aircraft travels on before it starts flying

rural /ˈrʊərəl/ *adjective*
not near cities or large towns: *The service is ideal for people who live in rural areas.*

rush ¹ /rʌʃ/ *verb* (**rushes, rushing, rushed**)

1 to go somewhere quickly: *Emma rushed into the room.*

2 to do something quickly: *Foreign banks rushed to buy as many dollars as they could.*

3 to take someone to a place quickly: *They rushed him to a hospital.*

rush ² /rʌʃ/ *noun*

in a rush quickly: *The men left in a rush.*

'rush hour *noun*
a period of the day when most people are travelling to or from their job: *Try to avoid travelling during the evening rush hour.*

rust /rʌst/ *uncountable noun*
a red-brown substance that forms on iron or steel when it is wet: *The old car was red with rust.* ● **rust** *verb* (**rusts, rusting, rusted**) *Iron rusts if you do not keep it dry.*

rustle /ˈrʌsəl/ *verb* (**rustles, rustling, rustled**)
to make soft sounds while moving: *The leaves rustled in the wind.* ● **rustle** *noun* *We listened to the rustle of leaves outside.*

rusty /ˈrʌsti/ *adjective* (**rustier, rustiest**)
having some rust on it: *The house has a rusty iron gate.*

rut /rʌt/ *noun*
a deep, narrow mark that the wheels of a vehicle make in the ground: *He drove slowly over the ruts in the road.*

in a rut having a particular way of doing things that is difficult to change: *I don't like being in a rut.*

ruthless /ˈruːθləs/ *adjective*
cruel and not caring if your actions harm other people: *a ruthless dictator*

r

Ss

sack¹ /sæk/ *noun*
a large bag made of thick paper or rough material: *a sack of potatoes*
get the sack to be told that you must leave your job

sack² /sæk/ *verb* (**sacks, sacking, sacked**)
to tell someone to leave their job: *He was sacked for stealing from the company.*

sacred /'seɪkrɪd/ *adjective*
having a special religious meaning: *The eagle is sacred to Native Americans.*

sacrifice /'sækrɪˌfaɪs/ *verb* (**sacrificing, sacrificed**)
1 to give up something valuable or important in order to get something else for yourself or for other people: *She sacrificed family life for her career.*
● **sacrifice** *noun* *The family made many sacrifices so that they could send the children to a good school.*
2 to kill an animal in a special religious ceremony in order to say thank you to a god: *The priest sacrificed a chicken.*

sad /sæd/ *adjective* (**sadder, saddest**)
1 unhappy: *I'm sad that Jason's leaving.*
▶ **sadly** *adverb* *'My girlfriend is moving away', he said sadly.*
▶ **sadness** *uncountable noun* *I left with a mixture of sadness and joy.*
2 making you feel unhappy: *It was a sad ending to a great story.* □ *I have some sad news for you.*

saddle /'sædəl/ *noun*
1 a leather seat that you put on the back of an animal: *He put a saddle on the horse.*
2 a seat on a bicycle or a motorcycle

saddle

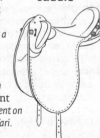

safari /sə'fɑːri/ *noun*
a trip to look at or hunt wild animals: *She went on a seven-day African safari.*

safe¹ /seɪf/ *adjective* (**safer, safest**)
1 not dangerous: *We must try to make our roads safer.*
2 not in danger: *Where's Sophie? Is she safe?*
▶ **safely** *adverb* *'Drive safely', he said, waving goodbye.*

safe² /seɪf/ *noun*
a strong metal box with a lock, where you keep money or other valuable things: *Who has the key to the safe?*

safety¹ /'seɪfti/ *uncountable noun*
the state of not being in danger: *We need to improve safety on our roads.*

safety² /'seɪfti/ *adjective*
intended to make something less dangerous: *There are child safety locks on all the gates.*

sag /sæg/ *verb* (**sags, sagging, sagged**)
to hang down loosely or to have a fold in the middle: *The dress won't sag or lose its shape after washing.*

said /sed/ → see **say**

sail¹ /seɪl/ *noun*
a large piece of cloth on a boat, that catches the wind and moves the boat along

sail² /seɪl/ *verb* (**sails, sailing, sailed**)
1 a boat sails when it moves over water: *The ferry sails between Seattle and Bremerton.*
2 to use a boat's sails to move it across water: *I'd like to buy a big boat and sail around the world.*

sailing /'seɪlɪŋ/ *uncountable noun*
the activity or sport of sailing boats: *There was swimming and sailing on the lake.*

sailor /'seɪlə/ *noun*
someone who works on a ship or who sails a boat

saint /seɪnt/ *noun*
in certain religions, someone who has died, and whose life was a perfect example of the way people should live: *Every church here was named after a saint.*

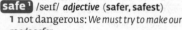

sake /seɪk/ *noun*
for something's sake/for someone's sake to help something or someone, or because of something or someone: *For safety's sake never stand directly behind a horse.* □ *Please do a good job, for Stan's sake.*

for the sake of something or someone because of something or someone: *For the sake of peace, I am willing to forgive them.* □ *They stayed together for the sake of the children.*

salad /'sæləd/ *noun*
a mixture of foods, especially vegetables, that you usually serve cold: *She ordered a pasta and a green salad.*
→ Look at picture on P3

salary /'sæləri/ *noun* (**salaries**)
the money that you earn from your employer: *The lawyer was paid a huge salary.*

> **LANGUAGE HELP**
> Pay, **salary**, or **wages**? Use the noun **pay** to talk in general about the money people get from their employer for doing their job. Professional people and office workers receive a **salary**, which is paid every month. People who do physical work, for example in a factory, receive **wages**, or **a wage**.

sale /seɪl/ *noun*
1 when you sell something for money: *He made a lot of money from the sale of the business.*
2 a time when a shop sells things at less than their normal price: *Did you know the bookshop was having a sale?*
for sale available for people to buy: *The house had a 'For Sale' sign in the garden.*
on sale available for less than the normal price: *She bought the coat on sale at a department store.*

salesman /'seɪlzmən/ *noun* (**salesmen**)
a man whose job is to sell things: *He's an insurance salesman.*

salesperson /'seɪlzpɜːsən/ *noun* (**salespeople** or **salespersons**)
a person whose job is to sell things: *Be sure to ask the salesperson for help.*

saleswoman /'seɪlzwʊmən/ *noun* (**saleswomen**)
a woman whose job is to sell things: *She spent three years as a saleswoman.*

saliva /sə'laɪvə/ *uncountable noun*
the liquid in your mouth that helps you

to swallow food □ *They tested his saliva.*

salmon /'sæmən/ *noun* (**salmon**)
1 a large fish with silver skin
2 *uncountable* the pink flesh of this fish that you can eat: *He gave them a plate of salmon.*

salon /'sælɒn/ *noun*
a place where you go to have your hair cut, or to have beauty treatments: *The club has a beauty salon and two swimming pools.*

salt /sɔːlt/ *uncountable noun*
a white substance that you use to improve the flavour of food: *Now add salt and pepper.*
→ Look at picture on P3

salty /'sɔːlti/ *adjective* (**saltier, saltiest**)
containing salt or tasting of salt: *Ham and bacon are salty foods.*

salute /sə'luːt/ *verb* (**salutes, saluting, saluted**)
to make a special sign to show your respect for someone, for example by raising your right hand to your head, like a soldier: *The sailors saluted as the captain entered the room.* □ *The two guards saluted the major.*

salute

same /seɪm/ *adjective*
1 very similar: *The houses are all the same.*
2 used to show that you are talking about only one thing, and not two different ones: *Jason works at the same office as Gabrielle.* □ *He gets up at the same time every day.*

sample /'sɑːmpəl/ *noun*
a small amount of something that shows you what the rest of it is like: *We're giving away 2,000 free samples of the perfume.* □ *The doctor took a blood sample.*

sand /sænd/ *uncountable noun*
a powder made of very small pieces of stone that you find in some deserts and on most beaches: *They walked across the sand to the water's edge.*

sandal /'sændəl/ *noun*
a light shoe that you wear in warm weather: *He put on a pair of old sandals.*

sandwich /'sænwɪdʒ/ *noun*
two slices of bread with another food between them: *an egg sandwich*
→ Look at picture on P3

sandy /'sændi/ *adjective* (**sandier, sandiest**)
covered with sand: *sandy beaches*

sane /seɪn/ *adjective* (**saner, sanest**)
thinking and behaving normally and reasonably; not mad: *He seemed perfectly sane.*

sang /sæŋ/ → see **sing**

sank /sæŋk/ → see **sink**

sarcasm /'sɑːkæzəm/ *uncountable noun*
the use of words or phrases that are the opposite of what you really mean in order to be rude to someone: *'How nice of you to join us', he said with heavy sarcasm.*

sarcastic /sɑː'kæstɪk/ *adjective*
saying the opposite of what you really mean in order to be rude to someone: *He made some very sarcastic comments.*

sardine /sɑː'diːn/ *noun*
a small sea fish that you can eat: *They opened a can of sardines.*

sat /sæt/ → see **sit**

satellite /'sætəlaɪt/ *noun*
a piece of electronic equipment that is sent into space in order to receive and send back information: *The rocket carried two communications satellites.*

'satellite dish *noun*
a piece of equipment that people put on their house in order to receive television signals from a satellite
→ Look at picture on P5

,satellite navi'gation *uncountable noun*
a system that uses information from a satellite (= an object that moves around the Earth in space) to help you to find your way: *Many of the boats have satellite navigation.*

,satellite 'television *uncountable noun*
a system of broadcasting television programs that are sent to your television from a satellite (= an object that moves around the Earth in space): *We have access to 49 satellite television channels.*

satin /'sætɪn/ *noun*
a smooth, shiny cloth: *a satin dress*

satire /'sætaɪə/ *noun*
1 *uncountable* the use of humour to criticize people's behaviour or ideas: *He loved the book's humour and satire.*
2 a play, a film or a piece of writing that uses humour to criticize people's behaviour or ideas: *The film is a satire on American politics.*

satisfaction /ˌsætɪs'fækʃən/ *uncountable noun*
the feeling of being pleased to do or to get something: *It gives me a real sense of satisfaction when I help someone.*

satisfactory /ˌsætɪs'fæktəri/ *adjective*
good enough for a particular purpose: *I never got a satisfactory answer.*

satisfied /'sætɪsfaɪd/ *adjective*
happy because you have what you wanted: *Doctors are satisfied with his condition.*

satisfy /'sætɪsfaɪ/ *verb* (**satisfies, satisfying, satisfied**)
to give someone enough of what they want or need: *Milk alone should satisfy your baby's hunger.*

satisfying /'sætɪsfaɪɪŋ/ *adjective*
making you feel happy because you have what you want, or you are doing what you want: *Taking care of children can be very satisfying.*

satnav /'sætˌnæv/ *noun*
a piece of equipment in a car that tells you the best way of getting to a place: *We didn't have a satnav, so we had to use a map.*

Saturday /'sætədeɪ, -di/ *noun*
the day after Friday and before Sunday: *He called her on Saturday morning.* ☐ *Every Saturday, Dad made soup.*

sauce /sɔːs/ *noun*
a thick liquid that you eat with other food: *The pasta is cooked in a garlic and tomato sauce.*

saucepan /'sɔːspən/ *noun*
a deep metal cooking pot, usually with a long handle and a lid

saucepan

saucer /'sɔːsə/ *noun*
a small curved plate that you put under a cup

sauna /'sɔːnə/ *noun*
a very hot room that is filled with steam, where people relax: *The hotel has a sauna and a swimming pool.*

sausage /'sɒsɪdʒ/ *noun*
a mixture of very small pieces of meat, spices and other foods, inside a long thin skin: *They ate sausages for breakfast.*

savage /'sævɪdʒ/ *adjective*
very cruel or violent: *This was a savage attack on a young girl.*

save [1] /seɪv/ *verb* (**saves, saving, saved**)
1 to help someone to escape from a dangerous or a bad situation: *We must save these children from disease and death.*
2 (*also* **save up**) to gradually collect money by spending less than you get: *Tim and Barbara are now saving for a house.* □ *I was saving money to go to college.* □ *Taylor was saving up for something special.*
3 to use less of something: *Going through the city by bike saves time.* □ *We're trying to save water.*
4 to keep something because you will need it later: *Save the vegetable water for making the sauce.*
5 to give a computer an instruction to store some information: *It's important to save frequently when you are working on a document.*

save [2] /seɪv/ *noun*
the act of stopping someone from scoring a goal in a sports game: *The goalkeeper made some great saves.*

savings /'seɪvɪŋz/ *plural noun*
all the money that you have saved, especially in a bank: *Her savings were in the First National Bank.*

savoury /'seɪvəri/ *adjective*
having a salty flavour rather than a sweet one: *We had all sorts of sweet and savoury snacks at the party.*

saw [1] /sɔː/ → see **see**

saw [2] /sɔː/ *noun*
a metal tool for cutting wood ● **saw** *verb* (**saws, sawing, sawed** or **sawn**) *He escaped by sawing through the bars of his jail cell.* □ *I sawed the dead branches off the tree.*

saxophone /'sæksəˌfəʊn/ *noun*
a musical instrument made of metal that

you play by blowing into it

say [1] /seɪ/ *verb* (**says, saying, said**)
1 to speak words: *She said that they were very pleased.* □ *I packed and said goodbye to Charlie.*
2 to give information in writing or in numbers: *The clock said four minutes past eleven.*

LANGUAGE HELP

say or **tell**? Use **say** with the actual words that someone speaks, or before **that** with reported speech. *He said 'I don't feel well.' He said that he didn't feel well.* Remember: You **say something to someone**. *What did she say to you?* You **tell someone something**. *He told Alison the news.*

say [2] /seɪ/ *noun*
have your say in something to have the right to give your opinion about something: *He should have a say in the decisions that affect his life.*

saying /'seɪɪŋ/ *noun*
something that people often say, that gives advice about life: *Remember that old saying: 'Forgive and forget.'*

scab /skæb/ *noun*
a hard, dry cover that forms over the surface of a wound: *After a few days, the spots become dry and form scabs.*

scaffolding /'skæfəldɪŋ/ *uncountable noun*
a frame of metal bars that people can stand on when they are working on the outside of a building: *Builders have put up scaffolding around the tower.*

scald /skɔːld/ *verb* (**scalds, scalding, scalded**)
to burn yourself with very hot liquid or steam: *A patient scalded herself in the bath.*

scale [1] /skeɪl/ *noun*
1 a set of levels or numbers that you use to measure things: *The earthquake measured 5.5 on the Richter scale.*
2 one of the small, flat pieces of hard skin that cover the body of animals like fish and snakes
3 the size or level of something: *He doesn't realize the scale of the problem.*
4 a set of musical notes that are played in a fixed order: *the scale of F major* □ *Celia was practising her scales on the piano.*

scales

bathroom scales

scales

kitchen scales

musical scale

C D E F G A B C

scales /skeɪlz/ *plural noun*
a machine that you use for weighing people or things: *He weighed himself on the bathroom scales.*

scalp /skælp/ *noun*
the skin under the hair on your head: *Try this treatment for beautiful thick hair and a healthy scalp.*

scan /skæn/ *verb* (**scans, scanning, scanned**)
1 to look through a piece of writing quickly to find important or interesting information: *She scanned the front page of the newspaper.*
2 to make an electronic copy of a picture or a document using a special piece of equipment (= a scanner): *She scanned the images into her computer.*

scandal /'skændəl/ *noun*
a situation or an event that people think is shocking: *It was a financial scandal.*

scanner /'skænə/ *noun*
1 a machine that you use to make an electronic copy of something, such as a picture or a document: *Scan your photos using any desktop scanner.*
2 a machine that gives a picture of the inside of something: *His bag was passed through the airport X-ray scanner.*

scar /skɑː/ *noun*
a mark that is left on the skin by an old wound: *He had a scar on his forehead.* ● **scar** *verb* (**scars, scarring, scarred**) *He was scarred for life during a fight.*

scarce /skeəs/ *adjective* (**scarcer, scarcest**)
not enough in number or quantity: *Food was scarce and expensive.* □ *Jobs are becoming scarce.*

scarcely /'skeəsli/ *adverb*
used for emphasizing that something is only just true: *He could scarcely breathe.*

scare [1] /skeə/ *verb* (**scares, scaring, scared**)
to frighten or worry someone: *The thought of failure scares me.*

scare [2] /skeə/ *noun*
1 when someone or something frightens or worries you: *You gave us a terrible scare!*
2 a situation where many people are afraid or worried about something: *The new drug was the subject of a recent health scare.*

scared /skeəd/ *adjective*
frightened or worried: *I'm not scared of him.*

scarf /skɑːf/ *noun* (**scarves**)
a piece of cloth that you wear around your neck or head: *He loosened the scarf around his neck.*

scary /'skeəri/ *adjective* (**scarier, scariest**)
frightening (*informal*): *The film is too scary for children.*

scatter /'skætə/ *verb* (**scatters, scattering, scattered**)
to throw or drop things over an area so that they spread over it: *She scattered the flowers over the grave.*

scene /siːn/ *noun*
1 a part of a play, a film or a book that happens in the same place: *This is the opening scene of 'Tom Sawyer'.*
2 a place when you are describing what is there: *The photographs show scenes of everyday life in the village.* □ *It's a scene of complete horror.*

S

3 the place where an event happened: *Firefighters rushed to the scene of the car accident.*

scenery /'si:nəri/ *uncountable noun*
1 the land, water or plants that you can see around you in a country area: *Most visitors come for the island's beautiful scenery.*
2 the objects or the backgrounds in a theatre that show where the action in the play is happening: *The actors will move the scenery themselves.*

scent /sent/ *noun*
the pleasant smell that something has: *This perfume gives off a heavy scent of roses.*
▶ **scented** *adjective* scented soap

schedule /'ʃedju:l/ *noun*
a plan that gives a list of the times when things will happen: *For best results, plan a training schedule.*
behind schedule after the planned time: *The project is about three months behind schedule.*

scheme /ski:m/ *verb* (**schemes, scheming, schemed**)
to make secret plans to do something: *The family was scheming to stop the wedding.* ▢ *She thinks that everyone is scheming against her.*

scholar /'skɒlə/ *noun*
a person who studies an academic subject and who knows a lot about it (*formal*): *The library is full of scholars and researchers.*

scholarship /'skɒləʃɪp/ *noun*
money to help you to continue studying: *He won a scholarship to the Pratt Institute of Art.*

school /sku:l/ *noun*
1 a place where people go to learn: *The school was built in the 1960s.*
2 *uncountable* your time in school or college: *Parents want their kids to do well in school.* ▢ *Jack eventually graduated from school in 1998.*

schoolteacher /'sku:lti:tʃə/ *noun*
a teacher in a school

science /'saɪəns/ *uncountable noun*
the study of natural things: *He studied plant science at university.*

science fiction *uncountable noun*
stories in books, magazines and films about things that happen in the future or in other parts of the universe

scientific /ˌsaɪən'tɪfɪk/ *adjective*
relating to science: *He spends a lot of time conducting scientific research.*

scientist /'saɪəntɪst/ *noun*
someone whose job is to teach or do research in science: *Scientists have discovered a new gene.*

sci-fi /'saɪfaɪ/ *uncountable noun*
short for **science fiction** (*informal*)

scissors /'sɪzəz/ **scissors**
plural noun
a small tool for cutting with two sharp parts that are joined together: *Cut the card using scissors.*

scoop /sku:p/ *verb* (**scoops, scooping, scooped**)
to remove something from a container with your hand or with a spoon: *He was scooping dog food out of a can.*
scoop something up to put your hands under something and lift it: *Use both hands to scoop up the leaves.*

scooter /'sku:tə/ *noun*
1 a small light motorcycle with a low seat
2 a child's vehicle with a long handle and two wheels joined by a long board

scorch /skɔ:tʃ/ *verb* (**scorches, scorching, scorched**)
to burn something slightly: *Many of my plants were scorched by the sun.*

score¹ /skɔ:/ *verb* (**scores, scoring, scored**)
1 to get a goal or a point in a sport or a game: *Patten scored his second goal of the game.*
2 to achieve a particular amount on a test: *Kelly scored 88 on the test.*

score² /skɔ:/ *noun*
1 the number of points that someone has won in a game or a test: *Hogan won, with a score of 287.*
2 the result of a game: *The final score was 4–1.*

scorn /skɔ:n/ *uncountable noun*
a strong feeling of not liking or respecting someone or something: *Her words attracted scorn and anger.*

scornful /'skɔ:nfəl/ *adjective*
showing that you do not like or respect someone or something: *He is deeply scornful of politicians.*
▶ **scornfully** *adverb* They laughed scornfully.

s

scout /skaʊt/ *verb* (**scouts, scouting, scouted**)
to go around an area in order to search for something: *She's scouting for locations to open a restaurant.*

Scout /skaʊt/ *noun*
a member of the Scouts (= an organization that teaches boys practical skills, and encourages them to help other people)

scowl /skaʊl/ *verb* (**scowls, scowling, scowled**)
to make an angry face: *He scowled, and slammed the door.*

scramble /'skræmbəl/ *verb* (**scrambles, scrambling, scrambled**)
to move quickly over rocks or up a hill, using your hands to help you: *We scrambled over the rocks to the beach.*

scrap [1] /skræp/ *noun*
a very small piece or amount of something: *A scrap of red paper was found in her handbag.*

scrap [2] /skræp/ *verb* (**scraps, scrapping, scrapped**)
to get rid of something or cancel it: *The government has scrapped plans to build a new airport.*

scrape /skreɪp/ *verb* (**scrapes, scraping, scraped**)
1 to accidentally rub a part of your body against something hard and rough, and damage it slightly: *She fell, scraping her hands and knees.*
2 to remove something from a surface by moving a sharp object over it: *She scraped the frost off the car windows.*

scratch [1] /skrætʃ/ *verb* (**scratches, scratching, scratched**)
1 to rub your fingernails against the skin on a part of your body: *He scratched his head thoughtfully.* □ *My arms are very itchy and I can't stop scratching.*
2 to make small cuts on someone's skin or on the surface of something: *The branches scratched my face.*

scratch [2] /skrætʃ/ *noun* (**scratches**)
a small cut made by a sharp object: *He had scratches on his face and neck.*

scream /skri:m/ *verb* (**screams, screaming, screamed**)
to give a loud, high cry because you are hurt or frightened: *Women were screaming in*

the houses nearest the fire. ● **scream** *noun*
Rose gave a loud scream.

screech /skri:tʃ/ *verb* (**screeches, screeching, screeched**)
to make an unpleasant high sound: *Two police cars screeched into the car park.*

screen /skri:n/ *noun*
1 a flat surface on a piece of electronic equipment, such as a television or a computer, where you see pictures or words
2 the flat area on the wall of a cinema, where you see the film: *The cinema has 20 screens.*

screensaver /'skri:nseɪvə/ *noun*
a moving picture that appears on a computer screen when the computer is not being used

screw [1] /skru:/ *noun*
a small metal object with a sharp end, that you use to join things together: *Each shelf is attached to the wall with screws.*

screw [2] /skru:/ *verb* (**screws, screwing, screwed**)
1 to join one thing to another thing using a screw: *I screwed the shelf on the wall myself.*
2 to turn something in order to attach it to something else: *Make sure you screw the lid on tightly.*

screwdriver

screwdriver /'skru:draɪvə/ *noun*
a tool that you use for turning screws

scribble /'skrɪbəl/ *verb* (**scribbles, scribbling, scribbled**)
to write or draw something quickly and roughly: *She scribbled a note to her mother.*

script /skrɪpt/ *noun*
the written words that actors speak in a play, a film or a television programme: *Jenny's writing a film script.*

scroll /skrəʊl/ *verb* (**scrolls, scrolling, scrolled**)
to move the text on a computer screen up or down to find the information that you need: *I scrolled down to find 'United States of America'.*

scrub /skrʌb/ *verb* (**scrubs, scrubbing, scrubbed**)
to rub something hard in order to clean it:

s

Surgeons must scrub their hands and arms with
soap and water.

scruffy /'skrʌfi/ *adjective* (**scruffier,
scruffiest**)
dirty and messy: *The man was pale, scruffy
and unshaven.*

sculptor /'skʌlptə/ *noun*
an artist who makes solid works of
art out of stone, metal or wood: *The
sculptor carved the swan from a solid block
of ice.*

sculpture /'skʌlptʃə/ *noun*
1 a piece of art that is made into a
shape from a material like stone or
wood: *There were stone sculptures of different
animals.*
2 *uncountable* the art of creating
objects (= sculptures) from a substance
like stone or wood: *Both of them studied
sculpture.*

sea /siː/ *noun*
a large area of salty water that is part of
an ocean or is surrounded by land: *They
swam in the warm Caribbean Sea.*

seafood /'siːfuːd/ *noun*
fish and other small animals from the
sea that you can eat: *Let's find a seafood
restaurant.*

seagull /'siːgʌl/ *noun*
a common type of bird with white or grey
feathers that lives near the sea

seal¹ /siːl/ *verb* (**seals, sealing, sealed**)
to close an envelope by folding part of it
and sticking it down: *He sealed the envelope
and put on a stamp.*

seal² /siːl/ *noun*
a large animal with a rounded body and
short fur that eats fish and lives near the
sea

seam /siːm/ *noun*
a line where two pieces of cloth are joined
together

search¹ /sɜːtʃ/ *verb* (**searches, searching,
searched**)
1 to look carefully for something or
someone: *Police are already searching for the
men.*
2 to look carefully in a place for
something or someone: *The police are
searching the town for the missing men.*

search² /sɜːtʃ/ *noun* (**searches**)
an attempt to find something or someone

by looking for them carefully: *The search
was stopped because of the heavy snow.*

'search ,engine *noun*
a computer program that you use to
search for information on the Internet

seaside /'siːsaɪd/ *noun*
an area that is close to the sea, especially
where people go for their holidays

season /'siːzən/ *noun*
1 one of the four parts of a year that each
have their own typical weather
conditions: *Autumn is my favourite season.*
2 a time each year when something
happens: *The football season begins again
soon.*

seat /siːt/ *noun*
something that you can sit on: *We had
front-row seats at the concert.* □ *The car has
comfortable leather seats.*
take a seat to sit down (*formal*): *'Take a
seat', he said.*

'seat belt *noun*
a long belt that you fasten around your
body in a vehicle to keep you safe: *Please
fasten your seat belts.*

seaweed /'siːwiːd/ *uncountable noun*
a plant that grows in the sea

second¹ /'sekənd/ *noun*
a measurement of time. There are sixty
seconds in one minute: *For a few seconds
nobody spoke.*

second² /'sekənd/ *adjective*
the person or thing that you count as
number two in a series: *It was the second day
of his visit to Florida.* ●**second** *adverb* Emma
came in second in the race.

secondary /'sekəndri/ *adjective*
less important than something else:
*Money is of secondary importance to them.
Happiness comes first.*

'secondary school *noun*
a school for students between the ages of
11 and 18: *They take examinations after five
years of secondary school.*

second-hand /'sekənd,hænd/ *adjective*
already used by another person; not new:
They could just afford a second-hand car.

secondly /'sekəndli/ *adverb*
used when you want to talk about
a second thing, or give a second reason
for something: *Firstly, involve your children
in planning the holiday, and secondly, ask your*

travel agent for family-friendly suggestions.

secrecy /'si:krəsi/ *uncountable noun*
a situation in which you do not tell anyone about something: *They met in complete secrecy.*

secret¹ /'si:krɪt/ *adjective*
with only a small number of people knowing about something, and not telling anyone else about it: *They tried to keep their marriage secret.*

secret² /'si:krɪt/ *noun*
something that only a small number of people know and that they do not tell anyone else about: *Can you keep a secret?*

secretarial /ˌsekrə'teəriəl/ *adjective*
relating to typing letters, answering the telephone and other work done in an office: *I was doing temporary secretarial work.*

secretary /'sekrətri/ *noun* (**secretaries**)
1 a person whose job is to type letters, answer the telephone, and do other office work
2 a person with an important position in the government: *The Foreign Secretary will meet with the president tomorrow.*

secretive /'si:krətɪv/ *adjective*
not sharing your knowledge, feelings or intentions: *She's very secretive about how much money she has.*

section /'sekʃən/ *noun*
a particular part of something: *It is wrong to blame one section of society for all these problems.* □ *He works in the research section of the company.*

secure /sɪ'kjʊə/ *adjective*
1 well protected, so that people cannot enter or leave: *We'll make our home as secure as possible.*
▶ **securely** *adverb He locked the heavy door securely.*
2 properly fixed in position: *The farmer made sure that the fence was always secure.*
▶ **securely** *adverb He fastened his belt securely.*
3 a secure job will not end soon: *For the moment, his job is secure.*
4 feeling safe and happy, and not worried about life: *She felt secure when she was with him.*

security /sɪ'kjʊərɪti/ *uncountable noun*
1 everything that you do to protect a place: *They are improving airport security.*
2 a feeling of being safe and free from worry: *He loves the security of a happy home life.*

see /si:/ *verb* (**sees, seeing, saw, seen**)
1 to notice something using your eyes: *The fog was so thick we couldn't see anything.* □ *Have you seen my keys?*
2 to visit or meet someone: *I saw him yesterday.*
3 to watch a play, film or sports match: *I saw a great film last night.*
4 to understand something: *Oh, I see what you're saying.*
5 to find out information or a fact about something: *She looked around to see if anyone was listening.*
6 to experience a particular event: *I have seen many changes here over the past decade.*

I'll/we'll see used for saying that you will decide something later: *'Can we go swimming tomorrow?' — 'We'll see. Maybe.'*

let's see used when you are trying to remember something: *Let's see. Where did I leave my purse?*

see someone off to go with someone who is leaving, to the station or airport, to say goodbye to them: *Ben saw Jackie off on her plane.*

see you used for saying goodbye to someone (*informal*): *'Talk to you later.' — 'All right. See you.'*

> **LANGUAGE HELP**
> See note at **look.**

seed /si:d/ *noun*
the small, hard part of a plant from which a new plant grows: *Plant the seeds in small plastic pots.*

seek /si:k/ *verb* (**seeks, seeking, sought**)
to try to find or get something (*formal*): *They are seeking work in hotels and bars.*

seem /si:m/ *verb* (**seems, seeming, seemed**)
to give the impression of being a particular thing or of being a particular way: *The thunder seemed quite close.* □ *They seemed a perfect couple to everyone who knew them.*

seen /si:n/ → see **see**

'see-saw *noun*
a long board that children play on. One child sits at each end, and they go up and down.

segment /'segmənt/ *noun*
one part of something: *These people come from the poorer segments of society.*

segregation /ˌsegrɪˈgeɪʃən/ *uncountable noun*
the official practice of separating people, especially based on race or religion: *racial segregation in schools*

seize /siːz/ *verb* (**seizes, seizing, seized**)
to take hold of something quickly and firmly: *He seized my arm and pulled me closer.*

seldom /ˈseldəm/ *adverb*
not very often: *They seldom speak to each other.* □ *I've seldom felt so happy.*

select /sɪˈlekt/ *verb* (**selects, selecting, selected**)
to choose one particular person or thing from a group of similar people or things: *Only three players were selected for the Olympic team.* □ *Select 'Save' from the File menu.*

selection /sɪˈlekʃən/ *noun*
a set of people or things that someone has chosen, or that you can choose from: *The singer will perform a selection of his favourite songs.* □ *Choose from a selection of delicious dishes prepared by our chefs.*

self /self/ *noun* (**selves**)
your own personality or nature: *You're looking like your usual self again.*

self-'confident *adjective*
behaving confidently because you feel sure of your abilities or value: *She's become a very self-confident young woman.*
▶ **self-confidence** *uncountable noun* *I lost all my self-confidence.*

self-'conscious *adjective*
easily embarrassed because you feel that everyone is judging you: *I felt a bit self-conscious in my bikini.*

self-con'trol *uncountable noun*
the ability to control yourself and your feelings: *She was told she must learn self-control.*

self-de'fence *uncountable noun*
the use of force to protect yourself against someone who is attacking you: *Use your gun only in self-defence.*

self-em'ployed *adjective*
working for yourself, rather than for someone else: *If you are self-employed, it is easy to change the time you start work.*

selfie /ˈselfi/ *noun*
a photograph that someone takes of themselves.

selfish /ˈselfɪʃ/ *adjective*
caring only about yourself, and not about other people: *I realize now that I've been very selfish.*
▶ **selfishly** *adverb* *Someone has selfishly finished all the milk.*
▶ **selfishness** *uncountable noun* *Julie's selfishness shocked us.*

self-re'spect *uncountable noun*
feeling confident about your own ability and value: *They have lost their jobs, their homes and their self-respect.*

self-'study *uncountable noun*
study that you do on your own, without a teacher: *She's started a self-study course.*

sell /sel/ *verb* (**sells, selling, sold**)
1 to let someone have something that you own in return for money: *Emily sold the paintings to an art gallery.* □ *The directors sold the business for £14.8 million.*
2 to be available for people to buy: *The shop sells newspapers and sweets.*

sell out to not have any tickets left because they have all been sold: *Football games often sell out fast.*

sell out of something to sell all of your supply of something: *The supermarket sold out of milk yesterday.*

Sellotape /ˈseləˌteɪp/ *uncountable noun*
a sticky strip of plastic used for sticking things together (*trademark*)

selves /selvz/ → see **self**

semester /səˈmestə/ *noun*
half of a school or a college year: *Spring semester starts on February 22nd.*

semicircle /ˈsemiˌsɜːkəl/ *noun*
one half of a circle: *They sit in a semicircle and share stories.*

semicolon /ˌsemiˈkəʊlɒn/ *noun*
the mark (;) that you use in writing to separate different parts of a sentence

semifinal /ˌsemiˈfaɪnəl/ *noun*
one of the two games in a competition that are played to decide who will play in the final part: *The football team lost in their semifinal yesterday.*

seminar /ˈsemɪnɑː/ *noun*
a class at a college or university in which the teacher and a small group of students discuss a topic: *Students are asked to prepare material for the weekly seminars.*

send /send/ *verb* (**sends, sending, sent**)
1 to make a message or a package go to someone: *I sent her an email this morning.*

□ *Hannah sent me a letter last week.*
2 to make someone go somewhere: *His parents sent him to the supermarket to buy a few things.*

send for someone to send someone a message asking them to come and see you: *If her temperature goes up, send for the doctor.*

senior /'si:njə/ *adjective*
having an important job in an organization: *He was a senior official in the Italian government.*

senior citizen *noun*
an older person, especially someone over 65: *We want to improve healthcare services for senior citizens.*

sensation /sen'seɪʃən/ *noun*
a physical feeling: *Floating can be a pleasant sensation.*

be a sensation to cause great excitement or interest: *The film was an overnight sensation.*

sensational /sen'seɪʃənəl/ *adjective*
causing great excitement and interest: *a sensational victory*

sense /sens/ *noun*
1 *plural* your physical ability to see, smell, hear, touch and taste: *We are studying the five senses at school.*
2 a feeling of something: *She felt a sense of relief as she crossed the finish line.*
3 *uncountable* the ability to think carefully about something and to do the right thing: *Now that he's older, he has a bit more sense.*
4 one of the possible meanings of a word: *This noun has four senses.*

make sense to be able to be understood: *Do these figures make sense to you?*

sense of humour *noun*
the ability to find things funny and not to be serious all the time: *She has a good sense of humour.*

sensible /'sensɪbəl/ *adjective*
based on reasons rather than emotions: *It might be sensible to get a lawyer.* □ *The sensible thing is to leave them alone.*

▸ **sensibly** /'sensɪbli/ *adverb He sensibly decided to hide for a while.*

LANGUAGE HELP
If you want to talk about someone whose emotions are strongly affected by their experiences, use **sensitive**. *He's a highly sensitive child.*

sensitive /'sensɪtɪv/ *adjective*
1 easily affected by something: *This chemical is sensitive to light.* □ *He is very sensitive to the cold.*
2 showing that you understand other people's feelings: *The classroom teacher must be sensitive to a child's needs.*
3 easily worried and offended about something when people talk about it: *Young people are sensitive about their appearance.*

sent /sent/ → see **send**

sentence /'sentəns/ *noun*
1 a group of words that tells you something or asks a question: *After I've written each sentence, I read it aloud.*
2 the punishment that a person receives in a law court: *He was given a four-year sentence.* ● **sentence** *verb* (**sentences, sentencing, sentenced**) *The court sentenced him to five years in prison.*

sentimental /ˌsentɪ'mentəl/ *adjective*
feeling or showing too much pity or love: *I'm trying not to be sentimental about the past.*

separate¹ /'sepərət/ *adjective*
apart and not connected to another thing: *Use separate surfaces for cutting raw meats and cooked meats.* □ *In this gym, men and women have separate exercise rooms.*

▸ **separately** /'sepərətli/ *adverb Cook each vegetable separately.*

separate² /'sepəˌreɪt/ *verb* (**separates, separating, separated**)
1 to move people or things apart: *The police tried to separate the two groups.*
2 to decide to live apart: *Her parents separated when she was very young.*

▸ **separated** /'sepəˌreɪtid/ *adjective Rachel's parents are separated.*

3 to exist between two people, groups or things: *The white fence separated the garden from the field.*

September /sep'tembə/ *noun*
the ninth month of the year: *Her son was born in September.*

sequence /'si:kwəns/ *noun*
a number of events or things that come one after another: *This is the sequence of events that led to the murder.*

sergeant /'sɑːdʒənt/ *noun*
an officer in the army or the police: *A police sergeant patrolling the area noticed the fire.*

s

serial /'sɪəriəl/ *noun*

a story that is told in a number of parts on television or radio, or in a magazine or newspaper: *The book was filmed as a six-part TV serial.*

series /'sɪəriːz/ *noun* (**series**)

1 a number of things or events that come one after another: *There will be a series of meetings with political leaders.*

2 a set of radio or television programmes: *The long-running TV series is filmed in Manchester.*

serious /'sɪəriəs/ *adjective*

1 very bad; making people worried or afraid: *Crime is a serious problem in our society.*
▸ **seriously** *adverb* *This law could seriously damage my business.*
▸ **seriousness** *uncountable noun* *They don't realize the seriousness of the crisis.*

2 important that people need to think about carefully: *This is a very serious matter.*

3 not joking, and really meaning what you say: *You really are serious about this, aren't you?*
▸ **seriously** *adverb* *'I followed him home,' he said. 'Seriously?'*

seriously /'sɪəriəsli/ *adverb*

take someone/something seriously to believe that someone or something is important and that they deserve attention: *The company takes all complaints seriously.*

sermon /'sɜːmən/ *noun*

a talk that a religious leader gives as part of a religious service: *Cardinal Murphy will deliver the sermon on Sunday.*

servant /'sɜːvənt/ *noun*

someone who works at another person's home, doing work like cooking or cleaning: *The family employed several servants.*

serve /sɜːv/ *verb* (**serves**, **serving**, **served**)

1 to give people food and drinks: *The restaurant serves breakfast, lunch and dinner.*

2 to help customers in a shop or a bar and to provide them with what they want to buy: *Noah served me coffee and chocolate cake.*

3 to do useful work for your country, an organization or a person: *He spoke of the fine character of those who serve their country.*

server /'sɜːvə/ *noun*

a computer that stores information and supplies it to a number of computers on a network: *They couldn't send any emails because the mail server was down.*

service /'sɜːvɪs/ *noun*

1 something that the public needs, such as transport or energy supplies: *There is a regular local bus service to Yorkdale.*

2 *uncountable* the help that people in a restaurant or a shop give you: *We always receive good service in that restaurant.*

3 *uncountable* the time that you spend working for someone else: *Most employees had long service with the company.*

4 a religious ceremony: *After the service, his body was taken to a cemetery.*

session /'seʃən/ *noun*

a period of a particular activity: *The two leaders arrived for a photo session.*

set¹ /set/ *noun*

1 a number of things that belong together: *The table and chairs are normally bought as a set.* □ *I got a chess set for my birthday.*

2 the place where a film is made: *The place looked like the set of a James Bond movie.*

set² /set/ *verb* (**sets**, **setting**, **set**)

1 to put something somewhere carefully: *She set the vase down gently on the table.*

2 to make a clock ready to use: *I set my alarm clock for seven o'clock every morning.*

3 to decide what a date or a price will be: *They have finally set the date of their wedding.*

4 when the sun sets, it goes down in the sky: *They watched the sun set behind the hills.*

5 to prepare the table for a meal by putting plates, glasses, knives, forks, and spoons on it: *Could you set the table for dinner, please?*

set fire to something/set something on fire to make something burn: *Angry protestors threw stones and set cars on fire.* □ *I struck a match and set fire to the papers.*

set off to start going somewhere: *Nick set off for his farmhouse in Connecticut.*

set someone free to cause someone to be free: *They agreed to set the prisoners free.*

set something up to start or arrange something: *He plans to set up his own business.*

set³ /set/ *adjective*

1 fixed and not able to be changed: *The kids have to be home at a set time every evening.*

2 happening in a particular place or time: *The play is set in a small seaside town.*

'set square *noun*

a thin flat piece of plastic or metal with three straight sides, used for drawing

363

lines and measuring angles.

settle /'setəl/ *verb* (**settles, settling, settled**)

1 to decide what to do about an argument or a problem by talking about it: *They agreed to try again to settle the dispute.*
2 to start living in a place permanently: *He visited Paris and eventually settled there.*
3 to sit down and make yourself comfortable: *Brandon settled in front of the television.*
settle down to become calm after being excited: *Come on, kids. Time to settle down and go to sleep now.*
settle in to become used to living in a new place, doing a new job, or going to a new school: *I enjoyed school once I settled in.*

settled /'setəld/ *adjective*
decided and arranged: *We feel the matter is now settled.*

settlement /'setəlmənt/ *noun*
1 an official agreement between two people or groups after they have disagreed about something: *Officials are hoping for a peaceful settlement of the crisis.*
2 a place where people have come to live and have built homes: *The village is a settlement of just fifty houses.*

seven /'sevən/
the number 7

seventeen /ˌsevən'tiːn/
the number 17
▸ **seventeenth** /ˌsevən'tiːnθ/ *adjective, adverb* *I had a big party for my seventeenth birthday.*

seventh¹ /'sevənθ/ *adjective, adverb*
counted as number seven in a series: *I was the seventh child in the family.*

seventh² /'sevənθ/ *noun*
one of seven equal parts of something (¹/₇)

seventy /'sevənti/
the number 70
▸ **seventieth** /'sevəntiəθ/ *adjective, adverb* *It's my grandad's seventieth birthday next week.*

several /'sevrəl/ *adjective*
used for talking about a number of people or things that is not large but is greater than two: *I spent several years in France.* □ *There were several blue boxes on the table.*
● **several** *pronoun* *The cakes were delicious, and we ate several.*

severe /sɪ'vɪə/ *adjective* (**severer, severest**)
1 very bad: *The business is having severe financial problems.*
▸ **severely** *adverb* *An aircraft crashed on the runway and was severely damaged.*
2 very strong: *A severe sentence is necessary for this type of crime.*
▸ **severely** *adverb* *They want to punish dangerous drivers more severely.*

sew /səʊ/ *verb* (**sews, sewing, sewed, sewn**)
to join pieces of cloth together using a needle and thread: *Anyone can sew a button onto a shirt.*
▸ **sewing** *uncountable noun* *She lists her hobbies as cooking, sewing and going to the cinema.*

sewer /'suːə/ *noun*
a large pipe under the ground that carries waste and rain water away: *The rain water drains into the city's sewer system.*

sewn /səʊn/ → see **sew**

sex /seks/ *noun* (**sexes**)
1 one of the two groups, male and female, into which you can divide people and animals: *This movie appeals to both sexes.*
2 the characteristic of being either male or female: *We can identify the sex of your unborn baby.*
3 *uncountable* the physical activity by which people can produce children: *He was very open in his attitudes about sex.*
have sex to perform the act of sex

sexual /'sekʃuəl/ *adjective*
1 connected with sex: *The clinic can provide information about sexual health.*
2 relating to the differences between male and female people: *There are laws against sexual discrimination.*
3 relating to the biological process by which people and animals produce young: *Girls usually reach sexual maturity earlier than boys.*
▸ **sexually** *adverb* *These organisms can reproduce sexually.*

sexy /'seksi/ *adjective* (**sexier, sexiest**)
sexually attractive: *She is the sexiest woman I have ever seen.*

shabby /'ʃæbi/ *adjective* (**shabbier, shabbiest**)
old and in bad condition: *His clothes were old and shabby.*

shade /ʃeɪd/ *noun*

1 one of the different forms of a particular colour: *The walls were painted in two shades of green.*

2 *uncountable* an area where direct sunlight does not reach: *Alexis was reading in the shade of a tree.*

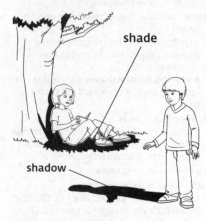

shade

shadow

shadow /ˈʃædəʊ/ *noun*

a dark shape on a surface that is made when something blocks the light: *The long shadows of the trees fell across their path.*

shady /ˈʃeɪdi/ *adjective* (**shadier, shadiest**)

not in bright sunlight: *We stopped in a shady place under some trees.*

shake /ʃeɪk/ *verb* (**shakes, shaking, shook, shaken**)

1 to move quickly backward and forward or up and down: *My whole body was shaking with fear.*

2 to hold something and move it quickly up and down: *Always shake the bottle before you pour out the medicine.* • **shake** *noun We gave the children a gentle shake to wake them.*

3 to move your head from side to side to say 'no': *'Did you see Crystal?' Kathryn shook her head.*

shake hands to say hello or goodbye to someone by holding their right hand in your own right hand and moving it up and down: *Michael shook hands with Burke.* ☐ *The two men shook hands.*

shaky /ˈʃeɪki/ *adjective* (**shakier, shakiest**)

not able to control your voice or your body because you are ill or afraid: *Her voice was shaky and she was close to tears.*

▸ **shakily** *adverb* '*I don't feel well', she said shakily.*

shall /ʃəl, STRONG ʃæl/ *modal verb*

1 used with 'I' and 'we' in questions to make offers or suggestions: *Shall I get the keys?* ☐ *Well, shall we go?*

2 usually used with 'I' and 'we', when you are talking about something that will happen to you in the future (*formal*): *We shall be landing in Paris in sixteen minutes.* ☐ *I shall know more tomorrow.*

shallow /ˈʃæləʊ/ *adjective* (**shallower, shallowest**)

not deep: *The river is very shallow here.*

shame /ʃeɪm/ *noun*

1 *uncountable* the very uncomfortable feeling that you have when you have done something wrong or stupid: *I was filled with shame.*

2 something that you feel sad or disappointed about: *It was a shame about the weather, but the party was still a great success.*

shameful /ˈʃeɪmfʊl/ *adjective*

very bad: *The government's treatment of the refugees was shameful.*

shampoo /ʃæmˈpuː/ *noun*

a liquid soap that you use for washing your hair: *Don't forget to pack a towel, soap, and shampoo.* • **shampoo** *verb* (**shampoos, shampooing, shampooed**) *I shampooed my hair and dried it, then I got dressed.*

shan't /ʃɑːnt/

short for 'shall not'

shape /ʃeɪp/ *noun*

1 the form or appearance of the outside edges or surfaces of something: *Pasta comes in all different shapes and sizes.*

2 a something such as a circle, a square or a triangle • **shape** *verb* (**shapes, shaping, shaped**) *Shape the dough into a ball and place it in the bowl.*

in bad shape in a bad state of health or in a bad condition: *The company is in bad shape.*

in (good) shape in a good state of health or in a good condition: *He's 76 and still in good shape.*

share ¹ /ʃeə/ *verb* (**shares, sharing, shared**)

to have or use something with another person: *Jose shares an apartment with six other students.* ☐ *Maria and I shared a dessert.*

share ² /ʃeə/ *noun*

1 the part of something that you do or

shapes

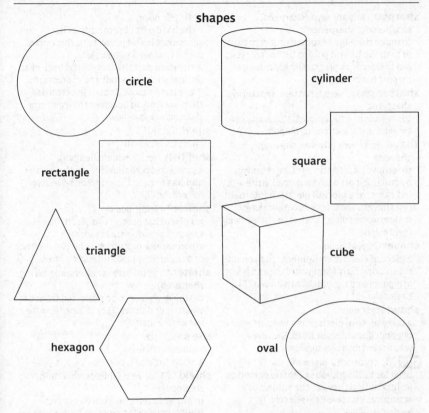

circle

cylinder

rectangle

square

triangle

cube

hexagon

oval

have: *I do my share of the housework.* ☐ *I need my share of the money now.*

2 one of the equal parts that the value of a company is divided into, which people can buy so that they own a part of the company and have a part of its profit: *I've bought shares in my brother's new company.*

shareholder /ˈʃeəhəʊldə/ *noun*
a person who owns shares (= parts of a company's value)

shark /ʃɑːk/ *noun*
a very large fish which often has very sharp teeth and may attack people

sharp /ʃɑːp/ *adjective, adverb* (**sharper, sharpest**)

1 very thin and able to cut through things very easily: *Cut the skin off the mango using a sharp knife.* ☐ *You'll need a sharp pencil and a rubber.*

2 changing direction suddenly: *I came to a*

sharp bend in the road and had to brake quickly.
▶ **sharply** *adverb After a mile, the road turns sharply to the right.*

3 good at noticing and understanding things: *Dan's very sharp, and a quick thinker.*

4 sudden and angry: *His sharp reply surprised me.*
▶ **sharply** *adverb 'Why didn't you tell me?' she asked sharply.*

5 big or strong and sudden: *There's been a sharp rise in oil prices.* ☐ *I felt a sharp pain in my right leg.*
▶ **sharply** *adverb Unemployment rose sharply last year.*

6 very clear and easy to see: *Digital TV offers sharper images than analogue TV.*

7 exactly: *Be in my office tomorrow morning at eight o'clock sharp.*

8 used for describing a note that is slightly higher than another note: *The scale of G major has an F sharp in it.*

s

sharpen /'ʃɑːpən/ *verb* (**sharpens, sharpening, sharpened**)

to make the edge of something very thin or to make its end pointed: *What's the best way to sharpen a knife?* □ *Mike had to sharpen the pencils every morning.*

shatter /'ʃætə/ *verb* (**shatters, shattering, shattered**)

to break into small pieces: *Megan dropped the glass, and it shattered on the floor.*

shave /ʃeɪv/ *verb* (**shaves, shaving, shaved**)

to remove hair from your face or body by cutting it off using a special knife (= a razor) or a piece of electric equipment (= a shaver): *Samuel had a bath and shaved.* □ *Many women shave their legs.* ● **shave** *noun* *I need a shave.*

shaver /'ʃeɪvə/ *noun*

a piece of electric equipment that you use for shaving hair from your face and body: *In 1937 the company introduced the world's first electric shaver.*

shawl /ʃɔːl/ *noun*

a large piece of cloth that a woman wears over her shoulders or head: *She wore a yellow shawl round her shoulders.*

she /ʃi, STRONG ʃiː/ *pronoun*

used for talking about a female person or animal when they are the subject of a sentence: *She's seventeen years old.*

shed /ʃed/ *noun*

a small building where you store things: *The house has a large shed in the backyard.*

she'd /ʃiːd, ʃɪd/

1 short for 'she had'
2 short for 'she would'

sheep /ʃiːp/ *noun* (**sheep**)

a farm animal with thick hair called wool, that is kept for its wool or for its meat

sheet /ʃiːt/ *noun*

1 a large piece of cloth that you sleep on or cover yourself with in bed: *Once a week, we change the sheets.*
2 a piece of something flat such as paper: *Sean folded the sheets of paper and put them in his briefcase.*

shelf /ʃelf/ *noun* (**shelves**)

a long flat piece of wood on a wall or in a cupboard that you can keep things on: *Dad took a book from the shelf.*

shell /ʃel/ *noun*

1 the hard part of something that surrounds it and protects it: *They cracked the nuts and removed their shells.*
2 the hard part that covers the back of an animal such as a snail and protects it
3 the hard part of a small sea creature that you find on beaches: *I have gathered shells since I was a child.*

she'll /ʃiːl, ʃɪl/

short for 'she will'

shellfish /'ʃelfɪʃ/ *noun* (**shellfish**)

a small creature that lives in the ocean and has a shell: *The restaurant serves local fish and shellfish.*

shelter[1] /'ʃeltə/ *noun*

1 a place that protects you from bad weather or danger: *a bus shelter*
2 **uncountable** protection from bad weather or danger: *They took shelter under a tree.*

shelter[2] /'ʃeltə/ *verb* (**shelters, sheltering, sheltered**)

to stay in a place to be protected from bad weather or danger: *They sheltered from the rain under a tree.*

she's /ʃiːz, ʃɪz/

1 short for 'she is'
2 short for 'she has'

shield[1] /ʃiːld/ *verb* (**shields, shielding, shielded**)

to protect someone from danger or injury: *I shielded my eyes from the sun with my hands.*

shield[2] /ʃiːld/ *noun*

a large piece of metal or leather that soldiers carried in the past to protect their bodies

shift[1] /ʃɪft/ *verb* (**shifts, shifting, shifted**)

to move something from one place to another: *Please would you help me shift the table over to the window?*

shift[2] /ʃɪft/ *noun*

one of the fixed periods of work in a factory or a hospital: *Nick works night shifts at the hospital.*

shin /ʃɪn/ *noun*

the front part of your leg between your knee and your ankle: *Ken suffered a bruised left shin.*

shine /ʃaɪn/ *verb* (**shines, shining, shone**)

1 to give out bright light: *Today it's warm and the sun is shining.*

2 to point a light somewhere: *The guard shone a light in his face.*

3 to reflect light: *The sea shone in the silver moonlight.*

shiny /ˈʃaɪni/ *adjective* (**shinier, shiniest**)
bright and reflecting light: *Her blonde hair was shiny and clean.*

ship¹ /ʃɪp/ *noun*
a large boat that carries people or goods: *The ship was ready to sail.*

ship² /ʃɪp/ *verb* (**ships, shipping, shipped**)
to send goods somewhere: *Our company ships orders worldwide.*

shirt /ʃɜːt/ *noun*
a piece of clothing with a collar and buttons, that you wear on the top part of your body

shiver /ˈʃɪvə/ *verb* (**shivers, shivering, shivered**)
to shake because you are cold, frightened or sick: *She shivered with cold and fear.*
● **shiver** *noun She gave a small shiver.*

shock¹ /ʃɒk/ *noun*
1 when you suddenly feel very upset because something unpleasant has happened: *William never recovered from the shock of his brother's death.*
2 → see **electric shock**

shock² /ʃɒk/ *verb* (**shocks, shocking, shocked**)
to be very unpleasant and suddenly make someone feel very upset: *After forty years as a police officer, nothing shocks me.*
▶ **shocked** *adjective She was deeply shocked when she heard the news.*

shocking /ˈʃɒkɪŋ/ *adjective*
very bad or morally wrong, and making you feel very upset and surprised: *Everyone found the photos shocking.*

shoe /ʃuː/ *noun*
things that you wear on your feet: *I need a new pair of shoes.* ▢ *I don't usually wear high-heeled shoes.*

shoelace /ˈʃuːleɪs/ *noun*
a long, thick string that you use to fasten your shoe: *He began to tie his shoelaces.*

shone /ʃɒn/ → see **shine**

shook /ʃʊk/ → see **shake**

shoot¹ /ʃuːt/ *verb* (**shoots, shooting, shot**)
1 to kill or injure a person or an animal by

shoes

shoe — laces

shoe — heel

boot — sole

trainer

slipper

sandal

firing a gun at them: *The gunmen shot two policemen before they escaped.* ▢ *A man was shot dead during the robbery.*
2 to fire a bullet from a weapon: *He raised his arms above his head, and shouted, 'Don't shoot!'*
3 to make a film: *Tim wants to shoot his new film in Mexico.*
4 to kick or throw the ball toward the goal or net in football or basketball: *Brennan shot and missed.*

shoot² /ʃuːt/ *noun*
a new part that is growing from a plant or tree: *It was spring, and new shoots began to appear.*

shop¹ /ʃɒp/ *noun*
a place where you buy things: *Paul and his wife run a flower shop.*

shop² /ʃɒp/ *verb* (**shops, shopping, shopped**)
to go to shops and buy things: *He always shops on Saturday mornings.*
▶ **shopper** *noun* *The streets were filled with crowds of shoppers.*

ˈshop aˌssistant (American: **clerk**) *noun*
a person who works in a shop
→ Look at picture on P7

shopping /ˈʃɒpɪŋ/ *uncountable noun*
the activity of going to shops to buy things: *I'll do the shopping this afternoon.*

ˈshopping ˌcentre (American: **mall**) *noun*
a large building with lots of shops and restaurants inside it

ˈshopping ˌtrolley *noun*
a large metal or plastic basket on wheels that you put your shopping in while you are in a shop

shore /ʃɔː/ *noun*
the land along the edge of the sea or a lake: *They walked slowly down to the shore.*

short /ʃɔːt/ *adjective* (**shorter, shortest**)
1 not lasting very long: *Last year we all went to Brighton for a short holiday.*
2 not tall: *She's a short woman with grey hair.*
3 measuring only a small amount from one end to the other: *The restaurant is only a short distance away.* □ *She has short, curly hair.*
be short for something to be a shorter way of saying something: *Her name's Jo — it's short for Josephine.*
be short of something not having enough of something: *His family is very short of money.*

shortage /ˈʃɔːtɪdʒ/ *noun*
when there is not enough of something: *In this town there is a great shortage of cheap housing.*

shorten /ˈʃɔːtən/ *verb* (**shortens, shortening, shortened**)
to make something shorter: *The treatment shortens the length of the illness.*

shortly /ˈʃɔːtli/ *adverb*
soon: *'Please take a seat. Dr Garcia will see you shortly.'*

shorts /ʃɔːts/ *plural noun*
trousers with very short legs: *She was wearing pink shorts and a black t-shirt.*

ˈshort-term *adjective*
lasting only for a short time, or having an effect soon: *This is only a short-term solution.*

shot¹ /ʃɒt/ → see **shoot**

shot² /ʃɒt/ *noun*
1 an act of firing a gun: *The man was killed with a single shot.*
2 in sports, when you kick, hit or throw the ball, to try to score a point: *Grant missed two shots at the goal.*
3 a photograph: *The photographer got some great shots of the bride.*

should /ʃəd, STRONG ʃʊd/ *modal verb*
1 used for saying what is the right thing to do: *I should exercise more.* □ *You shouldn't stay up so late.*
2 used for saying that something is probably true or will probably happen: *The doctor said I should be fine by next week.* □ *You should have no problems with this exercise.*
3 used in questions when you are asking someone for advice: *Should I ask for more help?* □ *What should I do?*

shoulder /ˈʃəʊldə/ *noun*
one of the two parts of your body between your neck and the tops of your arms: *She put her arm round his shoulders.*
→ Look at picture on P1

shouldn't /ˈʃʊdənt/
short for 'should not'

should've /ˈʃʊdəv/
short for 'should have'

shout /ʃaʊt/ *verb* (**shouts, shouting, shouted**)
to say something very loudly: *'She's alive!' he shouted.* □ *Andrew ran out of the house, shouting for help.* ● **shout** *noun* *There were angry shouts from the crowd.*

shove /ʃʌv/ *verb* (**shoves, shoving, shoved**)
to push someone or something roughly: *The woman shoved the other customers out of the way.*

shovel /ˈʃʌvəl/ *noun*
a flat tool with a handle that is used for lifting and moving earth or snow: *I'll need the coal shovel.*
● **shovel** (**shovels, shovelling, shovelled**) *verb* *He had to shovel the snow away from the door.*

shovel

s

show [1] /ʃəʊ/ *verb* (**shows, showing, showed, shown**)

1 to prove that a situation exists: *Research shows that certain foods can help prevent headaches.*

2 to let someone see something: *She showed me her engagement ring.*

3 to teach someone how to do something: *Claire showed us how to make pasta.*

4 to be easy to notice: *When I feel angry, it shows.*

show off to try to make people admire you: *He spent the entire evening showing off.*

show something off to show something to a lot of people because you are proud of it: *Naomi was showing off her engagement ring.*

show up to arrive at the place where you agreed to meet someone: *We waited until five, but he didn't show up.*

show [2] /ʃəʊ/ *noun*

1 a programme on television or radio: *I never missed his TV show when I was a kid.*

2 a performance in a theatre: *How about going to see a show tomorrow?*

'**show ,business** *uncountable noun*

the entertainment industry of films, theatre and television: *His show business career lasted more than 45 years.*

shower /ˈʃaʊə/ *noun*

1 a short period of rain: *A few showers are expected in the south on Saturday.*

2 a thing that you stand under, that covers you with water so you can wash yourself: *I was in the shower when the phone rang.*
→ Look at picture on P4

3 an occasion when you wash yourself by standing under the water that comes from a shower: *I think I'll take a shower.*
● **shower** (**showers, showering, showered**) *verb* *I was late and there wasn't time to shower.*

shown /ʃəʊn/ → see **show**

shrank /ʃræŋk/ → see **shrink**

shriek /ʃriːk/ *verb* (**shrieks, shrieking, shrieked**)

to give a short, very loud cry: *Gwen shrieked with excitement when she heard the news.*
● **shriek** *noun* *He heard the boy shriek in terror.*

shrimp /ʃrɪmp/ *noun* (**shrimp**) (*American*)
→ see **prawn**: *Add the shrimp and cook for 30 seconds.*

shrine /ʃraɪn/ *noun*

a religious place where people go to remember a holy person or event: *They visited the holy shrine of Mecca.*

shrink /ʃrɪŋk/ *verb* (**shrinks, shrinking, shrank** or **shrunk**)

to become smaller in size: *Dad's trousers shrank after just one wash.*

shrub /ʃrʌb/ *noun*

a small bush: *This books tells you how to choose shrubs for your garden.*

shrug /ʃrʌg/ *verb* (**shrugs, shrugging, shrugged**)

to move your shoulders up to show that you do not know or care about something: *Melissa just shrugged and replied, 'I don't know.'*
● **shrug** *noun* *'Who cares?' said Anna with a shrug.*

shrunk /ʃrʌŋk/ → see **shrink**

shudder /ˈʃʌdə/ *verb* (**shudders, shuddering, shuddered**)

to shake because you are frightened or cold, or because you feel disgust: *Some people shudder at the idea of injections.*
● **shudder** *noun* *'It was terrifying', she says with a shudder.*

shuffle /ˈʃʌfəl/ *verb* (**shuffles, shuffling, shuffled**)

1 to walk without lifting your feet off the ground: *Moira shuffled across the kitchen.*

2 to mix up playing cards before you begin a game: *Aunt Mary shuffled the cards.*

shut /ʃʌt/ *verb* (**shuts, shutting, shut**)

to close something: *Please shut the gate.*
□ *Lucy shut her eyes and fell asleep at once.*
● **shut** *adjective* *The police have told us to keep our doors and windows shut.* □ *Her eyes were shut and she seemed to be asleep.*

shut down to close and stop working

shut up used for telling someone, in a rude way, to stop talking: *Just shut up, will you?*

shutter /ˈʃʌtə/ *noun*

a wooden or metal cover on the outside of a window: *She opened the shutters and looked out of the window.*

shuttle /ˈʃʌtəl/ *noun*

1 → see **space shuttle**

2 a plane, bus, or train that makes regular trips between two places: *There is a free shuttle between the airport terminals.*

shy /ʃaɪ/ *adjective* (**shyer, shyest**)

nervous and embarrassed about talking

s

to people that you do not know well: *She was a shy, quiet girl.* □ *I was too shy to say anything.*

▶ **shyly** *adverb* *The children smiled shyly.*

▶ **shyness** *uncountable noun* *His shyness made it difficult for him to make friends.*

sibling /'sɪblɪŋ/ *noun*
your brother or sister (*formal*): *I often had to take care of my five younger siblings.*

sick[1] /sɪk/ *adjective* (**sicker, sickest**)
not well: *He's very sick. He needs a doctor.*

be sick of something to be very annoyed by something that has been happening for a long time (*informal*): *I am sick of all your complaints!*

off sick not at work because you are sick: *Tom is off sick today.*

sickness /'sɪknəs/ *uncountable noun*
the state of being unwell or unhealthy: *Grandpa had only one week of sickness in fifty-two years.*

side /saɪd/ *noun*
1 a position to the left or right of something: *On the left side of the door there's a door bell.*
2 any part of an object that is not its front, back, top or bottom: *He took me along the side of the house and into the garden.*
3 the edge of something: *We parked on the side of the road.*
4 one of the flat surfaces of something: *You should write on both sides of the paper.*
5 the part of your body from under your arm to the top of your leg: *Hold your arms by your sides and bend your knees.*
6 a group of people who are fighting in a war or playing against another group in a game: *Both sides want the war to end.*

on someone's side supporting someone in an argument: *Whose side are you on?*
side by side next to each other.: *The children were sitting side by side on the sofa.*
take someone's side to support someone in an argument: *Mum took my side in the argument.*

sidebar /'saɪdbɑː/ *noun*
the narrow area at the side of a web page where you find more information or links to other pages.

sidewalk /'saɪdwɔːk/ *noun* (*American*)
→ see **pavement**

sideways /'saɪdweɪz/ *adverb*
from or towards the side: *Pete looked sideways at her.* □ *Alfred gave him a sideways look.*

siege /siːdʒ/ *noun*
a situation in which soldiers or police officers surround a place in order to force the people there to come out: *The siege has been going on for three days.*

sieve /sɪv/ *noun*
a tool with a fine metal net, that you use for separating solids from liquids: *Press the soup through a sieve into a bowl.* ● **sieve** *verb* (**sieves, sieving, sieved**) *Sieve the flour.*

sigh /saɪ/ *verb* (**sighs, sighing, sighed**)
to let out a deep breath because you are disappointed, tired or pleased: *He sighed with relief.* ● **sigh** *noun* *She sat down with a sigh.*

sight /saɪt/ *noun*
1 *uncountable* the ability to see: *Grandpa has lost the sight in his right eye.*
2 the act of seeing something: *Liz can't bear the sight of blood.*
3 *plural* places that are interesting to see and that tourists often visit: *We saw the sights of Paris.*

catch sight of someone/something to suddenly see someone or something for a short period of time: *He caught sight of Helen in the crowd.*
in sight/within sight/out of sight used for saying that you can or cannot see something: *At last the town was in sight.*
lose sight of someone/something used for saying that you can no longer see someone or something: *The man ran off and I lost sight of him.*

sightseeing /'saɪtsiːɪŋ/ *uncountable noun*
the activity of travelling around visiting the interesting places that tourists usually visit: *During our holiday, we had a day's sightseeing in Venice.*

sign[1] /saɪn/ *noun*
1 a mark, a shape or a movement that has a particular meaning: *In maths, + is a plus sign and = is an equals sign.* □ *They gave me a sign to show that everything was OK.*
2 an object with words or pictures on it that warn you about something, or give you information or an instruction: *road signs* □ *The sign said, 'Welcome to Glasgow.'*
3 something that shows that something else exists or is happening: *Matthew showed no sign of fear.*

sign[2] /saɪn/ *verb* (**signs, signing, signed**)
to write your name on a document: *World*

leaders have signed an agreement to protect the environment.

signal /'sɪgnəl/ *noun*
a movement, a light, or a sound that gives a particular message to the person who sees or hears it: *The captain gave the signal for the soldiers to attack.* ● **signal** *verb* (**signals, signalling, signalled**) *Mandy signalled to Jesse to follow her.*

signature /'sɪgnətʃə/ *noun*
your name, written in your own special way: *I put my signature at the bottom of the page.*

significance /sɪg'nɪfɪkəns/ *uncountable noun*
the importance or meaning of something: *What do you think is the significance of this event?*

significant /sɪg'nɪfɪkənt/ *adjective*
important or large: *There has been a significant increase in the price of oil.*
▶ **significantly** *adverb* *The temperature dropped significantly.*

Sikh /siːk/ *noun*
a person who follows the Indian religion called Sikhism: *Rebecca's husband is a Sikh.* □ *a Sikh temple*

silence /'saɪləns/ *noun*
when no one is speaking: *They stood in silence.* □ *There was a long silence before Sarah replied.*

silent /'saɪlənt/ *adjective*
1 not speaking: *Jessica was silent because she did not know what to say.*
▶ **silently** *adverb* *She and Ned sat silently, enjoying the peace.*
2 completely quiet, with no sound at all: *The room was silent except for the TV.*
▶ **silently** *adverb* *The thief moved silently across the room.*

silhouette /ˌsɪluˈet/ *noun*
the dark shape that you see when someone or something has a bright light behind them: *She could see the distant silhouette of a castle.*

silk /sɪlk/ *uncountable noun*
a smooth, shiny cloth that is made from very thin threads: *Pauline was wearing a beautiful silk dress.*

silky /'sɪlki/ *adjective* (**silkier, silkiest**)
smooth, soft and shiny, like silk: *This shampoo makes your hair beautifully silky.*

silly /'sɪli/ *adjective* (**sillier, silliest**)
not behaving in a sensible or serious way: *'Don't be so silly, darling!'*

silver [1] /'sɪlvə/ *uncountable noun*
a valuable pale grey metal that is used for making jewellery: *He bought her a bracelet made from silver.*

silver [2] /'sɪlvə/ *adjective*
shiny and pale grey in colour: *He had thick silver hair.*

silver medal *noun*
an award made of silver metal that you get as second prize in a competition: *Gillingham won the silver medal in the 200 metres.*

SIM card /'sɪm ˌkɑːd/ *noun*
a small piece of electronic equipment in a mobile phone that connects it to a particular phone network. SIM is short for 'Subscriber Identity Module'.

similar /'sɪmɪlə/ *adjective*
the same in some ways but not in every way: *This cake tastes similar to carrot cake.* □ *Nowadays, cars all look very similar.*

similarity /ˌsɪmɪ'lærɪti/ *noun* (**similarities**)
something that is the same about two people or things: *There are many similarities between the two country's cultures.*

simile /'sɪmɪli/ *noun*
an expression that describes a person or a thing by comparing it with another person or thing, using the words 'like' or 'as'. An example of a simile is 'She swims like a fish'.

simmer /'sɪmə/ *verb* (**simmers, simmering, simmered**)
to cook gently in water that is just boiling: *Let the soup simmer for 15-20 minutes.*

simple /'sɪmpəl/ *adjective* (**simpler, simplest**)
1 easy to understand: *The recipes in the book are simple and easy to follow.* □ *Just follow the simple instructions below.*
▶ **simply** *adverb* *He explained his views simply and clearly.*
2 having all the basic necessary things, but nothing more: *He ate a simple dinner of rice and beans.* □ *Amanda was wearing a simple black silk dress.*
▶ **simply** *adverb* *Her house is decorated simply.*

S

simplicity /sɪm'plɪsɪti/ *uncountable noun*
the quality of being simple: *I love the simplicity of his designs.*

simplify /'sɪmplɪfaɪ/ *verb* (**simplifies, simplifying, simplified**)
to make something easier to understand or to do: *This program simplifies the task of searching for information.*
▸ **simplified** *adjective* *We read a simplified version of Shakespeare's 'Hamlet'.*

simply /'sɪmpli/ *adverb*
used to emphasize what you are saying: *Your behaviour is simply unacceptable.*

sin /sɪn/ *noun*
an action or a type of behaviour that breaks a religious law: *They believe that lying is a sin.* ● **sin** *verb* (**sins, sinning, sinned**) *The Bible says that we have all sinned.*

since¹ /sɪns/ *preposition*
used for talking about a time or an event that started in the past, and that has continued from then until now: *My uncle has lived in India since 1995.* ● **since** *adverb* *They worked together in the 1980s, and have been friends ever since.* ● **since** *conjunction* *I've lived here since I was six years old.*

since² /sɪns/ *conjunction*
because: *I'm always on a diet, since I put on weight easily.*

sincere /sɪn'sɪə/ *adjective*
honest and really meaning what you say.: *Do you think Ryan's being sincere?*

sincerely /sɪn'sɪəli/ *adverb*
used for showing that you really mean or feel something: *'Well done!' he said sincerely.*
Yours sincerely written before your signature at the end of a formal letter when you have addressed it to someone by their name: *Yours sincerely, Robbie Weinz.*

sing /sɪŋ/ *verb* (**sings, singing, sang, sung**)
to make music with your voice: *I love singing.* □ *My brother and I used to sing this song.*

singer /'sɪŋə/ *noun*
a person who sings, especially as a job: *My mother was a singer in a band.*

single /'sɪŋɡəl/ *adjective*
1 used for showing that you are talking about only one thing: *She hasn't said a single word about what happened.* □ *We sold over two hundred pizzas in a single day.*
2 not married: *Joseph is a single man in his early twenties.*

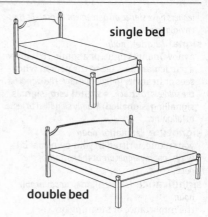

single bed

double bed

3 for one person only: *Would you like to reserve a single or a double room?*

singular /'sɪŋɡjʊlə/ *adjective*
used for describing the form of a word that you use when you are talking about one person or thing: *The singular form of 'mice' is 'mouse'.* ● **singular** *noun* *What is the singular of 'geese'?*

sink¹ /sɪŋk/ *noun*
a large fixed container in a kitchen or a bathroom that you can fill with water: *The sink was filled with dirty dishes.* □ *The bathroom has a toilet, a shower and a sink.*
→ Look at picture on P4

sink² /sɪŋk/ *verb* (**sinks, sinking, sank, sunk**)
1 to go below the surface of the water: *The boat hit the rocks and began to sink.*
2 to move slowly down, to a lower level: *The sun was sinking in the west.*

sip /sɪp/ *verb* (**sips, sipping, sipped**)
to drink something slowly, taking a small amount at a time: *Jessica sipped her drink slowly.* ● **sip** *noun* *Harry took a sip of tea.*

sir /sɜː/ *noun*
used as a polite way of talking to a man: *Excuse me sir, is this your car?*
Dear Sir written at the beginning of a formal letter or a business letter when you are writing to a man: *Dear Sir, Thank you for your letter.*

siren /'saɪərən/ *noun*
a piece of equipment in a fire engine or a police car that makes a long, loud noise to warn people about something: *In the distance I could hear a siren.*

sister /ˈsɪstə/ *noun*
a girl or woman who has the same parents as you: *This is my sister Sarah.*
→ Look at picture on P8

'sister-in-law *noun* (**sisters-in-law**)
the sister of your husband or wife, or the woman who is married to your brother
→ Look at picture on P8

sit /sɪt/ *verb* (**sits, sitting, sat**)
1 to have the lower part of your body resting on a chair and the upper part straight: *Mother was sitting in her chair in the kitchen.* ◻ *They sat watching television all evening.*
2 to move your body down until you are sitting on something: *Kelly sat down on the bed and took off her shoes.* ◻ *Mom sat down beside me.*
sit up to change the position of your body, so that you are sitting instead of lying down: *She felt dizzy when she sat up.*

site /saɪt/ *noun*
1 a place where a particular thing happens: *Dad works on a building site.* ◻ *This city was the site of a terrible earthquake.*
2 → see **website**: *The site contains advice for new teachers.*

'sitting room *noun*
a room in a house where people sit and relax

situated /ˈsɪtʃuˌeɪtɪd/ *adjective*
in a particular place: *The hotel is situated in the centre of Berlin.*

situation /ˌsɪtʃuˈeɪʃən/ *noun*
what is happening in a particular place at a particular time: *Army officers said the situation was under control.*

six /sɪks/
the number 6

sixteen /ˌsɪksˈtiːn/
the number 16
▶ **sixteenth** /ˌsɪksˈtiːnθ/ *adjective, adverb*
I'm having a party for my sixteenth birthday.

sixth¹ /sɪksθ/ *adjective, adverb*
counted as number six in a series: *The sixth round of the competition begins tomorrow.*

sixth² /sɪksθ/ *noun*
one of six equal parts of something (¹⁄₆)

sixty /ˈsɪksti/
the number 60
▶ **sixtieth** /ˈsɪkstiəθ/ *adjective, adverb* *Dad had a big party for his sixtieth birthday.*

size /saɪz/ *noun*
1 how big or small something is: *The size of the room is about 10 feet by 15 feet.* ◻ *The shelves contain books of various sizes.*
▶ **-sized** *adjective* *I work for a medium-sized company in Chicago.*
2 one of a series of particular measurements for clothes and shoes: *My sister is a size 12.* ◻ *What size are your feet?* ◻ *Do you have these shoes in a size nine?*

skate¹ /skeɪt/ *noun*
1 (*also* **ice-skate**) a boot with a long, sharp piece of metal on the bottom, for moving quickly and smoothly on ice
2 (*also* **roller-skate**) a boot with wheels on the bottom, for moving quickly on the ground

skate² /skeɪt/ *verb* (**skates, skating, skated**)
to move around wearing skates: *When the pond froze, we skated on it.*
▶ **skating** *uncountable noun* *They all went skating together in the winter.*
▶ **skater** *noun* *The ice-rink was full of skaters.*

skateboard /ˈskeɪtbɔːd/ *noun*
a narrow board with wheels at each end that you can stand on and ride

skeleton /ˈskelɪtən/ *noun*
all the bones in a person's or an animal's body: *a human skeleton*

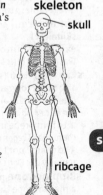

skeleton

skull

ribcage

sketch /sketʃ/ *noun* (**sketches**)
a drawing that you do quickly, without a lot of details: *He did a quick sketch of the building.* ● **sketch** *verb* (**sketches, sketching, sketched**) *She started sketching designs when she was six years old.*

ski¹ /skiː/ *noun*
a long, flat, narrow piece of wood, metal or plastic that you fasten to your boot so that you can move easily on snow or water

ski² /skiː/ *verb* (**skis, skiing, skied**)
to move over snow or water on skis: *They tried to ski down Mount Everest.*
▶ **skier** /ˈskiːə/ *noun* *My dad's a very good skier.*
▶ **skiing** *uncountable noun* *My hobbies are skiing and swimming.*
→ Look at picture on P6

S

skid /skɪd/ *verb* (**skids, skidding, skidded**)
to slide sideways: *The car skidded on the icy road.*

skill /skɪl/ *noun*
1 a job or an activity that needs special training and practice: *You're never too old to learn new skills.*
2 *uncountable* your ability to do something well: *He shows great skill on the football field.*

skilful /ˈskɪlfʊl/ *adjective*
able to do something very well: *He was a highly skilful football player.*
▶ **skilfully** *adverb* *The story is skilfully written.*

skilled /skɪld/ *adjective*
having the knowledge and ability to do something well: *We need more skilled workers.*

skim /skɪm/ *verb* (**skims, skimming, skimmed**)
to move quickly just above a surface: *We watched seagulls skimming the waves.*

skin /skɪn/ *noun*
1 *uncountable* the substance that covers the outside of a person's or an animal's body: *His skin is pale and smooth.* □ *a crocodile skin handbag*
2 the outer part that covers a fruit or a vegetable: *a banana skin*

skinny /ˈskɪni/ *adjective* (**skinnier, skinniest**)
extremely thin or too thin (*informal*): *He was a skinny little boy.*

skip /skɪp/ *verb* (**skips, skipping, skipped**)
1 to move forward quickly, jumping from one foot to the other: *We skipped down the street, talking and laughing.*
2 to jump repeatedly over a rope: *She took the rope and began to skip.*
3 to decide not to do something that you usually do: *Don't skip breakfast.*

ˈskipping rope *noun*
a piece of rope that you jump over, with handles at each end that you use to turn the rope

skirt /skɜːt/ *noun*
a piece of clothing for women and girls that hangs down from the waist and covers part of the legs

skull /skʌl/ *noun*
the bones of a person's or an animal's head: *After the accident, they X-rayed his skull.*

sky /skaɪ/ *noun* (**skies**)
the space above the Earth that you can see when you stand outside and look upwards: *The sun was shining in the sky.* □ *Today we have clear blue skies.*

skyscraper /ˈskaɪskreɪpə/ *noun*
a very tall building in a city

slab /slæb/ *noun*
a thick, flat piece of something: *slabs of stone*

slack /slæk/ *adjective* (**slacker, slackest**)
1 loose: *Suddenly, the rope went slack.*
2 not busy: *The shop has busy times and slack periods.*

slam /slæm/ *verb* (**slams, slamming, slammed**)
1 to shut a door very noisily and roughly: *She slammed the door behind her.*
2 to close very noisily: *He walked out and the door slammed behind him.*
3 to put something down somewhere quickly and roughly: *Lauren slammed the phone down angrily.*

slang /slæŋ/ *uncountable noun*
informal words that you can use when you are talking to people you know very well: *'A quid' is slang for 'a pound (£1)'.*

slant /slɑːnt/ *verb* (**slants, slanting, slanted**)
to have one side higher than the other: *The roof of the house slants sharply.*

slap /slæp/ *verb* (**slaps, slapping, slapped**)
to hit someone with the flat inside part of your hand: *I slapped him hard across the face.*
● **slap** *noun* *She gave him a slap on the face.*

slash [1] /slæʃ/ *verb* (**slashes, slashing, slashed**)
to make a long, deep cut in something: *Someone slashed my car tyres in the night.*

slash [2] /slæʃ/ *noun* (**slashes**)
a line (/) that separates numbers, letters or words in writing

slaughter /ˈslɔːtə/ *verb* (**slaughters, slaughtering, slaughtered**)
1 to kill a very large number of people violently: *So many innocent people have been slaughtered.* ● **slaughter** *uncountable noun* *The slaughter of women and children was common.*
2 to kill animals for their meat: *The farmers here slaughter their own sheep.*
● **slaughter** *uncountable noun* *The sheep were taken away for slaughter.*

slave [1] /sleɪv/ *noun*
a person who belongs to another person

and who works for them without being paid

▶ **slavery** /'sleɪvəri/ *uncountable noun* The United States abolished slavery in 1865.

slave [2] /sleɪv/ *verb* (**slaves, slaving, slaved**) (*also* **slave away**)
to work very hard: *He was slaving away in the hot kitchen.*

'slave trade *noun*
the business of buying and selling slaves (= servants who are forced to work for someone): *Many people made money from the slave trade.*

sledge /sledʒ/ *noun*
an object that you sit on in order to travel over snow: *We pulled the children across the snow on a sledge.*

sleek /sliːk/ *adjective* (**sleeker, sleekest**)
used to describe hair or fur that is smooth and shiny

sleep [1] /sliːp/ *noun*
1 *uncountable* a person's or an animal's natural state of rest when their eyes are closed, and their body is not active: *You should try to get as much sleep as possible.*
2 a period of sleeping: *Good morning, Pete. Did you have a good sleep?*
go to sleep to start sleeping: *Be quiet and go to sleep!*

LANGUAGE HELP
When you go to bed at night, you **go to sleep** or **fall asleep**. If you have difficulty sleeping, you can say that you cannot **get to sleep**.

sleep [2] /sliːp/ *verb* (**sleeps, sleeping, slept**)
to rest with your eyes closed and with no activity in your mind or body: *I didn't sleep well last night — it was too hot.*

'sleeping bag *noun*
a large warm bag for sleeping in when you go camping

sleepless /'sliːpləs/ *adjective*
without sleep: *I have sleepless nights worrying about her.*

sleepover /'sliːpəʊvə/ *noun*
an occasion when a child stays at a friend's home for the night: *Molly is having a sleepover tonight.*

sleepy /'sliːpi/ *adjective* (**sleepier, sleepiest**)
very tired and almost asleep: *The pills made me sleepy.*

sleet /sliːt/ *uncountable noun*
a mixture of snow and rain: *The snow and sleet will continue overnight.*

sleeve /sliːv/ *noun*
one of the two parts of a piece of clothing that cover your arms: *Rachel wore a blue dress with long sleeves.*

slender /'slendə/ *adjective*
used to describe a person who is thin in a graceful, attractive way: *She was tall and slender, like her mother.*

slept /slept/ → see **sleep**

slice /slaɪs/ *noun*
a thin piece of something that you cut from a larger piece: *Would you like a slice of bread?* ▢ *Nicole had a cup of coffee and a large slice of chocolate cake.* ● **slice** *verb* (**slices, slicing, sliced**) *I blew out the candles and Mum sliced the cake.*

slide [1] /slaɪd/ *verb* (**slides, sliding, slid**)
to move quickly and smoothly over a surface: *She slid across the ice on her stomach.*

slide [2] /slaɪd/ *noun*
a large metal frame that children can play on. They climb the steps at one side, and move down a smooth slope on their bottom.

slight /slaɪt/ *adjective*
small and not important or serious: *The sun was shining and there was a slight breeze.* ▢ *The company has announced a slight increase in sales.*

slightly /'slaɪtli/ *adverb*
just a little: *We've moved to a slightly larger house.*

slim /slɪm/ *adjective* (**slimmer, slimmest**)
thin in an attractive way: *The young woman was tall and slim.*
slim down to lose weight and become thinner: *I've slimmed down a size or two.*

slime /slaɪm/ *uncountable noun*
a thick, wet substance that looks or smells unpleasant: *The rocks are slippery with mud and slime.*

sling [1] /slɪŋ/ *verb* (**slings, slinging, slung**)
to throw something in a rough way: *She slung the sack over her shoulder.*

sling [2] /slɪŋ/ *noun*
a piece of cloth that you wear around your neck and arm, to hold up your arm when it is broken or injured: *Emily had her arm in a sling.*

s

slip¹ /slɪp/ *verb* (**slips, slipping, slipped**)
1 to accidentally slide and fall: *He slipped on the wet grass.* □ *I slipped on a patch of ice as I was crossing the road.*
2 to slide out of position: *Grandpa's glasses slipped down his nose.*
3 to go somewhere quickly and quietly: *In the morning she quietly slipped out of the house.*
4 to put something somewhere quickly and quietly: *I slipped the letter into my pocket.*
slip up to make a mistake: *We slipped up a few times, but no-one noticed.*

slip² /slɪp/ *noun*
1 a small mistake: *Even a tiny slip could spoil everything.*
2 a small piece of paper: *He wrote our names on slips of paper.*

slipper /'slɪpə/ *noun*
a loose, soft shoe that you wear indoors: *She put on a pair of slippers and went downstairs.*

slippery /'slɪpəri/ *adjective*
smooth or wet, and difficult to walk on or to hold: *Be careful — the floor is slippery.* □ *Motorists were warned about the slippery roads.*

slit /slɪt/ *verb* (**slits, slitting, slit**)
to make a long narrow cut in something: *He slit open the envelope.* ● **slit** *noun Make a slit about half an inch long.*

slither /'slɪðə/ *verb* (**slithers, slithering, slithered**)
to move along the ground, sliding from side to side, like a snake: *Robert slithered down into the water.*

slogan /'sləʊɡən/ *noun*
a short phrase that you can remember easily, that is used in advertisements and by political parties: *His campaign slogan was 'Time for Action'.*

slope¹ /sləʊp/ *noun*
the side of a mountain, hill or valley: *A steep slope leads to the beach.* □ *The house was built on a slope.*

slope² /sləʊp/ *verb* (**slopes, sloping, sloped**)
1 having one end higher than the other: *The land sloped down sharply to the river.*
▶ **sloping** *adjective Our house has a sloping roof.*
2 to lean to the right or to the left rather than being straight: *John's writing slopes backwards.*

sloppy /'slɒpi/ *adjective* (**sloppier, sloppiest**)
done in a careless and lazy way: *All teachers hate sloppy work from their students.*

slot /slɒt/ *noun*
a long, narrow hole in something: *He dropped a coin into the slot and pressed the button.* □ *Please place your credit card in the slot.*

slouch /slaʊtʃ/ *verb* (**slouches, slouching, slouched**)
to sit, stand or walk with your shoulders and head drooping down: *Try not to slouch when you are sitting down.*

slow¹ /sləʊ/ *adjective* (**slower, slowest**)
1 not moving or happening quickly: *His bike was heavy and slow.* □ *The investigation was a long and slow process.* □ *They danced to the slow rhythm of the music.*
▶ **slowly** *adverb He spoke slowly and clearly.* □ *She walks very slowly now.*
2 showing a time that is earlier than the correct time: *The clock is five minutes slow.*

slow² /sləʊ/ *verb* (**slows, slowing, slowed**)
slow down to start to move or happen more slowly: *The bus slowed down for the next stop.*

slowdown /'sləʊdaʊn/ *noun*
a reduction in speed or activity: *There has been a slowdown in the economy.*

slow 'motion also **slow-motion**
uncountable noun
when film or television pictures are shown much more slowly than normal: *They played it again in slow motion.*

slug /slʌɡ/ *noun*
a small animal with a long soft body and no legs that moves very slowly

slug

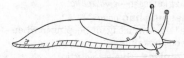

slum /slʌm/ *noun*
an area of a city where the buildings are in bad condition and the people are very poor: *More than 2.4 million people live in the city's slums.*

slump /slʌmp/ *verb* (**slumps, slumping, slumped**)
1 to fall suddenly and by a large amount: *The company's profits slumped by 41% in a single*

year. • **slump** *noun* *There has been a slump in house prices.*

2 to fall or sit down suddenly and heavily: *She slumped into a chair and burst into tears.*

slur /slɜː/ *verb* (**slurs, slurring, slurred**)
to speak without saying each word clearly, because you are drunk, ill or very tired: *He was slurring his words and I couldn't understand what he was saying.*

▶ **slurred** *adjective* *Her speech was slurred and she was very pale.*

sly /slaɪ/ *adjective*
showing that you know something that other people do not know or that was meant to be a secret: *He gave a sly smile.*

▶ **slyly** *adverb* *Anna grinned slyly.*

smack /smæk/ *verb* (**smacks, smacking, smacked**)
to hit someone with your hand: *He smacked me on the side of the head.*

small /smɔːl/ *adjective* (**smaller, smallest**)
1 not large in size or amount: *My daughter is small for her age.* ▫ *Fry the onions in a small amount of butter.*

2 young: *I have two small children.*

3 not very serious or important: *It's a small problem, and we can easily solve it.*

sm'all-sc'ale *adjective*
small in size: *Most of the world's coffee beans are grown by small-scale farmers.*

smart /smɑːt/ *adjective* (**smarter, smartest**)
1 right for a formal occasion or activity; clean and tidy: *He looked very smart in his new uniform.* ▫ *Members must wear a smart jacket and tie in the restaurant.*

▶ **smartly** *adverb* *a tall, smartly dressed young man*

2 (*American*) clever or intelligent: *He's a very smart, intelligent player.*

smartphone /ˈsmɑːtfəʊn/ *noun*
a type of mobile phone that can do many of the things that a computer does

smash /smæʃ/ *verb* (**smashes, smashing, smashed**)
1 to break something into many pieces: *The gang started smashing windows in the street.*

2 to break into many pieces: *I dropped the bottle and it smashed on the floor.* • **smash** *noun* *I heard the smash of glass and I shouted, 'Get down!'*

smear /smɪə/ *verb* (**smears, smearing, smeared**)
to spread a sticky substance all over a surface: *My little sister smeared jam all over her face.* • **smear** *noun* *There were smears of oil on his face.*

smell [1] /smel/ *noun*
the quality of something that you notice when you breathe in through your nose: *I just love the smell of freshly baked bread.* ▫ *There was a horrible smell in the refrigerator.*

smell [2] /smel/ *verb* (**smells, smelling, smelled**)
1 to have a quality that you notice by breathing in through your nose: *The room smelled of lemons.* ▫ *The soup smells delicious!*

2 to smell unpleasant: *My girlfriend says my feet smell.*

3 to notice something when you breathe in through your nose: *As soon as we opened the front door, we could smell smoke.*

smelly /ˈsmeli/ *adjective* (**smellier, smelliest**)
having an unpleasant smell: *smelly socks*

smile /smaɪl/ *verb* (**smiles, smiling, smiled**)
to curve up the corners of your mouth because you are happy or you think that something is funny: *When he saw me, he smiled.* ▫ *The children were all smiling at her.*
• **smile** *noun* *She gave a little smile.*

smoke [1] /sməʊk/ *uncountable noun*
the black or white clouds of gas that you see in the air when something burns: *Thick black smoke blew over the city.*

smoke [2] /sməʊk/ *verb* (**smokes, smoking, smoked**)
1 to suck the smoke from a cigarette into your mouth and blow it out again: *He smokes 20 cigarettes a day.*

2 to regularly smoke cigarettes: *Do you smoke?*

▶ **smoker** *noun* *Smokers have a much higher risk of developing this disease.*

▶ **smoking** *uncountable noun* *Smoking is banned in many restaurants.*

smoky /ˈsməʊki/ *adjective* (**smokier, smokiest**)
with a lot of smoke in the air: *The bar was dark, noisy and smoky.*

smooth /smuːð/ *adjective* (**smoother, smoothest**)
1 flat, with no rough parts, lumps or holes: *The baby's skin was soft and smooth.*

s

☐ *The surface of the water is as smooth as glass.*
2 without lumps: *Stir the mixture until it is smooth.*
3 without sudden changes in direction or speed: *The pilot made a very smooth landing.*
▸ **smoothly** *adverb* *The boat was travelling smoothly through the water.*
4 happening without any problems: *We hope for a smooth move to our new home.*
▸ **smoothly** *adverb* *I hope your trip goes smoothly.*

smother /'smʌðə/ *verb* (**smothers, smothering, smothered**)
1 to cover a fire with something in order to stop it burning: *She tried to smother the flames with a blanket.*
2 to cover something with too much of a substance: *Don't smother the pasta in sauce.*

smudge /smʌdʒ/ *noun*
a dirty mark: *There was a dark smudge on his forehead.* ● **smudge** *verb* (**smudges, smudging, smudged**) *Jennifer rubbed her eyes, smudging her make-up.*

smudge

smug /smʌg/ *adjective*
very pleased with yourself, in a way that other people find annoying: *'I have everything I need', he said with a smug little smile.*
▸ **smugly** *adverb* *Sue smiled smugly and sat down.*

smuggle /'smʌgəl/ *verb* (**smuggles, smuggling, smuggled**)
to take things or people into a place or out of it illegally or secretly: *They smuggled goods into the country.*
▸ **smuggler** *noun* *The police arrested the diamond smugglers yesterday.*
▸ **smuggling** *uncountable noun* *A pilot was arrested and charged with smuggling.*

snack /snæk/ *noun*
a simple meal that is quick to prepare and to eat: *The children have a snack when they come in from school.* ● **snack** *verb* (**snacks, snacking, snacked**) *During the day, I snack on fruit and drink lots of water.*

snag /snæg/ *noun*
a small problem or difficulty: *There is one possible snag in his plans.*

snail /sneɪl/ *noun*
a small animal with a long, soft body, no legs and a round shell on its back

snail

snake /sneɪk/ *noun*
a long, thin animal with no legs, that slides along the ground

snap /snæp/ *verb* (**snaps, snapping, snapped**)
1 to break with a short, loud noise: *The rope snapped, and he fell to his death.*
2 to break something in this way: *Angrily, Matthew snapped the plastic pen in two.*
● **snap** *noun* *I heard a snap and a crash as the tree fell.*
3 to speak to someone in a sharp, angry way: *Sorry, I didn't mean to snap at you.*
4 to try to bite someone: *The dog snapped at my ankle.*

snatch /snætʃ/ *verb* (**snatches, snatching, snatched**)
to take something away quickly and roughly: *Michael snatched the cards from Archie's hand.*

sneak /sni:k/ *verb* (**sneaks, sneaking, sneaked**)
1 to go somewhere very quietly: *He sneaked out of his house late at night.*
2 to secretly have a quick look at something: *She sneaked a look at her watch.*

sneaker /'sni:kə/ *noun* (American)
→ see **trainer**: *a pair of sneakers*

sneer /snɪə/ *verb* (**sneers, sneering, sneered**)
to show on your face that you do not like someone or something: *'I don't need any help from you', he sneered.* ☐ *I could see her sneering at me.*

sneeze /sniːz/ *verb* (**sneezes, sneezing, sneezed**)
to suddenly take in your breath and then blow it down your nose noisily, for example, because you have a cold: *Cover your nose and mouth when you sneeze.*
● **sneeze** *noun* *The disease is passed from person to person by a sneeze.*

sniff /snɪf/ *verb* (**sniffs, sniffing, sniffed**)
to suddenly and quickly breathe in air through your nose: *She dried her eyes and sniffed.* ● **sniff** *noun* *I could hear quiet sobs and sniffs.*

snigger /ˈsnɪɡə/ *verb* (**sniggers, sniggering, sniggered**)
to laugh quietly in an unpleasant way: *Three kids started sniggering.* ● **snigger** *noun* *I heard a snigger, and looked around.*

snip /snɪp/ *verb* (**snips, snipping, snipped**)
to cut something quickly using sharp scissors: *Snip off the dead flowers with a pair of scissors.*

snob /snɒb/ *noun*
someone who feels that they are better than other people because of their behaviour or social class: *Her parents did not like him because they were snobs.*

snooker /ˈsnuːkə/ *uncountable noun*
a game that is played on a special table. Players use a long stick to hit a white ball so that it knocks coloured balls into holes around the edge of the table.

snore /snɔː/ *verb* (**snores, snoring, snored**)
to make a loud noise each time you breathe when you are asleep: *His mouth was open, and he was snoring.* ● **snore** *noun* *We heard loud snores coming from the next room.*

snorkel /ˈsnɔːkəl/ *noun*
a tube that a person swimming just under the surface of the sea can breathe through
▶ **snorkelling** *uncountable noun* *We went snorkelling at the nearby beach.*

snort /snɔːt/ *verb*
(**snorts, snorting, snorted**)
to breathe air noisily out through your nose: *Harrell snorted with laughter.* ● **snort** *noun* *Yana gave a snort of laughter.*

snout /snaʊt/ *noun*
the long nose of an animal such as a pig: *Two alligators rest their snouts on the water's surface.*

snow /snəʊ/ *uncountable noun*
soft white frozen water that falls from the sky: *Six inches of snow fell.* ● **snow** *verb* (**snows, snowing, snowed**) *It snowed all night.*

snowball /ˈsnəʊbɔːl/ *noun*
a ball of snow

snowboard /ˈsnəʊbɔːd/ *noun*
a board that you stand on and travel down slopes that are covered with snow
▶ **snowboarding** *uncountable noun* *He loves skiing and snowboarding.*
▶ **snowboarder** *noun* *He's one of the world's top snowboarders.*

snowman /ˈsnəʊmæn/ *noun* (**snowmen**)
a large shape like a person that is made out of snow

snowy /ˈsnəʊi/ *adjective* (**snowier, snowiest**)
covered with snow: *snowy mountains*

snuggle /ˈsnʌɡəl/ *verb* (**snuggles, snuggling, snuggled**)
to get into a warm, comfortable position, especially by moving closer to another person: *Jane snuggled up against his shoulder.*

so¹ /səʊ/ *adverb*
1 used for talking about something that has just been mentioned: *'Do you think they will stay together?' — 'I hope so.'* □ *If you don't like it, then say so.*
2 used when you are saying that something is also true: *I enjoy Ann's company and so does Martin.* □ *They had a wonderful time and so did I.*
3 used in conversations to introduce a new subject: *So how was your day?*
4 used in front of adjectives and adverbs to make them stronger: *I'm surprised they're married — they seemed so different.*
or so used when you are giving an approximate amount: *A ticket will cost you £20 or so.*

so² /səʊ/ *conjunction*
1 used for introducing the result of a situation: *I am shy and so I find it hard to talk to people.*

snorkel

S

2 (also **so that**) used for introducing the reason for doing something: *Come to dinner so we can talk about what happened.* ▫ *They moved to the corner of the room so that nobody would hear them.*

soak /səʊk/ *verb* (**soaks, soaking, soaked**)
1 to put something into a liquid and leave it there: *Soak the beans for 2 hours.*
2 to make something very wet: *The water soaked his jacket.*
▸ **soaked** /səʊkt/ *adjective* *The tent got completely soaked in the storm.*
▸ **soaking** *adjective* *My raincoat was soaking wet.*
3 to pass through something: *Blood soaked through the bandages.*
soak something up to take in a liquid: *Use a towel to soak up the water.*

soap /səʊp/ *uncountable noun*
a substance that you use with water for washing yourself or for washing clothes: *a bar of soap*

'soap ,opera *noun*
a popular television series about the daily lives and problems of a group of people who live in a particular place

soar /sɔː/ *verb* (**soars, soaring, soared**)
1 to quickly increase: *Prices soared in the first half of the year.*
2 to go quickly upwards: *A golden eagle soared overhead.*

sob /sɒb/ *verb* (**sobs, sobbing, sobbed**)
to cry in a noisy way: *She began to sob.* ● **sob** *noun* *She heard quiet sobs from the next room.*

sober /'səʊbə/ *adjective*
1 not drunk: *He was completely sober.*
2 plain and not bright: *He dresses in sober grey suits.*

'so-called *adjective*
used for showing that you think a word or expression is in fact wrong: *This so-called miracle never actually happened.*

soccer /'sɒkə/ *uncountable noun*
→ see **football**: *My father played soccer for Manchester United.*
→ Look at picture on P6

sociable /'səʊʃəbəl/ *adjective*
friendly, and enjoying talking to other people: *She was extremely sociable.*

social /'səʊʃəl/ *adjective*
1 relating to society: *He sings about social problems like poverty.*

▸ **socially** *adverb* *It wasn't socially acceptable to eat in the street.*
2 relating to enjoyable activities that involve meeting other people: *We organize social events.*
▸ **socially** *adverb* *We have known each other socially for a long time.*

socialism /'səʊʃə,lɪzəm/ *uncountable noun*
a set of political principles whose general aim is to create a system in which everyone has equal chances to gain wealth and to own the country's main industries

socialist /'səʊʃəlɪst/ *adjective*
based on socialism or to do with socialism: *He's a member of the Socialist Party.*
● **socialist** *noun* *His grandparents were socialists.*

socialize /'səʊʃə,laɪz/ *verb* (**socializes, socializing, socialized**)
to meet other people socially, for example at parties: *I like socializing and making new friends.*

'social life *noun* (**social lives**)
the time someone spends with their friends: *I was popular and had a busy social life.*

,social 'networking *uncountable noun*
the activity of contacting friends, sharing information and making new friends using links on particular websites: *Have you used a social networking site such as MySpace or Facebook?*

'social ,worker *noun*
a person whose job is to help people who have social problems

society /sə'saɪɪti/ *noun* (**societies**)
1 all the people in a country, when you think about their general behaviour or problems: *These are common problems in today's society.* ▫ *We live in an unequal society.*
2 an organization for people who have the same interest or aim: *He's a member of the American Historical Society.*

sock /sɒk/ *noun*
a piece of clothing that covers your foot and ankle and that you wear inside shoes: *a pair of red socks*

socket /'sɒkɪt/ *noun*
a hole that something fits into to make a connection: *He took the light bulb out of the socket.* ▫ *There's an electric socket by every seat on the train.*

soda /'səʊdə/ *uncountable noun*
water with bubbles that is used for mixing with other drinks: *orange juice and soda*

sodium /'səʊdiəm/ *uncountable noun*
a silvery white chemical element such as salt, that combines with other chemicals

sofa /'səʊfə/ *noun*
a long, comfortable seat with a back, and usually with arms, that two or three people can sit on
→ Look at picture on P5

soft /sɒft/ *adjective* (**softer**, **softest**)
1 pleasant to touch, and not rough or hard: *Body lotion will keep your skin soft.* □ *She wiped the baby's face with a soft cloth.*
2 changing shape easily when pressed: *Add milk to form a soft dough.*
3 very gentle: *There was a soft tapping on my door.* □ *Her skin was glowing in the soft light.*
▶ **softly** *adverb She walked into the softly lit room.*

soft 'drink *noun*
a cold drink that does not contain alcohol, such as lemonade or fruit juice: *Can I get you some tea or coffee, or a soft drink?*

soften /'sɒfən/ *verb* (**softens**, **softening**, **softened**)
to become, or make something less hard: *Soften the butter in a small saucepan.*

software /'sɒftweə/ *uncountable noun*
computer programs. Compare with **hardware**: *He writes computer software.*

soggy /'sɒgi/ *adjective* (**soggier**, **soggiest**)
unpleasantly wet: *The cheese and tomato sandwiches were soggy.*

soil /sɔɪl/ *noun*
the substance on the surface of the Earth in which plants grow: *The soil here is good for growing vegetables.*

solar /'səʊlə/ *adjective*
used for describing power that is obtained from the sun's light and heat: *The visitor centre runs on solar power.*

sold /səʊld/ → see **sell**

soldier /'səʊldʒə/ *noun*
a member of an army

sole [1] /səʊl/ *adjective*
used for describing the only thing or person of a particular type: *Their sole aim is to win.*
▶ **solely** *adverb The money that you earn belongs solely to you.*

sole [2] /səʊl/ *noun*
the lower surface of your foot or of a shoe or sock: *Wear shoes with thick soles.*

solemn /'sɒləm/ *adjective*
very serious rather than cheerful or amusing: *His face looked solemn.*
▶ **solemnly** *adverb Her listeners nodded solemnly.*

solicitor /sə'lɪsɪtə/ *noun*
a lawyer who gives legal advice, prepares legal documents, and arranges for people to buy and sell land

solid [1] /'sɒlɪd/ *adjective*
1 hard; not like liquid or gas: *The pure oil is solid at room temperature.* □ *The lake was frozen solid.*
2 with no holes or space inside: *They had to cut through 50 feet of solid rock.*

solid [2] /'sɒlɪd/ *noun*
a hard substance: *Solids turn to liquids at certain temperatures.*

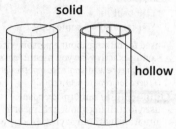

solid

hollow

solitary /'sɒlɪtri/ *adjective*
1 spending a lot of time alone: *Paul was a shy, solitary man.*
2 done alone: *He spent his evenings in solitary reading.*

solo /'səʊləʊ/ *noun*
a piece of music or a dance performed by one person: *The music teacher asked me to sing a solo.* ● **solo** *adjective He has just recorded his first solo album.* ● **solo** *adverb Lindbergh flew solo across the Atlantic.*

solution /sə'luːʃən/ *noun*
a way of dealing with a problem: *They both want to find a peaceful solution to the conflict.*

solve /sɒlv/ *verb* (**solves**, **solving**, **solved**)
to find an answer to a problem or a question: *They have not solved the problem of unemployment.*

some /səm, STRONG sʌm/ *adjective*
1 used for talking about an amount of

S

something or a number of people or things: *Would you like some orange juice?* □ *He went to buy some books.* □ *Some of the workers will lose their jobs.* □ *Put some of the sauce onto a plate.* ● **some pronoun** *The apples are ripe, and we picked some today.*

2 used for showing that you do not know exactly which person or thing you are talking about: *She wanted to talk to him about some problem she was having.*

somebody /'sʌmbədi/ **pronoun**
→ see **someone**

someday /'sʌmdeɪ/ **adverb**
a time in the future that you do not yet know: *Someday I hope to become a pilot.*

somehow /'sʌmhaʊ/ **adverb**
used when you do not know or cannot say how something was done or will be done: *We'll manage somehow, I know we will.*
□ *I somehow managed to finish the race.*

someone /'sʌmwʌn/ **pronoun**

LANGUAGE HELP
You can also say **somebody**.

used for talking about a person without saying exactly who you mean: *I got a call from someone who wanted to rent the flat.*
□ *I need someone to help me.*

something /'sʌmθɪŋ/ **pronoun**
used for talking about a thing or a situation, without saying exactly what it is: *He knew that there was something wrong.*
□ *Was there something you wanted to ask me?*

sometime /'sʌmtaɪm/ **adverb**
used for talking about a time in the future or the past that you do not yet know: *We will finish sometime next month.*
□ *Why don't you come and see me sometime?*

sometimes /'sʌmtaɪmz/ **adverb**
on some occasions rather than all the time: *I sometimes sit out in the garden and read.*
□ *Sometimes he's a little rude.*

somewhat /'sʌmwɒt/ **adverb**
a little (*formal*): *She behaved somewhat differently when he was there.*

somewhere /'sʌmweə/ **adverb**
used for talking about a place without saying exactly where you mean: *I've seen him before somewhere.* □ *I needed somewhere to live.*

son /sʌn/ **noun**
your male child: *Sam is the seven-year-old son*

of Eric Davies. □ *I have two daughters and a son.*
→ Look at picture on P8

song /sɒŋ/ **noun**
1 words and music sung together: *She sang a Spanish song.*
2 the pleasant musical sounds that a bird makes: *It's lovely to hear a blackbird's song in the evening.*

'son-in-law noun (**sons-in-law**)
the husband of your daughter

soon /suːn/ **adverb** (**sooner, soonest**)
after a short time: *I'll call you soon.* □ *He arrived sooner than I expected.*

as soon as used for saying that one t hing happens immediately after something else: *As soon as the weather improves we will go.*

soothe /suːð/ **verb** (**soothes, soothing, soothed**)
1 to make someone who is angry or upset feel calmer: *He sang to her to soothe her.*
▶ **soothing adjective** *Put on some nice soothing music.*
2 to make a painful part of your body feel better: *Use this lotion to soothe dry skin.*
▶ **soothing adjective** *Cold tea is very soothing for burns.*

sophisticated /sə'fɪstɪˌkeɪtɪd/ **adjective**
1 complicated and highly developed: *Bees use a very sophisticated communication system.*
2 knowing about things like culture and fashion: *Claude was a charming, sophisticated man.*

sore /sɔː/ **adjective** (**sorer, sorest**)
painful and uncomfortable: *I had a sore throat and a cough.*

sorrow /'sɒrəʊ/ **uncountable noun**
a feeling of deep sadness: *Words cannot express my sorrow.*

sorry /'sɒri/ **adjective** (**sorrier, sorriest**)
1 feeling regret, sadness or disappointment: *I'm sorry he's gone.*
feel sorry for someone to feel sadness for someone: *I felt sorry for him because nobody listened to him.*
sorry/I'm sorry
1 used for apologizing for something that you have done: '*You're making too much noise.*' — '*I'm sorry.*' □ *Sorry I took so long.*
2 used when you have not heard what someone has said: '*My name's Thea.*' — '*Sorry?*'
3 used to express your regret and sadness

when you hear sad or unpleasant news: *'Robert's sick today.' — 'I'm sorry to hear that.'*

sort¹ /sɔːt/ *noun*
a type or kind of person or thing: *What sort of school did you go to?*

sort² /sɔːt/ *verb* (**sorts, sorting, sorted**)
to separate things into different groups: *He sorted the materials into their folders.*

sort of used when your description of something is not very accurate (*informal*): *'What's a sub?' — 'Well, it's sort of a sandwich.'*

sort someone/something out
1 to separate people or things into different groups: *Sort out all your bills as quickly as possible.*
2 to deal with a problem successfully: *The two countries have sorted out their disagreement.*

sought /sɔːt/ → see **seek**

soul /səʊl/ *noun*
1 the part of you that consists of your mind, character, thoughts and feelings. Many people believe that your soul continues existing after your body is dead: *She prayed for the soul of her dead husband.*
2 *uncountable* → see **soul music**: *The show stars American soul singer Anita Baker.*

'soul ,music *uncountable noun*
a type of pop music performed mainly by African-American musicians, which often expresses deep emotions

sound¹ /saʊnd/ *noun*
something that you hear: *Peter heard the sound of a car engine outside.*

sound² /saʊnd/ *verb* (**sounds, sounding, sounded**)
1 used for describing a noise: *They heard something that sounded like a huge explosion.*
2 used for describing how someone seems when they speak: *She sounds very angry.*
3 used for describing your opinion of something: *It sounds like a wonderful idea to me.*
4 to produce a sound: *The fire alarm sounded at about 3.20 a.m.*

sound³ /saʊnd/ *adjective* (**sounder, soundest**)
1 in good condition: *The building is perfectly sound.*
2 sensible; that you can trust: *Our experts will give you sound advice.*

sound⁴ /saʊnd/ *adverb*
sound asleep in a deep sleep: *He was lying in bed, sound asleep.*

soundly /'saʊndli/ *adverb*
sleep soundly to sleep deeply, without waking during your sleep: *How can he sleep soundly at night?*

soup /suːp/ *uncountable noun*
a liquid food made by boiling meat, fish or vegetables in water: *home-made chicken soup*
→ Look at picture on P3

sour /'saʊə/ *adjective*
1 with a sharp, unpleasant taste like the taste of a lemon: *The stewed apple was sour.*
2 tasting bad; not fresh: *I can smell sour milk.*

source /sɔːs/ *noun*
1 the person, place or thing that something comes from: *Many adults use television as their major source of information.* □ *We are developing new sources of energy.*
2 the place where a river or a stream begins: *the source of the Tiber*

south /saʊθ/ also **South** *uncountable noun*
the direction that is on your right when you are looking at the sun in the morning: *The town lies ten miles to the south.* □ *We organize vacations in the south of Mexico.*
● **south** *adjective, adverb* *We live on the south coast of Ireland.* □ *I drove south on the M1 motorway.*
▶ **southern** /'sʌðən/ *adjective* *The Everglades National Park stretches across southern Florida.*

south-east /ˌsaʊθ'iːst/ *uncountable noun*
the direction that is between south and east: *The train left Colombo for Galle, 70 miles to the south-east.* ● **south-east** *adjective* also an adjective: *South-east Asia*
▶ **south-eastern** *adjective* *The city is on the south-eastern edge of the United States.*

southerly /'sʌðəli/ *adjective*
1 to or towards the south: *We travelled in a southerly direction towards Italy.*
2 blowing from the south: *a strong southerly wind*

south-west /ˌsaʊθ'west/ *uncountable noun*
the direction that is between south and west: *He lives about 500 miles to the south-west of Johannesburg.* ● **south-west** *adjective*

S

also an adjective: *south-west France*

▶ **south-western** *adjective* *They come from a small town in the south-western part of the country.*

souvenir /ˌsuːvəˈnɪə/ *noun*
something that you buy or keep to remind you of a place or an event: *The cup was a souvenir of the summer of 2002.*

sovereignty /ˈsɒvrɪnti/ *uncountable noun*
the power that a country has to govern itself or another country: *It is important to protect our national sovereignty.*

sow /səʊ/ *verb* (**sows, sowing, sowed, sown**)
to plant seeds in the ground: *Sow the seed in a warm place in early March.*

soya /ˈsɔɪə/ *uncountable noun*
used for describing flour, oil or sauce that is made using **soya beans**: *soya sauce*

'soya bean *noun*
a bean that can be eaten, or used for making flour, oil or sauce

spa /spɑː/ *noun*
1 a place where water comes out of the ground: *Buxton is a spa town that is famous for its water.*
2 a place where people go to exercise and have special treatments in order to improve their health: *Hotel guests may use the health spa.*

space¹ /speɪs/ *noun*
1 an area that is empty: *They cut down trees to make space for houses.* □ *The space under the bed could be used as a storage area.*
2 a period of time: *They've come a long way in a short space of time.*
3 *uncountable* the area beyond the Earth's atmosphere, where the stars and planets are: *The six astronauts will spend ten days in space.*

space² /speɪs/ *verb* (**spaces, spacing, spaced**) (*also* **space something out**)
to separate a series of things so that they are not all together: *Write the words down, spacing them evenly.* □ *He talks quite slowly and spaces his words out.*

spacecraft /ˈspeɪskrɑːft/ *noun* (**spacecraft**)
a vehicle that can travel in space: *This is the world's largest and most expensive spacecraft.*

spaceship /ˈspeɪsʃɪp/ *noun*
→ see **spacecraft**

'space ˌshuttle *noun*
a vehicle that is designed to travel into space and back to Earth several times

space shuttle

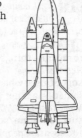

spacious /ˈspeɪʃəs/ *adjective*
large, with a lot of space: *The house has a spacious kitchen and dining area.*

spade /speɪd/ *noun*
a tool that is used for digging: *a garden spade*

spaghetti /spəˈgeti/ *uncountable noun*
a type of pasta (= a food made from flour and water) that looks like long pieces of string

spam /spæm/ *uncountable noun*
advertising messages that are sent automatically by email to large numbers of people: *Spam is becoming a major problem for many Internet users.*

span¹ /spæn/ *noun*
1 a period of time: *The batteries had a life span of six hours.*
2 the total width of something from one side to the other: *The butterfly has a 2-inch wing span.*

span² /spæn/ *verb* (**spans, spanning, spanned**)
1 to last for a particular period of time: *His professional career spanned 16 years.*
2 to stretch right across something such as a river: *There is a footbridge that spans the little stream.*

spanner /ˈspænə/ *noun*
a metal tool that you use for turning small pieces of metal (= nuts) to make them tighter

spare¹ /speə/ *adjective*
used for describing extra things that you keep in case you need them: *It's useful to have a spare pair of glasses.* □ *I'll give you the spare key.*

spare² /speə/ *verb* (**spares, sparing, spared**)
to make time or money available: *I can only spare 35 minutes for this meeting.*

spare 'time *uncountable noun*
the time when you do not have to work: *In her spare time she read books on cooking.*

spark /spɑːk/ *noun*
1 a very small piece of burning material that comes out of something that is burning: *Sparks flew out of the fire in all directions.*
2 a flash of light caused by electricity: *I saw a spark when I connected the wires.*

sparkle /'spɑːkəl/ *verb* (**sparkles, sparkling, sparkled**)
to shine clearly and brightly, with a lot of very small points of light: *The jewels on her fingers sparkled.* □ *His bright eyes sparkled.*

sparkling /'spɑːklɪŋ/ *adjective*
containing bubbles: *a glass of sparkling water*

sparrow /'spærəʊ/ *noun*
a small very common brown bird

sparse /spɑːs/ *adjective* (**sparser, sparsest**)
spread out in small amounts over an area: *He was a fat little man in his fifties, with sparse hair.*
▶ **sparsely** *adverb* *This is a sparsely populated mountain region.*

speak /spiːk/ *verb* (**speaks, speaking, spoke, spoken**)
1 to use your voice in order to say something: *He opened his mouth to speak.* □ *I called the hotel and spoke to Louie.* □ *He often speaks about his mother.*
▶ **spoken** *adjective* *They took tests in written and spoken English.*
2 to make a speech: *He will speak at the Democratic Convention.*
3 to know a foreign language and be able to have a conversation in it: *He speaks English.*
speak up to speak more loudly: *I'm quite deaf — you'll have to speak up.*

> **LANGUAGE HELP**
> See note at **talk**.

speaker /'spiːkə/ *noun*
1 a piece of electrical equipment that sound comes out of: *I bought a pair of speakers for my computer.*
2 a person who makes a speech: *Bruce Wyatt will be the guest speaker at next month's meeting.*

spear /spɪə/ *noun*
a weapon consisting of a long pole with a sharp metal point at the end

special /'speʃəl/ *adjective*
1 better or more important than other

people or things: *You're very special to me.*
□ *My special guest will be Zac Efron.*
2 different from normal: *In special cases, a child can be educated at home.*

specialist /'speʃəlɪst/ *noun*
a person who knows a lot about a particular subject: *Peckham is a cancer specialist.*

speciality /ˌspeʃi'ælɪti/ *noun* (**specialities**)
1 a particular type of work that someone does, or a subject that they know a lot about: *My father's speciality was the history of Germany.*
2 a special food or product that is always very good in a particular place: *Paella is a speciality of the restaurant.*

specialize /'speʃəˌlaɪz/ *verb* (**specializes, specializing, specialized**)
to concentrate a lot of your time and energy on a subject: *He's a professor who specializes in Russian history.*

specially /'speʃəli/ *adverb*
1 only for a particular person: *This soap is specially designed for sensitive skin.*
2 more than usual (*informal*): *On his birthday I got up specially early.*

species /'spiːʃiz/ *noun* (**species**)
a related group of plants or animals: *Many species could disappear from our Earth within the next 200 years.*

specific /spɪ'sɪfɪk/ *adjective*
1 particular: *Do you have pain in any specific part of your body?* □ *There are several specific problems.*
2 exact and clear: *She refused to be more specific about her plans.*

specifically /spɪ'sɪfɪkli/ *adverb*
used for showing that something is being considered separately: *The show is specifically for children.*

specify /'spesɪfaɪ/ *verb* (**specifies, specifying, specified**)
to explain something in an exact and detailed way: *Does the recipe specify the size of egg to be used?*

specimen /'spesɪmɪn/ *noun*
an example or a small amount of something: *Job applicants have to give a specimen of handwriting.*

speck /spek/ *noun*
a very small mark or piece of something: *There was a speck of dirt on his collar.*

S

spectacle /'spektəkəl/ *noun*
a big, wonderful sight or event: *The fireworks were an amazing spectacle.*

spectacles /'spektəkəlz/ *plural noun* (formal)
→ see **glasses**: *a pair of spectacles*

spectacular /spek'tækjʊlə/ *adjective*
big and dramatic: *We had spectacular views of Mount Everest.*
▶ **spectacularly** *adverb* *Our sales increased spectacularly.*

spectator /spek'teɪtə/ *noun*
someone who watches a sports event: *Thirty thousand spectators watched the game.*

speculate /'spekjʊˌleɪt/ *verb* (speculates, speculating, speculated)
to make guesses about something: *Everyone has been speculating about why she left.*
▶ **speculation** /ˌspekjʊ'leɪʃən/ *uncountable noun* *There has been a lot of speculation about the future of the band.*

sped /sped/ → see **speed**

speech /spiːtʃ/ *noun* (speeches)
1 *uncountable* the ability to speak or the act of speaking: *We are studying the development of speech in children.* □ *The medicine can affect speech.*
2 *uncountable* the way in which you speak: *His speech became slow and unclear.*
3 a formal talk that someone gives to a group of people: *The president gave a speech to the nation.*

speech

The president gave a speech to the nation.

'speech marks *plural noun*
→ see **quotation marks**

speed¹ /spiːd/ *noun*
1 how fast something moves or is done: *He drove off at high speed.* □ *He invented a way to measure wind speeds.*

2 *uncountable* very fast movement or travel: *Speed is essential for all athletes.*

speed² /spiːd/ *verb* (speeds, speeding, sped or speeded)

> **LANGUAGE HELP**
> Use **sped** in meaning **1** and **speeded** for the phrasal verb.

1 to move or travel somewhere quickly, usually in a vehicle: *Trains speed through the tunnel at 186 mph.*
2 to drive a vehicle faster than the legal speed limit: *Police stopped him because he was speeding.*
▶ **speeding** *uncountable noun* *He was fined for speeding.*

speed something up to make something happen more quickly than before: *We need to speed up a solution to the problem.*

speed up to happen more quickly than before: *My breathing speeded up a bit.*

'speed ˌlimit *noun*
the highest speed at which you are legally allowed to drive on a particular road

speedy /'spiːdi/ *adjective* (speedier, speediest)
happening or done very quickly: *We wish Bill a speedy recovery.*

spell¹ /spel/ *verb* (spells, spelling, spelled or spelt)
1 to write or speak each letter of a word in the correct order: *He spelled his name.* □ *How do you spell 'potato'?*
2 to know the correct order of letters in words: *He can't spell his own name.*

spell² /spel/ *noun*
a set of magic words: *They say that a witch cast a spell on her.*

spelling /'spelɪŋ/ *noun*
the correct order of the letters in a word: *I'm not sure about the spelling of his name.*

spend /spend/ *verb* (spends, spending, spent)
1 to pay money for things that you want or need: *I have spent all my money.*
2 to use your time doing something: *She spends hours working on her garden.*

spent /spent/ → see **spend**

sphere /sfɪə/ *noun*
an object that is completely round in shape, like a ball: *A tennis ball is a regular sphere shape.*

spice /spaɪs/ *noun*
a part of a plant that you put in food to give it flavour: *herbs and spices*

spicy /'spaɪsi/ *adjective* (**spicier, spiciest**)
strongly flavoured with spices: *Thai food is hot and spicy.*

spider /'spaɪdə/ *noun*
a small animal with eight legs

spike /spaɪk/ *noun*
a long piece of metal with a sharp point: *There was a high wall around the building with iron spikes at the top.*

spill /spɪl/ *verb* (**spills, spilling, spilled** or **spilt**)
to accidentally make a liquid flow over the edge of a container: *He always spilled the drinks.* ▢ *Oil spilt into the sea.*

spin /spɪn/ *verb* (**spins, spinning, spun**)
1 to turn quickly around a central point: *The disc spins 3,600 times a minute.* ▢ *He spun the steering wheel and turned the car around.*
2 to make thread by twisting together pieces of wool or cotton: *It's a machine for spinning wool.*

spinach /'spɪnɪdʒ, -ɪtʃ/ *uncountable noun*
a vegetable with large dark green leaves

spine /spaɪn/ *noun*
the row of bones down a person's or an animal's back: *He suffered injuries to his spine.*

spiral /'spaɪərəl/ *noun*
a shape that winds around and around, with each curve above or outside the one before
● **spiral** *adjective*
a spiral staircase

spirit /'spɪrɪt/ *noun*
1 the part of you that is not physical and that consists of your character and feelings: *The human spirit is hard to destroy.*
2 the part of a person that some people believe remains alive after their death: *He is gone, but his spirit is still with us.*
3 *plural* your feelings at a particular time, especially feelings of happiness or unhappiness: *At supper, everyone was in high spirits.*
4 *plural* strong alcoholic drinks: *I don't drink beer, wine, or spirits.*

spiritual /'spɪrɪtʃuəl/ *adjective*
1 relating to people's thoughts and beliefs, rather than to their bodies: *She is a very spiritual person.*
2 relating to people's religious beliefs: *He is the spiritual leader of the world's Catholics.*

spit /spɪt/ *verb* (**spits, spitting, spat**)
to force a small amount of liquid or food out of your mouth: *Spit out that gum.*

spite /spaɪt/ *uncountable noun*
a feeling that makes you do something because you want to hurt or upset someone: *I said those things out of spite I suppose.*
in spite of something used to introduce a fact that makes the rest of what you are saying seem surprising: *He hired her in spite of her lack of experience.*

splash /splæʃ/ *verb* (**splashes, splashing, splashed**)
1 to hit water in a noisy way: *People were splashing around in the water.*
2 if a liquid splashes, it moves or hits something, making a noise: *A little wave splashed in my face.* ● **splash** *noun* (**splashes**) *There was a splash as something fell into the water.*

splendid /'splendɪd/ *adjective*
very good: *The book includes some splendid photographs.*

splinter /'splɪntə/ *noun*
a thin, sharp piece of wood or glass that has broken off from a larger piece: *We found splinters of the glass in our clothes.*

split /splɪt/ *verb* (**splits, splitting, split**)
1 to break into two or more parts: *The ship split in two during a storm.*
2 to divide something into two or more parts: *Split the chicken in half.*
3 to break, producing a long crack or tear: *My trousers split while I was climbing over the wall.*
4 to share something between two or more people: *Let's split the bill.*
split up to stop being in a relationship together: *His parents split up when he was ten.*

spoil /spɔɪl/ *verb* (**spoils, spoiling, spoiled** or **spoilt**)
1 to prevent something from being successful: *Don't let mistakes spoil your life.*
2 to give children everything they want or ask for: *Grandparents often like to spoil their grandchildren.*

spoke¹ /spəʊk/ → see **speak**

spoke² /spəʊk/ *noun*
a bar that connects the outer ring of a wheel to the centre: *Her feet got caught in the spokes of the bike wheel.*

spoken /'spəʊkən/ → see **speak**

spokesman /'spəʊksmən/ *noun* (**spokesmen**)
a man who speaks as the representative of a group or an organization: *A spokesman said that food is on its way to the region.*

spokesperson /'spəʊkspɜːsən/ *noun* (**spokespersons** or **spokespeople**)
a person who speaks as the representative of a group or an organization: *a White House spokesperson*

spokeswoman /'spəʊkswʊmən/ *noun* (**spokeswomen**)
a woman who speaks as a representative of a group or an organization: *A hospital spokeswoman said he was recovering well.*

sponge /spʌndʒ/ *noun*
a piece of a very light soft material with lots of little holes in it, that you use for washing yourself or for cleaning things: *He wiped the table with a sponge.*

sponsor /'spɒnsə/ *verb* (**sponsors, sponsoring, sponsored**)
1 to pay for an event: *A local bank is sponsoring the race.*
2 to agree to give money to someone who is doing something to raise money, if they succeed in doing it: *The children asked friends and family to sponsor them.*

spontaneous /spɒn'teɪniəs/ *adjective*
done because someone suddenly wants to do it: *He gave her a spontaneous hug.*
▸ **spontaneously** *adverb* *People spontaneously stood up and cheered.*

spooky /'spuːki/ *adjective* (**spookier, spookiest**)
seeming frightening (*informal*): *The house has a slightly spooky atmosphere.*

spoon /spuːn/ *noun*
a long object with a round end that is used for eating, serving or mixing food: *He stirred his coffee with a spoon.*

spoonful /'spuːnfəl/ *noun*
an amount of food that a spoon holds: *He took a spoonful of the stew and ate it.*

sport /spɔːt/ *noun*
a game or other activity that needs physical effort and skill: *Basketball is my*

spoons

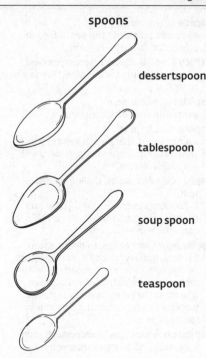

dessertspoon

tablespoon

soup spoon

teaspoon

favourite sport. ☐ *She is very good at sports.*
→ Look at pictures on P6

sports centre *noun*
a building where you can go to do sports and other activities

spot¹ /spɒt/ *noun*
1 a small, round coloured area on a surface: *The leaves are yellow with orange spots.*
2 a particular place: *This is one of the country's top tourist spots.*
3 a small red lump or mark on a person's skin: *I've got a big spot on my nose.*
on the spot immediately: *They offered him the job on the spot.*

spot² /spɒt/ *verb* (**spots, spotting, spotted**)
to notice something or someone: *I didn't spot the mistake in his essay.*

spotlight /'spɒtlaɪt/ *noun*
a powerful light that can be directed so that it lights up a small area

spotty /'spɒti/ *adjective*
1 with small red lumps on your skin: *a spotty face*
2 with a pattern of spots: *a spotty dress*

spouse /spaʊs/ *noun*
someone's husband or wife: *You and your spouse must both sign the contract.*

sprang /spræŋ/ → see **spring**

spray /spreɪ/ *noun*
1 a lot of small drops of water that are thrown into the air: *We were hit by spray from the waterfall.*
2 a liquid that comes out of a can or other container in very small drops when you press a button: *hair spray* • **spray** *verb* (**sprays, spraying, sprayed**) *Firefighters sprayed water on the fire.*

spread /spred/ *verb* (**spreads, spreading, spread**)
1 (*also* **spread something out**) to open something out over a surface: *She spread a towel on the sand and lay on it.* □ *He spread the papers out on a table.*
2 (*also* **spread something out**) to stretch out parts of your body until they are far apart: *Sit on the floor, and spread your legs.* □ *David spread out his hands.*
3 to put a substance all over a surface: *She was spreading butter on the bread.*
4 to gradually reach a larger area: *Information technology has spread across the world.* • **spread** *noun We closed schools to stop the spread of the disease.*

spread out same meaning as **spread 1, 2**

spreadsheet /'spredʃiːt/ *noun*
a computer program that deals with numbers. Spreadsheets are mainly used for financial planning.

spring¹ /sprɪŋ/ *noun*
1 the season between winter and summer when the weather becomes warmer and plants start to grow again: *They are getting married next spring.*
2 a long piece of metal that goes round and round. It goes back to the same shape after you pull it: *The springs in the bed were old and soft.*
3 a place where water comes up through the ground: *The town is famous for its hot springs.*

spring² /sprɪŋ/ *verb* (**springs, springing, sprang, sprung**)
to jump suddenly or quickly: *He sprang to his feet.*

spring onion *noun*
a small onion with long green leaves
→ Look at picture on P2

sprinkle /'sprɪŋkəl/ *verb* (**sprinkles, sprinkling, sprinkled**)
to drop a bit of liquid or powder over the surface of something: *Sprinkle the meat with salt before you cook it.*

sprinkler /'sprɪŋklə/ *noun*
a machine that spreads drops of water over an area of grass or onto a fire

sprint /sprɪnt/ *verb* (**sprints, sprinting, sprinted**)
to run as fast as you can over a short distance: *Sergeant Adams sprinted to the car.*
• **sprint** *noun Rob Harmeling won the sprint.*

sprout¹ /spraʊt/ *verb* (**sprouts, sprouting, sprouted**)
to start to grow out of the ground: *It only takes a few days for beans to sprout.*

sprout² /spraʊt/ *noun* (*also* **Brussels sprout**)
a small round green vegetable

sprung /sprʌŋ/ → see **spring**

spun /spʌn/ → see **spin**

spy¹ /spaɪ/ *noun* (**spies**)
a person whose job is to find out secret information about another country or organization: *He used to be a spy.*

spy² /spaɪ/ *verb* (**spies, spying, spied**)
1 to try to find out secret information about another country or organization: *The two countries are still spying on one another.*
2 to watch someone secretly: *He spied on her while she was on her way to work.*

square¹ /skweə/ *noun*
1 a shape with four straight sides that are all the same length: *Cut the cake into squares.*
2 an open place with buildings around it in a town or city: *The restaurant is in the town square.*
3 the number you get when you multiply a number by itself: *The square of 4 is 16.*

square² /skweə/ *adjective*
1 used for describing a shape that has four straight sides that are all the same length: *They sat at a square table.*
2 used for talking about the area of something: *The house covers an area of 3,000 square feet.*

s

square 'root *noun*

a number that you multiply by itself to produce another number: *The square root of 36 is 6.*

squash ¹ /skwɒʃ/ *verb* (**squashes, squashing, squashed**)

to push or press someone or something hard: *Robert was squashed against a fence by a car.*

squash ² /skwɒʃ/ *uncountable noun*

1 a game in which two players hit a small rubber ball against the walls of a court: *I play squash once a week.*

2 a drink that is made from fruit juice, sugar, and water: *a glass of orange squash*

squeak /skwiːk/ *verb* (**squeaks, squeaking, squeaked**)

to make a short, high sound: *My boots squeaked as I walked.* ● **squeak** *noun I heard a squeak, like a mouse.*

squeal /skwiːl/ *verb* (**squeals, squealing, squealed**)

to make a long, high sound: *Jennifer squealed with pleasure.* ● **squeal** *noun There was a squeal of brakes as the car suddenly stopped.*

squeeze /skwiːz/ *verb* (**squeezes, squeezing, squeezed**)

1 to press something firmly, usually with your hands: *He squeezed her arm gently.*

● **squeeze** *noun She took my hand and gave it a squeeze.*

2 to get a soft substance out of a container by pressing: *Joe squeezed some toothpaste out of the tube.*

squid /skwɪd/ *noun*

> **LANGUAGE HELP**
> The plural can also be **squid**.

1 a sea animal that has a long soft body and many soft arms called tentacles

2 *uncountable* this animal eaten as food: *Cook the squid for 2 minutes.*

squirrel /'skwɪrəl/ *noun*

a small animal with a long thick tail. Squirrels live mainly in trees.

squirt /skwɜːt/ *verb* (**squirts, squirting, squirted**)

1 to make a liquid come out of a narrow opening very quickly: *Norman squirted tomato sauce onto his plate.*

2 to come out of a narrow opening very quickly: *The mustard squirted all over the front*

of my shirt. ● **squirt** *noun It needs a little squirt of oil.*

stab /stæb/ *verb* (**stabs, stabbing, stabbed**)

to push a knife or sharp object into someone's body: *Someone stabbed him in the stomach.*

stable ¹ /'steɪbəl/ *adjective* (**stabler, stablest**)

1 not likely to change suddenly: *The price of oil has remained stable this month.*

▸ **stability** /stə'bɪlɪti/ *uncountable noun It was a time of political stability.*

2 firmly fixed in position: *Make sure the ladder is stable.*

stable ² /'steɪbəl/ *noun* (*also* **stables**)

a building in which horses are kept

stack /stæk/ *noun*

a pile of things: *There were stacks of books on the floor.* ● **stack** *verb* (**stacks, stacking, stacked**) *He asked me to stack the dirty dishes.*

stadium /'steɪdiəm/ *noun*

a large sports pitch with rows of seats all around it: *a football stadium*

staff /stɑːf/ *noun*

the people who work for an organization: *The hospital staff were very good.* □ *staff members*

stag /stæg/ *noun*

an adult male deer (= a large wild animal that eats grass and leaves, and has horns that look like branches)

stage /steɪdʒ/ *noun*

1 one part of an activity or process: *We are completing the first stage of the plan.*

2 the area in a theatre where people perform: *The band walked onto the stage.*

stagger /'stægə/ *verb* (**staggers, staggering, staggered**)

to walk as if you are going to fall, for example because you are ill: *He staggered back and fell over.*

stain /steɪn/ *noun*

a mark on something that is difficult to remove: *How do you remove tea stains?*

● **stain** *verb* (**stains, staining, stained**) *Some foods can stain the teeth.*

▸ **stained** *adjective His clothing was stained with mud.*

stair /steə/ *noun*

one of a set of steps inside a building: *Terry was sitting on the bottom stair.*

staircase /'steəkeɪs/ *noun*
a set of stairs inside a building: *They walked down the staircase together.*

stairs /steəz/ *plural noun*
a set of steps inside a building that go from one level to another: *Nancy began to climb the stairs.* □ *We walked up the stairs to the second floor.*

stale /steɪl/ *adjective* (**staler, stalest**)
no longer fresh: *stale bread*

stalk /stɔ:k/ *noun*
the thin part of a flower, leaf or fruit that joins it to the plant or tree: *A single flower grows on each long stalk.*

stammer /'stæmə/ *verb* (**stammers, stammering, stammered**)
to find it difficult to speak without repeating words or sounds: *'F-f-forgive me',* I stammered.

stamp¹ /stæmp/ *noun*
1 a small piece of paper that you stick on an envelope before you post it: *She put a stamp on the corner of the envelope.*
2 a small block of wood or metal with words, numbers or a pattern on it. You put ink on it, then press it onto a piece of paper: *a date stamp*

stamp

stamp² /stæmp/ *verb* (**stamps, stamping, stamped**)
to press a mark or a word onto an object using a stamp: *They stamp a special number on new cars.*

stamp your foot to put your foot down very hard on the ground: *I stamped my foot in anger.*

stand¹ /stænd/ *verb* (**stands, standing, stood**)
1 to be on your feet: *She was standing beside my bed.*
2 (*also* **stand up**) to move so that you are on your feet: *Becker stood and shook hands with Ben.* □ *When I walked in, they all stood up.*
3 to be in a place: *The house stands alone on top of a hill.*

can't stand someone/something used for saying that you dislike someone or something very strongly (*informal*): *I can't stand that awful man.* □ *I can't stand that smell.*

stand aside/stand back to move a short distance away: *I stood aside to let her pass me.*

stand by
1 to be ready to help: *Police officers are standing by in case of trouble.*
2 to not do anything to stop something bad from happening: *I will not stand by and watch people suffering.*

stand for something to be a short form of a word: *U.S. stands for United States.*

stand out to be very easy to see: *The black necklace stood out against her white dress.*

stand up same meaning as **stand 2**

stand up for someone/something to support a person or a belief: *Nelson Mandela stood up for his people and his beliefs.*

stand up to someone to defend yourself against someone who is more powerful than you: *He was too afraid to stand up to her.*

stand² /stænd/ *noun*
1 a small structure where you can buy things like food, drink and newspapers: *I bought a magazine from a newspaper stand.*
2 a small piece of furniture that you use to hold a particular thing: *Take the television set off the stand.*

standard¹ /'stændəd/ *noun*
1 a level of quality: *The standard of his work is very low.*
2 *plural* moral principles that guide people's behaviour: *My father always had high moral standards.*

standard² /'stændəd/ *adjective*
usual and normal: *It's just a standard size car.*

standby /'stændbaɪ/ *noun*
something or someone that is always ready to be used if they are needed: *Canned*

S

vegetables are a good standby.

on standby ready to be used if needed: *Five ambulances are on standby.*

stank /stæŋk/ → see **stink**

staple /'steɪpəl/ *noun*
a small piece of bent wire that holds sheets of paper together firmly. You put the staples into the paper using a stapler.
● **staple** *verb* (**staples, stapling, stapled**) *Staple some sheets of paper together.*

staple /'steɪpəl/ *adjective*
important in people's lives: *Rice is the staple food of more than half the world's population.*

stapler /'steɪplə/ *noun*
a small piece of equipment that is used for attaching sheets of paper together

star¹ /stɑː/ *noun*
1 a large ball of burning gas in space. Stars look like small points of light in the sky: *Stars lit the sky.*
2 a shape that has four, five or more points sticking out of it in a regular pattern: *How many stars are there on the American flag?*
3 a famous actor, musician or sports player: *He's one of the stars of the TV series 'Friends'.*

star² /stɑː/ *verb* (**stars, starring, starred**)
1 to have one of the most important parts in a play or a film: *Meryl Streep stars in the movie 'The Devil Wears Prada'.*
2 to have a famous actor or actress in one of the most important parts in a play or film: *The movie stars Brad Pitt.*

stare /steə/ *verb* (**stares, staring, stared**)
to look at someone or something for a long time: *Ben continued to stare out the window.* □ *She was staring at me angrily.*
● **stare** *noun Harry gave him a long stare.*

starfish /'stɑːfɪʃ/ *noun* (**starfish**)
a flat creature in the shape of a star, that lives in the sea

start /stɑːt/ *verb* (**starts, starting, started**)
1 to do something that you were not doing before: *Susanna started working in TV in 2005.*
2 to take place from a particular time: *The fire started in an upstairs room.* ● **start** *noun It was 1918, four years after the start of the Great War.*

3 to create something or cause it to begin: *She has started a child care centre in Leeds.*
4 to make an engine, a car or a machine begin to work: *He started the car and drove off.*

start off to do something as the first part of an activity: *She started off by clearing some space on the table.*

to start with used for introducing the first of a number of things: *To start with, you need her name and address.*

starter /'stɑːtə/ *noun*
a small amount of food that you eat as the first part of a meal: *There was a choice of three starters and three main courses on the menu.*

startle /'stɑːtəl/ *verb* (**startles, startling, startled**)
to suddenly surprise and frighten someone slightly: *The telephone startled him.*
▶ **startled** *adjective Martha gave her a startled look.*

starve /stɑːv/ *verb* (**starves, starving, starved**)
to suffer greatly or die from lack of food: *A number of the prisoners are starving.*
▶ **starvation** /stɑːˈveɪʃən/ *uncountable noun Over three hundred people died of starvation.*

starve yourself to eat very little or no food over a long period of time: *He was starving himself.*

starving /'stɑːvɪŋ/ *adjective*
very hungry (*informal*): *Does anyone have any food? I'm starving.*

state¹ /steɪt/ *noun*
1 a country, especially when it is considered politically: *a socialist state*
2 a smaller area that some large countries such as the United States are divided into: *Leaders of the Southern states are meeting in Louisville.*
3 the government of a country: *In Sweden, child care is provided by the state.*
4 the condition that someone or something is in: *After Daniel died, I was in a state of shock.*

the States the United States of America (*informal*): *She bought it in the States.*

state² /steɪt/ *verb* (**states, stating, stated**)
to say or write something in a formal or definite way: *Clearly state your address and telephone number.*

statement /'steɪtmənt/ *noun*
something that you say or write that gives information in a formal way: *I was very angry when I made that statement.*

static¹ /'stætɪk/ *adjective*
not moving or changing: *House prices were static last month.*

static² /'stætɪk/ *uncountable noun* (*also* **static electricity**)
electricity that collects on things such as your body or metal objects

station /'steɪʃən/ *noun*
1 a place where trains stop so that people can get on or off: *Ingrid went with him to the train station.*
2 a place in a town or a city where a lot of buses stop: *I walked to the bus station and bought a ticket.*
3 a company that broadcasts programmes on radio or television: *a local radio station*

stationary /'steɪʃənri/ *adjective*
not moving: *A bus crashed into the back of a stationary vehicle.*

> **LANGUAGE HELP**
>
> **stationary** or **stationery**? **Stationary** is an adjective; it means 'not moving'. **Stationery** is a noun; it means 'paper products used for writing and typing'.

stationery /'steɪʃənri/ *uncountable noun*
paper, envelopes and other materials or equipment used for writing and typing: *office stationery*

statistic /stə'tɪstɪk/ *noun*
a fact that is expressed in numbers: *Statistics show that wages are rising.*

statue /'stætʃuː/ *noun*
a large model of a person or an animal, made of stone or metal: *She gave me a stone statue of a horse.*

statue

status /'steɪtəs/ *uncountable noun*
the importance that people give to someone or something: *Older family members enjoy high status in many societies.*

stay /steɪ/ *verb* (**stays, staying, stayed**)
1 to continue to be where you are, and not to leave: *'Stay here', Trish said. 'I'll bring the car to you.'*
2 to live somewhere for a short time: *Gordon stayed at The Park Hotel, Milan.* □ *Can't you stay a for few more days?* ● **stay** *noun Please contact the hotel reception if you have any problems during your stay.*
3 to continue to be in a particular state or situation: *Exercise is one of the best ways to stay healthy.*

stay away to not go to a place: *Most workers stayed away from work during the strike.*

stay in to remain at home and not go out: *We decided to stay in and have dinner at home.*

stay up not to go to bed at your usual time: *I used to stay up late with my mum and watch films.*

steady /'stedi/ *adjective* (**steadier, steadiest**)
1 continuing or developing gradually and not likely to change quickly: *Despite these problems there has been steady progress.*
▶ **steadily** /'stedɪli/ *adverb Prices have been rising steadily.*
2 firm, and not moving around: *Hold the camera steady.* ● **steady** *verb* (**steadies, steadying, steadied**) *Two men were steadying the ladder.*

steak /steɪk/ *noun*
1 a large flat piece of beef without much fat on it: *There was a steak cooking on the grill.*
2 a large piece of fish that does not contain many bones: *fresh salmon steaks*

steal /stiːl/ *verb* (**steals, stealing, stole, stolen**)
to take something from someone without their permission: *They said he stole a small boy's bicycle.* □ *It's wrong to steal* □ *Give me back the money that you stole from me.*
▶ **stolen** /'stəʊlən/ *adjective We have now found the stolen car.*

steam¹ /stiːm/ *uncountable noun*
the hot gas that forms when water boils: *The heat converts water into steam.*

steam² /stiːm/ *verb* (**steams, steaming, steamed**)
to cook food in steam rather than in water: *Steam the carrots until they are slightly soft.*

steel /stiːl/ *uncountable noun*
a very strong metal that is made mainly from iron: *steel pipes* □ *the steel industry*

s

steep /stiːp/ *adjective* (**steeper, steepest**)

1 rising at a very sharp angle: *Some of the hills in San Francisco are very steep.*

▸ **steeply** *adverb* *The road climbs steeply.*

2 very big: *There have been steep price increases.*

▸ **steeply** *adverb* *Unemployment is rising steeply.*

steer /stɪə/ *verb* (**steers, steering, steered**)

to control a vehicle so that it goes in the direction that you want: *What is it like to steer a big ship?*

'steering wheel *noun*

the wheel in a car or other vehicle that the driver holds when he or she is driving

stem /stem/ *noun*

the long, thin part of a plant that the flowers and leaves grow on: *He cut the stem and gave her the flower.*

step¹ /step/ *noun*

1 the action of lifting your foot and putting it down in a different place: *I took a step towards him.* □ *She walked back a few steps.*

2 a raised flat surface that you put your feet on in order to walk up or down to a different level: *We went down some steps into the garden.* □ *A girl was sitting on the bottom step.*

3 one of a series of actions that you take in a process: *We have taken the first step towards peace.*

step by step progressing gradually from one stage to the next: *I am not rushing things. I'm taking it step by step.*

step² /step/ *verb* (**steps, stepping, stepped**)

1 to move somewhere by lifting your foot and putting it down in a different place: *He stepped carefully over the sleeping cat.*

2 to put your foot on something: *Neil Armstrong was the first man to step on the Moon.*

stepfather /'stepfɑːðə/ *noun*

the man who has married someone's mother but who is not their father.

stepmother /'stepmʌðə/ *noun*

the woman who has married someone's father but who is not their mother.

stereo /'steriəʊ/ *noun*

a machine that plays music, with two parts (= speakers) that the sound comes from: *a car stereo*

→ Look at picture on P5

sterile /'steraɪl/ *adjective*

1 completely clean: *Cover the cut with a* sterile bandage and keep it dry.

2 unable to produce babies: *The tests showed that George was sterile.*

stern /stɜːn/ *adjective* (**sterner, sternest**)

1 very severe: *Our rugby coach gave us a stern warning about our behaviour.*

▸ **sternly** *adverb* *'We will punish anyone who breaks the rules', she said sternly.*

2 very serious and not friendly: *Her father was a stern man.*

stew¹ /stjuː/ *noun*

a meal that you make by cooking meat and vegetables in liquid: *She gave him a bowl of beef stew.*

stew² /stjuː/ *verb* (**stews, stewing, stewed**)

to cook meat, vegetables, or fruit slowly in liquid: *Stew the apples for half an hour.*

steward /'stjuːəd/ *noun*

a man whose job is to look after passengers on a ship, a plane, or a train

stewardess /ˌstjuːə'des/ *noun* (**stewardesses**)

a woman whose job is to look after passengers on a ship, a plane, or a train

stick¹ /stɪk/ *noun*

1 a thin branch from a tree: *She put some dry sticks on the fire.*

2 a long thin piece of wood that is used for a particular purpose: *He picked up his walking stick and walked away.*

stick² /stɪk/ *verb* (**sticks, sticking, stuck**)

1 to join one thing to another using a sticky substance: *Now stick your picture on a piece of paper.*

2 to push a pointed object into something: *The doctor stuck the needle into Joe's arm.*

3 to put something somewhere (*informal*): *He folded the papers and stuck them in his desk.*

4 to become joined to something and be difficult to remove: *The paper sometimes*

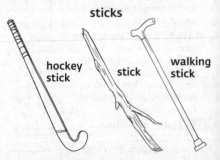

sticks

hockey stick

stick

walking stick

sticks to the bottom of the cake.

stick by someone to continue to give someone support: *All my friends stuck by me during the difficult times.*

stick out to continue further than the main part of something: *His two front teeth stick out slightly.*

stick something out to push something forwards or away from you: *She stuck out her tongue at him.*

stick to something to not change your mind about a promise or a decision: *We are waiting to see if he sticks to his promise.*

stick up for someone/something to support someone or something, and say that they are right: *My father always sticks up for me.*

sticker /'stɪkə/ *noun*
a small piece of paper with writing or a picture on one side, that you can stick onto a surface: *I bought a sticker that said, 'I love Florida'.*

sticky /'stɪki/ *adjective* (**stickier, stickiest**)
1 sticking to other things: *The floor was sticky with spilled orange juice.* ☐ *If the mixture is sticky, add more flour.*
2 involving problems (*informal*): *There were some sticky moments.*

stiff /stɪf/ *adjective* (**stiffer, stiffest**)
1 firm or not bending easily: *His jeans were new and stiff.*
▸ **stiffly** *adverb* *Moira sat stiffly in her chair.*
2 with muscles or joints that hurt when you move: *A hot bath is good for stiff muscles.*
bored stiff/worried stiff extremely bored or worried (*informal*): *Anna tried to look interested, but she was bored stiff.*

stifle /'staɪfəl/ *verb* (**stifles, stifling, stifled**)
to stop something from happening or continuing: *He stifled a laugh.*

still¹ /stɪl/ *adverb*
1 used for showing that a situation that existed in the past has continued and exists now: *Do you still live in Newcastle?* ☐ *Donald is still teaching at the age of 89.*
2 used for saying that something is true, despite something else: *She says she still loves him even though he treats her badly.*
3 used for making another word stronger: *It's good to travel, but it's better still to come home.*

still² /stɪl/ *adjective* (**stiller, stillest**)
1 not moving: *Please stand still and listen to me!*

2 without any wind: *It was a warm, still evening.*
3 without bubbles: *Would you like still or sparkling mineral water?*

stimulate /'stɪmjʊˌleɪt/ *verb* (**stimulates, stimulating, stimulated**)
1 to make something more active: *America is trying to stimulate its economy.*
2 to make someone feel full of ideas and enthusiasm: *Bill was stimulated by the challenge.*
▸ **stimulating** *adjective* *It is a stimulating book.*
▸ **stimulation** *uncountable noun* *Children need stimulation, not relaxation.*

sting /stɪŋ/ *verb* (**stings, stinging, stung**)
1 if a plant, an animal or an insect stings you, a pointed part of it is pushed into your skin so that you feel a sharp pain: *She was stung by a bee.*
2 to feel a sharp pain in a part of your body: *His cheeks were stinging from the cold wind.* ● **sting** *noun* *This won't hurt — you will just feel a little sting.*

stink /stɪŋk/ *verb* (**stinks, stinking, stank, stunk**)
to smell very bad: *We all stank and nobody cared.* ☐ *The kitchen stinks of fish.* ● **stink** *noun* *He was aware of the stink of onions on his breath.*

stir /stɜː/ *verb* (**stirs, stirring, stirred**)
1 to mix a liquid in a container using a spoon: *Stir the soup for a few seconds.*
2 to move slightly in your sleep: *Eileen shook him, and he started to stir.*

stitch¹ /stɪtʃ/ *verb* (**stitches, stitching, stitched**)
1 to sew cloth using a needle and thread: *Stitch the two pieces of fabric together.*
2 to use a special needle and thread to sew the skin of a wound together: *Jill washed and stitched the wound.*

stitch² /stɪtʃ/ *noun* (**stitches**)
1 a short line of thread that has been sewn in a piece of cloth: *Sew a row of straight stitches.*
2 a short line of thread that has been used for sewing the skin of a wound together: *He had six stitches in the cut.*

stock¹ /stɒk/ *noun*
1 *uncountable* the total amount of goods that a shop has available to sell: *Most of the stock was destroyed in the fire.*

S

2 one part of the value of a business that may be bought and sold: *She works for a bank, buying and selling stocks and shares.*

3 *uncountable* the total amount of goods that a shop has available to sell: *Most of the stock was destroyed in the fire.*

in stock available for you to buy: *Check that your size is in stock.*

out of stock not available for you to buy: *I'm sorry. The CD you are looking for is out of stock.*

stock² /stɒk/ *verb* (**stocks, stocking, stocked**)

to keep a supply of a particular product to sell: *The shop stocks everything from pens to TV sets.*

'stock exchange *noun*

a place where people buy and sell stocks in companies: *the New York stock exchange*

stocking /'stɒkɪŋ/ *noun*

a piece of women's clothing that fits closely over the foot and leg: *a pair of nylon stockings*

'stock market *noun*

the activity of buying shares (= parts of a company's value): *This book is a practical guide to investing in the stock market.*

stole /stəʊl/ → see **steal**

stolen /'stəʊlən/ → see **steal**

stomach /'stʌmək/ *noun*

1 the organ inside your body where food goes when you eat it: *He has stomach problems.*

2 the front part of your body below your waist: *The children lay down on their stomachs.*
→ Look at picture on P1

stone /stəʊn/ *noun*

1 *uncountable* a hard solid substance that is found in the ground and is often used for building: *a stone floor*

2 a small piece of rock that is found on the ground: *He removed a stone from his shoe.*

3 a piece of beautiful and valuable rock that is used in making jewellery: *He gave her a diamond ring with three stones.*

stood /stʊd/ → see **stand**

stool /stuːl/ *noun*

a seat with legs and no support for your arms or back: *Kate sat on a stool in the corner of the room.*

stop¹ /stɒp/ *verb* (**stops, stopping, stopped**)

1 to not do something any more: *Stop throwing those stones!* □ *She stopped eating and started to laugh.*

2 to prevent something from happening: *They are trying to find a way to stop the war.*

3 to not happen any more: *The rain has stopped.*

4 to be no longer working: *The clock stopped at 11.59 on Saturday night.*

5 to not move any more: *The car failed to stop at a traffic light.* □ *He stopped and waited for her.*

LANGUAGE HELP

stop doing or **stop to do something**? When an action comes to an end, you say that someone **stops doing** it. *She stopped reading and closed the book.* If you say that someone **stops to do** something, you mean that they interrupt their an activity in order to do that thing. *I stopped to read the notices on the bulletin board.*

---

stop² /stɒp/ *noun*

a place where buses or trains regularly stop so that people can get on and off: *Ann started to walk towards the bus stop.*

come to a stop to slow down and no longer move: *Do not open the door before the train comes to a stop.*

put a stop to something to prevent something from continuing: *Our leaders must put a stop to the war.*

storage /'stɔːrɪdʒ/ *uncountable noun*

when you keep something in a special place until it is needed: *This room is used for storage.*

store¹ /stɔː/ *noun*

1 a large shop that sells many different products: *The company has 100 stores across the country.* □ *This is my favourite high-street store.*

2 (*American*) a shop of any size: *a grocery store*

store² /stɔː/ *verb* (**stores, storing, stored**)

to put things somewhere and leave them there until they are needed: *Store the biscuits in a tin.*

storey /'stɔːri/ *noun*

one of the different levels of a building: *Our block of flats is 25 storeys high.*

storm /stɔːm/ *noun*

very bad weather, with heavy rain and strong winds: *There will be violent storms along the coast tonight.*

stormy /'stɔːmi/ *adjective* (**stormier, stormiest**)

with strong winds and heavy rain: *Expect a night of stormy weather, with heavy rain and strong winds.*

story /'stɔːri/ *noun* (**stories**)

1 a description of imaginary people and events, that is intended to entertain people: *I'm going to tell you a story about four little rabbits.*

2 a description of something that has happened: *The parents all had interesting stories about their children.*

stove /stəʊv/ *noun*

a piece of equipment that provides heat, either for cooking or for heating a room: *She put the saucepan on the gas stove.* ☐ *There's a wood-burning stove in the living room.*

straddle /'strædəl/ *verb* (**straddles, straddling, straddled**)

to put one leg on either side of something: *He sat down, straddling the chair.*

straight /streɪt/ *adjective, adverb* (**straighter, straightest**)

1 continuing in one direction; not bending or curving: *Keep the boat moving in a straight line.* ☐ *Grace had long straight hair.* ☐ *Stand straight and hold your arms out to the side.* ☐ *When he arrived, he went straight to his office.*

2 clear and honest: *She tells lies all the time. I can't get a straight answer from her.*

get something straight to make sure that you understand something properly (*informal*): *Now, let me get this straight: you say that you were here all evening?*

straighten /'streɪtən/ *verb* (**straightens, straightening, straightened**)

1 to make something neat or put it in its proper position: *She straightened a picture on the wall.*

2 (*also* **straighten up**) to make your back or body straight when you are standing: *The three men straightened and stood waiting.* ☐ *He straightened up and took his hands out of his pockets.*

3 to make something straight: *Straighten both legs.*

strain [1] /streɪn/ *noun*

1 the state of having to do more than you are able to do: *She couldn't cope with the stresses and strains of her career.*

2 an injury to a muscle in your body, caused by using it too much: *Avoid muscle strain by taking rests.*

strain [2] /streɪn/ *verb* (**strains, straining, strained**)

1 to injure a muscle by using it too much: *He strained his back playing tennis.*

2 to make a great effort to do something: *The music was so loud that I had to strain to hear what she was saying.*

3 to separate the liquid part of food from the solid parts: *Strain the soup and put it back into the pan.*

strange /streɪndʒ/ *adjective* (**stranger, strangest**)

1 unusual or unexpected: *There was something strange about the way she spoke.* ☐ *He was quite a strange man.*

▶ **strangely** *adverb* *She noticed he was acting strangely.*

2 that you have never been to before: *I was alone in a strange city.*

stranger /'streɪndʒə/ *noun*

someone who you have never met before: *We don't want a complete stranger staying with us.* ☐ *I've warned her not to talk to strangers.*

strangle /'stræŋgəl/ *verb* (**strangles, strangling, strangled**)

to kill someone by pressing their throat tightly so that they cannot breathe: *He tried to strangle a policeman.*

strap [1] /stræp/ *noun*

a long, narrow piece of leather or other material: *Nancy held the strap of her bag.* ☐ *Her shoes had elastic ankle straps.*

strap [2] /stræp/ *verb* (**straps, strapping, strapped**)

to fasten something somewhere with a strap: *She strapped the baby seat into the car.*

strategy /'strætədʒi/ *noun* (**strategies**)

a general plan or set of plans for the future: *Do you have a strategy for solving this type of problem?*

straw /strɔː/ *noun*

1 **uncountable** the dried, yellow stems of crops: *The floor of the barn was covered with straw.* ☐ *a straw hat*

2 a thin tube that you use to suck a drink into your mouth: *I drank from a bottle of lemonade with a straw in it.*

the last straw/the final straw the last in a series of bad events that makes you

S

feel that the situation is now impossible: *When both children started crying, it was the last straw for their mother.*

strawberry /ˈstrɔːbri/ *noun* (**strawberries**)

a small soft red fruit that has a lot of very small seeds on its skin: *strawberries and cream* → Look at picture on P2

stray [1] /streɪ/ *verb* (**strays, straying, strayed**)

to go away from where you are supposed to be: *Be careful not to stray into dangerous parts of the city.*

stray [2] /streɪ/ *adjective*

far away from home, or not having a home: *A stray dog came up to him.* ● **stray** *noun The dog was a stray.*

streak /striːk/ *noun*

a long mark on a surface: *There are dark streaks on the surface of the moon.*

stream [1] /striːm/ *noun*

1 a small narrow river: *There was a small stream at the end of the garden.*

2 a large number of things that come one after another: *The TV show caused a stream of complaints.*

stream [2] /striːm/ *verb* (**streams, streaming, streamed**)

to move somewhere in large amounts: *Tears streamed down their faces.* □ *Sunlight was streaming into the room.*

street /striːt/ *noun*

a road in a city or a town: *The streets were crowded with shoppers.* □ *He lives at 66 Bingfield Street.*

strength /streŋθ/ *noun*

1 *uncountable* how physically strong you are: *Swimming builds up the strength of your muscles.* □ *He threw the ball forward with all his strength.*

2 *uncountable* your confidence or courage: *He copes with his illness very well. His strength is amazing.*

3 how strong something is: *He checked the strength of the rope.*

4 the qualities and abilities that you have: *Make a list of your strengths and weaknesses.*

5 *uncountable* how deeply people feel or believe something: *He was surprised at the strength of his own feeling.*

strengthen /ˈstreŋθən/ *verb* (**strengthens, strengthening, strengthened**)

to make something stronger: *Cycling strengthens all the muscles of the body.*

stress [1] /stres/ *noun*

1 an unpleasant feeling of worry cause by difficulties in life: *She's away from work suffering from stress.* □ *I cannot think clearly when I'm under stress.*

2 when you say a word or part of a word slightly more loudly: *The stress is on the first part of the word 'animal'.*

stress [2] /stres/ *verb* (**stresses, stressing, stressed**)

1 to make it clear that something is very important: *He stressed that the problem was not serious.*

2 to say something slightly more loudly: *She stressed the words 'very important'.*

stressed /strest/ *adjective*

feeling very worried because of difficulties in your life: *What situations make you feel stressed?*

stressful /ˈstresfʊl/ *adjective*

making you feel worried or upset: *She's got a very stressful job.*

stretch [1] /stretʃ/ *verb* (**stretches, stretching, stretched**)

1 to cover all of a particular distance: *The queue of cars stretched for several miles.*

2 to put your arms or legs out very straight: *He yawned and stretched.*

3 to become longer and thinner: *Can you feel your leg muscles stretching?*

stretch out to lie with your legs and body in a straight line: *The bath was too small to stretch out in.*

stretch something out to hold out a part of your body straight: *He stretched out his hand to touch me.*

stretch [2] /stretʃ/ *noun* (**stretches**)

a length or area of land or water: *It's a very dangerous stretch of road.*

stretcher /ˈstretʃə/ *noun*

a long piece of strong material with a pole along each side, used for carrying an injured or ill person: *They put him on a stretcher and lifted him into the ambulance.*

strict /strɪkt/ *adjective* (**stricter, strictest**)

1 very clear; that you must obey completely: *She gave them strict instructions not to get out of the car.* □ *The school's rules are very strict.*

▶ **strictly** *adverb The number of new members each year is strictly controlled.*

2 expecting rules to be obeyed and people to behave properly: *My parents were very strict.*
▶ **strictly** *adverb* *They brought their children up very strictly.*

stride /straɪd/ *verb* (**strides, striding, strode**)
to walk with long steps: *The farmer came striding across the field.* ● **stride** *noun* *He crossed the street with long, quick strides.*

strike¹ /straɪk/ *verb* (**strikes, striking, struck**)
1 to hit something (*formal*): *She took two steps forward and struck him across the face.* □ *His head struck the bottom when he dived into the pool.*
2 to have a quick and violent effect: *A storm struck the northeastern United States on Saturday.*
3 to come suddenly into your mind: *A thought struck her. Was she jealous of her mother?*
4 when a clock strikes, it makes a sound so that people know what the time is: *The clock struck nine.*
5 to stop working, usually in order to try to get more money: *Workers have the right to strike.*
strike a match to make a match produce a flame by moving it against something rough: *Duncan struck a match and lit the fire.*

strike² /straɪk/ *noun*
a period of time when workers stop working, usually in order to try to get more money: *Staff at the hospital went on strike yesterday.*

string /strɪŋ/ *noun*
1 very thin rope that is made of twisted threads: *He held out a small bag tied with string.*
2 a number of things on a piece of thread: *She wore a string of pearls around her neck.*
3 one of the thin pieces of wire that are stretched across a musical instrument that make sounds when the instrument is played: *Suddenly one of his guitar strings snapped.*

stringed instrument *noun*
any musical instrument that has strings

strip¹ /strɪp/ *noun*
1 a long, narrow piece of something: *The rugs are made from strips of fabric.*
2 a long narrow area of something: *He owns a narrow strip of land along the coast.*

strip² /strɪp/ *verb* (**strips, stripping, stripped**) (*also* **strip off**)
to take off your clothes: *They stripped and jumped into the pool.* □ *The children were stripping off and running into the sea.*

stripe /straɪp/ *noun*
a long line that is a different colour from the areas next to it: *She wore a blue skirt with white stripes.*

striped /straɪpt/ *adjective*
having stripes: *a striped tie*

strode /strəʊd/ → see **stride**

stroke¹ /strəʊk/ *verb* (**strokes, stroking, stroked**)
to move your hand slowly and gently over someone or something: *Carla was stroking her cat.*

stroke² /strəʊk/ *noun*
1 a movement or mark that you make with a pen or a brush: *She added a few brush strokes to the painting.*
2 a movement that you make with your arms when you are swimming or playing some sports: *I turned and swam a few strokes further out to sea.*
3 a serious illness where the blood does not flow through your brain properly: *He had a stroke last year, and now he can't walk.*

stroll /strəʊl/ *verb* (**strolls, strolling, strolled**)
to walk in a slow, relaxed way: *We love strolling along by the river.* ● **stroll** *noun* *After dinner, I took a stroll around the city.*

strong /strɒŋ/ *adjective* (**stronger** /ˈstrɒŋgə/, **strongest** /ˈstrɒŋgɪst/)
1 healthy, with good muscles: *I'm not strong enough to carry him.*
2 confident and determined: *You have to be strong and do what you believe is right.*
3 not breaking easily: *This strong plastic will not crack.*
▶ **strongly** *adverb* *The wall was very strongly built.*
4 that you will not change easily: *She has strong views on environmental issues.* □ *He has strong beliefs and ideas.*
▶ **strongly** *adverb* *Obviously you feel very strongly about this.*
5 containing a lot of a particular substance in order to be effective: *a cup of strong coffee* □ *The doctor gave me some strong painkillers.*

S

6 easily noticed: *Onions have a strong flavour.* □ *There was a strong smell of paint in the house.*
▶ **strongly** *adverb* *He smelled strongly of sweat.*

struck /strʌk/ → see **strike**

structure /'strʌktʃə/ *noun*
1 the way in which something is made, built or organized: *The typical family structure was two parents and two children.*
2 something that consists of parts that are connected together in an ordered way: *She had beautiful bone structure and great big eyes.* □ *This week's lesson is about the structure of the human brain.*
3 something that has been built: *This modern brick and glass structure was built in 1905.*

struggle¹ /'strʌgəl/ *verb* (**struggles, struggling, struggled**)
1 to try hard to do something that you find very difficult: *She struggled to find the right words.*
2 to try very hard to get away from someone who is holding you: *I struggled, but she was too strong for me.*

struggle² /'strʌgəl/ *noun*
1 something that is very difficult to do: *Losing weight was a terrible struggle.*
2 a long and difficult attempt to achieve something such as freedom: *The movie is about a young boy's struggle to survive.*

stubborn /'stʌbən/ *adjective*
determined to do what you want: *I am a very stubborn and determined person.*
▶ **stubbornly** *adverb* *He stubbornly refused to tell her the truth.*

stuck¹ /stʌk/ → see **stick**

stuck² /stʌk/ *adjective*
unable to move: *His car was stuck in the snow.*
be/get stuck
1 to want to get away from somewhere boring or from an unpleasant situation, but to be unable to do so: *I don't want to get stuck in another job like that.* □ *The airport's closed, so we're stuck in this hotel.*
2 to be unable to continue doing something because it is too difficult: *The teacher will help if you get stuck.*

student /'stjuːdənt/ *noun*
a person who is studying at a university or a college: *Warren's eldest son is an art student.*

studies /'stʌdiz/ *plural noun*
the activity of learning about a particular subject: *In 1924, he went to Paris where he continued his studies in painting, sculpture and drawing.*

studio /'stjuːdiəʊ/ *noun*
1 a room where someone paints, draws or takes photographs: *She was in her studio, painting on a large canvas.*
2 a room where people make radio or television programmes, record CDs, or make films: *a New York recording studio*

study¹ /'stʌdi/ *verb* (**studies, studying, studied**)
1 to spend time learning about a particular subject: *She spends most of her time studying.* □ *He studied History and Economics at university.*
2 to look at or consider something very carefully: *Debbie studied her friend's face.*

study² /'stʌdi/ *noun* (**studies**)
1 the activity of studying: *'What is the study of animals called?' — 'Zoology.'*
2 a room in a house that is used for reading, writing and studying: *We sat together in his study.*

stuff¹ /stʌf/ *uncountable noun*
things in general (*informal*): *He pointed to a bag. 'That's my stuff.'* □ *There is a huge amount of useful stuff on the Internet.*

stuff² /stʌf/ *verb* (**stuffs, stuffing, stuffed**)
1 to push something somewhere quickly and roughly: *I stuffed the money into my pocket.*
2 to put a mixture of one type of food inside another type of food: *Stuff the mushrooms with cheese and put them in the oven for 5 minutes.* □ *stuffed olives*

stuffy /'stʌfi/ *adjective* (**stuffier, stuffiest**)
warm; without enough fresh air: *It was hot and stuffy in the classroom.*

stumble /'stʌmbəl/ *verb* (**stumbles, stumbling, stumbled**)
to nearly fall down while you are walking or running: *He stumbled on the pavement and almost fell.*

stump /stʌmp/ *noun*   **tree stump**
a small part of
something that
remains when the
rest of it has been
removed or
broken off:
a tree stump

stun /stʌn/ *verb* (**stuns, stunning, stunned**)
1 to shock or surprise someone so much that they are unable to speak: *We were stunned by his sudden death.*
2 to make you unconscious for a short time: *The blow to his head stunned him.*

stung /stʌŋ/ → see **sting**

stunk /stʌŋk/ → see **stink**

stunning /'stʌnɪŋ/ *adjective*
extremely beautiful: *She was 55 and still a stunning woman.*

stunt /stʌnt/ *noun*
a dangerous piece of action in a film: *This movie has some amazing stunts.*

stupid /'stjuːpɪd/ *adjective* (**stupider, stupidest**)
not sensible: *I'll never do anything so stupid again.* □ *I made a stupid mistake.*
▶ **stupidly** *adverb* *I'm sorry. I behaved stupidly.*
▶ **stupidity** /stjuː'pɪdɪti/ *uncountable noun*
I was surprised by his stupidity.

sturdy /'stɜːdi/ *adjective* (**sturdier, sturdiest**)
strong; unlikely to be easily hurt or damaged: *She was a short, sturdy woman.*
□ *Bring a hat, sunscreen and wear sturdy shoes.*
▶ **sturdily** *adverb* *The table was strong and sturdily built.*

stutter /'stʌtə/ *verb* (**stutters, stuttering, stuttered**)
to have difficulty speaking because you find it hard to say the first sound of a word: *'I ... I'm sorry', he stuttered.* ● **stutter** *noun* *He spoke with a stutter.*

style /staɪl/ *noun*
1 the way in which something is done: *Children have different learning styles.* □ *I prefer the Indian style of cooking.*
2 the design of something: *These kids want everything in the latest style.*

stylish /'staɪlɪʃ/ *adjective*
attractive and fashionable: *She was an attractive, stylish woman.*

subject /'sʌbdʒɪkt/ *noun*
1 the thing that is being discussed in a conversation or a book: *I'd like to hear the president's own views on the subject.*
2 an area of knowledge that you study in school, university or college: *Maths is my favourite subject.*
3 in grammar, the noun that talks about the person or thing that is doing the action expressed by the verb. For example,

in 'My cat keeps catching birds', 'my cat' is the subject.
4 the person or thing that is shown in a piece of art: *Spring flowers are a perfect subject for painting.*

subjective /səb'dʒektɪv/ *adjective*
based on personal opinions and feelings rather than on facts: *Art is very subjective.*

submarine /ˌsʌbmə'riːn/ *noun*
a type of ship that can travel below the surface of the sea: *a nuclear submarine*

submit /səb'mɪt/ *verb* (**submits, submitting, submitted**)
to formally send something to someone, so that they can consider it: *They submitted their reports yesterday.*

subscription /səb'skrɪpʃən/ *noun*
an amount of money that you pay regularly in order to belong to an organization or to receive a service: *Members pay a subscription every year.*

subsidy /'sʌbsɪdi/ *noun* (**subsidies**)
money that a government pays in order to help an industry or a business: *farming subsidies*

substance /'sʌbstəns/ *noun*
a solid, a powder, a liquid or a gas: *The waste contained several unpleasant substances.*

substantial /səb'stænʃəl/ *adjective*
very large (*formal*): *A substantial number of people disagree with the new plan.*

substitute [1] /'sʌbstɪˌtjuːt/ *verb* (**substitutes, substituting, substituted**)
to make one person or thing take the place of another person or thing: *You can substitute wholewheat flour for white flour.*
□ *Goalkeeper Aidan Davison was substituted at half-time because of an injury.* ● **substitute** *noun* *Many teachers worry that pupils are using calculators as a substitute for thinking.* □ *Jefferson entered as a substitute for the injured player.*

subtle /'sʌtəl/ *adjective* (**subtler, subtlest**)
1 not immediately obvious: *Subtle changes take place in all living things.*
▶ **subtly** *adverb* *The truth is subtly different.*
2 pleasant and delicate in smell, taste, sound or colour: *Brown, grey or subtle shades of purple suit you best.*

subtract /səb'trækt/ *verb* (**subtracts, subtracting, subtracted**)
to take one number away from another number. For example, if you subtract

S

3 from 5, you get 2.

▶ **subtraction** /səb'trækʃən/ *uncountable noun* She's ready to learn subtraction.

suburb /'sʌbɜːb/ *noun*
one of the areas on the edge of a city where many people live: *Anna was born in a suburb of Philadelphia.* □ *His family lives in the suburbs.*

suburban /sə'bɜːbən/ *adjective*
in or relating to the suburbs: *They have a comfortable suburban home.*

subway /'sʌbweɪ/ *noun*
1 a path that goes under a road so that people can cross safely
2 *uncountable* (American)
→ see **the underground**

succeed /sək'siːd/ *verb* (**succeeds, succeeding, succeeded**)
to get the result that you wanted: *We have already succeeded in starting our own company.* □ *Do you think he will succeed?*

success /sək'ses/ *noun* (**successes**)
1 *uncountable* when you do well and get the result that you wanted: *Hard work is the key to success.* □ *We were surprised by the play's success.*
2 someone or something that does very well, or that is admired very much: *We hope the movie will be a success.*

successful /sək'sesful/ *adjective*
doing or getting what you wanted: *Kate's job application was successful.*
▶ **successfully** *adverb* The disease can be successfully treated with drugs.

such /sʌtʃ/ *adjective*
1 like this or like that: *How could you do such a thing?*
2 used for making an uncountable or plural noun stronger: *These roads are not designed for such heavy traffic.*
such a/such an used for making a noun stronger: *It was such a pleasant surprise.*
such as used for introducing an example: *Avoid fatty food such as butter and red meat.*

suck /sʌk/ *verb* (**sucks, sucking, sucked**)
1 to hold something in your mouth for a long time: *They sucked their sweets noisily.* □ *Many young children suck their thumbs.*
2 to pull liquid into your mouth through your lips: *The baby sucked the milk from his bottle.*

sudden /'sʌdən/ *adjective*
happening quickly and unexpectedly: *He was shocked by the sudden death of his father.* □ *It was all very sudden.*

▶ **suddenly** *adverb* Suddenly, she looked ten years older. □ *Her expression suddenly changed.*
all of a sudden quickly and unexpectedly: *All of a sudden she didn't look tired anymore.*

sue /suː/ *verb* (**sues, suing, sued**)
to start a legal case against someone, usually in order to get money from them because they have harmed you: *The couple are suing the company for $4.4 million.*

suffer /'sʌfə/ *verb* (**suffers, suffering, suffered**)
1 to feel pain, sadness or worry: *She was very sick, and suffering great pain.* □ *He has suffered terribly the last few days.*
2 to be affected by an illness: *He was suffering from cancer.*
▶ **sufferer** *noun* asthma sufferers

suffering /'sʌfərɪŋ/ *noun*
the pain, sadness or worry that someone feels: *They began to recover from their pain and suffering.*

sufficient /sə'fɪʃənt/ *adjective*
as much of something as you need or want: *The food we have is sufficient for 12 people.*
▶ **sufficiently** *adverb* She recovered sufficiently to go on holiday.

suffix /'sʌfɪks/ *noun* (**suffixes**)
a letter or a group of letters, for example '-ly' or '-ness', that is added to the end of a word in order to form a different word, often of a different word class. For example, the suffix '-ly' is added to 'quick' to form 'quickly'. Compare with **prefix**.

suffocate /'sʌfəˌkeɪt/ *verb* (**suffocates, suffocating, suffocated**)
to die because there is no air to breathe: *He either suffocated, or froze to death.*

suffragist /'sʌfrədʒɪst/ *noun*
a person who believes that all adults in a particular country should have the right to vote. Suffragists often fight for women to be allowed to vote.

sugar /'ʃʊgə/ *uncountable noun*
a sweet substance used for making food and drinks taste sweet: *Do you take sugar in your coffee?* □ *a bag of brown sugar*

suggest /sə'dʒest/ *verb* (**suggests, suggesting, suggested**)
to tell someone what you think they should do: *I suggest you ask him some questions about his past.* □ *I suggested we go for a walk in the park.*

suggestion /sə'dʒestʃən/ *noun*
something that you tell someone they should do: *Do you have any suggestions for improving the service we provide?* ◻ *May I make a suggestion?*

suicide /'suːɪsaɪd/ *noun*
the act of killing yourself: *She tried to commit suicide several times.* ◻ *It was obviously a case of attempted suicide.*

suit¹ /suːt/ *noun*
1 a jacket and trousers or a jacket and skirt that are both made from the same cloth: *a dark business suit*
2 a piece of clothing that you wear for a particular activity: *The divers wore special rubber suits.*

suit² /suːt/ *verb* (**suits, suiting, suited**)
1 to make you look attractive: *Green suits you.* ◻ *Isabel's soft woollen dress suited her very well.*
2 to be convenient for you: *With online shopping, you can do your shopping when it suits you.*

suitable /'suːtəbəl/ *adjective*
right for a particular purpose or occasion: *This film is suitable for young children.*
▶ **suitably** *adverb* *He was suitably dressed for the occasion.*

suitcase /'suːtkeɪs/ *noun*
a case for carrying your clothes when you are travelling: *It did not take Andrew long to pack a suitcase.*

sulk /sʌlk/ *verb* (**sulks, sulking, sulked**)
to be silent for a while because you are angry about something: *He turned his back and sulked.*
▶ **sulky** *adjective* *I was a sulky, 14-year-old teenager.*

sum /sʌm/ *noun*
1 an amount of money: *Large sums of money were lost.*
2 in mathematics, the number that you get when you add two or more numbers together: *Fourteen is the sum of eight and six.*

summarize /'sʌmə,raɪz/ *verb* (**summarizes, summarizing, summarized**)
to give the most important points about something: *Now summarize the article in three sentences.*

summary /'sʌməri/ *noun* (**summaries**)
a short description of something that gives the main points but not the details: *Here is a short summary of the news.*

summer /'sʌmə/ *noun*
the season between spring and autumn. In the summer the weather is usually warm or hot: *I went to France this summer.* ◻ *It was a perfect summer's day.*

summit /'sʌmɪt/ *noun*
1 a meeting between the leaders of two or more countries: *The topic will be discussed at next week's Washington summit.*
2 the top of a mountain: *He wanted to be the first man to reach the summit of Mount Everest.*

summon /'sʌmən/ *verb* (**summons, summoning, summoned**)
to order someone to come to you (*formal*): *The queen summoned her guards.* ◻ *Suddenly we were summoned to his office.*

sun /sʌn/ *noun*
1 the ball of fire in the sky that gives us heat and light: *The sun was now high in the sky.* ◻ *Suddenly, the sun came out.*
2 the heat and light that comes from the sun: *They went outside to sit in the sun.*

sunbathe /'sʌnbeɪθ/ *verb* (**sunbathes, sunbathing, sunbathed**)
to sit or lie in a place where the sun shines on you, so that your skin becomes browner: *Frank sunbathed at the pool every morning.*
▶ **sunbathing** *uncountable noun* *The beach is perfect for sunbathing.*

sunburn /'sʌnbɜːn/ *uncountable noun*
pink sore skin that you get when you have spent too much time in the sun: *Sunburn can damage your skin.*

sunburned /'sʌnbɜːnd/ also **sunburnt** *adjective*
having pink, sore skin because you have

S

spent too much time in the sun: *A badly sunburned face is extremely painful.*

sundae /'sʌndeɪ/ *noun*
a tall glass of ice cream (= a frozen sweet food) with cream and nuts or fruit on top: *We had ice cream sundaes for dessert.*

Sunday /'sʌndeɪ, -di/ *noun*
the day after Saturday and before Monday: *We went for a walk on Sunday.*

sunflower /'sʌnflaʊə/ *noun*
a very tall plant with large yellow flowers

sung /sʌŋ/ → see **sing**

sunglasses /'sʌnglɑːsɪz/ *plural noun*
dark glasses that you wear to protect your eyes from bright light: *She put on a pair of sunglasses.*

sunk /sʌŋk/ → see **sink**

sunlight /'sʌnlaɪt/ *uncountable noun*
the light that comes from the sun: *Sunlight filled the room.*

sunny /'sʌni/ *adjective* (**sunnier, sunniest**)
1 with the sun shining brightly: *The weather was warm and sunny.*
2 being brightly lit by the sun: *a sunny window seat*

sunrise /'sʌnraɪz/ *uncountable noun*
the time in the morning when the sun first appears in the sky: *The rain began before sunrise.*

sunscreen /'sʌnskriːn/ *uncountable noun*
a cream that protects your skin from the sun: *Use a sunscreen when you go outside and remember to wear a hat.*

sunset /'sʌnset/ *uncountable noun*
the time in the evening when the sun goes down: *The party began at sunset.*

sunshine /'sʌnʃaɪn/ *uncountable noun*
the light and heat that comes from the sun: *She was sitting outside a cafe in bright sunshine.*

suntan /'sʌntæn/ *noun*
when your skin becomes darker because you have been outside in the sun: *They want to go to the Bahamas and get a suntan.*

super /'suːpə/ *adjective, adverb*
1 very good: *That was a super concert.*
2 having a lot of a particular quality: *Beverly Hills, home of the rich and the super rich*

superb /suː'pɜːb/ *adjective*
very good: *There is a superb golf course 6 miles away.*

▶ **superbly** *adverb The orchestra played superbly.*

superior¹ /suː'pɪərɪə/ *adjective*
better than other similar people or things: *We want to create superior products for our customers.* □ *superior quality coffee*

▶ **superiority** /suː,pɪərɪ'brɪtɪ/ *uncountable noun Belonging to a powerful organization gives them a feeling of superiority.*

superior² /suː'pɪərɪə/ *noun*
a person who has a higher position than you at work: *They do not have much communication with their superiors.*

superlative /suː'pɜːlətɪv/ *adjective*
in grammar, the form of an adjective or an adverb that shows that something has more of a quality than anything else in a group. For example, 'biggest' is the superlative form of 'big'. Compare with **comparative**. ● **superlative** *noun His writing contains many superlatives.*

supermarket /'suːpəmɑːkɪt/ *noun*
a large shop that sells all kinds of food and other products for the home: *We mostly do our food shopping in the supermarket.*

superstition /,suːpə'stɪʃən/ *noun*
a belief that things such as good and bad luck exist, even though they cannot be explained: *Many people have superstitions about numbers.*

superstitious /,suːpə'stɪʃəs/ *adjective*
believing in things that cannot be explained: *Jean was superstitious and believed that the colour green brought bad luck.*

supervise /'suːpə,vaɪz/ *verb* (**supervises, supervising, supervised**)
to make sure that an activity is done correctly: *She cooks the supper, supervises the children's homework, and puts them to bed.*

▶ **supervision** /,suːpə'vɪʒən/ *uncountable noun Young children need close supervision.*

▶ **supervisor** *noun He got a job as a supervisor at a factory.*

supper /'sʌpə/ *noun*
a meal that people eat in the evening: *Would you like to join us for supper?*

supplement /'sʌplɪmənt/ *verb* (**supplements, supplementing, supplemented**)
to add one thing to another thing in order to improve it: *Some people do extra jobs to supplement their incomes.* ● **supplement**

noun *These classes are a supplement to school study.*

supplier /sə'plaɪə/ *noun*
a company that sells something such as goods or equipment to customers: *We are one of the country's biggest food suppliers.*

supplies /sə'plaɪz/ *plural noun*
food, equipment and other important things that are provided for people: *What happens when there are no more food supplies?*

supply /sə'plaɪ/ *verb* (**supplies, supplying, supplied**)
to give someone an amount of something: *The pipeline will supply Greece with Russian natural gas.* ● **supply uncountable noun** *The brain needs a constant supply of oxygen.*

support¹ /sə'pɔːt/ *verb* (**supports, supporting, supported**)
1 to agree with someone or their ideas, and perhaps help them because you want them to succeed: *We haven't found any evidence to support that idea.*
▶ **supporter noun** *the president's supporters*
2 to provide someone with money or the things that they need: *I have three children to support.*
3 to be under an object and holding it up: *Thick wooden posts supported the roof.*

support² /sə'pɔːt/ *noun*
1 *uncountable* actions that help someone: *She gave me a lot of support when my husband died.*
2 *uncountable* actions or words that show that you agree with someone: *The president gave his full support to the reforms.*
3 a bar or another object that supports something: *Each piece of metal was on wooden supports.*

supportive /sə'pɔːtɪv/ *adjective*
kind and helpful to someone at a difficult or unhappy time in their life: *They were always supportive of each other.*

suppose /sə'pəʊz/ *verb* (**supposes, supposing, supposed**)
1 used before talking about a situation that could happen: *Suppose someone gave you a cheque for £6 million. What would you do with it?*
2 to imagine that something is probably true: *I suppose you'll be going back to New York.*
be supposed to do something used when someone expects you to do

something, especially when this does not happen: *She was supposed to be home at six.*
I suppose used for showing that you are slightly uncertain about something: *I suppose you're right.* □ *'Is that the right way?' — 'Yeah. I suppose so.'*

sure /ʃʊə/ *adjective* (**surer, surest**)
1 certain: *He was not sure that he wanted to be a teacher.* □ *I'm not sure where he lives.*
2 used as an informal way of saying 'yes' or 'all right': *'Can you show me where she lives?' — 'Sure.'*
for sure definitely true: *One thing's for sure, women still love Barry Manilow.*
make sure to check that something is the way that you want it to be: *He looked in the bathroom to make sure that he was alone.*

surely /'ʃʊəli/ *adverb*
used for showing that you think something should be true: *You surely haven't forgotten Dr Walters?*

surf¹ /sɜːf/ *uncountable noun*
the mass of white bubbles on the top of waves in the sea: *We watched the surf rolling onto the white sandy beach.*

surf² /sɜːf/ *verb* (**surfs, surfing, surfed**)
to ride on big waves in the sea on a special board: *I'm going to buy a board and learn to surf.*
▶ **surfer noun** *This small fishing village continues to attract surfers.*
▶ **surfing uncountable noun** *My favourite sport is surfing.*
surf the Internet to spend time looking at different websites on the Internet: *No one knows how many people surf the Net.*

surface /'sɜːfɪs/ *noun*
the flat top part or the outside of something: *There were pen marks on the table's surface.* □ *Small waves moved on the surface of the water.*

surfboard /'sɜːfbɔːd/ *noun*
a long narrow board that people use for surfing (= riding on waves in the sea).

surge /sɜːdʒ/ *verb* (**surges, surging, surged**)
to move forward suddenly: *The crowd surged forward into the shop.* ● **surge noun** *a surge in prices*

surgeon /'sɜːdʒən/ *noun*
a doctor who is specially trained to perform operations: *a heart surgeon*

S

surgery /'sɜːdʒəri/ *uncountable noun*
a process in which a doctor cuts open a patient's body in order to repair, remove or replace a diseased or damaged part: *His father just had heart surgery.*

surgical /'sɜːdʒɪkəl/ *adjective*
relating to the process in which a doctor cuts open a patient's body to repair, remove or replace a diseased or damaged part: *a collection of surgical instruments*

surname /'sɜːneɪm/ *noun*
the name that you share with other members of your family: *'And what's your surname, please?' — 'Mitchell.'*

surplus /'sɜːpləs/ *noun* (**surpluses**)
more than you need of a particular thing: *The world has a surplus of food, but still people are hungry.* ● **surplus** *adjective* *Few people have large sums of surplus cash.*

surprise /sə'praɪz/ *noun*
1 an unexpected event, fact or piece of news: *I have a surprise for you: we are moving to Switzerland!* ● **surprise** *adjective Baxter arrived this afternoon, on a surprise visit.*
2 *uncountable* the feeling that you have when something that you do not expect happens: *The prime minister has expressed surprise at his comments.* ● **surprise** *verb* (**surprises, surprising, surprised**) *We'll do the job ourselves and surprise everyone.* □ *It surprised me that he should make such a stupid mistake.*

surprised /sə'praɪzd/ *adjective*
having a feeling of surprise when something happens, because you did not expect it to happen: *I was surprised at how easy it was.*

surprising /sə'praɪzɪŋ/ *adjective*
not expected and making you feel surprised: *It is not surprising that children learn to read at different rates.*
▶ **surprisingly** *adverb The party was surprisingly good.*

surrender /sə'rendə/ *verb* (**surrenders, surrendering, surrendered**)
to stop fighting because you cannot win: *The army finally surrendered.*

surround /sə'raʊnd/ *verb* (**surrounds, surrounding, surrounded**)
to be or go all around something: *Bodyguards surrounded the president.*
□ *The cottage was surrounded by a low wall.*

surround

The cottage was surrounded by a low wall.

surroundings /sə'raʊndɪŋz/ *plural noun*
everything around you or the place where you live: *He soon felt at home in his new surroundings.*

survey /'sɜːveɪ/ *noun*
the process of finding out information about a lot of different people, in a formal way, by asking them questions: *They conducted a survey to see how students study.*

survival /sə'vaɪvəl/ *uncountable noun*
when someone or something still exists after a difficult or dangerous time: *Many of these companies are now struggling for survival.*

survive /sə'vaɪv/ *verb* (**survives, surviving, survived**)
to still exist after a difficult or dangerous time: *It's a miracle that anyone survived.*
□ *He survived heart surgery.*
▶ **survivor** *noun There were no survivors of the plane crash.*

suspect /sə'spekt/ *verb* (**suspects, suspecting, suspected**)
1 to think that something is true although you are not certain about it: *He suspected that she was telling lies.*
2 to believe that someone probably did something wrong: *The police did not suspect him of anything.* ● **suspect** *noun* /'sʌspekt/ *Police have arrested a suspect.*

suspend /sə'spend/ *verb* (**suspends, suspending, suspended**)
1 to delay something or stop it from happening for a period of time: *The company will suspend production at the end of June.*
2 to be hanging from a high place: *Three television screens were suspended from the ceiling.*

suspense /sə'spens/ *uncountable noun*
a state of excitement about something that is going to happen very soon: *The suspense ended when the judges gave their decision.*

S

suspicion /sə'spɪʃən/ *noun*
a belief or a feeling that someone has done something wrong: *Don't do anything that might cause suspicion.*

suspicious /sə'spɪʃəs/ *adjective*
1 not trusting someone or something: *He was suspicious of me at first.*
▸ **suspiciously** *adjective* *'What is it you want me to do?' Adams asked suspiciously.*
2 making you feel that something is wrong: *Please contact the police if you see any suspicious person in the area.*
▸ **suspiciously** *adverb* *Has anyone been acting suspiciously over the last few days?*

sustain /sə'steɪn/ *verb* (**sustains, sustaining, sustained**)
1 to continue something for a period of time: *He has difficulty sustaining relationships.*
2 to have something bad happen to you (*formal*): *The aircraft sustained some damage.*

sustainable /sə'steɪnəbəl/ *adjective*
using natural products in a way that does not damage the environment: *The government introduced its program of sustainable development in 2006.*
▸ **sustainability** /sə,steɪnə'bɪlɪti/ *uncountable noun* *environmental sustainability*

swallow [1] /'swɒləʊ/ *verb* (**swallows, swallowing, swallowed**)
to make something go from your mouth down into your stomach: *Polly took a bite of the apple and swallowed it.*

swallow [2] /'swɒləʊ/ *noun*
a type of small bird with pointed wings and a split tail

swam /swæm/ → see **swim**

swan /swɒn/ *noun*
a large white bird with a very long neck, that lives on rivers and lakes

swap /swɒp/ *verb* (**swaps, swapping, swapped**)
1 to give something to someone and to receive a different thing back from them: *We swapped phone numbers.*
2 to remove one thing and replace it with another thing: *He swapped his jeans and t-shirt for a suit and tie.*

sway /sweɪ/ *verb* (**sways, swaying, swayed**)
to move slowly from one side to the other: *The people swayed from side to side, singing.*
□ *The tall grass was swaying in the wind.*

swear /sweə/ *verb* (**swears, swearing, swore, sworn**)
1 to use language that is considered to be offensive: *It's wrong to swear and shout.*
2 to promise in a serious way that you will do something: *I swear to do everything I can to help you.*

sweat /swet/ *verb* (**sweats, sweating, sweated**)
to produce liquid from your skin when you are hot, ill or afraid: *It's really hot. I'm sweating.* ● **sweat** *uncountable noun* *Both horse and rider were dripping with sweat.*

sweater /'swetə/ *noun*
a warm piece of clothing that covers the upper part of your body and your arms

sweatshirt /'swetʃɜːt/ *noun*
a loose, warm piece of clothing, made of thick cotton, that covers the upper part of your body

sweaty /'sweti/ *adjective* (**sweatier, sweatiest**)
covered with sweat: *hot, sweaty hands*
□ *sweaty socks*

sweep /swiːp/ *verb* (**sweeps, sweeping, swept**)
1 to push dirt off an area using a brush with a long handle: *The owner of the shop was sweeping his floor.* □ *She was in the kitchen sweeping food off the floor.*
2 to push objects off something with a quick smooth movement of your arm: *She swept the cards from the table.*

sweet [1] /swiːt/ *adjective* (**sweeter, sweetest**)
1 containing a lot of sugar: *a cup of sweet tea* □ *If the sauce is too sweet, add some salt.*
2 having a pleasant smell: *I recognized the sweet smell of her perfume.*
3 having a pleasant, smooth and gentle sound: *The young girl's voice was soft and sweet.*
4 kind and gentle toward other people: *He was a sweet man.*
▸ **sweetly** *adverb* *I just smiled sweetly and said no.*
5 attractive in a simple way (*informal*): *a sweet little baby*

sweet [2] /swiːt/ *noun*
a food such as a chocolate that contains a lot of sugar: *Eat more fruit and vegetables and fewer sweets.*

S

sweetcorn /'swi:tkɔ:n/ *uncountable noun*
a long round vegetable covered in small yellow seeds. The seeds are also called sweetcorn.

swell /swel/ *verb* (**swells, swelling, swelled, swollen**) (*also* **swell up**)
to become larger and thicker than normal: *Do your legs swell at night?* □ *His eye swelled up.*

swept /swept/ → see **sweep**

swerve /swɜ:v/ *verb* (**swerves, swerving, swerved**)
to suddenly change direction: *Her car swerved off the road.*

swift /swift/ *adjective* (**swifter, swiftest**)
1 happening very quickly or without delay: *We need to make a swift decision.*
▶ **swiftly** *adverb* *We have to act as swiftly as we can.*
2 moving very quickly: *With a swift movement, Matthew sat up.*
▶ **swiftly** *adverb* *Lenny moved swiftly and silently across the grass.*

swim /swim/ *verb* (**swims, swimming, swam, swum**)
to move through water by making movements with your arms and legs: *She learned to swim when she was 10.* □ *I swim a mile a day.* ● **swim** *noun* *When can we go for a swim?*
▶ **swimmer** *noun* *I'm a good swimmer.*

swimming /'swimɪŋ/ *uncountable noun*
the activity of swimming, especially as a sport or for pleasure: *Swimming is a great form of exercise.*
→ Look at picture on P6

'swimming ,costume *noun*
a piece of clothing that is worn for swimming, especially by women and girls: *Don't forget to pack a swimming costume and a towel.*

'swimming pool *noun*
a large hole filled with water that people can swim in

'swimming trunks *noun*
a piece of clothing that is worn for swimming by men and boys: *The boys changed into their swimming trunks.*

swimsuit /'swimsu:t/ *noun*
→ see **swimming costume**

swing¹ /swiŋ/ *verb* (**swings, swinging, swung**)
to move repeatedly backwards and forwards or from side to side through the air: *Amber walked beside him, her arms swinging.*

swing² /swiŋ/ *noun*
a seat, hanging by two ropes, that you can sit on and move forwards and backwards through the air: *I took the kids to the park to play on the swings.*

switch¹ /swɪtʃ/ *noun* (**switches**)
a small control for turning electricity on or off: *She shut the dishwasher and pressed the switch.*

switch² /swɪtʃ/ *verb* (**switches, switching, switched**)
1 to change to something different: *Companies are switching to cleaner fuels.*
□ *A friend encouraged Chris to switch jobs.*
2 to replace one thing with another thing: *They switched the keys, so Karen had the key to my room and I had the key to hers.*

switch something off to stop electrical equipment from working by operating a switch: *She switched off the coffee machine.*

switch something on to make electrical equipment start working by operating a switch: *He switched on the lamp.*

swollen¹ /'swəʊlən/ *adjective*
larger and thicker than normal: *My eyes were swollen and I could hardly see.*

swollen² /'swəʊlən/ → see **swell**

sword /sɔ:d/ *noun*
a weapon with a handle and a long sharp blade

swore /swɔ:/ → see **swear**

sworn /swɔ:n/ → see **swear**

swum /swʌm/ → see **swim**

swung /swʌŋ/ → see **swing**

syllable /'sɪləbəl/ *noun*
a part of a word that contains a single vowel sound and that is pronounced as a unit. So, for example, 'book' has one syllable, and 'reading' has two syllables.

syllabus /'sɪləbəs/ *noun* (**syllabuses**)
a list of the subjects to be covered in a school, university or college course: *The course syllabus consists mainly of novels by American writers.*

symbol /'sɪmbəl/ *noun*
a number, a letter or a shape that represents a particular thing: *The chemical symbol for hydrogen is 'H'.*

symmetrical symmetrical
/sɪ'metrɪkəl/
adjective
having two
halves that are
exactly the same:
*The rows of windows
were perfectly symmetrical.*

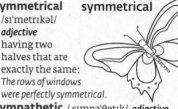

sympathetic /ˌsɪmpə'θetɪk/ *adjective*
kind and able to understand other
people's feelings: *Try talking about your
problem with a sympathetic teacher.*
▶ **sympathetically** /ˌsɪmpə'θetɪkli/
adverb *She nodded sympathetically.*

sympathize /'sɪmpəˌθaɪz/ *verb*
(**sympathizes, sympathizing, sympathized**)
to show that you are sorry for someone
who is in a bad situation: *It's terrible when
a parent dies. I sympathize with you.*

sympathy /'sɪmpəθi/ *uncountable noun*
the feeling of being sorry for someone
who is in a bad situation, or the act of
showing them that you feel sorry for
them: *I get no sympathy from my family when
I'm sick.* □ *I have great sympathy for these
refugees.*

symphony /'sɪmfəni/ *noun* (**symphonies**)
a piece of music that has been written to
be played by an orchestra: *Beethoven's Ninth
Symphony*

symphony orchestra *noun*
a large orchestra that plays classical
music: *the London Symphony Orchestra*

symptom /'sɪmptəm/ *noun*
something that is wrong with you that

is a sign of a particular illness: *All these
patients have flu symptoms.*

synagogue /'sɪnəgɒg/ *noun*
a building where Jewish people go to pray

syndrome /'sɪndrəʊm/ *noun*
a medical condition: *No one knows what
causes Sudden Infant Death Syndrome.*

synonym /'sɪnənɪm/ *noun*
a word or an expression that means the
same as another word or expression:
'Afraid' is a synonym for 'frightened'.

synthetic /sɪn'θetɪk/ *adjective*
made from chemicals or artificial
substances rather than from natural
ones: *synthetic rubber*

syringe /sɪ'rɪndʒ/ *noun*
a small tube with a thin hollow needle at
the end that is used for putting medicine
into a part of the body or for taking blood
from your body

syrup /'sɪrəp/ *noun*
a sweet liquid made by cooking sugar
with water: *tinned fruit with syrup*

system /'sɪstəm/ *noun*
1 a way of working, organizing or doing
something that follows a plan: *You need a
better system for organizing your DVDs.*
2 a set of equipment, parts or
instruments: *There's something wrong with
the computer system.* □ *a heating system*
3 a network of things that are linked
together so that people or things can
communicate with each other or
travel from one place to another:
Australia's road and rail system

S

Tt

table /'teɪbəl/ *noun*

1 a piece of furniture with a flat top that you put things on or sit at: *Mum was sitting at the kitchen table.*

2 a set of facts or numbers that you arrange in neat rows: *See the table on page 104.*

tablecloth /'teɪbəlklɒθ/ *noun*

a cloth that you use to cover a table

tablespoon /'teɪbəlspuːn/ *noun*

a large spoon that you use when you are cooking

tablet /'tæblət/ *noun*

1 a small solid piece of medicine that you swallow: *The doctor gave me a sleeping tablet to help me sleep.*

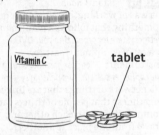

Vitamin C — **tablet**

2 a small, flat computer that you use by touching the screen

'table ˌtennis *uncountable noun*

a game in which one or two players on either side of a table hit a small light ball across a low net across the table

tabloid /'tæblɔɪd/ *noun*

a newspaper that has small pages, short news stories, and a lot of photographs

tackle /'tækəl/ *verb* (**tackles, tackling, tackled**)

1 to deal with a problem: *We discussed the best way to tackle the situation.*

2 to try to take the ball away from someone in a sports game: *Foley tackled the defender.* ●**tackle** *noun A great tackle from Beckham saved the game.*

tactful /'tæktfʊl/ *adjective*

very careful not to do or say anything that will upset or embarrass other people: *Dan obviously heard our argument but he was too tactful to mention it.*

▸**tactfully** *adverb Tactfully, Jessica changed the subject.*

tactic /'tæktɪk/ *noun*

the way that you choose to do something when you are trying to succeed in a particular situation: *Things weren't going well, so I decided to change my tactics.*

tadpole /'tædpəʊl/ *noun*

a small water animal that looks like a black fish, and that develops into a frog or a toad (= a small green or brown animal with long back legs)

tag /tæg/ *noun*

a small piece of cardboard or cloth that is attached to something. It has information written on it: *The staff all wear name tags.* □ *There's no price tag on this purse.*

tail /teɪl/ *noun*

1 the long thin part at the end of an animal's body: *The dog wagged its tail.*

2 the end or the back of something: *The plane's tail hit the runway while it was landing.*

tailor /'teɪlə/ *noun*

a person whose job is to make and repair clothes

take /teɪk/ *verb* (**takes, taking, took, taken**)

1 to hold or remove something: *Let me take your coat.* □ *He took a pen from his pocket.*

2 to carry something with you: *Don't forget to take a map with you.*

3 to transport someone somewhere: *Michael took me to the airport.*

4 to steal something: *They took my wallet.*

5 to need an amount of time: *The sauce takes 25 minutes to prepare.*

6 to accept something that someone offers you: *Sylvia has taken a job in Tokyo teaching English.* □ *I think you should take my advice.*

7 to choose to travel along a road: *Take a right at the traffic lights.*

8 to use a vehicle to go from one place to another: *She took the train to New York.*

9 used for saying that someone does something: *She was too tired to take a bath.* ◻ *Betty took a photograph of us.*

10 to study a subject at school: *Students can take European history and American history.*

11 to do an examination: *She took her driving test yesterday and passed.*

12 to swallow medicine: *I try not to take pills of any kind.*

take after someone to look or behave like an older member of your family: *Your mum was a clever, brave woman. You take after her.*

take off used for saying that an aeroplane leaves the ground and starts flying: *We took off at 11 o'clock.*

take someone out to take someone somewhere enjoyable: *Sophia took me out to lunch today.*

take something away to remove something: *The waitress took away the dirty dishes.*

take something back to return something: *If you don't like it, I'll take it back to the shop.*

take something off to remove clothes: *Come in and take off your coat.*

take something over to get control of something: *I'm going to take over this company one day.*

take something up to start doing an activity: *Peter took up tennis at the age of eight.*

take time off to not go to work for a time: *My husband was ill and I had to take time off work to look after him.*

take up something to use an amount of time or space: *I don't want to take up too much of your time.* ◻ *The round wooden table takes up most of the kitchen.*

> **LANGUAGE HELP**
> See note at **bring**.

takeaway /'teɪkəˌweɪ/ (American: **takeout**) *noun*

1 hot cooked food that you buy from a shop or a restaurant and eat somewhere else: *a Chinese takeaway* ● **takeaway** *adjective a takeaway pizza*

2 a shop or a restaurant which sells hot cooked food that you eat somewhere else

taken /'teɪkən/ → see **take**

takeoff /'teɪkɒf/ also **take-off** *noun*
the time when an aircraft leaves the ground and starts to fly: *What time is takeoff?*

takeout /'teɪkaʊt/ *uncountable noun* (American)
→ see **takeaway**

tale /teɪl/ *noun*
a story: *It's a tale about the friendship between two boys.*

talent /'tælənt/ *noun*
your natural ability to do something well: *Both her children have a talent for music.* ◻ *He's got lots of talent, but he's rather lazy.*

talented /'tæləntɪd/ *adjective*
having a natural ability to do something well: *Howard is a talented pianist.*

talk¹ /tɔːk/ *verb* (**talks, talking, talked**)
to say words, or speak to someone about your thoughts, ideas or feelings: *After the fight, Mark was too upset to talk.* ◻ *Tom didn't talk until he was three years old.* ◻ *They were all talking about the film.* ◻ *I talked to him yesterday.*

> **LANGUAGE HELP**
> **Talk** or **speak**? When you **speak**, you say things: *Did someone speak?* **Talk** is used for describing a conversation or discussion: *I talked about it with my family at dinner.*

talk² /tɔːk/ *noun*

1 when two or more people talk together: *I had a long talk with my father.*

2 when someone speaks to a group of people: *She gave a brief talk on the history of the building.*

3 *plural* formal discussions between different groups, to try to reach an agreement: *peace talks*

tall /tɔːl/ *adjective* (**taller, tallest**)

1 higher than other people or things: *John is very tall.* ◻ *The lighthouse is a tall square tower.*

2 used when you are asking or talking about the height of someone or something: *'How tall are you?' — 'I'm six foot five.'*

tambourine /ˌtæmbə'riːn/ *noun*
a round musical instrument that you shake or hit with your hand

tame /teɪm/ *adjective* (**tamer, tamest**)
used for describing an animal that is not afraid of humans

tan¹ /tæn/ *noun*
when your skin has become darker

t

because you have spent time in the sun:
She is tall and blonde, with a tan.

tan² /tæn/ *verb* (**tans, tanning, tanned**)
to become darker because you have spent
time in the sun: *I have very pale skin that
never tans.*

▸ **tanned** *adjective* *Becky's skin was deeply
tanned.*

tangle /'tæŋgəl/ *noun*
a mass of something that has become
twisted together in a messy way: *A tangle
of wires connected the two computers.*

● **tangle** *verb* (**tangles, tangling, tangled**)
Her hair is curly and tangles easily.

tank /tæŋk/ *noun*
1 a large container for holding liquid or
gas: *a fuel tank*
2 a heavy, strong military vehicle, with
large guns. It moves on metal tracks that
are fixed over the wheels.

tanker /'tæŋkə/ *noun*
a large ship or lorry that carries large
amounts of gas or liquid: *an oil tanker*

tantrum /'tæntrəm/ *noun*
an occasion when a child gets very angry
and upset and cannot control themselves:
Isabel had a tantrum in the cafe.

tap¹ /tæp/ *verb* (**taps, tapping, tapped**)
to hit or touch something quickly and
lightly: *He tapped the table nervously with his
fingers.* □ *Karen tapped on the bedroom door
and went in.*

tap² /tæp/ *noun*
1 (*American*: **faucet**) an object that controls
the flow of a liquid or a gas from a pipe:
*When people turn the tap on, they have good,
drinkable water.*
→ Look at picture on P4
2 when someone hits or touches
something quickly and lightly: *There was
a tap on the door.*

tape¹ /teɪp/ *noun*
1 *uncountable* a sticky strip of plastic used
for sticking things together: *Attach the
picture to the cardboard using sticky tape.*
2 a long narrow plastic strip that you use
to record music, sounds or moving
pictures

tape² /teɪp/ *verb* (**tapes, taping, taped**)
1 to record music, sounds or moving
pictures on a tape: *Ms Pringle secretly taped
her conversation with her boss.*

2 to stick two things together using tape:
I taped the envelope shut.

'tape re,corder also **tape-recorder** *noun*
a machine that you use for recording and
playing sound or music

tar /tɑː/ *uncountable noun*
a thick, black, sticky substance that is
used for making roads: *It was so hot that the
tar melted on the roads.*

target /'tɑːgɪt/ *noun*
1 something that you try to hit with a
weapon or other object: *One of the missiles
missed its target.*
2 the result that you are trying to
achieve: *We failed to meet our sales targets last
year.*

tarmac /'tɑːmæk/ *uncountable noun*
a black substance used for making road
surfaces (*trademark*)

tart /tɑːt/ *noun*
a case made of flour, fat and water
(= pastry) that you fill with fruit or
vegetables and cook in an oven: *We had
apple tarts, served with fresh cream.*

task /tɑːsk/ *noun*
a piece of work that you have to do: *I had
the task of cleaning the kitchen.*

taskbar /'tɑːskbɑː/ also **task bar** *noun*
a narrow strip at the bottom of a
computer screen that shows you which
windows are open

taste¹ /teɪst/ *noun*
1 *uncountable* your ability to recognize the
flavour of things with your tongue: *Over
the years my sense of taste has disappeared.*
2 the particular quality that something
has when you put it in your mouth, for
example whether it is sweet or salty: *I like
the taste of chocolate.* □ *This medicine has a
nasty taste.*
3 *uncountable* someone's choice in all the
things that they like or buy: *Will's got great
taste in clothes.*
4 a small amount of food or drink that
you try in order to see what the flavour is
like: *Have a taste of this pie.*

taste² /teɪst/ *verb* (**tastes, tasting,
tasted**)
1 to have a particular flavour: *The water
tasted of metal.* □ *The pizza tastes delicious.*
2 to eat or drink a small amount of food
or drink in order to see what the flavour is

like: *Don't add salt until you've tasted the food.*
3 to be aware of the flavour of something that you are eating or drinking: *Can you taste the onions in this dish?*

tasteful /'teɪstfʊl/ *adjective*
attractive, having a good design and being of good quality: *Sarah was wearing a purple suit and tasteful jewellery.*
▸ **tastefully** *adverb* *They live in a large and tastefully decorated home.*

tasteless /'teɪstləs/ *adjective*
1 unattractive, badly designed and of poor quality: *Jim's house is full of tasteless furniture.*
2 that upsets people: *That was a very tasteless remark.*
3 having no flavour: *The fish was tasteless.*

tasty /'teɪsti/ *adjective* (**tastier, tastiest**)
having a pleasant flavour and being good to eat: *The food here is tasty and good value.*

tattoo /tæ'tuː/ *noun*
a design on a person's skin made with a needle and coloured ink: *He has a tattoo on his arm.* ●**tattoo** *verb* (**tattoos, tattooing, tattooed**) *She has had three small stars tattooed on one of her shoulders.*

taught /tɔːt/ → see **teach**

tax¹ /tæks/ *noun* (**taxes**)
an amount of money that you have to pay to the government so that it can pay for public services such as roads and schools: *No one enjoys paying tax.* □ *The government has promised not to raise taxes this year.*

tax² /tæks/ *verb* (**taxes, taxing, taxed**)
to make a person or a company pay a part of their income to the government: *We are the most heavily taxed people in Europe.*

taxation /tæk'seɪʃən/ *uncountable noun*
when a government takes money from people and spends it on things such as education, health and defence: *The council wants major changes in taxation.*

taxi /'tæksi/ *noun*
a car that you can hire, with its driver, to take you where you want to go: *We took a taxi back to our hotel.*

'taxi rank *noun*
a place where taxis wait for passengers, for example at an airport

taxpayer /'tækspeɪə/ *noun*
a person who pays tax: *The government has wasted taxpayers' money.*

tea /tiː/ *uncountable noun*
1 a drink that you make by pouring boiling water on the dry leaves of a plant called the tea bush: *I made myself a cup of tea and sat down to watch TV.* □ *Would you like some tea?*
→ Look at picture on P3
2 the chopped dried leaves of the plant that tea is made from
3 a meal that some people eat in the late afternoon or the early evening

teach /tiːtʃ/ *verb* (**teaches, teaching, taught**)
1 to give someone instructions so they know about something or know how to do it: *She taught me to read.* □ *George taught him how to ride a horse.*
2 to give lessons in a subject at a school or a college: *Christine teaches biology at Piper High.* □ *Mrs Green has been teaching part-time for 16 years.*
▸ **teacher** *noun* *I was a teacher for 21 years.*
→ Look at picture on P7
▸ **teaching** *uncountable noun* *The quality of teaching in the school is excellent.*

team /tiːm/ *noun*
1 a group of people who play a particular sport or game against other groups of people: *Kate was in the school hockey team.*
2 any group of people who work together: *A team of doctors visited the hospital yesterday.*

teamwork /'tiːmwɜːk/ *uncountable noun*
the ability that a group of people have to work well together: *She knows the importance of teamwork.*

teapot /'tiːpɒt/ *noun*
a container that is used for making and serving tea
→ Look at picture on P4

tear¹ /tɪə/ *noun*
a drop of the liquid that comes out of your eye when you are crying: *Her eyes filled with tears.*
burst into tears to suddenly start crying: *She burst into tears and ran from the kitchen.*
in tears crying: *By the end of the film, we were all in tears.*

tear² /teə/ *verb* (**tears, tearing, tore, torn**)
to pull something into pieces or make a hole in it: *I tore my coat on a nail.* □ *She tore the letter into several pieces.* ●**tear** *noun* *I looked through a tear in the curtains.*
tear something up to tear something

t

such as a piece of paper into small pieces: *He tore up the letter and threw it in the fire.*

tease /ti:z/ *verb* (**teases, teasing, teased**)
to laugh at someone or make jokes about them in order to embarrass or annoy them: *Amber's brothers are always teasing her.*

teaspoon /'ti:spu:n/ *noun*
a small spoon that you use for putting sugar into tea or coffee: *Use a teaspoon to remove the seeds from the fruit.*

technical /'teknɪkəl/ *adjective*
involving machines, processes and materials that are used in science and industry: *We still have to solve a number of technical problems.*
▶ **technically** /'teknɪkli/ *adverb* *It is a very technically advanced car.*

technician /tek'nɪʃən/ *noun*
someone who works with scientific or medical equipment or machines: *Joseph works as a laboratory technician at St Thomas's Hospital.*

technique /tek'ni:k/ *noun*
a special way of doing something practical: *Doctors have recently developed these new techniques.*

technology /tek'nɒlədʒi/ *noun*
(**technologies**)
the way that scientific knowledge is used in a practical way: *Computer technology has developed fast during the last 10 years.*

teddy bear /'tedi ˌbeə/ *noun* (*also* **teddy**)
a soft toy that looks like a bear

tedious /'ti:diəs/ *adjective*
continuing for too long, and not interesting: *The film was very tedious.*

teenage /'ti:neɪdʒ/ *adjective*
aged between thirteen and nineteen years old: *Taylor is a typical teenage girl.*

teenager /'ti:neɪdʒə/ *noun*
someone who is between thirteen and nineteen years old

teens /ti:nz/ *plural noun*
in your teens between thirteen and nineteen years old: *I met my husband when I was in my teens.*

teeth /ti:θ/
the plural of **tooth**
→ Look at picture on P1

telephone¹ /'telɪ,fəʊn/ *noun*
the piece of equipment that you use for speaking to someone who is in another

place: *He got up and answered the telephone.*
on the telephone speaking to someone by telephone: *Linda was on the telephone for three hours this evening.*

telephone² /'telɪ,fəʊn/ *verb* (**telephones, telephoning, telephoned**)
to speak to someone using a telephone: *I telephoned my boyfriend to say I was sorry.* □ *He telephoned for a taxi to take him to the airport.*

telescope /'telɪ,skəʊp/ *noun*
an instrument shaped like a tube. It has special glass inside it that makes things that are far away look bigger and nearer when you look through it.

telescope

television /'telɪ,vɪʒən, -'vɪʒ-/ *or* **TV** *noun*
1 a piece of electrical equipment with a screen on which you watch moving pictures with sound: *She turned the television on.*
2 *uncountable* the moving pictures and sounds that you watch and listen to on a television: *Michael spends too much time watching television.* □ *What's on television tonight?* □ *My favourite television programme is about to start.*

tell /tel/ *verb* (**tells, telling, told**)
1 to give someone information: *I told Rachel I got the job.* □ *I called Anna to tell her how angry I was.* □ *Claire made me promise to tell her the truth.* □ *He told his story to The Times.*
2 to order someone to do something: *The police officer told him to get out of his car.*
3 to be able to judge correctly what is happening or what is true: *I could tell that Tom was tired and bored.*
tell someone off to speak to someone in an angry or serious way because they have done something wrong: *He never listened to us when we told him off.*

> **LANGUAGE HELP**
> See note at **say**.

telly /'teli/ *noun* (**tellies**) (*informal*)
→ see **television**

temper /'tempə/ *noun*
have a temper to become angry very easily: *Their mother had a terrible temper.*
in a temper angry: *I was in a temper last*

night because I was so tired and couldn't sleep.

lose your temper to suddenly become angry: *Simon lost his temper and hit me.*

temperature /'temprətʃə/ *noun*
1 how hot or cold something is: *At night here, the temperature drops below freezing.*
2 *uncountable* how hot someone's body is: *The baby's temperature continued to rise.*

have a temperature to have a temperature that is higher than it should be

take someone's temperature to use an instrument (= a thermometer) to measure the temperature of someone's body: *The nurse took my temperature.*

temple /'tempəl/ *noun*
a building where people pray to their god or gods: *We visited the biggest Sikh temple in India.*

temporary /'tempərəri/ *adjective*
lasting for only a certain time: *His job here is only temporary.*
▸ **temporarily** /'tempərərəli/ *adverb Her website was temporarily shut down yesterday.*

tempt /tempt/ *verb* (**tempts, tempting, tempted**)
to make someone want something, even though it may be wrong or harmful: *Credit cards can tempt people to buy things they can't afford.* □ *I was tempted to lie, but in the end I told the truth.*
▸ **tempting** *adjective The berries look tempting to children, but they're poisonous.*

temptation /temp'teɪʃən/ *uncountable noun*
the feeling that you want to do something or have something, when you know that it is wrong: *Exercise regularly and resist the temptation to eat snacks.*

tempted /'temptɪd/ *adjective*
feeling that you would like to do something although it may not be a good idea: *I was tempted to buy a car, but I paid off my debts instead.*

ten /ten/
the number 10

tenant /'tenənt/ *noun*
someone who pays money to use a house or an office: *Each tenant in the flat pays £200 a week.*

tend /tend/ *verb* (**tends, tending, tended**)
tend to to usually do or be something: *Women tend to live longer than men.*

tendency /'tendənsi/ *noun* (**tendencies**)
something that usually happens, or

something a person usually does: *Laura has a tendency to gossip.*

tender /'tendə/ *adjective* (**tenderer, tenderest**)
1 kind and gentle: *Her voice was tender.*
▸ **tenderly** *adverb He kissed her tenderly.*
2 easy to cut or bite: *Cook for about 2 hours, until the meat is tender.*
3 painful when touched: *My cheek felt very tender.*

tennis /'tenɪs/ *uncountable noun*
a game for two or four players, who use rackets (= special bats) to hit a ball across a net between them
→ Look at picture on P6

tense¹ /tens/ *adjective* (**tenser, tensest**)
1 anxious and nervous, and not feeling relaxed: *The team were very tense before the game.*
2 when your muscles are tight and not relaxed: *A bath can relax tense muscles.*

tense² /tens/ *noun*
the form of a verb that shows whether something is happening in the past, present or future

tension /'tenʃən/ *uncountable noun*
a feeling of worry and anxiety that makes it impossible for you to feel relaxed: *Physical exercise can reduce tension.*

tent /tent/ *noun*
a shelter made of cloth that is held up by poles and ropes. You sleep in a tent when you go camping.

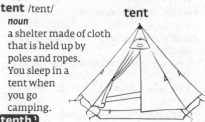
tent

tenth¹
/tenθ/ *adjective, adverb*
counted as number ten in a series: *She's having a party for her tenth birthday.*

tenth² /tenθ/ *noun*
one of ten equal parts of something ($\frac{1}{10}$): *She won the race by a tenth of a second.*

term /tɜːm/ *noun*
1 a special word or expression that is used by experts in a particular subject: *Sodium chloride is the scientific term for table salt.*
2 one of the periods of time that a school, college or university year is divided into: *The school's headteacher, Mrs Johnson, will retire at the end of the term.*
3 *plural* the conditions that all of the

people involved in an arrangement must agree to: *The terms of the agreement are quite simple.*

terminal /'tɜ:mɪnəl/ *noun*
a place where people begin or end a trip by bus, aircraft or ship: *Port Authority is the world's busiest bus terminal.*

terminate /'tɜ:mɪˌneɪt/ *verb* (**terminates, terminating, terminated**)
to end something (*formal*): *His contract was terminated early.*

terrace /'terɪs/ *noun*
1 a flat area next to a building, where people can sit: *Our house has a terrace overlooking the sea.*
2 a line of houses that are joined together by their side walls

terraced house /ˌterɪst 'haʊs/ *noun*
one of a row of houses that are joined together by both of their side walls

terrible /'terɪbəl/ *adjective*
1 extremely bad: *I have a terrible singing voice.*
▸ **terribly** *adverb* *Our team played terribly today.*
2 causing great pain or sadness: *Thousands of people suffered terrible injuries.*
▸ **terribly** *adverb* *These people have suffered terribly during the war.*

terrific /tə'rɪfɪk/ *adjective*
very good (*informal*): *What a terrific idea!*

terrify /'terɪfaɪ/ *verb* (**terrifies, terrifying, terrified**)
to make someone feel extremely afraid: *Flying terrifies him.*
▸ **terrified** *adjective* *Jacob is terrified of spiders.*

terrifying /'terɪˌfaɪɪŋ/ *adjective*
making you very afraid: *That was a terrifying experience.*

territory /'terətri/ *noun* (**territories**)
all the land that a particular country owns

terror /'terə/ *uncountable noun*
very great fear: *I shook with terror.*

terrorism /'terəˌrɪzəm/ *uncountable noun*
the use of violence to force a government to do something: *We need new laws to fight terrorism.*

terrorist /'terərɪst/ *noun*
a person who uses violence to achieve their aims: *terrorist attacks* ◻ *The president called for all nations to come together to defeat terrorism.*

test /test/ *verb* (**tests, testing, tested**)
1 to use or touch something to find out what condition it is in, or how well it works: *Test the temperature of the water with your wrist before you put your baby in the bath.* ◻ *The drug has only been tested on mice.* ● **test** *noun* *The car achieved great results in crash tests.*
2 to ask someone questions to find out how much they know about something: *The students were tested on grammar, spelling and punctuation.* ● **test** *noun* *Only 15 of the 25 students passed the test.*

test tube *noun*
a long thin glass container that is used in scientific experiments

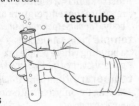
test tube

text[1] /tekst/ *noun*
1 *uncountable* all the words in a book, document, newspaper or magazine: *You can insert text, delete text or move text around.*
2 an academic or scientific book or short piece of writing: *The bookshelves were filled with religious texts.*
3 → see **text message**: *The new system can send a text to a mobile phone.*

text[2] /tekst/ *verb* (**texts, texting, texted**)
to send someone a text message on a mobile phone: *Mary texted me when she got home.*

textbook /'tekstbʊk/ *also* **text book** *noun*
a book containing facts about a particular subject that is used by people studying that subject: *Amy was in the library reading a textbook on international law.*

textile /'tekstaɪl/ *noun*
any type of cloth: *the textile industry*

texting /'tekstɪŋ/ *uncountable noun*
→ see **text messaging**

text message *noun*
a message that you write and send using a mobile phone: *Lauren sent her boyfriend a text message asking him to meet her at the restaurant at eight.*

text messaging *uncountable noun*
sending messages in writing using a mobile phone: *Text messaging started to become widely used in 1998.*

texture /'tekstʃə/ *noun*
the way that something feels when you touch it: *The cheese has a soft, creamy texture.*

than /ðən, STRONG ðæn/ *preposition*
used when you are comparing two people or things: *Tom is taller than his dad.* □ *Children learn faster than adults.* □ *They talked on the phone for more than an hour.* ● **than** *conjunction* *He should have helped her more than he did.*

thank /θæŋk/ *verb* (**thanks, thanking, thanked**)
to say 'thank you' to someone to show that you are grateful to them for something: *I thanked them for all their kindness to me.*

thankful /'θæŋkfʊl/ *adjective*
grateful and glad that something has happened: *I'm so thankful that they are all safe.*

thankfully /'θæŋkfʊli/ *adverb*
used in order to express approval or happiness about something: *Thankfully, she was not injured.*

thanks /θæŋks/
1 *exclamation* used when you want to show that you are grateful for something (*informal*): *Thanks for the information.* □ *'Tea?' —'No thanks.'*
2 *plural noun* things that you say when you are grateful to someone for something: *I would like to express my thanks to the wonderful hospital staff.*
thanks to someone/something
because of a particular person or thing: *Thanks to Sean's courage, his dad survived.*

Thanksgiving /ˌθæŋks'ɡɪvɪŋ/ *uncountable noun*
in the United States, a public holiday on the fourth Thursday in November, when families have a special meal together: *I travelled back to my grandmother's house a few days before Thanksgiving.*

thank you /'θæŋkjuː/ *exclamation*
used when you want to show that you are grateful for something that someone has done for you: *Thank you very much for inviting me to your birthday party.* □ *'Would you like a cup of coffee?' —'Thank you, I'd love one.'*

that[1] /ðæt, ðət, STRONG ðæt/ *adjective*
used for talking about someone or something that is a distance away from you in position or time: *Look at that guy over there.*

not that not as much as might be possible: *Well, actually, it's not that expensive.*

that[2] /ðæt, ðət, STRONG ðæt/ *pronoun*
1 used for talking about someone or something that is a distance away from you in position or time: *What's that?*
2 used for talking about something that you have mentioned before: *They said you wanted to talk to me. Why was that?*
3 used for showing which person or thing you are talking about: *There's the girl that I told you about.* □ *He hates the town that he lives in.*
that's that used for saying that you have finished with a particular subject (*informal*): *If that's your final decision, I guess that's that.*

that[3] /ðæt, ðət, STRONG ðæt/ *conjunction*
1 used for joining two parts of a sentence: *He said that he and his wife were coming to New York.* □ *I felt sad that he was leaving.*
2 used after 'so' and 'such' to talk about the result of something: *I shouted so that they could hear me.*

thatched /θætʃd/ *adjective*
with a roof made of straw (= the yellow stems of dried crops): *The cottage has small windows and a thatched roof.*

that's /ðæts/
short for 'that is'

thaw /θɔː/ *verb* (**thaws, thawing, thawed**)
1 to warm something that is frozen until it becomes soft or liquid: *How long does it take to thaw a frozen chicken?*
2 to become warm enough to become soft or liquid: *We will leave when the snow thaws.*

the *article*

LANGUAGE HELP
Pronounce **the** /ði/ before a vowel (= a, e, i, o or u). Pronounce **the** /ðə/ before a consonant (= all the other letters).

1 used before a noun when it is clear which person or thing you are talking about: *The office staff here are all British.* □ *It's always hard to think about the future.* □ *The doctor's on his way.*
2 used before a singular noun to talk about things of that type in general: *The computer has developed very fast in recent years.*
3 used with adjectives and plural nouns to talk about all people of a particular type or nationality: *the British and the French*
4 used in front of dates: *The meeting should*

t

take place on the fifth of May.
5 used in front of superlative adjectives
and adverbs: *Daily walks are the best exercise.*

theatre /'θɪːətə/ *noun*
a place where you go to see plays or
shows: *Last night, we went to the theatre to see
a play by Chekhov.*

theft /θeft/ *noun*
the crime of stealing: *Martinez was arrested
for car theft and assault.*

their /ðeə/ *adjective*
1 used for showing that something
belongs to or relates to the group of
people, animals or things that you
are talking about: *Janis and Kurt have
announced their engagement.* ◻ *They took off
their coats.*
2 used instead of 'his or her' to show that
something belongs or relates to a person,
without saying if that person is a man or
a woman. Some people think this use is
incorrect: *Each student works at their own
pace.*

theirs /ðeəz/ *pronoun*
used for showing that something belongs
or relates to the group of people, animals
or things that you are talking about: *The
people at the table next to theirs were talking
loudly.*

them /ðəm, STRONG ðem/ *pronoun*
1 used for talking about more than one
person, animal or thing: *I've lost my keys.
Have you seen them?*
2 used instead of 'him or her', to talk
about a person without saying whether
that person is a man or a woman: *If anyone
calls, tell them I'm out.*

theme /θiːm/ *noun*
the most important idea of a piece of
writing or a discussion, or its subject:
Progress was the main theme of his speech.

themselves /ðəm'selvz/ *pronoun*
1 used for talking about people, animals
or things that you have just talked about:
They all seemed to be enjoying themselves.
2 used for saying that certain people did
something, and not anyone else: *My
parents designed our house themselves.*

then /ðen/ *adverb*
1 at a particular time in the past or in the
future: *I bought this flat in 2005. Since then,
house prices have fallen.*

2 used for saying that one thing happens
after another: *Add the onion and then the
garlic.*
3 used for starting the second part of a
sentence that begins with 'if': *If you are not
sure about this, then you must say so.*

theory /'θɪəri/ *noun* (**theories**)
an idea or a set of ideas that tries to
explain something: *The Big Bang Theory
explains the beginning of the universe.*

therapist /'θerəpɪst/ *noun*
a person who helps people who have
emotional or physical problems: *Scott saw
a therapist after his marriage ended in 2004.*

therapy /'θerəpi/ *noun* (**therapies**)
1 *uncountable* the process of talking to a
person with special training about your
problems and your relationships so that
you can understand them and then
change the way you feel and behave: *He
returned to work, but he was still having therapy.*
2 a treatment for a particular illness or
condition: *Scientists are working on a therapy
to slow down the aging process.*

there [1] /ðə/ *pronoun*
used with the verb 'be' to say that
something exists or is happening: *There is
a swimming pool in the garden.* ◻ *Are there any
biscuits left?*

there [2] /ðə, STRONG ðeə/ *adverb*
1 used for talking about a place that has
already been mentioned: *I'm going back to
California. My family have lived there for many
years.*
2 used for talking about a place that you
are pointing to or looking at: *'Where is
Mr Hernandez?'* — *'He's sitting over there.'*
◻ *There she is, at the corner of the street.*
3 used when you are speaking on the
telephone, to ask if someone is available
to speak to you: *Hello, is Tony there, please?*
here/there you are used when you are
offering something to someone.
(*informal*): *'There you are, Mr Walters,' she said,
giving him his documents.*

therefore /'ðeəfɔː/ *adverb*
used when you are talking about the
result of an action or a situation: *Matthew
is injured and therefore will not play in Saturday's
game.*

there's /ðəz/
short for 'there is'

thermometer /θəˈmɒmɪtə/ *noun*
an instrument for measuring how hot or cold something is

thermometer

these /ðiːz/ *adjective*
1 used for talking about people or things that are near you, especially when you touch them or point to them: *These scissors are heavy.* ●**these** *pronoun Do you like these?*
2 used for talking about someone or something that you have already mentioned: *These people need more support.*
3 used for introducing people or things that you are going to talk about: *If you're looking for a builder, these phone numbers will be useful.*

they /ðeɪ/ *pronoun*
1 used when you are talking about more than one person, animal or thing: *She said goodbye to the children as they left for school.* □ *'Where are your toys?'* — *'They're in the garden.'*
2 used instead of 'he or she' when you are talking about a person without saying whether that person is a man or a woman: *'Someone phoned. They said they would call back later.'*

they'd /ðeɪd/
1 short for 'they had'
2 short for 'they would'

they'll /ðeɪəl/
short for 'they will'

they're /ðeə, ðeɪə/
short for 'they are'

they've /ðeɪv/
short for 'they have', especially when 'have' is an auxiliary verb

thick /θɪk/ *adjective* (**thicker, thickest**)
1 having a large distance between one side and the other: *I cut a thick slice of bread.*
2 used for saying or asking how wide or deep something is: *The book is two inches thick.* □ *How thick are these walls?*
▶**thickness** *uncountable noun The cooking time depends on the thickness of the steaks.*
3 consisting of a lot of hairs growing closely together: *Jessica has thick dark curly hair and brown eyes.*
4 difficult to see through: *The crash happened in thick fog.*

5 not flowing easily: *Cook the sauce until it is thick and creamy.*

thief /θiːf/ *noun* (**thieves** /θiːvz/)
a person who steals something from another person: *The thieves took his camera.*

thigh /θaɪ/ *noun*
the top part of your leg, above your knee: *She's broken her thigh bone.*
→ Look at picture on P1

thin /θɪn/ *adjective* (**thinner, thinnest**)
1 having a small distance between one side and the other: *His arms and legs were very thin.* □ *The book is printed on very thin paper.*
2 having no extra fat on your body: *Bob was a tall, thin man.*
3 flowing easily: *The soup was thin and tasteless.*

thing /θɪŋ/ *noun*
1 an object: *What's that thing in the middle of the road?*
2 *plural* possessions: *She told him to take all his things and not to return.*
3 something that happens or something that you think or talk about: *They were driving home when a strange thing happened.* □ *We had so many things to talk about.*
4 *plural* used for talking about life in general: *How are things with you?*

think /θɪŋk/ *verb* (**thinks, thinking, thought**)
1 to believe something or have an opinion about it: *I think that it will snow tomorrow.* □ *What do you think of my idea?*
2 to use your mind to consider something: *She closed her eyes for a moment, trying to think.* □ *What are you thinking about?*
think of/about doing something to consider doing something: *I'm thinking of going to college next year.*

t

think of something used for saying that something comes into your mind: *I know who he is but I can't think of his name.*

think something over to consider something carefully before you make a decision about it: *They've offered her the job but she said she needs time to think it over.*

third¹ /θɜːd/ *adjective, adverb*

the item in a series that you count as number three: *My office is the third door on the right.* ☐ *Katie came third in the race.*

third² /θɜːd/ *noun*

one of three equal parts of something (¹/₃)

thirst /θɜːst/ *uncountable noun*

the feeling that you want to drink something: *Drink water to satisfy your thirst.*

thirsty /'θɜːsti/ *adjective* (**thirstier, thirstiest**)

wanting to drink something: *Drink some water whenever you feel thirsty.*

thirteen /,θɜː'tiːn/

the number 13

▸ **thirteenth** /,θɜː'tiːnθ/ *adjective, adverb* *It's my thirteenth birthday tomorrow.*

thirty /'θɜːti/

the number 30

▸ **thirtieth** /'θɜːtiəθ/ *adjective, adverb* *We celebrated the thirtieth anniversary of my parents' wedding.*

this¹ /ðɪs/ *adjective*

1 used for talking about a person or a thing that is near you, especially when you touch them or point to them: *I like this room much better than the other one.*

2 used for talking about someone or something that you have already mentioned: *How can we solve this problem?*

3 used for talking about the next day, month or season: *We have tickets for this Sunday's performance.* ☐ *We're getting married this June.*

this² /ðɪs/ *pronoun*

1 used for talking about a person or a thing that is near you, especially when you touch them or point to them: *'Would you like a different one?' – 'No, this is great.'*

2 used for introducing someone or something that you are going to talk about: *This is what I will do. I will telephone Anna and explain.*

this is used for saying who you are when you are speaking on the telephone: *Hello, this*

is John Thompson. Can I speak to David, please?

thorn /θɔːn/ *noun*

a sharp point on some plants and trees: *He removed a thorn from his foot.*

thorough /'θʌrə/ *adjective*

done completely, and with great attention to detail: *There will be a thorough investigation into the cause of the crash.*

▸ **thoroughly** *adverb* *The food must be thoroughly cooked.*

those /ðəʊz/ *adjective*

1 used when you are talking about people or things that are a distance away from you in position or time, especially when you point to them: *What are those buildings?*

● **those** *pronoun* *Those are nice shoes.*

2 used for talking about people or things that have already been mentioned: *I don't know any of those people you mentioned.*

though /ðəʊ/ *conjunction*

1 although, or despite the fact that: *I love him though I do not know him.* ☐ *Ashley plays in adult tennis games even though she is only 15.*

2 but: *I think I left home at about seven thirty, though I could be wrong.*

thought¹ /θɔːt/ → see **think**

thought² /θɔːt/ *noun*

1 an idea or an opinion: *The thought of Nick made her sad.* ☐ *I just had a thought. Why don't you have a party?* ☐ *What are your thoughts about the political situation?*

2 *uncountable* the activity of thinking, especially deeply and carefully: *Alice was deep in thought.*

thoughtful /'θɔːtfʊl/ *adjective*

1 quiet and serious because you are thinking about something: *Nancy paused, looking thoughtful.*

▸ **thoughtfully** *adverb* *Daniel nodded thoughtfully.*

2 thinking and caring about other people's feelings: *Ben is a thoughtful and caring boy.*

thoughtless /'θɔːtləs/ *adjective*

not caring or thinking about other people's feelings: *It was thoughtless of me to forget your birthday.*

thousand /'θaʊzənd/

LANGUAGE HELP
The plural form is **thousand** after a number.

the number 1,000: *Over five thousand people attended the conference.*

thousands of a very large number of things or people: *I have been there thousands of times.*

thread ¹ /θred/ *noun*

thread

a long, very thin piece of cotton, nylon or silk that you use for sewing: *a needle and thread*

needle

thread ² /θred/ *verb* (**threads, threading, threaded**)

to put a piece of thread through the hole in the top of a needle so that you can sew with it: *I threaded a needle and sewed the button on the shirt.*

threat /θret/ *noun*

1 when you say that something bad will happen to someone if they do not do what you want: *The two boys made death threats against a teacher.*

2 something that can harm someone or something: *Stress is a threat to people's health.*

threaten /'θretən/ *verb* (**threatens, threatening, threatened**)

1 to say that you will hurt someone if they do not do what you want: *Army officers threatened to destroy the town.* □ *If you threaten me, I will go to the police.*

▶ **threatening** *adjective* *He was arrested for using threatening behaviour toward police officers.*

2 to be likely to harm people or things: *The fire threatened more than 1,000 homes.*

three /θri:/

the number 3: *We waited three months before going back.*

three-dimensional /ˌθri:daɪˈmenʃənəl, -dɪm-/ *adjective*

1 solid rather than flat. The short form '3D' is also used: *We made a three-dimensional model.*

2 looking deep or solid rather than flat: *The software generates three-dimensional images.*

threw /θru:/ → see **throw**

thrill ¹ /θrɪl/ *noun*

a sudden feeling of great excitement: *I can remember the thrill of opening my birthday presents when I was a child.*

thrill ² /θrɪl/ *verb* (**thrills, thrilling, thrilled**)

to give you a feeling of great excitement:

Manchester United thrilled the crowd with a 5-3 victory.

thrilled /θrɪld/ *adjective*

very happy and excited about something: *I was so thrilled to get a good mark for my maths exam.*

thriller /'θrɪlə/ *noun*

an exciting book, film or play about a crime: *The book is a historical thriller.*

thrilling /'θrɪlɪŋ/ *adjective*

very exciting and enjoyable: *It was a thrilling finish to the tournament.*

thrive /θraɪv/ *verb* (**thrives, thriving, thrived**)

to do well and be successful, healthy or strong: *Some plants thrive in the shade.* □ *Their national film industry is thriving. It produces thousands of films each year.*

throat /θrəʊt/ *noun*

1 the back of your mouth and inside your neck, where you swallow: *He spent two days at home with a sore throat.*

2 the front part of your neck: *Mr Williams grabbed him by the throat.*

throb /θrɒb/ *verb* (**throbs, throbbing, throbbed**)

1 to beat regularly and very strongly, or to make a regular sound, like your heart: *His heart throbbed with excitement.* □ *The ship's engines throbbed.*

2 to beat regularly with pain: *Kevin's head throbbed.*

throne /θrəʊn/ *noun*

the special chair where a king or a queen sits on important official occasions

through /θru:/ *preposition*

1 from one side of something to the other side: *The bullet went through the front windscreen.* □ *We walked through the crowd.* □ *Alice looked through the window.* ● **through** *adverb* *There was a hole in the wall and water was coming through.*

2 from the beginning until the end of a period of time: *She kept quiet all through breakfast.*

3 because of: *I only succeeded through hard work.*

throughout /θru:ˈaʊt/ *preposition*

1 during all of a particular period of time: *It rained heavily throughout the game.*

2 in all parts of a place: *Thousands of children throughout Africa suffer from the*

t

condition. ● **throughout** *adverb* The flat is painted white throughout.

throw /θrəʊ/ *verb* (**throws, throwing, threw, thrown**)

to move your hand or arm quickly and let go of an object that you are holding, so that it moves through the air: *The crowd began throwing stones at the police.* ● **throw** *noun* That was a good throw.

throw something away or **throw something out** to get rid of something that you do not want: *I never throw anything away.* □ *I've decided to throw out all the clothes I never wear.*

thrown /θrəʊn/ → see **throw**

thud /θʌd/ *noun*
the sound that a heavy object makes when it hits the ground: *She tripped and fell with a thud.*

thumb /θʌm/ *noun*
the short thick finger on your hand: *O'Donnell missed the game because of a broken thumb.*
→ Look at picture on P1

thump /θʌmp/ *verb* (**thumps, thumping, thumped**)
1 to hit something hard with your hand: *Kazuo thumped the table with his fist.*
2 used for saying that someone's heart beats strongly and quickly because they are afraid or excited: *Her heart was thumping loudly in her chest.*

thunder /'θʌndə/ *uncountable noun*
the loud noise that you sometimes hear from the sky during a storm: *Last night there was thunder and lightning.*

thunderstorm /'θʌndə,stɔːm/ *noun*
a very noisy storm: *The tree was hit by lightning during a thunderstorm last night.*

Thursday /'θɜːzdeɪ, -di/ *noun*
the day after Wednesday and before Friday: *On Thursday Barbara invited me to her house for lunch.* □ *We go to the supermarket every Thursday morning.*

tick /tɪk/ *verb* (**ticks, ticking, ticked**)
1 to make a regular series of short sounds: *An alarm clock ticked loudly on the bedside table.* ● **tick** *noun* I could hear the tick of the clock in the hall.
2 (*American*: **check**) to put a written mark ✔ on a piece of paper to show that something is correct or that it has been done: *Tick the*

correct answer. ● **tick** (*American*: **check mark**) *noun* Put a tick in the box.

ticket /'tɪkɪt/ *noun*
a small piece of paper that shows that you have paid to go somewhere or to do something: *Where are the tickets for tonight's game?* □ *He had a first-class plane ticket for London.*

tickle /'tɪkəl/ *verb* (**tickles, tickling, tickled**)
to move your fingers lightly over a part of someone's body to make them laugh: *Stephanie was cuddling the baby and tickling her toes.*

tide /taɪd/ *noun*
the regular change in the level of the sea towards the land and away from the land that happens twice a day: *The tide was going out.*

tidy¹ /'taɪdi/ *adjective* (**tidier, tidiest**)
1 liking everything to be in its correct place: *I'm not a very tidy person.*
2 neat, and arranged in an organized way: *The room was neat and tidy.*

tidy² /'taɪdi/ *verb* (**tidies, tidying, tidied**) (*also* **tidy up**)
to organize a place by putting things in their proper places: *She tidied her room.* □ *You relax while I tidy up the house.*

tie¹ /taɪ/ *verb* (**ties, tying, tied**)
1 (*also* **tie up**) to fasten or fix something, using string or a rope: *He tied the dog to the fence.* □ *She tied the ends of the two ropes together.* □ *She tied her scarf over her head.* □ *His hands were tied with rope.* □ *I bent down to tie my shoelaces.* □ *The woman tied up her dog outside the shop.*
2 to have the same number of points at the end of a game: *The teams tied 2-2.*

tie² /taɪ/ *noun*
1 a long narrow piece of cloth that you wear around your neck with a shirt: *Jason took off his jacket and loosened his tie.*
2 when teams have the same number of points at the end of a game: *The first game ended in a tie.*
3 a connection that you have with people or a place: *Quebec has close ties to France.*

tiger /'taɪgə/ *noun*
a large wild animal of the cat family. Tigers are orange with black stripes.

tight /taɪt/ *adjective, adverb* (**tighter, tightest**)

1 small, and fitting closely to your body: *Amanda was wearing a tight black dress.*

▶ **tightly** *adverb* *Her jacket fastened tightly at the waist.*

2 very firm or firmly: *He kept a tight hold of her arm.* □ *Richard put his arms around her and held her tight.* □ *Just hold tight to my hand and don't let go.*

▶ **tightly** *adverb* *The children hugged me tightly.*

tighten /'taɪtən/ *verb* (**tightens, tightening, tightened**)

to make something tighter: *She tightened the belt on her robe.* □ *He tightened the last screw.*

tights /taɪts/ *plural noun*

a piece of tight clothing that covers the lower body, worn by women, girls and dancers

tile /taɪl/ *noun*

a flat, square object that is used for covering floors, walls or roofs

till¹ /tɪl/ *preposition*

until: *They had to wait till Monday to phone the bank.* ● **till** *conjunction* *I didn't leave home till I was nineteen.*

till² /tɪl/ *noun*

a machine that holds money in a shop

tilt /tɪlt/ *verb* (**tilts, tilting, tilted**)

to have one end higher than the other: *The boat tilted as Eric leaned over the side.*

timber /'tɪmbə/ *uncountable noun*

wood that is used for building and making things: *There are timber floors throughout the house.*

time¹ /taɪm/ *noun*

1 *uncountable* something that we measure in minutes, hours, days and years: *Time passed, and still Mary did not come back.* □ *I've known Mr Martin for a long time.* □ *Listen to me. I haven't got much time.*

2 used when you are talking about a particular point in the day, that you describe in hours and minutes: *'What time is it?' — 'Eight o'clock.'* □ *He asked me the time.*

3 the point in the day when something happens: *Departure times are 08.15 from London, and 10.15 from Birmingham.* □ *It's time to go home.*

4 used for talking about a particular period of time in the past: *At that time there were no cars.*

5 used for talking about an experience that you had: *Sarah and I had a great time at the party.*

6 used for talking about how often you do something: *Try to exercise at least three times a week.*

7 *plural* used after numbers when you are showing how much bigger or smaller one thing is than another: *The sun is 400 times bigger than the moon.*

all the time continually or very often: *We can't be together all the time.*

at a time together: *Patients may have two visitors at a time.*

at times sometimes: *Every job is boring at times.*

for the time being now, but only for a short time: *The situation is calm for the time being.*

from time to time sometimes but not often: *Her daughters visited her from time to time.*

in a few minutes'/days'/weeks' time after a few minutes/days/weeks: *Presidential elections will be held in a few days' time.*

in time not late: *I arrived just in time for my flight to Bristol.*

on time not late or early: *The train arrived at the station on time at eleven thirty.*

take your time to do something slowly: *'Take your time,' Ted told him. 'I'm in no hurry.'*

times used when you are multiplying numbers. Three times five is written 3 x 5: *Four times six is 24.*

LANGUAGE HELP

Do not say 'one time a day/week/month/year' or 'two times a day/week/month/year'; instead, say '**once a day/week/month/year**' or '**twice a day/week/month/year**'.

---

time² /taɪm/ *verb* (**times, timing, timed**)

to measure how long an activity lasts: *Practise your speech and time yourself, so that you don't talk for too long.*

timeline /'taɪmlaɪn/ also **time line** *noun*

a picture that shows the order of historical events: *The timeline shows important events from the Earth's creation to the present day.*

timetable /'taɪmteɪbəl/ *noun*

a list of the times when trains, buses or planes arrive and depart, or when

t

something happens: *Have you checked the bus timetable?* □ *a school timetable*

'time zone *noun*
one of the areas that the world is divided into for measuring time: *We were tired after a long flight across several time zones.*

timid /'tɪmɪd/ *adjective*
shy and nervous, and lacking confidence in yourself: *I was a timid child.*
▸ **timidly** *adverb* *The little boy stepped forward timidly.*

timing /'taɪmɪŋ/ *uncountable noun*
the skill of judging the right moment to do something: *'Am I too early?' — 'No, your timing is perfect.'*

tin /tɪn/ *noun*
1 *uncountable* a type of soft metal: *a tin can*
2 a metal container used for keeping food or drink fresh: *a tin of soup*

tin-opener /'tɪn,əʊpənə/ *noun*
a tool that you use for opening tins

tiny /'taɪni/ *adjective* (**tinier, tiniest**)
extremely small: *The living room is tiny.*

tip¹ /tɪp/ *noun*
1 the end of something long and narrow: *He pressed the tips of his fingers together.*
2 a useful piece of advice: *The article gives tips on applying for jobs.*
3 money that you give someone to thank them for a job they have done for you: *I gave the waiter a tip.*

tip² /tɪp/ *verb* (**tips, tipping, tipped**)
1 to move so that one end is higher than the other: *The pram can tip backwards if you hang bags on the handles.*
2 to pour something somewhere: *I picked up the bowl of cereal and tipped it over his head.*
3 to give someone some money to thank them for a job they have done for you: *At the end of the meal, he tipped the waiter.*
tip something over to make something fall over: *He tipped the table over.*

tiptoe¹ /'tɪptəʊ/ *verb* (**tiptoes, tiptoeing, tiptoed**)
to walk somewhere very quietly on your toes: *Emma got out of bed and tiptoed to the window.*

tiptoe² /'tɪptəʊ/ *noun*
on tiptoe on your toes and not putting your heels on the ground: *She stood on tiptoe to look over the wall.*

tire /taɪə/ *verb* (**tires, tiring, tired**)
to make you feel that you want to rest or sleep: *If driving tires you, take the train instead.*

tired /taɪəd/ *adjective*
feeling that you want to rest or sleep: *Michael is tired after his long flight.*
tired of something not wanting something to continue because you are bored with it: *I'm tired of waiting for him.*

tiring /'taɪərɪŋ/ *adjective*
making you feel tired so that you want to rest or sleep: *It was a long and tiring day.*
□ *Travelling is tiring.*

tissue /'tɪʃuː, 'tɪsjuː/ *noun*
1 *uncountable* one of the substances that humans, animals and plants are made of: *brain tissue*
2 *uncountable* (*also* **tissue paper**) thin paper that you use for wrapping things that break easily: *The parcel was wrapped in pink tissue paper.*
3 a piece of thin, soft paper that you use to wipe your nose: *He passed me a box of tissues.*

title /'taɪtəl/ *noun*
1 the name of a book, a play, a film or a piece of music: *What is the title of the poem?*
2 a word such as 'Mr' or 'Dr' that is used in front of someone's own name

to¹ *preposition*

PRONUNCIATION HELP
To is usually pronounced /tə/ before a consonant and /tʊ/ before a vowel, but pronounced /tuː/ when you are emphasizing it.

1 used when you are talking about the position or direction of something: *Two friends and I drove to Wales.* □ *She went to the window and looked out.* □ *The bathroom is to the right.*
2 used for saying that someone receives something: *He picked up the knife and gave it to me.*
3 used when you are talking about how something changes: *The shouts of the crowd changed to laughter.*
4 used before the last thing in a range: *I worked there from 1990 to 1996.* □ *I can count from 1 to 100 in Spanish.*
5 used when you are saying how many minutes there are until the next hour:

t

At twenty to six I was waiting by the entrance to the station.

to²

1 used before the infinitive (= the simple form of a verb): *We just want to help.* □ *It was time to leave.*

2 used for giving the reason for doing something: *I went out to buy some milk.*

toad /təʊd/ *noun*
a small brown or green animal with long legs, that lives in water

toast¹ /təʊst/ *noun*
1 *uncountable* slices of bread that you have heated until they are brown: *a slice of toast*
2 when you lift up your glass, wish someone happiness, and drink: *We drank a toast to the bride and groom.*

toast² /təʊst/ *verb* (**toasts, toasting, toasted**)
1 to lift up your glass, wish someone happiness, and drink: *We all toasted the baby's health.*
2 to heat bread so that it becomes brown: *Mum made us some delicious toasted sandwiches.*

toaster /ˈtəʊstə/ *noun*
a piece of electrical equipment that you use to heat bread
→ Look at picture on P4

tobacco /təˈbækəʊ/ *uncountable noun*
the dried leaves of a plant that people smoke in cigarettes

today /təˈdeɪ/ *adverb*
1 used when you are talking about the actual day on which you are speaking or writing: *How are you feeling today?* ● **today** *uncountable noun Today is Friday, September 14th.*
2 used when you are talking about the present period of history: *More people have cars today.*

toddler /ˈtɒdlə/ *noun*
a young child who has only just learned to walk: *Toddlers love activities that involve music and singing.*

toe /təʊ/ *noun*
one of the five parts at the end of your foot: *He is in hospital with a broken toe.*

toenail /ˈtəʊneɪl/ *noun*
one of the hard parts that cover the ends of each of your toes

toffee /ˈtɒfi/ *noun*
a sticky brown sweet

together /təˈgeðə/ *adverb*
1 with each other: *We went on long walks together.* □ *Richard and I went to school together.*
2 touching each other or making a single object, group or mixture: *Beat the butter and sugar together.* □ *He joined the two pieces of wood together.* □ *We added all the numbers together.*
3 in the same place and very near to each other: *The trees grew close together.* □ *Carol and Nick live together in Manhattan.*
4 at the same time: *Patrick and Amanda arrived at the party together.*

toilet /ˈtɔɪlət/ *noun*
1 a large bowl with a seat that you use when you want to get rid of waste from your body: *She flushed the toilet and went back into the bedroom.*
→ Look at picture on P4
2 (*American*: **restroom**) (*also* **toilets**) a room that contains one or more toilets: *She ran to the toilet and locked the door.*

'toilet ˌpaper or **toilet tissue** *uncountable noun*
the thin, soft paper that you use for cleaning yourself after using the toilet

toiletries /ˈtɔɪlətriz/ *plural noun*
the things that you use when you are washing or taking care of your body, such as soap and toothpaste

token /ˈtəʊkən/ *noun*
a round, flat piece of metal or plastic that you use in a machine instead of money: *The machine uses plastic tokens rather than coins.*

told /təʊld/ → see **tell**

tolerant /ˈtɒlərənt/ *adjective*
happy for other people to say, think and do what they like even though you do not agree with them: *We all need to be tolerant of different points of view.*
▶ **tolerance** *uncountable noun They promote tolerance of all religions.*

tolerate /ˈtɒləˌreɪt/ *verb* (**tolerates, tolerating, tolerated**)
to accept something or someone although you do not like them very much: *The college will not tolerate such behaviour.*

toiletries

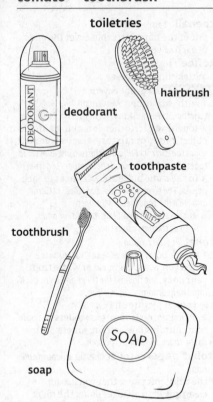

hairbrush

deodorant

toothpaste

toothbrush

SOAP

soap

tomato /tə'mɑ:təʊ/ *noun* (**tomatoes**)
a soft, red fruit that you can eat raw in salads or cook like a vegetable
→ Look at picture on P2

tomb /tu:m/ *noun*
a stone grave where the body of a dead person is placed: *In Xian, we visited the emperor's tomb.*

tombstone /'tu:mstəʊn/ *noun*
a large stone on a person's grave, with words written on it, telling their name and the date that they were born and died

tomorrow /tə'mɒrəʊ/ *adverb*
1 the day after today: *Bye, see you tomorrow.*
•**tomorrow** *uncountable noun What's on your schedule for tomorrow?*
2 the future: *What is the world going to be like tomorrow?* •**tomorrow** *uncountable noun The children of today are the adults of tomorrow.*

ton /tʌn/ *noun*
a unit of weight. There are 2240 pounds

(= 1016 kilos) in a British ton: *Hundreds of tons of oil spilled into the sea.*

tone /təʊn/ *noun*
1 the particular quality of a sound: *Lisa has a deep tone to her voice.*
2 the quality in someone's voice that shows what they are feeling or thinking: *I didn't like his tone of voice; he sounded angry.*

tongue /tʌŋ/ *noun*
the soft part inside your mouth that moves when you speak or eat
→ Look at picture on P1

tonight /tə'naɪt/ *adverb*
the evening of today: *I'm at home tonight.*
□ *Tonight he showed what a great player he is.*
•**tonight** *uncountable noun Tonight is a very important night for him.*

too /tu:/ *adverb*
1 also: *I like swimming and tennis too.* □ *'Can we come too?'* □ *'I'm excited about the party.'* — *'Me too.'*
2 more than you want or need: *She talks too much.* □ *Sorry, I can't stop. I'm too busy.*

LANGUAGE HELP
See note at **also**.

took /tʊk/ → see **take**

tool /tu:l/ *noun*
anything that you hold in your hands and use to do a particular type of work: *Do you have the right tools for the job?*

toolbar /'tu:lbɑ:/ *noun*
a narrow strip across a computer screen that contains pictures (= icons) that represent different things that the computer can do

toot /tu:t/ *verb* (**toots, tooting, tooted**)
if a car horn toots, or if you toot it, it makes a short sound: *The cars passed by with their horns tooting.* □ *The driver behind tooted his horn.* •**toot** *noun The driver gave me a wave and a toot.*

tooth /tu:θ/ *noun* (**teeth**)
1 one of the hard white objects in your mouth, that you use for biting and eating: *Brush your teeth at least twice a day.*
2 *plural* the parts of a comb that stick out in a row on its edge

toothache /'tu:θeɪk/ *uncountable noun*
a pain in your tooth

toothbrush /'tu:θbrʌʃ/ *noun*
(**toothbrushes**)

a small brush that you use for cleaning your teeth

toothpaste /'tuːθpeɪst/ *uncountable noun*
a thick substance that you put on a toothbrush and use for cleaning your teeth

top¹ /tɒp/ *noun*
1 the highest point of something: *We climbed the path up to the top of the hill.*
2 the lid of something: *He twisted the top off the bottle and handed it to her.*
3 a piece of clothing that you wear on the upper half of your body (*informal*): *I was wearing a black skirt and a red top.*
on top of something on the highest part of something: *There was a clock on top of the television.*

top² /tɒp/ *adjective*
highest: *I can't reach the top shelf.*

topic /'tɒpɪk/ *noun*
a particular subject that you discuss or write about: *What is the topic of your essay?*

torch /tɔːtʃ/ *noun* (**torches**)
1 a small electric light that you carry in your hand
2 a long stick or object that has a flame at one end: *Wood carried the Olympic Torch in Sydney in 2002.*

tore /tɔː/ → see **tear**

torn /tɔːn/ → see **tear**

tornado /tɔːˈneɪdəʊ/ *noun* (**tornadoes** or **tornados**)
a storm with strong winds that spin around very fast and cause a lot of damage

tortoise /'tɔːtəs/ *noun*
an animal with a shell on its back. Tortoises move very slowly.

torture /'tɔːtʃə/ *verb* (**tortures, torturing, tortured**)
to deliberately cause someone terrible pain • **torture** *uncountable noun* *The use of torture is prohibited by international law.*

toss /tɒs/ *verb* (**tosses, tossing, tossed**)
1 to throw something: *Kate tossed the ball to Jessica.*
2 (*also* **toss something about/around**) to make something move up and down, or from side to side, quickly and suddenly: *The strong winds tossed the plane up and down.* □ *The huge waves tossed the boat about.*
toss a coin to decide something by throwing a coin into the air and guessing which side of the coin will face upwards when it lands: *We tossed a coin to decide who should go first.*

total¹ /'təʊtəl/ *noun*
the number that you get when you add several numbers together: *Add all the amounts together, and subtract ten from the total.* □ *The three companies have a total of 1,776 employees.*

total² /'təʊtəl/ *adjective*
1 when you add all the numbers together: *The total cost of the project was £240 million.*
2 complete: *When I failed all my exams, I felt like a total failure.*
▶ **totally** *adverb* *I accept that I am totally to blame.*

totalitarian /'təʊtælɪteəriən/ *adjective*
used for describing a political system in which there is only one political party that controls everything: *He promised that the country would never return to its totalitarian past.*

touch¹ /tʌtʃ/ *verb* (**touches, touching, touched**)
1 to put your hand onto something: *Her little hands gently touched my face.*
2 to be so close to another thing or person that there is no space between the two: *Their knees were touching.* □ *Her feet just touched the floor.*

touch² /tʌtʃ/ *noun* (**touches**)
1 when someone puts their hand onto something: *She felt the touch of his hand on her arm.*
2 *uncountable* your ability to tell what something is like when you feel it with your hands: *A baby's sense of touch is fully developed at birth.*
be/keep/stay in touch to write or speak to someone regularly: *My brother and I keep in touch by phone.*
get in touch to write to someone or telephone them: *We'll get in touch with you if we have any news of your brother.*
lose touch to gradually stop writing or speaking to someone: *When he went to college, I lost touch with him.*

tough /tʌf/ *adjective* (**tougher, toughest**)
1 strong and determined: *Paul has a reputation as a tough businessman.*
2 difficult to do: *We will have to make some tough decisions.*

t

3 strong, and difficult to break or cut: *The bag is made from a tough and waterproof nylon material.* □ *The meat was tough and chewy.*

tour [1] /tʊə/ *noun*
1 a trip to several different places in order to perform a concert or a show: *The band is planning a national tour.* □ *Next year, the orchestra will be going on tour.*
2 a trip to an interesting place or around several interesting places: *Michael took me on a tour of the nearby islands.* □ *We went on a tour of the new office building.*

tour [2] /tʊə/ *verb* (**tours, touring, toured**)
1 to go to several different places in order to perform a concert or a show: *A few years ago the band toured Europe.*
2 to go on a trip around a place: *Tour the museum with a guide for £5 per person.*

'tour guide *noun*
someone whose job is to help people who are on holiday, or to show them round a place: *A tour guide will organize activities every day.*

tourism /'tʊərɪzəm/ *uncountable noun*
the business of providing hotels, restaurants, trips and activities for people who are on holiday: *Tourism is the island's main industry.*

tourist /'tʊərɪst/ *noun*
a person who is visiting a place on holiday: *About 75,000 tourists visit the town each year.*

'tourist infor'mation *uncountable noun*
details of hotels and places to visit in an area

'tourist infor'mation ,centre *noun*
a place that provides details of hotels and places to visit in an area for people who are on holiday

tournament /'tʊənəmənt/ *noun*
a sports competition. Each player who wins a game plays another game, until just one person or team remains. They win the competition: *Tiger Woods won the tournament in 2000.*

tow /təʊ/ *verb* (**tows, towing, towed**)
to pull another vehicle along behind: *He uses the lorry to tow his trailer.*

towards /tə'wɔːdz/ also **toward**
preposition
1 in the direction of something or someone: *They drove towards Lake Ladoga in silence.*

2 used for describing the way you feel about something or someone: *How do you feel towards the man who stole your handbag?*
3 just before a particular time: *We're having another meeting towards the end of the month.*
4 to help pay for something: *My husband's parents gave us £50,000 towards our first house.*

towel /'taʊəl/ *noun*
a piece of thick soft cloth that you use to dry yourself: *I've put clean towels in the bathroom.*
→ Look at picture on P4

tower /'taʊə/ *noun*
a tall, narrow building, or a tall part of another building: *He looked up at the clock in the church tower. It was ten o'clock.*

town /taʊn/ *noun*
a place with many streets, buildings and shops, where people live and work: *Larry comes from a small town near the Canadian border.* □ *We met in town at around eight.*

toxic /'tɒksɪk/ *adjective*
poisonous: *The leaves of the plant are highly toxic.*

toy /tɔɪ/ *noun*
an object that children play with: *Sophie went to sleep holding her favourite toy.*

trace /treɪs/ *verb* (**traces, tracing, traced**)
1 to find someone or something after looking for them: *The police quickly traced the owner of the car.*
2 to copy a picture by covering it with a piece of thin paper and drawing over the lines: *Linda learned to draw by tracing pictures in books.*

track [1] /træk/ *noun*
1 a rough road or path: *We walked along a track in the forest.*
2 a piece of ground that is used for races: *The university's facilities include a 400-metre running track.*
3 one of the metal lines that trains travel along: *a railway track*
4 one of the songs or pieces of music on a CD: *I only like two of the tracks on this CD.*
5 *plural* the marks that an animal leaves on the ground: *William found fresh bear tracks in the snow.*

keep track of someone/something to have information about someone or something all the time: *Keep track of what you spend while you're on holiday.*

lose track of someone/something to no longer know where someone or something is or what is happening: *I'm sorry I'm late. I lost track of time.*

track² /træk/ *verb* (**tracks, tracking, tracked**)
to try to find animals or people by following the signs or marks that they leave behind: *We all got up early to track deer in the woods.*

track someone/something down to find someone or something after a difficult or long search: *She spent years trying to track down her parents.*

tractor /'træktə/ *noun*
a vehicle that a farmer uses to pull farm machinery

trade /treɪd/ *verb* (**trades, trading, traded**)
1 to buy and sell goods: *We have been trading with this company for over thirty years.* ● **trade** *uncountable noun* *Texas has a long history of trade with Mexico.*
2 to give someone one thing and get something else from them in exchange: *He traded his car for a motorcycle.*

trademark /'treɪdmɑːk/ *noun*
a special name or symbol that a company owns and uses on its products: *Kodak is a trademark of Eastman Kodak Company.*

tradition /trə'dɪʃən/ *noun*
a type of behaviour or a belief that has existed for a long time: *Afternoon tea is a British tradition.*
▸ **traditional** /trə'dɪʃənəl/ *adjective* *The band plays a lot of traditional Scottish music.*
▸ **traditionally** *adverb* *Christmas is traditionally a time for families.*

traffic /'træfɪk/ *uncountable noun*
1 all the vehicles that are on a particular road at one time: *There was heavy traffic on the roads.* ◻ *Yesterday, traffic was light on the motorway.*
2 the movement of ships, trains or aircraft between one place and another: *No air traffic was allowed out of the airport.*

'traffic jam *noun*
a long line of vehicles that cannot move forward, or can only move very slowly

'traffic lights *plural noun*
coloured lights that control the flow of traffic

tragedy /'trædʒɪdi/ *noun* (**tragedies**)
1 an extremely sad event or situation: *They have suffered a terrible personal tragedy.*
2 a type of serious play, that usually ends with the death of the main character: *the tragedies of Shakespeare*

tragic /'trædʒɪk/ *adjective*
extremely sad: *It was a tragic accident.*
▸ **tragically** /'trædʒɪkli/ *adverb* *He died tragically in a car accident.*

trail /treɪl/ *noun*
1 a series of marks that is left by someone or something as they move around: *Everywhere in the house was a sticky trail of orange juice.*
2 a path through the countryside: *He was walking along a trail through the trees.*

trailer /'treɪlə/ *noun*
1 a large container on wheels that is pulled by a lorry or other vehicle
2 (*American*) → see **caravan**

train¹ /treɪn/ *noun*
a long vehicle that is pulled by an engine along a railway: *We caught the early-morning train.* ◻ *He came to Glasgow by train.*

train² /treɪn/ *verb* (**trains, training, trained**)
1 to learn the skills that you need in order to do something: *Stephen is training to be a teacher.*
▸ **training** *uncountable noun* *Kennedy had no formal training as an artist.*
2 to prepare for a sports competition: *She spent six hours a day training for the race.*
▸ **training** *uncountable noun* *He keeps fit through exercise and training.*

trainer /'treɪnə/ (*American*: **sneaker**) *noun*
a shoe that you wear for running and other sports, or with informal clothes: *a pair of trainers*

traitor /'treɪtə/ *noun*
someone who harms a group that they belong to by helping its enemies: *Traitors were sending messages to the enemy.*

tram /træm/ *noun*
an electric vehicle that travels along rails in the surface of a street: *You can get to the beach by tram.*

transfer /træns'fɜː/ *verb* (**transfers, transferring, transferred**)
to make something or someone go from

t

one place to another: *Transfer the meat to a dish.* ● **transfer** *noun* /'trænsfɜ:/ *Arrange for the transfer of medical records to your new doctor.*

transform /træns'fɔ:m/ *verb* (**transforms, transforming, transformed**)
to change someone or something completely: *The railway transformed America.* □ *Your body transforms food into energy.*
▶ **transformation** /ˌtrænsfə'meɪʃən/ *noun* The TV show follows the transformation of a bedroom into an office.

transitive /'trænzɪtɪv/ *adjective*
used for describing a verb that has a direct object

translate /trænz'leɪt/ *verb* (**translates, translating, translated**)
to say or write something again in a different language: *A small number of Kadare's books have been translated into English.*
▶ **translator** *noun* She works as a translator.

translation /trænz'leɪʃən/ *noun*
a piece of writing or speech that has been put into a different language: *a translation of the Bible*

transparent /træns'pærənt/ *adjective*
used for describing an object or a substance that you can see through: *We used a sheet of transparent plastic.*

transplant /'trænsplɑ:nt/ *noun*
a medical operation in which a part of a person's body is replaced because it has a disease: *a heart transplant*

transport [1] /'trænspɔ:t/ *uncountable noun*
a system for taking people or things from one place to another in a vehicle: *We will spend the money on improving public transport.*

transport [2] /træns'pɔ:t/ *verb* (**transports, transporting, transported**)
to take people or goods from one place to another in a vehicle: *Buses transported passengers to the town.*

trap [1] /træp/ *noun*
1 a piece of equipment for catching animals: *Nathan's dog got caught in a trap.*
2 a trick that is intended to catch someone: *He hesitated, wondering if there was a trap in the question.*

trap [2] /træp/ *verb* (**traps, trapping, trapped**)
1 to catch animals using traps: *They*

survived by trapping and killing wild animals.
2 to trick someone so that they do or say something that they do not want to do or say: *Were you trying to trap her into confessing?*
3 to prevent someone from moving: *The car turned over, trapping both men.*

trash /træʃ/ *uncountable noun* (American)
→ see **rubbish**

travel [1] /'trævəl/ *verb* (**travels, travelling, travelled**)
to go from one place to another, often to a place that is far away: *I've been travelling all day.* □ *People often travel hundreds of miles to get here.*

travel [2] /'trævəl/ *uncountable noun*
the activity of travelling: *He hated air travel.*

> **LANGUAGE HELP**
>
> **travel**, **journey** or **trip**? The uncountable noun **travel** is used for talking about the general activity of travelling. If you want to talk about a particular occasion when someone goes somewhere, use **journey**: *a journey by train from Berlin.* Use **trip** to talk about the whole experience of going somewhere, staying there and returning: *He suggested I cancel my trip to China.*

travel agency *noun* (**travel agencies**)
a company or a shop that sells holidays

travel agent *noun*
a person who works for a company or a shop that sells holidays

traveller /'trævələ/ *noun*
a person who is on a trip or a person who travels a lot: *airline travellers*

tray /treɪ/ *noun*
a flat piece of wood, plastic or metal that is used for carrying things, especially food and drinks

tread /tred/ *verb* (**treads, treading, trod, trodden**)
to walk in a particular way: *There is no safety railing here, so tread carefully.*

treasure /'treʒə/ *uncountable noun*
a collection of valuable old objects in children's stories, such as gold coins and jewellery: *buried treasure*

treat /tri:t/ *verb* (**treats, treating, treated**)
1 to behave towards someone or something in a particular way: *Stop treating me like a child.*

2 to try to make a patient well again: *Doctors treated the boy for a minor head wound.*
3 to buy or arrange something special for someone: *She treated him to ice cream.*
● **treat** *noun* *Lesley returned from town with a special treat for him.*

treatment /'triːtmənt/ *noun*
1 medical attention that is given to an ill or injured person or animal: *Many patients are not getting the medical treatment they need.*
2 *uncountable* the way you behave towards someone or deal with them: *We don't want any special treatment.*

treaty /'triːti/ *noun* (**treaties**)
a written agreement between countries: *a treaty on global warming*

tree /triː/ *noun*
a tall plant that lives for a long time. It has a hard central part (= a trunk), branches and leaves: *apple trees*

trek /trek/ *verb* (**treks, trekking, trekked**)
to go on a journey across difficult country, usually on foot: *We trekked through the jungle.*
● **trek** *noun* *We went on a trek through the desert.*

tremble /'trembəl/ *verb* (**trembles, trembling, trembled**)
to shake slightly: *Lisa was white and trembling with anger.* □ *He felt the earth tremble under him.*

tremendous /trɪ'mendəs/ *adjective*
1 very big or very great: *My students have all made tremendous progress recently.*
▶ **tremendously** *adverb* *I thought they played tremendously well, didn't you?*
2 very good: *I thought her performance was absolutely tremendous.*

trend /trend/ *noun*
a change or a development towards something different: *The restaurant is responding to the trend toward healthier eating.*

trendy /'trendi/ *adjective* (**trendier, trendiest**)
fashionable and modern (*informal*): *a trendy Manchester nightclub*

trial /'traɪəl/ *noun*
1 a formal meeting in a law court, at which people decide whether someone is guilty of a crime: *New evidence showed that the witness lied at the trial.* □ *He is on trial for murder.*

2 an experiment in which you test something by using it or doing it for a period of time to see how well it works: *The drug is being tested in clinical trials.*

triangle /'traɪæŋɡəl/ *noun*
a shape with three straight sides
▶ **triangular** /traɪ'æŋɡjʊlə/ *adjective*
a triangular roof

tribe /traɪb/ *noun*
used for talking about a group of people of the same race, language and culture, especially in a developing country. Some people disapprove of this use: *three hundred members of the Xhosa tribe*
▶ **tribal** /'traɪbəl/ *adjective* *tribal lands*

tribute /'trɪbjuːt/ *noun*
something that you say, do or make to show that you admire and respect someone: *The song is a tribute to Roy Orbison.*

trick¹ /trɪk/ *verb* (**tricks, tricking, tricked**)
to do something dishonest in order to make someone do something: *Stephen is going to be very upset when he finds out how you tricked him.* □ *They tricked him into signing the contract.*

trick² /trɪk/ *noun*
1 something dishonest that you do in order to make someone do something
2 a clever or skilful action that someone does in order to entertain people: *a card trick*

trickle /'trɪkəl/ *verb* (**trickles, trickling, trickled**)
to flow slowly in small amounts: *A tear trickled down the old man's cheek.* ● **trickle** *noun* *There was not even a trickle of water.*

tricky /'trɪki/ *adjective* (**trickier, trickiest**)
difficult: *Parking can be tricky in the town centre.*

tricycle /'traɪsɪkəl/ *noun*
a bicycle with three wheels

trigger /'trɪɡə/ *noun*
the part of a gun that you pull to make it shoot: *A man pointed a gun at them and pulled the trigger.*

trim /trɪm/ *verb* (**trims, trimming, trimmed**)
to cut off small amounts of something in order to make it look tidy: *My friend trims my hair every eight weeks.* ● **trim** *noun* *His hair needed a trim.*

t

trio /'tri:əʊ/ *noun*
a group of three people, especially musicians or singers

trip [1] /trɪp/ *noun*
a journey that you make to a particular place and back again: *She has just returned from a trip to Switzerland.*

trip [2] /trɪp/ *verb* (**trips, tripping, tripped**)
to knock your foot against something and fall or nearly fall: *She tripped and broke her hip.*

triple [1] /'trɪpəl/ *adjective*
consisting of three things or parts: *The property includes a triple garage.*

triple [2] /'trɪpəl/ *verb* (**triples, tripling, tripled**)
to become three times as large: *I got a fantastic new job and my salary tripled.*

triplet /'trɪplət/ *noun*
one of three children that are born at the same time to the same mother

triumph /'traɪʌmf/ *noun*
1 a great success: *The championships were a personal triumph for the coach.*
2 *uncountable* a feeling of great satisfaction after a great success: *She felt a sense of triumph.*

trivial /'trɪviəl/ *adjective*
not important or serious: *I was not interested in the trivial details of his life.*

trod /trɒd/ → see **tread**

trodden /'trɒdən/ → see **tread**

trolley /'trɒli/ (*American*: **cart**) *noun*
a large container with wheels that you use for moving heavy things such as shopping or luggage: *a supermarket trolley* □ *She pushed her cases on a trolley.*

trombone /trɒm'bəʊn/ *noun*
a metal musical instrument that you play by blowing into it and sliding part of it backwards and forwards: *Her husband plays the trombone.*

troops /tru:ps/ *plural noun*
soldiers: *35,000 troops from a dozen countries are already there.*

trophy /'trəʊfi/ *noun* (**trophies**)
a prize, such as a silver cup, that is given to the winner of a competition: *The special trophy for the best rider went to Chris Read.*

tropical /'trɒpɪkəl/ *adjective*
belonging to or typical of the hot, wet areas of the world: *tropical diseases*

tropics /'trɒpɪks/ *plural noun*
the tropics the hottest parts of the world, where it is hot and wet

trot /trɒt/ *verb* (**trots, trotting, trotted**)
1 to move at a speed between walking and running: *I trotted down the steps and out to the garden.*
2 used for saying that an animal such as a horse moves fairly fast, taking quick small steps: *My horse was soon trotting around the field.*

trouble [1] /'trʌbəl/ *noun*
1 problems or difficulties: *I had trouble parking.* □ *You've caused us a lot of trouble.*
2 *uncountable* a situation where people are arguing or fighting: *Police were sent to the city to prevent trouble.*
in trouble having broken a rule or a law, and likely to be punished: *He was in trouble with his teachers.*

trouble [2] /'trʌbəl/ *verb* (**troubles, troubling, troubled**)
1 to make someone feel worried: *Is anything troubling you?*
2 to disturb someone: *Sorry to trouble you, but can I borrow your pen?*

trousers /'traʊzəz/ (*American*: **pants**) *plural noun*
a piece of clothing that covers the body from the waist downwards, and that covers each leg separately (*formal*): *He was dressed in a shirt, dark trousers and boots.*
→ Look at picture on P2

truck /trʌk/ *noun* (*American*)
→ see **lorry**

true /tru:/ *adjective* (**truer, truest**)
based on facts, and not invented or imagined: *Everything she said was true.* □ *The film is based on a true story.*
come true to actually happen: *When I was 13, my dream came true and I got my first horse.*

truly /'tru:li/ *adverb*
really and completely: *We want a truly democratic system.* □ *Believe me, Susan, I am truly sorry.*
Yours truly (*American*)
→ see **Yours faithfully**

trumpet /'trʌmpɪt/ *noun*
a metal musical instrument that you blow: *I played the trumpet in the school orchestra.*

trunk /trʌŋk/ *noun*
1 the large main stem of a tree from which the branches grow: *The tree trunk was more than two metres across.*
2 (*American*) the **boot** of a car
3 a large, strong box that is used for storing things: *Maloney unlocked his trunk and took out some clothing.*
4 the long nose of an elephant
5 *plural* → see **swimming trunks**

trunk

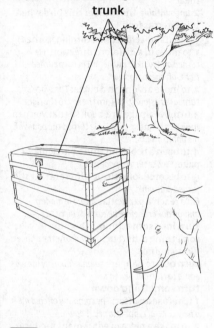

trust /trʌst/ *verb* (**trusts, trusting, trusted**)
1 to believe that someone is honest and that they will not deliberately do anything to harm you: *'I trust you completely,' he said.* ● **trust** *uncountable noun* *He destroyed my trust in men.* □ *There was a shared feeling of trust amongst the members of the team.*
2 to believe that someone will do something: *I trust you to keep this secret.*

trustworthy /'trʌstwɜːði/ *adjective*
responsible and able to be trusted completely: *He is a trustworthy leader.*

truth /truːθ/ *uncountable noun*
all the facts about something, rather than things that are imagined or

invented: *There is no truth in this story.* □ *Are you telling me the truth?*

truthful /'truːθfʊl/ *adjective*
honest: *She was always completely truthful with us.* □ *The truthful answer is that I don't know.*
▶ **truthfully** *adverb* *I answered all their questions truthfully.*
▶ **truthfulness** *uncountable noun* *I can say, with absolute truthfulness, that I did my best.*

try /traɪ/ *verb* (**tries, trying, tried**)
1 to make an effort to do something: *He tried to help her at work.* □ *She doesn't seem to try hard enough.* □ *I must try and see him.* ● **try** *noun* (**tries**) *It was a good try.*
2 to use or do something new or different in order to discover what it is like: *You could try a little cheese melted on the top.*
● **try** *noun* *All we're asking is that you give it a try.*
3 to go to a particular place or person because you think that they may be able to give you what you need: *Have you tried the local music shops?*
4 to decide in a law court if someone is guilty of a crime: *They were arrested and tried for murder.*

try something on to put on a piece of clothing in order to see if it fits you or if it looks nice: *Try on the shoes to make sure they fit.*

try something out to test something in order to find out how useful or effective it is: *I want to try the boat out next weekend.*

> **LANGUAGE HELP**
> **Try and** is often used instead of **try to** in spoken English. *Just try and stop me!*

'T-shirt also **tee-shirt** *noun*
a simple shirt with no collar and short sleeves

tsunami /tsʊ'nɑːmi/ *noun*
a very large wave that flows onto the land and can cause a lot of damage

tub /tʌb/ *noun*
a deep container: *We ate four tubs of ice cream between us.*

tuba /'tjuːbə/ *noun*
a large round metal musical instrument with one wide end, that produces very low notes when you blow into it

t

the Tube /ðə ˈtjuːb/ *noun*
the underground railway in London: *I took the Tube and then the train.*

tube /tjuːb/ *noun*
1 a long hollow object that is usually round, like a pipe: *He is fed by a tube that enters his nose.*
2 a long, thin container that you can press in order to force the substance out: *a tube of toothpaste*

tuck /tʌk/ *verb* (**tucks, tucking, tucked**)
to put something somewhere so that it is safe, comfortable or tidy: *He tucked his shirt inside his trousers.*

Tuesday /ˈtjuːzdeɪ, -di/ *noun*
the day after Monday and before Wednesday: *He phoned on Tuesday, just before you arrived.* □ *Work on the project will start next Tuesday.*

tug /tʌg/ *verb* (**tugs, tugging, tugged**)
to give something a quick, strong pull: *A little boy tugged at his sleeve excitedly.* ● **tug** *noun* *I felt a tug at my sleeve.*

tulip /ˈtjuːlɪp/ *noun*
a flower that grows in the spring and is shaped like a cup

tumble /ˈtʌmbəl/ *verb* (**tumbles, tumbling, tumbled**)
to fall with a rolling movement: *A small boy tumbled off the step.*

tummy /ˈtʌmi/ *noun* (**tummies**)
your stomach: *Your baby's tummy should feel warm, but not hot.*

tumour /ˈtjuːmə/ *noun*
an unusual lump that has grown in a person's or an animal's body: *a brain tumour*

tuna /ˈtjuːnə/ *noun* (**tuna** or **tunas**) or **tuna fish**
1 a large fish that lives in warm seas
2 *uncountable* this fish when it is eaten as food: *She opened a can of tuna.*

tune [1] /tjuːn/ *noun*
a series of musical notes that is pleasant to listen to: *She was humming a little tune.*
in tune/out of tune producing/not producing exactly the right notes: *It was just an ordinary voice, but he sang in tune.*

tune [2] /tjuːn/ *verb* (**tunes, tuning, tuned**)
to adjust a musical instrument so that it produces the right notes: *We tune our guitars before we go on stage.*

tune something up same meaning as **tune**: *Others were quietly tuning up their instruments.*

tunnel /ˈtʌnəl/ *noun*
a long passage that has been made under the ground, usually through a hill or under the sea

turkey /ˈtɜːki/ *noun*
1 a large bird that is kept on a farm for its meat
2 *uncountable* the meat of this bird when it is eaten as food

turn [1] /tɜːn/ *verb* (**turns, turning, turned**)
1 to move in a different direction: *He turned and walked away.* □ *Then we turned right, off the motorway.*
2 to move around in a circle: *The wheels turned very slowly.* □ *Turn the key to the right.*
3 to move a page in a book so that you can look at the next page: *He turned the pages of his photo album.*
4 to open a book and find a particular page: *Please turn to page 236.*
5 to become something different: *The sky turned pale pink.*
6 to reach a particular age: *He made a million dollars before he turned thirty.*

turn into something to become something different: *In the story, the prince turns into a frog.*

turn out to happen: *I didn't know my life was going to turn out like this.*

turn something down
1 to refuse an offer: *The company offered me a new contract, but I turned it down.*
2 to make a piece of equipment produce less sound or heat: *Please turn the TV down!* □ *I'll turn down the central heating.*

turn something off to make a piece of equipment stop working: *The light's a bit bright. Can you turn it off?* □ *When the bath was full, she turned off the tap.*

turn something on to make a piece of equipment start working: *I turned on the television.*

turn something out to switch off a light: *Remember to turn the lights out when you leave the building.*

turn something over to move something so that the top part is on the bottom: *Liz picked up the envelope and turned it over.* □ *The car turned over and landed in a river.*

turn something up to make a piece of

equipment produce more sound or heat: *I turned the volume up.*

turn to someone to ask someone for their help: *She turned to him for support when she lost her job.*

turn up to arrive: *They finally turned up at nearly midnight.*

turn² /tɜːn/ *noun*

1 a move in a different direction: *You can't do a right-hand turn here.*

2 the time when you can do something: *Tonight it's my turn to cook.*

take turns to do something one after the other several times: *It's a long way to Washington, so we took turns driving.*

turning /'tɜːnɪŋ/ *noun*
a place where two roads join: *Take the next turning on the right.*

turnip /'tɜːnɪp/ *noun*
a round white vegetable that grows under the ground

turnover /'tɜːnəʊvə/ *noun*
the value of the goods or services that are sold by a company during a particular period of time: *The company had a turnover of £3.8 million.*

turquoise /'tɜːkwɔɪz/ *adjective*
of a light greenish-blue colour: *the clear turquoise sea* ● **turquoise** *noun The door is painted a bright turquoise.*

turtle /'tɜːtəl/ *noun*
an animal that has a thick shell around its body and lives in water: *Seabirds and turtles live on the island.*

tusk /tʌsk/ *noun*
a very long, curved, pointed tooth that grows beside the mouth of an elephant (= a very large grey animal that lives in Africa and Asia)

tutor /'tjuːtə/ *noun*
someone who gives private lessons to one student or a very small group of students: *a maths tutor*

TV /ˌtiː 'viː/ *noun* (**TVs**)
→ see **television**: *The TV was on.* □ *What's on TV?* □ *They watch too much TV.*
→ Look at picture on P5

tweezers /'twiːzəz/ *plural noun*
a small tool that you use for picking up or removing small objects. Tweezers consist of two thin pieces of metal joined

together at one end: *a pair of tweezers*

twelfth¹ /twelfθ/ *adjective, adverb*
the item in a series that you count as number twelve: *They're celebrating the twelfth anniversary of the revolution.* □ *She came twelfth in the competition.*

twelfth² /twelfθ/ *noun*
one of twelve equal parts of something ($^1/_{12}$): *She will get a twelfth of her father's money.*

twelve /twelv/
the number 12

twenty /'twenti/
the number 20

24-7 /ˌtwentifɔː'sevən/ also **twenty-four seven** *adverb*
all the time; twenty-four hours a day, seven days a week (*informal*): *I feel like sleeping 24-7.* ● **24-7** *adjective a 24-7 radio station*

twice /twaɪs/ *adverb*
two times: *He visited me twice last week.* □ *I phoned twice a day.* □ *Budapest is twice as big as my home town.*

twig /twɪg/ *noun*
a small thin branch of a tree or a bush

twilight /'twaɪlaɪt/ *uncountable noun*
the time just before night when the light of the day has almost gone: *They returned at twilight.*

twin /twɪn/ *noun*
one of two people who were born at the same time to the same mother: *Sarah was looking after the twins.*

twinkle /'twɪŋkəl/ *verb* (**twinkles, twinkling, twinkled**)
to shine with a light that continuously becomes brighter and then weaker: *Lights twinkled across the valley.*

twirl /twɜːl/ *verb* (**twirls, twirling, twirled**)
to turn or make something turn around several times very quickly: *Bonnie twirled her empty glass in her fingers.* □ *The dancers twirled around the dance floor.*

twist /twɪst/ *verb* (**twists, twisting, twisted**)
1 to turn something to make it into a different shape: *She sat twisting the handles of the bag, and looking worried.*

2 to turn part of your body such as your head or your shoulders while keeping the rest of your body still: *She twisted her head around to look at him.*

t

3 to injure a part of your body by turning it too suddenly, or in an unusual direction: *He fell and twisted his ankle.*
4 to turn something so that it moves around: *She was twisting the ring on her finger.*

twitch /twɪtʃ/ *verb* (**twitches, twitching, twitched**)
to make a little jumping movement: *Her right eye began to twitch.* •**twitch** *noun* (**twitches**) *He had a nervous twitch.*

two /tuː/
the number 2

two-dimensional /ˌtuːdaɪˈmenʃənəl, -dɪm-/ *adjective*
used for describing an object or a figure that is flat

type¹ /taɪp/ *noun*
a particular kind of something: *I like most types of music.* □ *Have you done this type of work before?*

type² /taɪp/ *verb* (**types, typing, typed**)
to write something using a machine like a computer: *I can type your essays for you.* □ *You should learn to type properly.*

typewriter /ˈtaɪpraɪtə/ *noun*
a machine with keys that you press in order to print writing onto paper

typical /ˈtɪpɪkəl/ *adjective*
1 used for describing a good example of a type of person or thing: *Tell me about your typical day.* □ *In some ways, Jo is just a typical 12-year old.*
2 showing the usual qualities or characteristics of someone or something: *The bear had thick, white fur, typical of polar bears.*

typically /ˈtɪpɪkəli/ *adverb*
1 used for saying that something is a good example of a particular type of person or thing: *The food is typically American.*
2 usually: *The day typically begins with swimming.*

typist /ˈtaɪpɪst/ *noun*
someone who works in an office typing letters and other documents

tyrant /ˈtaɪərənt/ *noun*
someone who has a lot of power and treats people in a cruel and unfair way: *His staff all thought he was a tyrant.*

tyre /ˈtaɪə/ *noun*
a thick round piece of rubber that fits around the wheels of cars and bicycles

t

Uu

ugly /'ʌgli/ *adjective* (uglier, ugliest)
very unpleasant to look at: *The museum is a rather ugly building.*

ultimate /'ʌltɪmət/ *adjective*
used for describing the final result of a long series of events: *Our ultimate goal is to win the gold medal.*

ultimately /'ʌltɪmətli/ *adverb*
finally, after a long series of events: *Who, ultimately, is going to pay?*

umbrella
/ʌm'brelə/
noun
a thing that you hold over your head to protect yourself from the rain: *She put up her umbrella and headed back to the car.*

umbrella

umpire /'ʌmpaɪə/ *noun*
a person who watches a game such as tennis or cricket to make sure that the players do not break the rules: *The umpire's decision is final.*

unable /ʌn'eɪbəl/ *adjective*
not able to do something: *After the car accident, Jacob was unable to walk.*

unacceptable /ˌʌnək'septəbəl/ *adjective*
used for describing something that is so bad or wrong that you cannot accept it or allow it: *This behaviour is unacceptable and will be punished.*

unanimous /juː'nænɪməs/ *adjective*
with everyone agreeing about something: *Their decision was unanimous.*
▶ **unanimously** *adverb* *The board unanimously approved the project last week.*

unattractive /ˌʌnə'træktɪv/ *adjective*
not beautiful or attractive: *I felt lonely and unattractive.* □ *The walls were painted an unattractive orange colour.*

unavailable /ˌʌnə'veɪləbəl/ *adjective*
busy and unable to meet you or talk to you: *The actress was making a film in Canada, and was unavailable for comment.*

unavoidable /ˌʌnə'vɔɪdəbəl/ *adjective*
impossible to avoid or prevent: *The accident was unavoidable.*

unaware /ˌʌnə'weə/ *adjective*
not knowing about or not seeing someone or something: *Many people are unaware that they have the disease.* □ *She said she was unaware of the incident.*

unbearable /ʌn'beərəbəl/ *adjective*
used for describing something that is so unpleasant that you cannot deal with it: *The pain was unbearable.*
▶ **unbearably** /ʌn'beərəbli/ *adverb*
In the afternoon, the sun became unbearably hot.

unbelievable /ˌʌnbɪ'liːvəbəl/ *adjective*
1 very hard to believe: *The film was good, but the plot was unbelievable.*
2 very good or very bad (*informal*): *It's a beautiful island, with unbelievable views.*
□ *The pain was unbelievable.*
▶ **unbelievably** /ˌʌnbɪ'liːvəbli/ *adverb*
Jarrod is an unbelievably brave guy.

unborn /ʌn'bɔːn/ *adjective*
not born yet: *This disease can harm an unborn child.*

uncertain /ʌn'sɜːtən/ *adjective*
not sure; not decided: *If you're uncertain about anything, you must ask.*

uncertainty /ʌn'sɜːtənti/ *uncountable noun*
a feeling that bad things might happen: *a time of political uncertainty*

uncle /'ʌŋkəl/ *noun*
the brother of your mother or father, or the husband of your aunt: *My uncle was the mayor of Liverpool.* □ *An email from Uncle Fred arrived.*
→ Look at picture on P8

unclear /ʌnˈklɪə/ *adjective*

1 not known: *It is unclear who tried to kill the president.*

2 not understanding or being sure about something: *People are unclear about the present situation.*

uncomfortable /ʌnˈkʌmftəbəl/ *adjective*

1 slightly worried or embarrassed, and not relaxed and confident: *The request for money made them feel uncomfortable.* □ *She was uncomfortable with the situation.*

▶ **uncomfortably** /ʌnˈkʌmftəbli/ *adverb*
Sam's face was uncomfortably close.

2 not pleasant to sit on, lie on or wear: *This is an extremely uncomfortable chair.*

uncommon /ʌnˈkɒmən/ *adjective*

not happening very often: *It's not uncommon to get rain, snow and sun, all in one day.*

unconscious /ʌnˈkɒnʃəs/ *adjective*

not awake and not aware of what is happening around you because of illness or a serious injury: *When the ambulance arrived, he was unconscious.*

▶ **unconsciousness** *uncountable noun*
Breathing in this gas can cause unconsciousness and death.

uncontrollable /ʌnkənˈtrəʊləbəl/ *adjective*

impossible to stop or control: *She felt an almost uncontrollable excitement.*

▶ **uncontrollably** /ʌnkənˈtrəʊləbli/ *adverb I started shaking uncontrollably.*

uncountable /ʌnˈkaʊntəbəl/ *adjective*

used for describing nouns such as 'gold' or 'information' that have only one form and that cannot be used with 'a' or 'an'

uncover /ʌnˈkʌvə/ *verb* (**uncovers, uncovering, uncovered**)

1 to take away something that is on top of another thing: *Uncover the dish and cook the chicken for about 15 minutes.*

2 to find out about something secret: *They want to uncover the truth of what happened that night.*

undecided /ʌndɪˈsaɪdɪd/ *adjective*

not having decided about something yet: *Mary is still undecided about her future.*

under /ˈʌndə/ *preposition*

1 below something: *There are hundreds of tunnels under the ground.* □ *The two girls were sitting under a tree.* □ *There was a big splash and she disappeared under the water.*

2 less than a particular age or amount: *Sarah has three children under ten years of age.*

● **under** *adverb Children (14 years and under) get into the show free.*

undergo /ʌndəˈgəʊ/ *verb* (**undergoes, undergoing, underwent, undergone**)

to have an unpleasant experience: *Mia is undergoing treatment for cancer.*

undergraduate /ʌndəˈgrædʒʊət/ *noun*

a university or college student who has not yet passed their final exams: *More than 55 per cent of undergraduates are female.*

underground *adjective, adverb*

PRONUNCIATION HELP

adverb /ʌndəˈgraʊnd/; adjective /ˈʌndəgraʊnd/

---

below the surface of the ground: *The new library has an underground car park for 143 vehicles.* □ *Much of the castle is built underground.*

the underground (*American*: **subway**) in a city, the railway system in which electric trains travel below the ground in tunnels: *The underground is the best way of getting to work in Milan.*

underline /ʌndəˈlaɪn/ *verb* (**underlines, underlining, underlined**)

to draw a line under a word or a sentence: *She underlined her name.*

underneath /ʌndəˈniːθ/ *preposition*

below or under something: *The bomb exploded underneath a van.* ● **underneath** *adverb He was wearing a blue sweater with a white T-shirt underneath.*

underpants /ˈʌndəˌpænts/ *plural noun*

a short piece of underwear that covers the area between a man's or a boy's waist and the top of his legs: *Richard packed a spare shirt, socks and underpants.*

understand /ʌndəˈstænd/ *verb* (**understands, understanding, understood**)

1 to know what something means: *Toni can speak and understand Russian.* □ *'Do you understand what I'm telling you, Sean?'*

2 to know why or how something happens: *The children are too young to understand what is going on.* □ *I don't understand why you're so afraid of her.*

3 to believe that something is true

because you have heard it or read it somewhere: *I understand that you're leaving tomorrow.*

understanding[1] /ˌʌndə'stændɪŋ/ *noun*
when you know about something: *Children need to have an understanding of right and wrong.*

understanding[2] /ˌʌndə'stændɪŋ/ *adjective*
kind to other people and thinking about how they feel: *He was very understanding when we told him about our mistake.*

understood /ˌʌndə'stʊd/
→ see **understand**

undertake /ˌʌndə'teɪk/ *verb* (**undertakes, undertaking, undertook, undertaken**)
to start doing some work: *The company has undertaken two large projects in Dubai.*

undertook /ˌʌndə'tʊk/ → see **undertake**

underwater /ˌʌndə'wɔːtə/ *adjective, adverb*
below the surface of the sea, a river or a lake: *The divers were using underwater cameras.* □ *Submarines are able to travel at high speeds underwater.*

underwear /'ʌndə,weə/ *uncountable noun*
clothes that you wear next to your skin, under your other clothes: *I bought some new underwear for the children.*

underwent /ˌʌndə'went/ → see **undergo**

undid /ʌn'dɪd/ → see **undo**

undo /ʌn'duː/ *verb* (**undoes, undoing, undid, undone**)
to untie something or make it loose: *I managed to undo a corner of the package.* □ *I undid the buttons of my shirt.*

undoubtedly /ʌn'daʊtɪdli/ *adverb*
used for emphasizing that something is true: *Hanley is undoubtedly a great player.*

undress /ʌn'dres/ *verb* (**undresses, undressing, undressed**)
to take off your clothes or another person's clothes: *Emily undressed, got into bed and turned off the light.* □ *Often young babies don't like being undressed and bathed.*
▸ **undressed** *adjective Fifteen minutes later Brandon was undressed and in bed.*

uneasy /ʌn'iːzi/ *adjective*
anxious or afraid about something: *Emma looked uneasy and refused to answer questions.*
▸ **uneasily** /ʌn'iːzɪli/ *adverb Meg looked at her watch and moved uneasily on her chair.*

unemployed /ˌʌnɪm'plɔɪd/ *adjective*
able to work but without a job: *Millions of people are unemployed.* □ *This course helps young unemployed people to find work.*
the unemployed people who are able to work but are without a job: *We want to create jobs for the unemployed.*

unemployment /ˌʌnɪm'plɔɪmənt/ *uncountable noun*
when people who want to work cannot work, because there are not enough jobs: *Robert's family live in an area of high unemployment.*

unequal /ʌn'iːkwəl/ *adjective*
not equal in quality or quantity: *Unequal pay is a serious problem in this industry.*

uneven /ʌn'iːvən/ *adjective*
not flat or smooth: *The ground was uneven and he fell off his bike.*

unexpected /ˌʌnɪk'spektɪd/ *adjective*
surprising, because you did not expect it to happen: *Scientists have made an unexpected discovery.*
▸ **unexpectedly** *adverb April was unexpectedly hot.*

unfair /ʌn'feə/ *adjective*
not treating people in an equal way or in the right way: *It's unfair to expect a child to behave like an adult.* □ *They claimed that the test was unfair.*
▸ **unfairly** *adverb She feels they treated her unfairly.*
▸ **unfairness** *uncountable noun I joined the police to tackle unfairness in society.*

unfamiliar /ˌʌnfə'mɪliə/ *adjective*
that you do not know; strange: *The woman's voice was unfamiliar to me.*

unfit /ʌn'fɪt/ *adjective*
1 not good enough for a particular purpose: *The water was unfit for drinking.*
2 not healthy or strong: *Many children are so unfit they cannot do even basic exercises.*

unfold /ʌn'fəʊld/ *verb* (**unfolds, unfolding, unfolded**)
1 to open something that has been folded, to make it flat: *Mum unfolded the piece of paper.*
2 to open out and become flat: *The sofa unfolds to form a double bed.*

unfortunate /ʌn'fɔːtʃʊnət/ *adjective*
1 unlucky: *We were very unfortunate to lose the game.*

2 that you wish had not happened:
We've made some unfortunate mistakes in the past.

unfortunately /ʌnˈfɔːtʃʊnətli/ *adverb*
used for showing that you are sorry about something: *Unfortunately, I don't have time to stay.*

unfriendly /ʌnˈfrendli/ *adjective*
not friendly; behaving in an unkind or unpleasant way: *The people he met there were unfriendly and rude.*

ungrateful /ʌnˈɡreɪtfʊl/ *adjective*
not showing that you want to thank someone who has helped you or been kind to you

unhappy /ʌnˈhæpi/ *adjective* (**unhappier, unhappiest**)
1 sad: *Christopher was a shy, unhappy man.*
▶ **unhappily** *adverb Jean shook her head unhappily.*
▶ **unhappiness** *uncountable noun There was a lot of unhappiness in my childhood.*
2 not pleased about something or satisfied with it: *We were unhappy with the way we played on Friday.*

unhealthy /ʌnˈhelθi/ *adjective* (**unhealthier, unhealthiest**)
1 ill or not in good physical condition: *The man looked pale and unhealthy.*
2 likely to make you ill or harm your health: *Avoid unhealthy foods such as hamburgers and chips.*

unhelpful /ʌnˈhelpfʊl/ *adjective*
not helping you or making things better: *Josh was rude and unhelpful to Della.*

uniform /ˈjuːnɪˌfɔːm/ *noun*
the special clothes that some people wear to work, and that some children wear at school: *The police wear blue uniforms.* ▫ *Daniel was dressed in his school uniform.*

uniform

police officer's uniform

school uniform

unimportant /ˌʌnɪmˈpɔːtənt/ *adjective*
not important: *Abigail always remembers unimportant details*

union /ˈjuːnjən/ *noun*
1 a workers' organization that tries to improve working conditions for the workers: *Ten new members joined the union last week.*
2 *uncountable* a group of people or countries that have joined together: *the European Union*

unique /juːˈniːk/ *adjective*
different from every other person or thing: *Each person's signature is unique.*

unit /ˈjuːnɪt/ *noun*
1 a single, complete thing that can belong to something larger: *The building is divided into twelve units.*
2 a measurement: *A centimetre is a unit of measurement.*

unite /juːˈnaɪt/ *verb* (**unites, uniting, united**)
to join together and act as a group: *The world must unite to fight this disease.* ▫ *Only the president can unite the people.*

universal /juːnɪˈvɜːsəl/ *adjective*
including or affecting everyone: *Love is a universal emotion.*
▶ **universally** /juːnɪˈvɜːsəli/ *adverb Reading is universally accepted as being good for kids.*

universe /ˈjuːnɪˌvɜːs/ *noun*
the universe everything that exists in space, including the Earth, the sun, the moon, the planets and the stars: *Can you tell us how the universe began?*

university /juːnɪˈvɜːsɪti/ *noun* (**universities**)
a place where you can study after you leave school: *I started my degree at St Andrews University in 1999.* ▫ *Robert's mother is a university professor.*

unjust /ʌnˈdʒʌst/ *adjective*
not fair or right: *He was an unjust ruler, responsible for the deaths of thousands of people.*
▶ **unjustly** *adverb Megan was unjustly accused of stealing money.*

unkind /ʌnˈkaɪnd/ *adjective* (**unkinder, unkindest**)
unpleasant and unfriendly: *Tyler was unkind to his sister all evening.*

unknown /ʌnˈnəʊn/ *adjective*
1 not known: *The child's age is unknown.*

2 not famous: *Ten years ago he was an unknown writer but now he is a celebrity.*

unleaded /ʌnˈledɪd/ *adj*
unleaded fuel contains a smaller amount of lead (= a metal) than most types of fuel: *He filled up his car with unleaded petrol.*

unless /ənˈles/ *conjunction*
used for saying what will happen if another thing does not happen: *Ryan says he won't go to the party, unless I go too.*

unlike /ʌnˈlaɪk/ *preposition*
different from: *You're so unlike your father!*

unlikely /ʌnˈlaɪkli/ *adjective* (**unlikeliest**)
not likely to happen: *The boys are unlikely to arrive before nine o'clock.*

unload /ʌnˈləʊd/ *verb* (**unloads, unloading, unloaded**)
to remove goods from a ship or a vehicle: *We unloaded everything from the car.* □ *The men started unloading the lorry.*

unlock /ʌnˈlɒk/ *verb* (**unlocks, unlocking, unlocked**)
to open something using a key: *Taylor unlocked the car and got in.*

unlucky /ʌnˈlʌki/ *adjective* (**unluckier, unluckiest**)
1 having something bad happen to you when it is not your fault: *Michael was unlucky to break his leg in the tournament in Rotterdam.*
2 bringing bad luck: *Four is an unlucky number in East Asia.*

unmarried /ʌnˈmærid/ *adjective*
not married: *an unmarried couple*

unmistakable /ˌʌnmɪsˈteɪkəbəl/ also **unmistakeable** *adjective*
very obvious and easy to recognize: *A few minutes later, we heard Shirley's unmistakable voice.*

unnatural /ʌnˈnætʃərəl/ *adjective*
different from what you usually expect: *His eyes were an unnatural shade of blue.*

unnecessary /ʌnˈnesəsri/ *adjective*
not needed or that you do not need to do: *It is unnecessary to spend huge amounts of money on Christmas presents.*

unofficial /ˌʌnəˈfɪʃəl/ *adjective*
not organized or approved by an official person or group: *Unofficial reports say that one police officer was killed.*

unpack /ʌnˈpæk/ *verb* (**unpacks, unpacking, unpacked**)
to take things out of a suitcase or a box: *He unpacked his bag.* □ *Bill helped his daughter to unpack.*

unpaid /ʌnˈpeɪd/ *adjective*
1 without receiving any money for something: *Most of the work I do is unpaid.*
2 not yet paid: *His telephone was disconnected because of an unpaid bill.*

unpleasant /ʌnˈplezənt/ *adjective*
1 making you feel upset or uncomfortable: *The plant has an unpleasant smell.*
▶ **unpleasantly** *adverb She stayed until the water became unpleasantly cold.*
2 very unfriendly and rude: *He is such an unpleasant man!*

unplug /ʌnˈplʌɡ/ *verb* (**unplugs, unplugging, unplugged**)
to take a piece of electrical equipment from its electrical supply, so that it stops working: *Whenever there's a storm, I unplug my computer.*

unpopular /ʌnˈpɒpjʊlə/ *adjective*
not liked by most people; not popular: *It was an unpopular decision.* □ *I was very unpopular at school.*

unpredictable /ˌʌnprɪˈdɪktəbəl/ *adjective*
always behaving in a way that you do not expect: *Jim was unpredictable — he could get angry about anything.* □ *The British weather is unpredictable.*

unprepared /ˌʌnprɪˈpeəd/ *adjective*
not ready for something: *I'm totally unprepared for my English exam tomorrow.*

unreasonable /ʌnˈriːzənəbəl/ *adjective*
not fair or sensible: *It's unreasonable to expect a child to behave well all the time.*

unreliable /ˌʌnrɪˈlaɪəbəl/ *adjective*
that you cannot trust or depend on: *My old car is very slow and unreliable. It's always breaking down.* □ *The law protects people from unreliable builders.*

unruly /ʌnˈruːli/ *adjective*
difficult to control: *Police arrested 60 people after the unruly crowd began throwing rocks and bottles.*

unsafe /ʌnˈseɪf/ *adjective*
dangerous; not safe: *The building is unsafe and beyond repair.* □ *The water here is unsafe to drink.*

u

unsatisfactory /ˌʌnsætɪsˈfæktəri/ *adjective*
not good enough: *His boss said that his work was unsatisfactory.* □ *Our accommodation was unsatisfactory.*

unsteady /ʌnˈstedi/ *adjective*
likely to fall: *My grandma is unsteady on her feet.*

unsuccessful /ˌʌnsəkˈsesfʊl/ *adjective*
failing to do what you wanted and tried to do: *They tried to save the man's life, but they were unsuccessful.*

unsuitable /ʌnˈsuːtəbəl/ *adjective*
not right for someone or something: *This film is unsuitable for children.*

unsure /ʌnˈʃʊə/ *adjective*
not certain about something: *Police are unsure exactly when the items were stolen.*

unsympathetic /ˌʌnsɪmpəˈθetɪk/ *adjective*
not kind or helpful to someone who is having problems: *Jane's husband was unsympathetic and she felt she had no one to talk to.*

untidy /ʌnˈtaɪdi/ *adjective*
not well arranged: *The place quickly became untidy.* □ *He was a thin man with untidy hair.* □ *Clothes were thrown in the luggage in an untidy heap.*

untie /ʌnˈtaɪ/ *verb* (**unties, untying, untied**)
to open a knot, or something that is tied with a knot: *She untied the laces on one of her shoes.* □ *They untied his hands.*

until /ənˈtɪl, ʌnˈtɪl/ *preposition*
1 happening before a particular time and then stopping at that time: *Until 2004, Julie lived in Canada.* • **until** *conjunction* I waited until it got dark.
2 not happening before a particular time and only starting to happen at that time: *I won't arrive in Dublin until Saturday.* • **until** *conjunction* They won't be safe until they get out of the country.

> **LANGUAGE HELP**
> You only use **until** when you are talking about time. When you are talking about place or position, use **as far as** or **up to**: *Will you come with us as far as the village? We walked up to the gate, but we didn't go in.*

untrue /ʌnˈtruː/ *adjective*
not true or correct: *Bryant said the story was untrue.*

unusual /ʌnˈjuːʒʊəl/ *adjective*
not happening very often or not seen or heard very often: *It's unusual for our teacher to make a mistake.*
▸ **unusually** /ʌnˈjuːʒʊəli/ *adverb* It was an unusually cold winter.

unwanted /ʌnˈwɒntɪd/ *adjective*
not wanted or loved: *Delete unwanted emails from your computer.* □ *Emily felt unwanted and unloved.*

unwelcome /ʌnˈwelkəm/ *adjective*
used for describing something or someone that you are not happy to have or to see: *We were clearly unwelcome guests.*

unwell /ʌnˈwel/ *adjective*
not well; ill: *Grandpa was feeling unwell and had to stay at home.*

unwilling /ʌnˈwɪlɪŋ/ *adjective*
not happy or keen to do something: *Many people are unwilling to change their email addresses.*

unwind /ʌnˈwaɪnd/ *verb* (**unwinds, unwinding, unwound**)
1 to loosen and straighten something that has been wrapped around something else: *She unwound the scarf from her neck.*
2 to do something relaxing after you have been working hard or worrying about something: *You need to unwind after a busy day at work.*

unwise /ʌnˈwaɪz/ *adjective*
not sensible: *It would be unwise of me to comment.*
▸ **unwisely** *adverb* She understands that she acted unwisely.

unwrap /ʌnˈræp/ *verb* (**unwraps, unwrapping, unwrapped**)
to take off the paper or plastic that is around something: *I untied the ribbon and unwrapped the small box.*

unzip /ʌnˈzɪp/ *verb* (**unzips, unzipping, unzipped**)
1 to undo the metal strip (= a zip) that fastens a piece of clothing: *Pete unzipped his leather jacket and sat down.*
2 to make a computer file go back to its original size after it has been zipped (= reduced in size using a special program): *Use the 'Unzip' command to unzip the file.*

up¹ /ʌp/ *preposition*
1 towards a higher place: *They were climbing*

up a mountain road. □ *I ran up the stairs.*
2 along a road: *A dark blue lorry came up the road.*

up² /ʌp/ *adjective, adverb*
1 towards a higher place: *Keep your head up.*
2 from sitting or lying down to standing: *He stood up and went to the window.*
3 to the place where someone or something is: *He came up to me and gave me a big hug.*
4 not in bed: *'Did I wake you?' — 'No, I'm up.'*
be up to come to an end: *When the half-hour was up, Brian left.*
be up against someone/something to have a difficult person or situation to deal with: *They were up against a good team, but did very well.*
be up to someone to do something to be the person who must do or decide something: *It's up to you to solve your own problems.*
What's up? used for asking someone what is wrong (*informal*): *'What's up?' I said to him. 'Nothing much,' he answered.*

upbringing /'ʌpbrɪŋɪŋ/ *noun*
the way that your parents treat you and the things that they teach you when you are growing up: *I had a strict upbringing.*

update¹ /ʌp'deɪt/ *verb* (**updates, updating, updated**)
to make something more modern or add new information to it: *We update our news reports regularly.*

update² /'ʌpdeɪt/ *noun*
the most recent information about a particular situation: *Now here's a weather update.*

upgrade¹ /ʌp'greɪd/ *verb* (**upgrades, upgrading, upgraded**)
to improve something or replace it with a better version: *The road into town is being upgraded.* □ *I recently upgraded my computer.*

upgrade² /'ʌpgreɪd/ *noun*
a piece of equipment or a program that makes a computer more powerful: *a software upgrade*

uphill /ʌp'hɪl/ *adverb*
up, towards the top of a slope: *He ran uphill a long way.*

upload /ʌp'ləʊd/ *verb* (**uploads, uploading, uploaded**)
to move a document or a program from

your computer to another one, using the Internet: *Next, upload the files on to your website.*

upon /ə'pɒn/ *preposition*
on (*formal*): *The decision was based upon science and fact.*

upper /'ʌpə/ *adjective*
in a higher position: *There is a good restaurant on the upper floor of the building.* □ *The soldier was shot in the upper back.*

upper case /ʌpə 'keɪs/ *uncountable noun*
the larger form of letters at the beginning of sentences or people's names. These are also called 'capital letters'. Compare with **lower case**: *Typing an email using upper case is like shouting at someone instead of talking to them.*

upright /'ʌpraɪt/ *adjective*
standing up and not lying down: *John offered Andrew a seat, but he remained upright.* □ *The ladder was upright against the wall.*

upset¹ /ʌp'set/ *adjective*
unhappy because something bad has happened: *After Grandma died, I was very, very upset.* □ *Marta looked upset.*
have an upset stomach to have a mild illness that affects your stomach, often because of something that you have eaten: *Paul was sick last night with an upset stomach.*

upset² /ʌp'set/ *verb* (**upsets, upsetting, upset**)
1 to make you feel worried or unhappy: *What you said in your letter really upset me.*
2 to make your plans go wrong: *Heavy rain upset our plans for a barbecue on the beach.*

upsetting /ʌp'setɪŋ/ *adjective*
making you feel unhappy or worried: *The death of a family pet is always upsetting.*

upside down /ʌpsaɪd 'daʊn/ *adverb*
with the bottom part of something at the top: *The painting was hanging upside down.*

upside down

upstairs
/ʌp'steəz/
adverb
on or to a higher floor of a building: *He went*

u

upstairs and changed his clothes. □ The restaurant is upstairs. • **upstairs** *adjective* Mark lived in the upstairs flat.

up-to-'date also **up to date** *adjective*
1 most recent: *Our company uses the most up-to-date technology.*
2 having the latest information about something: *We'll keep you up to date with any news.* □ *We need some up-to-date weather information.*

upwards /'ʌpwədz/ or **upward** *adverb*
moving or looking up: *She turned her face upwards.*

urban /'ɜːbən/ *adjective*
relating to a city or a town: *We are recruiting young adults from both rural and urban areas all over the country.*

urge¹ /ɜːdʒ/ *verb* (**urges, urging, urged**)
to try hard to persuade someone to do something: *Doctors urged my uncle to change his diet.*

urge² /ɜːdʒ/ *noun*
a strong feeling that you want to do or have something: *He felt a sudden urge to phone Mary.*

urgent /'ɜːdʒənt/ *adjective*
needing attention as soon as possible: *The refugees have an urgent need for food and water.* □ *I've got to take an urgent telephone call.*
▶ **urgently** *adverb* *These people urgently need medical supplies.*

URL /,ju: ɑːr 'el/ *noun* (**URLs**)
an address that shows where you can find a particular page on the World Wide Web

us /əs, STRONG ʌs/ *pronoun*
used for talking about yourself and the person or people with you: *William's girlfriend has invited us for lunch.* □ *Heather went to the kitchen to get drinks for us.*

USB /,ju: es 'biː/ *noun* (**USBs**)
a part of a computer where you can attach another piece of equipment. **USB** is short for 'Universal Serial Bus'.

use¹ /juːz/ *verb* (**uses, using, used**)
1 to do something with a particular thing: *They wouldn't let him use the phone.* □ *She used the money to buy food for her family.*
2 (also **use up**) to finish something so that none of it is left: *She used all the shampoo.* □ *If you use up the milk, please buy some more.*

use² *noun*
1 *uncountable* the action of using something: *We encourage the use of computers in the classroom.*
2 the way in which you can use something: *Bamboo has many uses — it provides food, shelter and medicine.*
have the use of something to be allowed to use something that belongs to someone else: *My older sister has the use of Mum's car one night a week.*
it's no use doing something something that you say when you stop doing something because you believe that it is impossible to succeed: *'It's no use asking him what happened,' said Kate. 'He won't tell us.'*
make use of something to use something for a particular purpose: *You can make use of the leisure facilities in the nearby hotel.*

used¹ /juːst/ *adjective*
be used to something to be familiar with something because you have done it many times before: *I'm used to hard work.* □ *I am used to travelling First Class.*
get used to something to become familiar with something: *This is how we do things here. You'll soon get used to it.*

used² /juːzd/ *adjective*
not new: *If you are buying a used car, you will need to check it carefully.*

used to /'juːs tə/ *modal verb*
used for talking about something that was true in the past but is not true now: *I used to live in Los Angeles.* □ *He used to be one of my teachers.*

useful /'juːsfʊl/ *adjective*
helpful: *The book is full of useful advice about growing fruit and vegetables.*
▶ **usefully** *adverb* *The students used their extra time usefully, doing homework or playing sports.*

useless /'juːsləs/ *adjective*
1 not helpful or useful in any way: *My leather jacket is useless in the rain.*
2 not having the result you would like: *Christina knew it was useless to argue with the police officer.*
3 very bad at something (*informal*): *I was always useless at maths.*

user /'juːzə/ *noun*
a person who uses something: *Some young*

Internet users spend up to 70 hours a week online.
□ *I'm a regular user of the underground.*

user-'friendly *adjective*
well designed and easy to use: *This is a well designed and user-friendly website.*

username /'juːzəˌneɪm/ *noun*
the name that you type onto your screen each time you open a particular computer program or website: *You have to log in with a username and a password.*

usual /'juːʒəl/ *adjective*
happening or found most often: *It is a large city with the usual problems.* □ *February was warmer than usual.*
as usual happening in the way that it normally does: *Dad's late, as usual.*

usually /'juːʒəli/ *adverb*
in the way that most often happens: *We usually eat in the kitchen.*

utensil /juːˈtensəl/ *noun*
a tool or an object that you use when you are preparing or eating food: *Always wash cooking utensils thoroughly.*

uterus /'juːtərəs/ *noun* (**uteruses**)
the part of the female body where babies grow

utter¹ /'ʌtə/ *verb* (**utters, uttering, uttered**)
to say something or to make a sound

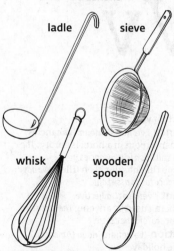

utensils

ladle   sieve

whisk   wooden
             spoon

(formal): *He finally uttered the words 'I'm sorry.'*
□ *He uttered a cry of pain.*

utter² /'ʌtə/ *adjective*
complete: *This is utter nonsense.*

utterly /'ʌtəli/ *adverb*
completely or very: *Their behaviour was utterly stupid.* □ *Patrick felt completely and utterly alone.*

u

Vv

v.
short for **versus**

vacancy /'veɪkənsi/ *noun* (**vacancies**)
1 when a room in a hotel is empty: *The hotel still has a few vacancies.*
2 a job that has not been filled: *We have a vacancy for an assistant.*

vacant /'veɪkənt/ *adjective*
not being used by anyone: *They saw two vacant seats in the centre.*

vacation /və'keɪʃən/ *noun* (American)
→ see **holiday**

vaccinate /'væksɪ‚neɪt/ *verb* (**vaccinates, vaccinating, vaccinated**)
to give a person or an animal a substance to prevent them from getting a disease: *Has your child been vaccinated against measles?*
▶ **vaccination** /‚væksɪ'neɪʃən/ *noun* I got my flu vaccination last week

vaccine /'væksi:n/ *noun*
a substance containing a very small amount of the thing that causes a particular disease. It is given to people to prevent them from getting that disease: *The flu vaccine is free for those aged 65 years and over.*

vacuum¹ /'vækju:m/ *verb* (**vacuums, vacuuming, vacuumed**)
to clean a room or a surface using a vacuum cleaner: *I had to vacuum the carpet and clean the bathrooms.*

vacuum² /'vækju:m/ *noun*
a space that contains no air or other gas: *When the machine is switched on, a vacuum is created.*

'vacuum ‚cleaner
noun (also **vacuum**)
an electric machine that cleans surfaces by sucking up dust and dirt

vacuum cleaner

vagina /və'dʒaɪnə/ *noun*
the passage that leads from the outside of a woman's or girl's body to the uterus (= the place where babies grow)

vague /veɪg/ *adjective* (**vaguer, vaguest**)
not explaining things clearly: *The description was pretty vague.*

vaguely /'veɪgli/ *adverb*
slightly: *The voice on the phone was vaguely familiar.*

vain /veɪn/ *adjective* (**vainer, vainest**)
1 not successful: *She made a vain attempt at a smile.*
2 too proud of the way you look: *He was so vain he spent hours in front of the mirror.*
in vain without success: *She tried in vain to open the door.*

valentine /'væləntaɪn/ *noun* (also **valentine card, valentine's card**)
a card that you send to someone who you are in love with, or who you like very much, on Valentine's Day, February 14: *I didn't receive any valentine cards this year.*

valid /'vælɪd/ *adjective*
used for saying that a ticket can be used and will be accepted: *All tickets are valid for two months.*

valley /'væli/ *noun*
a low area of land between hills: *a steep mountain valley*

valuable /'væljʊəbəl/ *adjective*
1 very useful: *Television can be a valuable tool in the classroom.*
2 worth a lot of money: *Do not leave any valuable items in your hotel room.*

value¹ /'vælju:/ *noun*
1 *uncountable* the importance or usefulness of something: *They didn't recognize the value of language learning.*
2 how much money you can get if you sell something: *The value of the house rose by £50,000 in a year.*
3 *uncountable* how much money

something is worth compared with its price: *This restaurant is extremely good value.*
4 *plural* the moral principles and beliefs of a person or group: *The countries of South Asia share many common values.*

value² /'vælju:/ *verb* (**values, valuing, valued**)
to think that something or someone is important: *I value my sister's opinion.*

valve /vælv/ *noun*
an object that controls the flow of air or liquid through a tube

vampire /'væmpaɪə/ *noun*
a monster in stories that comes out at night and sucks the blood of living people

van /væn/ *noun*
a vehicle like a large car or a small lorry with space for carrying things in the back

vandal /'vændəl/ *noun*
someone who deliberately damages property: *The street lights were broken by vandals.*

vandalism /'vændə,lɪzəm/ *uncountable noun*
the act of deliberately damaging property: *What can be done to stop school vandalism?*

vandalize /'vændə,laɪz/ *verb* (**vandalizes, vandalizing, vandalized**)
to damage something on purpose: *The walls were vandalized with spray paint.*

vanilla /və'nɪlə/ *uncountable noun*
a flavour used in some sweet foods, such as ice cream

vanish /'vænɪʃ/ *verb* (**vanishes, vanishing, vanished**)
to go away suddenly or in a way that cannot be explained: *He vanished ten years ago and was never seen again.*

vapour /'veɪpə/ *uncountable noun*
tiny drops of water or other liquids in the air: *Water vapour rises from Earth and falls again as rain.*

variable /'veəriəbəl/ *adjective*
changing quite often: *The quality of his work is very variable.*

variation /,veəri'eɪʃən/ *noun*
1 a similar thing in a slightly different form: *This is a delicious variation on an omelette.*
2 a change or difference in a level or

amount: *Can you explain the wide variation in your prices?*

varied /'veərid/ *adjective*
consisting of different types of things: *Your diet should be varied.*

variety /və'raɪɪti/ *uncountable noun*
when something consists of things that are different from each other: *Susan wanted variety in her lifestyle.*

various /'veəriəs/ *adjective*
of several different types: *He spent the day doing various jobs around the house.*

varnish /'vɑːnɪʃ/ *uncountable noun*
a thick, clear liquid that is painted onto things to give them a shiny surface

vary /'veəri/ *verb* (**varies, varying, varied**)
1 to be different from each other: *The bowls are handmade, so they vary slightly.*
2 to change something or make it different: *Be sure to vary the topics you write about.*
3 to become different or changed: *Here in the village, the temperature never varied a great deal.*

vase /vɑːz/ *noun*
a container that is used for holding flowers: *There was a small vase of flowers on the table.*

vast /vɑːst/ *adjective* (**vaster, vastest**)
extremely large: *Australia is a vast continent.* □ *Suddenly they have a vast amount of cash.*

vegetable /'vedʒtəbəl/ *noun*
a plant that you can cook and eat
→ Look at picture on P2

vegetarian¹ /,vedʒɪ'teəriən/ *noun*
someone who never eats meat or fish: *When did you decide to become a vegetarian?*

vegetarian² /,vedʒɪ'teəriən/ *adjective*
not containing meat or fish: *They did not follow a strict vegetarian diet.* □ *a vegetarian dish*

vegetation /,vedʒɪ'teɪʃən/ *uncountable noun*
plants, trees and flowers (*formal*): *tropical vegetation*

vehicle /'viːɪkəl/ *noun*
a machine that carries people or things from one place to another: *There are too many vehicles on the road.* □ *The car hit another vehicle that was parked nearby.*

v

veil /veɪl/ *noun*
a piece of thin soft cloth that women sometimes wear over their heads to cover their faces: *She wore a veil over her face.*

vein /veɪn/ *noun*
a thin tube in your body that carries blood to your heart. Compare with **artery**.

velvet /'velvɪt/ *noun*
soft cloth that is thick on one side: *red velvet curtains*

vent /vent/ *noun*
a hole that allows clean air to come in, and smoke or gas to go out: *Vents in the walls allow fresh air to enter the house.*

ventilate /'ventɪˌleɪt/ *verb* (**ventilates, ventilating, ventilated**)
to allow fresh air to get into a room: *You must ventilate the room well when painting.*
▶ **ventilation** /ˌventɪ'leɪʃən/ *uncountable noun* *The only ventilation came from one small window.*

venue /'venjuː/ *noun*
the place where an event or an activity will happen: *Fenway Park will be used as a venue for the rock concert.*

verb /vɜːb/ *noun*
a word such as 'sing', 'feel' or 'eat' that is used for saying what someone or something does

verbal /'vɜːbəl/ *adjective*
used for showing that something is expressed in speech: *We will not tolerate verbal abuse.*
▶ **verbally** *adverb* *We complained both verbally and in writing.*

verdict /'vɜːdɪkt/ *noun*
the decision that is given in a court of law: *The jury delivered a verdict of 'not guilty'.*

verge /vɜːdʒ/ *noun*
be on the verge of something to be about to do something very soon: *Carole was on the verge of tears (= she was nearly crying).*

verify /'verɪfaɪ/ *verb* (**verifies, verifying, verified**)
to check that something is true (*formal*): *We haven't yet verified his information.*

versatile /'vɜːsəˌtaɪl/ *adjective*
having many different skills or uses: *He was one of our most versatile athletes.*

verse /vɜːs/ *noun*
1 *uncountable* poetry: *The story was written in verse.*
2 one of the groups of lines in a poem or song

version /'vɜːʃən, -ʒən/ *noun*
1 a particular form of something: *He is bringing out a new version of his book.*
2 someone's own description of an event: *Her version of the story was different from Jack's.*

versus /'vɜːsəs/ *preposition*
used for showing that two teams or people are on different sides in a sports event. The short forms **vs.** and **v.** are also used: *It will be Scotland versus Belgium in tomorrow's game.*

vertebrate /'vɜːtɪˌbrət/ *noun*
an animal that has a spine (= bones in its back) Compare with **invertebrate**.

vertical /'vɜːtɪkəl/ *adjective*
standing or pointing straight up: *The climber moved up a vertical wall of rock.*

very /'veri/ *adverb*
used before an adjective or an adverb to make it stronger: *The answer is very simple.* □ *I'm very sorry.*

vest /vest/ *noun*
1 a piece of clothing that you wear under your shirt or t-shirt in order to keep warm
2 (*American*) → see **waistcoat**

vet /vet/ (*American:* **veterinarian**) *noun*
a person whose job is to treat ill or injured animals (*informal*)
→ Look at picture on P7

veterinarian /ˌvetərɪ'neərɪən, ˌvetrɪ-/ *noun* (*American*)
→ see **vet**

veto[1] /'vi:təu/ *verb* (**vetoes, vetoing, vetoed**)
to stop something from happening: *The president vetoed the proposal.*

veto[2] /'vi:təu/ *uncountable noun* (**vetoes**)
the power that someone has to stop something from happening: *The president has power of veto over the matter.*

via /'vaɪə, 'vi:ə/ *preposition*
through one place on the way to another: *I'm flying to New York via Sweden.*

vibrate /vaɪ'breɪt/ *verb* (**vibrates, vibrating, vibrated**)
to shake with repeated small, quick movements: *There was a loud bang and the ground seemed to vibrate.*
▸ **vibration** /vaɪ'breɪʃən/ *noun Vibrations from the train made the house shake.*

vice /vaɪs/ *noun*
1 *uncountable* criminal activity connected with sex and drugs
2 a bad habit or weakness: *My only vice is spending too much on clothes.*

vice versa /ˌvaɪsə 'vɜ:sə/ *adverb*
showing the opposite of what you have said: *The government exists to serve us, and not vice versa.*

vicious /'vɪʃəs/ *adjective*
1 violent and cruel: *He was a cruel and vicious man.*
2 cruel and intended to upset someone: *That wasn't true; it was just a vicious rumour.*

victim /'vɪktɪm/ *noun*
someone who has been hurt or killed: *The driver apologized to the victim's family.*

victorious /vɪk'tɔ:rɪəs/ *adjective*
describing someone who has won in a war or a competition: *The French team was victorious in all four games.*

victory /'vɪktəri/ *noun* (**victories**)
a success in a war or a competition: *The team are celebrating their victory.*

video /'vɪdiəu/ *noun*
1 an event that has been recorded, that you can watch on a television using a special machine: *We watched a video of my first birthday party.*
2 a film that you can watch at home: *You can rent a video for £3 and watch it at home.*
3 *uncountable* the system of recording films and events in this way: *She has watched the show on video.*

4 (*also* **video recorder**) a machine for playing videos

'video game *noun*
an electronic game that you play on your television or on a computer screen

view /vju:/ *noun*
1 an opinion that you have about something: *We have similar views on politics.*
2 everything that you can see from a place: *From our hotel room we had a great view of the sea* □ *He stood up to get a better view of the blackboard.*
on view in a public place for people to look at: *Her paintings are on view at the Portland Gallery.*

viewer /'vju:ə/ *noun*
a person who is watching a particular programme on television: *Twelve million viewers watch the show every week.*

vigorous /'vɪgərəs/ *adjective*
using a lot of energy: *You should have an hour of vigorous exercise three times a week.*
▸ **vigorously** *adverb He shook his head vigorously.*

village /'vɪlɪdʒ/ *noun*
a very small town in the countryside

villain /'vɪlən/ *noun*
someone who deliberately harms other people or breaks the law: *They called him a villain and a murderer.*

vine /vaɪn/ *noun*
a plant that grows up or over things: *a grape vine*

vinegar /'vɪnɪgə/ *noun*
a sour, sharp-tasting liquid that is used in cooking

vinyl /'vaɪnɪl/ *uncountable noun*
a strong plastic that is used for making things like floor coverings and furniture: *vinyl floor covering*

viola /vi'əulə/ *noun*
a musical instrument with four strings that produces low notes. You hold it under your chin, and play it by moving a long stick (= a bow) across the strings: *She plays the viola in several different orchestras.*

violate /'vaɪəˌleɪt/ *verb* (**violates, violating, violated**)
to break an agreement or a law (*formal*): *The company has violated international law.*
▸ **violation** /ˌvaɪə'leɪʃən/ *noun This is a violation of the law.*

v

violence /'vaɪələns/ *uncountable noun*
behaviour that is intended to hurt or kill people: *Twenty people died in the violence.*

violent /'vaɪələnt/ *adjective*
using physical force to hurt or kill other people: *These men have committed violent crimes.*
▶ **violently** *adverb* *The woman was violently attacked while out walking.*

violet [1] /'vaɪəlɪt/ *noun*
1 a small plant that has purple or white flowers in the spring
2 a blue-purple colour: *The sky turned purple and violet as the sun set.*

violet [2] /'vaɪəlɪt/ *adjective*
of a blue-purple colour: *a violet dress*

violin /,vaɪə'lɪn/ *noun*
a musical instrument made of wood with four strings. You hold it under your chin, and play it by moving a long stick (= a bow) across the strings: *Lizzie plays the violin.*

VIP /,viː aɪ 'piː/ *noun* (**VIPs**)
someone who receives better treatment than ordinary people because they are famous or important. VIP is short for 'very important person'.

virtual /'vɜːtʃuəl/ *adjective*
1 used for showing that something is nearly true: *He was a virtual prisoner in his own home.*
▶ **virtually** /'vɜːtʃuəli/ *adverb* *She does virtually all the cooking.*
2 made by a computer to seem like real objects and activities: *The virtual world sometimes seems more attractive than the real one.*

virtual re'ality *uncountable noun*
a situation that is produced by a computer to seem almost real to the person who is using it: *a virtual reality game*

virtue /'vɜːtʃuː/ *noun*
1 *uncountable* good thoughts and behaviour: *The priests talked to us about virtue.*
2 a good quality or way of acting: *His greatest virtue is patience.*

virus /'vaɪərəs/ *noun* (**viruses**)
1 a very small living thing that can enter your body and make you ill: *There are thousands of different types of virus, and they change all the time.*

2 a program that enters a computer system and changes or destroys the information that is there: *You should protect your computer against viruses.*

visa /'viːzə/ *noun*
an official document or a stamp in your passport that allows you to enter a particular country

visibility /,vɪzɪ'bɪlɪti/ *uncountable noun*
how far or how clearly you can see in particular weather conditions: *Visibility was poor.*

visible /'vɪzɪbəl/ *adjective*
able to be seen: *The warning lights were clearly visible.*

vision /'vɪʒən/ *noun*
1 what you imagine or hope a future situation or society will be like: *I have a vision of world peace.*
2 *uncountable* your ability to see clearly with your eyes: *He's suffering from loss of vision.*

visit /'vɪzɪt/ *verb* (**visits, visiting, visited**)
1 to go to see someone in order to spend time with them: *He wanted to visit his brother.* ▫ *In the evenings, friends often visit.*
● **visit** *noun* *I recently had a visit from an English relative.*
2 to go to a place for a short time: *He'll be visiting four cities on his trip.*

visitor /'vɪzɪtə/ *noun*
someone who is visiting a person or place: *We had some visitors from Australia.*

visual /'vɪʒuəl/ *adjective*
relating to sight, or to things that you can see: *The film's visual effects are amazing.*

vital /'vaɪtəl/ *adjective*
very important: *It is vital that children attend school regularly.*

vitamin /'vɪtəmɪn/ *noun*
a substance in food that you need in order to stay healthy: *These problems are caused by lack of vitamin D.*

vivid /'vɪvɪd/ *adjective*
1 very clear and detailed: *I had a very vivid dream last night.*
▶ **vividly** *adverb* *I can vividly remember the first time I saw him.*
2 very bright in colour: *She was dressed in a vivid pink jacket.*

vocabulary /vəʊ'kæbjʊləri/ *noun* (**vocabularies**)

1 all the words a person knows in a particular language: *He has a very large vocabulary.*

2 all the words in a language: *English has the biggest vocabulary of any language.*

vocal /'vəʊkəl/ *adjective*

1 giving your opinion very strongly: *Local people were very vocal about the problem.*

2 using the human voice, especially in singing: *She has an interesting vocal style.*

voice /vɔɪs/ *noun*
the sound that comes from someone's mouth when they speak or sing: *She spoke in a soft voice.* □ *Lucinda sings in the choir and has a beautiful voice.*

voicemail /'vɔɪsmeɪl/ *uncountable noun*
an electronic system that records spoken messages: *a voicemail message*

volcano /vɒl'keɪnəʊ/ *noun* (volcanoes)
a mountain that throws out hot liquid rock and fire: *The volcano erupted last year.*

volcano

volleyball /'vɒli,bɔːl/ *uncountable noun*
a game in which two teams hit a large ball over a high net with their arms or hands

volt /vəʊlt/ *noun*
a unit used for measuring electricity

volume /'vɒljuːm/ *noun*

1 the amount of space that an object contains: *What is the volume of a cube with sides 3 cm long?*

2 one book in a series of books: *We read the first volume of his autobiography.*

3 *uncountable* how loud or quiet a sound is: *He turned down the volume.*

voluntary /'vɒləntri/ *adjective*

1 done because someone wants to, and not because they must: *Participation is completely voluntary.*

▸ **voluntarily** /'vɒləntərəli/ *adverb*
I would never leave here voluntarily.

2 used for describing work that is done by people who are not paid, but who do it because they want to: *I do voluntary work with disabled children.*

volunteer¹ /,vɒlən'tɪə/ *noun*
someone who does work without being paid, because they want to do it: *She helps in a local school as a volunteer.*

volunteer² /,vɒlən'tɪə/ *verb* (volunteers, volunteering, volunteered)
to offer to do something that you do not have to do, or that you will not be paid for: *Mary volunteered to clean up the kitchen.*

vomit¹ /'vɒmɪt/ *verb* (vomits, vomiting, vomited)
if you vomit, food and drink comes up from your stomach and out through your mouth: *Milk made him vomit.*

vomit² /'vɒmɪt/ *uncountable noun*
food and drink that comes up from your stomach and out of your mouth when you vomit

vote¹ /vəʊt/ *noun*
a choice made by a particular person or group in a meeting or an election: *Mr Reynolds won the election by 102 votes to 60.*

vote² /vəʊt/ *verb* (votes, voting, voted)
to show your choice officially at a meeting or in an election: *The workers voted to strike.*

▸ **voter** *noun* *The region has 2.1 million registered voters.*

vow /vaʊ/ *verb* (vows, vowing, vowed)
to make a serious promise or decision that you will do something: *She vowed to continue the fight.* □ *I vowed that someday I would go back to Europe.* ● **vow** *noun* *I made a vow to be more careful in the future.*

vowel /'vaʊəl/ *noun*

1 a sound such as the ones written as **a**, **e**, **i**, **o** and **u**, and sometimes **y**

2 one of the letters **a**, **e**, **i**, **o** and **u**

voyage /'vɔɪɪdʒ/ *noun*
a long trip on a ship or in a spacecraft: *They began the long voyage down the river.*

vs.
short for **versus**

vulnerable /'vʌlnərəbəl/ *adjective*
weak and without protection: *Older people are particularly vulnerable to colds and flu in cold weather.*

Ww

wade /weɪd/ *verb* (**wades, wading, waded**)
to walk through water with difficulty:
I waded across the river to reach them.

wade

waffle /'wɒfəl/ *noun*
a flat, sweet cake with a pattern of
squares on it

wag /wæg/ *verb* (**wags, wagging, wagged**)
when a dog wags its tail, it moves it from
side to side

wage /weɪdʒ/ *noun*
the amount of money that is paid to
someone for the work that they do: *His
wages have gone up.*

> **LANGUAGE HELP**
> See note at **salary**.

wagon /'wægən/ *noun*
a strong vehicle with four wheels, usually
pulled by animals

waist /weɪst/ *noun*
1 the middle part of your body: *Ricky put his
arm around her waist.*
→ Look at picture on P1
2 the part of a pair of trousers that goes
around the middle part of your body:
The waist of these trousers is a little tight.

waistcoat /'weɪstkəʊt/ (*American*: **vest**)
noun
a piece of clothing without sleeves that

people usually wear over a shirt

wait /weɪt/ *verb* (**waits, waiting,
waited**)
1 to spend time doing very little, before
something happens: *I walked to the street
corner and waited for the school bus.* □ *I waited
to hear what she said.* □ *We had to wait a week
before we got the results.* ● **wait** *noun There
was a four-hour wait at the airport.*
2 to be ready for someone to use, have or
do: *There'll be a car waiting for you.*
can't wait/can hardly wait to be very
excited about something: *We can't wait to
get started.*
something can wait used to say that
something is not very important, so you
will do it later: *I want to talk to you, but it can
wait.*

waiter /'weɪtə/ *noun*
a man whose job is to serve food in a
restaurant
→ Look at picture on P7

'waiting room *noun*
a room where people can sit down while
they wait: *She sat for half an hour in the
dentist's waiting room.*

waitress /'weɪtrəs/ *noun* (**waitresses**)
a woman whose job is to serve food in a
restaurant
→ Look at picture on P7

wake /weɪk/ *verb* (**wakes, waking, woke,
woken**)
1 (*also* **wake up**) to stop sleeping: *It was cold
and dark when I woke at 6.30.* □ *We woke up
early to a perfect summer morning.*
2 (*also* **wake someone up**) to make
someone stop sleeping: *Betty woke me when
she left.* □ *She went upstairs to wake Jack up.*

walk [1] /wɔ:k/ *verb* (**walks, walking,
walked**)
to move forwards by putting one foot in
front of the other: *She walked two miles to
school every day.* □ *We walked into the hall.*
□ *I walked a few steps toward the fence.*

w

walk out to leave a situation suddenly, to show that you are angry or bored: *Several people walked out of the meeting in protest.*

walk² /wɔːk/ *noun*
a trip that you make by walking, usually for pleasure: *I went for a walk after lunch.*

wall /wɔːl/ *noun*
1 one of the sides of a building or a room: *His bedroom walls are covered with pictures of cars.*
2 a long narrow structure made of stone or brick that divides an area of land: *He sat on the wall in the sun.*

wallet /'wɒlɪt/ *noun*
a small case in which you can keep money and cards

wallpaper /'wɔːlpeɪpə/ *uncountable noun*
coloured or patterned paper that is used for decorating the walls of rooms
● **wallpaper** *verb* (**wallpapers, wallpapering, wallpapered**) *Every wall was wallpapered with a different colour.*

walnut /'wɔːlnʌt/ *noun*
a nut that is hard and round, with a rough texture

walnut

wander /'wɒndə/ *verb* (**wanders, wandering, wandered**)
to walk around, often without intending to go in any particular direction: *When he got bored he wandered around the park.*

want /wɒnt/ *verb* (**wants, wanting, wanted**)
to feel a need for something: *I want a drink.* □ *People wanted to know who she was.*

war /wɔː/ *noun*
a period of fighting between countries or groups: *He spent part of the war in France.*

ward /wɔːd/ *noun*
a room in a hospital that has beds for many people: *They took her to the children's ward.*

wardrobe /'wɔːdrəʊb/ (*American*: **closet**) *noun*
a cupboard where you hang your clothes
→ Look at picture on P5

warehouse /'weəhaʊs/ *noun*
a large building where goods are stored before they are sold

warfare /'wɔːfeə/ *uncountable noun*
the activity of fighting a war: *His men were trained in desert warfare.*

warm¹ /wɔːm/ *adjective* (**warmer, warmest**)
1 having some heat, but not hot: *On warm summer days, she would sit outside.* □ *Because it was warm, David wore only a white cotton shirt.*
2 made of a material that protects you from the cold: *You need to wear warm clothes when you go out today.*
▸ **warmly** *adverb* *Remember to dress warmly on cold days.*
3 friendly: *She was a warm and loving mother.*
▸ **warmly** *adverb* *We warmly welcome new members.*

warm² /wɔːm/ *verb* (**warms, warming, warmed**)
warm something up to make something less cold: *He blew on his hands to warm them up.*

warmth /wɔːmθ/ *uncountable noun*
1 the heat that something produces: *Feel the warmth of the sun on your skin.*
2 friendly behaviour towards other people: *They treated us with warmth and kindness.*

'warm-up *noun*
a period of gentle exercise that you do to prepare yourself for a particular sport or activity: *Training consists of a 20-minute warm-up, followed by ball practice.*

warn /wɔːn/ *verb* (**warns, warning, warned**)
to tell someone about something such as a possible danger: *They warned him of the dangers of sailing alone.*

warning /'wɔːnɪŋ/ *noun*
something that tells people of a possible danger: *It was a warning that we should be careful.* □ *Suddenly and without warning, a car crash changed her life.*

warrant /'wɒrənt/ *noun*
a legal document that allows someone to do something: *Police have a warrant for his arrest.*

warranty /'wɒrənti/ *noun* (**warranties**)
a promise by a company that if you buy something that does not work, they will repair it or replace it: *The TV comes with a twelve-month warranty.*

wary /'weəri/ *adjective* (**warier, wariest**)
careful because you do not know much about something or someone, and you

w

think they may be dangerous: *People teach their children to be wary of strangers.*

was /wəz, STRONG wɒz/ → see **be**

wash¹ /wɒʃ/ *verb* (**washes, washing, washed**)
1 to clean something using water and soap: *She finished her dinner and washed the dishes.* □ *It took a long time to wash the dirt out of his hair.*
2 to clean your body using soap and water: *I haven't washed for days.* □ *She washed her face with cold water.*
wash up to wash dishes: *You cooked, so I'll wash up.*

wash² /wɒʃ/ *uncountable noun*
in the wash being washed (*informal*): *Your jeans are in the wash.*

washbasin /'wɒʃbeɪsən/ *noun*
a large bowl in a bathroom for washing your hands and face
→ Look at picture on P4

washing /'wɒʃɪŋ/ *uncountable noun*
clothes and other things that you need to wash, or that you have just washed: *a bag full of dirty washing*

'washing machine *noun*
a machine that you use to wash clothes in: *Dan put his shirts in the washing machine.*
→ Look at picture on P4

,washing-'up *uncountable noun*
when you wash the plates, cups and other things that you have used for cooking and eating a meal: *Martha offered to do the washing-up.*

,washing-'up ,liquid *uncountable noun*
a thick liquid that you put into hot water to wash dirty dishes

wasn't /'wɒzənt/
short for 'was not'

wasp /wɒsp/ *noun*
an insect with wings and yellow and black stripes across its body. Wasps can sting people.

waste¹ /weɪst/ *verb* (**wastes, wasting, wasted**)
to use too much of something such as time, money or energy doing something that is not important: *She didn't want to waste time looking at old cars.* □ *I decided not to waste money on a hotel room.* ● **waste** *noun* *It is a waste of time complaining about it.*

waste² /weɪst/ *uncountable noun*
material that is no longer wanted

because the valuable or useful part of it has been taken out: *Waste materials such as paper and aluminium cans can be recycled.*

waste'paper ,basket *noun*
a container where you put things like paper that you do not need any more

watch¹ /wɒtʃ/ *verb* (**watches, watching, watched**)
1 to look at someone or something for a period of time: *A man stood in the doorway, watching me.* □ *I stayed up late to watch the film.*
2 to take care of someone or something for a period of time: *Could you watch my bags? I need to go to the bathroom.*
keep watch to keep looking and listening so that you can warn other people of danger: *Josh climbed a tree to keep watch.*

watch for something or **watch out for something** to pay attention so that you will notice something if it happens: *You should watch carefully for signs of the illness.* □ *Police warned shoppers to watch out for thieves.*

watch out used for warning someone to be careful: *You must watch out because this is a dangerous city.*

> **LANGUAGE HELP**
> See note at **look**.

watch² /wɒtʃ/ *noun* (**watches**)
a small clock that you wear on your wrist: *Dan gave me a watch for my birthday.*

water¹ /'wɔːtə/ *uncountable noun*
a clear, thin liquid that has no colour or taste. It falls from clouds as rain: *Could I have a glass of water, please?*

water² /'wɔːtə/ *verb* (**waters, watering, watered**)
1 to pour water over plants in order to help them to grow: *Make sure you water the plants before you go on holiday.*
2 when your eyes water, tears appear in them: *His eyes were watering in the smoke.*

watercolour /'wɔːtəkʌlə/ *noun*
1 a coloured paint that is mixed with water and used for painting pictures: *Campbell painted with watercolours.*
2 a picture that has been painted with watercolours: *a watercolour by Andrew Wyeth*

waterfall /'wɔːtəfɔːl/ *noun*
a place where water flows over the edge of

w

a steep part of hills or mountains, and falls into a pool below

watermelon /'wɔːtəˌmelən/ *noun*
a large, heavy fruit with green skin, pink flesh and black seeds

waterproof /'wɔːtəˌpruːf/ *adjective*
not letting water pass through: *You'll need to take waterproof clothing when you go camping.*

watt /wɒt/ *noun*
a unit of measurement of electrical power: *The lamp takes a 60-watt lightbulb.*

wave¹ /weɪv/ *verb* (**waves, waving, waved**)
1 to hold your hand up and move it from side to side, usually in order to say hello or goodbye to someone: *Jessica saw Lois and waved to her.* □ *She waved her hand in the air.*
2 to hold something up and move it from side to side: *More than 4,000 people waved flags and sang songs.*

wave

wave² /weɪv/ *noun*
1 a higher part of water on the surface of the sea. Waves are caused by the wind blowing on the surface of the water: *I fell asleep to the sound of waves hitting the rocks.*
2 when you hold your hand up and move it from side to side: *Steve stopped him with a wave of his hand.*
3 the form in which things such as sound, light and radio signals travel: *sound waves* □ *radio waves*

wavelength /'weɪvleŋθ/ *noun*
the size of a radio wave that a particular radio station uses to broadcast its programmes: *She found the station's wavelength on her radio.*

on the same wavelength finding it easy to understand someone because you share similar interests or opinions: *We often finished each other's sentences — we were on the same wavelength.*

wavy /'weɪvi/ *adjective* (**wavier, waviest**)
not straight or curly, but curving slightly: *She had short, wavy, brown hair.*

wax /wæks/ *uncountable noun*
a solid, slightly shiny substance that is used for making candles (= sticks that you burn for light) and polish for furniture: *The candle wax melted in the heat.*

way /weɪ/ *noun*
1 the action that you take to do something: *One way of making friends is to go to an evening class.* □ *She smiled in a friendly way.*
2 the route that you take in order to get to a place: *Do you know the way to the post office?*
3 a direction: *Which way do we go now — left or right?*

a long way a long distance: *It's a long way from New York to Nashville.*

by the way used when you are going to talk about something different: *By the way, how is your back?*

get your way/have your way to do what you want to do without anyone stopping you: *He likes to get his own way.*

in the way in the same place as you, and stopping you from doing something: *Please can you move? You're in the way.*

out of the way no longer stopping another person from doing something: *Get out of the way of the ambulance!*

we /wɪ, STRONG wiː/ *pronoun*
used for talking about both yourself and one or more other people as a group: *We said we would be friends for ever.* □ *We bought a bottle of lemonade.*

weak /wiːk/ *adjective* (**weaker, weakest**)
1 not healthy, or not having strong muscles: *I was too weak to move.*
▸ **weakly** *adverb* *'I'm all right', Max said weakly.*
▸ **weakness** *uncountable noun* *Symptoms of the disease include weakness in the arms.*
2 containing very little of a particular substance: *We drank weak coffee.*
3 not having much determination, and easy to influence: *He was weak, but he was not a bad man.*
▸ **weakness** *uncountable noun* *Some people think that crying is a sign of weakness.*

w

weaken /ˈwiːkən/ *verb* (**weakens, weakening, weakened**)
to become less strong: *The economy weakened in early 2001.*

weakness /ˈwiːknəs/ *noun* (**weaknesses**)
when you like something very much: *Stephen had a weakness for chocolate.*

wealth /welθ/ *uncountable noun*
a large amount of money, property or other valuable things: *He used his wealth to help others.*

wealthy /ˈwelθi/ *adjective* (**wealthier, wealthiest**)
having a large amount of money, property or valuable possessions: *She's going to be a very wealthy woman someday.*

weapon /ˈwepən/ *noun*
an object such as a gun, that is used for killing or hurting people: *He was charged with carrying a dangerous weapon.*

wear¹ /weə/ *verb* (**wears, wearing, wore, worn**)
to have something such as clothes, shoes or jewellery on your body: *He was wearing a brown shirt.*

wear down to become flatter or smoother because of rubbing against something: *The heels on my shoes have worn down.*

wear off to disappear slowly: *The excitement of having a new job soon wore off.*

wear someone out to make someone feel extremely tired (*informal*): *The kids wore themselves out playing football.*

> **LANGUAGE HELP**
> After getting up in the morning, you **get dressed** by **putting on** your clothes. *I got up, got dressed, and went downstairs. He put on his shoes and socks.* When you **are dressed**, you **are wearing** your clothes, or you **have** them **on**. *Cheryl was wearing a short black dress. Edith still had her hat on.*

wear² /weə/ *uncountable noun*
1 used to talk about clothes that are suitable for a certain time or place: *Jeans are perfect for everyday wear.*
2 the damage or change that is caused by something being used a lot: *The suit showed signs of wear.*

weary /ˈwɪəri/ *adjective* (**wearier, weariest**)
very tired: *Rachel looked pale and weary.*
be weary of something to have become tired of something: *They were all growing a bit weary of the game.*

weather /ˈweðə/ *uncountable noun*
the temperature and conditions outside, for example if it is raining, hot or windy: *The weather was bad.* □ *I like cold weather.* □ *Have you heard the weather forecast* (= information about what the weather is going to be like) *this morning?*

weave /wiːv/ *verb* (**weaves, weaving, wove, woven**)
to make cloth by crossing threads over and under each other: *We gathered wool and learned how to weave it into cloth.*

web /web/ *noun*
the thin net made by a spider from a string that comes out of its body: *a spider's web*

web

the Web /web/ *uncountable noun* (*also* **the World Wide Web**)
a computer system that helps you find information. You can use it anywhere in the world. It is also called the **World Wide Web**: *The handbook is available on the Web.*

webcam /ˈwebkæm/ *noun*
a camera on a computer that produces images that can be seen on a website

ˈweb page *noun*
a set of information that you can see on a computer screen as part of a website

website /ˈwebsaɪt/ *also* **web site** *noun*
a set of information about a particular subject that is available on the Internet

wedding /ˈwedɪŋ/ *noun*
a marriage ceremony and the party that often takes place after the ceremony: *Many couples want a big wedding.*

w

Wednesday /'wenzdeɪ, -di/ *noun*
the day after Tuesday and before
Thursday: *Come and have supper with us on
Wednesday.*

weed¹ /wiːd/ *noun*
a plant that grows where you do not want
it: *The garden was full of weeds.*

weed² /wiːd/ *verb* (**weeds, weeding,
weeded**)
to remove the weeds from an area: *Try not
to walk on the flowerbeds while you are weeding.*

week /wiːk/ *noun*
1 a period of seven days: *I thought about it
all week.*
2 the hours that you spend at work
during a week: *I work a 40-hour week.*

weekday /'wiːkdeɪ/ *noun*
any of the days of the week except
Saturday and Sunday

weekend /ˌwiːk'end/ *noun*
Saturday and Sunday: *I had dinner with Tim
last weekend.*

weekly /'wiːkli/ *adjective, adverb*
happening once a week or every week:
We do the weekly shopping every Thursday.
□ *They are paid weekly.*

weep /wiːp/ *verb* (**weeps, weeping, wept**)
to cry: *She wept tears of joy.*

weigh /weɪ/ *verb* (**weighs, weighing,
weighed**)
1 to have a particular weight: *She weighs
nearly 10 stone.*
2 to measure how heavy something or
someone is: *Lisa weighed the boxes for postage.*

weight /weɪt/ *noun*
1 how heavy a person or thing is: *What is
your height and weight?*
2 an object that people lift as a form of
exercise: *I was in the gym lifting weights.*
lose weight, gain/put on weight to
become thinner or become fatter: *I'm lucky
because I never put on weight.*

weird /wɪəd/ *adjective* (**weirder, weirdest**)
strange (*informal*): *He's a very weird guy.*

welcome¹ /'welkəm/ *verb* (**welcomes,
welcoming, welcomed**)
to act in a friendly way when someone
arrives somewhere: *She was there to welcome
him home.* ● **welcome** *noun* *They gave him a
warm welcome.*

welcome² /'welkəm/ *exclamation*
used for being friendly to someone who

has just arrived somewhere: *Welcome to
Washington!*

welcome³ /'welkəm/ *adjective*
you're welcome used for answering
someone who has thanked you for
something: *'Thank you for dinner.' — 'You're
welcome.'*

welfare /'welfeə/ *uncountable noun*
the health and happiness of a person or a
group: *I don't believe he is thinking of Emma's
welfare.*

well¹ /wel/ *exclamation*
used before you begin to speak, or when
you are surprised about something: *Well,
it's a pleasure to meet you.* □ *Well, I didn't expect
to see you here!*

oh well used for showing that you accept
a situation, even though you are not very
happy about it: *Oh well, I suppose it could be
worse.*

well² /wel/ *adverb* (**better, best**)
1 in an effective way: *The team played well
last week.* □ *He speaks English well.* □ *Did you
sleep well last night?*
2 in a complete way: *Mix the butter and sugar
well.* □ *Do you know him well?*
as well also: *Everywhere he went, I went as well.*
as well as and also: *Adults as well as children
will enjoy the film.*
do well to be successful: *If she does well in
her exams, she will go to college.*
may/might as well used for saying that
you will do something because there is
nothing better to do: *Anyway, you're here now
— you may as well stay.*
well done! said to someone when they
have done something good: *This is excellent
work. Well done!*

well³ /wel/ *adjective*
healthy: *'How are you?' — 'I'm very well, thank
you.'* □ *He said he wasn't feeling well.*

well⁴ /wel/ *noun*
a deep hole in the ground from which
people take water or oil: *The women and
children were carrying water from the well.*

we'll /wɪl, STRONG wiːl/
short for 'we shall' or 'we will'

well-be'haved *adjective*
behaving in a correct way: *well-behaved
children*

well 'done *adjective*
cooked thoroughly: *I like lamb well done.*

W

wellies /'weliːz/ *plural noun* (informal)
→ see **wellingtons**

wellingtons /'welɪŋtənz/ *plural noun* (also **wellington boots**)
long rubber boots that you wear to keep your feet dry

well-'known *adjective*
famous: *She was a very well-known author.*

well-'off *adjective*
rich (informal): *She comes from a reasonably well-off family.*

went /went/ → see **go**

wept /wept/ → see **weep**

were [1] /wə, STRONG wɜː/ → see **be**

were [2] /wə, STRONG wɜː/
sometimes used instead of 'was' in conditional sentences or after the verb 'wish' (formal): *Jerry wished he were back in Britain.*

we're /wɪə/
short for 'we are'

weren't /wɜːnt/
short for 'were not'

west [1] /west/ also **West** *uncountable noun*
the direction that is in front of you when you look at the sun in the evening: *Many of the buildings in the west of the city are on fire.*
the West the United States, Canada and the countries of Western Europe: *relations between Japan and the West*

west [2] /west/ also **West** *adjective, adverb*
1 towards the west: *We are going west to Glasgow.*
2 coming from the west

westerly /'westəli/ *adjective*
1 to the west or towards the west: *They walked in a westerly direction along the riverbank.*
2 blowing from the west: *a strong westerly wind*

western [1] /'westən/ also **Western** *adjective*
1 in or from the west of a place: *Western Europe*
2 used for describing things, people or ideas that come from the United States, Canada and the countries of Western Europe: *They need billions of dollars from Western governments.*

western [2] /'westən/ also **Western** *noun*
a film about life in the western United States in the past

wet [1] /wet/ *adjective* (**wetter, wettest**)
1 covered in liquid: *He dried his wet hair with a towel.*
2 raining: *It's cold and wet outside.*

wet [2] /wet/ *verb* (**wets, wetting, wet** or **wetted**)
to put water or some other liquid over something: *She wet a cloth and wiped the child's face.*

we've /wɪv, STRONG wiːv/
short for 'we have'

whale /weɪl/ *noun*
a very large mammal that lives in the sea

what /wɒt/ *pronoun*
used in questions when you ask for information: *What do you want?* □ *'Has something happened?' — 'Yes.' — 'What?'*
● **what** *adjective What time is it?* ● **what** *conjunction I want to know what happened to Norman.*

what (a/an) used in exclamations to make an opinion or a reaction stronger: *What a horrible thing to do!* □ *What pretty hair she has!*

what about...? used when you make a suggestion, an offer or a request: *What about going to see a film?*

what if...? used at the beginning of a question when you ask about something that might happen: *What if this doesn't work?*

whatever /wɒt'evə/ *conjunction*
1 used for talking about anything or everything of a particular type: *Frank was free to do whatever he wanted.* ● **whatever** *adjective He has to accept whatever punishment they give him.*
2 used to say that something is the case in all situations: *I will always love you, whatever happens.*

what's /wɒts/
short for 'what is' or 'what has'

wheat /wiːt/ *uncountable noun*
a crop that is grown for food. It is made into flour and used for making bread.

wheel [1] /wiːl/ *noun*
1 one of the round objects under a vehicle that allow it to move along the ground: *The car's wheels slipped on the wet road.*
2 the round object on a vehicle that you turn to make the vehicle go in different directions: *He sat down behind the wheel and started the engine.*

w

wheel [2] /wi:l/ *verb* (**wheels, wheeling, wheeled**)

to push an object along on its wheels: *He wheeled his bike into the alley.*

wheelbarrow /'wi:lbærəʊ/ *noun*

an open container with one wheel and two handles, that is used for moving things such as bricks, earth or plants

wheelbarrow

wheelchair

/'wi:ltʃeə/ *noun*

a chair with wheels that you use if you cannot walk very well

when [1] /wen/ *pronoun*

used for asking questions about the time at which things happen: *When are you going home?* □ *When did you get married?*

when [2] /wen/ *conjunction*

1 used for talking about something that happens during a situation: *When I met Jill, I was living on my own.*

2 used for introducing the part of the sentence where you mention the time at which something happens: *I asked him when he was coming back.*

whenever /wen'evə/ *conjunction*

used for talking about any time or every time that something happens: *Whenever I talked to him, he seemed quite nice.* □ *You can stay at my house whenever you like.*

where [1] /weə/ *pronoun*

used for asking questions about the place someone or something is in: *Where did you meet him?* □ *Where's Anna?*

where [2] /weə/ *conjunction*

used for talking about the place in which something happens: *People were looking to see where the noise was coming from.* □ *He knew where Henry was.* ●**where** *pronoun* *This is the room where I work.*

where's /weəz/

short for 'where is'

wherever /weər'evə/ *conjunction*

1 used for saying that something happens in any place or any situation: *Some people enjoy themselves wherever they are.*

2 used when you say that you do not

know where a person or a place is: *I'd like to be with my children, wherever they are.*

whether /'weðə/ *conjunction*

1 used when you are talking about a choice between two or more things: *They now have two weeks to decide whether or not to buy the house.*

2 used for saying that something is true in any of the situations that you mention: *You are part of this family whether you like it or not.*

which [1] /wɪtʃ/ *adjective*

used for talking about a choice between two or more possible people or things: *I want to know which school you went to.* □ *'You go down that road.' — 'Which one?'* □ *Which teacher do you like best?*

which [2] /wɪtʃ/ *pronoun*

1 used when you want to show the exact thing that you are talking about: *Police followed a car which didn't stop at a red light.*

2 used for talking about something that you have just said: *She spoke extremely good English, which was not surprising.*

whichever /wɪtʃ'evə/ *adjective*

any person or thing: *Whichever way we do this, it isn't going to work.* ●**whichever** *conjunction* *You can order by phone or from our website — whichever you prefer.*

while [1] /waɪl/ *conjunction*

used for saying that two things are happening at the same time: *His wife got up while he was in bed asleep.*

while [2] /waɪl/ *noun*

a period of time: *They walked on in silence for a while.*

whine /waɪn/ *verb* (**whines, whining, whined**)

1 to make a long, high noise that sounds sad or unpleasant: *He could hear the dog barking and whining in the background.*

2 to complain in an annoying way about something unimportant: *People were complaining and whining.*

whip [1] /wɪp/ *noun*

a long, thin piece of material attached to a handle. It is used for hitting people or animals.

whip [2] /wɪp/ *verb* (**whips, whipping, whipped**)

1 to hit a person or an animal with a whip: *Mr Melton whipped the horse several times.*

w

2 to stir cream very fast until it is thick or stiff: *Whip the cream until it is thick.*

whirl /wɜːl/ *verb* (**whirls, whirling, whirled**)
to turn around very quickly: *She whirled around to look at him.*

whisk¹ /wɪsk/ *verb* (**whisks, whisking, whisked**)
1 to take or move someone or something somewhere quickly: *He whisked her across the dance floor.*
2 to stir eggs or cream very fast

whisk² /wɪsk/ *noun*
a kitchen tool used for whisking eggs or cream

whisker /'wɪskə/ *noun*
one of the long, stiff hairs that grow near the mouth of an animal such as a cat or a mouse

whisky /'wɪski/ *uncountable noun*
a strong alcoholic drink made from grain: *a bottle of whisky*

whisper /'wɪspə/ *verb* (**whispers, whispering, whispered**)
to say something very quietly: *'Be quiet,' I whispered.* □ *He whispered in her ear.*
● **whisper** *noun* *People were talking in whispers.*

whistle¹ /'wɪsəl/ *verb* (**whistles, whistling, whistled**)
to make musical sounds by blowing your breath out between your lips: *He was whistling softly to himself.*

whistle² /'wɪsəl/ *noun*
a small tube that you blow into in order to produce a loud sound: *The guard blew his whistle and the train started to move.*

whistle

white¹ /waɪt/ *adjective* (**whiter, whitest**)
1 having the colour of snow or milk: *He had nice white teeth.*
2 having a pale skin: *A family of white people moved into a house up the street.*
3 white wine is a pale-yellow colour: *a glass of white wine*
4 white coffee or tea has milk in it

white² /waɪt/ *noun*
1 the colour of snow or milk: *He was dressed in white from head to toe.*
2 a person with pale skin: *The school has brought blacks and whites together.*

whiteboard /'waɪtbɔːd/ *noun*
a shiny, white board that you can draw or write on, using special pens. Teachers often use whiteboards.
→ Look at picture on P13

whizz /wɪz/ *verb* (**whizzes, whizzing, whizzed**)
to move somewhere very fast (*informal*): *Stewart felt a bottle whizz past his head.*

who /huː/ *pronoun*
used in questions when you ask about the name of a person or a group of people: *Who's there?* □ *Who is the strongest man around here?* □ *'You remind me of someone.' — 'Who?'*
● **who** *conjunction* *Police have not found out who did it.*

who'd /huːd/
1 short for 'who had'
2 short for 'who would'

whoever /huː'evə/ *conjunction*
1 used for talking about someone when you do not know who they are: *Whoever wins the prize is going to be famous for life.*
2 used for talking about any person: *You can have whoever you like visit you.*

whole /həʊl/ *noun*
all of something: *This is a problem for the whole of society.* ● **whole** *adjective* *We spent the whole summer in Italy that year.*
on the whole in general: *On the whole I agree with him.*

who'll /huːl/
short for 'who will' or 'who shall'

whom /huːm/ *pronoun*
used in formal or written English instead of 'who' when it is the object of a verb or a preposition: *The book is about her husband, Denis, whom she married in 1951.* □ *To whom am I speaking?*

who's /huːz/
short for 'who is' or 'who has'

whose /huːz/ *pronoun*
1 used in questions to ask about the person that something belongs to: *'Whose is this?' — 'It's mine.'* ● **whose** *adjective* *Whose daughter is she?* □ *I can't remember whose idea it was.*

w

2 used when you mention something that belongs to the person or the thing mentioned before: *That's the driver whose car was blocking the street.*

who've /huːv/
short for 'who have'

why /waɪ/ *pronoun*
used in questions when you ask about the reasons for something: *Why is she here?* □ *Why are you laughing?* ● **why** *conjunction* *He wondered why she was late.* ● **why** *adverb* *I liked him - I don't know why.*

Why not?
1 used for agreeing with a suggestion: *'Would you like to spend the afternoon with me?' – 'Why not?'*
2 used for introducing a suggestion: *Why not give Jenny a call?*

wicked /'wɪkɪd/ *adjective*
very bad: *That's a wicked lie!*

wide /waɪd/ *adjective* (**wider, widest**)
1 having a large distance from one side to the other: *The bed is too wide for this room.*
2 as far as possible: *'It was huge,' he announced, spreading his arms wide.*
3 used to talk or ask about how much something measures from one side to the other: *The lake was over a mile wide.*

widen /'waɪdən/ *verb* (**widens, widening, widened**)
to make something bigger from one side or edge to the other: *They are planning to widen the road.*

widespread /'waɪdspred/ *adjective*
happening over a large area, or to a great extent: *Food shortages are widespread.*

widow /'wɪdəʊ/ *noun*
a woman whose husband has died: *She became a widow a year ago.*

widower /'wɪdəʊə/ *noun*
a man whose wife has died

width /wɪdθ/ *noun*
the distance from one side of something to the other: *Measure the full width of the window.*

wife /waɪf/ *noun* (**wives**)
the woman a man is married to: *He married his wife, Jane, 37 years ago.*
→ Look at picture on P8

wig /wɪg/ *noun*
a covering of artificial hair that you wear on your head

wiggle /'wɪgəl/ *verb* (**wiggles, wiggling, wiggled**)
to make something move up and down or from side to side in small quick movements: *She wiggled her finger.*

wild /waɪld/ *adjective* (**wilder, wildest**)
1 used for describing animals or plants that live or grow in nature, and are not taken care of by people: *We could hear the calls of wild animals in the jungle.*
2 uncontrolled or excited: *The crowds went wild when they saw him.*
▸ **wildly** *adverb* *As she finished each song, the crowd clapped wildly.*

wilderness /'wɪldənəs/ *noun* (**wildernesses**)
a desert or other area of natural land that is not used by people: *There will be no wilderness left on the planet within 30 years.*

wildlife /'waɪldlaɪf/ *uncountable noun*
used for talking about the animals and other living things that live in nature: *The area is rich in wildlife.*

will¹ /wɪl/ *modal verb*

> **LANGUAGE HELP**
> When you are speaking, you can use the short forms **I'll** for **I will** and **won't** for **will not.**

1 used for talking about things that are going to happen in the future: *I'm sure things will get better.* □ *The concert will finish at about 10.30 p.m.* □ *One day I will come to visit you in York.*
2 used when you are asking someone to do something: *Please will you be quiet?*
3 used when you offer to do something: *No, don't call a taxi. I'll drive you home.*

will² /wɪl/ *noun*
1 the ability that someone has to decide to do something difficult: *I have a strong will and I'm sure I'll succeed.*
2 a legal document that says who will receive someone's money when they die: *He left £8 million in his will to the University of Edinburgh.*

willing /'wɪlɪŋ/ *adjective*
happy to do something: *He was a natural and willing learner.* □ *She's willing to answer questions.*
▸ **willingly** *adverb* *Bryant talked willingly to the police.*
▸ **willingness** *uncountable noun* *She showed her willingness to work hard.*

W

win /wɪn/ *verb* (**wins, winning, won**)
1 to do better than everyone else involved in a race, a game, or a competition: *He does not have a chance of winning the fight.* □ *The four local teams all won their games.* ● **win** *noun They played eight games without a win.*
2 to get a prize because you have done better than everyone else: *The first correct entry wins the prize.*

wind [1] /wɪnd/ *noun*
air that moves: *A strong wind was blowing from the north.*

wind [2] /waɪnd/ *verb* (**winds, winding, wound**)
1 to have a lot of bends: *From here, the river winds through attractive countryside.*
2 to wrap something long around something else several times: *She wound the rope around her waist.*
3 to turn part of a clock or a watch several times in order to make it work: *Did you remember to wind the clock?*

wind instrument /wɪnd ˌɪnstrəmənt/ *noun*
any musical instrument that you blow into to produce sounds

windmill /'wɪndmɪl/ *noun*
a building with long, flat parts on the outside that turn as the wind blows to make machinery move inside. Windmills are used for grinding grain or to pump water.

window /'wɪndəʊ/ *noun*
1 a space in the wall of a building or in the side of a vehicle that has glass in it: *He looked out of the window.*
→ Look at picture on P5
2 one of the work areas that a computer screen can be divided into: *Open the document in a new window.*

windscreen /'wɪndskriːn/ (American: **windshield**) *noun*
the glass window at the front of a car or other vehicle

windscreen wiper *noun*
a thing that cleans rain from a vehicle's windscreen

windshield /'wɪndʃild/ *noun* (American)
→ see **windscreen**

windsurfing /'wɪndˌsɜːfɪŋ/ *uncountable noun*
a sport in which you move across water on a long narrow board with a sail on it

windy /'wɪndi/ *adjective* (**windier, windiest**)
with a lot of wind: *It was a wet and windy day.*

wine /waɪn/ *uncountable noun*
an alcoholic drink made from grapes (= small green or purple fruit): *a bottle of white wine*

wing /wɪŋ/ *noun*
1 one of the two parts of the body of a bird or an insect that it uses for flying: *The bird flapped its wings.*
2 one of the long flat parts at the side of an aeroplane that support it while it is flying

wing

wink /wɪŋk/ *verb* (**winks, winking, winked**)
to look at someone and close one eye quickly, usually as a sign that something is a joke or a secret ● **wink** *noun I gave her a wink.*

winner /'wɪnə/ *noun*
the person who wins a prize, a race or a competition: *She will present the prizes to the winners.*

winter /'wɪntə/ *noun*
the season between autumn and spring. In the winter the weather is usually cold: *In winter the nights are long and cold.*

wipe /waɪp/ *verb* (**wipes, wiping, wiped**)
1 to rub the surface of something with a cloth to remove dirt or liquid from it: *I'll just wipe my hands.* ● **wipe** *noun The table's dirty - could you give it a wipe, please?*
2 to remove dirt or liquid from

something by using a cloth or your hand: *Gary wiped the sweat from his face.*

wipe something out to destroy something completely: *The disease wiped out thousands of birds.*

wire /waɪə/ *noun*

1 a long, thin piece of metal: *Eleven birds were sitting on a telephone wire.* □ *a wire fence*

2 a long thin piece of wire that carries electricity: *A wire connects the device to your mobile phone.*

wireless /'waɪələs/ *adjective*

using radio waves (= a form of power that travels through the air) instead of wires: *I have a wireless Internet connection for my laptop.*

wisdom /'wɪzdəm/ *uncountable noun*

the ability to use your experience and knowledge to make sensible decisions or judgements: *He has the wisdom that comes from old age.*

wise /waɪz/ *adjective* (**wiser, wisest**)

able to use your experience and knowledge to make sensible decisions and judgements: *She's a wise woman.*

▸ **wisely** *adverb* *They spent their money wisely.*

wish¹ /wɪʃ/ *noun* (**wishes**)

1 something that you would like: *Her wish is to become a doctor.*

2 when you say in your mind that you want something, and then hope that it will happen: *Did you make a wish?*

3 *plural* polite and friendly feelings that you express to someone: *Please give him my best wishes.*

wish² /wɪʃ/ *verb* (**wishes, wishing, wished**)

1 to want to do something (*formal*): *I wish to leave a message.*

2 to want something to be true, even though you know that it is impossible or unlikely: *I wish I could do that.*

wish for something to say in your mind that you want something, and then hope that it will happen: *Every birthday I closed my eyes and wished for a guitar.*

wish someone something to express the hope that someone will be lucky or happy: *I wish you both a good trip.*

wit /wɪt/ *uncountable noun*

the ability to use words or ideas in an amusing and clever way: *He writes with great wit.*

witch /wɪtʃ/ *noun* (**witches**)

a woman in children's stories who has magic powers that she uses to do bad things

with /wɪð/ *preposition*

1 together in one place: *Her son and daughter were with her.*

2 used for saying that two people or groups are both involved in a discussion, a fight or an argument: *We didn't discuss it with each other.* □ *About a thousand students fought with police.*

3 using something: *Turn the meat over with a fork.* □ *I don't allow my children to eat with their fingers.*

4 carrying something: *A woman came in with a cup of coffee.*

5 having a feature or a possession: *He was tall, with blue eyes.*

withdraw /wɪð'drɔ:/ *verb* (**withdraws, withdrawing, withdrew, withdrawn**)

1 to remove or take something away from a place (*formal*): *He reached into his pocket and withdrew a sheet of paper.*

2 to leave the place where you are fighting and return nearer home: *The army will withdraw as soon as the war ends.*

3 to take money out of a bank account: *He withdrew £750 from his account.*

4 to stop taking part in an activity or an organization: *She's the second tennis player to withdraw from the games.*

withdrawn /wɪð'drɔ:n/ → see **withdraw**

withdrew /wɪð'dru:/ → see **withdraw**

within /wɪ'ðɪn/ *preposition*

1 inside or surrounded by a place, an area or an object (*formal*): *The sports fields must be within the city.*

2 less than a particular distance from a place: *The man was within a few feet of him.*

3 before the end of a particular length of time: *Within twenty-four hours I had the money.*

without /wɪ'ðaʊt/ *preposition*

1 used for showing that someone or something does not have or use the thing mentioned: *I prefer tea without milk.* □ *You shouldn't drive without a seat belt.*

2 used for saying that the second thing mentioned does not happen: *He left without speaking to me.* □ *They worked without stopping.*

w

3 used for saying that someone else is not in the same place as you are, or they are not involved in the same action as you: *I told Frank to start dinner without me.*

witness /'wɪtnəs/ *noun* (**witnesses**)
1 a person who saw a particular event such as an accident or a crime: *Witnesses say they saw an explosion.*
2 someone who appears in a court of law to say what they know about a crime or other event: *Eleven witnesses appeared in court.* ● **witness** *verb* (**witnesses, witnessing, witnessed**) *Anyone who witnessed the attack should call the police.*

witty /'wɪti/ *adjective* (**wittier, wittiest**)
amusing in a clever way: *His books were very witty.*

wives /waɪvz/
the plural of **wife**

wizard /'wɪzəd/ *noun*
a man in children's stories who has magic powers

wobble /'wɒbəl/ *verb* (**wobbles, wobbling, wobbled**)
a person or thing wobbles when they make small movements from side to side as if they are going to fall: *The bike wobbled, but I didn't fall.*

wobbly /'wɒbli/ *adjective* (**wobblier, wobbliest**)
not steady, and moving from side to side: *He sat on a wobbly plastic chair.*

woke /wəʊk/ → see **wake**

woken /'wəʊkən/ → see **wake**

wolf /wʊlf/ *noun* (**wolves**)
a wild animal that looks like a large dog

woman /'wʊmən/ *noun* (**women**)
an adult female human being: *She was a tall, dark woman, with an unusual face.*

women /'wɪmɪn/
the plural of **woman**

won /wʌn/ → see **win**

wonder [1] /'wʌndə/ *verb* (**wonders, wondering, wondered**)
to think about something, and try to guess or understand more about it: *I wondered what the noise was.*

wonder [2] /'wʌndə/ *noun*
1 a very surprising and unexpected thing: *It's a wonder that we're still friends.*
2 *uncountable* a feeling of great surprise

and pleasure: *My eyes opened wide in wonder at the view.*
3 something that causes people to feel great surprise or admiration: *He loved to read about the wonders of nature.*

wonderful /'wʌndəfʊl/ *adjective*
extremely good: *The cold air felt wonderful on his face.* □ *It's wonderful to see you.*

won't /wəʊnt/
short for 'will not'

wood /wʊd/ *noun*
1 *uncountable* the hard material that trees are made of: *Some houses are made of wood.*
2 (also **woods**) a large area of trees growing near each other: *We went for a walk in the woods.*

wooden /'wʊdən/ *adjective*
made of wood: *She sat in a wooden chair.*

woodwind /'wʊdwɪnd/ *noun*
the group of musical instruments that are mainly made of wood, that you play by blowing into them

wool /wʊl/ *uncountable noun*
1 the hair that grows on sheep and on some other animals
2 a material made from animal's wool that is used for making things such as clothes: *The socks are made of wool.*

woollen /'wʊlən/ *adjective*
made from wool: *thick woollen socks*

woolly /'wʊli/ *adjective*
made from wool or looking like wool: *a woolly hat*

word /wɜːd/ *noun*
a unit of language with meaning: *The Italian word for 'love' is 'amore'.*
a word something that you say: *John didn't say a word all the way home.*
have a word with someone to have a short conversation with someone: *Could I have a word with you in my office, please?*
in other words said before you repeat something in a different way: *Ray is in charge of the office. In other words, he's my boss.*
word for word using exactly the same words: *I learned the song word for word.*

'Word ˌdocument *noun*
a document that you create on a computer using a program for writing text (*trademark*)

wore /wɔː/ → see **wear**

w

work¹ /wɜːk/ *verb* (**works, working, worked**)

1 to have a job and earn money for it: *He worked as a teacher for 40 years.* □ *I can't talk to you right now — I'm working.*

2 to do an activity that uses a lot of your time or effort: *You should work harder at school.*

3 to operate correctly: *My mobile phone isn't working.*

4 to be successful: *Our plan worked perfectly.*

5 to use or control a machine: *Do you know how to work the DVD player?*

work out

1 to develop in a way that is good for you: *I hope everything works out for you in Australia.*

2 to do physical exercises in order to make your body healthy: *I work out at a gym twice a week.*

work something out to discover the solution to a problem by thinking: *It took me some time to work out the answer.*

work out

They were working out at the gym.

work² /wɜːk/ *noun*

1 *uncountable* the job that you do to earn money: *I start work at 8.30 a.m. and finish at 7 p.m.*

2 *uncountable* the place where you do your job: *I'm lucky. I can walk to work.*

3 *uncountable* any activity that uses a lot of your time or effort: *I did some work in the garden this weekend.*

4 a painting, a book or a piece of music that someone has produced: *My uncle bought me the complete works of William Shakespeare for Christmas.* □ *a work of art*

worker /'wɜːkə/ *noun*

1 a person who works, who is not a manager: *His parents were factory workers.*

2 used for saying how well or badly someone works: *He is a hard worker.*

workforce /'wɜːkfɔːs/ *noun*

1 the total number of people in a country or a region who are able to do a job and who are available for work: *Half the workforce is unemployed.*

2 the total number of people who are employed by a particular company: *The company employs a very large workforce.*

workout /'wɜːkaʊt/ *noun*

a period of physical exercise or training: *She does a 35-minute workout every day.*

workplace /'wɜːkpleɪs/ *noun*

the place where you work: *This new law will make the workplace safer for everyone.*

workshop /'wɜːkʃɒp/ *noun*

1 a time when people share their knowledge or experience on a particular subject: *A music workshop for beginners will be held in the town hall.*

2 a place where people make or repair things: *He works as a mechanic in the workshop.*

world /wɜːld/ *noun*

1 the planet that we live on: *Scotland is a beautiful part of the world.*

2 a particular area of activity, and the people who are involved in it: *We have the latest news from the fashion world.*

worldwide /ˌwɜːldˈwaɪd/ *adverb*

throughout the world: *His books have sold more than 20 million copies worldwide.*

● **worldwide** *adjective* *They made £20 billion in worldwide sales last year.*

World Wide Web *noun*

a computer system that allows you to see information from all over the world on your computer. The short forms **WWW** and the **Web** are often used.

worm /wɜːm/ *noun*

a small animal with a long, thin body, no bones and no legs

worn¹ /wɔːn/ → see **wear**

worn² /wɔːn/ *adjective*

used for describing something that is damaged or thin because it is old and you have used it a lot: *There was a worn blue carpet on the floor.*

worn out also **worn-out** *adjective*

1 damaged after being used a lot: *old, worn-out tyres*

W

2 very tired after hard work: *After the race, he was worn out.*

worry¹ /'wʌri/ *verb* (**worries, worrying, worried**)

1 to keep thinking about problems that you have or about unpleasant things that might happen: *Don't worry, I'm sure he'll be fine.* □ *I worry about her all the time.* □ *They worry that he works too hard.*

▸ **worried** *adjective* *He seemed very worried.*
2 to make someone anxious: *'Why didn't you tell us?' — 'I didn't want to worry you.'*

worry² /'wʌri/ *noun* (**worries**)

1 *uncountable* the state or feeling of anxiety and unhappiness caused by the problems that you have or by thinking about unpleasant things that might happen: *Modern life is full of worry.*
2 a problem that you keep thinking about and that makes you unhappy: *My parents had a lot of worries.*

worse /wɜːs/ *adjective, adverb*

1 a form of the adjective **bad**, used for saying that one thing is of a lower standard than another thing: *The situation is even worse than we imagined.*
2 a form of the adverb **badly**, used for saying that one thing is done or happens in a way that is of a lower standard than another thing: *I feel even worse than I did yesterday.*

worship /'wɜːʃɪp/ *verb* (**worships, worshipping, worshipped**)

1 to show your respect to God or a god, for example, by saying prayers: *He likes to worship in his own home.* □ *We talked about different ways of worshipping God.* ● **worship** *uncountable noun* *This was his family's place of worship.*
2 to love or admire someone or something very much: *She worshipped him for many years.*

worst¹ /wɜːst/ *adjective, adverb*

1 a form of the adjective **bad**, used for saying that one thing is of the lowest possible standard: *That was the worst meal I've ever had.*
2 a form of the adverb **badly**, used for saying that one thing is done or happens in a way that is of the lowest possible standard: *The areas outside the city were worst affected by the fires.*

worst² /wɜːst/ *noun*
the most unpleasant thing that could

happen or does happen: *Many people still fear the worst.*

worth¹ /wɜːθ/ *adjective*

1 to have a particular value: *The picture is worth £500.*
2 to be pleasant or useful, and a good thing to have: *He decided to see if the house was worth buying.*

worth² /wɜːθ/ *uncountable noun*
used for saying how much of something you can buy for a particular amount of money: *I put twenty pounds' worth of petrol in the car.*

worthless /'wɜːθləs/ *adjective*
having no value or use: *He had nothing but a worthless piece of paper.*

worthwhile /ˌwɜːθ'waɪl/ *adjective*
enjoyable or useful, and worth the time, money or effort that you spend on it: *The president's trip was worthwhile.*

would /wəd STRONG wʊd/ *modal verb*

1 used for asking questions in a polite way: *Would you mind if I opened the window?*
2 often used in questions with 'like', when you are making a polite offer or invitation: *Would you like a drink?*
3 used for talking about situations that are not real: *If I had more money, I would go travelling.*
4 used when you are saying what someone believed, hoped or expected to happen: *We all hoped you would come.*
5 used for saying that someone was willing to do something. You use **would not** to say that someone refused to do something: *He said he would help her.* □ *She wouldn't say where she bought her shoes.*
6 used for talking about something that someone often did in the past: *He would sit by the window, watching people go by.*

wouldn't /'wʊdənt/
short for 'would not'

would've /'wʊdəv/
short for 'would have'

wound¹ /waʊnd/ → see **wind**

wound² /wuːnd/ *noun*
damage to part of your body caused by a gun or something sharp like a knife: *The wound is healing nicely.* ● **wound** *verb* (**wounds, wounding, wounded**) *He killed one man with a knife and wounded five other people.*

injured or **wounded**? When someone is hurt accidentally, for example in a car accident, or when they are playing sport, you say that they **are injured**. *A man was injured in the explosion.*
Wounded is normally used for talking about soldiers who are injured in battle, or someone who has been physically attacked. *A wounded soldier*

wow /waʊ/ *exclamation*
used for saying that you think something is very good or surprising (*informal*): *I thought, 'Wow, what a good idea.'*

wrap /ræp/ *verb* (**wraps, wrapping, wrapped**)
1 (*also* **wrap something up**) to fold paper or cloth tightly around something to cover it: *Diana is wrapping up the presents.*
2 to put something such as a piece of paper or cloth around another thing: *She wrapped a cloth around her hand.*

wrapper /ˈræpə/ *noun*
a piece of paper or plastic that covers something that you buy, especially food: *There were sweet wrappers on the floor.*

ˈwrapping ˌpaper *uncountable noun*
special paper that is used for covering presents

wreck [1] /rek/ *verb* (**wrecks, wrecking, wrecked**)
to completely destroy or ruin something: *The storm wrecked the garden.*

wreck [2] /rek/ *noun*
something such as a ship, a car, a plane or a building that has been destroyed, usually in an accident: *They discovered the wreck of a sailing ship.*

wrestle /ˈresəl/ *verb* (**wrestles, wrestling, wrestled**)
to fight someone by trying to throw them to the ground. Some people wrestle as a sport: *My father taught me to wrestle.*

wriggle /ˈrɪɡəl/ *verb* (**wriggles, wriggling, wriggled**)
to twist and turn your body, or part of your body, with quick movements: *She pulled off her socks and wriggled her toes.*

wrinkle [1] /ˈrɪŋkəl/ *noun*
one of the lines that form on your face as you grow old

wrinkle [2] /ˈrɪŋkəl/ *verb* (**wrinkles, wrinkling, wrinkled**)
to develop folds or lines: *Her stockings wrinkled at the ankles.*
▸ **wrinkled** *adjective* His suit was wrinkled and he looked very tired.

wrist /rɪst/ *noun*
the part between your hand and your arm that bends when you move your hand: *She fell over and broke her wrist.*

write /raɪt/ *verb* (**writes, writing, wrote, written**)
1 to use a pen or a pencil to produce words, letters or numbers: *Write your name and address on a postcard and send it to us.*
□ *I'm teaching her to read and write.*
2 to create something such as a book, a poem or a piece of music: *She wrote articles for French newspapers.*
3 to give someone information, ask them something or express your feelings in a letter or an email: *She wrote to her aunt asking for help.* □ *I wrote a letter to the manager.*

write something down to record something on a piece of paper using a pen or a pencil: *He took out a small notebook and wrote down the number.*

writer /ˈraɪtə/ *noun*
a person whose job is to write books, stories or articles: *She enjoys reading detective stories by American writers.*

writing /ˈraɪtɪŋ/ *uncountable noun*
1 something that has been written or printed: *Joe tried to read the writing on the next page.*
2 used for describing any piece of written work, especially when you are considering the style of language used in it: *The writing is very funny.*
3 the activity of writing, especially of writing books for money: *She was bored with writing books about the same thing.*
4 the way that you write with a pen or a pencil: *It's difficult to read your writing.*

written /ˈrɪtən/ → see **write**

wrong [1] /rɒŋ/ *adjective*
1 not as it should be: *Pain is the body's way of telling us that something is wrong.* □ *What's wrong with him?*
2 chosen by mistake: *He went to the wrong house.*

w

3 not the best or most suitable: *I made the wrong decision.*

4 not correct: *I did not know if Mark's answer was right or wrong.* ● **wrong** *adverb I must have added it up wrong.*

▶ **wrongly** *adverb He is an innocent man who was wrongly accused of stealing.*

5 bad: *She was wrong to leave her child alone.*

go wrong to stop progressing, and become worse: *We will do everything to make sure that nothing goes wrong.*

wrong ² /rɒŋ/ *uncountable noun*
activities or actions that are considered to be morally bad: *He can't tell the difference between right and wrong.*

wrote /rəʊt/ → see **write**

WWW /ˌdʌblju: dʌblju: ˈdʌblju:/
short for **World Wide Web**. It appears at the beginning of website addresses in the form **www.**

Xx

Xmas /ˈeksməs, ˈkrɪsməs/ *noun* (**Xmases**)
short for **Christmas**

'X-ray ¹ also **x-ray** *noun*
a picture of the inside of someone's body
that is made by using a special type of
light: *She had a chest X-ray at the hospital.*

'X-ray ² *verb* (**X-rays, X-raying, X-rayed**)
also **x-ray**
to take an X-ray picture of someone or
something: *All hand luggage must be x-rayed.*

xylophone /ˈzaɪləˌfəʊn/ *noun*
a musical instrument with a row of
wooden bars of different lengths that you
play with special hammers

xylophone

Yy

yacht /jɒt/ *noun*
a large boat with sails or a motor, used for racing or for pleasure trips

yam /jæm/ *noun*
a vegetable that is similar to a sweet potato: *Peel and boil the yams, and then mash them.*

yank /jæŋk/ *verb* (**yanks, yanking, yanked**)
to pull someone or something hard: *She yanked open the drawer.*

yard /jɑːd/ *noun*
1 a unit for measuring length. There are 91.4 centimetres in a yard: *The bomb exploded 500 yards from where he was standing.*
2 (*American*) a **garden** next to a house

yarn /jɑːn/ *uncountable noun*
thick cotton or wool thread: *She brought me a bag of yarn and some knitting needles.*

yawn /jɔːn/ *verb* (**yawns, yawning, yawned**)
to open your mouth very wide and breathe in more air than usual because you are tired: *She yawned, and stretched lazily.*
● **yawn** *noun Sophia woke and gave a huge yawn.*

yeah /jeə/
yes (*informal*): *'Don't forget your library book.' — 'Oh, yeah.'* □ *'Anybody want my ice cream?' — 'Um, yeah, sure.'*

year /jɪə/ *noun*
1 a period of twelve months, beginning on the first of January and ending on the thirty-first of December: *The year was 1840.* □ *We had an election last year.*
2 any period of twelve months: *The castle has more than 650,000 visitors a year.*
3 the period of time in the year when schools or universities are open: *the 2009/2010 academic year*
4 *plural* used for talking about a long time: *I lived here years ago.*
all year round for the whole year: *The hotel is open all year round.*

yearly /'jɪəli/ *adjective, adverb*
happening once a year or every year: *The company dinner is a yearly event.* □ *Students may pay fees yearly or each term.*

yeast /jiːst/ *uncountable noun*
the substance that makes bread rise: *Add the yeast to the flour in the bowl.*

yell /jel/ *verb* (**yells, yelling, yelled**)
to shout loudly: *'Eva!' he yelled.* ● **yell** *noun I heard a yell and the sound of something falling.*

yellow /'jeləʊ/ *adjective*
of the colour of lemons or butter: *She was wearing a yellow dress.* ● **yellow** *noun Her favourite colour is yellow.*

Yellow 'Pages *uncountable noun*
a book that has the telephone numbers for businesses and organizations in a particular area (*trademark*): *I looked for a plumber in the Yellow Pages.*

yes /jes/
1 used for giving a positive answer to a question: *'Are you a friend of Nick's?' — 'Yes.'*
2 used for accepting an offer or a request, or for giving permission: *'More coffee?' — 'Yes please.'* □ *'Could you help me, please?' — 'Yes, of course.'* □ *'Can I borrow your pen?' — 'Yes, of course.'*

yesterday /'jestə,deɪ, -di/ *adverb*
used for talking about the day before today: *She left yesterday.* ● **yesterday** *uncountable noun In yesterday's game, the Cowboys were the winners.*

yet¹ /jet/ *adverb*

1 used when something has not happened up to the present time, although it probably will happen: *They haven't finished yet.* □ *They haven't yet set a date for their wedding.*

2 used in questions to ask if something has happened before the present time: *Have they finished yet?*

3 not now, but at a later time: *Don't get up yet.* □ *You can't go home yet.*

yet² /jet/ *conjunction*

but: *He's a champion tennis player yet he is very modest.*

yield /jiːld/ *verb* (**yields, yielding, yielded**)

1 to produce crops, fruit or vegetables: *Each tree yields about 20 kilos of apples.*

2 to finally agree to do what someone wants you to do: *Finally, he yielded to his parents' demands.*

yoga /ˈjəʊɡə/ *uncountable noun*

a type of exercise in which you move your body into various positions in order to become more fit, and to relax your body and your mind: *I do yoga twice a week.*

yogurt /ˈjɒɡət/ also **yoghurt** *noun*

a thick, liquid food that is made from milk: *Frozen yogurt is £2 per cup.*

→ Look at picture on P3

yolk /jəʊk/ *noun*

the yellow part in the middle of an egg

you /juː/ *pronoun*

1 the person or people that you are talking to or writing to: *Hurry up! You are really late.* □ *I'll call you tonight.*

2 any person; people in general: *Getting good results gives you confidence.* □ *In those days you did what you were told.*

you'd /juːd/

1 short for 'you had'

2 short for 'you would'

you'll /juːl/

short for 'you will'

young¹ /jʌŋ/ *adjective* (**younger** /ˈjʌŋɡə/, **youngest** /ˈjʌŋɡɪst/)

not having lived for very long: *There is plenty of information on this for young people.* □ *a field of young corn*

young² /jʌŋ/ *plural noun*

an animal's babies: *You can watch birds feed their young with this wireless camera.*

the young people who are young: *Everyone from the young to the elderly can enjoy yoga.*

youngster /ˈjʌŋstə/ *noun*

a young person, especially a child: *The children's club will keep the youngsters occupied.*

your /jɔː/ *adjective*

1 belonging to or relating to the person or people that you are talking or writing to: *Are you taller than your brother?* □ *I left your newspaper on your desk.*

2 belonging to or relating to people in general: *You should always wash your hands after touching raw meat.*

you're /jɔː/

short for 'you are'

yours /jɔːz/ *pronoun*

something that belongs or relates to the person or people that you are talking to: *I believe Paul is a friend of yours.*

Yours/Yours sincerely/Yours faithfully (American: **Yours truly**) written at the end of a letter before you sign your name: *I hope to see you soon. Yours, George.*

yourself /jɔːˈself/ *pronoun* (**yourselves**)

1 the person that you are talking or writing to: *Be careful with that knife - you might cut yourself.*

2 used for making 'you' stronger: *You don't know anything about it — you said so yourself.*

3 done by you, and not by anyone else: *Don't do all of that yourself - let me help you.*

youth /juːθ/ *noun* (**youths** /juːðz/)

1 *uncountable* the period of someone's life when they are a child, before they become an adult: *In my youth, my ambition was to be a dancer.*

2 *uncountable* the quality or state of being young: *Youth is not an excuse for bad behaviour.*

3 a young man: *A 17-year-old youth was arrested yesterday.*

the youth young people when they are considered as a group: *The youth of today are just as caring as we were.*

you've /juːv/

short for 'you have'

yo-yo /ˈjəʊjəʊ/ *noun*

a round wooden or plastic toy that you hold in your hand. You make it go up and down on a piece of string.

y

Zz

zebra /ˈzebrə, ˈziː-/ *noun* (**zebras** or **zebra**)
a wild horse with black and white stripes
that lives in Africa

zebra crossing /ˌzebrə ˈkrɒsɪŋ/ *noun*
a place on the road that is painted with
black and white lines, where vehicles
should stop so that people can cross the
road safely

zero /ˈzɪərəʊ/ *uncountable noun*
1 the number 0
2 the temperature of 0°C, at which water
freezes: *a few degrees above zero*

zigzag /ˈzɪgzæg/ also **zig-zag** *noun*
a line that has angles in it like a lot of Ws

zinc /zɪŋk/ *uncountable noun*
a blue-white metal

zip ¹ /zɪp/ *noun*
a long metal or plastic object with two
rows of teeth that join together, and a
small part that you pull in order to open
and close clothes or bags

zip ² /zɪp/ *verb* (**zips, zipping, zipped**)
to use a special program to reduce the size
of a computer file so that it is easier to send
it to someone using the Internet: *This is how
to zip files so that you can send them via email.*
zip something up to fasten something
such as a piece of clothing using its zip:
He zipped up his jeans.

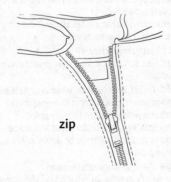
zip

'zip code *noun* (*American*)
→ see **postcode**

zone /zəʊn/ *noun*
an area where something particular
happens: *The area is a disaster zone.*

zoo /zuː/ *noun*
a park where animals are kept and
people can go to look at them: *He took his
son to the zoo.*

zoom /zuːm/ *verb* (**zooms, zooming,
zoomed**)
to go somewhere very quickly (*informal*):
Lorries zoomed past at 70 miles per hour.

zucchini /zuːˈkiːni/ *noun* (*American*)
(**zucchini** or **zucchinis**)
→ see **courgette**

Thesaurus

Vocabulary-building is an important part of learning a language. One way of doing this is by finding **synonyms** or **near-synonyms** of words that you already know. **Synonyms** are words that have similar meanings and this thesaurus gives you synonyms for 20 of the most over-used words in English.

If, for example, you feel that you are using words like *good*, *bad* and *nice* too often, using words from this thesaurus will make your writing more interesting and will allow you to express yourself more creatively and accurately in English.

Guide to thesaurus entries

The main word is in a blue box.

This tells you the word class of a word.

Synonyms – these are words that have a similar meaning to the main word.

Where a word has several meanings, these are ordered according to how common they are.

good¹

1 ADJECTIVE: pleasant or enjoyable
- ▶ **great**
  *We had a **great** time at Martin's party.*
- ▶ **lovely**
  *Thank you both for a **lovely** evening!*
- ▶ **nice**
  *The chocolate-chip cookies were really **nice**.*
- ▶ **pleasant**
  *I have many **pleasant** memories of this place.*

2 ADJECTIVE: of a high quality or level
- ▶ **awesome** (informal)
  *Both teams played well. It was an **awesome** game.*
- ▶ **cool** (informal)
  *She was wearing really **cool** boots.*
- ▶ **excellent**
  *The food in the hotel was **excellent**.*
- ▶ **great**
  *It's a **great** movie – you've got to see it.*

The number helps you find the correct entry for the word in the main dictionary.

The definition tells you what the main word means.

Labels tell you whether the word is used in serious situations or not.

Example sentences show you how the synonyms are used in sentences, and help you to understand them.

about

1 PREPOSITION: used for introducing a particular subject

▶ **concerning** (formal)
*For more information **concerning** the class, please contact the number below.*

▶ **on**
*Jackson has written a number of books **on** birds.*

▶ **regarding**
*He refused to give any information **regarding** his financial situation.*

2 ADVERB: used in front of a number to show that the number is not exact

▶ **almost**
*We have been married for **almost** three years now.*

▶ **approximately**
*They spent **approximately** £150 million.*

▶ **around**
*My salary was **around** £45,000.*

▶ **nearly**
*He worked for the company for **nearly** 20 years – 19 years and 10 months, to be exact.*

▶ **roughly**
*The disease kills **roughly** half a million people a year.*

bad

1 ADJECTIVE: unpleasant or harmful

▶ **damaging**
*Everyone knows that smoking is **damaging** to the health.*

▶ **nasty**
*I got a huge phone bill later that month, which was a **nasty** surprise.*

▶ **unhealthy**
*Try to avoid **unhealthy** foods, such as hamburgers, chips and biscuits.*

▶ **unpleasant**
*There was a very **unpleasant** smell – like old milk or cheese – coming from the fridge.*

2 ADJECTIVE: of a very low standard, quality or amount

▶ **defective**
*The company promises to repair or replace any **defective** equipment.*

▶ **faulty**
*The cause of the accident was **faulty** brakes.*

▶ **inferior**
*She paid less but she got an **inferior** product.*

▶ **poor**
*We were disappointed by the **poor** quality of the food.*

3 ADJECTIVE: painful or not working properly because of illness or injury

▶ **acute**
*He was in **acute** pain.*

▶ **intense**
*The pain was so **intense**, I nearly fainted.*

▶ **painful**
*Her toe was swollen and **painful**.*

▶ **serious**
*She suffered a **serious** head injury and was in hospital for many months.*

▶ **severe**
*I get **severe** headaches and no painkiller helps.*

▶ **terrible**
*For months I had **terrible** backache and couldn't walk.*

4 ADJECTIVE: rude or offensive

▶ **obscene**
*I read some advice on how to deal with **obscene** phone calls.*

▶ **offensive**
*He was extremely **offensive** so I asked him to say sorry.*

▶ **rude**
*The boys were telling **rude** jokes and laughing loudly.*

big

1 ADJECTIVE: large in size

▶ **enormous**
*She has an **enormous** house with eight bedrooms.*

▶ **giant**
*They have a **giant** TV screen that fills a whole wall.*

▶ **gigantic**
*The waves there are **gigantic** and great for surfing.*

▶ **huge**
*Emily was wearing a **huge** hat that hid most of her face.*

▶ **large**
*Can I have a **large** coffee and a chocolate muffin, please?*

▶ **vast**
*Australia is a **vast** continent.*

2 ADJECTIVE: important or serious

▶ **grave** (formal)
*These weapons are a **grave** danger to the world.*

▶ **great**
*The **great** advantage of plastic is that it is strong.*

▶ **major**
*Thousands of people are now without homes so this is a **major** problem.*

▶ **urgent**
*The refugees have an **urgent** need for food and water.*

call

1 VERB: to say something in a loud voice

▶ **cry**
'See you soon!' she **cried**, as she walked up the street.

▶ **cry out**
'You're wrong, you're all wrong!' Henry **cried out**.

▶ **scream**
Someone was **screaming** 'Help me!'.

▶ **shout**
He **shouted**, 'Don't shoot!'

▶ **yell**
'Eva, come back!' he **yelled**.

2 VERB: to telephone someone

▶ **call back**
I'm busy now – can I **call** you **back** later?

▶ **contact**
Here's my number if you need to **contact** me.

▶ **phone**
He **phoned** Laura to see if she was better.

▶ **ring**
He **rang** me at my mother's.

3 VERB: to make a short visit somewhere

▶ **call on**
I thought I might **call on** Jane while I'm in town.

▶ **drop by**
I'll **drop by** on my way home from work and give you the book.

▶ **drop in**
If you're passing my house, why not **drop in** for a cup of coffee?

▶ **visit**
I plan to **visit** my brother while I'm in New York.

difficult

ADJECTIVE: not easy to do, understand or deal with

▶ **complex**
Crime is a very **complex** problem.

▶ **complicated**
The situation is **complicated** and there's no easy way to explain it.

▶ **hard**
I found the exam very **hard**.

▶ **tough**
It was a **tough** decision because I knew I would upset someone whatever I did.

enjoy

VERB: to like doing something

▶ **adore**
I **adore** reading.

▶ **appreciate**
Everyone can **appreciate** this sort of art.

▶ **be fond of**
He's very **fond of** music.

▶ **like**
Do you **like** swimming?

▶ **love**
I really **love** cooking – it's my passion.

funny

1 ADJECTIVE: amusing and likely to make you smile or laugh

▶ **amusing**
Diana told an **amusing** story about her last boss.

▶ **comical**
James looked very **comical** in his hat.

▶ **hilarious**
It was a **hilarious** film – I've never laughed so much in my life.

▶ **witty**
I think you will enjoy Guy's company – he's very **witty**.

2 ADJECTIVE: strange, surprising or confusing

▶ **mysterious**
He was suffering from a **mysterious** illness that his doctor couldn't cure.

▶ **odd**
His behaviour was a little **odd** and it was worrying his parents.

▶ **peculiar**
He has a rather **peculiar** sense of humour.

▶ **unusual**
It's **unusual** for it to be so hot in April.

▶ **weird**
The other kids thought I was **weird** because I dressed differently.

go¹

1 VERB: to move or travel somewhere

▶ **drive**
I **drove** into town in my mother's car.

▶ **fly**
Jerry **flew** to Los Angeles this morning.

▶ **run**
I had to **run** to catch my train.

▶ **travel**
We're **travelling** around Europe this summer.

▶ **walk**
I usually **walk** to work.

2 VERB: to leave the place where you are

▶ **depart**
Flight 43 will **depart** from London Heathrow at 11:45 a.m.

► **exit**
Exit the motorway at Junction 24.
► **go away**
Just go away and leave me alone!
► **leave**
My flight leaves in less than an hour.
► **set off**
Nick set off for school at 8.
► **take off**
The plane took off on time.

good¹

1 ADJECTIVE: pleasant or enjoyable
► **great**
We had a great time at Martin's party.
► **lovely**
Thank you both for a lovely evening!
► **nice**
The chocolate-chip cookies were really nice.
► **pleasant**
I have many pleasant memories of this place

2 ADJECTIVE: of a high quality or level
► **awesome** (informal)
Both teams played well. It was an awesome game.
► **cool** (informal)
She was wearing really cool boots.
► **excellent**
The food in the hotel was excellent.
► **great**
It's a great movie – you've got to see it.

3 ADJECTIVE: suitable for an activity
► **convenient**
Would it be more convenient for you to meet nearer your office?
► **handy**
It's very handy having a supermarket so nearby.
► **suitable**
Jeans are not suitable for a formal interview.

4 ADJECTIVE: skilful at doing something
► **capable**
She's a very capable teacher.
► **competent**
A competent driver should be able to deal with situations like these.
► **skilful**
He was probably the most skilful player in the team.
► **skilled**
An employer has to pay more for skilled workers.
► **talented**
Both children are talented musicians.

great

1 ADJECTIVE: very large
► **enormous**
It's an enormous apartment for one man!
► **gigantic**
There are gigantic rocks along the roadside.
► **great big**
They have a great big house in the country.
► **huge**
A huge crowd of people gathered in the square.
► **massive**
The explosion left a massive hole in the ground.
► **vast**
Australia is a vast continent.

2 ADJECTIVE: large in amount or degree
► **excessive**
It wasn't an excessive amount to spend on a coat.
► **huge**
She made a huge effort to help us.
► **immense**
We still have an immense amount of work to do.
► **incredible**
He works an incredible number of hours.
► **massive**
She spends a massive amount of money on clothes.
► **tremendous**
The students have all made tremendous progress.

3 ADJECTIVE: very important
► **major**
Traffic is a major problem in the city.
► **serious**
It's not a serious problem – we can fix it.
► **significant**
There has been a significant improvement in his work this term.

4 ADJECTIVE: very good
► **awesome** (informal)
We had an awesome evening – thank you so much!
► **excellent**
The food was excellent.
► **fantastic** (informal)
You look fantastic in that dress.
► **superb**
There is a superb golf course 6 miles away.
► **terrific**
What a terrific idea!
► **wonderful**
It was wonderful to see them after all these years.

happy

1 ADJECTIVE: feeling pleased and satisfied

▶ **cheerful**
*Paddy was always smiling and **cheerful**.*

▶ **content**
*She seems quite **content** with her life and doesn't want to change anything.*

▶ **glad**
*I'm so **glad** you came!*

▶ **pleased**
*I'm really **pleased** that we solved the problem.*

2 PHRASE: If you are **happy to do** something, you are willing to do it.

▶ **content**
*The old lady seemed **content** to sit and look out of the window.*

▶ **pleased**
*I'd be **pleased** to take you there myself.*

▶ **prepared**
*If you are **prepared** to wait, she can see you in an hour.*

▶ **ready**
*My parents are **ready** to help if we need them.*

many

1 ADJECTIVE: used for talking about a large number of people or things

▶ **numerous**
*I called her **numerous** times but she never answered.*

▶ **several**
*We've met on **several** occasions.*

▶ **various**
*I spent the day doing **various** jobs around the house.*

2 PHRASE: You use **many of** for talking about a large number of people or things.

▶ **a lot of**
***A lot of** these houses have been built in the last ten years.*

▶ **lots of**
***Lots of** my friends have left town.*

▶ **masses of** (informal)
*There were **masses of** people at the concert.*

▶ **plenty of**
*She has **plenty of** clothes.*

new

ADJECTIVE: recently created or invented

▶ **brand-new**
*There was a **brand-new** car in the drive.*

▶ **fresh**
*She saw **fresh** car tracks in the snow.*

▶ **latest**
*These stores only sell the **latest** fashions.*

▶ **recent**
*It's a fairly **recent** movie – it came out last year.*

▶ **up-to-date**
*Their problem is they don't have **up-to-date** technology.*

nice

ADJECTIVE: attractive, pleasant or enjoyable

▶ **appealing**
*The long beaches with their golden sand are very **appealing**.*

▶ **beautiful**
*This is probably the most **beautiful** town I've ever seen.*

▶ **charming**
*My father was a very **charming** man – everyone liked him.*

▶ **lovely**
*Mia, thank you for a **lovely** evening!*

▶ **pretty**
*It's a very **pretty** village.*

▶ **sweet**
*She has a very **sweet** little baby.*

really

ADVERB: used for giving a sentence a stronger meaning

▶ **extremely**
*It's **extremely** cold in the winter here.*

▶ **remarkably**
*She did **remarkably** well in her exams, considering how sick she was.*

▶ **seriously**
*Luckily, no one was **seriously** hurt in the accident.*

▶ **severely**
*The aircraft was **severely** damaged in the attack.*

▶ **so**
*I'm surprised they're married – they seemed **so** different.*

▶ **very**
*I was **very** sorry to hear your sad news.*

say¹

VERB: to speak words

▶ **announce**
*He has just **announced** his resignation.*

▶ **answer**
*I asked him but he didn't **answer**.*

▶ **mention**
*She didn't **mention** her mother at all.*

▶shout
*'She's alive!' he **shouted**.*

▶tell
*I **told** Rachel I got the job.*

▶whisper
*He **whispered** something in her ear.*

short

1 ADJECTIVE: not lasting very long

▶brief
*We only had time for a **brief** chat.*

▶hasty
*I don't want to make a **hasty** decision about such an important matter.*

▶little
*Shall we stop here for a **little** while?*

▶quick
*He took a **quick** look around the room and walked out again.*

2 ADJECTIVE: not tall

▶little
*Even at ten, she's still very **little**.*

▶small
*Her husband is **small** too.*

▶tiny
*Both parents are short and the children are **tiny**.*

3 ADJECTIVE: measuring only a small amount from one end to the other

▶little
*We just need a **little** piece of string.*

▶minute
*There are **minute** bones in the ear.*

▶tiny
*I was fascinated by the baby's **tiny** fingers.*

small

1 ADJECTIVE: not large in size or amount

▶little
*She bought a nice **little** cottage in the country.*

▶minute
*You only need a **minute** amount of glue.*

▶tiny
*I bought a **tiny** sweater for the baby.*

2 ADJECTIVE: not very serious or important

▶minor
*We just made one or two **minor** changes to the document.*

▶slight
*There has been a **slight** increase in sales.*

▶trivial
*They shouldn't get upset over something so **trivial**.*

▶insignificant
*He worries about **insignificant** details.*

sometimes

ADVERB: on some occasions but not all the time

▶frequently
*Here is a list of **frequently** asked questions.*

▶now and then
*I see her **now and then** when she's in town.*

▶occasionally
*We **occasionally** go to the cinema but not as much as we used to.*

▶often
*I **often** see Tom on my way to work.*

very

ADVERB: used before an adjective or an adverb to make it stronger

▶extremely
*I'm **extremely** fond of her and I would hate her to go.*

▶really
*It's a **really** good movie – you must see it.*

▶remarkably
*The book was **remarkably** successful.*

▶so
*He's **so** tall!*

▶truly
*This is a **truly** great achievement.*

Reference Pages

Irregular verbs

Infinitive	Past Tense	Past Participle	Infinitive	Past Tense	Past Participle
arise	arose	arisen	fall	fell	fallen
be	was, were	been	feed	fed	fed
beat	beat	beaten	feel	felt	felt
become	became	become	fight	fought	fought
begin	began	begun	find	found	found
bend	bent	bent	fly	flew	flown
bet	bet	bet	forbid	forbade	forbidden
bind	bound	bound	forget	forgot	forgotten
bite	bit	bitten	freeze	froze	frozen
bleed	bled	bled	get	got	gotten, got
blow	blew	blown	give	gave	given
break	broke	broken	go	went	gone
bring	brought	brought	grind	ground	ground
build	built	built	grow	grew	grown
burn	burned *or* burnt	burned *or* burnt	hang	hung *or* hanged	hung *or* hanged
burst	burst	burst	have	had	had
buy	bought	bought	hear	heard	heard
catch	caught	caught	hide	hid	hidden
choose	chose	chosen	hit	hit	hit
cling	clung	clung	hold	held	held
come	came	come	hurt	hurt	hurt
cost	cost *or* costed	cost *or* costed	keep	kept	kept
			kneel	kneeled *or* knelt	kneeled *or* knelt
creep	crept	crept			
cut	cut	cut	know	knew	known
deal	dealt	dealt	lay	laid	laid
dig	dug	dug	lead	led	led
dive	dived *or* dove	dived	lean	leaned	leaned
do	did	done	leap	leaped *or* leapt	leaped *or* leapt
draw	drew	drawn			
dream	dreamed *or* dreamt	dreamed *or* dreamt	learn	learned	learned
			leave	left	left
drink	drank	drunk	lend	lent	lent
drive	drove	driven	let	let	let
eat	ate	eaten	lie	lay	lain

Infinitive	Past Tense	Past Participle	Infinitive	Past Tense	Past Participle
light	lit *or* lighted	lit *or* lighted	spell	spelled *or* spelt	spelled *or* spelt
lose	lost	lost	spend	spent	spent
make	made	made	spill	spilled *or* spilt	spilled *or* spilt
mean	meant	meant			
meet	met	met	spit	spit *or* spat	spit *or* spat
pay	paid	paid			
put	put	put	spoil	spoiled *or* spoilt	spoiled *or* spoilt
quit	quit	quit			
read	read	read	spread	spread	spread
ride	rode	ridden	spring	sprang	sprung
ring	rang	rung	stand	stood	stood
rise	rose	risen	steal	stole	stolen
run	ran	run	stick	stuck	stuck
say	said	said	sting	stung	stung
see	saw	seen	stink	stank	stunk
seek	sought	sought	strike	struck	struck *or* stricken
sell	sold	sold			
send	sent	sent	swear	swore	sworn
set	set	set	sweep	swept	swept
shake	shook	shaken	swell	swelled	swollen
shine	shined *or* shone	shined *or* shone	swim	swam	swum
			swing	swung	swung
shoot	shot	shot	take	took	taken
show	showed	shown	teach	taught	taught
shrink	shrank	shrunk	tear	tore	torn
shut	shut	shut	tell	told	told
sing	sang	sung	think	thought	thought
sink	sank	sunk	throw	threw	thrown
sit	sat	sat	wake	woke *or* waked	woken *or* waked
sleep	slept	slept			
slide	slid	slid	wear	wore	worn
smell	smelled	smelled	weep	wept	wept
speak	spoke	spoken	win	won	won
speed	sped *or* speeded	sped *or* speeded	wind	wound	wound
			write	wrote	written

Key words

Here is a list of the most common and useful words you need to know.

a	all	association	best	cabinet
ability	allow	assume	better	call
able	all right	at	between	camera
about	almost	attack	beyond	camp
above	alone	attempt	bid	campaign
absolutely	along	attend	big	can
abuse	already	attention	bill	cancer
accept	also	attitude	billion	capital
according to	alternative	attract	bird	captain
account	although	audience	bit	car
accuse	always	August	bite	card
achieve	among	aunt	black	care
across	amount	author	blame	career
act	and	authority	block	careful
action	animal	available	blood	carry
active	announce	average	blow	case
activity	annual	avoid	blue	cash
actually	another	award	board	catch
add	answer	aware	boat	cause
addition	any	away	body	cell
address	anyone	baby	bomb	central
admit	anything	back	bond	centre
adopt	anyway	bad	book	century
adult	apart	bag	border	certainly
advance	apparently	balance	born	chair
advantage	appeal	ball	boss	challenge
advice	appear	ban	both	chance
affair	appearance	band	bottle	change
affect	apply	bank	bottom	channel
after	approach	bar	box	charge
afternoon	approve	base	boy	cheap
again	April	basic	brain	check
against	area	basis	break	chemical
age	aren't	battle	bridge	chief
agency	argue	be	brief	child
agent	argument	bear	bright	choice
ago	arm	beat	bring	choose
agree	army	beautiful	broad	church
agreement	around	because	brother	circle
ahead	arrest	become	brown	city
aid	arrive	bed	budget	claim
AIDS	art	before	build	class
aim	artichoke	begin	building	clean
air	artist	behaviour	burn	clear
aircraft	as	behind	business	close
airline	ask	believe	but	clothes
airport	aspect	below	buy	club
album	asset	benefit	by	coach

coast	cream	development	easy	examine
coffee	create	didn't	eat	example
cold	credit	die	economic	excellent
collapse	crime	diet	economy	except
colleague	criminal	difference	edge	exchange
collect	crisis	different	editor	exercise
collection	criticism	difficult	education	exist
college	cross	difficulty	effect	expect
colour	crowd	digital	effective	expensive
come	cry	dinner	effort	experience
comment	culture	direct	egg	expert
commercial	cup	direction	eight	explain
commit	customer	director	eighteen	express
commitment	cut	discover	eighth	extra
committee	daily	discuss	eighty	eye
common	damage	discussion	either	face
community	dance	disease	elect	fact
company	danger	dispute	election	factor
competition	dangerous	distance	eleven	factory
complain	dark	district	else	fail
complete	data	divide	email	failure
complex	date	division	emerge	fair
computer	daughter	do	emergency	fall
concerned	day	doctor	employee	family
condition	dead	document	encourage	famous
conduct	death	doesn't	end	fan
conference	debt	dog	energy	far
confidence	decade	dollar	engine	farmer
confident	December	door	English	fashion
confirm	decide	double	enjoy	fast
conflict	decision	doubt	enough	fat
consider	declare	down	ensure	father
constant	decline	dozen	enter	favour
contact	deep	Dr	entire	favourite
contain	defeat	dramatic	entry	fear
continue	defence	draw	environment	feature
contract	defend	dream	equipment	February
control	degree	dress	escape	fee
cook	delay	drink	especially	feed
cool	deliver	drive	establish	feel
copy	demand	driver	estimate	feeling
corner	deny	drop	European	female
correct	department	drug	even	festival
cost	depend	dry	evening	few
could	describe	due	event	field
count	design	during	eventually	fifteen
country	desire	duty	ever	fifth
couple	desk	each	every	fifty
course	despite	early	everybody	fight
court	destroy	earn	everyone	figure
cousin	detail	earth	everything	file
cover	determine	east	evidence	fill
crash	develop	eastern	exact	film

final	gain	help	individual	knowledge
finally	game	her	industrial	lack
financial	garden	here	industry	lady
find	gas	herself	inflation	land
fine	gather	high	influence	language
finger	general	highly	information	large
finish	generally	him	injury	largely
fire	generation	himself	inside	last
firm	get	his	insist	late
first	girl	history	instance	later
fish	give	hit	instead	latest
fit	glass	hold	institution	laugh
five	glasses	hole	insurance	launch
flat	go	holiday	intend	law
flight	goal	home	interest	lawyer
floor	god	hope	interested	lay
flow	going	horse	international	lead
flower	gold	hospital	Internet	leader
fly	gone	host	interview	leadership
focus	good	hot	into	leading
follow	goods	hotel	introduce	learn
following	government	hour	investigate	least
food	grand	house	investment	leave
foot	great	how	invite	leg
football	green	however	involve	legal
for	ground	huge	involved	length
force	group	human	island	less
foreign	grow	hundred	issue	let
forget	growth	hurt	it	letter
form	guard	husband	I.T.	level
formal	guess	I	item	liberal
former	guest	ice	its	lie
forty	guide	idea	itself	life
forwards	gun	identify	January	lift
four	guy	if	job	light
fourteen	hair	ignore	join	like
fourth	half	ill	joint	likely
free	hand	image	journalist	limit
freedom	handle	imagine	judge	line
frequent	hang	impact	July	link
fresh	happen	important	jump	list
Friday	happy	impossible	June	listen
friend	hard	improve	just	little
from	hardly	in	justice	live
front	have	incident	keep	loan
fruit	he	include	key	local
fuel	head	including	kick	long
full	health	income	kid	look
fully	health care	increase	kill	lose
fun	hear	increasingly	kind	loss
function	heart	indeed	king	lot
fund	heat	independent	kitchen	love
future	heavy	indicate	know	low

lunch	mix	no	original	player
machine	model	nobody	other	please
magazine	modern	none	otherwise	plus
main	moment	no one	our	point
mainly	Monday	nor	out	police
maintain	money	normal	outside	policy
major	month	north	over	political
majority	more	north-east	own	politician
make	morning	north-west	owner	politics
male	most	not	pack	poor
man	mother	note	package	popular
manage	motor	nothing	page	population
management	mountain	notice	pain	position
manager	mouth	novel	paint	positive
many	move	November	painting	possibility
March	movement	now	pair	possible
mark	movie	nuclear	paper	possibly
market	MP	number	parent	post
marriage	Mr	object	park	potential
marry	Mrs	obvious	part	pound
match	Ms	obviously	particular	power
material	much	occasion	particularly	powerful
matter	mum	occupy	partner	practice
may	murder	occur	party	practise
May	museum	October	pass	prefer
maybe	music	odd	past	prepare
me	must	of course	patient	prepared
mean	my	off	pattern	presence
means	myself	offer	pay	present
meanwhile	name	office	payment	president
measure	narrow	officer	peace	press
media	national	official	people	pressure
medical	natural	often	per cent	pretty
meet	nature	oh	perfect	prevent
meeting	near	oil	perform	previous
member	nearly	okay	performance	price
memory	necessary	old	perhaps	prime minister
mention	need	on	period	prince
message	neighbour-	once	person	princess
method	hood	one	personal	principle
middle	neither	online	phone	print
might	network	only	photo	prison
mile	never	open	photograph	prisoner
military	new	operate	physical	private
million	news	operation	pick	prize
mind	newspaper	opinion	picture	probably
mine	next	opportunity	piece	problem
minority	nice	option	pink	process
minute	night	or	place	produce
miss	nine	orange	plan	product
Miss	nineteen	order	plane	production
mission	ninety	organization	plant	professional
mistake	ninth	organize	play	professor

profit	recommend	role	seventeen	soldier
program	record	roll	seventh	solution
programme	red	room	seventy	some
progress	reduce	round	several	somebody
project	refer	route	severe	someone
promise	reflect	royal	shake	something
promote	reform	rule	shall	sometimes
property	refugee	run	shape	son
proposal	refuse	sad	share	song
propose	regard	safe	sharp	soon
protect	region	safety	she	sorry
protection	regular	sale	ship	sort
protest	reject	same	shock	sound
prove	relation	Saturday	shoot	source
provide	relationship	save	shop	south
public	release	say	short	south-east
publish	relief	scale	shot	south-west
pull	religious	scales	should	space
purchase	remain	scene	shoulder	speak
purple	remember	schedule	show	special
purpose	remove	scheme	side	specific
push	repeat	school	sight	speech
put	replace	science	sign	speed
quality	reply	scientist	significant	spend
quarter	report	score	similar	spirit
queen	reporter	screen	simple	split
question	represent	sea	simply	sport
quick	request	search	since	spot
quiet	require	season	sing	spread
quite	research	seat	single	spring
race	reserve	second	sir	square
radio	resident	secret	sister	stable
rain	resource	secretary	sit	staff
raise	respect	section	site	stage
range	respond	secure	situation	stand
rapid	response	security	six	standard
rate	responsibility	see	sixteen	star
rather	responsible	seed	sixth	start
reach	rest	seem	sixty	state
reaction	restaurant	sell	size	statement
read	result	send	skill	station
reader	return	senior	skin	stay
ready	reveal	sense	sleep	step
real	rich	sentence	slightly	stick
reality	ride	separate	slip	still
realize	right	September	slow	stone
really	ring	series	small	stop
reason	rise	serious	smile	store
recall	risk	serve	smoke	storey
receive	rival	service	so	story
recent	river	set	social	straight
recently	road	settle	society	strange
recognize	rock	seven	soft	street

strength	tend	top	variety	who
stress	tenth	total	various	whole
strike	terrible	touch	vehicle	whom
strong	test	tough	version	whose
structure	than	tour	very	why
struggle	thank	towards	victim	wide
student	thanks	town	victory	wife
study	thank you	track	video	wild
stuff	that	trade	view	will
style	the	train	village	willing
subject	theatre	transport	violence	win
succeed	their	travel	visit	wind
success	them	treat	voice	window
successful	themselves	treatment	volume	wing
such	then	tree	vote	winner
suffer	theory	trial	wait	wish
suggest	there	trip	walk	with
suit	therefore	trouble	wall	within
summer	these	true	want	without
sun	the Web	trust	war	woman
Sunday	they	truth	warm	wonder
supply	thing	try	warn	wonderful
support	think	Tuesday	waste	wood
suppose	third	turn	watch	word
sure	thirteen	TV	water	work
surface	thirty	twelfth	wave	world
surprise	this	twelve	way	worry
surround	those	twenty	we	worth
survive	though	twice	weak	would
suspect	thought	two	weapon	wound
system	thousand	type	wear	write
table	threat	uncle	weather	writer
take	threaten	under	website	writing
talk	three	understand	Wednesday	wrong
tape	through	unit	week	yard
target	throughout	university	weekend	year
task	throw	unless	weight	yellow
taste	Thursday	unlikely	welcome	yes
tax	ticket	until	well	yesterday
tea	tie	up	west	yet
teach	tight	upon	western	you
team	time	us	what	young
tear	title	use	whatever	your
technique	to	used	when	yourself
technology	today	used to	where	youth
telephone	together	useful	whether	
television	tomorrow	usual	which	
tell	tonight	usually	while	
ten	too	value	white	

Countries and oceans

Below is a list of the names of well-known places in the world.

Afghanistan /æfˈgænɪˌstɑːn/

Africa /ˈæfrɪkə/

Albania /ælˈbeɪniə/

Algeria /ælˈdʒɪəriə/

American Samoa /əˌmerɪkən səˈməʊə/

Andorra /ænˈdɔːrə/

Angola /æŋˈgəʊlə/

Antarctica /ænˈtɑːktɪkə/

Antigua and Barbuda /ænˈtiːgə ənd bɑːˈbuːdə/

the Arctic /ði ˈɑktɪk/

Argentina /ˌɑːdʒənˈtiːnə/

Armenia /ɑːˈmiːniə/

Asia /ˈeɪʒə/

the Atlantic /ði ətˈlæntɪk/

Australia /ɒˈstreɪliə/

Austria /ˈɒstriə/

Azerbaijan /ˌæzəbaɪˈdʒɑːn/

the Bahamas /ðə bəˈhɑːməz/

Bahrain /bɑːˈreɪn/

Bangladesh /ˌbæŋgləˈdeʃ/

Barbados /bɑːˈbeɪdɒs/

Belarus /ˌbeləˈrʊs/

Belgium /ˈbeldʒəm/

Belize /bəˈliːz/

Benin /beˈniːn/

Bhutan /buːˈtɑːn/

Bolivia /bəˈlɪviə/

Bosnia and Herzegovina /ˈbɒzniə ənd ˌhɜːsəgəʊˈviːnə/

Botswana /bɒtˈswɑːnə/

Brazil /brəˈzɪl/

Brunei /bruːˈnaɪ/

Bulgaria /bʌlˈgeəriə/

Burkina-Faso /bɜːˌkiːnəˈfæsəʊ/

Burma /ˈbɜːmə/

Burundi /bəˈrʊndi/

Cambodia /kæmˈbəʊdiə/

Cameroon /ˌkæməˈruːn/

Canada /ˈkænədə/

Cape Verde /ˌkeɪp ˈvɜːd/

the Caribbean /ðə ˌkærɪˈbiːən/

the Central African Republic /ðə ˌsentrəl ˌæfrɪkən rɪˈpʌblɪk/

Chad /tʃæd/

Chile /ˈtʃɪli/

(the People's Republic of) China /(ðə ˌpiːpəlz rɪˌpʌblɪk əv) ˈtʃaɪnə/

Colombia /kəˈlʌmbiə/

Comoros /ˈkɒməˌrəʊz/

(the Republic of) Congo /(ðə rɪˌpʌblɪk əv) ˈkɒŋgəʊ/

(the Democratic Republic of) Congo /(ðə deməˌkrætik rɪˌpʌblɪk əv) ˈkɒŋgəʊ/

Costa Rica /ˌkɒstə ˈriːkə/

Côte d'Ivoire /ˌkəʊt diːˈvwɑː/

Croatia /krəʊˈeɪʃə/

Cuba /ˈkjuːbə/

Cyprus /ˈsaɪprəs/

the Czech Republic /ðə ˈtʃek rɪˌpʌblɪk/

Denmark /ˈdenmɑːk/

Djibouti /dʒiˈbuːti/

Dominica /ˌdɒmiˈniːkə, dəˈmɪnɪkə/

the Dominican Republic /ðə dəˈmɪnɪkən rɪˌpʌblɪk/

East Timor /ˌiːst ˈtiːmɔː/

Ecuador /ˈekwəˌdɔː/

Egypt /ˈiːdʒɪpt/

El Salvador /el ˈsælvəˌdɔː/

England /ˈɪŋglənd/

Equatorial Guinea /ˌekwəˌtɔːriəl ˈgɪni/

Eritrea /ˌerɪˈtreɪə/

Estonia /eˈstəʊniə/

Ethiopia /ˌiːθiˈəʊpiə/

Europe /ˈjʊərəp/

Fiji /ˈfiːdʒiː/

Finland /ˈfɪnlənd/

France /ˈfrɑːns/

Gabon /gəˈbɒn/

Gambia /ˈgæmbiə/

Georgia /ˈdʒɔːdʒə/

Germany /ˈdʒɜːməni/

Ghana /ˈgɑːnə/

Great Britain /ˌgreɪt ˈbrɪtən/

Greece /griːs/

Greenland /ˈgriːnlənd/

Grenada /griˈneɪdə/

Guatemala /ˌgwætəˈmɑːlə/

Guinea /ˈgɪni/

Guinea-Bissau /ˌgɪnibiˈsaʊ/

Guyana /gaɪˈɑːnə/

Haiti /ˈheɪti/

Holland /ˈhɒlənd/

Honduras /hɒnˈdjʊərəs/

Hungary /ˈhʌŋgəri/

Iceland /ˈaɪslənd/

India /ˈɪndiə/

Indonesia /ˌɪndəˈniːziə/

Iran /ɪˈrɑːn, ɪˈræn/

Iraq /ɪˈrɑːk, ɪˈræk/

(the Republic of) Ireland /(ðə rɪˌpʌblɪk əv) ˈaɪələnd/

Israel /ˈɪzreɪəl/

Italy /ˈɪtəli/

Jamaica /dʒəˈmeɪkə/

Japan /dʒəˈpæn/

Jordan /ˈdʒɔːdən/

Kazakhstan /ˌkæzækˈstæn, ˌkɑːzɑːkˈstɑːn/

Kenya /ˈkenjə/

Kiribati /ˌkɪriˈbɑːti/

Kuwait /kuːˈweɪt/
Kyrgyzstan /ˌkɪəgiˈstɑːn/
Laos /laʊs/
Latvia /ˈlætviə/
Lebanon /ˈlebənən/
Lesotho /ləˈsəʊtəʊ/
Liberia /laɪˈbɪəriə/
Libya /ˈlɪbiə/
Liechtenstein /ˈlɪktənˌstaɪn/
Lithuania /ˌlɪθjuːˈeɪniə/
Luxembourg /ˈlʌksəmˌbɜːg/
Macedonia /ˌmæsiˈdəʊniə/
Madagascar /ˌmædəˈgæskə/
Malawi /məˈlɑːwi/
Malaysia /məˈleɪziə/
the Maldives /ðə ˈmɔːldiːvz/
Mali /ˈmɑːli/
Malta /ˈmɔːltə/
the Marshall Islands /ðə ˈmɑːʃəl ˌaɪləndz/
Mauritania /ˌmɒriˈteɪniə/
Mauritius /məˈrɪʃəs/
the Mediterranean /ðə ˌmedɪtəˈreɪniən/
Mexico /ˈmeksɪˌkəʊ/
Micronesia /ˌmaɪkrəʊˈniːziə/
Moldova /mɒlˈdəʊvə/
Monaco /ˈmɒnəˌkəʊ/
Mongolia /mɒnˈgəʊliə/
Montenegro /ˌmɒntiˈniːgrəʊ/
Morocco /məˈrɒkəʊ/
Mozambique /ˌməʊzæmˈbiːk/
Myanmar /ˈmjænmɑː/
Namibia /nəˈmɪbiə/
Nauru /nɑːˈuːruː, ˈnaʊruː/
Nepal /niˈpɔːl/
the Netherlands /ðə ˈneðələndz/
New Zealand /ˌnjuː ˈziːlənd/
Nicaragua /ˌnɪkəˈrægjʊə/
Niger /ˈnaɪdʒə, niːˈʒeə/

Nigeria /naɪˈdʒɪəriə/
Northern Ireland /ˌnɔːðən ˈaɪələnd/
North Korea /ˌnɔːθ kəˈriːə/
Norway /ˈnɔːweɪ/
Oman /əʊˈmɑːn/
the Pacific /ðə pəˈsɪfɪk/
Pakistan /ˌpɑːkiˈstɑːn, ˌpækiˈstɑːn/
Panama /ˈpænəˌmɑː, ˌpænəˈmɑː/
Papua New Guinea /ˌpæpjʊə njuː ˈgɪniː/
Paraguay /ˈpærəgwaɪ/
Peru /pəˈruː/
the Philippines /ðə ˈfɪləpiːnz/
Poland /ˈpəʊlənd/
Portugal /ˈpɔːtjʊgəl/
Puerto Rico /ˌpwɜːtə ˈriːkəʊ, ˌpweətə ˈriːkəʊ/
Qatar /kʌˈtɑː/
Romania /rəʊˈmeɪniə/
Russia /ˈrʌʃə/
Rwanda /rʊˈændə/
St Kitts and Nevis /sənt ˌkɪts ənd ˈniːvis/
St Lucia /sənt ˈluːʃə/
St Vincent and the Grenadines /sənt ˈvɪnsənt ənd ðə ˌgrenəˈdiːnz/
Samoa /səˈməʊə/
San Marino /ˌsæn məˈriːnəʊ/
São Tomé and Principe /ˌsaʊ təˈmeɪ ənd ˈprɪnsiˌpeɪ/
Saudi Arabia /ˌsaʊdi əˈreɪbiə/
Scotland /ˈskɒtlənd/
Senegal /ˌseniˈgɔːl/
Serbia /ˈsɜːbiə/
the Seychelles /ðə ˌseɪˈʃelz/
Sierra Leone /siːˈeərə liˌəʊn/
Singapore /ˌsɪŋəˈpɔː/
Slovakia /sləʊˈvækiə/
Slovenia /sləʊˈviːniə/

the Solomon Islands /ðə ˈsɒləmən ˌaɪləndz/
Somalia /səˈmɑːliə/
South Africa /ˌsaʊθ ˈæfrikə/
South Korea /ˌsaʊθ kəˈriːə/
Spain /speɪn/
Sri Lanka /ˌsriː ˈlæŋkə/
Sudan /suːˈdɑːn, suːˈdæn/
Suriname /ˌsʊəriˈnæm/
Swaziland /ˈswɑːziˌlænd/
Sweden /ˈswiːdən/
Switzerland /ˈswɪtsələnd/
Syria /ˈsɪriə/
Taiwan /taɪˈwɑːn/
Tajikistan /tɑːˌdʒiːkiˈstɑːn/
Tanzania /ˌtænzəˈniːə/
Thailand /ˈtaɪˌlænd/
Togo /ˈtəʊgəʊ/
Tonga /ˈtɒŋgə/
Trinidad and Tobago /ˌtrɪnidæd ənd təˈbeɪgəʊ/
Tunisia /tjuːˈnɪziə/
Turkey /ˈtɜːki/
Turkmenistan /tɜːkˌmeniˈstɑːn/
Tuvalu /ˌtuːvəˈluː/
Uganda /juːˈgændə/
Ukraine /juːˈkreɪn/
the United Arab Emirates /ðiː juːˌnaɪtid ˌærəb ˈemɪrəts/
the United Kingdom /ðiː juːˌnaɪtid ˈkɪŋdəm/
the United States of America /ðiː juːˌnaɪtid ˌsteɪts əv əˈmerikə/
Uruguay /ˈʊərəˌgwaɪ/
Uzbekistan /ʊzˌbekiˈstɑːn/
Vanuatu /ˌvænuːˈɑːtuː/
the Vatican City /ðə ˌvætikən ˈsɪti/
Venezuela /ˌveniˈzweɪlə/
Vietnam /ˌvjetˈnæm/
Wales /weɪlz/
Yemen /ˈjemən/
Zambia /ˈzæmbiə/
Zimbabwe /zɪmˈbɑːbweɪ/

Numbers and measurements

Cardinal numbers

1	one
2	two
3	three
4	four
5	five
6	six
7	seven
8	eight
9	nine
10	ten
11	eleven
12	twelve
13	thirteen
14	fourteen
15	fifteen
16	sixteen
17	seventeen
18	eighteen
19	nineteen
20	twenty
21	twenty-one
22	twenty-two
30	thirty
40	forty
50	fifty
60	sixty
70	seventy
80	eighty
90	ninety
100	a hundred
101	a hundred and one
1,000	a thousand
10,000	ten thousand
100,000	a hundred thousand
1,000,000	a million

Ordinal numbers

1st	first
2nd	second
3rd	third
4th	fourth
5th	fifth
6th	sixth
7th	seventh
8th	eighth
9th	ninth
10th	tenth
11th	eleventh
12th	twelfth
13th	thirteenth
14th	fourteenth
15th	fifteenth
16th	sixteenth
17th	seventeenth
18th	eighteenth
19th	nineteenth
20th	twentieth
21st	twenty-first
22nd	twenty-second
30th	thirtieth
40th	fortieth
50th	fiftieth
60th	sixtieth
70th	seventieth
80th	eightieth
90th	ninetieth
100th	hundredth
101st	hundred and first
200th	two hundredth
$1,000^{th}$	thousandth
$10,000^{th}$	ten thousandth
100,000	hundred thousandth
1,000,000	millionth

Roman numerals

I	one	VIII	eight	XV	fifteen	L	fifty
II	two	IX	nine	XVI	sixteen	C	a hundred
III	three	X	ten	XVII	seventeen	D	five hundred
IV	four	XI	eleven	XVIII	eighteen	M	a thousand
V	five	XII	twelve	XIX	nineteen	MM	2,000
VI	six	XIII	thirteen	XX	twenty	MMI	2001
VII	seven	XIV	fourteen	XL	forty	MMX	2010

Length

millimetre (mm)
centimetre (cm)
metre (m)
kilometre (km)
mile (= 1.61 kilometres)

Weight

milligram (mg)
gram (g)
kilogram (kg)
tonne

Capacity

millilitre (ml)
litre (l)
pint (= 0.57 litres)
gallon (= 4.55 litres)